The Essential Writing of

HUNTER S. THOMPSON

FEAR and LOATHING at ROLLING STONE

Edited and with a Foreword
by Jann S. Wenner
and with an Introduction
by Paul Scanlon

SIMON & SCHUSTER
NEW YORK LONDON TORONTO SYDNEY NEW DELHI

Simon & Schuster
1230 Avenue of the Americas
New York, NY 10020

First Simon & Schuster hardcover edition November 2011

Designed by Joy O'Meara

Manufactured in the United States of America

10 9 8 7 6 5 4 3 2 1

Library of Congress Cataloging-in-Publication Data

Thompson, Hunter S.
Fear and loathing at Rolling stone : the essential writing of Hunter S. Thompson / edited and with a foreword by Jann S. Wenner and with an introduction by Paul Scanlon.
p. cm.
I. Wenner, Jann. II. Rolling stone (San Francisco, Calif.) III. Title.
PN4874.T444F43 2011
070.1'7—dc23 2011032312

ISBN 978-1-4391-6595-9
ISBN 978-1-4391-7023-6 (ebook)

Contents

Foreword

Jann S. Wenner

The record shows that in 1970 we published Hunter S. Thompson's "The Battle of Aspen"; in 1971 he wrote about the stirrings of Mexican unrest in East Los Angeles, featuring a fiery lawyer named Oscar Zeta Acosta, who later that year emerged as Dr. Gonzo in "Fear and Loathing in Las Vegas."

In 1972, we began nonstop coverage of the Nixon-McGovern presidential campaign. Hunter took over my life then—and for many years after that when he was reporting (long, nocturnal telephone calls and frequent all-night strategy sessions), and especially when he was writing.

After "Fear and Loathing in Las Vegas," everything else he wrote was a full-on siege. Setting up the assignment was easy—Hunter was pretty much welcome everywhere and had the skills and instincts to run a presidential campaign if he had wanted. But then came the travel arrangements: hotels, tickets, researchers, rental cars. Later in the process, finding a place for him to hunker down and write—The Seal Rock Inn, Key West, Owl Farm, preferably isolated and with a good bar. Flying in IBM Selectric typewriters with the right typeface; booze and drugs (usually he had this part already done); arranging for a handler-assistant at his end. Back at *Rolling Stone*, I had to be available to read and edit copy as it came in eight-to-ten-page bursts via the Xerox telecopier (the Mojo Wire), a primitive fax using telephone lines that had a stylus that printed onto treated, smelly paper (at a rate of seven minutes per page). I had to talk to Hunter for hours, then track and organize the various scenes and sections. He would usually begin writing in the middle, then back up or skip around to write what he felt good about at the moment, reporting scenes that might fit somewhere later, or spinning out total fantasies

("Insert ZZ" or "midnight screed") that would also find a place—parts that were flights of genius. Generally the lede was easy, describing the invariably dramatic weather wherever he was writing from. Then a flurry of headlines and chapter headings and the transitions he had to produce on demand to create the flow and logic, and always, sooner or later, the conclusion, which we always called "the Wisdom."

He liked to work against a crisis, and if there wasn't a legitimate one, he made one. We never had a fight about the editing. I never tried to change or "improve" him, but since I had a pretty deep understanding of his style and his motives, I could tell where he was going and sit at his side and read the map to him. If I didn't personally supervise everything he wrote for *Rolling Stone,* he wouldn't finish. It was a bit like being a cornerman for Ali. Editing Hunter required stamina, but I was young, and this was once in a lifetime, and we were both clear on that.

We were deep into politics and shared the same ambition to have a voice in where the country was going (thus the "National Affairs Desk"). We became partners in this as well, as mad as it may have seemed at the time—a rock-and-roll magazine and a man known for writing about motorcycle gangs, joining forces to change the country. We used to read aloud what he had just written, get to certain phrases or sentences, and just exclaim to each other, "Hot fucking damn." It was scorching, original, and it was fun. He was my brother in arms.

• • •

Now those days are gone. I still feel deeply in debt to him, and I never seem to stop working for him. And so it goes. And here we are publishing yet another volume of his work.

After Hunter's death, we produced a special tribute issue of *Rolling Stone* based on memories and vignettes from nearly a hundred of his friends, colleagues, and coconspirators. It took ten days, with a half-dozen editors working around the clock against a hellacious deadline, and once again we were in service to Hunter S. Thompson, busting our asses on his behalf. He had again touched us in some magical, unforgettable way, even affecting those on our staff who had never met him.

That special issue was commissioned as a full-length book, *Gonzo: The Life of Hunter S. Thompson,* a one-hundred-fifty-thousand-word oral history. For now it stands as the definitive Hunter S. Thompson biography, and an essential companion to any understanding of his work and life; I edited it word by word, with much devotion.

I've always thought that Hunter had, in a sense, written his own autobiography in the pages of *Rolling Stone,* and that if there was a way to take his collected work and edit it properly, there would emerge a narrative of Hunter's great and wild life, a story about himself, who was, after all, his own greatest character.

This notion was among the things I discussed with Paul Scanlon, who was my trusted right-hand man and managing editor for many of our San Francisco years, when we sat down to edit this book. Paul knows the *Rolling Stone* lore thoroughly, was a tasteful and meticulous editor, and was a natural to work with me on this comprehensive look at Hunter's years with the magazine.

We've also included some correspondence between Hunter S. Thompson and me (actually a very small sample), as well as a couple of thoughtful—and hilarious—memos to the staff that bring yet another subtext and flavor to the arc of his work. Hunter lived a great life of genius, talent, and righteousness. It is reflected in these pages.

FEAR and LOATHING at ROLLING STONE

Introduction

Paul Scanlon

When I first met Hunter S. Thompson in 1971, I didn't know what to expect. I was familiar with his work, of course, and had read the wonderful account of his campaign to become sheriff of Pitkin County (Aspen), Colorado, in the pages of *Rolling Stone*. He had been in Los Angeles working on a piece about the murder of newspaperman Ruben Salazar. There had been talk—very vague talk—about his writing something about Las Vegas. Then, one fine spring day, he appeared in *Rolling Stone*'s San Francisco office. For me, and the magazine, nothing would ever be quite the same.

• • •

If you were a progressively minded college student in the 1960s, certain books were required reading: *One Flew Over the Cuckoo's Nest* by Ken Kesey, *A Confederate General from Big Sur* and *Trout Fishing in America* by Richard Brautigan, *The Kandy-Kolored Tangerine-Flake Streamline Baby* and *The Electric Kool-Aid Acid Test* by Tom Wolfe, and *Hell's Angels* by Hunter S. Thompson.

As an undergraduate majoring in journalism, I was drawn to the writing of Wolfe and a few others who were practicing what was not yet being called the "New Journalism." It's funny, but even at an überliberal school like San Francisco State, there was a schism—what was known in the day as a "generation gap"—between faculty and students over this new kind of writing. Our professors considered Wolfe and his ilk poseurs, inspiring some kind of journalistic vaudeville by applying fictional techniques to reporting. We thought our instructors intended to mold us into drones, destined to carve out careers at small-town dailies.

I guess it was my junior year when I pulled a copy of *The Nation* from the student lounge magazine rack and had my first encounter with the writing of Hunter Thompson. It was the first of his two-part report on traveling with the Hells Angels. The outlaw motorcycle club's Oakland chapter was a fixture in the Bay Area. Encountering a group of Angels was not uncommon, especially after they embraced LSD and began hanging out at dance-rock concerts in places like the Fillmore Auditorium and Winterland. Big Brother and the Holding Company became their "official" band. The rule of thumb was simple if you were nearby: keep your distance and try not to make eye contact. Even in their brief, acid-drenched benign phase, the Angels were downright scary, clearly capable of unpredictable violence.

So it was a revelation to me that there was a writer who could figure out a way to win their trust and run with these characters. Hunter Thompson clearly had the smarts and the courage to do so. Or he was a hell of a salesman and a little bit crazy. Whatever. That early installment in *The Nation* convinced me he was the real deal. Later that day, I wondered aloud to my fellow campus newspaper staffers what our faculty advisers would make of *him.*

• • •

Rolling Stone in the early 1970s was an exciting place to be. Social, cultural, and political unrest was in the air and we tried to cover that turbulence in ways that newspapers and newsweeklies did not. I was the managing editor for many of those years and was fortunate to work with some of the finest journalists in the land, including several on the magazine's masthead. My colleagues were a gifted bunch of renegades who had served apprenticeships in places like the *Los Angeles Times,* the *New York Post,* the *Detroit Free Press,* the *Cleveland Plain Dealer,* and the *Wall Street Journal.* Two of our most talented staffers came from the creative writing programs of San Francisco State and Stanford. Our first copy chief, who kept the place from coming unglued every two-week publishing cycle, was a Middle East scholar who had once roomed with Owsley Stanley III. We all shared a disdain for traditional, mainstream journalism and a penchant for hard work.

When Hunter entered our ranks he quickly became, in many ways, our team leader. He had already established his credentials as an outlaw journalist, and the Salazar piece would demonstrate his investigative zeal.

You had to like the guy. I think some of it came from his innate Southern charm and the contradictory fact that he was, well, a little shy. He was in town that spring to work on "Fear and Loathing in Las Vegas, Part I," and had set up shop in the basement of Jann Wenner's house. His visits to the office, a converted downtown warehouse with lots of exposed brick and wooden beams, were infrequent, but always memorable. Hunter was a big, hulking but graceful guy who clearly had charisma, and we responded to it.

Standing about six-foot-two, usually clad in khaki shorts, high-topped sneakers, a baseball cap, and either a parka or a safari jacket, he'd amble into the office with a bowlegged quickstep, making the zigzagging, seriocomic, dramatic entrance we had come to expect. There was a big, round oak table in the middle of the editorial department, a sort of central gathering spot, where he'd plop down his leather rucksack, open it, and wordlessly proceed to remove the contents, which varied, but usually included something edible, like a grapefruit, a carton of Dunhills, a large police flashlight, a bottle of Wild Turkey, and a can of liquid Mace.

Next, he'd open his mouth and speak. I called it "Hunter-ese." His delivery was something akin to a lawn sprinkler or a Gatling gun, a rapid-fire baritone mumble that was hard to understand at first. But once you caught on to the rhythms, you realized he was spitting out perfect sentences.

Late one morning, Hunter came in and handed some manuscript pages to a couple of editors and me, then turned and motored out with nary a word. He had given us copies of the first section of "Vegas," and by late afternoon most of the staff had read and digested them. We were flat knocked out. Between fits of laughter we ran our favorite lines back and forth to one another: "One toke? You poor fool. Wait until you see those goddamned bats!" Delivered in Hunter-ese, of course.

Between bouts of serious writing there was the usual goofing off and troublemaking. There were evenings of drug-fueled adventures that left more than a few staffers dazed and worn out. There were interesting characters who were part of his—and subsequently our—orbit, including Oscar Zeta Acosta, who was the model for the "three-hundred-pound Samoan attorney" in "Vegas," and his sometimes sidekick, a fellow named Savage Henry.

Early on we became familiar with Hunter's penchant for fright wigs, bizarre recordings of animals in their death throes that would somehow find their way onto the office public address system, and novelty store pranks. One evening Jann invited a few of us over to his place on some pretext or other. We walked in and saw Hunter standing there in a torn tie-dyed T-shirt covered in red splotches. Brandishing what looked like a giant horse syringe, he announced that he was going to inject 151 proof rum directly into his navel. He then jammed the "needle" into his belly and doubled over as he let out a series of wails and groans. One of my companions almost fainted.

But the fun and games—for Hunter and for the rest of us—always took second position to the work. We loved what we were doing, and none more than he. Once, reflecting on the scrambling years of his early career, he stated that he had "no taste for either poverty or honest labor, so writing is the only recourse left for me." His tongue, of course, was firmly in his cheek. He was serious about his craft and was an ongoing student of correct grammar and syntax, and enjoyed sharing that knowledge. One of our staff writers was quite talented but often taunted for the sloppiness of his copy. I stood by one day as Hunter patiently lectured him on the necessity of producing a clean manuscript and how it would complement his writing skills (Hunter was right). In fact, he went out of his way to be friendly and helpful, even solicitous, about our work. Hunter would somehow get wind of what I was assigning and often I'd find on my desk a note in his distinctive scrawl suggesting a source or a contact. The notes were always signed: OK/HST. He had a gift to inspire, and he lifted everybody's game.

He could have played the star, but the really good ones never do. *Hells Angels* brought notoriety, and his Kentucky Derby piece for *Scanlan's* as well as the early *Rolling Stone* appearances received attention. He chose to be a friend and colleague, and we responded in kind. When the sloppy manuscript guy heard that Hunter used swimming as a way to relax, he escorted Hunter to a scuba school a couple of blocks away where he could do laps when the pool was free.

When he was in town, Hunter became a low-key regular at Jerry's Inn, the staff watering hole across the street. He was very much at home there at the bar, and would love to engage us, one-on-one, in everything from his heroes, Scott Fitzgerald and Joseph Conrad; to classic sports-writers such as Jimmy Cannon or Red Smith; to the fortunes of the Oakland Raiders, the scruffy, mean-spirited pro football team on which he had a few friends. He also loved to talk shop, about articles we would read in *Esquire* and elsewhere, which I like to think validated a few of the hours we spent in Jerry's instead of in the office.

When Hunter embarked on the 1972 campaign trail, it signaled the end of one chapter and the beginning of another for both him and the magazine. At first there was no real blueprint other than establishing a presence with an office in Washington, D.C. But he quickly found himself reinventing the mission statement almost issue by issue, and pretty soon the assignment had become an endless road trip. He was always writing against extreme deadline and filing copy at the last possible minute, which became a crucible for both him and the magazine. I was mercifully out of the direct line of fire, with too many other things on my plate. But I was close enough to feel the terrible weight borne by Jann, associate editor David Felton, copy editor Charles Perry, and a heroic production staff. The now legendary Mojo Wire sat just a few feet from my office door. Night after night, in the midst of deadline frenzy, that infernal thing would be beeping away, signaling Hunter's presence at the other end, while Jann or Felton stood by, waiting for the copy to be slowly ejected. It was as if he was always in our midst. And in the final accounting, those articles solidified *Rolling Stone*'s commitment to political coverage, made Hunter a true celebrity (for good and ill), and eventually resulted in a great book. It was a miracle of journalism under pressure, and only Hunter could have pulled it off.

A few months after the election we were sitting in Jerry's. Hunter looked like hell and was clearly not in great spirits. For reasons that will ever elude me, I decided to give him a helpful lecture. Retire your alter ego Raoul Duke, I said. Or send him on a long vacation. Go back to being the journalist who wrote *Hells Angels*. Cut back a little on the drugs and the booze. He turned toward me as he reached into the pocket of his safari jacket. He gave me a look; nothing nasty, just *a look*. He extracted a tab of Mr. Natural blotter acid from the pocket, stared me in the eye, and swallowed it. I got the message. Our conversation resumed.

• • •

The last time I worked with Hunter was on his "interdicted dispatch" from a rapidly falling Saigon in 1975. We pretty much lost contact after that, although I'd occasionally run into him in New York. The last time I spoke to him was at a 1996 celebration of the twenty-fifth anniversary of *Fear and Loathing in Las Vegas* and the simultaneous publication of a Modern Library edition, an acknowledgment of his work by the literary establishment of which he was justly proud. It was a splendid evening. A lot of *Rolling Stone* alumni were there, and among the guests was Johnny Depp, Hunter's great friend who would portray Raoul Duke, Doctor of Journalism, in the movie version of *Vegas* in 1998.

One of my favorite memories of Hunter goes back to the spring of 1973, and it's actually on video tape. He had been sequestered at the Seal Rock Inn, on the western edge of San Francisco, finishing the final edits on *Fear and Loathing: On the Campaign Trail '72*. A group of video journalists who had been assigned to do a documentary on *Rolling Stone* for public television had taped him at the hotel as he was preparing to leave, and he obliged them with a few minutes of classic Hunter S. Thompson gibberish and shtick.

But when he got to the office to say his good-byes before heading home to Colorado, the video crew had preceded him and closed in, peppering him with stupid questions. Hunter and I tried to ignore them by poring over his fan mail, which in itself was something to behold. Finally, Hunter gave up. He started moving down the hallway, looking back over his shoulder at me, saying, "I have to meet a guy across the street!" By the time he reached the exit, he was shouting, "I HAVE TO MEET A GUY ACROSS THE STREET!" Across the street was Jerry's, naturally. The guy was me.

Hunter was a terrific writer whose unique talent and enthusiasm helped propel *Rolling Stone* forward at some crucial points in its early history. He was a swell drinking companion, a hell of a salesman, and yes, a little bit crazy. Crazy like a fox.

• • •

It's been forty years since Hunter Thompson embarked on the presidential campaign trail and almost seven years since he passed away, but somehow he still manages to consume many of us to this day. When I began work on this book, I figured his total output for *Rolling Stone* exceeded four hundred fifty thousand words. The main text, after some pretty serious editing, is still about two hundred ten thousand words.

The selection process was easy: practically everything. Only four articles were omitted; they simply weren't up to par with the other material. But this meant that cutting would be that much more difficult.

The campaign trail material was the least difficult to work with. It was specifically geared to the moment, and much of it had simply ceased being topical. But there were plenty of vignettes and colorful incidents, and the overall reporting has held up remarkably well.

A characteristic of Hunter's writing is the long digression, or the shorter but carefully designed tangent. If a digression got in the way of the main narrative, out it came. The best example is "Fear and Loathing at the Super Bowl." Almost half the article was a world-class digression on the Oakland Raiders, which had nothing to do with the contest itself. Of course if a digression or tangent was outrageously funny, it had to stay in. It would have been a crime to cut Hunter's adventures riding the Vincent Black Shadow motorcycle. Such is also the case with "Fear and Loathing in Las Vegas." The excerpt presented here is a stand-alone section from Part II in which Duke and his attorney have their way with a hapless delegate to the district attorneys' conference.

Curiously, the hardest article to cut was Hunter's first piece for the magazine, "The Battle of Aspen," which details his efforts to unseat the sheriff of Pitkin County, Colorado, through the use of "Freak Power." I made a moderate initial cut, but the second time around I struggled and finally gave up. The damn thing was too intricate and dense.

• • •

The arc of Hunter's relationship with *Rolling Stone* is pretty clear looking at the table of contents. His output from 1970 through 1972 was amazing, and Watergate and all things Nixon kept him involved through 1974. But when he was dispatched to the Ali-Foreman heavyweight championship fight in Zaire that year, he returned empty-handed. His trip to Saigon as the Vietnam War wound down yielded an abbreviated, unfinished piece. A later excursion to Grenada yielded nothing. In the meantime, he had become—and would continue to be—a popular speaker on college campuses. The money was good and the appearances were plentiful. The writing just wasn't there, for long periods.

When he would reappear in the pages of *Rolling Stone*, the results were often first-rate. In 1977, "The Banshee Screams for Buffalo Meat" was a paean to his friend and sometimes nemesis Oscar Acosta, who had apparently perished in a drug deal gone bad. His two-part profile and interview with Muhammad Ali the following year was insightful and hilarious. Who else would leap into Ali's hotel room wearing an African fright mask, sending the Champ into gales of laughter?

Another five-year absence ended with Hunter's last great piece of reporting when he was sent to cover the sensational Roxanne Pulitzer divorce trial. "A Dog Took My Place" features Hunter at his best, exploring the sex-and-drugs culture of well-heeled Palm Beach denizens in wide-eyed amazement and disdain.

The 1990s would produce two late masterpieces. "Fear and Loathing in Elko" is a sustained fantasia of nightmare imagery featuring Supreme Court justice Clarence Thomas and a cast of weirdos. It is mordantly funny and dark—in fact much darker than "Fear and Loathing in Las Vegas." "Polo Is My Life" would prove to be his last great piece of lyrical, expansive writing, involving his observations on a sport for the wealthy, the lost world of F. Scott Fitzgerald, and sex dolls. It should be noted that these two articles, like his first for *Rolling Stone*, were extremely difficult to cut.

The correspondence between Hunter and Jann starts with their very first exchange in 1969. There are backstage looks at the writer as he works, how "Vegas" came to be, the evolution of the 1972 campaign coverage, story ideas (mostly discarded), and the push-me, pull-you faxes required to produce Hunter's later work. Taken as a whole, the letters and memos are a kind of additional biography of the writer who did his signature work for *Rolling Stone.*

In the Beginning . . .

Hunter first wrote to Jann Wenner in January 1970, having already published his first book, Hell's Angels, *in 1966 to generally positive critical attention.* Rolling Stone, *then two years old, had gained national attention with a special issue on Altamont, the Rolling Stones' debacle of a free outdoor concert in December 1969, at which the Hells Angels (incredibly, hired as* security*) terrorized the crowd, stabbing one spectator to death. Early correspondence between editor and writer danced around the possibility of a story about Terry the Tramp, an Angel who'd recently died, until Hunter casually mentioned his nascent campaign for sheriff of Aspen, Colorado. "The Battle of Aspen"—both Hunter's run for office and his account of it in the magazine—inserted Hunter into the national conversation both politically and journalistically, and was the opening battle cry to an epic, righteous, and occasionally combustible partnership between Hunter and* Rolling Stone.

Undated letter from Hunter S. Thompson to Jann S. Wenner

Owl Farm
Woody Creek, Colorado
Jann Wenner
Rolling Stone

Your Altamont coverage comes close to being the best journalism I can remember reading, by anybody. When I cited it to a friend who teaches at UCLA's journalism school he said he'd never heard of *Rolling Stone* . . . and that sort of says it all, I think, except maybe to speculate that the trouble isn't really with print, but with the people who control print. And that's an old bitch, too, so fuck it. Anyway, *Rolling Stone* makes [Marshall] McLuhan suck wind. It's a hell of a good medium by any standard, from Hemingway to the Airplane. People like [founder of the *Los Angeles Free Press* Art] Kunkin and [author-journalist Paul] Krassner never came close to what you're doing . . . so don't fuck it up with pompous bullshit; the demise of *R.S.* would leave a nasty hole.

Which reminds me of that shitty ignorant slur you laid on Eric Von Schmidt's last album, *Who Knocked the Brains Out of the Sky?* It's one of the few really original things I've heard in five years and "Wooden Man" ranks with the best of The Band's stuff. Whoever wrote that sleazy rap is a waterhead with a shit ear. Dismissing Von Schmidt as a bad rock artist is like comparing Lenny Bruce to the Hells Angels & saying that Bruce didn't make it.

Sincerely,
Hunter S. Thompson

Undated letter from Jann S. Wenner to Hunter S. Thompson

746 Brannan Street
San Francisco 94103

Hunter:

Thanks for your note. Having once read your *Angels* book in galley proof forms (stole them when I worked at *Ramparts*) and having really dug it in its pre-cut form, I've been a fan of yours. Glad you are now a fan of ours. So, good to get your note.

The record review section has been a problem—a lot of prep-school masturbatory reviewers getting their rocks off in the past. We're weeding them out now, and bringing the section back under my control, so I apologize for past idiocies in that part of the paper.

How about doing something for us? What have you been writing lately? Send it to me. Maybe we can use it, or maybe you have some ideas for some new stuff. Let me know.

Two items for your interest: 1) We submitted Altamont (plus groupies, ups, Dylan, etc.) for a Pulitzer. I doubt it will happen, but what the hell; and 2) I found out yesterday that Terry the Tramp committed suicide—sleeping pills—he wanted to quit the Angels after Altamont, and that's how he did it. I think we'll be having a good story about it. Would you be interested in adding your thoughts?

Hope Woody Creek is as beautiful as it sounds.

Sincerely,
Jann Wenner

Letter from HST to JSW

Owl Farm
Woody Creek, Colorado

Feb 25 '70

Dear Jann . . .

Thanx for the note & good luck with the Pulitzer gig. If I had a vote you'd be in good shape . . . but you'll be dealing with a gang of crusty shitheads, so don't let it worry you if they don't give you a medal. And even if they do it'll probably be for the wrong reasons.

About writing something: Your news about *Terry the Tramp* depresses the shit out of me. When I think of all those worthless mean-souled fuckers who *should* commit suicide, it's rotten to hear that Terry was the one who did it. I have hours of tape-talk with the bastard & I was listening to them tonight & remembering how he always knew that Angel thing was a bad trip & how he wanted to get out of it . . . but he never knew how, or where to go. He was the only one of the Angels I ever felt next to for long enough to consider him a friend. I kept expecting him to show up out here & I'd have been happy to see him—but he never did.

And now, looking at your letter, I don't mind knowing he's dead so much as I hate to think of him sitting around deciding to do it. He should have gone out at about 120, head-on with a cop car. That's what he was looking for; and it's a bitch to know he had to go out on his knees.

Anyway, I'd like to write something about him. Maybe a long thing—because thinking about him puts me back in a scene that's beginning to look very rare. San Francisco in the mid-Sixties was a very special time . . . and Terry, to me, was a key figure. I remember taking him down to the Matrix to hear the Airplane before they ever got into the Fillmore . . . then taking him down to La Honda to meet Kesey . . . and those fuckarounds with the Berkeley peace freaks. So probably I could write a decent thing about him—as a freak-symbol of an era he never quite understood. What do you have room for? A short obit . . . or a long rambling truth-nut? Let me know quick—if you need it quick—and also say what you pay. I'll write the fucker anyway, if there's room, but I tend to bear down a little harder when I smell money.

Whatever you think: I'll do a short obit (say, 2500 words) for nothing . . . or a long (10–15,000 words) for money. I'd like to get into it, and it fits with the long-overdue book I'm supposed to be finishing right now for Random House . . . so if you can use a long piece it's no problem. Shit . . . I sound like a pawnbroker here (or a speed-dealer), but in fact there's no point in my zapping off a huge chunk of esoteric madness that nobody can use. I've done that all too often, and it gets old . . .

OK for now . . . and in any case keep *R.S.* on its rails. We are heading into a shitstorm on all fronts.

Ciao,
Hunter

Also—send any details or news clips about Terry—like if there's a funeral, etc. They would help if I do anything long or serious—Thanx

Letter from JSW to HST

March 30, 1970

Hunter Thompson
Owl Farm
Woody Creek, Colorado

Dear Hunter:

Sorry for taking so long to get back to you but just before your letter arrived I went to London for awhile and I've just gotten back.

In the meantime, Terry the Tramp has passed from memory and we have received a beautiful piece by one of our writers in London, Chuck Alverson. I think we will be using this piece for a special issue we will be doing this fall about the Sixties. This obviates the need for the Terry the Tramp piece.

However, I would like you to write some things for us. You say you're working on a book right now for Random House, and if Terry the Tramp fits into it, perhaps then something from your book would fit into *Rolling Stone*. Maybe you could send us the chapters or some chapters, and maybe we could run some of it. I'd enjoy reading them in any case.

Best regards,
Jann Wenner

Letter from HST to JSW

Owl Farm
Woody Creek, Colorado

Apr 10 '70

Dear Jann . . .

OK, I'll try to let you know whenever I have something suitable for *R.S.* God only knows when, or what, it will be. Between running for Sheriff and getting this new Wallposter off the ground, I don't have much time for heavy writing. But I have to do it—or else start looking around for a job; so I'll get something together pretty soon.

Meanwhile, how can I get on the list for the *Earth Times* [Jann had recently launched an environmental publication with this title]? Who's running it? If it's you, write me in & bill me, or we can trade straight across for 12 issues of the Wallposter—which is on firm enough footing at least until next Nov, when we plan to bring everything to a terrible climax. Until then, the WP is our forum. I'm enclosing the first two issues, FYI.

What I'm hoping for now is just sending out all kinds of queries, hoping to come up with a few good ideas about printing and distribution before June, when we'll have to get down to serious twice-a-month publication. So if you have any ideas—mainly about how to sell this thing on the coast, or maybe a name or so of some distributors, I'd appreciate hearing from you pretty soon. Thanks for anything you can send.

And meanwhile, put me on the list for the *Earth Times.*

Ciao . . .
Hunter S. Thompson

In re: Chuck Alverson in London—he's an old friend of mine from the SF era—he did one of the first big magazine stories on the Angels (in *True*)—say hello when you see him.

Letter from JSW to HST, April 16, 1970

Hunter S. Thompson
Owl Farm
Woody Creek, Colorado

Dear Hunter:

Thanks for your letter. Something suitable for *Rolling Stone*: how about the tale of your campaign to be elected Sheriff? That would be beautiful.

Wallposter is a gas. There's nothing I can do for you in the way of distribution, but if you would like to sell a lot of single copies through the mail at 25 cents each, we could give you a plug in Random Notes.

Enclosed are the first two issues of *Earth Times*. I'd really love to have your first-person piece on running for sheriff. It sounds like it would be beautiful, especially with a lot of general material about Aspen and the scene there worked into it. How about 2500 words?

Best,
Jann Wenner

P.S. Chuck Alverson is now traveling around the Mediterranean for us, doing a special issue on the hashish trails. He'll be in San Francisco in August, and would probably love to see you.

Letter from HST to JSW

Owl Farm
Woody Creek, Colorado

Apr 23 '70

Dear Jann . . .

OK . . . but first let me explain the X-factors in both the Sheriff's campaign piece and the 25-cent Wallposters.

First: I saw that photo/caption in the last issue of *R.S.* about the lad who was running for sheriff of Virginia City—and although it sounds fine, that scene is a long way from ours. This one is getting very grim. . . . and our real opposition goes by names like 1st National City Bank of NY, "First Boston," and the Aspen Ski Corp.—with directors like Rbt. McNamara, Paul Nitze & other Washington heavies. What we've been trying to do—since we lost last November's mayoral race by six (6) votes—is seize control of what the opposition regards as a working gold mine. And it is. The idea that a 29-year-old bike-racer head almost became the Mayor of Aspen last fall has put the fatbacks in a state of wild fear; at the moment they're trying to pass a new City Charter that would disenfranchise most of "our" voters & also bar most of "our" candidates from running for office. So—to destroy this New Charter—we have to mount a serious campaign almost instantly. The charter election (Yes, or No) is in June. And if we can beat them on that, I think we can generate a fucking landslide in November—not only in the Sheriff's race, but also in the crucial County Commissioner's contest—and also for the ballot proposition to change the name of Aspen, officially, to Fat City. This would wreck the bastards, and give us working control of the whole county.*

* we've just rented a large mid-town office—a log building with huge windows

Anyway, I trust you see the problem—both in timing and magnitude. My sheriff's gig is just a small part of the overall plot, which amounts to a sort of Freak Power takeover bid. It began last Nov. and won't end until Nov '70. So maybe you should ponder the timing of any article; For my own purposes, I'd rather do it sometime this summer, like August, when we're well underway. Or I can wait until after it's over . . . although chances are that I'll be somewhere in Chuck Alverson's territory by that time, if I lose. If I make a serious run at the sheriff's thing, I'll either win or have to move out. That's the tradition here—and it'll be especially true in my case. Last summer was heavy with violence, and this one looks nine times worse. Last year the dynamite action didn't even start until mid-July, but this year it's already heavy in April . . . and last fall's near-miss election has given the local freaks a huge shot of confidence for whatever lies ahead.

So . . . on the "Sheriff's Campaign" article, I'm inclined to look at it as part of a far larger thing. If Freak Power can win in Aspen, it can win in a lot of other places . . . and in that context I'd just as soon do the article fairly soon, maybe in time for August publication, so that what we've learned here might be put to use somewhere else, before November. The important thing here is not whether I win or not—and I hope to hell I don't—but the mechanics of seizing political power in an area with a potentially powerful freak population. (As a passing note, there, I suppose I should say that if I *do* win, I'll serve out the term—although not without the help of a carefully selected posse and a very special crew of deputies, most of whom are already chosen and working to register my constituents.) We found, last fall, that *registration* is the key to freak power.

And so much for all that. I can do the piece sooner, or later; I'd prefer sooner, but what the hell? We're into it anyway, and by autumn a hell of a lot of people are going to be leaving this town: The only question is Who they're going to be.

* * *

Well . . . 3 days later now, & I've just talked to [*Ramparts* and *Scanlan's* editor] Warren Hinckle about doing a piece on the Kentucky Derby for *Scanlan's*. I'm leaving in a few hours for Louisville, so I want to get this off quick.

Right now the political balance looks about 40/60 against us—but that's without the crazed brilliance that we'll naturally bring to any serious effort we decide to make. So I figure the real balance, right now, is roughly 50/50—which means, if we don't make any serious mistakes, we'll probably control the town & the county by November of 1970. This includes the Sheriff's race, the (more important) County Commissioner's race, and also the referendum to change the name of the town to "Fat City."

Meanwhile, we are being sued by the County Attorney, who claims that Wallposter #1 forced him to quit his job. He wants more money than the Meat Possum Press Ltd. [Hunter's loose collective of like-minded freaks] can ever earn, so fuck him—we welcome his action. In WP #4 we intend to go for his throat & goad him on to further frenzies.

So that's it for now; I'm off to the Derby. Let me know when you'd like the Sheriff article—and write the Random Notes Wallposter note however you see fit; we'll honor it. OK . . .

Hunter

Undated letter from JSW to HST

746 Brannan Street
San Francisco 94103

Hunter:

Aspen story as is sounds great. I would dig it—at length, long really, maybe 5000 words, whatever it is worth once you write it—on the whole thing. Last year's elections, this year's, the dynamite things, all the local color and personalities. It sounds superb for us. I would like it in June to run in July or something.

I don't want to wait until it's over. I'd like the story while it is still in progress. If you know of a local photographer, then we'd like him on the story as well. If not, we'll send our own photographer.

The whole thing really moves me, as freakpower or whatever you call it, but the story of how young turned-on people are trying to take over the town in a regular election in Aspen, the Aspen scene in general for a while, the specifics of the election, who is running against whom, the reaction of the local gentry. And registration.

Your story in *RS* should be part of the larger effort to get everyone to register for 1972.

So do it. We can use it as soon as you finish it. Rate is 5 cents a word. Let me know on the photos.

Jann

Rather than plug the Wallposter now, let's get it with the issue we run the above piece.

Letter from HST to JSW

Owl Farm
Woody Creek, Colorado

June 1 '70

Dear Jann . . .

OK, back now from the Derby & recovering from a massive fuck-around—with Wallposter #4 due at the (Denver) printer in 4 days, and nothing written. Not even a cover—and my art partner, Tom Benton, is in the hospital for a shoulder operation. So things are jangled here. Selah.

On the Aspen/politics piece, I'll aim at getting it to you around mid/late June. One of the main problems is that anything I write in *RS* is going to get back here pretty quick, so I have to consider that aspect before I get it on. Our county commissioner candidate hasn't been told, yet, that he's it . . . and I want to get him solidly committed before I announce for sheriff. Otherwise, he—and our whole liberal/money gang—will freak right out and leave me running a straight Freak-Power shot; and that won't work. The dropout Head mentality is a maddening thing to work with; they don't know Kent State from Kent cigarettes, and frankly they don't give a fuck. But I'll get a decent piece out of this scene—for good or ill. Let's look at June 20 or so.

As for photographs, we have some competent locals but they don't give a fuck either—but let's wait a while until you send somebody out. July 4 is always a bitch here: Violence, bombs, bikers, posses with shotguns, etc. So if I can't root up a batch of good photos by July 1, maybe you should send somebody out who can do this scene with a fresh eye. There are one or two local photogs who could get the stuff pretty easily, but if I can't prod them out of their lethargy we'd be better off with somebody interested. I'll let you know.

But frankly I'd just as soon have one of your people come out. Otherwise, I'll have to ride herd on the local fuckers & do everything for them except push the button. (And in fact I might do that. I used to take pictures for half a living. No reason why I shouldn't make a run at it this time . . . and if my own stuff bombs we can always use one of your people.)

Anyway, the thing is cooking. My only real problem is how to write it without screwing myself to the floor in November. We'll see . . .

Sincerely,
Hunter

The Battle of Aspen: Freak Power in the Rockies

October 1, 1970

Two hours before the polls closed we realized that we had no headquarters—no hole or Great Hall where the faithful could gather for the awful election-night deathwatch. Or to celebrate the Great Victory that suddenly seemed very possible.

We had run the whole campaign from a long oaken table in the Jerome Tavern on Main Street, working flat out in public so anyone could see or even join if they felt ready . . . but now, in these final hours, we wanted a bit of privacy; some clean, well-lighted place, as it were, to hunker down and wait . . .

We also needed vast quantities of ice and rum—and a satchel of brain-rattling drugs for those who wanted to finish the campaign on the highest possible note, regardless of the outcome. But the main thing we needed, with dusk coming down and the polls due to close at seven o'clock, was an office with several phone lines, for a blizzard of last-minute calls to those who hadn't yet voted. We'd collected the voting lists just before five—from our poll-watcher teams who'd been checking them off since dawn—and it was obvious, from a very quick count, that the critical Freak Power vote had turned out in force.

Joe Edwards, a twenty-nine-year-old head, lawyer, and bike-racer from Texas, looked like he might, in the waning hours of Election Day in November 1969, be the next mayor of Aspen, Colorado.

The retiring mayor, Dr. Robert "Buggsy" Barnard, had been broadcasting vicious radio warnings for the previous forty-eight hours, raving about long prison terms for vote-fraud and threatening violent harassment by "phalanxes of poll watchers" for any strange or freaky-looking scum who might dare to show up at the polls. We checked the laws and found that Barnard's radio warnings were a violation of the "voter intimidation" statutes, so I called the district attorney and tried to have the mayor arrested at once . . . but the DA said "Leave me out of it: police your own elections."

Which we did, with finely organized teams of poll watchers: two inside each polling place at all times, with six more just outside in vans or trucks full of beef, coffee, propaganda, checklists and bound xerox copies of all Colorado voting laws.

The idea was to keep massive assistance available, at all times, to our point men *inside* the official voting places. And the reasoning behind this rather heavy public act—which jolted a lot of people who wouldn't have voted for Edwards anyway—was our concern that the mayor and his cops would create some kind of ugly scene, early on, and rattle the underground grapevine with fear-rumors that would scare off a lot of our voters. Most of our people were fearful of *any* kind of legal hassle at the polls, regardless of their rights. So it seemed important that we should make it very clear, from the start, that we knew the laws and we weren't going to tolerate *any* harassment of our people. None.

Each poll watcher on the dawn shift was given a portable tape recorder with a microphone that he was instructed to stick in the face of any opposition poll watcher who asked anything beyond the legally allowable questions regarding Name, Age, and Residence. Nothing else could be asked, under penalty of an obscure election law relating to "frivolous challenge," a little brother to the far more serious charge of "voter intimidation."

And since the only person who had actually threatened to intimidate voters was the mayor, we decided to force the confrontation as soon as possible in Ward 1, where Buggsy had announced that he would personally stand the first poll-watching shift for the opposition. If the buggers wanted a confrontation, we decided to give it to them.

The polling place in Ward 1 was a lodge called the Cresthaus, owned by an old and infamous Swiss/Nazi who calls himself Guido Meyer. Martin Bormann went to Brazil, but Guido came to Aspen—arriving here several years after the Great War . . . and ever since then he has spent most of his energy (including two complete terms as city magistrate) getting even with this country by milking the tourists and having young (or poor) people arrested.

So Guido was watching eagerly when the mayor arrived in his parking lot at ten minutes to seven, creeping his Porsche through a gauntlet of silent Edwards people. We had mustered a half dozen of the scurviest looking *legal* voters we could find—and when the mayor arrived at the polls, these freaks were waiting to vote. Behind them, lounging around a coffee dispenser in an old VW van, were at least a dozen others, most of them large and bearded, and several so eager for violence that they had spent the whole night making chain-whips and loading up on speed to stay crazy.

Buggsy looked horrified. It was the first time in his long drug experience that he had ever laid eyes on a group of non-passive, super-aggressive Heads. What had got into them? Why were their eyes so wild? And why were they yelling: "You're fucked, Buggsy . . . We're going to croak you . . . Your whole act is doomed . . . We're going to beat your ass like a gong."

Who were they? All strangers? Some gang of ugly bikers or speed freaks from San Francisco? Yes . . . of course . . . that bastard Edwards had brought in a bunch of ringers. But then he looked again . . . and recognized, at the head of the group, his ex-drinkalong bar-buddy Brad Reed, the potter and known gun freak, 6′4″ and 220, grinning down through his beard and black hair-flag . . . saying nothing, just smiling . . .

Great God, he knew the others, too . . . there was Don Davidson, the accountant, smooth shaven and quite normal-looking in a sleek maroon ski parka, but not smiling at all . . . and who were those girls, those ripe blond bodies whose names he knew from chance meetings in friendlier times? What were they doing out here at dawn, in the midst of this menacing mob?

What indeed? He scurried inside to meet Guido, but instead ran into Tom Benton, the hairy artist and known Radical . . . Benton was grinning like a crocodile and waving a small black microphone, saying: "Welcome, Buggsy. You're late. The voters are waiting outside . . . Yes, did you see them out there? Were they friendly? And if you wonder what *I'm* doing here, I'm Joe Edwards' poll watcher . . . and the reason I have this little black machine here is that I want to tape every word you say when you start committing felonies by harassing our voters . . ."

The mayor lost his first confrontation almost instantly. One of the first obvious Edwards voters of the day was a blond kid who looked about seventeen. Buggsy began to jabber at him and Benton moved in with the microphone, ready to intervene . . . but before Benton could utter a word the kid began snarling at the mayor, yelling: "Go fuck yourself, Buggsy! *You* figure out how old I am. I know the goddamn law! I don't have to show you proof of *anything*! You're a *dying man*, Buggsy! Get out of my way. I'm ready to vote!"

The mayor's next bad encounter was with a very heavy young girl with no front teeth, wearing a baggy gray T-shirt and no bra. Somebody had brought her to the polls, but when she got there she was crying—actually shaking with fear—and she refused to go inside. We weren't allowed within one hundred feet of the door, but we got word to Benton, and he came out to escort the girl in. She voted, despite Buggsy's protests, and when she came outside again she was grinning like she'd just clinched Edwards' victory all by herself.

After that, we stopped worrying about the mayor. No goons had shown up with blackjacks, no cops were in evidence, and Benton had established full control of his turf around the ballot box. Elsewhere, in Wards 2 and 3, the freak-vote was not so heavy and things were going smoothly. In Ward 2, in fact, our official poll watcher (a drug person with a beard about two feet long) had caused a panic by challenging dozens of *straight* voters. The city attorney called Edwards and complained that some ugly lunatic in Ward 2 was refusing to let a seventy-five-year-old woman cast her ballot until she produced a birth certificate. We were forced to replace the man; his zeal was inspiring, but we feared he might spark a backlash.

This had been a problem all along. We had tried to mobilize a huge underground vote, without frightening the burghers into a counterattack. But it didn't work—primarily because most of our best people were also hairy, and very obvious. Our opening shot—the midnight registration campaign—had been ramrodded by bearded heads; Mike Solheim and Pierre Landry, who worked the streets and bars for head voters like wild junkies, in the face of near-total apathy.

• • •

Aspen is full of freaks, heads, fun-hogs, and weird night-people of every description . . . but most of them would prefer jail or the bastinado to the horror of actually registering to vote. Unlike the main bulk of burghers and businessmen, the dropout has to *make an effort* to use his long-dormant vote. There is not much to it, no risk and no more than ten minutes of small talk and time—but to the average dropout the idea of registering to vote is a very heavy thing. The psychic implications, "copping back into the system," etc., are fierce . . . and we learned, in Aspen, that there is no point even trying to convince people to take that step unless you can give them a very good reason. Like a very unusual candidate . . . or a fireball pitch of some kind.

The central problem that we grappled with last fall is the gap that separates the Head Culture from activist politics. Somewhere in the nightmare of failure that gripped America between 1965 and 1970, the old Berkeley-born notion of beating The System by fighting it gave way to a sort of numb conviction that it made more sense in the long run to Flee, or even to simply hide, than to fight the bastards on anything even vaguely resembling their own terms.

Our ten-day registration campaign had focused almost entirely on the Head/Dropout Culture: they wanted no part of activist politics, and it had been a hellish effort to convince them to register at all. Many had lived in Aspen for five or six years, and they weren't at all concerned with being *convicted* of vote fraud—they simply didn't want to be hassled. Most of us are living here because we like the idea of being able to walk out our front doors and smile at what we see. On my own front porch I have a palm tree growing in a blue toilet bowl . . . and on occasion I like to wander outside, stark naked, and fire my .44 Magnum at various gongs I've mounted on the nearby hillside. I like to load up on mescaline and turn my amplifier up to 110 decibels for a taste of "White Rabbit" while the sun comes up on the snow-peaks along the Continental Divide.

Which is not entirely the point. The world is full of places where a man can run wild on drugs and loud music and firepower—but not for long. I lived a block above Haight Street for two years, but by the end of '66 the whole neighborhood had become a cop-magnet and a bad sideshow. Between the narcs and the psychedelic hustlers, there was not much room to live.

The idea of asking young heads to "go clean" never occurred to us. They could go dirty, or even naked, for all we cared . . . all we asked them to do was first *register* and then *vote*. A year earlier these same people had seen no difference between Nixon and Humphrey. They were against the war in Vietnam, but the McCarthy crusade had never reached them. At the grass-roots of the Dropout Culture, the idea of going Clean for Gene was a bad joke. Both Dick Gregory and George Wallace drew unnaturally large chunks of the vote in Aspen. Robert Kennedy would probably have carried the town, if he hadn't been killed, but he wouldn't have won by much. The town is essentially Republican: GOP registrations outnumber Democrats by more than two to one . . . but the combined total of both major parties just about equals the number of registered Independents, most of whom pride themselves on being totally unpredictable. They are a jangled mix of Left/Crazies and Birchers: cheap bigots, dope dealers, Nazi ski instructors, and spaced-out "psychedelic farmers" with no politics at all beyond self-preservation.

• • •

At the end of that frenzied ten-day hustle (since we kept no count, no lists or records) we had no way of knowing how many half-stirred dropouts had actually registered, or how many of those would vote. So it was a bit of a shock all around when, toward the end of that Election Day, our poll watchers' tallies showed that Joe Edwards had already cashed more than 300 of the 486 *new* registrations that had just gone into the books.

The race was going to be very close. The voting lists showed roughly one hundred pro-Edwards voters who hadn't showed up at the polls, and we figured that one hundred phone calls might raise at least twenty-five of these laggards. At that point it looked like twenty-five might make the nut, particularly in a sharply divided three-way mayor's race in a town with only 1,623 registered voters.

So we needed those phones. But where? Nobody knew . . . until a girl who'd been working on the phone network suddenly came up with a key to a spacious two-room office in the old Elks Club building. She had once worked there, for a local businessman and ex-hipster named Craig, who had gone to Chicago on business.

We seized Craig's office at once, ignoring the howls and curses of the mob in the Elks bar—where the outgoing mayor's troops were already gathering to celebrate the victory of his handpicked successor. (Legally, there was nothing they could do to keep us out of the place, although later that night they voted to have Craig evicted . . . and he is now running for the state legislature on a Crush the Elks platform.) By six o'clock we had the new headquarters working nicely. The phone calls were extremely brief and direct: "Get off your ass, you bastard! We *need* you! Get out and vote!"

About six people worked the lists and the phones. Others went off to hustle the various shacks, lodges, hovels, and communes where we knew there were voters but no phones. The place filled up rapidly, as the word went out that we finally had a headquarters. Soon the whole second floor of the Elks Club was full of bearded freaks yelling frantically at each other; strange-looking people rushing up and down the stairs with lists, notebooks, radios, and cases of Budweiser . . .

Somebody stuck a purple spansule in my hand, saying, "Goddamn, you look tired! What you need is a hit of this excellent mescaline." I nodded absently and stuck the thing in one of the twenty-two pockets in my red campaign parka. Save this drug for later, I thought. No point getting crazy until the polls close . . . keep checking these stinking lists, squeeze every last vote out of them . . . keep calling, pushing, shouting at the bastards, threaten them . . .

There was something weird in the room, some kind of electric madness that I'd never noticed before. I stood against a wall with a beer in my hand and watched the machinery working. And after a while I realized what the difference was. For the first time in the campaign, these people really believed we were going to win—or at least that we had a good chance. And now, with less than an hour to go, they were working like a gang of coal miners sent down to rescue the survivors of a cave-in. At that point—with my own role ended—I was probably the most pessimistic person in the room: the others seemed entirely convinced that Joe Edwards would be the next mayor of Aspen . . . that our wild-eyed experiment with Freak Power was about to carry the day and establish a nationwide precendent.

• • •

We were in for a very long night—waiting for the ballots to be counted by hand—but even before the polls closed we knew we had changed the whole structure of Aspen's politics. The Old Guard was doomed, the liberals were terrorized, and the Underground had emerged, with terrible suddenness, on a very serious power trip. Throughout the campaign I'd been promising, on the streets and in the bars, that if Edwards won this mayor's race I would run for sheriff next year (November 1970) . . . but it never occurred to me that I would actually have to run; no more than I'd ever seriously believed we could mount a "takeover bid" in Aspen.

But now it was happening. Even Edwards, a skeptic from the start, had said on election eve that he thought we were going to "win big." When he said it, we were in his office, sorting out xerox copies of the Colorado election laws for our poll-watching teams, and I recall being stunned at his optimism.

"Never in hell," I said. "If we win at all it's going to be damn close—like twenty-five votes." But his comment had jangled me badly. Goddamn! I thought. Maybe we *will* win . . . and what then?

• • •

Finally, at around six thirty, I felt so useless and self-conscious just hanging around the action that I said what the hell, and left. I felt like Dagwood Bumstead pacing back and forth in some comic-strip version of a maternity-ward waiting room. Fuck this, I thought. I'd been awake and moving around like a cannonball for the last fifty hours, and now—with nothing else to confront—I felt the adrenaline sinking. Go home, I thought, eat this mescaline and put on the earphones, get away from this public agony . . .

At the bottom of the long wooden stairway from Craig's office to the street I paused for a quick look into the Elks Club bar. It was crowded and loud and happy . . . a bar full of winners, like always. They had never backed a loser. They were the backbone of Aspen: shop owners, cowboys, firemen, cops, construction workers . . . and their leader was the most popular mayor in the town's history, a two-term winner now backing his own handpicked successor, a half-bright young lawyer. I flashed the Elks a big smile and a quick V-fingered "victory" sign. Nobody smiled . . . but it was hard to know if they realized that their man was already croaked; in a sudden three-way race he had bombed early, when the local Contractors' Association and all their real estate allies had made the painful decision to abandon Oates, their natural gut-choice, and devote all their weight and leverage to stopping the "hippie candidate," Joe Edwards. By the weekend before Election Day, it was no longer a three-way campaign . . . and by Monday the only question left was how many mean-spirited, Right-bent shitheads could be mustered to vote *against* Joe Edwards.

Our program, basically, was to drive the real estate goons completely out of the valley: to prevent the State Highway Department from bringing a four-lane highway into the town and, in fact, *to ban all auto traffic from every downtown street.* Turn them all into grassy malls where everybody, even freaks, could do whatever's right. The cops would become trash collectors and maintenance men for a fleet of municipal bicycles, for anybody to use. No more huge, space-killing apartment buildings to block the view, from any downtown street, of anybody who might want to look up and see the mountains. No more land rapes, no more busts for "flute-playing" or "blocking the sidewalk" . . . fuck the tourists, dead-end the highway, zone the greedheads out of existence, and in general create a town where people could live like human beings, instead of slaves to some bogus sense of Progress that is driving us all mad.

• • •

After a savage, fire-sucking campaign we lost by only six (6) votes, out of 1,200. Actually we lost by one (1) vote, but five of our absentee ballots didn't get here in time—primarily because they were mailed (to places like Mexico and Nepal and Guatemala) five days before the election.

We came very close to winning control of the town, and that was the crucial difference between our action in Aspen and, say, Norman Mailer's campaign in New York—which was clearly doomed from the start. At the time of Edwards' campaign, we were not conscious of any precedent . . . and even now, in calm retrospect, the only similar effort that comes to mind is Bob Scheer's 1966 run for a U.S. Congress seat in Berkeley/Oakland—when he challenged liberal Jeffrey Cohelan and lost by something like 2 percent of the vote. Other than that, most radical attempts to get into electoral politics have been colorful, fore-doomed efforts in the style of the Mailer-Breslin gig.

This same essential difference is already evident in 1970, with the sudden rash of assaults on various sheriff's fiefs. Stew Albert got 65,000 votes in Berkeley, running on a neo-hippie platform, but there was never any question of his winning. Another notable exception was David Pierce, a thirty-year-old lawyer who was actually elected mayor of Richmond, California (population 100,000 plus), in 1964. Pierce mustered a huge black ghetto vote—mainly on the basis of his lifestyle and his promise to "bust Standard Oil." He served, and in fact ran, the city for three years—but in 1967 he suddenly abandoned everything to move to a monastery in Nepal. He is now in Turkey, en route to Aspen and then California, where he plans to run for governor.

Another was Oscar Acosta, a Brown Power candidate for sheriff of Los Angeles County, who pulled 110,000 votes out of something like two million.

Meanwhile in Lawrence, Kansas, George Kimball (defense minister for the local White Panther party) has already won the Democratic primary—running unopposed—but he expects to lose the general election by at least ten to one.

On the strength of the Edwards showing, I had decided to surpass my pledge and run for sheriff, and when both Kimball and Acosta visited Aspen recently, they were amazed to find that I actually expect to *win* my race. A preliminary canvass shows me running well ahead of the Democratic incumbent, and only slightly behind the Republican challenger.

The root point is that Aspen's political situation is so volatile—as a result of the Joe Edwards campaign—that *any* Freak Power candidate is now a possible winner.

In my case, for instance, I will have to work very hard—and spew out some really heinous ideas during my campaign—to get *less* than 30 percent of the vote in a three-way race. And an underground candidate who really wanted to win could assume, from the start, a working nut of about 40 percent of the electorate—with his chances of victory riding almost entirely on his Backlash Potential; or how much active fear and loathing his candidacy might provoke among the burghers who have controlled local candidates for so long.

The possibility of victory can be a heavy millstone around the neck of any political candidate who might prefer, in his heart, to spend his main energies on a series of terrifying, whiplash assaults on everything the voters hold dear. There are harsh echoes of the Magic Christian in this technique: the candidate first creates an impossible psychic maze, then he drags the voters into it and flails them constantly with gibberish and rude shocks. This was Mailer's technique, and it got him fifty-five thousand votes in a city of ten million people—but in truth it is more a form of vengeance than electoral politics. Which is not to say that it can't be effective, in Aspen or anywhere else, but as a political strategy it is tainted by a series of disastrous defeats.

In any event, the Magic Christian conceit is one side of the "new politics" coin. It doesn't work, but it's fun . . . unlike that coin's other face that emerged in the presidential campaigns of Gene McCarthy and Bobby Kennedy in 1968. In both cases, we saw establishment candidates *claiming conversion* to some newer and younger state of mind (or political reality) that would make them more in tune with a newer, younger, and weirder electorate that had previously called them both useless.

And it worked. Both conversions were hugely successful, for a while . . . and if the tactic itself seemed cynical, it is still hard to know, in either case, whether the tactic was father to the conversion, or vice-versa. Which hardly matters, for now. We are talking about political-action formats: if the Magic Christian concept is one, then the Kennedy-McCarthy format has to qualify as another . . . particularly as the national Democratic Party is already working desperately to make it work again in 1972, when the Demos' only hope of unseating Nixon will again be some shrewd establishment candidate on the brink of menopause who will suddenly start dropping acid in late '71 and then hit the rock-festival trail in the summer of '72. He will doff his shirt at every opportunity and his wife will burn her bra . . . and millions of the young will vote for him, against Nixon.

Or will they? There is still another format, and this is the one we stumbled on in Aspen. Why not challenge the establishment with a candidate they've never heard of? Who has never been primed or prepped or greased for public office? And whose lifestyle is already so weird that the idea of "conversion" would never occur to him?

In other words, why not run an honest freak and turn him loose, on *their* turf, to show up all the "normal" candidates for the worthless losers they are and always have been? Why defer to the bastards? Why assume they're intelligent? Why believe they won't crack and fold in a crunch? (When the Japs went into Olympic volleyball they ran a blitz on everybody using strange but maddeningly legal techniques like the "Jap roll," the "dink spike," and the "lightning belly pass" that reduced their taller opponents to screaming jelly.)

This is the essence of what some people call "the Aspen technique" in politics: neither opting out of the system, nor working within it . . . but calling its bluff, by using its strength to turn it back on itself . . . and by always assuming that the people in power are not smart. By the end of the Edwards campaign, I was convinced, despite my lifelong bias to the contrary, that the Law was actually on our side. Not the cops, or the judges or the politicians—but the actual Law, itself, as printed in the dull and musty lawbooks that we constantly had to consult because we had no other choice.

• • •

By noon on Election Day, the only real question was How Many Liberals Had Hung On. A few had come over, as it were, but those few were not enough to form the other half of the nervous power base we had counted on from the start. The original idea had been to lash together a one-shot coalition and demoralize the local money/politics establishment by winning a major election before the enemy knew what was happening. Aspen's liberals are a permanent minority who have never won *anything*, despite their constant struggles . . . and Aspen's fabled "underground" is a far larger minority that has never even *tried* to win anything.

So *power* was our first priority. The platform—or at least our public version of it—was too intentionally vague to be anything but a flexible, secondary tool for wooing the liberals and holding our coalition. On the other hand, not even the handful of people in the powernexus of Joe Edwards' campaign could guarantee that he would start sodding the streets and flaying the sheriff just as soon as he got elected. He was, after all, a lawyer—an evil trade, at best—and I think we all knew, although nobody ever said it, that we really had no idea what the bastard might do if he got elected. For all we knew he could turn into a vicious monster and have us all jailed for sedition.

None of us even *knew* Joe Edwards. For weeks we had joked about our "ghost candidate" who emerged from time to time to insist that he was the helpless creature of some mysterious Political Machine that had caused his phone to ring one Saturday at midnight, and told him he was running for mayor.

Which was more or less true. I had called him in a frenzy, full of booze and resentment at a rumor that a gaggle of local powermongers had already met and decided who Aspen's next mayor would be—a giddy old lady would run unopposed behind some kind of lunatic obscenity they called a "united front," or "progressive solidarity"—endorsed by Leon Uris, who is Aspen's leading stag movie fan, and who writes books, like *Exodus*, to pay his bills. I was sitting in Peggy Clifford's living room when I heard about it, and, as I recall, we both agreed that the fuckers had gone too far this time.

Someone suggested Ross Griffin, a retired ski bum and lifelong mountain beatnik who was going half straight at the time and talking about running for the city council . . . but a dozen or so trial-balloon calls convinced us that Ross wasn't quite weird enough to galvanize the street vote, which we felt would be absolutely necessary. (As it turned out, we were wrong: Griffin ran for the council and won by a huge margin in a ward full of Heads.)

But at the time it seemed necessary to come up with a candidate whose Strange Tastes and Para-Legal Behavior were absolutely beyond question . . . a man whose candidacy would torture the outer limits of political gall, whose name would strike fear and shock in the heart of every burgher, and whose massive unsuitability for the job would cause even the most apolitical drug-child in the town's most degenerate commune to shout, "Yes! I must *vote* for that man!"

Joe Edwards didn't quite fill that bill. He was a bit too straight for the acid-people, and a little too strange for the liberals—but he was the only candidate even marginally acceptable on both ends of our untried coalition spectrum. And twenty-four hours after our first jangled phone talk about "running for mayor," he said, "Fuck it, why not?"

The next day was Sunday, and *The Battle of Algiers* was playing at the Wheeler Opera House. We agreed to meet afterward, on the street, but the hookup was difficult, because I didn't know what he looked like. So we ended up milling around for a while, casting sidelong glances at each other, and I remember thinking, Jesus, could that be *him* over there? That scurvy-looking geek with the shifty eyes? Shit, he'll never win anything . . .

Finally, after awkward introductions, we walked down to the old Jerome Hotel and ordered some beers sent out to the lobby, where we could talk privately. Our campaign juggernaut, that night, consisted of me, Jim Salter, and Mike Solheim—but we all assured Edwards that we were only the tip of the iceberg that was going to float him straight into the sea-lanes of big-time power politics. In fact, I sensed that both Solheim and Salter were embarrassed to find themselves there—assuring some total stranger that all he had to do was say the word and we would make him mayor of Aspen.

None of us had even a beginner's knowledge of how to run a political campaign. Salter writes screenplays (*Downhill Racer*) and books (*A Sport and a Pastime*). Solheim used to own an elegant bar called Leadville, in Ketchum, Idaho, and his Aspen gig is housepainting. For my part, I had lived about ten miles out of town for two years, doing everything possible to avoid Aspen's feverish reality. My lifestyle, I felt, was not entirely suited for doing battle with any small-town political establishment. They had left me alone, not hassled my friends (with two unavoidable exceptions—both lawyers), and consistently ignored all rumors of madness and violence in my area. In return, I had consciously avoided writing about Aspen . . . and in my very limited congress with the local authorities I was treated like some kind of half-mad cross between a hermit and a wolverine, a thing best left alone as long as possible.

So the '69 campaign was perhaps a longer step for me than it was for Joe Edwards. He had already tasted political conflict and he seemed to dig it. But my own involvement amounted to the willful shattering of what had been, until then, a very comfortable truce . . . and looking back, I'm still not sure what launched me. Probably it was Chicago—that brain-raping week in August of '68. I went to the Democratic Convention as a journalist, and returned a raving beast.

For me, that week in Chicago was far worse than the worst bad acid trip I'd even heard rumors about. It permanently altered my brain chemistry, and my first new idea—when I finally calmed down—was an absolute conviction there was no possibility for any personal truce, for me, in a nation that could hatch and be proud of a malignant monster like Chicago. Suddenly, it seemed imperative to get a grip on those who had somehow slipped into power and caused the thing to happen.

But who were they? Was Mayor Daley a cause, or a symptom? Lyndon Johnson was finished, Hubert Humphrey was doomed, McCarthy was broken, Kennedy was dead, and that left only Nixon, that pompous, plastic little fart who would soon be our president. I went to Washington for his inauguration, hoping for a terrible shitrain that would pound the White House to splinters. But it didn't happen; no shitrain, no justice . . . and Nixon was finally in charge.

So in truth it was probably a sense of impending doom, of horror at politics in general, that goaded me into my role in the Edwards campaign. The reasons came later, and even now they seem hazy. Some people call politics fun, and maybe it is when you're winning. But even then it's a mean kind of fun, and more like the rising edge of a speed trip than anything peaceful or pleasant. Real happiness, in politics, is a wide-open hammer shot on some poor bastard who knows he's been trapped, but can't flee.

The Edwards campaign was more an uprising than a movement. We had nothing to lose: we were like a bunch of wild-eyed amateur mechanics rolling a homemade racing car onto the track at Indianapolis and watching it overtake a brace of big Offenhausers at the 450 pole. There were two distinct phases in the monthlong Edwards campaign. For the first two weeks we made a lot of radical noise and embarrassed our friends and discovered that most of the people we had counted on were absolutely useless.

So nobody was ready for the second phase, when the thing began coming together like a conquered jigsaw puzzle. Our evening strategy meetings in the Jerome Bar were suddenly crowded with people demanding a piece of the action. We were inundated with $5 and $10 contributions from people whom none of us knew. From Bob Krueger's tiny darkroom and Bill Noonan's angry efforts to collect enough money to pay for a full-page ad in Bill Dunaway's liberal *Aspen Times*, we suddenly inherited all the facilities of the "Center of the Eye" Photography School and an unlimited credit-line (after Dunaway fled to the Bahamas) from Steve Herron at the *Times*-owned radio station, then the only one in town. (Several months after the election a twenty-four-hour FM station began broadcasting—with daytime Muzak balanced off against a late-night freak-rock gig as heavy as anything in S.F. or L.A.) With no local television, the radio was our equivalent of a high-powered TV campaign. And it provoked the same kind of surly reaction that has been shrugged off, on both coasts, by U.S. Senate candidates such as Ottinger (N.Y.) and Tunney (Calif.).

That comparison is purely technical. The radio spots we ran in Aspen would have terrified political eunuchs like Tunney and Ottinger. Our theme song was Herbie Mann's "Battle Hymn of the Republic," which we ran over and over again—as a doleful background to very heavy raps and evil mockery of the retrograde opposition. They bitched and groaned, accusing us in their ignorance of "using Madison Avenue techniques," while in truth it was pure Lenny Bruce. But they didn't know Lenny; their humor was still Bob Hope, with a tangent taste for Don Rickles here and there among the handful of swingers who didn't mind admitting that they dug the stag movies on weekends at Leon Uris' home on Red Mountain.

We enjoyed skewering those bastards. Our radio wizard, an ex-nightclub comic, Phil Clark, made several spots that caused people to foam at the mouth and chase their tails in impotent rage. There was a thread of high, wild humor in the Edwards campaign, and that was what kept us all sane. There was a definite satisfaction in knowing that, even if we lost, whoever beat us would never get rid of the scars. It was necessary, we felt, to thoroughly terrify our opponents, so that even in hollow victory, they would learn to fear every sunrise until the next election.

• • •

This worked out nicely—or at least effectively, and by the spring of 1970 it was clear on all fronts that Aspen's traditional power structure was no longer in command of the town. The new city council quickly broke down to a permanent 3–4 split, with Ned Vare as the spokesman for one side and a Bircher-style dentist named Comcowich taking care of the other. This left Eve Homeyer, who had campaigned with the idea that the mayor was "only a figurehead," in the nasty position of having to cast a tie-breaking vote on every controversial issue. The first few were minor, and she voted her Agnew-style convictions in each case . . . but the public reaction was ugly, and after a while the council lapsed into a kind of nervous stalemate, with neither side anxious to bring *anything* to a vote. The realities of small-town politics are so close to the bone that there is no way to avoid getting cursed in the streets, by somebody, for any vote you cast. An alderman in Chicago can insulate himself almost completely from the people he votes against, but there is no escape in a place the size of Aspen.

The same kind of tension began popping up on other fronts: the local high school principal tried to fire a young teacher for voicing a left-wing political bias in the classroom, but her students went on strike and not only forced the teacher's reinstatement but very nearly got the principal fired. Shortly after that, Ned Vare and a local lawyer named Shellman savaged the State Highway Department so badly that all plans to bring the four-lane highway through town were completely de-funded. This drove the county commissioners into a filthy funk; the highway had been their pet project, but suddenly it was screwed, doomed . . . by the same gang of bastards who had caused all the trouble last fall.

We began organizing in mid-August—six weeks earlier than last time—and unless we can pace the thing perfectly we might find ourselves limp and burned out two weeks before the election. I have a nightmare vision of our whole act coming to a massive orgiastic climax on October 25: two thousand costumed freaks doing the schottische, in perfect unison, in front of the County Courthouse . . . sweating, weeping, chanting . . . "Vote NOW! Vote NOW!" Demanding the ballot *at once*, completely stoned on politics, too high and strung out to even recognize their candidate, Ned Vare, when he appears on the courthouse steps and shouts for them all to back off: "Go back to your homes! You can't vote for ten more days!" The mob responds with a terrible roar, then surges forward . . . Vare disappears . . .

I turn to flee, but the sheriff is there with a huge rubber sack that he quickly flips over my head and places me under arrest for felony conspiracy. The elections are canceled and J. Sterling Baxter places the town under martial law, with himself in total command . . .

Baxter is both the symbol and the reality of the Old/Ugly/Corrupt political machine that we hope to crack in November. He will be working from a formidable power base: a coalition of Buggsy's "Taxpayers" and Comcowich's right-wing suburbanites—along with heavy institutional support from both banks, the Contractors' Association, and the all-powerful Aspen Ski Corporation. He will also have the financing and organizing resources of the local GOP, which outnumbers the Democrats more than two to one in registrations.

The Democrats, with an eye on the probability of another Edwards-style uprising on the Left, are running a political transvestite, a middle-aged realtor whom they will try to promote as a "sensible alternative" to the menacing "extremes" posed by Baxter and Ned Vare. The incumbent sheriff is also a Democrat.

Vare is running as an Independent, and his campaign symbol, he says, will be "a tree." For the sheriff's campaign, my symbol will be either a horribly deformed cyclops owl, or a double-thumbed fist, clutching a peyote button, which is also the symbol of our general strategy and organizing cabal, the Meat Possum Athletic Club. At the moment I am registered as an Independent, but there is still the possibility—pending the outcome of current negotiations for campaign financing—that I may file for office as a Communist. It will make no difference which label I adopt; the die is already cast in my race—and the only remaining question is how many Freaks, Heads, criminals, anarchists, beatniks, poachers, Wobblies, bikers, and Persons of Weird Persuasion will come out of their holes and vote for me. The alternatives are depressingly obvious: my opponents are hopeless bums who would be more at home on the Mississippi State Highway Patrol . . . and, if elected, I promise to recommend them both for the kind of jobs they deserve.

Ned Vare's race is both more complex and far more important than mine. He is going after the dragon. Jay Baxter is the most powerful political figure in the county. He is *the* county commissioner; the other two are echoes. If Vare can beat Baxter, that will snap the spine of the local/money/politics establishment . . . and if Freak Power can do that in Aspen, it can also do it in other places. But if it *can't* be done here, one of the few places in America where we can work off a proven power base—then it is hard to imagine it working in any other place with fewer natural advantages. Last fall we came within six votes, and it will probably be close again this time. Memories of the Edwards campaign will guarantee a heavy turnout, with a dangerous backlash factor that could wipe us out completely unless the Head population can get itself together and actually *vote.* Last year perhaps the Heads voted; this year we will need them all. The ramifications of this election go far beyond any local issues or candidates. It is an experiment with a totally new kind of political muscle . . . and the results, either way, will definitely be worth pondering.

Editor's note: in November 1970, Thompson lost by 465 votes.

The Next Assignment . . .

Hunter's next story for the magazine was an investigation into the Los Angeles Police Department's involvement in the murder of Ruben Salazar, a Chicano activist and Los Angeles Times *columnist. It's during this time that Hunter first began working with Oscar Zeta Acosta, a local Chicano civil rights lawyer he'd met a few years earlier. Acosta, dubbed the "Brown Buffalo" by Hunter, would soon become better known as Dr. Gonzo in "Fear and Loathing in Las Vegas." (Hunter and Oscar's first trip together to Las Vegas was taken so the two could discuss the Salazar case in a secure location.) He became Hunter's attorney and aide de camp, wrote occasionally for* Rolling Stone, *and cultivated an office presence both feared and respected by other staffers.*

Undated early '71 letter from JSW to HST

746 Brannan Street
San Francisco 94103

Dear Hunter:

Thanks for the letter and the rambling unfinished excerpts. Of course I agree with you that nothing should be done with them other than our private inspection. Selah. However, the obvious point is that we should have some sort of propaganda to coincide with the next election, either a pre-election look at the issues and the candidates (!) (did I say that?) or an election-time fire-sucking tract, or an *immediate* post-election review of the trauma. What are your thoughts on this?

Finally, Vietnam or the Mexicans versus the L.A.P.D.: Which would you prefer to do? I'd rather have you go to Los Angeles as you're already backgrounded in it, and I think I can get Michael Herr to Vietnam for us for his final major take.

Letter from HST to JSW

Jan 27 '71

Owl Farm
Woody Creek, Colorado

Dear Jann . . .

We might be better off using some photos & captions (along with my letter—the one you mentioned running) along with a postscript & forecast (by me) that would tie that last election to the one coming up. I've begun to feel very guilty about losing that one—mainly because so many people all over the country were apparently looking to Aspen for a breakthrough. It's amazing to realize how many completely different kinds of people read that Aspen piece in the 10/1 issue. I've had letters from all over the fucking world. Anyway—we decided just tonight that [Ned] Vare will probably run for Mayor in the Spring & we'll need at least $2500 to pull it off properly. (At the moment, on the strength of a $250 donation from [*RS* board member] Arthur Rock's tall Houston girlfriend, Mary, we're mounting an eleventh-hour legal maneuver to postpone the election until November) . . . but we figure to lose this, so our real point is to mobilize the freaks *ahead* of the May election, so that when the postponement move fails we'll have our act together & ready for the showdown. And it *will* be the showdown, the *final act* if we lose—or a fine reprieve for Freak Power if we can put Vare over.

Also, I'd like to get something put together in the way of an Aspen article by then—even if it has to be just that letter.

Personally, & especially since I'm still writing about that election, I'd prefer something larger. I think the story is lost unless we can tie it to national politics in some way; and I don't mean just the article, but the whole Freak Power concept. Oscar Acosta, for instance, was shocked to find that only a handful of the freak-voters in Aspen bothered to vote for the Raza Unida candidates—which was *our* fault, for not pushing it more, but it blew Oscar's idea of forging a union of some kind between Chicanos & freak-anglos. What has to be done, I think, is a massive expansion of that "freak" concept—which I spent about half the campaign trying to do (see enc.), but a lot of people refuse to see that to be a freak in Nixon's America is actually the only honorable way to go . . .

And so much for that, too. The mention of Acosta brings up your notion of a Chicano story in LA . . . and that looks like a natural, I guess, except that I just about used up my white journalist's credit down there on that *Scanlan's* story, which Hinckle eventually killed & replaced with his own lead editorial in the "current" issue. So it might be extremely difficult for me to spend any productive time down there unless I really leaned on Oscar . . . and I guess I could do that, but the prospect doesn't make me real happy. I probably have as much or more access to the story down there as any gabacho journalist, but before I got into it I'd have to know more about what you wanted & it might also be a good idea to lay the whole gig on Oscar before we start—because without him I wouldn't go near that story. And even with him, it might be a problem.

Frankly, I'd much prefer to do the Vietnam thing—mainly because it looks like a fantastically good story that I could look right into. That's one I'd really *like* to do—and I don't get many of those. But I see the natural advantage in getting it from Herr, if you can . . . so let me know, & meanwhile I'll check with Oscar & see what's happening in LA.

Meanwhile, I'm still in the foul grip of the IRS & heading for a $3500 showdown on Feb 7—or actually only $1000 on that date, with the rest still hanging while I hassle with *Scanlan's* distributor. This is like having the hounds of hell on your neck while you're trying to think. My American Express card was just seized for expenses incurred on *Scanlan's* stories . . . but fuck all that for now. Let me know on the Vietnam/LA-Chicano thing, and also about the Aspen fotos & the idea of running a bit more than just my letter. OK for now.

HST

Letter from HST to JSW

Jan 30 '71

Owl Farm
Woody Creek, Colorado

Dear Jann . . .

This comes in the midst of a certain amount of work/priority/message chaos—some of which resulted from those fucking telegrams of yours that got here three days late. Jesus, you should know by now—don't *ever* fuck with Western Union.

Anyway, the nut of what's left hanging here is some ideas of consolidating *what we have* on Aspen, along with some hazy ideas on LA/Chicanos vs. Vietnam (with lengthy notes and samples) . . . along with a very definitely double-edged idea about the notion of doing a regular sort of *column* for *RS*—which is always a good idea, in abstract, but I remember I agreed to it once for *Ramparts*, & the idea of filling one page a month was never quite hashed out between [*Ramparts* editor Peter] Collier & myself—much less with that wiggy bastard Hinckle. But it *was* a *good idea*; I never denied that—although it was hard to lock into for $150 or $200 a month. Because what happens to anybody who gets into any kind of forced/regular writing is that he's bound to make a useless fool of himself now & then . . . and it's hard to set a price on that kind of reality.

But to hell with that for now; at best it's just a vague notion—maybe born of my continuing frustration at always having to dump about nine-tenths of everything worth writing about, the inevitable freelancer's compulsion to always fire your *best shot* . . . which kills a lot of fast raps & left jabs enroute to all those classic Kayos . . .

Right . . . but let's not forget that the KO's are where the main survival/nerve$ live, and we all have to scrape those evil fuckers once in a while, if only to pay the rent. Or maybe the real word is "dues." Which I suspect you might have a hard time understanding. No fault of your own—or anyone else's, for that matter . . . just some accident of history. But what the hell . . . ?

Strange Rumblings in Aztlan:
The Murder of Ruben Salazar

April 29, 1971

The . . . Murder . . . and Resurrection of Ruben Salazar by the Los Angeles County Sheriff's Department . . . Savage Polarization & the Making of a Martyr . . . Bad News for the Mexican-American . . . Worse News for the Pig . . . And Now the New Chicano . . . Riding a Grim New Wave . . . The Rise of the Batos Locos . . . Brown Power and a Fistful of Reds . . . Rude Politics in the Barrio . . . Which Side Are You On . . . Brother? . . . There Is No More Middleground . . . No Place to Hide on Whittier Boulevard . . . No Refuge from the Helicopters . . . No Hope in the Courts . . . No Peace with the Man . . . No Leverage Anywhere . . . and No Light at the End of This Tunnel . . . Nada . . .

Whittier Boulevard has not been a peaceful street, of late. And in truth it was *never* peaceful. Whittier is to the vast Chicano *barrio* in East Los Angeles what the Sunset Strip is to Hollywood. This is where the street action lives: the bars, the hustlers, the drug market, the whores—and also the riots, the trashings, killings, gassings, the sporadic bloody clashes with the hated, common enemy: the cops, the Pigs, the Man, that blue-crusted army of fearsome *gabacho* troops from the East L.A. Sheriff's Department.

The Hotel Ashmun is a good place to stay if you want to get next to whatever's happening on Whittier Boulevard. The window of no. 267 is about fifteen feet above the sidewalk and just a few blocks west of the Silver Dollar Cafe, a nondescript tavern that is not much different from any of the others nearby. There is a pool table in the rear, a pitcher of beer sells for $1, and the faded Chicano barmaid rolls dice with the patrons to keep the jukebox going. Low number pays, and nobody seems to care who selects the music.

We had been in there earlier, when not much was happening. It was my first visit in six months, since early September when the place was still rancid with the stench of CS gas and fresh varnish. But now, six months later, the Silver Dollar had aired out nicely. No blood on the floor, no ominous holes in the ceiling. The only reminder of my other visit was a thing hanging over the cash register that we all noticed immediately. It was black gas mask, staring blindly out at the room—and behind the gas mask was a stark handprinted sign that said: "In memory of August 29, 1970."

Nothing else, no explanation. But no explanation was necessary—at least not to anybody likely to be found drinking in the Silver Dollar. The customers are locals: Chicanos and barrio people—and every one of them is acutely aware of what happened in the Silver Dollar on August 29, 1970.

That was the day that Ruben, the prominent Mexican-American columnist for the *Los Angeles Times* and news director for bilingual KMEX-TV, walked into the place and sat down on a stool near the doorway to order a beer he would never drink. Because just about the time the barmaid was sliding his beer across the bar, a Los Angeles County sheriff's deputy named Tom Wilson fired a tear gas bomb through the front door and blew half of Ruben Salazar's head off. All the other customers escaped out the back exit to the alley, but Salazar never emerged. He died on the floor in a cloud of CS gas—and when his body was finally carried out, hours later, his name was already launched into martyrdom. Within twenty-four hours, the very mention of the name Ruben Salazar was enough to provoke tears and a fist-shaking tirade not only along Whittier Boulevard but all over East L.A.

Middle-aged housewives who had never thought of themselves as anything but lame-status "Mexican-Americans" just trying to get by in a mean Gringo world they never made suddenly found themselves shouting "Viva La Raza" *in public*. And their husbands—quiet Safeway clerks and lawn-care salesmen, the lowest and most expendable cadres in the Great Gabacho economic machine—were volunteering to *testify*; yes, to stand up in court, or wherever, and calling themselves Chicanos. The term "Mexican-American" fell massively out of favor with all but the old and conservative—and the rich. It suddenly came to mean "Uncle Tom." Or, in the argot of East L.A.—"Tio Taco." The difference between a Mexican-American and a Chicano was the difference between a Negro and a Black.

All this has happened very suddenly. Suddenly for most people. One of the basic laws of politics is that Action Moves Away from the Center. The middle of the road is only popular when nothing is happening. And nothing serious has been happening politically in L.A. for longer than most people can remember. Until six months ago the whole place was a colorful tomb, a vast slum of noise and cheap labor, a rifle away from the heart of downtown Los Angeles. The barrio, like Watts, is actually a part of the city core—while places like Hollywood and Santa Monica are separate entities. The Silver Dollar Cafe is a ten-minute drive from city hall. The Sunset Strip is a thirty-minute sprint on the Hollywood Freeway.

Whittier Boulevard is a hell of a long way from Hollywood, by any measure. There is no psychic connection at all. After a week in the bowels of East L.A., I felt vaguely guilty about walking into the bar in the Beverly Hills Hotel and ordering a drink—as if I didn't quite belong there and the waiters all knew it. I had been there before, under different circumstances, and felt totally comfortable. Or almost. There is no way to . . . well, to hell with that. The point is that this time I felt *different*. I was oriented to a completely different world—fifteen miles away.

• • •

My first night in the Hotel Ashmun was not restful. The others had left around five, then there was the junkie eruption at seven . . . followed an hour later by a thundering, low-fidelity outburst of wailing Norteño music from the jukebox in the Boulevard Cafe across the street . . . and then, about nine thirty, I was jerked up again by a series of loud whistles from the sidewalk right under my window, and a voice calling, "Hunter! Wake up, man! Let's get moving."

Holy Jesus! I thought. Only three people in the world know where I am right now, and they're all asleep. Who else could have tracked me to this place? I bent the metal slats of the venetian blind apart just enough to look down at the street and see Rudy Sanchez, Oscar's quiet little bodyguard, looking up at my window and waving urgently: "Come on out, man, it's time. Oscar and Benny are up the street at the Sweetheart.

That's the bar on the corner where you see all those people in front. We'll wait for you there, okay? You awake?"

"Sure I'm awake," I said. "I've been sitting here *waiting* for you lazy criminal bastards. Why do Mexicans need so much fucking sleep?"

Rudy smiled and turned away. "We'll be *waiting* for you, man. We're gonna be drinkin' a hell of a lot of Bloody Marys, and you know the rule we have down here."

"Never mind that," I muttered. "I need a shower."

But my room had no shower. And somebody, that night, had managed to string a naked copper wire across the bathtub and plug it into a socket underneath the basin outside the bathroom door. For what reason? Demon Rum, I had no idea. Here I was in the best room in the house, looking for the shower and finding only an electrified bathtub. And no place to righteously shave—in the best hotel on the strip. Finally I scrubbed my face with a hot towel and went across the street to the Sweetheart Lounge.

Oscar Acosta, the Chicano lawyer, was there; leaning on the bar, talking idly with some of the patrons. Of the four people around him—all in their late twenties—two were ex-cons, two were part-time dynamite freaks and known fire-bombers, and three of the four were veteran acid-eaters. Yet none of this surfaced in the conversation. The talk was political, but only in terms of the courtroom. Oscar was dealing with two hyperpolitical trials at the same time.

In one, the trial of the "Biltmore Six," he was defending six young Chicanos who'd been arrested for trying to burn down the Biltmore Hotel one night about a year ago, while Governor Ronald Reagan was delivering a speech there in the ballroom. Their guilt or innocence was immaterial at this point, because the trial had developed into a spectacular attempt to overturn the entire Grand Jury selection system. In the preceding months, Acosta had subpoenaed every superior court judge in Los Angeles County and cross-examined all 109 of them at length, under oath, on the subject of their "racism." It was a wretched affront to the whole court system, and Acosta was working overtime to make it as wretched as possible. Here were these 109 old men, these *judges*, compelled to take time out from whatever they were doing and go into another courtroom to take the stand and deny charges of "racism" from an attorney they all loathed.

Oscar's contention, throughout, was that all Grand Juries are racist, since all grand jurors have to be recommended by superior court judges—who naturally tend to recommend people they know personally or professionally. And that therefore no rat-bastard Chicano street crazy, for instance, could possibly be indicted by "a jury of his peers." The implications of a victory in this case were so obvious, so clearly menacing to the court system, that interest in the verdict had filtered all the way down to places like the Boulevard, the Silver Dollar, and the Sweetheart. The level of political consciousness is not normally high in these places—especially on Saturday mornings—but Acosta's very presence, no matter where he goes or what he seems to be doing, is so grossly political that anybody who wants to talk to him has to figure out some way to deal on a meaningful political level.

Acosta has been practicing law in the barrio for three years. I met him a bit earlier than that, in another era—which hardly matters here, except that it might be a trifle less than fair to run this story all the way out to the end without saying at least once, for the record, that Oscar is an old friend and occasional antagonist. I first met him, as I recall, in a bar called the Daisy Duck in Aspen, when he lumbered up to me and started raving about "ripping the system apart like a pile of cheap hay," or something like that . . . and I remember thinking, "Well, here's another one of those fucked-up, guilt-crazed dropout lawyers from San Francisco—some dingbat who ate one too many tacos and decided he was really Emiliano Zapata."

Which was okay, I felt, but it was a hard act to handle in Aspen in that high white summer of 1967. That was the era of *Sgt. Pepper's*, *Surrealistic Pillow*, and the original Buffalo Springfield. It was a good year for everybody—or for *most* people, anyway. There were exceptions, as always. Lyndon Johnson was one, and Oscar Acosta was another. For entirely different reasons. That was not a good summer to be either the president of the United States or an angry Mexican lawyer in Aspen.

Oscar didn't hang around long. He washed dishes for a while, did a bit of construction work, bent the county judge out of shape a few times, then took off for Mexico to "get serious." The next thing I heard, he was working for the public defender's office in L.A. That was sometime around Christmas of 1968, which was not a good year for anybody—

except Richard Nixon and perhaps Oscar Acosta. Because by that time Oscar was beginning to find his own track. He was America's only "Chicano lawyer," he explained in a letter, and he liked it. His clients were all Chicanos and most were "political criminals," he said. And if they were guilty it was only because they were "doing what had to be done."

That's fine, I said. But I couldn't really get into it. I was all *for it*, you understand, but only on the basis of a personal friendship. *Most* of my friends are into strange things I don't totally understand—and with a few shameful exceptions I wish them all well. Who am I, after all, to tell some friend he shouldn't change his name to Oliver High, get rid of his family, and join a Satanism cult in Seattle? Or to argue with another friend who wants to buy a single-shot Remington Fireball so he can go out and shoot cops from a safe distance?

Whatever's right, I say. Never fuck with a friend's head by accident. And if their private trips get out of control now and then—well, you do what has to be done.

Which more or less explains how I suddenly found myself involved in the murder of Ruben Salazar. I was up in Portland, Oregon, at the time, trying to cover the National American Legion Convention and the Sky River Rock Festival at the same time . . . and I came back to my secret room in the Hilton one night to find an "urgent message" to call Mr. Acosta in Los Angeles.

I wondered how he had managed to track me down in Portland. But I knew, somehow, what he was calling about. I had seen the *L.A. Times* that morning, with the story of Salazar's death, and even at a distance of two thousand miles it gave off a powerful stench. The problem was not just a gimp or a hole in the story; the whole goddamn thing was wrong. It made no sense at all.

The Salazar case had a very special hook in it: not that he was a Mexican or a Chicano, and not even Acosta's angry insistence that the cops had killed him in cold blood and that nobody was going to do anything about it. These were all proper ingredients for an outrage, but from my own point of view the most ominous aspect of Oscar's story was his charge that the police had deliberately gone out on the streets and killed a reporter who'd been giving them trouble. If this was true, it meant the ante was being upped drastically. When the cops declare open season on journalists, when they feel free to declare any scene of "unlawful protest" a free fire zone, that will be a very ugly day—and not just for journalists.

• • •

Ruben Salazar was killed in the wake of a Watts-style riot that erupted when hundreds of cops attacked a peaceful rally in Laguna Park, where five thousand or so liberal/student/activist type Chicanos had gathered to protest the drafting of "Aztlan citizens" to fight for the U.S. in Vietnam. The police suddenly appeared in Laguna Park, with no warning, and "dispersed the crowd" with a blanket of tear gas followed up by a Chicago-style mop-up with billyclubs. The crowd fled in panic and anger, inflaming hundreds of young spectators who ran the few blocks to Whittier Boulevard and began trashing every store in sight. Several buildings were burned to the ground; damage was estimated at somewhere around a million dollars. Three people were killed, sixty injured—but the central incident of that August 29, 1970, rally was the killing of Ruben Salazar.

And six months later, when the National Chicano Moratorium Committee felt it was time for another mass rally, they called it to "carry on the spirit of Ruben Salazar."

There is irony in this, because Salazar was nobody's militant. He was a professional journalist with ten years of experience on a variety of assignments for the neo-liberal *Los Angeles Times*. He was a nationally known reporter, winning prizes for his work in places like Vietnam, Mexico City, and the Dominican Republic. Ruben Salazar was a veteran war correspondent, but he had never shed blood under fire. He was good, and he seemed to like the work. So he must have been slightly bored when the *Times* called him back from the war zones, for a raise and a well-deserved rest covering "local affairs."

He focused on the huge barrio just east of city hall. This was a scene he had never really known, despite his Mexican-American heritage. But he locked into it almost instantly. Within months, he had narrowed his work for the *Times* down to a once-a-week column for the newspaper, and signed on as news director for KMEX-TV—the "Mexican-American station," which he quickly transformed into an energetic, aggressively political voice for the whole Chicano community. His coverage of police activities made the East Los Angeles Sheriff's Department so unhappy that they soon found themselves in a sort of running private argument with this man Salazar, this spic who refused to be reasonable. When Salazar got onto a routine story like some worthless kid named Ramirez getting beaten to death in a jail fight, he was likely to come up with almost anything—including a series of hard-hitting news commentaries strongly suggesting that the victim had been beaten to death by the jailers. In the summer of 1970 Ruben Salazar was warned three times, by the cops, to "tone down his coverage." And each time he told them to fuck off.

This was not common knowledge in the community until after he was murdered. When he went out to cover the rally that August afternoon, he was still a "Mexican-American journalist." But by the time his body was carried out of the Silver Dollar, he was a stone Chicano martyr. Salazar would have smiled at this irony, but he would not have seen much humor in the way the story of his death was handled by the cops and the politicians. Nor would he have been pleased to know that almost immediately after his death his name would become a battle cry, prodding thousands of young Chicanos who had always disdained "protest" into an undeclared war with the hated gringo police.

• • •

His paper, the *L.A. Times*, carried the account of its former foreign correspondent's death on its Monday front page: "Mexican-American newsman Ruben Salazar was killed by a bullet-like tear gas shell fired by a sheriff's deputy into a bar during rioting Saturday in East Los Angeles." The details were hazy, but the new, hastily revised police version was clearly constructed to show that Salazar was the victim of a Regrettable Accident which the cops were not aware of until many hours later. Sheriff's deputies had cornered an armed man in a bar, they said, and when he refused to come out—even after "loud warnings" (with a bullhorn) "to evacuate"—"the tear gas shells were fired and several persons ran out the back door."

At that time, according to the sheriff's nervous mouthpiece, Lt. Norman Hamilton, a woman and two men—one carrying a 7.65 automatic pistol—were met by deputies, who questioned them. "I don't know whether the man with the gun was arrested on a weapons violation or not," Hamilton added.

Ruben Salazar was not among those persons who ran out the back door. He was lying on the floor inside, with a huge hole in his head. But the police didn't know this, Lieutenant Hamilton explained, because "they didn't enter the bar until approximately 8 PM, when rumors began circulating that Salazar was missing," and "an unidentified man across the street from the bar" told a deputy, "I think there's an injured man in there." "At this point," said Hamilton, "deputies knocked down the door and found the body." Two and a half hours later, at 10:40 PM, the sheriff's office admitted that "the body" was Ruben Salazar.

"Hamilton could not explain," said the *Times*, "why two accounts of the incident given to the *Times* by avowed eyewitnesses differed from the sheriff's account."

For about twenty-four hours Hamilton clung grimly to his original story—a composite, he said, of firsthand police accounts. According to this version, Ruben Salazar had been "killed by errant gunfire . . . during the height of a sweep of more than seven thousand people in [Laguna] Park when police ordered everyone to disperse." Local TV and radio newscasts offered sporadic variations on this theme—citing reports "still under investigation" that Salazar had been shot accidentally by careless street snipers. It was tragic, of course, but tragedies like this are inevitable when crowds of innocent people allow themselves to be manipulated by a handful of violent, cop-hating anarchists.

By late Sunday, however, the sheriff's story had collapsed completely—in the face of sworn testimony from four men who were standing within ten feet of Ruben Salazar when he died in the Silver Dollar Cafe at 4045 Whittier Boulevard, at least a mile from Laguna Park. But the real shocker came when these men testified that Salazar had been killed—not by snipers or errant gunfire—by a cop with a deadly tear gas bazooka.

Acosta had no trouble explaining the discrepancy. "They're lying," he said. "They *murdered* Salazar and now they're trying to cover it up. The sheriff already panicked. All he can say is, 'No comment.' He's ordered every cop in the county to *say nothing* to anybody—especially the press. They've turned the East L.A. sheriff's station into a fortress. Armed guards all around it." He laughed. "Shit, the place looks like a prison—but with all the cops *inside*!"

Sheriff Peter J. Pitchess refused to talk to me when I called. The rude aftermath of the Salazar killing had apparently unhinged him completely. On Monday he called off a scheduled press conference and instead issued a statement, saying: "There are just too many conflicting stories, some from our own officers, as to what happened. The sheriff wants an opportunity to digest them before meeting with newsmen."

• • •

Indeed. Sheriff Pitchess was not alone in his inability to digest the garbled swill that his office was doling out. The official version of the Salazar killing was so crude and illogical—even after revisions—that not even the sheriff seemed surprised when it began to fall apart even before Chicano partisans had a chance to attack it. Which they would, of course. The sheriff had already got wind of what was coming: many eyewitnesses, sworn statements, firsthand accounts—all of them hostile.

The history of Chicano complaints against cops in East L.A. is not a happy one. "The cops never lose," Acosta told me, "and they won't lose this one either. They just murdered the only guy in the community they were really afraid of, and I guarantee you no cop will ever stand trial for it. Not even for manslaughter."

I could accept that. But it was difficult, even for me, to believe that the cops had killed him deliberately. I knew they were capable of it, but I was not quite ready to believe they had actually done it . . . because once I believed that, I also had to accept the idea that they are prepared to kill anybody who seemed to be annoying them. Even me.

As for Acosta's charge of murder, I knew him well enough to understand how he could make that charge *publicly* . . . I also knew him well enough to be sure he wouldn't try to hang that kind of monstrous bullshit on me. So our phone talk naturally disturbed me . . . and I fell to brooding about it, hung on my own dark suspicions that Oscar had told me the truth.

On the plane to L.A. I tried to make some kind of a case—either pro or con—from my bundle of notes and newsclips relating to Salazar's death. By that time at least six reportedly reliable witnesses had made sworn statements that differed drastically, on several crucial points, with the original police version—which nobody believed anyway. There was something very disturbing about the sheriff's account of that accident; it wasn't even a good *lie*.

Within hours after the *Times* hit the streets with the news that Ruben Salazar had in fact been killed by cops—rather than street snipers—the sheriff unleashed a furious assault on "known dissidents" who had flocked into East Los Angeles that weekend, he said, to provoke a disastrous riot in the Mexican-American community. He praised his deputies for the skillful zeal they displayed in restoring order to the area within two and a half hours, "thus averting a major holocaust of much greater proportions."

• • •

Meanwhile, evidence was building up that Ruben Salazar had been murdered—either deliberately or for no reason at all. The most damaging anti-cop testimony thus far had come from Guillermo Restrepo, a twenty-eight-year-old reporter and newscaster for KMEX-TV, who was covering the "riot" with Salazar that afternoon, and who had gone with him into the Silver Dollar Cafe "to take a leak and drink a quick beer before we went back to the station to put the story together." Restrepo's testimony was solid enough on its own to cast a filthy shadow on the original police version, but when he produced two *more* eyewitnesses who told exactly the same story, the sheriff abandoned all hope and sent his scriptwriters back to the sty.

Guillermo Restrepo is well known in East L.A.—a familiar figure to every Chicano who owns a TV set. Restrepo is the out-front public face of KMEX-TV news . . . and Ruben Salazar, until August 29, 1970, was the man behind the news—the editor.

They worked well together, and on that Saturday when the Chicano "peace rally" turned into a Watts-style street riot, both Salazar and Restrepo decided that it might be wise if Restrepo—a native Colombian—brought two of his friends (also Colombians) to help out as spotters and de facto bodyguards.

Their names were Gustavo Garcia, age thirty, and Hector Fabio Franco, also thirty. Both men appear in a photograph (taken seconds before Salazar was killed) of a sheriff's deputy pointing a shotgun at the front door of the Silver Dollar Cafe. Garcia is the man right in front of the gun. When the picture was taken, he had just asked the cop what was going on, and the cop had just told him to get back inside the bar if he didn't want to be shot.

The sheriff's office was not aware of this photo until three days after it was taken—along with a dozen others—by two *more* eyewitnesses, who also happened to be editors of *La Raza*, a militant Chicano newspaper that calls itself "the voice of the East L.A. barrio."

The photographs were taken by Raul Ruiz, a twenty-eight-year-old teacher of Latin American studies at San Fernando Valley State College. Ruiz was on assignment for *La Raza* that day when the rally turned into a street war with the police. He and Joe Razo—a thirty-three-year-old law student with an MA in psychology—were following the action along Whittier Boulevard when they noticed a task force of sheriff's deputies preparing to assault the Silver Dollar Cafe.

Their accounts of what happened there—along with Ruiz's photos—were published in *La Raza* three days after the sheriff's office said Salazar had been killed a mile away in Laguna Park, by snipers and/or "errant gunfire."

The *La Raza* spread was a bombshell. The photos weren't much individually, but together—along with the Ruiz-Razo testimony—they showed that the cops were still lying when they came up with their second (revised) version of the Salazar killing.

It also verified the Restrepo-Garcia-Franco testimony, which had already shot down the original police version by establishing, beyond any doubt, that Ruben Salazar had been killed, by a deputy sheriff, in the Silver Dollar Cafe. They were certain of *that*, but no more. They were puzzled, they said, when the cops appeared with guns and began threatening them. But they decided to leave anyway—by the back door, since the cops wouldn't let anybody out of the front—and that was when the shooting started, less than thirty seconds after Garcia was photographed in front of that shotgun barrel on the sidewalk.

The weakness in the Restrepo-Garcia-Franco testimony was so obvious that not even the cops could miss it. They knew nothing beyond what had happened *inside* the Silver Dollar at the time of Salazar's death. There was no way they could have known what was happening *outside*, or *why* the cops started shooting.

The explanation came almost instantly from the sheriff's office—once again from Lt. Hamilton. The police had received an "anonymous report," he said, that "a man with a gun" was inside the Silver Dollar

Cafe. This was the extent of their "probable cause," their reason for doing what they did. These actions, according to Hamilton, consisted of "sending several deputies" to deal with the problem . . . and they did so by stationing themselves in front of the Silver Dollar and issuing "a loud warning" with a bullhorn calling all those inside to come outside with their hands above their heads.

• • •

There was no response, Hamilton said, so a deputy then fired two tear gas projectiles into the bar through the front door. At this point two men and a woman fled out the back, and one of the men was relieved by waiting deputies of a 7.65 caliber pistol. He was not arrested—not even detained—and at that point a deputy fired two more tear gas projectiles through the front door of the place.

Again there was no response, and after a fifteen-minute wait one of the braver deputies crept up and skillfully slammed the front door—*without entering*, Hamilton added. The only person who actually entered the bar, according to the police version, was the owner, Pete Hernandez, who showed up about half an hour after the shooting and asked if he could go inside and get his rifle.

Why not? said the cops, so Hernandez went in the *back door* and got his rifle out of the rear storeroom—about fifty feet away from where Ruben Salazar's body lay in a fog of rancid CS gas.

Then, for the next two hours, some two dozen sheriff's deputies cordoned off the street in front of the Silver Dollar's front door. This naturally attracted a crowd of curious Chicanos, not all of them friendly—and one, an eighteen-year-old girl, was shot in the leg with the same kind of tear gas bazooka that had blown Ruben Salazar's head apart.

• • •

The Salazar inquest rumbled on for sixteen days, attracting large crowds and live TV coverage from start to finish. (In a rare demonstration of nonprofit unity, all seven local TV stations formed a combine of sorts, assigning the coverage on a rotating basis, so that each day's proceedings appeared on a different channel.) The *L.A. Times* coverage—by Paul Houston and Dave Smith—was so complete and often so rife with personal intensity that the collected Smith-Houston file reads like a finely detailed nonfiction novel. Read separately, the articles are merely good journalism. But as a document, arranged chronologically, the file is more than the sum of its parts. The main theme seems to emerge almost reluctantly, as both reporters are driven to the obvious conclusion that the sheriff, along with his deputies and all his official allies, have been *lying* all along. This is never actually stated, but the evidence is overwhelming.

A coroner's inquest is not a trial. Its purpose is to determine the circumstances surrounding a person's death—not who might have killed him, or why. If the circumstances indicate foul play, the next step is up to the DA. In California a coroner's jury can reach only two possible verdicts: that the death was "accidental," or that it was "at the hands of another." And in the Salazar case, the sheriff and his allies *needed* a verdict of "accidental." Anything else would leave the case open—not only to the possibility of a murder or manslaughter trial for the deputy, Tom Wilson, who finally admitted firing the death weapon; but also to the threat of a $1 million negligence lawsuit against the County by Salazar's widow.

The verdict finally hinged on whether or not the jury could believe Wilson's testimony that he fired into the Silver Dollar—at the *ceiling*—in order to ricochet a tear gas shell into the rear of the bar and force the armed stranger inside to come out the front door. But somehow Ruben Salazar had managed to get his head in the way of that carefully aimed shell. Wilson had never been able to figure out, he said, what went wrong.

Nor could he figure out how Raul Ruiz had managed to "doctor" those photographs that made it look like he and at least one other deputy were aiming their weapons straight into the Silver Dollar, pointing them directly at people's heads. Ruiz had no trouble explaining it. His testimony at the inquest was no different than the story he had told me just a few days after the murder. And when the inquest was over, there was nothing in the 2,025 pages of testimony—from 61 witnesses and 204 exhibits—to cast any serious doubt on the "Chicano Eyewitness Report" that Ruiz wrote for *La Raza* when the sheriff was still maintaining that Salazar had been killed by "errant gunfire" during the violence at Laguna Park.

• • •

The inquest ended with a split verdict. Smith's lead paragraph in the October 6 *Times* read like an obituary: "Monday the inquest into the death of newsman Ruben Salazar ended. The 16-day inquiry, by far the longest and costliest such affair in county history, concluded with a verdict that confuses many, satisfies few and means little. The coroner's jury came up with two verdicts: death was 'at the hands of another person' (four jurors) and death was by 'accident' (three jurors). Thus, inquests might appear to be a waste of time."

A week later, District Attorney Evelle Younger—a staunch Law & Order man—announced that he had reviewed the case and decided that "no criminal charge is justified," despite the unsettling fact two of the three jurors who had voted for the "death by accident" verdict were now saying they had made a mistake.

But by that time nobody really gave a damn. The Chicano community had lost faith in the inquest about midway through the second day, and all the rest of the testimony only reinforced their anger at what most considered an evil whitewash. When the DA announced that no charges would be filed against Wilson, several of the more moderate Chicano spokesmen called for a federal investigation. The militants called for an uprising. And the cops said nothing—at all.

• • •

The night before I left town I stopped by Acosta's place with Guillermo Restrepo. I had been there earlier, but the air was extremely heavy. As always, on stories like this, some of the troops were getting nervous about The Stranger Hanging Around. I was standing in the kitchen watching Frank put some tacos together and wondering when he was going to start waving the butcher knife in my face and yelling about the time I Maced him on my porch in Colorado (that had been six months earlier, at the end of a very long night during which we had all consumed a large quantity of cactus products; and when he started waving a hatchet around I'd figured Mace was the only answer . . . which turned him to jelly for about forty-five minutes, and when he finally came around he said, "If I ever see you in East Los Angeles, man, you're gonna wish you never heard the word 'Mace,' because I'm gonna carve it all over your fuckin' body.").

So I was not entirely at ease watching Frank chop hamburger on a meat block in the middle of East L.A. He hadn't mentioned the Mace, not yet, but I knew we would get to it sooner or later . . . and I'm sure we would have, except that suddenly out in the living room some geek was screaming: "What the hell is this goddamn gabacho pig writer doing here? Are we fuckin' *crazy* to be letting him hear all this shit? Jesus, he's heard enough to put every one of us away for five years!"

Longer than that, I thought. And at that point I stopped worrying about Frank. A firestorm was brewing in the main room—between me and the door—so I decided it was about time to drift around the corner and meet Restrepo at the Carioca. Frank gave me a big smile as I left.

• • •

"Losing Ruben was a goddamn disaster for the Movement," Acosta said recently. "He wasn't really *with* us, but at least he was interested. Hell, the truth is I never really liked the guy. But he was the only journalist in L.A. with real influence who would come to a press conference in the barrio. That's the truth. Hell, the only way we can get those bastards to listen to us is by renting a fancy hotel lounge over there in West Hollywood or some bullshit place like that—where *they* can feel comfortable—and hold our press conference there. With free coffee and snacks for the press. But even then about half the shitheads won't come unless we serve free booze, too. Shit! Do you know what that *costs*?"

• • •

This was the tone of our conversation that night when Guillermo and I went over to Oscar's pad for a beer and some talk about politics. The place was unnaturally quiet. No music, no grass, no bad-mouth *bato loco* types hunkered down on the pallets in the front room. It was the first time I'd seen the place when it didn't look like a staging area for some kind of hellish confrontation that might erupt at any moment.

But tonight it was deadly quiet. The only interruption was a sudden pounding on the door and voices shouting "Hey, man, open up. I got some *brothers* with me!" Rudy hurried to the door and peered out through the tiny eye-window. Then he stepped back and shook his head emphatically. "It's some guys from the project," he told Oscar. "I know them, but they're all fucked up."

"God*damn* it," Acosta muttered. "That's the last thing I need tonight. Get rid of them. Tell them I have to be in court tomorrow. Jesus! I *have* to get some sleep!"

Rudy and Frank went outside to deal with the brothers. Oscar and Guillermo went back to politics—while I listened, sensing a downhill drift on all fronts. *Nothing* was going right. He was expecting a decision on his Grand Jury challenge in the "Biltmore Six" case. "We'll probably lose that one, too," he said. "The bastards think they have us on the run now; they think we're demoralized—so they'll keep the pressure on, keep pushing." He shrugged. "And maybe they're right. Shit. I'm tired of arguing with them. How long do they expect me to keep coming down to their goddamn court-house and begging for justice? I'm tired of that shit. We're *all* tired." He shook his head slowly, then ripped the poptop of a Budweiser that Rudy brought in from the kitchen. "This legal bullshit ain't makin' it," he went on. "The way it looks now, I think we're just about finished with that game. You know at the noon recess today I had to keep a bunch of these goddamn *batos locos* from stomping the DA. Christ! That would fuck me for good. They'll send me to the goddamn pen for hiring thugs to assault the prosecutor!" He shook his head again. "Frankly, I think the whole thing is out of control. God only knows where it's heading, but I know it's going to be heavy. I think maybe the real shit is about to come down."

• • •

Later that week, the Los Angeles Board of Supervisors voted to use public funds to pay all legal expenses for several policemen recently indicted for "accidentally" killing two Mexican nationals—a case known in East L.A. as "the murder of the Sanchez brothers." It was a case of mistaken identity, the cops explained. They had somehow been given the wrong address of an apartment where they thought "two Mexican fugitives" were holed up, so they hammered on the door and shouted a warning to "come out of there with your hands over your head or we'll come in shooting." Nobody came out, so the cops went in shooting to kill.

But how could they have known that they'd attacked the wrong apartment? And how could they have known that neither one of the Sanchez brothers understood English? Even Mayor Sam Yorty and Police Chief Ed Davis admitted that the killings had been very unfortunate. But when the federal DA brought charges against the cops, both Yorty and Davis were publicly outraged. They both called press conferences and went on the air to denounce the indictments—in language that strangely echoed the American Legion outcry when Lt. Calley was charged with murdering women and children at My Lai.

The Yorty-Davis tirades were so gross that a District Court judge finally issued a "gag order" to keep them quiet until the case comes to trial. But they had already said enough to whip the whole barrio into a rage at the idea that Chicano tax dollars might be used to defend some "mad dog cops" who frankly admitted killing two Mexican nationals. It sounded like a replay of the Salazar bullshit: same style, same excuse, same result—but this time with different names, and blood on a different floor. "They'll put me in jail if I won't pay taxes," said a young Chicano watching a soccer game at a local playground, "then they take my tax money and use it to defend some killer pig. Hell, what if they had come to my address by mistake? I'd be dead as hell right now."

There was a lot of talk in the barrio about "drawing some pig blood for a change" if the supervisors actually voted to use tax funds to defend the accused cops. A few people actually called city hall and mumbled anonymous threats in the name of the "Chicano Liberation Front." But the supervisors hung tough. They voted on Thursday, and by noon the news was out: the city would pick up the tab.

• • •

At five fifteen on Thursday afternoon, the Los Angeles City Hall was rocked by a dynamite blast. A bomb had been planted in one of the downstairs restrooms. Nobody was hurt, and the damage was officially described as "minor." About $5,000 worth, they said—small potatoes, compared to the bomb that blew a wall out of the District Attorney's office last fall after Salazar died.

When I called the sheriff's office to ask about the explosion they said they couldn't talk about it. City hall was out of their jurisdiction. But they were more than willing to talk when I asked if it was true that the bomb had been the work of the Chicano Liberation Front.

"Where'd you hear that?"

"From the City News Service."

"Yeah, it's true," he said. "Some woman called up and said it was done in memory of the Sanchez brothers, by the Chicano Liberation Front. We've heard about those guys. What do *you* know about them?"

"Nothing," I said. "That's why I called the sheriff. I thought your intelligence network might know something."

"Sure they do," he said quickly. "But all that information is confidential."

First in a Series

By the summer of 1971, Hunter's relationship with the magazine was humming; he was an infrequent, if notorious, presence around the office and began to see himself as integrally involved in Rolling Stone*'s operations; to that effect, he initiated the first in an occasional and long-running series of "Memos from the Sports Desk"—short diatribes and mini manifestos covering issues of the day ranging from office politics to international conspiracies. The first such memo—on the emerging born-again menace infiltrating the local culture—featured the first* Rolling Stone *byline of Hunter's most infamous alter ego, Raoul Duke.*

Letter from HST to JSW

June 8 '71

Jann . . .

This (enc.) thing began as a one-graf note—sort of a quick edit joke. I'm not sure what it is now. Apparently I was more into it than I thought.

Which is true. This Jesus trip will tie us all in knots for at least the next year, unless we deal with it quick. I've seen what the Zen/Macro influence can do to Realpolitik—and this Jesus bullshit is simply a new twist in the old Big Answer game. These simple bastards refuse to accept the notion that they have to *do* something. They keep waiting for The Answer to turn up on some fucking scroll—or maybe a Tarot card.

Anyway, here's a Memo for you. I hesitate to even suggest what might be done with it. As the Sports Editor, I feel entitled to a certain modicum of craziness, but—even so—I'm not sure I'd like to see this in print with an italicized "editors note" saying "here's what crazy Hunter wrote this week." That last thing about the human drug-testing apparatus was all I need for this season.

OK for now.

HST

Memo from the Sports Desk: The So-Called "Jesus Freak" Scare

September 2, 1971

A recent emergency survey of our field-sources indicates a firestorm of lunacy brewing on the neo-religious front. Failure to prepare for this madness could tax our resources severely—perhaps to the breaking point. During the next few months we will almost certainly be inundated, even swamped, by a nightmare-blizzard of schlock, gibberish, swill, & pseudo-religious bullshit of every type and description. We can expect no relief until after Christmas. This problem will manifest itself in many treacherous forms—and we will have to deal with them all. To wit:

1) The mailroom will be paralyzed by wave after wave of pamphlets, records, warnings and half-mad screeds from Persons and/or Commercial Organizations attempting to cash in on this grisly shuck. So we have already made arrangements to establish an alternative mailroom, to handle our serious business.

2) We expect the main elevators to be jammed up, day and night, by a never-ending swarm of crazies attempting to drag huge wooden crosses and other over-sized gimcracks into the building. To circumvent this, we are even now in the process of installing a powerful glass/cube electric lift on the *exterior* of the building for employee/business & general editorial use. The ingress/egress door will be cut in the east wall, behind Dave Felton's cubicle. The ground-floor door will be disguised as a huge packing crate in the parking lot. An armed guard will be on duty at all times.

3) We expect the phone lines to be tied up almost constantly by hired and/or rabid *Jesus Freaks* attempting to get things like "Today's Prayer Message," etc., into our editorial columns. Our policy will be *not* to re-

ject these things: no, we will *accept* them. They will all be switched to a special automated phone extension in the basement of the building. Yail Bloor, the eminent theologist, has prepared a series of recorded replies for calls of this nature. Any callers who resist automation can leave their names & numbers, so Inspector Bloor can return their calls and deal with them personally between the hours of 2:00 and 6:00 AM.

These are only a few of the specific horrors that we will have to come to grips with between now and September. There will, of course, be others—less tangible and far more sensitive—such as Subversion of Key Personnel. As always, there will be a few brainless scumbags going under—succumbing, as it were—to the lure of this latest cult. We expect this, and when these organizational blow-holes appear, they will be *plugged* with extreme speed & savagery.

It is the view of the Sports Desk that a generation of failed dingbats and closet-junkies should under no circumstances be allowed to foul our lines of communication at a time when anybody with access to a thinking/nationwide audience has an almost desperate obligation to speak *coherently*. This is not the year for a mass reversion to atavistic bullshit—and particularly not in the pages of *Rolling Stone*.

We expect the pressure to mount in geometric progressions from now until December, & then to peak around Christmas. Meanwhile, it is well to remember the words of Dr. Heem, one of the few modern-day wizards who has never been wrong. Dr. Heem was cursed by Eisenhower, mocked by Kennedy, jeered by Tim Leary, and threatened by Eldridge Cleaver. But he is still on the stump . . . still hustling.

"The future of Christianity is far too fragile," he said recently, "to be left in the hands of the Christians—especially *pros*."

The Sports Desk feels very strongly about this. Further warnings will issue, as special problems arise. Which they will. We are absolutely certain of this, if nothing else. What we are faced with today is the same old Rising Tide that's been coming for the past five years or more . . . the same old evil, menacing, frog-eyed trip of a whole generation run amok from too many failures.

Which is fine. It was long overdue. And once again in the words of Dr. Heem, "Sometimes the old walls are so cock-eyed that you can't even fit a new window." But the trouble with the *Jesus Freak* outburst is that it is less a window than a gigantic ingrown hair. Horrible things have been done in the name of "Christianity": the Spanish Inquisition, the Salem Witch Trials, the Rape of the Congo, and the Conquest of the Incas, the Mayans, and the Aztecs. Entire civilizations have been done in by vengeful monsters claiming a special relationship with "God."

What we are dealing with now is nothing less than another Empire on the brink of collapse—more than likely of its own bad weight & twisted priorities. This process is already well underway. Everything Nixon stands for is doomed, now or later.

But it will sure as hell be *later* if the best alternative we can mount is a generation of loonies who've given up on everything except a revival of the same old primitive bullshit that caused all our troubles from the start. What a *horror* to think that all the fine, high action of the Sixties would somehow come down—ten years later—to a gross & mindless echo of Billy Sunday.

This is why the Sports Desk insists that these waterheads must be kept out of the building at all costs. We have serious business to deal with, and these fuckers will only be in the way.

Sincerely,
Raoul Duke

Handwritten Note Concerning Hunter's Invitation to National District Attorneys Conference

3/4

Jann

This just came—& I think it's a *must*.

I *insist* on doing this one. After all, I've been *invited*.

Right?

HST

Fear & Loathing in Las Vegas

Hunter's invitation to the National District Attorneys Association's institute on narcotics and dangerous drugs wasn't quite as impossible as it might seem on the surface; having nearly been elected sheriff of Aspen not long earlier, Hunter made sure his name was on various political and law enforcement mailing lists. When the invitation did show up, though, he wasted little time in seizing the moment. What eventually followed, of course, was Hunter's most sustained and compelling sui generis piece ever, begun in between stints working on the Salazar story.

"Working with Hunter was already a major hand-holding job," said Wenner. "It meant a minimum of two, maybe three people assigned to the task, including me. It was too much for any one person to handle, even that early on, because of the hours and the time Hunter took. He liked having a team of people working on his stuff. He liked the company, and he liked the crisis atmosphere. I could never change that pattern.

"But 'Vegas' was completely different. He did that on his own. It took him several months to write it. He'd send me pages. I'd change a word here or suggest a little thing there, but it was already completely formed. I'd ask him to write transitions to make the narrative more complete, but he politely and firmly refused. It was his pure fantasy, coming directly out of his own mind. There was no real reporting involved, except when he wanted to go back and do the District Attorneys Conference, which was hysterical and had pure gonzo potential."

Letter from HST to JSW

June 15 '71

Owl Farm
Woody Creek, Colorado

Dear Jann . . .

I'm sending today, under sep. cover, an accidental classic of a photo to go with the Vegas thing. As I noted in the margin, Acosta's name should *not* be mentioned without his permission. He's not opposed to use of the photo, but as of now he's concerned about seeing his name etched permanently in the caption. I understand this, and agreed that he would only be identified as "my attorney."

My own caption-ID is *personally* immaterial to me. The Raoul Duke byline, however, might not be entirely viable if Random House decides to use Vegas II in the American Dream book—by HST. This is an option that [Random House editor in chief James] Silberman bought—very cheap, I think—when he paid the Expense tab for both Vegas pieces (less $500 that was paid out in cash & remains un-reimbursed). What he paid was the Carte Blanche bill, but not in time to beat the computer that took my card. The swine cut me off last week—no warning at all, just a massive cut-off & a vicious letter from the Harbour Detective Agency, saying I should cut my card in half & send it back. I refused, of course, but that doesn't alter the fact that my number is now on the "to be arrested at once" list that circulates among CB dealers.

The fact that I blame you for this is probably unjust in the long run—but of course there was never any real question of "the long run." All I wanted to do was pay off my card, and talk about "Fiscal Responsibility" later.

Which is neither here nor there, for now. The deed is done. I am now naked of credit. And this ugly fact is going to put a bad crimp in my working-style for a long time to come. Selah . . .

* * *

As for Vegas, it's coming along very slowly. Silberman thinks it should go in the AmDream book, but I disagree. The Vegas stuff is too twisted, I think, to anchor a serious book. But what will probably happen, now, is that I'll have to pursuede [*sic*] Silberman of that and then trade him book rights on "The Battle of Aspen—An Epitaph for Freak Power?" for the entirety of Vegas. And this dealing will be subject in a lot of ways to The Schedule—my planned departure for Siagon [*sic*] on Sept 1.

So we'll have at least this to ponder when you get here. Sandy says you called Sunday & then today. I was far into madness on Sunday—[Hunter's friend and writer] Lucian Truscott showed up with a huge bag of mescaline—and today I was too cosmically pissed off to talk about anything. Especially money—which you seem to have indicated would be the subject under discussion. I had a terrible scene with the dentist earlier today: One of the side-horrors of Vegas II was that I bit down on something that cracked three of my teeth—a problem I was unaware of until I went in a few days ago for my routine 6-month cleaning.

Shit, I'll call you tomorrow. I'm vaguely concerned, among other things, about that "Jesus Freak memo" from the Sports Desk . . . if there's any possibility that it might be published, I want to talk about it first. (Meanwhile, I've prepared Sports Desk Memo #2—On the subject of "drug Lyrics in Rock Music.") The very nature of this format makes the writing a bit heavy. #1 began as a joke—and perhaps it ended that way. I can't be sure. Whenever I belch out my bias that strongly, it takes on an element of craziness . . . and I want to be careful of this. In the past two weeks I've received copies of two different books that used "selections" from "Hell's Angels," and in both cases I was shocked at what happens to my stuff when it's printed out of context. All it takes is a few cuts on the Humor to make the rest seem like the ravings of a dangerous lunatic.

Anyway, we can deal with these things when you get here. It's possible that Noonan will be gone, and if he is you can stay in his house—which would probably be preferable, from your end, to using the guest room here. Which is definitely available—complete with White Sound. But I'll talk to you tomorrow, before you get this, and get a fix on your travel dates.

OK for now . . .

HST

Letter from HST to JSW, July 30, 1971

7/30

Owl Farm
Woody Creek, Colorado

Jann/

Vegas is emerging from a bad case of stomach flu, combined with a water war that went a lot closer to the edge than I planned on.

It took me 2 days to bring the fucker under control—which included the croaking, tonight, of a "takeover bid" on the Owl Farm by M. Burns. (with [producer Bob] Rafelson)

Plenty of action out here—about 40 defecations a day & 20 vomitings, along with all the rest.

I feel very weak.

Ciao/
H

Undated letter from HST to JSW

Jann . . .

Vegas Two took a great leap forward yesterday; it finally developed a plotline. Only one big chunk still needs to be done—the Drug Conference itself. (Oh yeah—& there's also the ending.) Last week was totally consumed by the Water War. I won, but it cost me six full days of time & energy.

I figure Vegas will take another week, but let me know if you smell any deadlines I haven't been told about. October is a long way off, but I want to finish the fucker and get done with The Battle of Aspen.

I also want to decide, very soon, about this Washington gig—mainly because I have to know whether or not my house will be for rent this winter. I'd like to stay here as long as possible, but October 1 would probably be the deadline for getting it rented. In other words, I'd probably have to be *out* by then. There's a chance I could stretch that until Xmas by putting the tenant/family in the Iguana house, temporarily, but I haven't checked this out. Ideally, the Washington thing should be a one-year contract of sorts, from November to November. That would be the most convenient for a house/hq. lease in DC, and also from most other aspects. (Hell, I see where this kind of thing presents infinite complications, so I'll leave it alone for now) . . . but if you give it any thought in the meantime, keep in mind that my main considerations are:

1) Having enough money to move freely—not only in Washington, but also around the primaries (which means a fairly heavy airline/hotel tab for an extended period of time)

2) Being able to rent these houses, out here, so I won't have to worry about this end.

3) Having a certain amount of autonomy, inre: paying for information & that sort of thing. Dan Greene could provide a vast amount of sub rosa help, for instance, but not for very long unless we paid. (That Randy Agnew contact was a pure accident, resulting from my request that he track down the eyeball man, and he told me about it more on a gossip basis than a story lead.)

Anyway, I'm having dinner with [*New York Times* journalist] Max Frankel Tuesday night, and I'll warn him that I plan to be baying at his heels throughout the whole campaign. Actually—given the two-week deadline and some money to put people like Greene and maybe Bob Sherrill on a quiet-stringer basis, I think we could make the "Washington page" (or whatever) a sort of infamous press classic for the length of the whole campaign—not *competing* with the Fat City press, but riding herd on them; playing the Wolverine, as it were. A sort of Nader trip, focusing on the traditional & inevitable incest that seems to be the basis of the press/power relationship in Washington. Like a self-appointed ombudsman, hassling *everybody*—not just Nixon & Muskie—in the interest of that New/Dropout vote bloc we've talked about. The idea would be to approach the thing more as a lobby-interest than a straight observer—opening a news bureau with the undeclared option of using it, if necessary, as a de facto campaign headquarters. Which it would probably become, anyway, if we can put this Essalen [*sic*] idea together & come up with a platform.

Ciao,
H

Undated letter from HST to JSW

Saturday

Owl Farm
Woody Creek, Colorado

Jann . . .

Right after I hung up last night I realized you said the award was for "unstapled" journalism—but the word I got was *unstable*. Which made me wonder why you seemed so pleased. Or maybe I just felt guilty—one of those Freudian misunderstandings. Since I was working on the Las Vegas piece at the time, it figured. "Unstable," indeed! Those swine. Next year we should demand a Gonzo category—or maybe *RS* should give it. Of course. "The First Annual *Rolling Stone* Award for the Year's Finest Example of Pure Gonzo Journalism." First Prize: a gallon of raw ether. Second: a Pepper-Fogger, donated by the ELA Sheriff's Dept. Third: A free trip to the 1972 Mint 400 in Las Vegas to anybody with the balls to go out there and apply for "*Rolling Stone*" press credentials.

Ciao,
Hunter

Letter from HST to JSW

Monday Aug '71

Owl Farm
Woody Creek, Colorado

Jann . . .

Here's the *tentatively*-finished draft of Vegas II, Section One. I'm not sure it moves fast enough; maybe I need something rude & heavy injected up front . . . but right now I can't make that kind of judgement, so I might as well send this part off and wait a week or so before trying to read it objectively.

This is about 11,000 words, I think. I have maybe 10K more already written & waiting to be typed & chronologically fitted. My guess is that the whole of Vegas Two will run between 25 and 30K words. And that's plenty. Perhaps too much. The effectiveness of the story depends on its hi-speed pace. We can afford to slow it down a bit once we get to the book stage, but we can't afford anything slow or sluggish in the *RS* version . . . or readers will "take a break" & never come back.

You should read the first section with this in mind . . . keeping in mind, of course, that it's actually the middle (in book terms), so the crucial thing in this part is to build to a Climax, which should come at the end of Section Two . . . and then use Sec 3 at the Ending. I have a fairly clear notion of where I'm going . . . so what you should be thinking about right now is putting Alan on the phone with [Hunter's agent] Lynn [Nesbit] & Silberman, to work out the book-arrangements. That money is my down payment on the Owl Farm—120 acres & both houses, a deal that we just settled tonight.

OK for now . . .

HST

Undated 1971 letter from HST to JSW

Owl Farm
Woody Creek, Colorado

Jann/

Here's the rest of Vegas—minus a few graphs, but let's get it sorted out & cut before I start adding graphs. Otherwise, it will just keep growing.

Great rush & chaos here—the cops have a bench warrant for me—Sandy is vomiting all over the house—*seven* Dobermans underfoot, no sleep, *snowing* outside.

Send the $500 at once. I'm down to zero.

Thanx/
H

Letter from HST to JSW, September 14, 1971

9/14—Tues

Jann/

I'm making these final correx (galleys) on the plane to NY—going over it all again & finding typos I missed the first time.

No doubt I'll miss some on this round, too. All writers tend to read over their own mistakes. So you should definitely have somebody look at this for typos, missing words, etc.

One thing I want to add, up front, in Vegas I is a set of directions on *how* to read it . . . what music to play at top volume, what drugs to eat, ("read only between 2 & 6 a.m.," etc.)—Just a box, about 250 words, at the start. Do I have time to get this in?

Letter from HST to JSW

10/15/71

Owl Farm
Woody Creek, Colorado

Jann/

My mail today contained a wholly unreadable Xerox of the galleys for Vegas II. Totally worthless—& also totally unnecessary. I can't even read the fuckers, much less correct them. What's so fucking difficult about sending me some *galleys*? And whoever initialed these grey-hazy things should be fired. On G-45, I notice the word "teach"—in big black caps—spelled "TETCH." Uncorrected & apparently un-noticed . . . which makes me wonder what kind of typo-horrors might be lurking in that fog of grey shit I can't even begin to read or even see. (Jesus! I see another gross error just one inch down from "TETCH."

Fuck it—I refuse to search for any more. Only 2 of the 14 "galleys" are even initialed—it looks like even the proofreader gave up. (The "TETCH" pg. is *not* initialed). Jesus, what a mess. I'd appreciate another set of veloxes . . . along with some *galleys* I can read & work on.

Thanx
HST

Memo from the Sports Desk (Undated)

To all employees without exception

Why is the staff so fucking lazy? It's getting so I can't even walk fast through the hallways any more without stumbling over some freak on the nod.

Is it drugs? Has it come to that?

If so, by God, we're going to clean it up pretty damn fast. My attorney has worked out a series of disciplinary measures that will zap this thing where it lives.

Henceforth, anyone caught with narcotics, crazy pills, or other stupor inducing agents, will be dragged down to the basement and have his scrotum torn off . . . and, conversely, any offender *without* a scrotum will have one permanently attached to her.

We feel such measures are necessary, even vital, to the health of this organization. This is the unanimous opinion of the Sports Staff, & as editor, I mean to enforce it.

We will play no favorites. Beginning on the day after Christmas, any employee caught nodding out, jacking off, or otherwise squandering company time will pay the penalty.

This is a business—not a goddamn dude ranch, and any salaried person who feels he/she cannot abide by these new regulations had better get out *now*.

There will be no second warning. Copies of this notice will be posted in every corridor and they *shall not be defaced*.

Sincerely,
Raoul Duke
Sports Editor

Letter from HST to JSW, August 23, 1971

82371

Jann:

This thing is so fucking strange (to me) that I'm afraid to comment on it. I showed it to [Hunter's son] Juan, who's right in the middle of what Officer Bill says is the "impressionable age" . . . and he just smiled and tossed it aside after a quick scan. I got the feeling he thought I was putting him on. Anyway, don't lose the thing; I may need it later on. It was, by the way, part of Officer Bill's anti-drug package that I got in Vegas . . . and it strikes me as a good sample of the super-shrewd cop wisdom they were handing out there.

OK for now. Send it back if you don't see any place for it in the Vegas art stuff.

HST

Undated letter from National District Attorneys Association

National District Attorneys Association
211 East Chicago Avenue, Suite 1204
Chicago, Illinois 60611

To: All Las Vegas Drug Conference Attendees
From: Patrick F. Healy, Executive Director

It is my sincere pleasure to enclose your certificate of achievement in connection with your attendance at the Las Vegas Drug Conference.

If the NDAA can ever be of assistance to you, please feel free to call upon us.

Hunter writes to Jann as he nears completion of "Fear & Loathing in Las Vegas, Part II."

Jann . . .

The hole between our talk with the Georgia lawyer and "Back Door Beauty" should be properly and quite adequately filled by Steadman's art.

The hole between Back Door Beauty and "my attorney left at dawn" could use a slice of art, too . . . following the tape transcription.

The central problem here is that you're working overtime to treat this thing as Straight or at least Responsible journalism . . . whereas in truth we are dealing with a classic of irresponsible gibberish. You'd be better off trying to make objective, chronological sense of "Highway 61," *The Ginger Man*, "Mr. Tambourine Man," or even *Naked Lunch*.

Despite these onerous comparisons, I suspect the point still stands. And the real nut of the problem is that I seem to resent any attempts to tell me how I should write my Gonzo Journalism. I realize that this stance is rude & irrational, but I guess I tend to operate that way now and then.

This gibberish is no more "journalism" than Steadman's art is "illustration." Charlie [Perry, *RS* associate editor] was lamenting the fact—and I agreed—that one of Ralph's drawings would have been nicer if he'd included a herd of bats. But he didn't—so I offered to draw them in myself, with an ink pencil. Charlie was horrified. Which was exactly the right reaction. I wouldn't *touch* one of Ralph's drawings—and for the same reason, I can't work up much enthusiasm for treating "Fear & Loathing" like a news story. No doubt the holes and kinks *should* be filled, but for some reason I just can't work up much zeal for the job. Maybe after 12 or 20 hours of sleep I might think differently, but I wouldn't count on it. Let's keep in mind that this was never a commissioned work of journalism; it was a strange neo-fictional outburst that was deemed so rotten and wasteful, journalistically, that neither *RS* nor *Spts. Illustrated* would even reimburse me for my expenses. So I'm not in much of a mood, right now, to act grateful for any editorial direction. (No doubt I'm wrong and bullheaded on this score, but the way this thing developed has made me feel sort of personal about it; irrationally possessive, as it were—and at this stage of the action I'm not real hungry for advice about how the thing should be handled. It's been an instinct trip from the start, and I suspect it's going to stay that way—for good or ill.

Anyway, I've worked myself into such a stupor of crazed fatigue that I can't even sleep—and when I went into the office today Hank [Torgrimson, *RS* accountant] was ready to have me arrested for Stealing this typewriter. Things seem to be breaking down—after a long run of Good Work. So I think it's time to go home. I'll call you on Monday or Tuesday and see how things look then. But my general feeling is that you have a hell of a lot more important things to concern yourself with than perfecting the chronology of Vegas/Fear & Loathing. I have the feeling that it's a pretty fair piece of writing, as it stands, and I've developed a certain affection for it . . .

I *like* the bastard. So why not get on to more important things? (I'm not seriously opposed to any cutting or editing, but don't expect me to get wired on the idea of adding big sections that I didn't feel like including in the first place.)

OK for now. I'm in a massively rotten mood, trying to stay awake until plane time—seeing double, feeling bugs under my kneecaps, etc.

Under the circumstances I don't feel entirely ethical about billing you for *all* my SF trip expenses—so maybe I'll just seize your McIntosh amp & see if that balances—if not, I'll send a bill, & check for the amp. But don't cash it until we talk on the phone & I confirm a deposit of some kind. This last month has pretty well burned me out.

Anyway, I'm at the end of my wire—a bit on the wrong side of the edge, as it were. But I think all the Washington/book contract shit is settled—which is a pretty big step.

Fuck this—maybe I'll send another chunk(s) of Vegas II when I get back home—but let's not worry or count on it. We have enough, and 90% of it is absolutely right—on its own terms.

And that, after all, is the whole point.

Ciao,
H

Fear & Loathing in Las Vegas: A Savage Journey to the Heart of the American Dream, Part II . . . by Raoul Duke

November 25, 1971

About twenty miles east of Baker I stopped to check the drug bag. The sun was hot and I felt like killing something. Anything. Even a big lizard. Drill the fucker. I got my attorney's .357 Magnum out of the trunk and spun the cylinder. It was loaded all the way around: long, nasty little slugs—150 grains with a fine flat trajectory and painted asiac gold on the tips. I blew the horn a few times, hoping to call an iguana. Get the buggers moving. They were out there, I knew, in that goddamn sea of cactus—hunkered down, barely breathing, and every one of the stinking little bastards was loaded with deadly poison.

Three fast explosions knocked me off balance. Three deafening, double-action blasts from the .357 in my right hand. Jesus! Firing at nothing, for no reason at all. Bad craziness. I tossed the gun into the front seat of the Shark and stared nervously at the highway. No cars either way; the road was empty for two or three miles in both directions.

Fine luck. It would not *do* to be found in the desert under these circumstances: firing wildly into the cactus from a car full of drugs. And especially not now, on the lam from the Highway Patrol.

Awkward questions would arise: "Well now, Mister . . . ah . . . Duke; you understand, of course, that it *is* illegal to discharge a firearm of any kind while standing on a federal highway?"

"What? Even in self-defense? This goddamn gun has a *hair trigger*, officer. The truth is I only meant to fire *once*—just to scare the little bastards."

A heavy stare, then speaking very slowly: "Are you saying, Mister Duke . . . that you were *attacked* out here?"

"Well . . . no . . . not literally attacked, officer, but seriously *menaced*. I stopped to piss, and the minute I stepped out of the car these filthy little bags of poison were all around me. They moved like *greased lightning*!"

Would this story hold up?

No. They would place me under arrest, then routinely search the car—and when that happened all kinds of savage hell would break loose. They would never believe all these drugs were necessary to my work; that in truth I was a professional journalist on my way to Las Vegas to cover the National District Attorneys Conference on Narcotics and Dangerous Drugs.

"Just samples, officer. I got this stuff off a road man for the Neo-American Church back in Barstow. He started acting funny, so I worked him over."

Would they buy this?

No. They would lock me in some hell-hole of a jail and beat me on the kidneys with big branches—causing me to piss blood for years to come . . .

• • •

Luckily, nobody bothered me while I ran a quick inventory on the kit-bag. The stash was a hopeless mess, all churned together and half crushed. Some of the mescaline pellets had disintegrated into a reddish-brown powder, but I counted about thirty-five or forty still intact. My attorney had eaten all the reds, but there was quite a bit of speed left . . . no more grass, the coke bottle was empty, one acid blotter, a nice brown lump of opium hash and six loose amyls . . . Not enough for anything serious, but a careful rationing of the mescaline would probably get us through the four-day National District Attorneys Drug Conference.

On the outskirts of Vegas I stopped at a neighborhood pharmacy and bought two quarts of tequila, two fifths of Chivas Regal and a pint of ether. I was tempted to ask for some amyls. My angina pectoris was starting to act up. But the druggist had the eyes of a mean Baptist hysteric. I told him I needed the ether to get the tape off my legs, but by that time he'd already rung the stuff up and bagged it. He didn't give a fuck about ether.

I wondered what he would say if I asked him for $22 worth of Romilar and a tank of nitrous oxide. Probably he would have sold it to me. Why not? Free enterprise . . . Give the public what it needs—especially this bad-sweaty, nervous-talkin' fella with tape all over his legs and this terrible cough, along with angina pectoris and these godawful Aneuristic flashes every time he gets in the sun. *I mean this fella was in bad shape, officer. How the hell was I to know he'd walk straight out to his car and start abusing those drugs?*

How indeed? I lingered a moment at the magazine rack, then got a grip on myself and hurried outside to the car. The idea of going completely crazy on laughing gas in the middle of a DAs' drug conference had a definite warped appeal. But not on the *first day*, I thought. Save that for later. No point getting busted and committed before the conference even starts.

Another day, another convertible . . . & another hotel full of cops

The first order of business was to get rid of the Red Shark. It was too obvious. Too many people might recognize it, especially the Vegas police; although as far as *they* knew, the thing was already back home in L.A. It was last seen running full bore across Death Valley on Interstate 15. Stopped and warned in Baker by the CHP . . . then suddenly disappeared . . .

The last place they would look for it, I felt, was in a rental-car lot at the airport. I had to go out there anyway, to meet my attorney. He would be arriving from L.A. in the late afternoon.

I drove very quietly on the freeway, gripping my normal instinct for great speed and sudden lane changes—trying to remain inconspicuous—and when I got there I parked the Shark between two old Air Force buses in a "utility lot" about half a mile from the terminal. Very tall buses. Make it hard as possible for the fuckers. A little walking never hurt anybody.

By the time I got to the terminal I was pouring sweat. But nothing abnormal. I tend to sweat heavily in warm climates. My clothes are soaking wet from dawn to dusk. This worried me at first, but when I went to a doctor and described my normal daily intake of booze, drugs, and poison, he told me to come back when the sweating *stopped.* That would be the danger point, he said—a sign that my body's desperately overworked flushing mechanism had broken down completely. "I have great faith in the natural processes," he said. "But in *your* case . . . well . . . I find no precedent. We'll just have to wait and see, then work with what's left."

I spent about two hours in the bar drinking Bloody Marys for the V-8 nutritional content and watching the flights from L.A. I'd eaten nothing but grapefruit for about twenty hours and my head was adrift from its moorings.

You better watch yourself, I thought. There *are* limits to what the human body can endure. You don't want to break down and start bleeding from the ears right here in the terminal. Not in *this* town. In Las Vegas they *kill* the weak and deranged.

I realized this, and kept quiet even when I felt symptoms of a terminal blood sweat coming on. But this passed. I saw the cocktail waitress getting nervous, so I forced myself to get up and walk stiffly out of the bar. No sign of my attorney.

Down to the VIP car-rental booth, where I traded the Red Shark in for a White Cadillac Convertible. "This goddamn Chevy has caused me a lot of trouble," I told them. "I get the feeling that people are putting me down—especially in gas stations, when I have to get out & open the hood *manually*."

"Well . . . of *course*," said the man behind the desk. "What you need, I think, is one of our Mercedes 600 Towne-Cruiser Specials, with air-conditioning. You can even carry your own fuel, if you want; we make that available . . ."

"Do I look like a goddamn Nazi?" I said. "I'll have a natural *American* car, or nothing at all!"

They called up the white Coupe de Ville at once. Everything was automatic. I could sit in the red-leather driver's seat and make every inch of the car *jump*, by touching the proper buttons. It was a wonderful machine: ten grand worth of gimmicks and high-priced Special Effects. The rear windows leaped up with a touch, like frogs in a dynamite pond. The white canvas top ran up and down like a roller coaster. The dashboard was full of esoteric lights & dials & meters that I would never understand—but there was no doubt in my mind that I was into a *superior machine.*

The Caddy wouldn't get off the line quite as fast as the Red Shark, but once it got rolling—around eighty—it was pure smooth hell . . . all that elegant, upholstered weight lashing across the desert was like rolling through midnight on the old California Zephyr.

• • •

I drove straight to the hotel after renting the car. There was still no sign of my attorney, so I decided to check in on my own—if only to get off the street and avoid a public breakdown. I left the Whale in a VIP parking slot and shambled self-consciously into the lobby with one small leather bag—a handcrafted, custom-built satchel that had just been made for me by a leathersmith friend in Boulder.

Our room was at the Flamingo, in the nerve-center of the Strip: right across the street from Caesar's Palace and the Dunes—site of the Drug Conference. The bulk of the conferees were staying at the Dunes, but those of us who signed up fashionably late were assigned to the Flamingo.

The place was full of cops. I saw this at a glance. Most of them were just standing around trying to look casual, all dressed exactly alike in their cut-rate Vegas casuals: plaid Bermuda shorts, Arnie Palmer golf shirts, and hairless white legs tapering down to rubberized "beach sandals." It was a terrifying scene to walk into—a super stakeout of some kind. If I hadn't known about the conference my mind might have snapped. You get the impression that somebody was going to be gunned down in a blazing crossfire at any moment—maybe the entire Manson Family.

My arrival was badly timed. Most of the national DAs and other cop-types had already checked in. These were the people who now stood around the lobby & stared grimly at newcomers. What appeared to be the Final Stakeout was only about two hundred vacationing cops with nothing better to do. They didn't even *notice* each other.

I waded up to the desk and got in line. The man in front of me was a police chief from some small town in Michigan. His Agnew-style wife was standing about three feet off to his right while he argued with the desk clerk: "Look, fella—I *told* you I have a postcard here that says I have *reservations* in this hotel. Hell, I'm with the District Attorneys conference! I've already *paid* for my room."

"Sorry, sir. You're on the 'late list.' Your reservations were transferred to the . . . ah . . . Moonlight Motel, which is out on Paradise Boulevard and actually a very fine place of lodging and only sixteen blocks from here, with its own pool and . . ."

"You dirty little faggot! Call the manager! I'm tired of listening to this dogshit!"

The manager appeared and offered to call a cab. This was obviously the second or maybe even the third act in a cruel drama that had begun long before I showed up. The police chief's wife was crying; the gaggle of friends that he'd mustered for support were too embarrassed to back him up—even now, in this showdown at the desk, with this angry little cop firing his best and final shot. They *knew* he was beaten; he was going against the RULES, and the people hired to enforce those rules said "no vacancy."

After ten minutes of standing in line behind this noisy little asshole and his friends, I felt the bile rising. Where did this *cop*—of all people—get the nerve to argue with anybody in terms of Right & Reason? I had *been there* with these fuzzy little shitheads—and so, I sensed, had the desk clerk. He had the air of a man who'd been fucked around, in his time, by a fairly good cross-section of mean-tempered rule-crazy cops . . .

So now he was just giving their argument back to them: it doesn't matter who's right or wrong, man . . . or who's paid his bill & who hasn't . . . what matters right now is that for the first time in my life I can work out on a pig. "Fuck you, *officer*, I'm in charge here, and I'm telling you we don't have room for you."

I was enjoying this whipsong, but after a while I felt dizzy, bad nervous, and my impatience got the better of my amusement. So I stepped around the Pig and spoke directly to the desk clerk. "Say," I said, "I hate to interrupt, but I have a reservation and I wonder if maybe I could just sort of slide through and get out of your way." I smiled, letting him know I'd been digging his snake-bully act on the cop party that was now standing there, psychologically off-balance and staring at me like I was some kind of water-rat crawling up to the desk.

I looked pretty bad: wearing old Levi's and white Chuck Taylor

All-Star basketball sneakers . . . and my ten-peso Acapulco shirt had long since come apart at the shoulder seams from all that road-wind. My beard was about three days old, bordering on standard wino trim, and my eyes were totally hidden by Sandy Bull's Saigon-mirror shades.

But my voice had the tone of a man who *knows* he has a reservation. I was gambling on my attorney's foresight . . . but I couldn't pass a chance to put the horn into a cop:

. . . and I was right. The reservation was in my attorney's name. The desk clerk hit his bell to summon the bag boy. "This is all I have with me, right now," I said. "The rest is out there in that White Cadillac convertible." I pointed to the car that we could all see parked just outside the front door. "Can you have somebody drive it around to the room?"

The desk clerk was friendly. "Don't worry about a thing, sir. Just enjoy your stay here—and if there's anything you need, just call the desk."

I nodded & smiled, half watching the stunned reaction of the cop crowd right next to me. They were stupid with shock. Here they were arguing with every piece of leverage they could command, for a room they'd already *paid for*—and suddenly their whole act gets sideswiped by some crusty drifter who looks like something out of an upper-Michigan hobo jungle. And he checks in with a handful of *credit cards*! Jesus! What's happening in this world?

What indeed? The bag boy grinned. The desk clerk grinned. And the cop crowd eyed me nervously. They had just been blown off the track by a style of freak they'd never seen before. I left them there to ponder it, fuming & bitching at the gates of some castle they would never enter.

Getting Down to Business . . . Opening Day at the Drug Conference

"On behalf of the prosecuting attorneys of this country, I welcome you."

We sat in the rear fringe of a crowd of about 1,500 in the main ballroom of the Dunes Hotel. Far up in front of the room, barely visible from the rear, the executive director of the National District Attorneys Association—a middle-aged, well-groomed, successful GOP businessman type named Patrick Healy—was opening their Third National

Institute on Narcotics and Dangerous Drugs. His remarks reached us by way of a big, low-fidelity speaker mounted on a steel pole in our corner. Perhaps a dozen others were spotted around the room, all facing the rear and looming over the crowd . . . so that no matter where you sat or even tried to hide, you were always looking down the muzzle of a big speaker.

This produced an odd effect. People in each section of the ballroom tended to stare at the nearest voice-box, instead of watching the distant figure of whoever was actually talking far up front on the podium. This 1935 style of speaker placement totally depersonalized the room. There was something ominous and authoritarian about it. Whoever set up that sound system was probably some kind of sheriff's auxiliary technician on leave from a drive-in theater in Muskogee, Oklahoma, where the management couldn't afford individual car speakers and relied on ten huge horns, mounted on telephone poles in the parking area.

But the best technicians available to the National DAs convention in Vegas apparently couldn't handle it. Their sound system looked like something Ulysses S. Grant might have rigged up to address his troops during the siege of Vicksburg. The voices from up front crackled with a fuzzy, high-pitched urgency, and the delay was just enough to keep the words disconcertingly out of phase with the speaker's gestures.

"We must come to terms with the Drug Culture in this country . . . country . . . country! . . ." These echoes drifted back to the rear in confused waves. "The reefer butt is called a 'roach' because it resembles a cockroach . . . cockroach . . . cockroach . . ."

"What the fuck are these people talking about?" my attorney whispered. "You'd have to be crazy on acid to think a joint looked like a goddamn cockroach!"

I shrugged. It was clear that we'd stumbled into a prehistoric gathering. The voice of a "drug expert" named Bloomquist crackled out of the nearby speakers: ". . . about these flashbacks, the patient never knows; he thinks it's all over and he gets himself straightened out for six months . . . and then, darn it, the whole trip comes back on him."

Gosh darn that fiendish LSD! Dr. E. R. Bloomquist, MD, was the keynote speaker, one of the big stars of the conference. He is the author of a paperback book titled *Marijuana*, which—according to the cover—"tells it like it is." (He is also the inventor of the roach/cockroach theory . . .)

According to the book jacket, he is an "Associate Clinical Professor of Surgery (Anesthesiology) at the University of Southern California School of Medicine" . . . and also "a well known authority on the abuse of dangerous drugs." Dr. Bloomquist "has appeared on national network television panels, has served as a consultant for government agencies, was a member of the Committee on Narcotics Addiction and Alcoholism of the Council on Mental Health of the American Medical Association." His wisdom is massively reprinted and distributed, says the publisher. He is clearly one of the heavies on that circuit of second-rate academic hustlers who get paid anywhere from $500 to $1,000 a hit for lecturing to cop-crowds.

Dr. Bloomquist's book is a compendium of stale bullshit. On page 49 he explains the "four states of being" in the cannabis society: "Cool, Groovy, Hip & Square"—in that descending order. "The square is seldom if ever cool," says Bloomquist. "He is 'not with it,' that is, he doesn't know 'what's happening.' But if he manages to figure it out, he moves up a notch to 'hip.' And if he can bring himself to approve of what's happening, he becomes 'groovy.' And after that, with much luck and perseverence, he can rise to the rank of 'cool.' "

Bloomquist writes like somebody who once bearded Tim Leary in a campus cocktail lounge and paid for all the drinks. And it was probably somebody like Leary who told him with a straight face that sunglasses are known in the drug culture as "tea shades."

This is the kind of dangerous gibberish that used to be posted, in the form of mimeographed bulletins, in Police Dept. locker rooms.

Indeed:

> Know Your Dope Fiend. Your Life May Depend On It! *You will not be able to see his eyes because of Tea-Shades, but his knuckles will be white from inner tension and his pants will be crusted with semen from constantly jacking off when he can't find a rape victim. He will stagger and babble when questioned. He will not respect your badge. The Dope Fiend fears nothing. He will attack, for no reason, with every weapon at his command—including yours.* Beware. *Any officer*

apprehending a suspected marijuana addict should use all necessary force immediately. One stitch in time (on him) will usually save nine on you. Good luck.

"The Chief."

"If you don't know, come to learn . . . if you know, come to teach."

—motto on invitations to National DAs convention in Vegas, April 25–29, 1971

The first session—the opening remarks—lasted most of the afternoon. We sat patiently through the first two hours, although it was clear from the start that we weren't going to *learn* anything, and it was equally clear that we'd be crazy to try any *teaching*. It was easy enough to sit there with a head full of mescaline and listen to hour after hour of irrelevant gibberish . . . There was certainly no *risk* involved. These poor bastards didn't know mescaline from macaroni.

I suspect we could have done the whole thing on acid . . . except for some of the people; there were faces and bodies in that group who would have been absolutely unendurable on acid. The sight of a 344-pound police chief from Waco, Texas, necking openly with his 290-pound wife (or whatever woman he had with him) when the lights were turned off for a Dope Film was just barely tolerable on mescaline—which is mainly a sensual/surface drug that exaggerates reality, instead of altering it—but with a head full of acid, the sight of two fantastically obese human beings far gone in a public grope while a thousand cops all around them watched a movie about the "dangers of marijuana" would not be emotionally acceptable. The brain would reject it: the medulla would attempt to close itself off from the signals it was getting from the frontal lobes . . . and the middle-brain, meanwhile, would be trying desperately to put a different interpretation on the scene, before passing it back to the medulla and the risk of physical action.

Acid is a relatively *complex* drug, in its effects, while mescaline is pretty simple and straightforward—but in a scene like this, the difference was academic. There was simply no call, at this conference, for anything but a massive consumption of Downers: reds, grass, and booze, because the whole program had apparently been set up by people who had been in a Seconal stupor since 1964.

Here were more than a thousand top-level cops telling each other "we *must* come to terms with the drug culture," but they had no idea where to start. They couldn't even *find* the goddamn thing. There were rumors in the hallways that maybe the Mafia was behind it. Or perhaps the Beatles. At one point somebody in the audience asked Bloomquist if he thought Margaret Mead's "strange behavior," of late, might possibly be explained by a private marijuana addiction.

"I really don't know," Bloomquist replied. "But at her age, if she did smoke grass, she'd have one hell of a trip."

The audience roared with laughter at this remark.

• • •

My attorney was downstairs at the bar, talking to a sporty-looking cop about forty whose plastic name-tag said he was the DA from someplace in Georgia. "I'm a whiskey man, myself," he was saying. "We don't have much problem with drugs down where I come from."

"You will," said my attorney. "One of these nights you'll wake up and find a junkie tearing your bedroom apart."

"Naw!" said the Georgia man. "Not down in *my* parts."

I joined them and ordered a tall glass of rum, with ice.

"You're another one of these California boys," he said. "Your friend here's been tellin' me about dope fiends."

"They're everywhere," I said. "Nobody's safe. And sure as hell not in the South. They like the warm weather."

"They work in pairs," said my attorney. "Sometimes in gangs. They'll climb right into your bedroom and sit on your chest, with big bowie knives." He nodded solemnly. "They might even sit on your *wife's chest*—put the blade right down on her throat."

"Jesus God almighty," said the southerner. "What the hell's *goin' on* in this country?"

"You'd never believe it," said my attorney. "In L.A. it's out of control. First it was drugs, now it's witchcraft."

"Witchcraft? Shit, you can't mean it!"

"Read the newspapers," I said. "Man, you don't know trouble until you have to face down a bunch of these addicts gone crazy for human sacrifice!"

"Naw!" he said. "That's science fiction stuff!"

"Not where *we* operate," said my attorney. "Hell, in Malibu alone, these goddamn Satan-worshippers kill six or eight people *every day.*" He paused to sip his drink. "And all they want is the *blood,*" he continued. "They'll take people right off the *street* if they have to." He nodded. "Hell, yes. Just the other day we had a case where they grabbed a girl right out of a McDonald's hamburger stand. She was a waitress. About sixteen years old . . . with a lot of people watching, too!"

"What happened?" said our friend. "What did they *do* to her?" He seemed very agitated by what he was hearing.

"*Do*?" said my attorney. "Jesus Christ, man. They chopped her goddamn head off right there in the parking lot! Then they cut all kinds of holes in her and sucked out the blood!"

"God *almighty*!" the Georgia man exclaimed . . . "And nobody *did* anything?"

"What *could* they do?" I said. "The guy that took the head was about six-seven and maybe three hundred pounds. He was packing two Lugers, and the others had M-16s. They were all veterans . . ."

"The big guy used to be a major in the Marines," said my attorney. "We know where he lives, but we can't get near the house."

"Naw!" our friend shouted. "Not a major!"

"He wanted the pineal gland," I said. "That's how he got so big. When he quit the Marines he was just a *little guy.*"

"O my god!" said our friend. "That's horrible!"

"It happens every day," said my attorney. "Usually it's whole families. During the night. Most of them don't even wake up until they feel their heads going—and then, of course, it's too late."

The bartender had stopped to listen. I'd been watching him. His expression was not calm.

"Three more rums," I said. "With plenty of ice, and maybe a handful of lime chunks."

He nodded, but I could see that his mind was not on his work. He was staring at our name tags. "Are you guys with that police convention upstairs?" he said finally.

"We sure are, my friend," said the Georgia man with a big smile.

The bartender shook his head sadly. "I thought so," he said. "I never heard that kind of talk at this bar before. Jesus Christ! How do you guys *stand* that kind of work?"

My attorney smiled at him. "We *like* it," he said. "It's groovy."

The bartender drew back; his face was a mask of repugnance.

"What's wrong with you?" I said. "Hell, *somebody* has to do it."

He stared at me for a moment, then turned away.

"Hurry up with those drinks," said my attorney. "We're thirsty." He laughed and rolled his eyes as the bartender glanced back at him. "Only *two* rums," he said. "Make mine a Bloody Mary."

The bartender seemed to stiffen, but our Georgia friend didn't notice. His mind was somewhere else. "Hell, I really hate to hear this," he said quietly. "Because everything that happens in California seems to get down our way, sooner or later. Mostly Atlanta, but I guess that was back when the goddamn bastards were *peaceful.* It used to be that all we had to do was keep 'em under surveillance. They didn't roam around much . . ." He shrugged. "But now, Jesus, *nobody's* safe. They could turn up anywhere."

"You're right," said my attorney. "We learned that in California. You remember where Manson turned up, don't you? Right out in the middle of Death Valley. He had a whole *army* of sex fiends out there. We only got our hands on a few. Most of the crew got away; just ran off across the sand dunes, like big lizards . . . and every one of them stone naked, except for the weapons."

"They'll turn up somewhere, pretty soon," I said. "And let's hope we'll be ready for them."

The Georgia man whacked his fist on the bar. "But we can't just lock ourselves in the house and be prisoners!" he exclaimed. "We don't even know who these people are! How do you *recognize* them?

"You can't," my attorney replied. "The only way to do it is to take the bull by the horns—go to the mat with this scum!"

"What do you mean by that?" he asked.

"You *know* what I mean," said my attorney. "We've done it before, and can damn well do it again."

"Cut their goddamn heads off," I said. "Every one of them. That's what we're doing in California."

"*What?*"

"Sure," said my attorney. "It's all on the Q.T., but everybody who *matters* is with us all the way down the line."

"God! I had no idea it was that bad out there!" said our friend.

"We keep it quiet," I said. "It's not the kind of thing you'd want to talk about upstairs, for instance. Not with the press around."

Our man agreed. "Hell no!" he said. "We'd never hear the goddamn end of it."

"Dobermans don't talk," I said.

"What?"

"Sometimes it's easier to just rip out the backstraps," said my attorney. "They'll fight like hell if you try to take the head without dogs."

"God almighty!"

We left him at the bar, swirling the ice in his drink and not smiling. He was worried about whether or not to tell his wife about it. "She'd never understand," he muttered. "You know how women are."

I nodded. My attorney was already gone, scurrying through a maze of slot machines toward the front door. I said good-bye to our friend, warning him not to say anything about what we'd told him.

The Campaign Trail: '72

The idea of Hunter covering the 1972 presidential campaign for the magazine—from the early primaries on through Election Day—had been bandied about for months. Hunter's admiration for George McGovern (and contempt for McGovern's Democratic rivals, including Hubert Humphrey and Ed Muskie) was obvious, and rather than hiding it, he and Rolling Stone *intended to capitalize on it. Hunter and Jann—heavily stoned on pot—had an early meeting with McGovern's campaign manager, Frank Mankiewicz, to secure the campaign's cooperation and Hunter's access to its strategy and planning. Once Hunter and his assistant,* Rolling Stone *associate editor Timothy Crouse, joined up with the usual campaign press crew, though, they found themselves the target of the entrenched journalists' snickers, if not outright ridicule. The publication of Hunter's first stories from the campaign trail—filed via the first primitive fax machine in use, which Hunter dubbed the "Mojo Wire"—changed all that, but just to be sure, Hunter instructed Crouse to keep a separate notebook, noting every quirk, weirdness, and character weakness of their mainstream media cohorts. That notebook eventually became Crouse's classic* The Boys on the Bus. *As to Hunter's own campaign book: Mankiewicz famously dubbed it the "least factual, most accurate" account of the '72 election.*

Undated letter from HST to JSW

Jann . . .

Tonight I went into a huge 24-hr drugstore—one of a big chain around the DC area ("Drug Fair")—and when I asked the bearded clerk if they carried *RS* he said, "No, unfortunately."

"Why not?" I said.

He shrugged. "I get *mine* in the mail," he replied. "Who

handles it? We could probably sell a lot of them here, but nobody's pushing it."

So . . . that's FYI. DRUG FAIR, a chain of big all day & nite general store supermarkets that cater to a hell of a lot of potential *RS* readers. We have to break out of this widespread assumption that *RS* is an Underground, special interest "music rag." If *RS* is such a powerful goddamn "capitalist" operation (inre: Your Editorial), we might as well *act* like capitalists, instead of just talking about it . . . which means that if you want to *sell* something, you first have to make it available.

I've been here about 10 days now, constantly checking newsstands, & I've yet to find a single copy for sale. This is a definite bummer. I got thrown out of a fucking *rock club* tonight, despite Dan Greene's angry shouting about "What kind of asshole would keep an editor of *Rolling Stone* out of a music club just because he's wearing Levi's?" The doorman thought Greene was saying I was one of the Rolling Stones. "Look, fella," he said. "The rule here is No Levi's; I wouldn't give a damn if you were Mick Jaegger [*sic*]—you couldn't come in here wearing denims."

I'm thinking of taking the fucker to court, on grounds of financial discrimination . . . but in the meantime, we have to consider the fact that this doorman at one of the main downtown rock clubs (Ventura 21) has never even *heard* of *Rolling Stone*, much less seen it. And that's more your fault than his.

OK . . . that's it for now. I don't know what that useless fucking distributor does with those "2500 copies" he claims to be putting out for sale here, but he's sure as hell keeping them out of all the places where *I* go . . . and *all* of these places carry *Penthouse*. It's everywhere . . . along with the *National Enquirer*, the *Sporting News, Midnight, Sexology*, etc. Whoever distributes *Rolling Stone* in the Washington DC area should have his scrotum torn off. (Savage Henry said that, & you should probably warn the fucker that Mr. Henry might be stopping by to see him one of these nights unless he gets the goddamn book on the racks.) I'll load pro football player Dave Meggessey up on chemicals and send *him* over to check the books. A monster like that, full of mescaline, makes "My Attorney" seem like a bloodless cipher. He even scares *me*.

Selah . . .

HST

Undated '71 letter from JSW to HST

Hunter:

Re: Washington D.C. Gig

One thing I hate about political columns, etc., is that they are totally depersonalized; you never have a sense of the author, his point of view as a human being, who he is, etc., etc. [*Washington Post* writer Nicholas] von Hoffman and [*New York Herald Tribune* columnist Joseph] Alsop come closest to being real, but still not enough. That's why the first arrival/coming/D.C.-the-city-and-what-it's-like-joining-the-press-corps are excellent introductory things.

On the problem of D.C. distribution, apparently it's the next issue that the big push starts with, which is why you haven't seen much of it around. *Rolling Stone* staffer Peter Howard is coming down there himself on Dec 14 or so to personally supervise the fixing it up, and also he is under instructions to fucking lose money if necessary to get the goddamned thing out. Or, Savage Henry comes a-knocking.

Third column should be the Youth Vote. Let's presume the fucker exists; to question the matter at all would be foolish. To convince them, naturally we use *RS* in several ways, one of which is by excellent political coverage & reassembling certain facts. Also, when you start making your calls on Larry O'Brien, et al., they'll start to get the idea. Anyway, this column should explore the candidates' attitudes toward the youth vote, what the press and the columnists and professionals have been saying, how the press (a la that [Nat] Hentoff piece & apparently there was a good long *NYT* piece a few weeks ago and a *National Observer* piece, too) has been treating it, & you should talk to Lowenstein, etc. [Thomas] Braden once did a column on Lowenstein which was good and had good math in it. We don't need 23,000,000 votes, only a million or so as swing voters . . . then you've got all those facts being gathered by that girl at that Election news or something. There's also an outfit called the Youth Citizenship League that gathers this stuff . . . all registration by kids is heavily Democratic, and then we can throw in some of our philosophy—we'll talk about this.

Other matters:

1) Enclosed is a primary map. Please send me a memo on which ones are the important ones and which ones you want to/plan to cover, obviously N.H., Ill., Wisconsin, Mass., Calif., N.Y., Florida (?) . . . anyway, let's get together on a quick rundown of this. We have to discuss type of coverage, and which candidates to go with or what angle to do in each one, since they can get to be repetitive, etc.

2) Tim Crouse is available and anxious to work on some political things, so he can pick up some stories that you don't have the time for—for example, I thought I'd put him on the road with McCloskey for three days in N.H. after Xmas. Also, he can do some other Washington stories—like the Justice Dept. or the economist (which, by the way, is a reference to the guy who was thrown out of the Bureau of Labor Statistics for refusing to reinterpret, and he was young, and no one talked to him). I'd like to put Crouse on some of these kind of stories, possibly. This obviously we must also talk about.

Letter from HST to JSW

Nov 18 '71

Jann . . .

I'm interrupting VORTEX/Washington #1 to whip off this quick note inre: timing, deadlines, priorities, etc. What I've written so far is a slag heap of spotty gibberish with no real subject at all, and it suddenly occurs to me that I'd rather miss an issue than send something bad and/or useless.

It never occurred to me that so many media people in Washington would know who I was. I went into the city room of the *Wash/ Star* today, to cash a check (my checks are totally worthless here & I have no cash), and suddenly found myself socked into a long Q&A session that eventually became a formal interview for a series the *Star* is doing on "Intellectuals & Sports." None of these people had even read the Vegas stuff; their interest stemmed entirely from the HA book & two things in *Scanlan's*. As it happens, the spts ed. of the *Star* just came from the *SF Examiner* & is staffing his whole section with freaks. (See attached memo for two gratis subscriptions.) He offered the facilities of his office for anything I needed: phones, typewriters, work, etc.—so I now have a second office.

There are so many things happening that I can't even sleep. Coming out of Woody Creek into this scene has jacked me into a brutal adrenaline trip—compounded by the shock of finding myself treated like a public figure of sorts. Given this odd visibility factor, I suspect the new fact of a *RS* "bureau" in DC will soon be viewed more as a lobby gig than a news organization . . . because I'm already locked into the idea that I'm here to write a column with one hand and whip up a giant anti-Nixon Youth Vote with the other. There's no escaping it; my history is too public—so for christ's sake let's *create* that vote. We have a tremendous amount of latent sympathy (& potential energy) among young heads in the media. They seem puzzled at the idea that *RS* is "getting into politics," but they all seem to like it. Shit, today I got my first Job Application, which I'll forward as soon as I xerox it. Within a month or so, I suspect we'll be needing that extra room in *New York Post* bureau reporter Tony Prisendorf's office—more for a political hq. than anything journalistic, and now that I think on that I suspect we should be pretty careful. The point, however, is that a hell of a lot of people seem to want to "help" me. Too many, I think, but at this point I don't want to turn anybody off.

On more specific fronts, I'm already gearing down to make "The Real Nixon" VORTEX/Washington #2 (that name is off the top of my head & might not last, but let's use it for now as a sort of working title. It conveys a certain amount of urgency & bogus drama that fits in nicely with the activist side of this gig.). From here on in, it's going to be hard to defend the notion that I'm here to merely write a column.

I think, however, that we *have to* get away from that phrase "Youth Vote." It leaves out about two thirds of the people we're talking to. Ideally, we should come up with something about half-way between "Youth Vote" & "Freak Power." Something to embrace both the latent (& massive) Kesey-style voter with the 18–21 types.

* * *

Now a few important details:

I've had a long talk with the mgr. of the newsstand next door to the Nat. Press Bldg (see enc. note with name of the big boss for all six UNIVERSAL NEWS stores) & the man in store #2 says *RS* invariably sells out "in a few hours." I told him I wanted it there the next time I came around, so he gave me this man Siebert's name, which you should pass along to the distributor. OK for that. I haven't seen a copy of *RS* for sale since I got here—and that makes life unnecessarily difficult for me. There is—now that I think on it—a first-class FM rock station here that reaches almost the entire young/music type audience. I'll get the name & send it along. A few spots on that might work wonders. I'll check around for other possibilities & let you know.

Right now I have to get to bed. It's 6:30 a.m. & I have to get up before noon, in order to buy a bed & a TV set. (Today is Saturday.) My private phone number just got activated yesterday:

It's 726-8161. Don't give it to anybody; not even on the master Rollidex [*sic*]. The *RS* number is 882-2853 and rings here in the house, and that should be enough for all but the critical few. The point is that I want to have *one* phone I can always answer, without fear of being fucked around by lunatics . . . and the first time I start getting hassled on *that* number, I'll change it. So don't give it to anybody except [*RS* investor] Max [Palevsky], [Jann Wenner's secretary] Stephanie Franklin, etc.

What I'm doing at the moment is feeling my way around & trying to cope with all these unexpected reactions to my gig. The problem, oddly enough, is that things are working out better than I expected . . . but at the same time I'm swamped with vicious little details. The phone man, for instance, got here at 10:00 & left at 4:30. He's just back from Vietnam, & for a number of reasons that need no explanation it took him six hours to drill through a stone floor & then a stone wall, in order to put two phones in the Fear Room. And then he came back this morning: (to check the phones, he said, but what he really wanted was a copy of #95. Not for Vegas 1, but because of that story on Sly [Stone].) "I've been wondering why that sonofabitch is always late," he said . . . and then he said he's been reading "the Stone" for 2 yrs in Nam. I figure he'll be around again—which is okay, I think, because in a city that's 72% Black it might be nice to have a sharp black friend. When the bastard came back today he was wearing a hat that would have freaked even Sly.

And that's it for now. Hopefully, I'll get a column in by Tuesday—but I'm not optimistic about its potential coherence or heaviness. If it looks bad I'll simply hang it up and make the nut with something else. Don't worry, either way. This is going to be a good & extremely active gig, but I'll have to get grounded first. (I assume, by the way—based on the schedule you sent me—that the real deadline for VORTEX #1 is Dec 1, instead of Tuesday 11/22. Is that right?)

Send word,
HST

Undated letter from HST to JSW

Jann/

Can you put me on a list for *all new records* (at the Rm 1369 address)? That would give me some gravy to lay on Prisendorf for the office rent—for an album a day I can get an actual *office*, with a desk & a studio couch. Very cheap. He won't agree to anything that might hang him up—but if we keep it loose & informal, I think it will work . . . & a steady flow of "review albums" will make the nut.

Also, could Stephanie drop a note to the *Cellar Door* (the main Folk/Rock club here) & say I'll be a regular visitor. I've gone there twice & it cost me $28 the first time, $17 the second (Doug Kershaw & Al Cooper [*sic*])—I think a letter from the main office would cancel those rotten tabs. It's kind of a latter-day, high-powered Matrix, & I figure to stop there fairly often . . . & a letter from Hq. could save me $100 a month or so.

Thanx/

HST

Letter from JSW to Cellar Door

November 22, 1971

The Cellar Door
1201 34th Street, N.W.
Washington, D.C.

Gentlemen:

We have recently stationed a correspondent in Washington, D.C., Hunter S. Thompson, who is in the regular employ of *Rolling Stone*.

We would appreciate any and all courtesies, including admission and access to the backstage area, that you can provide.

Sincerely,
Jann Wenner
Editor

P.S. It is my understanding that there has been somebody in the Washington area claiming to be Raoul Duke, saying that he works for *Rolling Stone* too. There is, in fact, a real Raoul Duke who does work for us, but he is in semi-retirement in the Virgin Islands at the moment, and should anybody by the name of Raoul Duke claim admission to your club, you might as well just call the police.

cc: Hunter S. Thompson

Letter from JSW to HST

December 13, 1971

Hunter: Please return forthwith the various pre-recorded cassettes you stole from my house or else I'm going to give Acosta a first class ticket to Washington, D.C. and a huge quantity of ugly, bad LSD, plus your private number and your home address.

Yours,
[unsigned]

Undated letter from HST to JSW

You crazy dope addict bastard! Don't give me any more shit about "stealing your cassettes"! I did a lot of rotten things out there but I didn't steal your fucking cassettes. The next time you mention this thing, I'll put [HST attorney and longtime friend John] Clancy on you.

—& while we're into bummers, you should know that Lee Bailey just offered me a big chunk of stock in "Gallery."

Heavy duty, eh? First E.B. Williams & now Bailey. Are you ready for that?

Letter from HST to JSW, February 16, 1972

2/16

Royal Biscayne Hotel
555 Ocean Drive
Key Biscayne, Florida 33149

Jann/

—the Fla gig is so far running about 600% better than I could possibly have predicted. After 2 days of steady personal hassling with Lindsay, I think he's about ready to spring for the Freak Power trip.

—whatever happens, these fuckers will never forget that the campaign of '72 was "the one that *Rolling Stone* covered."

—terrible heavy showbiz; I feel like an alligator in the dog show. I have a clean '72 version of the Great Red Shark. But the thing that really brings them to their fucking knees is the telecopier.

The poor bastards are totally bamboozled. They can't grasp it. Here's some hopelessly out of control freak from Rolling Whatever, running around in a big red convertible with a fucking phone-transmitter in the trunk. It's wonderful—like putting a big red Twister on them.

OK for now. I'll call.

—H

Letter from JSW to HST

April 20, 1972

Hunter:

We can no longer go through this deadline scene as we have now with every one of your reports. The late deadlines on the Wisconsin piece and the Florida piece were quite understandable, but your latest piece should have been in no later than Friday evening. I am afraid that you literally have Dan Parker, Charles Perry, Robert Kingsbury, Cindy Ehrlich, Barbara Ziller, Paul, Hank and other members of the editorial staff quite angry about the situation.

Furthermore, the unvarying dullness of the layout and the continued proliferation of minor errors and improper structuring results only from the fact that you submit it so late. For everybody's good I think we have got to start considering Friday evening/Saturday early a.m. as the final deadline.

Sincerely,
Jann

bcc: Dan, Charles, Robert, Cindy, Barbara, Paul, Hank, Max, Jane (Wenner), Laurel

Memo to *RS* staff from HST

Fear & Loathing: CORRECTIONS, RETRACTIONS, APOLOGIES, COP-OUTS, ETC. (undated 1972)
[handwritten at top] Jann—this was written before I left to cover the Fla. primary

For various reasons that probably don't mean shit to anybody but me, I want to get straight—for the record, as it were—with regard to some of the most serious of the typographical errors that have marred the general style, tone & wisdom of "Fear & Loathing."

I have tried to blame various individuals in the San Francisco office for these things, but each time we trace one of the goddamn things back to its root, it turns out to have been my fault. This is mainly because I never seem to get my gibberish in to [*RS* copy chief Charlie Perry, aka "Smokestack El Ropo"] El Ropo, who has to cope with it, until the crack of dawn on deadline day—at which time I have to get him out of bed and keep him awake by means of ruses, shocks and warnings while I feed my freshly typed pages into the Mojo Wire, which zaps them across the nation to El Ropo at the rate of one page every four minutes.

This is a fantastic machine, and I carry it with me at all times. All I need is the Mojo Wire and a working telephone to send perfect Xerox copies of anything I've written to anybody else with a Mojo Wire receiver . . . and anybody with $50 a month can lease one of these things.

Incredible. What will they think of next?

The only real problem with the Mojo Wire is that it tends to miss or skip a line every once in a while, especially when we get one of those spotty phone connections. If you're playing "New Speedway Boogie" in the same room, for instance, the Mojo machine will pick up the noise and garble a name like "Jackson" so badly that El Ropo will get it as "Johnson" . . . or "Jackalong" . . . or maybe just a fuzzy grey blank.

Which would not be a problem if we had time to check back & forth on a different phone line—but by the time El Ropo can assemble my gibberish & read it I am usually checked out and driving like a bastard for the nearest airport.

So he has to read the whole thing several times, try to get a grip on the context, and then decide *what I really meant to say* in that line that came across garbled.

This is not always easy. My screeds tend to wander, without benefit of such traditional journalistic landmarks as "prior references" and "pyramid reverse-build foundations." I still insist "objective journalism" is a contradiction in terms. But I want to draw a very hard line between the inevitable reality of "subjective journalism" and the idea that any honestly subjective journalist might feel free to estimate a crowd at a rally for some candidate the journalist happens to like personally at 2000 instead of 612 . . . or to imply that a candidate the journalist views with gross contempt, personally, is a less effective campaigner than he actually is.

Hubert Humphrey, for instance: I don't mind admitting that I think sheep-dip is the only cure for everything Humphrey stands for. I consider him not only a living, babbling insult to the presumed intelligence of the electorate, but also a personally painful mockery of the idea that Americans can learn from history.

But if Hubert meets a crowd in Tampa and 77 ranking business leaders offer him $1000 each for his campaign, I will write that scene exactly as it happened—regardless of the immense depression it would plunge me into.

No doubt I would look around for any valid word or odd touches that might match the scene to my bias. If any of those 77 contributors were wearing spats or monocles I would take care to mention it. I would probably follow some of them outside to see if they had "America—Love it or Leave it" bumper stickers on their cars. And if they did I would definitely make note of it. If one of them grabbed a hummingbird out of the air and bit its head off, I think it's safe to say I would probably use that . . .

. . . but even if I did all that ugly stuff, and if the compilation of my selected evidence might pursuade a reader here and there to think that Humphrey was drawing his Florida support from a cabal of senile fascists . . . well . . . I probably wouldn't get much argument from any of the "objective" journalists on the tour, because even the ones who would flatly disagree with my interpretation of what happened would be extremely reluctant to argue that theirs or anyone else's was the flat objective truth.

You won't find many working reporters defending the concept of Pure Objectivity. They know better. The only zealous defenders of "objective" reporting are the Editors, Publishers and other diminished-capacity "news executives" who frequent National Journalism Conventions. Or semi-retired "commentators" like [CBS news analyst] Eric Sevareid, who have grown so far away from the sweaty midnight realities of politics that they might as well be looking down from some germ-free eiyre (sp) [aerie] in the Vatican, like the Pope or maybe Howard Hughes. Which is not to say they might not be Right from time to time. Even a *blind* pig finds an acorn once in a while. But it is a little hard on the senses to live thru a decade of getting the News from [NBC anchor] Chet Huntley, and then suddenly find him grinning out of the tube at you and spinning a salespitch for American Airlines.

On the other hand, it's also true that *I* will blow a fact here and there. A month ago I wrote that a registered independent in Colorado could vote in either the GOP or Democratic primary—which was true last year, but the law was recently changed. Somebody wrote to curse me for that one, and all I can do is apologize. In 1970 I knew every clause, twist, sub-section & constitutional precedent that had anything to do with voter-eligibility laws in Colorado. (When you run for office on the Freak Power ticket, the first thing you do is learn *all* the laws.) But when I moved to Washington and got into the Presidential Campaign I stopped keeping track of things like that.

Voter-eligibility laws are changing so fast all over the country this year that in many cases not even the city/county clerks and official registrars in charge of dealing with new voters really know who is eligible. Just because somebody tells you that you're not eligible to vote doesn't mean you aren't. During the Freak Power election in Aspen the county clerk formally and officially disqualified 88 out of 450 new voters. We took them all to court and won 87 out of 88 cases in six hours.

The only other serious error that I feel any need to explain or deal with at this time has to do with a statement about Nixon. What I wrote was: "There is still no doubt in my mind that he could never pass for human . . ."

But somebody cut the word "never." El Ropo denies it, but our relationship has never been the same. He says the printer did it. Which is understandable, I guess; it's a fairly heavy statement either way.

Is Nixon "human"? Probably so, in the technical sense. He is not a fish or a fowl. There is no real argument about that. Most juries would accept, prima facie, the idea that the President of the United States is a *mammal.*

He is surely not an Insect; and not of the lizard family. But "human" is something else. A mammal is not necessarily human. Rodents are mammals. An extremely intelligent Bayou Rat called "Honeyrunner" was once elected to the city council in DeFuniak Springs, Florida. Nobody called him "human," but they say he did okay on the job.

It would take a really sick and traitorous mind to compare the President of the United States to a Bayou Rat, regardless of intelligence. So maybe El Ropo was right. By almost any standard of responsible journalism the President must be referred to as "human." It is one of those ugly realities—like the Amnesty Question—that we will all have to face & accept.

About five years ago Tom Wicker wrote a column in the *New York Times* that focused—for reasons I no longer remember—on a whole wasps' nest of ominous flaws that he (Wicker) had only recently discovered in the character of Richard Milhous Nixon.

Wicker was shocked. He called up the memory of Conrad's "Lord Jim," and said that he'd always thought Richard Nixon was "one of us."

This is an impossible concept to explain to anybody who hasn't brooded over the Meaning & Truth of "Lord Jim." But to anyone who has, the idea that one of the most eminent journalistic gurus in the nation could ever have thought that "Richard Nixon was one of us" is genuinely unsettling.

Conrad's "one of us" idea was a sort of primitive version of today's far-flung belief that a very few people in this world radiate an almost unnaturally "good kaharma" (sp?) [*sic*]—and that only the ones who can radiate on this special level are capable of recognizing it in others. A sort of Aristocracy of Instinct . . .

Did Tom Wicker once see this special inner glow in Richard Nixon? He has come a long way since he wrote that thing, five years ago, but . . . well, what can you say? Wicker appears to be one of those fast-learning types. He is one of the few big-league journalists in America who still sees his job as a means of furthering his education. Which keeps him interesting . . . but it makes me a little nervous to know that Wicker might still be nursing some secret flash about Nixon being one of the world's special laid-back fireball truthseekers . . . while I still can't decide if the bugger is even *human*.

Which is neither here nor there, for now. Probably we'll never know anyway. And all I started out to do here was explain away a few of my worst mistakes.

The only other thing I had in mind was to say—to all the people who keep writing me those vicious goddamn letters—is that I get a really fine high boot out of reading them. I read them all, screening the best ones for good lines to steal. About a week ago I got one from somebody in Chicago, calling me a "Crypto-faggot Bulldog-nazi Honky-fascist Pig."

I can really get behind a letter like that. But most of the stuff is lame. I'm not running a goddamn "Dear Abbey" [*sic*] service here. Anybody with problems should write to David Felton, Bleeding Heart Editor, at the San Francisco office. He's *paid* to get down in the ditch with lunatics. And he *likes* it.

But I have more important things to do.

Politics.

Human Problems are secondary.

—30—

Letter from HST to JSW

Sept 17 '72

Dear Jann:

I think we should offer McGovern a full page, *free*, in every issue between now and the election. As far as I'm concerned he has a pretty weak goddamn case, but I think we should give him a chance to make it—especially in *RS*, because everything he's done since Miami has been subject to criticism by various *RS* writers, including me, and I suppose it's possible we've all been wrong.

So why don't we just give him a "house ad" in every issue from now until Nov 7? Let him do whatever he wants with it: solicit funds, denounce drugs, praise Muskie, etc. . . . whatever he wants.

Needless to say, we'll reserve all rights to comment, whenever necessary, on the content of the ads . . . Or at least I will.

OK for now. I have no plans to come to California anytime soon—unless McGov follows thru on his rumored plan to campaign out there with Humphrey. If that happens, I'll definitely make the trip. A horror like that would just about wrap the thing up for me, I think.

Hunter

Letter from HST to JSW

12/3

Jann/

—I will definitely need speed to get the campaign book done properly & on time—nevermind the fucking wisdom of it; just gather all you can & send it ASAP—with a bill, of course.

H

The Campaign Trail: Is This Trip Necessary?

January 6, 1972

Outside my new front door the street is full of leaves. My lawn slopes down to the sidewalk; the grass is still green, but the life is going out of it. Red berries wither on the tree beside my white colonial stoop. In the driveway my Volvo with blue leather seats and Colorado plates sits facing the brick garage. And right next to the car is a cord of new firewood: pine, elm, and cherry. I burn a vicious amount of firewood these days—even more than the Alsop brothers.

When a man gives up drugs he wants big fires in his life—all night long, every night, huge flames in the fireplace & the volume turned all the way up. I have ordered more speakers to go with my new McIntosh amp—and also a fifty-watt "boombox" for the FM car radio.

You want good strong seatbelts with the boombox, they say, because otherwise the bass riffs will bounce you around inside like a goddamn pingpong ball . . . a very bad act in traffic; especially along these elegant boulevards of Our Nation's Capital.

• • •

One of the best and most beneficial things about coming East now and then is that it tends to provoke a powerful understanding of the "Westward Movement" in U.S. history. After a few years on the Coast or even Colorado you tend to forget just exactly what it was that put you on the road, going west, in the first place. You live in L.A. a while and before long you start cursing traffic jams on the freeways in the warm Pacific dusk . . . and you tend to forget that in New York City you can't even *park*; forget about driving.

Even in Washington, which is still a relatively loose and open city in terms of traffic, it costs me about $1.50 an hour every time I park downtown . . . which is nasty: but the shock is not so much the money-cost as the rude understanding that it is no longer considered either sane or natural to *park* on the city streets. If you happen to find a spot beside an open parking meter you don't dare use it, because the odds are better than even that somebody will come along and either steal your car or reduce it to twisted rubble because you haven't left the keys in it.

There is nothing unusual, they tell me, about coming back to your car and finding the radio aerial torn off, the windshield wipers bent up in the air like spaghetti and all the windows smashed . . . for no particular reason except to make sure you know just exactly where it's at these days.

Where indeed?

"It's a Goddamn Jungle!"

Washington Post columnist Nicholas von Hoffman recently pointed out that the Nixon-Mitchell administration—seemingly obsessed with restoring Law and Order in the land, at almost any cost—seems totally unconcerned that Washington, D.C., has become the "Rape Capital of the World."

One of the most dangerous areas in town is the once-fashionable district known as Capitol Hill. This is the section immediately surrounding the Senate/Congress office buildings, a very convenient place to live for the thousands of young clerks, aides and secretaries who work up there at the pinnacle. The peaceful, tree-shaded streets on Capitol Hill look anything but menacing: brick colonial townhouses with cut glass doors and tall windows looking out on the Library of Congress and the Washington Monument . . . When I came here to look for a house or apartment, about a month ago, I checked around town and figured Capitol Hill was the logical place to locate.

"Good *God*, man!" said my friend from the liberal *New York Post*. "You can't live *there*! It's a goddamn jungle!"

Crime figures for "The District" are so heinous that they embarrass even J. Edgar Hoover. Rape is up 80 percent this year over 1970, and a recent rash of murders (averaging about one every day) has mashed the morale of the local police to a new low. Of the 250 murders this year, only 36 have been solved . . . and the *Washington Post* says the cops are about to give up.

Meanwhile, things like burglaries, street muggings, and random assaults are so common that they are no longer considered news. The *Washington Evening Star*, one of the city's three dailies, is located in the Southeast District—a few blocks from the Capitol—in a windowless building that looks like the vault at Fort Knox. Getting into the *Star* to see somebody is almost as difficult as getting into the White House. Visitors are scrutinized by hired cops and ordered to fill out forms that double as "hall passes." So many *Star* reporters have been mugged, raped, and menaced that they come & go in fast taxis, like people running the gauntlet—fearful, with good reason, of every sudden footfall between the street and the bright-lit safety of the newsroom guard station.

This kind of attitude is hard for a stranger to cope with. For the past few years I have lived in a place where I never even bothered to take the keys out of my car, much less try to lock up the house. Locks were more a symbol than a reality, and if things ever got serious there was always the .44 Magnum. But in Washington you get the impression—if you believe what you hear from even the most "liberal" insiders—that just about everybody you see on the street is holding at least a .38 Special, and maybe worse.

Not that it matters a hell of a lot at ten feet . . . but it makes you a trifle nervous to hear that nobody in his or her right mind would dare to walk alone from the Capitol Building to a car in the parking lot without fear of later on having to crawl, naked and bleeding, to the nearest police station.

There is no way to avoid "racist undertones" here. The simple heavy truth is that Washington is mainly a Black City, and that most of the violent crime is therefore committed by blacks—not always against whites, but often enough to make the relatively wealthy white population very nervous about random social contacts with their black fellow citizens. After only ten days in this town I have noticed the Fear/Syndrome clouding even my own mind: I find myself ignoring black hitchhikers, and every time I do it I wonder, Why the fuck did you do that? And I tell myself, Well, I'll pick up the next one I see. And sometimes I do, but not always . . .

My arrival in town was not mentioned by any of the society columnists. It was shortly after dawn, as I recall, when I straggled into Washington just ahead of the rush-hour, government-worker carpool traffic boiling up from the Maryland suburbs . . . humping along in the slow lane on U.S. Interstate 70S like a crippled steel pissant; dragging a massive orange U-Haul trailer full of books and "important" papers . . . feeling painfully slow & helpless because the Volvo was never made for this kind of work.

It's a quick little beast and one of the best ever built for rough-road, mud & snow driving . . . but not even this new, six-cylinder "super-Volvo" is up to hauling two thousand pounds of heavy swill across the country from Woody Creek, Colorado, to Washington, D.C. The odometer read 2155 when I crossed the Maryland line as the sun came up over Hagerstown.

• • •

"Welcome to Washington D.C." That's what the sign says. It's about twenty feet wide & ten feet tall—a huge stone plaque lit up by spotlights at the head of Sixteenth Street, just in from the Maryland line. The street is five lanes wide, with fat green trees on both sides and about 1,300 out-of-phase stoplights between here and the White House.

It is not considered fashionable to live in "The District" itself unless you can find a place in Georgetown, an aged-brick townhouse with barred windows, for $700 or so a month. Georgetown is Washington's lame answer to Greenwich Village. But not really. It's more like the Old Town section of Chicago, where the leading citizens are half-bright *Playboy* editors smoking tailor-made joints. The same people, in Georgetown, are trendy young lawyers, journalists, and bureaucrats who frequent a handful of pinepaneled bars and "singles only" discotheques where drinks cost $1.75 and there's No Cover Charge for girls wearing hotpants.

I live on the "black side" of Rock Creek Park, in what my journalistic friends call "a marginal neighborhood." Almost everybody else I know or have any professional contact with lives either in the green Virginia suburbs or over on the "white side" of the park, toward Chevy Chase and Bethesda, in Maryland.

The Underculture is scattered into various far-flung bastions, and the only thing even approximately a crossroads is the area around Dupont Circle, downtown. The only two people I know who live down there are Nicholas von Hoffman, a columnist for the *Washington Post*, and Jim Flug, Teddy Kennedy's hyperactive Legislative Assistant. But von Hoffman seems to have had a bellyful of Washington and now talks about moving out to the Coast, to San Francisco . . . and Flug, like everybody else even vaguely connected with Kennedy, is gearing down for a very heavy year: like maybe twenty hours a day on the telephone, and the other four on planes.

McGovern & the Press Wizards

With December winding down, there is a fast-swelling undercurrent of political angst in the air around Washington, a sense of almost boiling desperation about getting Nixon and his cronies out of power before they can finish the seizure that began about two years ago.

Jim Flug says he'd rather not talk about Kennedy running for president—at least not until he has to, and that time seems to be coming up fast. Teddy is apparently sincere about not planning to run, but it is hard for him or anyone else not to notice that almost everybody who "matters" in Washington is fascinated by the recent series of Gallup polls showing Kennedy creeping ever closer to Nixon—almost even with him now, and this rising tide has cast a very long shadow on the other Democratic candidates.

There is a sense of muted desperation in Democratic ranks at the prospect of getting stuck—and beaten once again—with some tried-and-half-true hack like Humphrey, Jackson, or Muskie . . . and George McGovern, the only candidate in either party worth voting for, is hung in a frustration limbo created mainly by the gross cynicism of the Washington press corps. "He'd be a fine president," they say, "but of course he can't possibly win."

Why not?

Well . . . the wizards haven't bothered to explain that, but their reasoning appears to be rooted in the hazy idea that the people who could make McGovern president—that huge & confused coalition of students, freaks, blacks, anti-war activists, & dazed dropouts—won't even bother to register, much less drag themselves to the polls on Election Day.

Maybe so . . . but it is hard to recall many candidates, in recent history, who failed to move what is now called "The McGovern Vote" to the polls if they *actually represented it*.

It sure as hell wasn't the AFL-CIO that ran LBJ out of the White House in 1968; and it wasn't Gene McCarthy either. It was the people who *voted* for McCarthy in New Hampshire that beat Johnson . . . and it wasn't George Meany who got shot with Bobby Kennedy in Los Angeles; it was a renegade "radical" organizer from the UAW.

It wasn't the big-time "Democratic bosses" who won the California primary for Bobby—but thousands of Niggers and Spics and white Peace Freaks who were tired of being gassed for not agreeing with The Man in the White House. Nobody had to drag them to the polls in California, and nobody would have had to drag them to the polls in November to beat Nixon.

But there was, of course, The Murder—and then the convention in Chicago, and finally a turnip called Humphrey. He appealed to "respectable" Democrats then and now—and if Humphrey or any of his greasy ilk runs in '72, it will be another debacle like the Eisenhower-Stevenson wipeout in 1956.

The people who turned out for Bobby are still around—along with several million others who'll be voting for the first time—but they won't turn out for Humphrey, or Jackson, or Muskie, or any other neo-Nixon hack. They will not even come out for McGovern if the national press wizards keep calling him a Noble Loser . . .

According to the Gallup polls, however, the underculture vote is holding up a fearful head of steam behind Ted Kennedy; and this drift has begun to cause genuine alarm among Big Wigs and "pros" in both parties. The mere mention of Kennedy's name is said to give Nixon bad cramps all over his body, such as it is. His thugs are already starting to lash Kennedy with vicious denunciations—calling him a "liar" and a "coward" and a "cheater."

And this is only December of 1971; the election is still ten months away.

The only person more nervous than Nixon about Kennedy's recent surge in the polls seems to be Kennedy himself. He won't even admit that it's happening—at least not for the record—and his top-level staffers, like Jim Flug, find themselves walking a public tightrope. They can see the thing coming—too soon, perhaps, but there's nothing they can do about that either. With the boss hunkered down, insisting he's not a candidate, his lieutenants try to keep their minds off the storm by working feverishly on Projects.

When I called Flug the other night, at the office, he was working late on a doomed effort to prevent Earl Butz from being confirmed, by the Senate, as Nixon's new Secretary of Agriculture.

"To hell with Butz," I said, "what about Rehnquist? Are they actually going to put a swine like that on the Supreme Court?"

"They have the votes," he replied.

"Jesus," I muttered, "is he as bad as all the rotten stuff I've read about him?"

"Worse," Flug said. "But I think he's in. We tried, but we can't get the votes."

Your New Supreme Court

Jim Flug and I are not close friends in any long-standing personal sense. I met him a few years ago when I went to Washington to do a lot of complicated research for an article about Gun Control Laws for *Esquire*—an article that finally died in a blaze of niggling between me and the editors about how to cut my "final version" down from thirty thousand words to a size that would fit in the magazine.

Flug had gone far out of his way to help me with that research. We talked in the dreary cafeteria in the Old Senate Office Building where we sat down elbow to elbow with Senator Roman Hruska, the statesman from Nebraska, and various other heavies whose names I forget now.

We idled through the line with our trays, then took our plastic-wrapped tuna fish sandwiches over to a small Formica table, along with coffee in styrofoam cups. Flug talked about the problems he was having with the Gun Control Bill—trying to put it into some form that might possibly pass the Senate. I listened, glancing up now and then toward the food-bar, half expecting to see somebody like Robert Kennedy pushing his tray through the line . . . until I suddenly remembered that Robert Kennedy was dead.

Meanwhile, Flug was outlining every angle and aspect of the Gun Control argument with the buzz-saw precision of a trial lawyer. He was totally *into* it: crouched there in his seat, wearing a blue pin-striped suit with a vest and oxblood cordovans—a swarthy, bright-eyed little man about thirty years old, mercilessly shredding every argument the National Rifle Association had ever mounted against federal gun laws. Later, when I learned he really was a lawyer, it ocurred to me that I would never under any circumstances want to tangle with a person like Flug in a courtroom . . . and I was careful not to tell him, even in jest, about my .44 Magnum fetish.

After lunch that day we went back to his office and he gave me an armload of fact sheets and statistics to back up his arguments. Then I left, feeling very much impressed with Flug's trip—and I was not surprised, a year later, when I heard that he had been the prime mover behind the seemingly impossible challenge to the Carswell Supreme Court nomination, one of the most impressive long shot political victories since McCarthy sent Lyndon back to the ranch.

Coming on the heels of Judge Haynsworth's rejection by the Senate, Carswell had seemed like a shoo-in . . . but a hard-core group of Senate staffers, led by Flug and Birch Bayh's assistants, had managed to dump Carswell, too.

Now, with Nixon trying to fill two *more* court vacancies, Flug said there was not a chance in hell of beating either one of them.

"Not even Rehnquist?" I asked. "Christ, that's like Lyndon Johnson trying to put Bobby Baker on the Court."

"I know," said Flug. "Next time you want to think about appealing a case to the U.S. Supreme Court, just remember who'll be up there."

"You mean *down* there," I said. "Along with all the rest of us." I laughed. "Well, there's always smack . . ."

Flug didn't laugh. He and a lot of others have worked too hard, for the past three years, to derail the kind of nightmare that the Nixon-Mitchell team is ready to ram down our throats. There is not much satisfaction in beating Haynsworth & Carswell, then having to swallow a third-rate yoyo like Powell and a vengeful geek like Rehnquist. What Nixon and Mitchell have done in three years—despite the best efforts of the sharpest and meanest young turks the Democratic opposition can call on—is reduce the U.S. Supreme Court to the level of a piss-poor bowling team in Memphis—and this disastrous, Nazi-bent shift of the federal government's Final Decision–making powers won't even *begin* to take effect until the spring of '72.

The effects of this takeover are potentially so disastrous—in terms of personal freedom and police power—that there is no point even speculating on the fate of some poor, misguided geek who might want to take his "Illegal Search & Seizure" case all the way up to the top. A helpful hint, however, might be found in the case of the Tallahassee newspaper reporter who went to Canada in 1967 to avoid the draft—and returned to find that he was no longer a citizen of the United States and he now has ninety days to leave the country. He appealed his case to the Supreme Court, but they refused to even hear it.

So now he has to go, but of course he has no passport—and international travel is not real easy without a passport. The federal immigration officials understand this, but—backed up by the Supreme Court—they have given him an ultimatum to vacate, anyway. They don't care where he goes; just get out—and meanwhile Chief Justice Burger has taken to answering his doorbell at night with a big six-shooter in his hand. You never know, he says, who might come crashing in.

Indeed. Maybe Rehnquist—far gone with an overdose of raw sowbelly and crazy for terminal vengeance on the first house he comes to.

More Bad Tendencies

This world is full of dangerous beasts—but none quite as ugly and uncontrollable as a lawyer who has finally flipped off the tracks of Reason. He will run completely amok—like a Priest into sex, or a narc-squad cop who suddenly desides to start sampling his contraband.

Yes . . . and . . . ah, where were we? I have a bad tendency to rush off on mad tangents and pursue them for fifty or sixty pages that get so out of control that I end up burning them, for my own good. One of the few exceptions to this rule occurred very recently, when I slipped up and let about two hundred pages go into print . . . which caused me a lot of trouble with the tax man, among others, and it taught me a lesson I hope I'll never forget.

Live steady. Don't fuck around. Give anything weird a wide berth—including people. It's not worth it. I learned this the hard way through brutal indulgence.

And it's also a nasty fact that I have to catch a plane for Chicago in three hours—to attend some kind of national Emergency Conference on New Voters, which looks like the opening shot in this year's version of the McCarthy-Kennedy uprising in '68—and since the conference starts at six o'clock tonight, I must make that plane . . .

. . . Back to Chicago; it's never dull out there. You never know exactly what kind of terrible shit is going to come down on you in that town, but you can always count on *something*. Every time I go to Chicago I come away with scars.

The Campaign Trail: The Million-Pound Shithammer

February 3, 1972

There are issues enough. What is gone is the popular passion for them. Possibly, hope is gone.

The failure of hope would be a terrible event; the blacks have never been cynical about America. But conversation you hear among the young now, on the South Side of Chicago, up in Harlem or in Bedford-Stuyvesant, certainly suggests the birth of a new cynicism. In the light of what government is doing, you might well expect young blacks to lose hope in the power elites, but this is something different—a cold personal indifference, a separation of man from man. What you hear and see is not rage, but injury, a withering of expectations.

—D.J.R. Bruckner, 1/6/72 in the *L.A. Times*

Bruckner's article was focused on the mood of Young Blacks, but unless you were reading very closely, the distinction was easy to miss. Because the mood amoung Young Whites is not much different—despite a lot of well-financed publicity about the potentially massive "youth vote."

These are the twenty-five million or so new voters between eighteen and twenty-five—going, maybe, to the polls for the first time—who supposedly hold the fate of the nation in the palms of their eager young hands. According to the people who claim to speak for it, this "youth vote" has the power to zap Nixon out of office with a flick of its wrist. Hubert Humphrey lost in '68 by 499,704 votes—a miniscule percentage of what the so-called "youth vote" could turn out in 1972.

But there are not many people in Washington who take this notion of the "youth vote" very seriously. Not even the candidates. The thinking here is that the young people who vote for the first time in '72 will split more or less along the same old lines as their parents, and that the addition of twenty-five million new (potential) voters means just another sudden mass that will have to be absorbed into the same old patterns . . . just another big wave of new immigrants who don't know the score yet, but who will learn it soon enough, so why worry?

Why indeed? The scumbags behind this thinking are probably right, once again—but it might be worth pondering, this time, if perhaps they might be right for the wrong reasons. Almost all the politicians and press wizards who denigrate the "so-called youth vote" as a factor in the '72 elections have justified their thinking with a sort of melancholy judgment on "the kids" themselves.

"How many will even register?" they ask. "And even then—even assuming a third of the *possibles* might register, how many of those will actually get out and vote?"

The implication, every time, is that the "youth vote" menace is just a noisy paper tiger. Sure, *some* of these kids will vote, they say, but the way things look now, it won't be more than 10 percent. That's the colleges; the other 90 percent are either military types, on the dole, or working people—on salary, just married, hired into their first jobs. Man, these people are already *locked down*, the same as their parents.

That's the argument . . . and it's probably safe to say, right now, that there is not a single presidential candidate, media guru, or backstairs politics wizard in Washington who honestly believes the "youth vote" will have more than a marginal, splinter-vote effect on the final outcome of the 1972 presidential campaign.

These kids are turned off from politics, they say. Most of 'em don't want to hear about it. All they want to do these days is lie around on waterbeds and smoke that goddamn marrywanna . . . yeah, and just between you and me, Fred, I think it's probably all for the best.

Among the half-dozen high-powered organizations in Washington who claim to speak for the "youth vote," the only one with any real muscle at this point is the National Association of Student Governments, which recently—after putting together an "Emergency Conference for New Voters" in Chicago last month—brought its leadership back to

D.C. and called a press conference in the Old Senate Office Building to announce the formation of a "National Youth Caucus."

The idea, said twenty-six-year-old Duane Draper—the main organizer—was to get student-type activists into power on the local level in every state where they might be able to influence the drift of the '72 election. The press conference was well attended. Edward P. Morgan of PBS was there, dressed in a snappy London Fog raincoat and twirling a black umbrella; the *New York Times* sent a woman, the *Washington Post* was represented by a human pencil, and the rest of the national press sent the same people they send to everything else that happens, officially, in this doomed sink-hole of a city.

As always, the "print people" stood or sat in a timid half circle behind the network TV cameras—while Draper and his mentor, Senator Fred Harris of Oklahoma, sat together at the front table and explained that the success of the Chicago rally had got the "youth vote" off to a running start. Harris didn't say much; he just sat there looking like Johnny Cash while Draper, a former student body president at the University of Oklahoma, explained to the jaded press that the "youth vote" would be an important and perhaps decisive factor in this year's election.

I came in about ten minutes late, and when question time came around I asked the same one I'd asked Allard Lowenstein at a similar press conference in Chicago: Would the Youth Caucus support Hubert Humphrey if he won the Democratic nomination?

Lowenstein had refused to answer that question in Chicago, saying, "We'll cross that bridge if we come to it." But in Washington Draper said "Yes," the Youth Vote could get behind Hubert if he said the right things—"if he takes the right positions."

"How about Jackson?" I asked.

This made for a pause . . . but finally Draper said the National Youth Caucus might support Jackson, too, "if he comes around."

"Around to what?" I asked. And by this time I was feeling very naked and conspicuous. My garb and general demeanor is not considered normal by Washington standards. Levi's don't make it in this town; if you show up wearing Levi's they figure you'll either be a servant or a messenger. This is particularly true at high-level press conferences, where any deviation from standard journalistic dress is considered rude and perhaps even dangerous.

In Washington all journalists dress like bank tellers—and those who don't have problems. Mister Nixon's press handlers, for instance, have made it ominously clear that I shall *not* be given White House press credentials. The first time I called, they said they'd never heard of *Rolling Stone*. "Rolling what?" said the woman.

"You'd better ask somebody a little younger," I said.

"Thank you," she hissed. "I'll do that." But the next obstacle up the line was the deputy White House press secretary, a faceless voice called Gerald Warren, who said Rolling Whatever didn't *need* White House press credentials—despite the fact they had been issued in the past, without any hassle, to all manner of strange and obscure publications, including student papers like the George Washington University *Hatchet*.

The only people who seem genuinely interested in the '72 elections are the actual participants—the various candidates, their paid staff people, the thousands of journalists, cameramen & other media-connected hustlers who will spend most of this year humping the campaign along . . . and of course all the *sponsors*, called "fat cats" in the language of Now-Politics, who stand to gain hugely for at least the next four years if they can muscle their man down the homestretch just a hair ahead of the others.

The fat-cat action is still one of the most dramatic aspects of a presidential campaign, but even in this colorful area the tension is leaking away—primarily because most of the really serious fat cats figured out, a few years back, that they could beat the whole rap—along with the onus of going down the tube with some desperate loser—by "helping" two candidates, instead of just one.

A good example of this, in 1972, will probably be Mrs. Rella Factor—widow of "Jake the Barber" and the largest single contributor to Hubert Humphrey's campaign in '68. She didn't get a hell of a lot of return for her investment last time around. But this year, using the new method, she can buy the total friendship of two, three, or perhaps even four presidential candidates, for the same price . . . by splitting up the nut, discreetly as possible, between Hubert, Nixon, and maybe—just for the natural randy hell of it—a chunk to Gene McCarthy, who appears to be cranking up a genuinely weird campaign this time.

• • •

I have a peculiar affection for McCarthy; nothing serious or personal, but I recall standing next to him in the snow outside the "exit" door of a shoe factory in Manchester, New Hampshire, in February of 1968 when the five o'clock whistle blew, and he had to stand there in the midst of those workers rushing out to the parking lot. I will never forget the pain in McCarthy's face as he stood there with his hand out, saying over and over again: "Shake hands with Senator McCarthy . . . shake hands with Senator McCarthy . . . shake hands with Senator McCarthy" . . . a tense plastic smile on his face, stepping nervously toward anything friendly, "Shake hands with Senator McCarthy" . . . but most of the crowd ignored him, refusing to even acknowledge his outstretched hand, staring straight ahead as they hurried out to their cars.

There was at least one network TV camera on hand that afternoon, but the scene was never aired. It was painful enough just being there, but to have put that scene on national TV would have been an act of genuine cruelty. McCarthy was obviously suffering; not so much because nine out of ten people refused to shake his hand, but because he really hated being there in the first place. But his managers had told him it was necessary, and maybe it was . . .

Later, when his outlandish success in New Hampshire shocked Johnson into retirement, I half expected McCarthy to quit the race himself, rather than suffer all the way to Chicago . . . and God only knows what kind of vengeful energy is driving him this time, but a lot of the people who said he was suffering from brain bubbles when he first mentioned that he might run again in '72 are beginning to take him seriously: not as a Democratic contender, but as an increasingly possible Fourth Party candidate with the power to put a candidate like Muskie through all kinds of terrible changes between August and November.

To Democratic chairman Larry O'Brien, the specter of a McCarthy candidacy in '72 must be something like hearing the Hound of the Baskervilles sniffing and pissing around on your porch every night. A left-bent Fourth Party candidate with a few serious grudges on his mind could easily take enough left/radical votes away from either Muskie or

Humphrey to make the Democratic nomination all but worthless to either one of them.

Nobody seems to know what McCarthy has in mind, but the possibilities are ominous, and anybody who thought he was kidding got snapped around fast last week when McCarthy launched a brutish attack on Muskie within hours after the Maine senator made his candidacy official.

The front page of the *Washington Post* carried photos of both men, along with a prominent headline and McCarthy's harsh warning that he was going to hold Muskie "accountable" for his hawkish stance on the war in Vietnam prior to 1968. McCarthy also accused Muskie of being "the most active representative of Johnson administration policy at the 1968 convention."

Muskie seemed genuinely shaken by this attack. He immediately called a press conference to admit that he'd been wrong about Vietnam in the past, but that now "I've had reason to change my mind." His new position was an awkward thing to explain, but after admitting his "past mistakes" he said that he now favored "as close to an immediate withdrawal from Vietnam as possible."

McCarthy merely shrugged. He had done his gig for the day, and Muskie was jolted. The senator focused all his efforts on the question of his altered Vietnam stance, but he was probably far more disturbed by McCarthy's ugly revenge-tainted reference to Muskie's role in the '68 Democratic Convention. This was obviously the main bone in McCarthy's throat, but Muskie ignored it and nobody asked Gene what he really meant by the charge . . . probably because there is no way to understand what happened to McCarthy in Chicago unless you were there and saw it yourself.

I have never read anything that comes anywhere close to explaining the shock and intensity I felt at that convention . . . and although I was right in the middle of it the whole time, I have never been able to write about it myself. For two weeks afterward, back in Colorado, I couldn't even talk about it without starting to cry—for reasons I think I finally understand now, but I still can't explain.

Because of this: because I went there as a journalist, with no real emotional attachment to any of the candidates and only the barest of illusions about the outcome . . . I was not personally involved in the thing, so there is no point in presuming to understand what kind of hellish effect Chicago must have had on Gene McCarthy.

I remember seeing him cross Michigan Avenue on Thursday night—several hours after Humphrey had made his acceptance speech out at the Stockyards—and then wandering into the crowd in Grant Park like a defeated general trying to mingle with his troops just after the Surrender. But McCarthy couldn't mingle. He could barely talk. He acted like a man in deep shock. There was not much to say. The campaign was over.

McCarthy's gig was finished. He had knocked off the president and then strung himself out on a fantastic six-month campaign that had seen the murder of Martin Luther King, the murder of Bobby Kennedy, and finally a bloody assault on his own campaign workers by Mayor Daley's police, who burst into McCarthy's private convention headquarters at the Chicago Hilton and began breaking heads. At dawn on Friday morning, his campaign manager, a seasoned old pro named Blair Clark, was still pacing up and down Michigan Avenue in front of the Hilton in a state so close to hysteria that his friends were afraid to talk to him because every time he tried to say something his eyes would fill with tears and he would have to start pacing again.

Perhaps McCarthy has placed that whole scene in its proper historical and poetic perspective, but if he has I didn't read it . . . or maybe he's been hanging onto the manuscript until he can find a right ending. McCarthy has a sharp sense of drama, along with his now kinky instinct for timing. But nobody appears to have noticed, until now, that he might also have a bull-sized taste for revenge.

• • •

Maybe not. In terms of classic journalism, this kind of wandering, unfounded speculation will have a nasty effect on that asshole from Ireland who sent word across The Waters to nail me for bad language and lack of objectivity. There have been numerous complaints, in fact, about the publisher allowing me to get away with calling our new Supreme Court Justice William Rehnquist a "swine."

Well . . . shit, what can I say? Objective Journalism is a hard thing to come by, these days. We all yearn for it, but who can point the way? The only man who comes to mind, right offhand, is my good friend and colleague on the Sports Desk, Raoul Duke. Most journalists only *talk* about objectivity, but Dr. Duke grabs it straight by the fucking throat. You will be hard pressed to find any argument, among professionals, on the question of Dr. Duke's Objectivity.

As for mine . . . well, my doctor says it swole up and busted about ten years ago. The only thing I ever saw that came close to Objective Journalism was the closed-circuit TV that watched shoplifters in the General Store at Woody Creek, Colorado. I always admired that machine, but I noticed that nobody paid much attention to it until one of those known, heavy, out-front shoplifters came into the place . . . but when that happened, everybody got so excited that the thief had to do something quick, like buy a green popsicle or a can of Coors and get out of the place immediately.

So much for objective journalism. Don't bother to look for it here—not under any byline of mine; or anyone else I can think of. With the possible exception of things like box scores, race results, and stock market tabulations, there is no such thing as Objective Journalism. The phrase itself is a gross contradiction in terms.

• • •

And so much for all that, too. There was at least one more thing I wanted to get into here, before trying to wind this down and get into something human. Like sleep, or that 550-watt Humm Box they have up there in the Ree-Lax Parlor at Silver Spring. Some people say they should outlaw the Humm Box, but I disagree.

Meanwhile, all that venomous speculation about what McCarthy is up to these days left a crucial question hanging: the odd truth that almost everybody in Washington who is paid to analyze & predict the behavior of Vote Blocs seems to feel that the much-publicized "Youth Vote" will not be a Major Factor in the '72 presidential campaign would be a hell of a lot easier to accept if it weren't for the actual figures.

What the experts appear to be saying is that the sudden addition of twenty-five million new voters between the ages of eighteen and twenty-five will not make much difference in the power-structure of American politics. No *candidate* will say this, of course. For the record, they are all very solicitous of the "youth vote." In a close election, even 10 percent of that bloc would mean two and a half million votes—a very serious figure when you stack it up against Nixon's thin margin over Humphrey in 1968.

Think of it: only *10 percent*! Two and a half million. Enough—even according to Nixon's own wizards—to swing almost *any* election. It is a general assumption, in the terms of contemporary presidential elections, that it would take something genuinely vile and terrifying to cause either one of the major party candidates to come away with less than 40 percent of the vote. Goldwater managed to do this in '64, but not by much. Even after allowing Johnson's TV sappers to cast him as a stupid, bloodthirsty ghoul who had every intention of blowing the whole world off its axis the moment he got his hands on "the button," Goldwater still got 27,178,188 votes, or 38.5 percent.

The prevailing wisdom today is that *any* candidate in a standard-brand, two-party election will get about 40 percent of the vote. The basic assumption here is that neither party would nominate a man more than 20 percent different from the type of person most Americans consider basically right and acceptable. Which almost always happens. There is no potentially serious candidate in either major party this year who couldn't pass for the executive vice president for mortgage loans in any hometown bank from Bangor to San Diego.

We are talking about a purely physical/image gig here, but even if you let the buggers jabber like magpies about anything that comes to their minds, not even a dangerous dingbat like Sam Yorty would be likely to alienate more than 45 or 50 percent of the electorate.

And even that far-left radical bastard, George McGovern—babbling a maddening litany of his most Far Out ideas—would be hard pressed to crank up any more than a 30 percent animosity quotient.

On balance, they are a pretty bland lot. Even Spiro Agnew—if you catch him between screeds—is not more than 20 percent different from Humphrey or Lindsay or Scoop Jackson. Four years ago, in fact, John Lindsay dug Agnew so much that he seconded his nomination for the vice-presidency. There are a lot of people who say we should forget about that this year "because John has already said he made a mistake about Agnew," but there are a lot of others who take Lindsay's "Agnew Mistake" very seriously—because they assume he would do the same thing again next week or next month, if he thought it would do him any good.

Nobody seems very worried about Lindsay right now; they are waiting to see what kind of action he can generate in Florida, a state full of transient and old/transplanted New Yorkers. If he can't make it there, he's done for. Which is just as well. But if he scores big in Florida, we will probably have to start taking him seriously—particularly if Muskie looks convincing in New Hampshire.

A Muskie-Lindsay ticket could be one of those "naturals," a marriage made in heaven and consummated by Larry O'Brien . . . Which gets us back to one of the main reasons why the political wizards aren't counting on much of a "youth vote" this year. It is hard to imagine even a zealot like Allard Lowenstein going out on the trail once again to whip up a campus-based firestorm for Muskie and Lindsay . . . particularly with Gene McCarthy lurking around with that ugly mouth of his, and those deep-bleeding grudges.

There is probably a lot of interesting talk going down around Humphrey headquarters these days: "Say . . . ah, Hube, baby. I guess you heard what your old buddy Gene did to Muskie the other day, right? Yeah, and we always thought they were *friends*, didn't we? [*Long pause, no reply from the candidate . . .*]

"So . . . ah . . . Hube? You still with me? Jesus Christ! Where's that goddamn sunlamp? We gotta get more of a tan on you, baby. You look *gray*. [*Long pause, no reply from the candidate . . .*] "Well, Hube, we might just as well face this thing. We're comin' up fast on what just might be a real nasty little problem for you . . . let's not try to kid ourselves, Hube, he's a really *mean* sonofabitch. [*Long pause, etc . . .*] You gonna have to be *ready*, Hube. You announce next Thursday at noon, right? So we might as well figure that crazy fucker is gonna come down on you like a million-pound shithammer that same afternoon. He'll probably stage a big scene at the Press Club—and we know who's gonna be there, don't we Hube? Yeah, every bastard in the business. Are you ready for that, Hube Baby? Can you handle it? [*Long pause, no reply, etc.—heavy breathing.*] Okay, Hube, tell me this: What does the bastard know? What's the worst he can spring on you?"

• • •

Jesus! This gibberish could run on forever, and even now I can see myself falling into the old trap that plagues every writer who gets sucked into this rotten business: you find yourself getting fascinated by the rules and strange quirks of the game. Even now, before I've even finished this one article, I can already feel the compulsion to start handicapping politics and primaries like it was all just another fat Sunday of pro football: pick Pittsburgh by 6 points in the early game, get Kansas City even with Oakland later on . . . win one, lose one . . . then flip the dial and try to get ahead by conning somebody into taking the Rams even against San Francisco.

After several weeks of this you no longer give a flying fuck who actually wins; the only thing that matters is the point spread. You find yourself screeching crazily at the screen, pleading for somebody to rip the lungs out of that junkie bastard who just threw an interception and then didn't even *pretend* to tackle the pig who ran it back for 6 points to beat the spread.

There is something perverse and perverted about dealing with life on this level. But on the other hand, it gets harder to convince yourself, once you start thinking about it, that it could possibly make any real difference to you if the 49ers win or lose . . . although every once in a while you stumble into a situation where you find yourself really *wanting* some team to get stomped all over the field, severely beaten and humiliated . . .

This happened to me on the last Sunday of the regular NFL season when two slobbering drunk sportswriters from the *Alexandria Gazette* got me thrown out of the press box at Robert F. Kennedy Stadium in Washington. I was there as a special guest of Dave Burgin, sports editor of the *Washington Star* . . . but when Burgin tried to force a bit of dignity on the scene, they ejected him too.

We were halfway down the ramp to the parking lot before I understood what had happened. "That gin-soaked little Nazi from the *Gazette* got pissed off when you didn't doff your hat for the national anthem," Burgin explained. "He kept bitching about you to the guy in charge of the press box, then he got that asshole who works for him all cranked up and they started talking about having you arrested."

"Jesus creeping shit," I muttered. "Now I know why I got out of sportswriting. Christ, I had no idea what was happening. You should have warned me."

"I was afraid you'd run amok," he said. "We'd have been in bad trouble. All those guys are from things like the *Norfolk Ledger* and the *Army-Navy Times.* They would have stomped us like rats in a closet."

I couldn't understand it. "Hell, I'd have taken the goddamn hat off if I thought it was causing trouble. I barely even remember the national anthem. Usually I don't even stand up."

"I didn't think you were going to," he said. "I didn't want to say anything, but I knew we were doomed."

"But I *did* stand," I said. "I figured, hell, I'm Dave's guest—why not stand and make it easy for him? But I never even thought about my goddamn hat."

Actually, I was happy to get out of that place. The Redskins were losing, which pleased me, and we were thrown out just in time to get back to Burgin's house for the 49er game on TV. If they won this one, they would go against the Redskins next Sunday in the playoffs—and by the end of the third quarter I had worked myself into a genuine hate frenzy; I was howling like a butcher when the 49ers pulled it out in the final moments with a series of desperate maneuvers, and the moment the gun sounded I was on the phone to TWA, securing a seat on the Christmas Nite Special to San Francisco. It was extremely important, I felt, to go out there and do everything possible to make sure the Redskins got the mortal piss beaten out of them.

• • •

Which worked out. Not only did the 49ers stomp the jingo bastards and knock them out of the playoffs, but my seat companion for the flight from Dallas to San Francisco was Edward Bennett Williams, the legendary trial lawyer, who is also president of the Washington Redskins.

"Heavy duty for you people tomorrow," I warned him. "Get braced for a serious beating. Nothing personal, you understand. Those poor bastards couldn't have known what they were doing when they croaked a Doctor of Journalism out of the press box."

He nodded heavily and called for another drink. "It's a goddamn shame," he muttered. "But what can you really expect? You lie down with pigs and they'll call you a swine every time."

"What? Did you call me a *swine*?"

"Not me," he said. "But this world is full of slander."

We spent the rest of the evening on politics. He is backing Muskie, and as he talked I got the feeling that he felt he was already at a point where, sooner or later, we would all be. "Ed's a good man," he said. "He's honest. I respect the guy." Then he stabbed the padded seat arm between us two or three times with his forefinger. "But the main reason I'm working for him," he said, "is that he's the only guy we have who can beat Nixon." He stabbed the arm again. "If Nixon wins again, we're in real trouble." He picked up his drink, then saw it was empty and put it down again. "That's the real issue this time," he said. "Beating Nixon. It's hard to even guess how much damage those bastards will do if they get in for another four years."

I nodded. The argument was familiar. I had even made it myself, here and there, but I was beginning to sense something very depressing about it. How many more of these goddamn elections are we going to have to write off as lame but "regrettably necessary" hold actions? And how many more of these stinking, double-downer sideshows will we have to go through before we can get ourselves straight enough to put together some kind of national election that will give me and the forty million I tend to agree with a chance to vote *for* something, instead of always being faced with that old familiar choice between the lesser of two evils?

I have been through three presidential elections now, but it has been twelve years since I could look at a ballot and see a name I wanted to vote *for*. In 1964 I refused to vote at all, and in '68 I spent half a morning in the county courthouse getting an absentee ballot so I could vote, out of spite, for Dick Gregory.

Now, with another one of these big bogus showdowns looming down on us, I can already pick up the stench of another bummer. I understand, along with a lot of other people, that the big thing, this year, is Beating Nixon. But that was also the big thing, as I recall, twelve years ago in 1960—and as far as I can tell, we've gone from bad to worse to rotten since then, and the outlook is for more of the same.

Not even James Reston, the swinging Calvinist, claims to see any light at the end of the tunnel in '72. Reston's first big shot of the year dealt mainly with a grim "memo" by former JFK strategist Fred Dutton, who is now a Washington lawyer.

There are hints of hope in the Reston-Dutton prognosis, but not for the next four years. Here is the rancid nut of it: "The 1972 election probably is fated to be a dated, weakening election, an historical curio, belonging more to the past than to the new national three- or four-party trend of the future."

Reston either ignored or overlooked, for some reason, the probability that Gene McCarthy appears to be gearing up almost exactly the kind of "independent third force in American politics" that both Reston and Dutton see as a wave of the future.

An even grimmer note comes with Reston's offhand dismissal of Ed Muskie, the only man—according to E. B. Williams—who can possibly save us from more years of Nixon. And as if poor Muskie didn't already have enough evil shit on his neck, the eminently reasonable, fine old liberal journal, the *Washington Post,* called Muskie's official "new beginning/I am now a candidate" speech on national TV a meaningless rehash of old bullshit and stale clichés raked up from old speeches by . . . yes . . . Himself, Richard Milhous Nixon.

In other words, the weight of the evidence filtering down from the high brainrooms of both the *New York Times* and the *Washington Post* seems to say we're all fucked. Muskie is a bonehead who steals his best lines from old Nixon speeches. McGovern is doomed because everybody who knows him has so much respect for the man that they can't bring themselves to degrade the poor bastard by making him run for president . . . John Lindsay is a dunce, Gene McCarthy is crazy, Humphrey is doomed and useless, Jackson should have stayed in bed . . . and, well, that just about wraps up the trip, right?

Not entirely, but I feel The Fear coming on, and the only cure for that is to chew up a fat black wad of blood-opium about the size of a young meatball and then call a cab for a fast run down to that strip of X-film houses on 14th Street . . . peel back the brain, let the opium take hold, and get locked into serious pornography.

As for politics, I think Art Buchwald said it all last month in his "Fan letter to Nixon."

"I always wanted to get into politics, but I was never light enough to make the team."

The Campaign Trail: Fear and Loathing in New Hampshire

March 2, 1972

It was just before midnight when I left Cambridge and headed north on U.S. 93 toward Manchester—driving one of those big green rented Auto/Stick Cougars that gets rubber for about twenty-nine seconds in Drive, and spits hot black divots all over the road in First or Second . . . a terrible screeching and fishtailing through the outskirts of Boston heading north to New Hampshire, back on the Campaign Trail . . . running late, as usual: left hand on the wheel and the other on the radio dial, seeking music, and a glass of iced Wild Turkey spilling into my crotch on every turn.

Not much of a moon tonight, but a sky full of very bright stars. Freezing cold outside; patches of ice on the road and snow on the sidehills . . . running about seventy-five or eighty through a landscape of stark naked trees and stone fences; not many cars out tonight, and no lights in the roadside farmhouses. People go to bed early in New England.

• • •

Four years ago I ran this road in a different Mercury, but I wasn't driving then. It was a big yellow sedan with a civvy-clothes cop at the wheel. Sitting next to the cop, up front, were two of Nixon's best speechwriters: Ray Price and Pat Buchanan.

There were only two of us in back: just me and Richard Nixon, and we were talking football in a very serious way. It was late—almost midnight then, too—and the cop was holding the big Merc at exactly sixty-five as we hissed along the highway for more than an hour between some American Legion hall in a small town near Nashua where Nixon had just made a speech and the airport up in Manchester where a Learjet was waiting to whisk the candidate and his brain trust off to Key Biscayne for a Think Session.

It was a very weird trip; probably one of the weirdest things I've ever done and especially weird because both Nixon and I enjoyed it. We had a good talk, and when we got to the airport, I stood around the Learjet with Dick and the others, chatting in a very relaxed way about how successful his swing through New Hampshire had been . . . and as he climbed into the plane it seemed only natural to thank him for the ride and shake hands . . .

But suddenly I was seized from behind and jerked away from the plane. Good God, I thought as I reeled backward, here we go . . . "Watch out!" somebody was shouting. "Get the cigarette!" A hand lashed out of the darkness to snatch the cigarette out of my mouth, then other hands kept me from falling and I recognized the voice of Nick Ruwe, Nixon's chief advance man for New Hampshire, saying, "Goddamn it, Hunter, you almost blew up the plane!"

I shrugged. He was right. I'd been leaning over the fuel tank with a burning butt in my mouth. Nixon smiled and reached out to shake hands again, while Ruwe muttered darkly and the others stared down at the asphalt.

The plane took off and I rode back to the Holiday Inn with Nick Ruwe. We laughed about the cigarette scare, but he was still brooding. "What worries me," he said, "is that nobody else noticed it. Christ, those guys get paid to *protect* the Boss . . ."

"Very bad show," I said, "especially when you remember that I did about three king-size Marlboros while we were standing there. Hell, I was flicking the butts away, lighting new ones . . . you people are lucky I'm a sane, responsible journalist; otherwise I might have hurled my flaming Zippo into the fuel tank."

"Not you," he said. "Egomaniacs don't do that kind of thing." He smiled. "You wouldn't do anything you couldn't live to write about, would you?"

"You're probably right," I said. "Kamikaze is not my style. I much prefer subtleties, the low-key approach—because I am, after all, a professional."

"We know. That's why you're along."

• • •

Actually, the reason was very different: I was the only one in the press corps, that evening, who claimed to be as seriously addicted to pro football as Nixon himself. I was also the only out-front, openly hostile Peace Freak; the only one wearing old Levi's and a ski jacket, the only one (no, there was *one* other) who'd smoked grass on Nixon's big Greyhound press bus, and certainly the only one who habitually referred to the candidate as "the Dingbat."

So I still had to credit the bastard for having the balls to choose *me*—out of the fifteen or twenty straight/heavy press types who'd been pleading for two or three weeks for even a five-minute interview—as the one who should share the backseat with him on this Final Ride through New Hampshire.

But there was, of course, a catch. I had to agree to talk about *nothing except football.* "We want the boss to relax," Ray Price told me, "but he can't relax if you start yelling about Vietnam, race riots, or drugs. He wants to ride with somebody who can talk football." He cast a baleful eye at the dozen or so reporters waiting to board the press bus, then shook his head sadly. "I checked around," he said. "But the others are hopeless—so I guess you're it."

"Wonderful," I said. "Let's do it."

We had a fine time. I enjoyed it—which put me a bit off balance, because I'd figured Nixon didn't know any more about football than he did about ending the war in Vietnam. He had made a lot of allusions to football on the stump, but it had never occurred to me that he actually *knew* anything more about football than he knew about the Grateful Dead.

But I was wrong. Whatever else might be said about Nixon—and there is still no doubt in my mind that he could pass for Human—he is a goddamn stone fanatic on every facet of pro football. At one point in our conversation, when I was feeling a bit pressed for leverage, I mentioned a down & out pass—in the waning moments of a Super Bowl mismatch between Green Bay and Oakland—to an obscure, second-string Oakland receiver named Bill Miller that had stuck in my mind because of its pinpoint style & precision.

He hesitated for a moment, lost in thought, then he whacked me on the thigh and laughed: "That's right, by God! The Miami boy!"

• • •

That was four years ago. LBJ was Our President and there was no real hint, in the winter of '68, that he was about to cash his check. Johnson seemed every bit as tough and invulnerable then as Nixon seems today . . . and it is slightly unnerving to recall that Richard Nixon, at that point in his campaign, appeared to have about as much chance of getting himself elected to the White House as Hubert Humphrey appears to have today.

When Nixon went into New Hampshire, he was viewed, by the pros, as just another of these stubborn, right-wing waterheads with nothing better to do. The polls showed him comfortably ahead of George Romney, but according to most of the big-time press wizards who were hanging around Manchester at the time, the Nixon-Romney race was only a drill that would end just as soon as Nelson Rockefeller came in to mop up both of them. The bar at the Wayfarer Motor Inn was a sort of unofficial press headquarters, where the press people hovered in nervous anticipation of the Rockefeller announcement that was said to be coming "at any moment."

So I was not entirely overcome at the invitation to spend an hour alone with Richard Nixon. He was, after all, a born loser—even if he somehow managed to get the Republican nomination, I figured he didn't have a sick goat's chance of beating Lyndon Johnson.

I was as guilty as all the others, that year, of treating the McCarthy campaign as a foredoomed exercise in noble futility. We had talked about it a lot—not only in the Wayfarer bar, but also in the bar of the Holiday Inn where Nixon was staying—and the press consensus was that the only Republican with a chance to beat Johnson was Nelson Rockefeller . . . and the only other possible winner was Bobby Kennedy, but of course he had already dropped out.

• • •

I was remembering all this as I cranked the big green Cougar along U.S. 93 once again, four years later, to cover another one of those flakey New Hampshire primaries. The electorate in this state is notoriously perverse and unpredictable. In 1964, for instance, it was a thumping victory in the New Hampshire primary that got the Henry Cabot Lodge steamroller off to a roaring start . . . and in '68, Gene McCarthy woke up on the morning of Election Day to read in the newspapers that the last-minute polls were nearly unanimous in giving him between 6 and 8 percent of the vote . . . and even McCarthy was stunned, I think, to wake up twenty-four hours later and find himself with 42 percent.

Strange Country & a Hitchhiker

Strange country up here; New Hampshire and Vermont appear to be the East's psychic answer to Colorado and New Mexico—big lonely hills laced with back roads and old houses where people live almost aggressively by themselves. The insularity of the old-timers, nursing their privacy along with their harsh right-wing politics, is oddly similar and even receptive to the insularity of the newcomers, the young dropouts and former left-wing activists—people like Andy Kopkind and Ray Mungo, co-founder of the Liberation News Service—who've been moving into these hills in ever increasing numbers since the end of the Sixties. The hitchhikers you find along these narrow twisting highways look exactly like the people you see on the roads around Boulder or Aspen or Taos.

• • •

The girl riding with me tonight is looking for an old boyfriend who moved out of Boston and is now living, she says, in a chicken coop in a sort of informal commune near Greenville, N.H. It is five or six degrees above zero outside and she doesn't even have a blanket, much less a sleeping bag, but this doesn't worry her. "I guess it sounds crazy," she explains. "We don't even sleep together. He's just a friend. But I'm happy when I'm with him because he makes me like myself."

Jesus, I thought. We've raised a generation of stone desperate cripples. She is twenty-two, a journalism grad from Boston University, and now—six months out of college—she talks so lonely and confused that she is eagerly looking forward to spending a few nights in a frozen chicken coop with some poor bastard who doesn't even know she's coming.

The importance of Liking Yourself is a notion that fell heavily out of favor during the coptic, anti-ego frenzy of the Acid Era—but nobody guessed, back then, that the experiment might churn up this kind of hangover: a whole subculture of frightened illiterates with no faith in anything.

The girl was not interested in whatever reasons I might have for going up to Manchester to spend a few days with the McGovern campaign. She had no plans to vote in *any* election, for president or anything else.

She tried to be polite, but it was obvious after two or three minutes of noise that she didn't know what the fuck I was talking about, and cared less. It was boring; just another queer hustle in a world full of bummers that will swarm you every time if you don't keep moving.

Like her ex-boyfriend. At first he was only stoned all the time, but now he was shooting smack and acting very crazy. He would call and say he was on his way over, then not show up for three days—and then he'd be out of his head, screaming at her, not making any sense.

It was too much, she said. She loved him, but he seemed to be drifting away. We stopped at a donut shop in Marlborough and I saw she was crying, which made me feel like a monster because I'd been saying some fairly hard things about "junkies" and "loonies" and "doom-freaks."

• • •

Once they let you get away with running around for ten years like a king hoodlum, you tend to forget now and then that about half the people you meet live from one day to the next in a state of such fear and uncertainty that about half the time they honestly doubt their own sanity.

These are not the kind of people who really need to get hung up in depressing political trips. They are not ready for it. Their boats are rocking so badly that all they want to do is get level for long enough to think straight and avoid the next nightmare.

This girl I was delivering up to the chicken coop was one of those people. She was terrified of almost everything, including me, and this made me very uncomfortable.

We couldn't find the commune. The directions were too vague: "Go far to the dim yellow light, then right at the big tree . . . proceed to the fork and then slow to the place where the road shines . . ."

After two hours of this I was half crazy. We had been back and forth across the same grid of backroads two or three times, with no luck . . . but finally we found it, a very peaceful-looking place in a cold hill in the woods. She went inside the main building for a while, then came back out to tell me everything was okay.

I shrugged, feeling a little sad because I could tell by the general vibrations that things were not really "okay." I was tempted to take her into Manchester with me, but I knew that would only compound the problem for both of us . . . checking into the Wayfarer at three thirty, then up again at seven for a quick breakfast and then into the press bus for a long day of watching McGovern shake hands with people at factory gates.

Could she handle that madness? Probably not. And even if she could, why do it? A political campaign is a very narrow ritual, where anything weird is unwelcome. I am trouble enough by myself; they would never tolerate me if I showed up with a nervous blonde nymphet who thought politics was some kind of game played by old people, like bridge.

No, it would never do. But on my way into Manchester, driving like a werewolf, it never occurred to me that maybe I was not quite as sane as I'd always thought I was. There is something seriously bent, when you think on it, in the notion that a man with good sense would race out of his peaceful home and fly off in a frenzy like some kind of electrified turkey buzzard to spend three or four days being carried around the foulest sections of New England like a piece of meat, to watch another man, who says he wants to be president, embarrassing a lot of people by making them shake his hand outside factory gates at sunrise.

Harold Hughes Is Your Friend

Manchester, New Hampshire, is a broken-down mill town on the Merrimack River with an aggressive Chamber of Commerce and America's worst newspaper. There is not much else to say for it, except that Manchester is a welcome change from Washington, D.C.

I checked into the Wayfarer, just before dawn, and tried to get some music on my high-powered waterproof Sony, but there was nothing worth listening to. Not even out of Boston or Cambridge. So I slept a few hours and then joined the McGovern caravan for a tour of the Booth Fisheries, in Portsmouth.

It was a wonderful experience. We stood near the time clock as the shifts changed & McGovern did his handgrabbing thing. There was no way to avoid him, so the workers shuffled by and tried to be polite. McGovern was blocking the approach to the drinking fountain, above which hung a sign saying "Dip Hands in Hand Solution Before Returning to Work."

The place was like a big aircraft hangar full of fish, with a strange cold gaseous haze hanging over everything—and a lot of hissing & humming from the fish-packing machines on the assembly line. I have always liked seafood, but after thirty minutes in that place I lost my appetite for it.

The next drill was the official opening of the new McGovern headquarters in Dover, where a large crowd of teenagers and middle-aged liberals were gathered to meet the candidate. This age pattern seemed to prevail at every one of McGovern's public appearances: the crowds were always a mix of people either under twenty or over forty. The meaning of this age diversion didn't hit me until I looked back on my notes and saw how consistent it was . . . even at the Massachusetts Rad/Lib Caucus, where I guessed the median age to be thirty-three; that figure was a rough mathematical compromise, rather than a physical description. In both Massachusetts and New Hampshire, the McGovern/McCarthy crowds were noticeably barren of people between twenty-five and thirty-five.

• • •

After Dover, the next speech was scheduled for the main auditorium at the Phillips Exeter Academy for Boys, an exclusive prep school about twenty-five miles up the road. The schedule showed a two-hour break for dinner at the Exeter Inn, where the McGovern press party took over about half the dining room.

I can't recommend the food at that place, because they wouldn't let me eat. The only other person barred from the dining room that night was Tim Crouse, from the *Rolling Stone* bureau in Boston. Neither one of us was acceptably dressed, they said—no ties, no three-button herringbone jackets—so we had to wait in the bar with James J. Kilpatrick, the famous neo-Nazi newspaper columnist. He made no attempt to sit with us, but he made sure that everybody in the room knew exactly who he was. He kept calling the bartender "Jim," which was not his name, and the bartender, becoming more & more nervous, began addressing Kilpatrick as "Mr. Reynolds."

Finally Kilpatrick lost his temper. "My name's not Reynolds, goddamn it! I'm James J. Kilpatrick of the *Washington Evening Star.*" Then he hauled his paunch off the chair and reeled out to the lobby.

The Exeter stop was not a happy one for McGovern, because word had just come in from Frank Mankiewicz, his campaign manager in Washington, that McGovern's old friend and staunch liberal ally from Iowa—Senator Harold Hughes—had just announced that he was endorsing Ed Muskie.

This news hit the campaign caravan like a dung-bomb. Hughes had been one of the few senators that McGovern was counting on to hang tough. The Hughes-McGovern–Fred Harris (D-Okla.) axis has been the closest thing in the Senate to a Populist power bloc for the past two years. Even the Muskie endorsement-hustlers who've been crisscrossing the nation putting pressure on local politicians to come out for Big Ed hadn't bothered with Hughes, because they considered him "untouchable." If anything, he was thought to be more radical and intransigent than McGovern himself.

Hughes had grown a beard; he didn't mind admitting that he talked to trees now and then—and a few months earlier he had challenged the party hierarchy by forcing a public showdown between himself and Larry O'Brien's personal choice for the chairmanship of the all-important Credentials Committee at the national convention.

• • •

Dick Dougherty, a former *L.A. Times* newsman who is handling McGovern's national press action, was so shaken by the news of Hughes' defection that he didn't even try to explain it when reporters began asking Why? Dougherty had just got the word when the crowded press limo left Dover for Exeter, and he did his best to fend off our questions until he could talk to the candidate and agree on what to say. But in terms of campaign morale, it was as if somebody had slashed all the tires on every car in the caravan, including the candidate's. When we got to the

Exeter Inn I half expected to see a filthy bearded raven perched over the entrance, croaking "Nevermore . . ."

By chance, I found George downstairs in the men's room, hovering into a urinal and staring straight ahead at the gray marble tiles.

"Say . . . ah . . . I hate to mention this," I said. "But what about this thing with Hughes?"

He flinched and quickly zipped his pants up, shaking his head and mumbling something about "a deal for the vice presidency." I could see that he didn't want to talk about it, but I wanted to get his reaction before he and Dougherty could put a story together.

"Why do you think he did it?" I said.

He was washing his hands, staring down at the sink. "Well . . ." he said finally. "I guess I shouldn't say this, Hunter, but I honestly don't know. I'm surprised; we're *all* surprised."

He looked very tired, and I didn't see much point in prodding him to say anything else about what was clearly a painful subject. We walked upstairs together, but I stopped at the desk to get a newspaper while he went into the dining room. This proved to be my undoing because the doorkeeper would no doubt have welcomed me very politely if I'd entered with the senator . . . but as it happened, I was shunted off to the bar with Crouse & James J. Kilpatrick, who was wearing a vest & a blue pin-striped suit.

Enter, the Shadow

I had not come to New Hampshire with any illusions about McGovern or his trip—which was, after all, a long-shot underdog challenge that even the people running his campaign said was not much better than thirty to one.

What depressed me, I think, was that McGovern was the only alternative available, this time around, and I was sorry I couldn't get up for it. I agreed with everything he said, but I wish he would say a lot more—or maybe something different.

Ideas? Specifics? Programs? Etc.?

Well . . . that would take a lot of time and space I don't have now, but for openers I think maybe it is no longer enough to have been "against the War in Vietnam since 1963"—especially when your name is not one of the two senators who voted against the Gulf of Tonkin resolution in 1964 and when you're talking to people who got their first taste of tear gas at anti-war rallies in places like Berkeley and Cambridge in early '65.

A lot of blood has gone under the bridge since then, and we have all learned a hell of a lot about the realities of Politics in America. Even the politicians have learned—but, as usual, the politicians are usually much slower than the people they want to lead.

This is an ugly portent for the twenty-five million or so new voters between eighteen and twenty-five who may or may not vote in 1972. And many of them probably *will* vote. The ones who go to the polls in '72 will be the most committed, the most idealistic, the "best minds of my generation," as Ginsberg said it fourteen years ago in "Howl." There is not much doubt that the hustlers behind the "Youth Vote" will get a lot of people out to the polls in '72. If you give twenty-five million people a new toy, the odds are pretty good that a lot of them will try it at least once.

But what about next time? Who is going to explain, in 1976, that all the people who felt they got burned in '72 should "try again" for another bogus challenger? Four years from now there will be two entire generations—between the ages of twenty-two and forty—who will not give a hoot in hell about *any* election, and their apathy will be rooted in personal experience. Four years from now it will be very difficult to convince anybody who has gone from Johnson-Goldwater to Humphrey-Nixon to Nixon-Muskie that there is any possible reason for getting involved in another bullshit election.

• • •

This is the gibberish that churned in my head on the drive back from Manchester. Every now and then I would pass a car with New Hampshire plates and the motto "Live Free or Die" inscribed above the numbers.

The highways are full of good mottoes. But T. S. Eliot put them all in a sack when he coughed up that line about . . . what was it? Have these dangerous drugs fucked my memory? Maybe so. But I think it went something like this:

"Between the Idea and the Reality . . . Falls the Shadow."

The Shadow? I could almost *smell* the bastard behind me when I made the last turn into Manchester. It was late Tuesday night, and tomorrow's schedule was calm. All the candidates had zipped off to Florida—except for Sam Yorty, and I didn't feel ready for that.

The next day, around noon, I drove down to Boston. The only hitchhiker I saw was an eighteen-year-old kid with long black hair who was going to Reading—or "Redding," as he said it—but when I asked him who he planned to vote for in November, he looked at me like I'd said something crazy.

"What election?" he asked.

"Never mind," I said. "I was only kidding."

One of the favorite parlor games in Left/Liberal circles from Beverly Hills to Chevy Chase to the Upper East Side and Cambridge has been—for more than a year now—a sort of guilty, half-public breast-beating whenever George McGovern's name is mentioned. He has become the Willy Loman of the Left; he is liked but not *well*-liked, and his failure to make the big charismatic breakthrough has made him the despair of his friends. They can't figure it out.

A few weeks ago I drove over to Chevy Chase—to the "White side" of Rock Creek Park—to have dinner with McGovern and a few of his heavier friends. The idea was to have a small, loose-talking dinner and let George relax after a week on the stump in New Hampshire. He arrived looking tired and depressed. Somebody handed him a drink and he slumped down on the couch, not saying much but listening intently as the talk quickly turned to "the McGovern problem."

For more than a year now, he's been saying all the right things. He has been publicly opposed to the war in Vietnam since 1963; he's for amnesty now; his alternative military spending budget would cut Pentagon money back to less than half of what Nixon proposes for 1972. Beyond that, McGovern has had the balls to go into Florida and say that if he gets elected he will probably pull the plug on the $5 billion Space Shuttle program, thereby croaking thousands of new jobs in the depressed Cape Kennedy–Central Florida area.

He has refused to modify his stand on the school busing issue, which Nixon-Wallace strategists say will be the number one campaign argument by midsummer—one of those wild-eyed fire-and-brimstone issues that scares the piss out of politicians because there is no way to dodge it . . . but McGovern went out of his way to make sure people understood he was for busing. Not because it's desirable, but it's "among the prices we are paying for a century of segregation in our housing patterns."

This is not the kind of thing people want to hear in a general election year—especially not if you happen to be an unemployed anti-gravity systems engineer with a deadhead mortgage on a house near Orlando . . . or a Polish millworker in Milwaukee with three kids the government wants to haul across town every morning to a school full of *Niggers*.

McGovern is the only major candidate—including Lindsay and Muskie—who invariably gives a straight answer when people raise these questions. He lines out the painful truth, and his reward has been just about the same as that of any other politician who insists on telling the truth: he is mocked, vilified, ignored, and abandoned as a hopeless loser by even his good old buddies like Harold Hughes.

On the face of it, the "McGovern problem" looks like the ultimate proof-positive for the liberal cynics' conviction that there is no room in American politics for an honest man. Which is probably true: if you take it for granted—along with McGovern and most of his backers—that "American politics" is synonymous with the traditional Two Party system: the Democrats and the Republicans, the Ins and the Outs, the Party in Power and the Loyal Opposition.

That's the term National Democratic Party chairman Larry O'Brien has decided to go with this year—and he says he can't for the life of him understand why Demo Party headquarters from coast to coast aren't bursting at the seams with dewy-eyed young voters completely stoned on the latest Party Message.

Getting It On in D.C.

The most recent Gallup poll says Nixon & Muskie are running Head to Head, but on closer examination the figures had Muskie trailing by a bare 1 percent—so he quickly resigned his membership in the "Caucasians Only" Congressional Country Club in the horsey suburbs near

Cabin John, Maryland. He made this painful move in late January, about the same time he began hammering Nixon's "end the war" proposal.

Watching Muskie on TV that week, I remembered the words of ex-senator Ernest Gruening (D-Alaska) when he appeared at the Massachusetts Rad/Lib Caucus in his role as the official spokesman for McGovern. Gruening was one of the two senators who voted against the Gulf of Tonkin resolution in 1964—the resolution that gave LBJ carte blanche to do Everything Necessary to win the war in Vietnam. (Wayne Morse of Oregon was the only other "nay" vote: . . . and both Gruening and Morse were defeated when they ran for reelection in 1966.)

In Worchester, Ernest Gruening approached the stage like a slow-moving golem. He is eighty-five years old, and his legs are not real springy—but when he got behind the podium he spoke like the Grim Reaper.

"I've known Ed Muskie for many years," he said. "I've considered him a friend . . . but I can't help remembering that, for all those years, while we were getting deeper and deeper into that war, and while more and more boys were dying . . . Ed Muskie stayed silent."

Gruening neglected to say where McGovern had been on the day of the Tonkin Gulf vote . . . but I remember somebody saying, up on the press platform near the roof of the Assumption College gym, that "I can forgive McGovern for blowing that Tonkin thing, because the Pentagon lied—but what's his excuse for not voting against that goddamn wire-tapping bill?" *The Omnibus Crime Control & Safe Streets Act of 1968, a genuinely oppressive piece of legislation—even Lyndon Johnson was shocked by it, but he couldn't quite bring himself to veto the bugger—for the same reasons cited by the many senators who called the bill "frightening" while refusing to vote against it because they didn't want to be on record as having voted against "safe streets and crime control." (The bare handful of senators who actually voted against the bill explained themselves in very ominous terms. For details, see* Justice *by Richard Harris.)*

• • •

I had thought about this, but I had also thought about all the other aspects of this puzzling and depressing campaign—which seemed, a few months ago, to have enough weird and open-ended possibilities that I actually moved from Colorado to Washington for the purpose of "covering the campaign." It struck me as a right thing to do, at the time—especially in the wake of the success we'd had with two back-to-back Freak Power runs at the heavily entrenched Money/Politics/Yahoo establishment in Aspen.

But things are different in Washington. It's not that everybody you talk to is aggressively hostile to any idea that might faze their well-ordered lifestyles; they'd just rather not think about it. And there is no sense of life in the Underculture. On the national/reality spectrum, Washington's Doper/Left/Rock/Radical community is somewhere between Toledo and Biloxi. "Getting it on" in Washington means killing a pint of Four Roses and then arguing about Foreign Aid, over chicken wings, with somebody's drunken congressman.

The latest craze on the local highlife front is mixing up six or eight aspirins in a fresh Coca-Cola and doing it all at once. Far more government people are into this stuff than will ever admit to it. What seems like mass paranoia, in Washington, is really just a sprawling, hyper-tense boredom—and the people who actually live and thrive here, in the great web of government, are the first ones to tell you, on the basis of long experience, that the name or even the party affiliation of the next president won't make any difference at all, except on the surface.

The leaves change, they say, but the roots stay the same. So just lie back and live with it. To crank up a noisy bad stance out in a place like San Francisco and start yelling about "getting things done in Washington" is like sitting far back in the end zone seats at the Super Bowl and screaming at the Miami linebackers "Stop Duane Thomas!"

Dope Saves the Cowboys

That is one aspect of the '72 Super Bowl that nobody has properly dealt with: What was it like for those humorless, god-fearing Alger-bent Jesus Freaks to go out on that field in front of one hundred thousand people in New Orleans and get beaten like gongs by the only certified dope freak in the NFL? Thomas ran through the Dolphins like a mule through corn-stalks.

It was a fine thing to see; and it was no real surprise when the Texas cops busted him, two weeks later, for Possession of Marijuana . . . and the Dallas coach said Yes, he'd just as soon trade Duane Thomas for almost anybody.

They don't get along. Tom Landry, the Cowboys' coach, never misses a chance to get up on the platform with Billy Graham whenever The Crusade plays in Dallas. Duane Thomas calls Landry a "plastic man." He tells reporters that the team's general manager, Tex Schramm, is "sick, demented, and vicious." Thomas played his whole season, last year, without ever uttering a sentence to anyone on the team: not the coach, the quarterback, his blockers—nobody; dead silence.

All he did was take the ball and run every time they called his number—which came to be more and more often, and in the Super Bowl Thomas was the whole show. But the season is now over; the purse is safe in the vault; and Duane Thomas is facing two to twenty for possession.

Nobody really expects him to serve time, but nobody seems to think he'll be playing for Dallas next year, either . . . and a few sporting people who claim to know how the NFL works say he won't be playing for *anybody* next year; that the commissioner is outraged at this mockery of all those government-sponsored "Beware of Dope" TV shots that dressed up the screen last autumn.

We all enjoyed those spots, but not everyone found them convincing. Here was a White House directive saying several million dollars would be spent to drill dozens of Name Players to stare at the camera and try to stop grinding their teeth long enough to say they hate drugs of any kind . . . and then the best running back in the world turns out to be a goddamn uncontrollable drug-sucker.

The Five W's

Which is neither here nor there, for right now. We seem to have wandered out on another tangent. But why not? Every now and then you have to get away from that ugly, Old Politics trip, or it will drive you kicking the walls and hurling AR 3 speakers into the fireplace.

This world is full of downers, but where is the word to describe the feeling you get when you come back tired and crazy from a week on the road to find twenty-eight fat newspapers on the desk: seven *Washington Posts*, seven *Washington Stars*, seven *New York Times*, six *Wall Street Journals*, and one *Suck* . . . to be read, marked, clipped, filed, correlated . . . and then chopped, burned, mashed, and finally hurled out in the street to freak the neighbors.

After two or three weeks of this madness, you begin to feel As One with the man who said "No news is good news." In twenty-eight papers, only the rarest kind of luck will turn up more than two or three articles of any interest . . . but even then the interest items are usually buried deep around paragraph 16 on the Jump (or "Cont. on . . .") page . . .

The *Post* will have a story about Muskie making a speech in Iowa. The *Star* will say the same thing, and the *Journal* will say nothing at all. But the *Times* might have enough room on the jump page to include a line or so that says something like: "When he finished his speech, Muskie burst into tears and seized his campaign manager by the side of the neck. They grappled briefly, but the struggle was kicked apart by an oriental woman who seemed to be in control."

• • •

Now that's good journalism. Totally objective; very active, and straight to the point. But we need to know more. *Who* was that woman? *Why* did they fight? *Where* was Muskie taken? *What* was he saying when the microphone broke?

Jesus, what's the other one? Every journalist in America knows the "Five W's." But I can only remember four. "Who, What, Why, Where," . . . and, yes, of course . . . "When!"

But what the hell? An item like that tends to pinch the interest gland, so you figure it's time to move out. Pack up the $419 Abercrombie & Fitch elephant-skin suitcase; send the phones and the scanner and the tape viewers by Separate Float, load everything into the weightless Magnesium Kitbag . . . then call for a high-speed cab to the airport; load on and zip off to wherever The Word says it's happening.

The public expects no less. They want a man who can zap around the nation like a goddamn methedrine bat: racing from airport to airport, from one crisis to another—sucking up the news and then spewing it out by the "Five W's" in a package that makes perfect sense. Why not? With the truth so dull and depressing, the only working alternative is wild bursts of madness and filigree. Or fly off and write nothing at all; get a room on the edge of Chicago and shoot up for about sixteen straight days—then wander back to Washington with a notebook full of finely honed insights on "The Mood of the Midwest."

Meanwhile, I am hunkered down in Washington—waiting for the next plane to anywhere and wondering what in the name of sweet Jesus ever brought me here in the first place. This is not what us journalists call a "happy beat."

At first I thought it was *me*; that I was missing all the action because I wasn't plugged in. But then I began reading the press wizards who are plugged in, and it didn't take long to figure out that most of them were just filling space because the contracts said they had to write a certain amount of words every week.

At that point I tried talking to some of the people that even the wizards said were "right on top of things." But they all seemed very depressed; not only about the '72 election, but about the whole, long-range future of politics and democracy in America.

Which is not exactly the kind of question we really need to come to grips with right now. The nut of the problem is that covering this presidential campaign is so fucking dull that it's just barely tolerable . . . and the only thing worse than going out on the campaign trail and getting hauled around in a booze-frenzy from one speech to another is having to come back to Washington and write about it.

The Campaign Trail: The View from Key Biscayne

March 16, 1972

One of the main marks of success in a career politician is a rooty distrust of The Press—and this cynicism is usually reciprocated, in spades, by most reporters who have covered enough campaigns to command a fat job like chronicling the Big Apple. Fifty years ago H. L. Mencken laid down the dictum that "The only way a reporter should look at a politician is *down*."

This notion is still a very strong factor in the relationship between politicians and the big-time press. On lower levels you find a tendency—among people like "national editors" on papers in Pittsburgh and Omaha—to treat *successful* politicians with a certain amount of awe and respect. But the prevailing attitude among journalists with enough status to work presidential campaigns is that all politicians are congenital thieves and liars.

This is usually true. Or at least as valid as the consensus opinion among politicians that The Press is a gang of swine. Both sides will agree that the other might occasionally produce an exception to prove the rule, but the overall bias is rigid . . . and, having been on both sides of that ugly fence in my time, I tend to agree. . . .

Which is neither here nor there, for right now. We seem to have wandered off again, and this time I can't afford the luxury of raving at great length about anything that slides into my head. So, rather than miss another deadline, I want to zip up the nut with a fast and extremely pithy five hundred words because that's all the space available, and in two hours I have to lash my rum-soaked red convertible across the Rickenbacker Causeway to downtown Miami and then to the airport—in order to meet John Lindsay in either Tallahassee or Atlanta, depending on which connection I can make: it is nearly impossible to get either in or out of Miami this week. All flights are booked far in advance, and the hotel/motel space is so viciously oversold that crowds of angry tourists are "becoming unruly"—according to the *Miami Herald*—in the lobbies of places that refuse to let them in.

Fortunately, I have my own spacious suite attached to the new National Affairs office in the Royal Biscayne Hotel.

When things got too heavy in Washington I had no choice but to move the National Affairs desk to a place with better working conditions. Everybody agreed that the move was long overdue. After three months in Washington I felt like I'd spent three years in a mine-shaft underneath Butte, Montana. My relations with the White House were extremely negative from the start; my application for press credentials was rejected out of hand. I wouldn't be needing them, they said. Because *Rolling Stone* is a music magazine, and there is not much music in the White House these days.

And not much on Capitol Hill either, apparently. When I called the Congressional Press Gallery to ask about the application (for press credentials) that I'd filed in early November '71, they said they hadn't got around to making any decision on it yet—but I probably wouldn't be needing that one either. And where the hell did I get the gall to apply for "press" status at the Democratic and Republican National Conventions this summer?

Where indeed? They had me dead to rights. I tried to save face by arguing that political science has never conclusively *proven* that music and politics can't mix—but when they asked for *my* evidence I said, "Shucks, you're probably right. Why shit in your own bed, eh?"

"What?"

"Never mind," I said. "I didn't really want the goddamn things, anyway."

Which was true. Getting barred from the White House is like being blackballed at the Playboy Club. There are definite advantages to having your name on the Ugly List in places like that.

The Campaign Trail:
The Banshee Screams in Florida

April 13, 1972

The whistle-stops were uneventful until his noon arrival in Miami, where Yippie activist Jerry Rubin and another man heckled and interrupted him repeatedly. The Senator at one point tried to answer Rubin's charges that he had once been a hawk on (Vietnam) war measures. He acknowledged that he had made a mistake, as did many other senators in those times, but Rubin did not let him finish.

Muskie ultimately wound up scolding Rubin and fellow heckler Peter Sheridan, who had boarded the train in West Palm Beach with press credentials apparently obtained from Rolling Stone*'s Washington correspondent, Dr. Hunter S. Thompson.*

—*Miami Herald*, 2/20/72

Chitty and the Boohoo

This incident has haunted me ever since it smacked me in the eyes one peaceful Sunday morning a few weeks ago as I sat on the balmy screened porch of the National Affairs Suite here in the Royal Biscayne Hotel. I was slicing up grapefruit and sipping a pot of coffee while perusing the political page of the *Herald* when I suddenly saw my name in the middle of a story on Ed Muskie's "Sunshine Special" campaign train from Jacksonville to Miami.

Several quick phone calls confirmed that something very ugly had happened on that train, and that I was being blamed for it. A New York reporter assigned to the Muskie camp warned me to "stay clear of this place . . . they're really hot about it. They've pulled your pass for good."

"Wonderful," I said. "That's one more summer that I have an excuse to avoid. But what happened? Why do they blame *me*?"

"Jesus Christ!" he said. "That crazy sonofabitch got on the train wearing *your* press badge and went completely crazy. He drank about ten martinis before the train even got moving, then he started abusing people. He cornered some poor bastard from one of the Washington papers and called him a Greasy Faggot and a Community Buttfucker . . . then he started pushing him around and saying he was going to throw him off the train at the next bridge . . . we couldn't believe it was happening. He scared one of the network TV guys so badly that he locked himself in one of the lavatories for the rest of the trip."

"Jesus, I hate to hear this," I said. "But nobody really thought it was *me*, did they?"

"Hell, yes, they did," he replied. "The only people on the train who even know what you look like were me and—and—." (He mentioned several reporters whose names needn't be listed here.) "But everybody else just looked at that ID badge he was wearing, and pretty soon the word was all the way back to Muskie's car that some thug named Thompson from a thing called *Rolling Stone* was tearing the train apart. They were going to send Rosey Grier up to deal with you, but Dick Stewart [Muskie's press secretary] said it wouldn't look good to have a three-hundred-pound bodyguard beating up journalists on the campaign train."

"That's typical Muskie-staff thinking," I said. "They've done everything else wrong; why balk at stomping a reporter?"

He laughed. "Actually," he said, "the rumor was that you'd eaten a lot of LSD and gone wild—that you couldn't help yourself."

"What do you mean, me?" I said. "I wasn't even *on* that goddamn train. The Muskie people deliberately didn't wake me up in West Palm Beach. They didn't like my attitude from the day before. My friend from the University of Florida newspaper said he heard them talking about it down in the lobby when they were checking off the press list and waking up all the others."

"Yeah, I heard some of that talk," he said. "Somebody said you seemed very negative."

"I was," I said. "That was one of the most degrading political experiences I've ever been subjected to."

"That's what the Muskie people said about your friend," he replied. "Abusing reporters is one thing: hell, we're all used to that—but about halfway to Miami I saw him reach over the bar and grab a whole bottle of gin off the rack. Then he began wandering from car to car, drinking out of the bottle and getting after those poor goddamn girls. That's when it really got bad."

"What girls?" I said.

"The ones in those little red, white, and blue hotpants outfits," he replied. "All those so-called 'Muskie volunteers' from Jacksonville Junior College, or whatever . . ."

"You mean the barmaids? The ones with the straw boaters?"

"Yeah," he said. "The cheerleaders. Well, they went all to goddamn pieces when your friend started manhandling them. Every time he'd come into a car the girls would run out the door at the other end. But every once in a while he'd catch one by an arm or a leg and start yelling stuff like 'Now I gotcha, you little beauty! Come on over here and sit on poppa's face!' "

"Jesus!" I said. "Why didn't they just put him off the train?"

"How? You don't stop a chartered Amtrak train on a main line just because of a drunken passenger. What if Muskie had ordered an emergency stop and we'd been rammed by a freight train? No presidential candidate would risk a thing like that."

I could see the headlines in every paper from Key West to Seattle:

Muskie Campaign Train Collision Kills 34;
Demo Candidate Blames "Crazy Journalist"

"Anyway," he said, "we were running late for that big rally at the station in Miami—so the Muskie guys figured it was better to just *endure* the crazy sonofabitch, rather than cause a violent scene on a train full of bored reporters. Christ, the train was *loaded* with network TV crews, all of them bitching about how Muskie wasn't doing anything worth putting on the air . . ." He laughed. "Hell, yes, we *all* would have loved a big brawl on the train. Personally, I was bored stupid. I didn't get a quote worth filing out of the whole goddamn trip." He laughed again. "Actually, Muskie *deserved* that guy. He was a goddamn nightmare to be trapped on a train with, but at least he wasn't dull. Nobody was dozing off like they did on Friday. Hell, there was no way to get away from that brute! All you could do was keep moving and hope he wouldn't get hold of you."

Both the *Washington Star* and *Women's Wear Daily* reported essentially the same tale: a genuinely savage person had boarded the train in West Palm Beach, using a fraudulent press pass, then ran amok in the lounge car—getting in "several fistfights" and finally "heckling the Senator unmercifully" when the train pulled into Miami and Muskie went out on the caboose platform to deliver what was supposed to have been the climactic speech of his triumphant whistle-stop tour.

It was at this point—according to press reports both published & otherwise—that my alleged friend, calling himself "Peter Sheridan," cranked up his act to a level that caused Senator Muskie to "cut short his remarks."

When the "Sunshine Special" pulled into the station at Miami, "Sheridan" reeled off the train and took a position on the tracks just below Muskie's caboose platform, where he spent the next half hour causing the senator a hellish amount of grief—along with Jerry Rubin, who also showed up at the station to ask Muskie what had caused him to change his mind about supporting the War in Vietnam.

Rubin had been in Miami for several weeks, making frequent appearances on local TV to warn that "Ten Thousand naked hippies" would be among those attending the Democratic National Convention at Miami Beach in July. "We will march to the convention center," he announced, "but there will be no violence—at least not by us."

To questions regarding his presence in Florida, Rubin said he "decided to move down here, because of the climate," and that he was also registered to vote in Florida—as a Republican. Contrary to the rancid suspicions of the Muskie staff people, Sheridan didn't even recognize Rubin, and I hadn't seen him since the Counter-Inaugural Ball, which ran opposite Nixon's inauguration in 1969.

When Rubin showed up at the train station that Saturday afternoon to hassle Muskie, the senator from Maine was apparently the only person in the crowd who didn't know who he was. His first response to Rubin's heckling was, "Shut up, young man—I'm talking."

"You're not a damn bit different from Nixon," Rubin shouted back . . .

And it was at this point, according to compiled press reports and a firsthand account by Monte Chitty of the University of Florida *Alligator*, that Muskie seemed to lose his balance and fall back from the rail.

What happened, according to Chitty, was that "the Boohoo reached up from the track and got hold of Muskie's pants leg—waving an empty glass through the bars around the caboose platform with his other hand and screaming: 'Get your lying ass back inside and make me another drink, you worthless old fart!' "

"It was really embarrassing," Chitty told me later on the phone. "The Boohoo kept reaching up and grabbing Muskie's legs, yelling for more gin . . . Muskie tried to ignore him, but the Boohoo kept after him and after awhile it got so bad that even Rubin backed off. He was acting just like he did the night before—only six times worse."

"The Boohoo," of course, was the same vicious drunkard who had terrorized the Muskie train all the way from Palm Beach, and he was still wearing a press badge that said "Hunter S. Thompson—*Rolling Stone*."

Chitty and I had met him the night before, about two thirty, in the lobby of the Ramada Inn where the press party was quartered. We were heading out to the street to look for a sandwich shop, feeling a trifle bent & very hungry . . . and as we passed the front desk, here was this huge wild-eyed monster, bellowing at the desk clerk about "All this chicken-shit" and "All these pansies around here trying to suck up to Muskie" and "Where the fuck can a man go in this town to have a good time, anyway?"

A scene like that wouldn't normally interest me, but there was something very special about this one—something abnormally crazy in the way he was talking. There was something very familiar about it. I listened for a moment and then recognized the Neal Cassady speed-booze-acid rap—a wild combination of menace, madness, genius, and fragmented coherence that wreaks havoc on the mind of any listener.

This is not the kind of thing you expect to hear in the lobby of a Ramada Inn, and especially not in West Palm Beach—so I knew we had no choice but to take this man along with us.

"Don't mind if I do," he said. "At this hour of the night I'll fuck around with just about anybody."

He had just got out of jail, he explained as we walked five or six blocks through the warm midnight streets to a twenty-four-hour hamburger place called the Copper Penny. Fifteen days for vagrancy, and when he'd hit the bricks today around four he just happened to pick up a newspaper and see that Ed Muskie was in town . . . and since he had this friend who "worked up-top," he said, for Big Ed . . . well, he figured he'd just drift over to the Ramada Inn and say hello.

But he couldn't find his friend. "Just a bunch of pansies from CBS and the *New York Times*, hanging around the bar," he said. "I took a few bites out of that crowd and they faded fast—just ran off like curs. But what the shit can you expect from people like that? Just a bunch of low-life ass-kissers who get paid for hanging around with politicians."

Just for the quick hell of it, I'd like to explain, or at least insist—despite massive evidence to the contrary—that this geek we met in the lobby of the Ramada Inn and who scared the shit out of everybody when he got on Muskie's train the next day for the run from Palm Beach to Miami, was in fact an excellent person, with a rare sense of humor that unfortunately failed to mesh, for various reasons, with the prevailing humors on Muskie's "Sunshine Special."

Just how he came to be wearing my press badge is a long and tangled story, but as I recall it had something to do with the fact that "Sheridan" convinced me that he was one of the original ranking Boohoos of the Neo-American Church and also that he was able to rattle off all kinds of obscure and pithy tales about his experiences in places like Millbrook, the Hog Farm, La Honda, and Mike's Pool Hall in San Francisco . . .

. . . which would not have meant a hell of a lot if he hadn't also been an obvious aristocrat of the Freak Kingdom. There was no doubt about it. This bastard was a serious, king-hell *crazy*. He had that rare weird electricity about him—that extremely wild & heavy *presence* that you only see in a person who has abandoned all hope of ever behaving "normally."

All of which is basic to any understanding of what happened on the Muskie campaign train—and which also explains why his "up-top friend" (who *WWD* later identified as Rich Evans, one of Muskie's chief tacticians) was not immediately available to take care of his old buddy, Pete Sheridan—who was fresh out of jail on a vagrancy rap, with no place to sleep and no transportation down to Miami except the prospect of hanging his thumb out in the road and hoping for a ride.

"To hell with that," I said. "Take the train with *us*. It's the presidential express—a straight shot into Miami and all the free booze you can drink. Why not? Any friend of Rich's is a friend of Ed's, I guess—but since you can't find Rich at this hour of the night, and since the train is leaving in two hours, well, perhaps you should borrow this little orange press ticket, just until you get aboard."

"I think you're right," he said.

"I am," I replied. "And besides, I paid thirty dollars for the goddamn thing and all it got me was a dozen beers and the dullest day of my life."

He smiled, accepting the card. "Maybe I can put it to better use," he said.

Which was true. He did—and I was subsequently censured very severely, by other members of the campaign press corps, for allowing my "credentials" to fall into foreign hands. There were also ugly rumors to the effect that I had somehow conspired with this monster "Sheridan"—and also with Jerry Rubin—to "sabotage" Muskie's wind-up gig in Miami, and that "Sheridan's" beastly behavior at the train station was the result of a carefully laid plot by me, Rubin, and the International Yippie brain trust.

• • •

This theory was apparently concocted by Muskie staffers, who told other reporters that they had known all along that I was up to something rotten—but they tried to give me a break, and now look what I done to 'em. Planted a human bomb on the train.

A story like this one is very hard to spike, because people involved in a presidential campaign are so conditioned to devious behavior on all fronts—including the press—that something like that fiasco in the Miami train station is just about impossible for them to understand except in terms of a conspiracy. Why else, after all, would I *give my credential* to some booze-maddened jailbird?

Well . . . why indeed?

Several reasons come quickly to mind, but the main one could only be understood by somebody who has spent twelve hours on a train with Ed Muskie and his people, doing whistle-stop speeches through central Florida.

We left Jacksonville around nine, after Muskie addressed several busloads of black teenagers and some middle-aged ladies from one of the local union halls who came down to the station to hear Senator Muskie say, "It's time for the *good* people of America to get together behind somebody they can trust—namely me."

After that, we went down to Delano—about a two-hour run—where Muskie addressed a crowd of about two hundred white teenagers who'd been let out of school to hear the candidate say, "It's about time the good people of America got *together* behind somebody they can trust—namely me."

And then we eased down the tracks to Sebring, where a feverish throng of about 150 senior citizens were on hand to greet the Man from Maine and pick up his finely honed message. As the train rolled into the station, Roosevelt Grier emerged from the caboose and attempted to lead the crowd through a few stanzas of "Let the Sunshine In."

Then the candidate emerged, acknowledging Grier's applause and smiling for the TV cameramen who had been let off a hundred yards up the track so they could get ahead of the train and set up . . . in order to film Muskie socking it to the crowd about how "It's about time we *good* people, etc., etc. . . ."

Meanwhile, the Muskie girls—looking very snappy in their tricolored pre-war bunny suits—were mingling with the folks; saying cheerful things and handing out red, white, and blue buttons that said "Trust Muskie" and "Believe Muskie."

Meanwhile, back on the train, a goodly chunk of the press roster were over the hump into serious boozing. A few had already filed, but most had scanned the prepared text of Big Ed's "whistlestop speech" and said to hell with it. Now, as the train headed south again, the Muskie girls were passing out sandwiches and O. B. McClinton, "the Black Irishman of Country Music," was trying to lure people into the lounge car for a "singalong thing."

• • •

It took awhile, but they finally collected a crowd. Then one of Muskie's college-type staffers took charge. He told the Black Irishman what to play, cued the other staff people, then launched into about nineteen straight choruses of Big Ed's newest campaign song: "He's got the whole state of Florida . . . In his hands . . ."

I left at that point. The scene was pure Nixon—so much like a pep rally at a Young Republican Club that I was reminded of a conversation I'd had earlier with a reporter from Atlanta. "You know," he said, "it's taken me half the goddamn day to figure out what it is that bothers me about these people." He nodded toward a group of clean-cut young Muskie staffers at the other end of the car. "I've covered a lot of Democratic campaigns," he continued, "but I've never felt out of place before—never personally uncomfortable with the people."

"I know what you mean," I said.

"Sure," he said. "It's obvious—and I've finally figured out *why.*" He chuckled and glanced at the Muskie people again. "You know what it is?" he said. "It's because these people act like goddamn Republicans! That's the problem. It took me awhile, but I finally figured it out."

• • •

On Monday morning, the day before the Florida primary, I flew down to Miami with Frank Mankiewicz, who runs the McGovern campaign.

We hit the runway in Key Biscayne at just over two hundred miles an hour in a strong crosswind, bouncing first on the left wheel and then—about one hundred yards down the runway—on the right wheel . . . then another long bounce, and finally straightening out just in front of the main terminal at Miami's International Airport.

Nothing serious. But my Bloody Mary was spilled all over Monday's *Washington Post* on the armrest. I tried to ignore it and looked over at Frank Mankiewicz (who was sitting next to me) . . . but he was still snoring peacefully.

I poked him. "Here we are," I said. "Down home in Fat City again. What's the schedule?"

Now he was wide awake, checking his watch. "I think I have to make a speech somewhere," he said. "I also have to meet Shirley MacLaine somewhere. Where's a telephone? I have to make some calls."

Soon we were shuffling down the corridor toward the big baggage-claim merry-go-round. Mankiewicz had nothing to claim. He has learned to travel light. His "baggage," as it were, consisted of one small canvas bag that looked like an oversize shaving kit.

My own bundle—two massive leather bags and a Xerox telecopier strapped into a fiberglass Samsonite suitcase—would be coming down the baggage-claim chute any moment now. I tend to travel heavy; not for any good reason, but mainly because I haven't learned the tricks of the trade.

"I have a car waiting," I said. "A fine bronze-gold convertible. Why? Do you need a ride?"

"Maybe," he said. "But I have to make some calls first. You go ahead, get your car and all that goddamn baggage, and I'll meet you down by the main door."

I nodded and hurried off. The Avis counter was only about fifty yards away from the wall-phone where Mankiewicz was setting up shop with a handful of dimes and a small notebook. He made at least six calls and a page of notes before my bags arrived . . . and by the time I began arguing with the car rental woman the expression on Mankiewicz's face indicated that he had everything under control.

I was impressed by this show of efficiency. Here was the one-man organizing vortex, main theorist and central intelligence behind the McGovern for President campaign—a small, rumpled little man who looked like an out-of-work "Pre-owned Car" salesman—putting McGovern's Florida Primary action together from a public wall-phone in the Miami airport.

Mankiewicz—a forty-seven-year-old Los Angeles lawyer who was director of the Peace Corps before he became Bobby Kennedy's press secretary in 1968—has held various job-titles since the McGovern campaign got underway last year. For a while he was the "Press Secretary," then he was called the "Campaign Manager"—but now he appears to feel comfortable with the title of "Political Director." Which hardly matters, because he has become George McGovern's alter ego. There are people filling all the conventional job-slots, but they are essentially front-men. Frank Mankiewicz is to McGovern what John Mitchell is to Nixon—the Man behind the Man.

Two weeks before voting day in New Hampshire, Mankiewicz was telling his friends that he expected McGovern to get 38 percent of the vote. This was long before Ed Muskie's infamous "breakdown scene" on that flatbed truck in front of the Manchester *Union Leader*.

When Frank laid his prediction on his friends in the Washington Journalism Establishment, they figured he was merely doing his job—trying to con the press and hopefully drum up a last-minute surge for

McGovern, the only candidate in the '72 presidential race who had any real claim on the residual loyalties of the so-called Kennedy Machine.

Beyond that, Mankiewicz was a political columnist for the *Washington Post* before he quit to run McGovern's campaign—and his former colleagues were not inclined to embarrass him by publicizing such a claim. Journalists, like The Rich, are inclined to protect Their Own . . . even those who go off on hopeless tangents.

So Frank Mankiewicz ascended to the Instant-Guru level on the morning of March 8, when the final New Hampshire tally showed McGovern with 37 percent of the Democratic primary vote, and "front-runner" Ed Muskie with only 46 percent.

New Hampshire in '72 jolted Muskie just as brutally as New Hampshire in '68 jolted LBJ. He cursed the press and hurried down to Florida, still talking like "the champ," and reminding everybody within reach that he had, after all, *Won* in New Hampshire.

Just like LBJ, who beat McCarthy by almost 20 points and then quit before the next primary four weeks later in Wisconsin.

But Muskie had only *one* week before the deal would go down in Florida, and he was already in . . . he came down and hit the streets with what his handlers called a "last-minute blitz" . . . shaking many hands and flooding the state with buttons, flyers & handbills saying "Trust Muskie" and "Believe Muskie" and "Muskie Talks Straight" . . .

When Muskie arrived in Florida for The Blitz, he looked and acted like a man who'd been cracked. Watching him in action, I remembered the nervous sense of impending doom in the face of Floyd Patterson when he weighed in for his championship re-match with Sonny Liston in Las Vegas. Patterson was so obviously crippled, in his head, that I couldn't raise a bet on him among the hundred or so veteran sportswriters in the ringside seats on fight night.

I was sitting next to Rocky Marciano in the first row, and just before the fight began I bought two tall paper cups full of beer, because I didn't want to have to fuck around with drink-vendors after the fight got underway.

"*Two*?" Marciano asked with a grin.

I shrugged, and drank one off very quickly as Floyd came out of his corner and turned to wax the first time Liston hit him. Then, with a minute still to go in the first round, Liston bashed him again and Patterson went down for the count. The fight was over before I touched my second beer.

• • •

Muskie went the same way to Florida—just as Mankiewicz had predicted, forty-eight hours earlier, in the living room of his suburban Washington home. "Muskie is already finished," he said then. "He had no *base.* Nobody's really *for* Muskie. They're only for the front-runner, the man who says he's the only one who can beat Nixon—but not even Muskie himself believes that anymore; he couldn't even win a majority of the Democratic vote in New Hampshire, on his own turf."

• • •

The Florida primary is over now. George Wallace stomped everybody, with 42 percent of the vote in a field of eleven. Ed Muskie, the erstwhile national front-runner, finished a sick fourth, with only 9 percent . . . and then he went on all the TV networks to snarl about how this horrible thing would never have happened except that Wallace is a Beast and a Bigot.

Which is at least half true, but it doesn't have much to do with why Muskie got beaten like a gong in Florida. The real reason is that the Man from Maine, who got the nod many months ago as the choice of the Democratic Party's ruling establishment, is running one of the stupidest and most incompetent political campaigns since Tom Dewey took his dive and elected Truman in 1948.

If I had any vested interest in the Democratic Party, I would do everything possible to have Muskie committed at once. Another disaster at the polls might put him around the bend. And unless all the other Democratic candidates are killed in a stone-blizzard between now and April 4, Muskie is going to absorb another serious beating in Wisconsin.

I am probably not the only person who has already decided to be almost anywhere except in Ed Muskie's headquarters when the polls close on election night. The place will probably be dead empty, and all the windows taped . . . TV crews hunkered down behind overturned ping-pong tables, hoping to film the ex-front-runner from a safe distance when he comes crashing into the place to blame his sixth-place finish on some kind of unholy alliance between Ti-Grace Atkinson and Judge

Crater. Nor is there any reason to believe he will forbear physical violence at that time. With his dream finished and his nerves completely shot, he might start laying hands on people . . .

Hopefully, some of his friends will be there to restrain the wiggy bastard. All we can be sure of, however, is the list of those who will *not* be there, under any pretense at all . . . Senator Harold Hughes will not be there, for instance, and neither will Senator John Tunney . . . Nor will any of the other senators, governors, mayors, congressmen, labor leaders, liberal pundits, fascist lawyers, fixers from ITT, and extremely powerful Democratic National committeewomen who are already on the record as full-bore committed to stand behind Big Ed.

None of those people will be there when Muskie sees the first returns from Wisconsin and feels the first rush of pus into his brain. At that point he will have to depend on his friends, because that suitcase full of endorsements he's been dragging around won't be worth the price of checking it into a bus station locker.

Except perhaps for Birch Bayh. There is something that doesn't quite meet the eye connected with this one. It makes no sense at all, on its face. Why would one of Ted Kennedy's closest friends and allies in the Senate suddenly decide to jump on the Muskie bandwagon when everybody else is struggling to get off gracefully?

Maybe Birch is just basically a nice guy—one of those down-home, warm-hearted Hoosiers you hear so much about. Well . . . why not? Maybe he and Big Ed are lifelong buddies. But if that were so, you'd think Bayh might have offered to fix Muskie up with some high-life political talent back then when it might have made a difference.

But times are tricky now, and you never know when even one of your best friends might slap a ruinous lawsuit on you for some twisted reason that nobody understands. Almost everybody you meet these days is nervous about the nasty drift of things.

It is becoming increasingly possible, for instance, that Hubert Humphrey will be the Democratic presidential nominee this year—which would cause another Nixon-Humphrey campaign. And a thing like that would probably have a serious effect on my nerves. I'd prefer no election at all to another Humphrey nightmare. Six months ago it seemed out of the question. But no longer.

Frank Mankiewicz was right. For months he's been telling anybody who asked him that the Democratic race would boil down, after the first few primaries, to a Humphrey-McGovern battle. But nobody took him seriously. We all assumed he was just talking up Humphrey's chances in order to slow Muskie down and thus keep McGovern viable.

But apparently he was serious all along. Humphrey is the bookies' choice in Wisconsin, which would finish Muskie and make Hubert the high rider all the way to the Oregon and California primaries in early June.

The "other race" in Wisconsin is between McGovern and Lindsay, which might strike a lot more sparks than it has so far if anybody really believed the boneheads who run the Democratic Party would conceivably nominate either one of them. But there is a definite possibility that the Democratic Convention this year might erupt into something beyond the control of anybody; the new delegate-selection rules make it virtually impossible for old-style bosses like Mayor Daley to treat delegates like sheep hauled in to be dipped.

A candidate like Lindsay or McGovern might be able to raise serious hell in a deadlocked convention, but the odds are better than even that Hubert will peddle his ass to almost anybody who wants a chunk of it, then arrive in Miami with the nomination sewed up and Nixon waiting to pounce on him the instant he comes out of his scumbag.

Another Nixon-Humphrey horror would almost certainly cause a "Fourth Party" uprising and guarantee Nixon's reelection—which might bring the hounds of hell down on a lot of people for the next four very long years.

But personally I think I'd be inclined to take that risk. Hubert Humphrey is a treacherous, gutless old ward-heeler who should be put in a goddamn bottle and sent out with the Japanese Current. The idea of Humphrey running for president again makes a mockery of a lot of things that it would take me too long to explain or even list here. And Hubert Humphrey wouldn't understand what I was talking about anyway. He was a swine in '68 and he's worse now. If the Democratic Party nominates Humphrey again in '72, the party will get exactly what it deserves.

The Campaign Trail: Bad News from Bleak House: Total Failure in Milwaukee . . . with a Few Quick Thoughts on the Shocking Victory of Double-George . . .

April 27, 1972

Failure comes easy at a time like this. After eight days in this fantastic dungeon of a hotel, the idea of failing totally and miserably in my work seems absolutely logical. It is a fitting end to this gig—not only for me, but for everyone else who got trapped here, especially journalists.

The Wisconsin primary is over now. It came to a shocking climax a few hours ago when George McGovern and George Wallace ran a blitz on everybody.

The results were such a jolt to the Conventional Wisdom that now—with a cold gray dawn bloating up out of Lake Superior and Hubert Humphrey still howling in his sleep despite the sedatives in his room directly above us—there is nobody in Milwaukee this morning, including me, who can even pretend to explain what really went down last night. The McGovern brain trust will deny this, but the truth of the matter is that less than twenty-four hours ago it was impossible to get an even-money bet in McGovern headquarters that their man would finish first. Not even Warren Beatty, who is blossoming fast in his new role as one of McGovern's most valuable and enthusiastic organizers, really believed that George would finish any better than a close second.

A week earlier it would have been considered a sign of madness, among those who knew the score, to bet McGovern any better than a respectable third—but toward the end of the final week the word went out that George had picked up a wave and was showing surprising strength in some of the blue-collar, hard-hat wards that had been more or less conceded to either Humphrey or Muskie. David Broder of the *Washington Post* is generally acknowledged to be the ranking wizard on the campaign trail this year, and five days before the election he caused serious shock waves by offering to bet—with me, at least—that McGovern would get more than 30 percent, and Wallace less than 10.

He lost both ends of that bet, as it turned out—and I mean to hunt the bastard down and rip his teeth out if he tries to welsh—but the simple fact that Broder had that kind of confidence in McGovern's strength was seen as a main signal by the professional pols and newsmen who'd been saying all along that the Wisconsin primary was so hopelessly confused that nobody in his right mind would try to predict the outcome.

The lead article in Sunday's *Washington Post* echoed the unanimous conviction of all the five or six hundred big-time press/politics wizards who were gathered here for what they all called "the crunch"—the showdown, the first of the national primaries that would finally separate the sheep from the goats, as it were.

After a month of intense research by some of the best political journalists in America, the *Post* had finally concluded that (1) "The Wisconsin primary election seems likely to make dramatic changes in the battle for the 1972 presidential nomination" . . . and (2), that "an unusually high degree of uncertainty remains as the contest nears its climax."

In other words, nobody had the vaguest idea what would happen here, except that some people were going to get hurt—and the smart-money consensus had Muskie and Lindsay as the most likely losers. The fact that Lindsay was almost totally out of money made him a pretty safe bet to do badly in Wisconsin, but Muskie—coming off a convincing victory in Illinois that at least partially redeemed his disastrous failure in Florida—looked pretty good in Wisconsin, on paper, but there was still something weak and malignant in the spine of the Muskie campaign. There was a smell of death about it. He talked like a farmer with terminal cancer trying to borrow money on next year's crop.

Two weeks before the election the polls had Muskie running more or less even with Humphrey and well ahead of McGovern—but not even his staffers believed it; they kept smiling, but their morale had been cracked beyond repair in Florida, when Muskie called a meeting the day after the primary to announce that he was quitting the race. They had managed to talk him out of it, agreeing to work without pay until after Wisconsin, but when word of the candidate's aborted withdrawal leaked out to the press . . . well, that was that. Nobody published it, nobody mentioned it on TV or radio—and, from that point on, the only thing that kept the Muskie campaign alive was a grim political version of the old vaudeville idea that "the show must go on."

Midway in the final week of the campaign even Muskie himself began dropping hints that he knew he was doomed. At one point, during a whistlestop tour of small towns in the Fox River Valley near Green Bay, he fell into a public funk and began muttering about "needing a miracle" . . . and then, when the sense of depression began spreading like a piss-puddle on concrete, he invited the campaign-press regulars to help him celebrate his fifty-eighth birthday at a small hotel on a snowy night in Green Bay. But the party turned sour when his wife mashed a piece of the birthday cake in the face of a *Newsweek* reporter, saying, "One good turn deserves another, eh?"

• • •

The final straw, for Muskie, was the result of an unpublished but carefully leaked poll, taken by Oliver Quayle at the behest of Senator Jackson and the local AFL-CIO that showed Muskie losing 70 percent of his support in Wisconsin in a period of two weeks. According to the Quayle poll, the onetime front-runner slipped from 39 percent to 13 percent, while McGovern was virtually doubling *his* figure from 12 percent to 23 percent in the same period—which put McGovern ahead of Humphrey, who had dropped about 5 points to 19 percent.

The same poll showed George Wallace with 12 percent, which convinced both the governor and organized labor that it would not be necessary to mount a serious effort to short-circuit the Wallace threat. Both the governor and the state labor bosses had been worried about Wallace stomping into Wisconsin and embarrassing everybody by pulling off another one of those ugly, Florida-style upsets.

It is still very hard to understand how the polls and the pols and especially a wizard like Broder could have so drastically underestimated the Wallace vote. Perhaps the threat of an anti-Wallace backlash by organized labor led the visiting press to think the other was safely boxed in. Wisconsin's Big Labor brain trust had come up with a theory that said Wallace got a huge boost, in Florida, by the fact that the liberal opposition got so hysterical about him that he got twice as many votes as he would have if the other candidates had simply ignored him and done their own things.

So they decided to turn the other cheek in Wisconsin. They ignored the Wallace rallies that, night after night, packed halls in every corner of the state. That was all Wallace did—except for a few TV spots—and every one of his rallies attracted far more people than the hall could hold.

I went to one at a place called Serb Hall on the South Side of Milwaukee—a neighborhood the pols said was locked up for Muskie. Serb Hall is a big yellow-brick place that looks like an abandoned gymnasium, across the street from Sentry Supermarket on Oklahoma Street, about five miles from downtown Milwaukee. One half of the hall is a "Lounge & Bowling Alley," and the other half is a fair-sized auditorium with a capacity of about three hundred.

The Serb Hall rally was a last-minute addition to the Wallace schedule. His main rally that night was scheduled for a much bigger hall in Racine, about fifty miles south, at seven thirty . . . but one of his handlers apparently decided to get him warmed up with a five o'clock gig at Serb Hall, despite the obvious risk involved in holding a political rally at that hour of the evening in a neighborhood full of Polish factory-workers just getting off work.

I got there at four thirty, thinking to get in ahead of the crowd and maybe chat a bit with some of the early arrivals at the bar . . . but at four thirty the hall was already packed and the bar was so crowded that I could barely reach in to get a beer. When I reached in again to pay for it, somebody pushed my hand back and a voice said "It's already taken care of, fella—you're a *guest* here."

For the next two hours I was locked in a friendly, free-wheeling conversation with about six of my hosts who didn't mind telling me that they were there because George Wallace was the most important man in America. "This guy is the real thing," one of them said. "I never cared anything about politics before, but Wallace ain't the same as the others. He don't sneak around the bush. He just comes right out and *says* it."

It was the first time I'd ever seen Wallace in person. There were no seats in the hall; everybody was standing. The air was electric even before he started talking, and by the time he was five or six minutes into his spiel, I had a sense that the bastard had somehow levitated himself and was hovering over us. It reminded me of a Janis Joplin concert. Anybody who doubts the Wallace appeal should go out and catch his act sometime. He jerked this crowd in Serb Hall around like he had them all on wires. They were laughing, shouting, whacking each other on the back . . . It was a flat-out fire-and-brimstone *performance*.

• • •

Ah yes . . . I can hear the Mojo wire humming frantically across the room. Crouse is stuffing page after page of gibberish into it. Greg Jackson, the ABC correspondent, had been handling it most of the day and whipping us along like Bear Bryant, but he had to catch a plane for New York, and now we are left on our own.

The pressure is building up. The copy no longer makes sense. Huge chunks are either missing or too scrambled to follow from one sentence to another. Crouse just fed two consecutive pages into the machine upside-down, provoking a burst of angry yelling from whoever is operating the receiver out there on the Coast.

And now the bastard is beeping . . . beeping . . . beeping, which means it is hungry for this final page, which means I no longer have time to crank out any real wisdom on the meaning of the Wisconsin primary. But that can wait, I think. We have a three-week rest now, before the next one of these goddamn nightmares . . . which gives me a bit of time to think about what happened here. Meanwhile, the only thing we can be absolutely sure of is that George McGovern is no longer the hopelessly decent loser that he has looked like up to now.

The real surprise of this campaign, according to Theodore White on CBS-TV last night, is that "George McGovern has turned out to be one of the great field organizers of American politics."

But Crouse is dealing with that story, and the wire is beeping again. So this page will have to go, for good or ill . . . and the minute it finishes we will flee this hotel like rats from a burning ship.

The only other problem will be to figure out the meaning of the strange relationship between George McGovern and George Wallace . . . but that will take some time. Selah.

The Campaign Trail:
More Late News from Bleak House

May 11, 1972

Yet I had planted thee a noble vine, wholly a right seed: How then art thou turned into a degenerate plant of a strange vine to me?

—Jeremiah 2:21

The arrival of Secret Service personnel has changed the campaign drastically. Sometime around seven on Friday night—three days before the Wisconsin primary—I left my dreary suite in the Sheraton-Schroeder Hotel and drove across town to McGovern headquarters at the Milwaukee Inn, a comfortably obscure sort of motor hotel in a residential neighborhood near Lake Michigan. The streets were still icy from a snowstorm earlier in the week, and my rented purple Mustang had no snow tires.

The car was extremly unstable—one of those Detroit "scrap" classics, apparently assembled by junkies to teach the rest of us a lesson. I had already been forced to remove the air filter, in order to manipulate the automatic choke by hand, but there was no way to cure the unnerving accelerator delay. It was totally unpredictable. At some stoplights the car would move out normally, but at others it would try to stall, seeming to want more gas—and then suddenly leap ahead like a mule gone amok from a bad sting.

Every red light was a potential disaster. Sometimes I would take off slowly, with the rest of the traffic . . . but at about every third light the goddamn worthless machine would hang back for a second or so, as if to give the others a head start, and then come thundering off the line at top speed with no traction at all and the rear end fishtailing all over the street about halfway to the next corner.

By the time I got to the Milwaukee Inn, I had all three lanes of State Street to myself. Anybody who couldn't get safely ahead of me was lagging safely behind. I wondered if anyone had taken my license number, in order to turn me in as a dangerous drunk or a dope addict. It was entirely possible that by the time I got back to the car every cop in Milwaukee would be alerted to grab me on sight.

Sheriff! Sheriff!

I was brooding on this as I entered the dining room and spotted Frank Mankiewicz at a table near the rear. As I approached the table, he looked up with a nasty grin and said, "Ah ha, it's you; I'm surprised you have the nerve to show up over here—after what you wrote about me."

I stared at him, trying to get my brain back in focus. Conversation ceased at every table within ten feet of us, but the only one that really concerned me was a knot of four Secret Service men who suddenly shifted into Deadly Pounce position at their table just behind Mankiewicz and whoever else he was eating with.

I had come down the aisle very fast, in my normal fashion, not thinking about much of anything except what I wanted to ask Mankiewicz—but his loud accusation about me having "the nerve to show up" gave me a definite jolt. Which might have passed in a flash if I hadn't realized, at almost the same instant, that four thugs with wires in their ears were so alarmed at my high-speed appearance that they were about to beat me into a coma on pure instinct, and ask questions later.

This was my first confrontation with the Secret Service. They had not been around in any of the other primaries, until Wisconsin, and I was not accustomed to working in a situation where any sudden move around a candidate could mean a broken arm. Their orders are to *protect the candidate*, period, and they are trained like high-strung guard dogs to reach with Total Force at the first sign of danger. Never hesitate. First crack the wrist, then go for the floating rib . . . and if the "assassin" turns out to be just an oddly dressed journalist: well, that's what the SS boys call "tough titty." Memories of Sirhan Sirhan are still too fresh, and there is no reliable profile on potential assassins . . . so *everybody* is suspect, including journalists.

All this flashed through my head in a split second. I saw it all happening, but my brain had gone limp from too much tension. First the car, now this . . . and perhaps the most unsettling thing of all was the fact that I'd never seen Mankiewicz even *smile*.

But now he was actually laughing, and the SS guards relaxed. I tried to smile and say something, but my head was still locked in neutral.

"You better stay away from my house from now on," Mankiewicz was saying. "My wife hates your guts."

Jesus, I thought. What's happening here? Somewhere behind me I could hear a voice saying "Hey, Sheriff! Hello there! Sheriff!"

I glanced over my shoulder to see who was calling, but all I saw was a sea of unfamiliar faces, all staring at me . . . so I turned quickly back to Mankiewicz, who was still laughing.

"What the hell are you talking about?" I said. "What did I do to your wife?"

He paused long enough to carve a bite out of what looked like a five- or six-pound Prime Rib on his plate, then he looked up again. "You called me a rumpled little man," he said. "You came over to my house and drank my liquor and then you said I was a rumpled little man who looked like a used car salesman."

"Sheriff! Sheriff!" That goddamn voice again; it seemed vaguely familiar, but I didn't want to turn around and find all those people staring at me.

Then the fog began to lift. I suddenly understood that Mankiewicz was *joking*—which struck me as perhaps the most shocking and peculiar development of the entire '72 campaign. The idea that anybody connected with the McGovern campaign might actually laugh in public was almost beyond my ken. In New Hampshire nobody had ever even smiled, and in Florida the mood was so down that I felt guilty even hanging around.

Even Mankiewicz, in Florida, was acting like a man about to take the bastinado . . . so I was puzzled and even a little nervous to find him grinning like this in Milwaukee.

Was he stoned? Had it come down to that?

"*Sheriff! Sheriff!*"

I spun around quickly, feeling a sudden flash of anger at some asshole mocking me in these rude and confusing circumstances. By this time I had forgotten even what I'd wanted to ask Mankiewicz. The night was turning into something out of Kafka.

"*Sheriff!*"

I glared at the table behind me, but nobody blinked. Then I felt a hand on my belt, poking at me . . . and my first quick instinct was to knock the hand away with a full-stroke hammer-shot from about ear level; really crack the bastard . . . and then immediately apologize: "Oh! Pardon *me*, old sport! I guess my nerves are shot, eh?"

Which they almost were, about thirty seconds later, when I realized that the hand on my belt—and the voice that had been yelling "Sheriff"—belonged to George McGovern. He was sitting right behind me, an arm's length away, having dinner with his wife and some of the campaign staffers.

Now I understood the Secret Service presence. I'd been standing so close to McGovern that every time I turned around to see who was yelling "Sheriff!" I saw almost every face in the room except the one right next to me.

He twisted around in his chair to shake hands, and the smile on his face was the smile of a man who has just cranked off a really wonderful joke.

"God damn!" I blurted. "It's you!" I tried to smile back at him, but my face had turned to rubber and I heard myself babbling: "Well . . . ah . . . how does it look?" Then quickly: "Excellent, eh? Yeah, I guess so. It certainly does look . . . ah . . . but what the hell, I guess you know all this . . ."

He said a few things that I never really absorbed, but there was nothing he could have said, at that moment, as eloquent or as meaningful as that incredible smile on his face.

The most common known source of ibogaine is from the roots of Tabernanthe Iboga, a shrub indigenous to West Africa. As early as 1869, roots of T.I. were reported effective in combating sleep or fatigue and in maintaining alertness when ingested by African natives.

Extracts of T.I. are used by natives while stalking game; it enables them to remain motionless for as long as two days while retaining mental alertness. It has been used for centuries by natives of Africa, Asia, and South America in conjunction with fetishistic and mythical ceremonies. In 1905 the gross effects of chewing large quantities of T.I. roots were described . . . "Soon his nerves get tense in an extraordinary way; an epileptic-like madness comes over him, during which he becomes unconscious and pronounces words which are interpreted by the older members of the group as having a prophetic meaning and to prove that the fetish has entered him."

At the turn of the century, iboga extracts were used as stimulants, aphrodisiacs, and inebriants. They have been available in European drugstores for over 30 years. Much of the research with ibogaine has been done with animals. In the cat, for example, 2–10 mg./kg. given intravenously caused marked excitation, dilated pupils, salivation, and tremors leading to a picture of rage. There was an alerting reaction, obvious apprehension and fear, and attempts to escape . . . In human studies, at a dose of 300 mg. given orally, the subject experiences visions, changes in perception of the environment, and delusions or alterations of thinking. Visual imagery became more vivid, with animals often appearing. Ibogaine produces a state of drowsiness in which the subject does not wish to move, open his eyes, or be aware of his environment. Since there appears to be an inverse relationship between the presence of physical symptoms and the richness of the psychological experience, the choice of environment is an important consideration. Many are disturbed by lights or noises . . . Dr. Claudio Naranjo, a psychotherapist, is responsible for most current knowledge regarding ibogaine effects in humans. He states: "I have been more impressed by the enduring effects resulting from ibogaine than by those from sessions conducted with any other drug."

—from a study by PharmChem Laboratories, Palo Alto, California

Not much has been written about the Ibogaine Effect as a serious factor in the presidential campaign, but toward the end of the Wisconsin primary race—about a week before the vote—word leaked out that some of Muskie's top advisers had called in a Brazilian doctor who was said to be treating the candidate with "some kind of strange drug" that nobody in the press corps had ever heard of.

It had been common knowledge for many weeks that Humphrey was using an exotic brand of speed known as "Wallot" . . . and it had long been whispered that Muskie was into something very heavy, but it was hard to take the talk seriously until I heard about the appearance of a mysterious Brazilian doctor. That was the key.

I immediately recognized the Ibogaine Effect—from Muskie's tearful breakdown on the flatbed truck in New Hampshire, the delusions and altered thinking that characterized his campaign in Florida; and finally the condition of "total rage" that gripped him in Wisconsin.

There was no doubt about it: the Man from Maine had turned to massive doses of ibogaine as a last resort. The only remaining question was "when did he start?" But nobody could answer this one, and I was not able to press the candidate himself for an answer because I was permanently barred from the Muskie campaign after that incident on the Sunshine Special in Florida . . . and that scene makes far more sense now than it did at the time.

Muskie has always taken pride in his ability to deal with hecklers; he has often challenged them, calling them up to the stage in front of big crowds and then forcing the poor bastards to debate with him in a blaze of TV lights.

But there was none of that in Florida. When the Boohoo began grabbing at his legs and screaming for more gin, Big Ed went all to pieces . . . which gave rise to speculation, among reporters familiar with his campaign style in '68 and '70, that Muskie was not himself. It was noted, among other things, that he had developed a tendency to roll his eyes wildly during TV interviews, that his thought-patterns had become strangely fragmented, and that not even his closest advisers could predict when he might suddenly spiral off into babbling rages, or neo-comatose funks.

In retrospect, however, it is easy to see why Muskie fell apart on that caboose platform in the Miami train station. There he was—far gone in a bad ibogaine frenzy—suddenly shoved out in a rainstorm to face a sullen crowd and some kind of snarling lunatic going for his legs while he tried to explain why he was "the only Democrat who can beat Nixon."

It is entirely conceivable—given the known effects of ibogaine—that Muskie's brain was almost paralyzed by hallucinations at the time; that he looked out at that crowd and saw gila monsters instead of people, and that his mind snapped completely when he felt something large and apparently vicious clawing at his legs.

We can only speculate on this, because those in a position to know have flatly refused to comment on rumors concerning the senator's disastrous experiments with ibogaine. I tried to find the Brazilian doctor on election night in Milwaukee, but by the time the polls closed he was long gone. One of the hired bimbos in Muskie's Holiday Inn headquarters said a man with fresh welts on his head had been dragged out the side door and put on a bus to Chicago, but we were never able to confirm this.

Humphrey's addiction to Wallot has not stirred any controversy, so far. He has always campaigned like a rat in heat, and the only difference now is that he is able to do it eighteen hours a day instead of ten. The main change in his public style, since '68, is that he no longer seems aware that his gibberish is not taken seriously by anyone except Labor Leaders and middle-class Blacks.

At least half the reporters assigned to the Humphrey campaign are convinced that he's senile. When he ran for president four years ago he was a hack and a fool, but at least he was consistent.

Now he talks like an eighty-year-old woman who just discovered speed. He will call a press conference to announce that if elected he will "have all our boys out of Vietnam within ninety days"—then rush across town, weeping and jabbering the whole way, to appear on a network TV show and make a fist-shaking emotional appeal for every good American to stand behind the president and "applaud" his recent decision to resume heavy bombing in North Vietnam.

Humphrey will go into a Black neighborhood in Milwaukee and drench the streets with tears while deploring "the enduring tragedy" that life in Nixon's America has visited on "these beautiful little children"—and then act hurt and dismayed when a reporter who covered his Florida campaign reminds him that "In Miami you were talking just a shade to the Left of George Wallace and somewhere to the Right of Mussolini."

Humphrey seems genuinely puzzled by the fast-rising tide of evidence that many once-sympathetic voters no longer believe anything he says. He can't understand why people snicker when he talks about "the politics of joy" and "punishing welfare chiselers" in almost the same breath . . . and God only knows what must have gone through his head when he picked up the current issue of *Newsweek* and found Stewart Alsop quoting *Rolling Stone* to the effect that "Hubert Humphrey is a treacherous, gutless old ward-heeler who should be put in a goddamn bottle and sent out with the Japanese Current."

Alsop made it clear that he was not pleased with that kind of language. He called it "brutal"—then wound up his column by dismissing the Humphrey candidacy in terms far more polite than mine, but no less final. Both Stewart and his demented brother, Joseph, have apparently concluded—along with almost all the other "prominent & influential" Gentleman Journalists in Washington—that the Democratic primaries have disintegrated into a series of meaningless brawls not worth covering. On the "opinion-shaping" level of the journalism Establishment in both Washington and New York, there is virtually unanimous agreement that Nixon's opponent in '72 will be Ted Kennedy.

McGovern's solid victory in Wisconsin was dismissed, by most of the press wizards, as further evidence that the Democratic Party has been taken over by "extremists": George McGovern on the Left and George Wallace on the Right, with a sudden dangerous vacuum in what is referred to on editorial pages as "the vital Center."

The root of the problem, of course, is that most of the big-time Opinion Makers decided a long time ago—along with all those Democratic senators, congressmen, governors, mayors, and other party pros—that the candidate of the "vital Center" in '72 would be none other than that fireball statesman from Maine, Ed Muskie. By the summer of '71 the party bosses had convinced themselves that Ed Muskie was the "only Democrat with a chance of beating Nixon."

This was bullshit, of course. Sending Muskie against Nixon would have been like sending a three-toed sloth out to seize turf from a wolverine. Big Ed was an adequate senator—or at least he'd seemed like one until he started trying to explain his "mistake" on the war in Vietnam—but it was stone madness from the start to ever think about exposing him to the kind of bloodthirsty thugs that Nixon and John Mitchell would sic on him. They would have him screeching on his knees by sundown on Labor Day. If I were running a campaign against Muskie, I would arrange for some anonymous creep to buy time on national TV and announce that twenty-two years ago he and Ed spent a summer working as male whores at a Peg House somewhere in the North Woods.

Nothing else would be necessary.

The idea that George McGovern has the Democratic nomination locked up by mid-April will not be an easy thing for most people to accept—especially since it comes from Frank Mankiewicz, the tall and natty "political director" for McGovern's campaign.

Total candor with the press—or anyone else, for that matter—is not one of the traits most presidential candidates find entirely desirable in their key staff people. Skilled professional liars are as much in demand in politics as they are in the advertising business . . . and the main function of any candidate's press secretary is to make sure the press gets nothing but Upbeat news. There is no point, after all, in calling a press conference to announce that nobody on the staff will be paid this month because three or four of your largest financial backers just called to say they are pulling out and abandoning all hope of victory.

When something like this happens, you quickly lock all the doors and send your press secretary out to start whispering, off the record, that your opponent's California campaign coordinator just called to ask for a job.

This kind of devious bullshit is standard procedure in most campaigns. Everybody is presumed to understand it—even the reporters who can't keep a straight face while they're jotting it all down for page one of the early edition: "Sen. Mace Denies Pullout Rumors; Predicts Total Victory in All States."

The best example of this kind of coverage in the current campaign has been the stuff coming out of the Muskie camp. In recent weeks the truth has been so painful that some journalists have gone out of their way to give the poor bastards a break and not flay them in print any more than absolutely necessary.

One of the only humorous moments in the Florida primary campaign, for instance, came when one of Muskie's state campaign managers, Chris Hart, showed up at a meeting with representatives of the other candidates to explain why Big Ed was refusing to take part in a TV debate. "My instructions," he said, "are that the senator should never again be put in a situation where he has to think quickly."

By nightfall of that day every journalist in Miami was laughing at Hart's blunder, but *nobody* published it; and none of the TV reporters ever mentioned it on the air. I didn't even use it myself, for some reason, although I heard about it in Washington while I was packing to go back to Florida.

I remember thinking that I should call Hart and ask him if he actually said a thing like that, but when I got there I didn't feel up to it. Muskie was obviously in deep trouble, and Hart had been pretty decent to me when I'd showed up at headquarters to sign up for that awful trip on the Sunshine Special . . . so I figured what the hell? Let it rest.

The other press people might have had different reasons for not using Hart's quote, but I can't say for sure because I never asked. Looking back on it, I think it must have been so obvious that the Muskie campaign was doomed that nobody felt mean enough to torment the survivors over something that no longer seemed important.

Muskie is finished. His only hope now is to do something like take a long vacation in New Zealand until July and get the ibogaine out of his system so he can show up in Miami and pray for a deadlocked convention. At that point, he can offer himself up for sacrifice as a "compromise candidate," make a deal with George Wallace for the VP slot, then confront the convention with a Muskie-Wallace "unity ticket."

Which might make the nut. If nothing else, it would command a lot of support from people like me who feel that the only way to save the Democratic Party is to destroy it. I have tried to explain this to George McGovern, but it's not one of the subjects he really enjoys talking about. McGovern is very nervous about the possibility of boxing himself into the role of a McCarthy-type "spoiler" candidate, which he was beginning to look like until he somehow won a big chunk of the hard-hat vote in New Hampshire and sensed the first strange seed of a coalition that might make him a serious challenger instead of just another martyr.

There was only a hint of it in New Hampshire, but in Wisconsin it came together with a decisiveness that nobody could quite understand in the alcoholic chaos of election night . . .

The only glaring weakness in McGovern's sweep was his failure to break Humphrey's grip on the Black wards in Milwaukee—where The Hube had campaigned avidly, greeting all comers with the Revolutionary Drug Brothers handshake. It was like Nixon flashing the peace sign, or Agnew chanting "Right on!" at a minstrel show.

The real shocker, however, came when McGovern carried the Polish south side of Milwaukee, which Muskie had planned on sweeping by at least ten to one. He was, after all, the first Pole to run for the presidency of the United States, and he had campaigned on the south side under his original Polish name . . . but when the deal went down he might as well have been an Arab, for all they cared in places like Serb Hall.

Which more or less makes the point, I think. And if it doesn't, well . . . political analysis was never my game anyway. All I do is wander around and make bets with people, and so far I've done pretty well.

As for betting on the chance that Mankiewicz is right and that McGovern will actually win on the first ballot in Miami . . . I think I'd like some odds on that one, and right now they should be pretty easy to get. McGovern right now is the only one of the Democratic candidates with any chance at all of getting the nomination . . . and if anybody wants to put money on Muskie, Humphrey, or Wallace, get in touch with me immediately.

The Campaign Trail: Crank-Time on the Low Road

June 8, 1972

Apologia

One of my clearest memories of the Nebraska primary is getting off the elevator on the wrong floor in the Omaha Hilton and hearing a sudden burst of song from a room down one of the hallways . . . twenty to thirty young voices in ragged harmony, kicking out the jams as they swung into the final, hair-raising chorus of "The Hound and the Whore."

I had heard it before, in other hallways of other hotels along the campaign trail—but never this late at night, and never at this level of howling intensity:

O the Hound chased the Whore across the mountains
Boom! Boom! Boom!
O the Hound chased the Whore into the sea . . .
Boom! Boom! Boom!

A very frightening song under any circumstances—but especially frightening if you happen to be a politician running for very high stakes and you know the people singing that song are *not on your side*. I have never been in that situation, myself, but I imagine it is something like camping out in the North Woods and suddenly coming awake in your tent around midnight to the horrible snarling and screaming sounds of a werewolf killing your guard dog somewhere out in the trees beyond the campfire.

I was thinking about this as I stood in the hallway outside the elevator and heard all those people singing "The Hound and the Whore" . . . in a room down the hall that led into a wing of the hotel that I knew had been blocked off for The Candidate's national staff. But there is nothing in my notes to indicate which one of the candidates was quartered in that wing—or even which floor I was on when I first heard the song. All I remember for sure is that it was one floor either above or below mine, on the eleventh. But the difference is crucial—because McGovern's people were mainly down on the tenth, and the smaller Humphrey contingent was above me on the twelfth.

It was a Monday night, as I recall, just a few hours before the polls opened on Tuesday morning—and at that point the race seemed so even that both camps were publicly predicting a victory and privately expecting defeat. So even in retrospect there is no way to be certain which staff was doing the singing.

And my own head was so scrambled at that hour that I can't be sure of anything except that we had just come back from a pre-dawn breakfast at the Omaha Toddle House with Jack Nicholson, Julie Christie, Goldie Hawn, Warren Beatty, and Gary Hart, McGovern's national campaign manager who had just picked up a check for roughly $40,000 gross from another one of Beatty's fund-raising spectacles.

This one had been over in Lincoln, the state capital town about sixty miles west of Omaha, where a friendly crowd of some 7,500 had packed the local civic center for a concert by Andy Williams and Henry Mancini . . . which apparently did the trick, because twenty-four hours later Lincoln delivered 2–1 for McGovern and put him over the hump in Nebraska.

I understand these things, and as a certified member of the national press corps I am keenly aware of my responsibility to keep calm and *endure* two hours of Andy Williams from time to time—especially since I went over to Lincoln on the press bus and couldn't leave until the concert was over anyway—but I'm beginning to wonder just how much longer I can stand it: this endless nightmare of getting up at the crack of dawn to go out and watch the candidate shake hands with workers coming in for the day shift at the Bilbo Bear & Sprocket factory, then following him across town for another press-the-flesh gig at the local Slaughterhouse . . . then back on the bus and follow the candidate's car through traffic for forty-five minutes to watch him eat lunch and chat casually with the folks at a basement cafeteria table in some high-rise Home for the Aged.

Both Humphrey and McGovern have been doing this kind of thing about eighteen hours a day for the past six months—and one of them will keep doing it eighteen hours a day for five more months until November. According to the political pros, there is no other way to get elected: go out and meet the voters on their own turf, shake their hands, look them straight in the eye, and introduce yourself . . . there is no other way.

The only one of the candidates this year who has consistently ignored and broken every rule in the Traditional Politicians book is George Wallace. He doesn't do plant gates and coffee klatches. Wallace is a performer, not a mingler. He campaigns like a rock star, working always on the theory that one really *big* crowd is better than forty small ones.

• • •

But to hell with these theories. This is about the thirteenth lead I've written for this goddamn mess, and they are getting progressively worse . . . which hardly matters now, because we are down to the deadline again and it will not be long before the Mojo Wire starts beeping and the phones start ringing and those thugs out in San Francisco will be screaming for Copy. Words! Wisdom! Gibberish!

Anything! The presses roll at noon—three hours from now, and the paper is ready to go except for five blank pages in the middle. The "center-spread," a massive feature story. The cover is already printed, and according to the Story List that is lying out there on the floor about ten feet away from this typewriter, the center-spread feature for this issue will be A Definitive Profile of George McGovern and Everything He Stands For—written by me.

Looking at it fills me with guilt. This room reeks of failure, once again. Every two weeks they send me a story list that says I am lashing together some kind of definitive work on a major subject . . . which is true, but these projects are not developing quite as fast as we thought they would. There are still signs of life in a few of them, but not many. Out of twenty-six projects—a year's work—I have abandoned all hope for twenty-four, and the other two are hanging by a thread.

There is no time to explain, now, why this is not a profile of George McGovern. That story blew up on us in Omaha, on the morning of the primary, when George and most of his troupe suddenly decided that Nixon's decision to force a showdown with Hanoi made it imperative for the senator to fly back to Washington at once.

Nobody could say exactly why, but we all assumed he had something special in mind—some emergency move to get control of Nixon. No time for long mind-probing interviews. Humphrey was leaving too, and there were two or three cynics in the press corps who suggested that this left McGovern no choice. If Humphrey thought the War-Scare was important enough to make him rush back to the Capitol instead of hanging around Omaha on Election Day, then McGovern should be there too—or Hubert might say his Distinguished Opponent cared more about winning the Nebraska Primary than avoiding World War Three.

As it turned out, neither Humphrey nor McGovern did anything dramatic when they got back to Washington—or at least nothing public—and a week or so later the *New York Times* announced that the mines in Haiphong harbor had been set to de-activate themselves on the day before Nixon's trip to Moscow for the summit meeting.

Maybe I missed something. Perhaps the whole crisis was solved in one of those top-secret confrontations between the Senate and the White House that we will not be able to read about until the records are opened seventy-five years from now.

But there is no point in haggling any longer with this. The time has come to get full-bore into heavy Gonzo Journalism, and this time we have no choice but to push it all the way out to the limit. The phone is ringing again and I can hear Crouse downstairs trying to put them off:

"What the hell are you guys worried about? He's up there cranking out a page every three minutes . . . What? . . . No, it won't make much sense, but I guarantee you we'll have plenty of words. If all else fails we'll start sending press releases and shit like that . . . Sure, why worry? We'll start sending almost immediately."

Only a lunatic would do this kind of work: twenty-three primaries in five months; stone drunk from dawn till dusk and huge speed-blisters all over my head. Where is the meaning? That light at the end of the tunnel?

Crouse is yelling again. They want more copy. He has sent them all of his stuff on the Wallace shooting, and now they want mine. Those halfwit sons of bitches should subscribe to a wire service; get one of those big AP tickers that spits out fifty words a minute, twenty-four hours a day . . . a whole grab-bag of weird news; just rip it off the top and print whatever comes up. Just the other day the AP wire had a story about a man from Arkansas who entered some kind of contest and won a two-way journey—all expenses paid—anywhere he wanted to go. Any place in the world: Mongolia, Easter Island, the Turkish Riviera . . . but his choice was Salt Lake City, and that's where he went.

Is this man a registered voter? Has he come to grips with the issues? Has he bathed in the blood of the lamb?

• • •

So much for all that. The noise level downstairs tells me Crouse will not be able to put them off much longer. So now we will start getting serious: first Columbus, Ohio, and then Omaha. But mainly in Columbus, only because this thing began—in my head, at least—as a fairly straight and serious account of the Ohio primary.

Then we decided to combine it with the ill-fated "McGovern Profile" and arranged to meet George in Nebraska. I flew out from Washington and Wenner flew in from the Coast—just in time to shake hands with the candidate on his way to the airport.

No—I want to be fair about it: there was a certain amount of talk, and on the evidence, it seems to have worked out.

But not in terms of "The Profile," which still had five blank pages. So I came back to Washington and grappled with it for a few days, and Crouse came from Boston to help beat the thing into shape . . . but nothing worked; no spine, no hope, to hell with it. We decided to bury the bugger and pretend none of that stuff ever happened. Tim flew back to Boston, and I went off to New York in a half-crazed condition to explain myself and my wisdom at the Columbia School of Journalism.

Later that day George Wallace was shot at a rally in Maryland about twelve minutes away from my house. It was the biggest political story of the year, and those five goddamn pages were still blank. Crouse flew back immediately from Boston, and I straggled back to New York, but by the time we got there it was all over.

• • •

After the Ohio polls closed, I had left Pat Caddell, McGovern's voter-analysis wizard, muttering to himself in the hallway outside the

Situation Room—where he and Frank Mankiewicz and about six others had been grappling all night with botched returns from places like Toledo and Youngstown and Cincinnati.

"Goddamn it," he was saying. "I still can't believe it happened! They *stole* it from us!" He shook his head and kicked a tin spittoon next to the elevator. "We *won* this goddamn election! We had a lock on the nomination tonight, we had it nailed down—but the bastards *stole* it from us!"

Which was more or less true. If McGovern had been able to win Ohio with his last-minute, half-organized blitz it would have snapped the psychic spine of the Humphrey campaign . . . because Hubert had been formidably strong in Ohio, squatting tall in the pocket behind his now-familiar screen of Organized Labor and Old Blacks.

By dawn on Wednesday it was still "too close to call," officially—but sometime around five Harold Himmelman, the national overseer for Ohio, had picked up one of the phones in the situation room and been jolted half out of his chair by the long-awaited tallies from midtown Cleveland. McGovern had already won three of the four congressional districts in Cuyahoga County (metropolitan Cleveland), and all he needed to carry the state, now—along with the thirty-eight additional convention delegates reserved for the statewide winner—was a half-respectable showing in the twenty-first, the heartland of the black vote, a crowded urban fiefdom bossed by Congressman Louis Stokes.

Ten seconds after he picked up the phone Himmelman was screaming: "What? Jesus Christ! No! That can't be right!" (pause . . .) Then: "Awww, shit! That's impossible!"

He turned to Mankiewicz: "It's all over. Listen to this . . ." He turned back to the phone: "Give that to me again . . . okay, yeah, I'm ready." He waited until Mankiewicz got a pencil, then began feeding the figures: "A hundred and nine to one! A hundred and twenty-seven to three! . . . Jesus . . ." Mankiewicz flinched, then wrote down the numbers.

It is 5:05 AM the following morning, and Frank Mankiewicz is calling the Secretary of State, getting him out of bed to protest what he gently but repeatedly refers to as "these fantastic irregularities" in the vote-counting procedure. McGovern's slim lead has suddenly fallen apart: the phones are ringing constantly, and every call brings a new horror story.

In Cincinnati the vote-counters have decided to knock off and rest for twelve hours, a flagrant violation of Sec. 350529 of the State Election Code, which says the counting must go on, without interruption, until all the votes are tallied. In Toledo McGovern is clinging to a precarious 11-vote lead—but in Toledo and everywhere else the polling places are manned by local (Democratic) party hacks not friendly to McGovern, and any delay in the counting will give them time to . . . ah . . .

Mankiewicz studiously avoids using words like "fraud" or "cheat" or "steal." Earlier that day Pierre Salinger had gone on the air to accuse the Humphrey forces of "vote fraud," but the charge was impossible to substantiate at the time, and Humphrey was able to broadcast an embarrassing counterattack while the polls were still open.

In Cleveland, in fact, 127 polling places had remained open until midnight—on the basis of an emergency directive from state Supreme Court.

A Puff Adder in Omaha

Another Wednesday morning, another hotel room, another grim bout with the *CBS Morning News* . . . and another postmortem press conference scheduled for ten o'clock. Three hours from now. Call room service and demand two whole grapefruits, along with a pot of coffee and four glasses of V-8 juice.

These goddamn Wednesday mornings are ruining my health. Last night I came out of a mild ibogaine coma just about the time the polls closed at eight. No booze on Election Day—at least not until the polls close; but they always seem to leave at least one loophole for serious juicers. In Columbus it was the bar at the airport, and in Omaha we had to rent a car and drive across the Missouri River to Council Bluffs, which is also across the state line into Iowa. Every year, on Election Day, the West End bars in Council Bluffs are jammed with boozers from Omaha.

Which is fine, for normal people, but when you drink all day with a head full of ibogaine and then have to spend the next ten hours analyzing election returns . . . there will usually be problems.

Last week—at the Neil House Motor Hotel in Columbus, Ohio—some lunatic tried to break into my room at six in the morning. But fortunately I had a strong chain on the door. In every reputable hotel there is a sign above the knob that warns: "For Our Guests' Protection—Please Use Door Chain at All Times, Before Retiring."

I always use it. During four long months on the campaign trail I have had quite a few bad experiences with people trying to get into my room at strange hours—and in almost every case they object to the music. One out of three will also object to the typewriter, but that hasn't been the case here in Omaha . . .

McGovern and Friend

Sen. George McGovern (D-SD), shown here campaigning in Nebraska where he has spent 23 hours a day for the past six days denying charges by local Humphrey operatives that he favors the legalization of Marijuana, pauses between denials to shake hands for photographers with his "old friend" Hunter S. Thompson, the notorious National Correspondent for Rolling Stone *who was recently identified by* Newsweek *magazine as a vicious drunkard and known abuser of hard drugs.*

A thing like that would have finished him here in Nebraska. No more of that "Hi, sheriff" bullshit; I am now the resident puff adder . . . and the problem is very real. In Ohio, which McGovern eventually lost by a slim nineteen-thousand-vote margin, his handlers figure perhaps ten thousand of those were directly attributable to his public association with Warren Beatty, who once told a reporter somewhere that he favored legalizing grass. This was picked up by the worthless asshole Sen. Henry Jackson (D. Wash.) and turned into a major issue.

So it fairly boggles the mind to think what Humphrey's people might do with a photo of McGovern shaking hands with a person who once ran for sheriff of Aspen on the Freak Power ticket, with a platform embracing the use and frequent enjoyment of Mescaline by the sheriff and all his deputies at any hour of the day or night that seemed Right.

No, this would never do. Not for George McGovern—at least not in May of '72, and probably never. He has spent the past week traveling around Nebraska and pausing at every opportunity to explain that he is flatly opposed to the legalization of marijuana. He is also opposed to putting people in prison for mere *possession*, which he thinks should be reclassified as a misdemeanor instead of a felony.

And even this went down hard in Nebraska. He came into this state with a comfortable lead, and just barely escaped with a 6 percentage-point (41 percent to 35 percent) win over Hubert Humphrey—who did everything possible, short of making the accusations on his own, to identify McGovern as a Trojan Horse full of dope dealers and abortionists.

• • •

Jackson had raised the same issues in Ohio, but George ignored them—which cost him the state and thirty-eight delegates, according to his staff thinkers—so when Hubert laid it on him again, in Nebraska, McGovern decided to "meet them head on." For almost a week, every speech he made led off with an angry denial that he favored either legalized grass or Abortion On Demand . . . and in the dawn hours of Saturday morning, three days before the election, he called his media wizard Charlie Guggenheim back from a vacation in the Caribbean to make a Special Film designed—for statewide exposure on Sunday night—to make goddamn sure that The Folks understood that George McGovern was just a regular guy, like them, who would no more tolerate marijuana than would send his wife to an abortionist.

And it worked. I watched it in McGovern's Omaha Hilton "press suite" with a handful of reporters and Dick Dougherty, a former *L.A. Times* reporter who writes many of George's major speech/statements, but who is usually kept out of the public eye because of his extremely seedy and unsettling appearance. On Sunday night, however, Dougherty came out of wherever he usually stays to watch The Man on the TV set in the pressroom. We found him hunkered there with a plastic glass of Old Overholt and a pack of Home Run cigarettes, staring at the tube and saying over and over again: "Jesus, that's fantastic! Christ, look at that camera angle! God damn, this is really a hell of a film, eh?"

I agreed. It was a first-class campaign film: the lighting was fantastic, the sound was as sharp and clear as diamonds bouncing on a magnesium tabletop, the characters and the dialogue made Turgenev seem like a punk. McGovern sat in the round and masterfully defused every ugly charge that had ever been leveled at him. He spoke like a combination of

Socrates, Clarence Darrow, and God. It was a flat-out masterpiece, both as a film and a performance—and when it ended I joined in the general chorus of praise.

"Beautiful," somebody muttered.

"Damn fine stuff," said somebody else.

Dougherty was grinning heavily. "How about *that*?" he said.

"Wonderful," I replied. "No doubt about it. My only objection is that I disagree with almost everything he said."

He stood up quickly and backed off a few steps. "Jesus Christ," he snapped. "You're really a goddamn *nit-picker*, aren't you?"

Nightmare in Fat City?

McGovern told a Flint (Mich.) press conference that while "Wallace is entitled to be treated with respect at the convention (in Miami), I don't propose to make any deals with him . . ." Humphrey (in Michigan) attacked Wallace more personally than McGovern, but when a question about wooing Wallace delegates was thrown at him, Humphrey said, "I will seek support wherever I can get it, if I can convince them to be for me."

—*Washington Post*, May 14, '72

Quotes like this are hard to come by—especially in presidential elections, where most candidates are smart enough to know better than to call a press conference and then announce—on the record—an overweening eagerness to peddle his ass to the highest bidder.

Only Hubert Humphrey would do a thing like that . . . and we can only assume that now, in his lust for the White House—after suffering for twenty-four years with a case of Political Blueballs only slightly less severe than Richard Nixon's—that the Hube has finally cracked; and he did it in public.

With the possible exception of Nixon, Hubert Humphrey is the purest and most disgusting example of a Political Animal in American politics today. He has been going at it hammer and tongs about twenty-five hours a day since the end of World War II—just like Richard Nixon, who launched his own career as a Red-baiting California congressman about the same time Hubert began making headlines as the Red-baiting mayor of Minneapolis. They are both career anti-Communists: Nixon's gig was financed from the start by Big Business, and Humphrey's by Big Labor . . . and what both of them stand for today is the de facto triumph of a One Party System in American politics.

George Meany, the aging ruler of the AFL-CIO, was one of the first to announce his whole-hearted support of Nixon's decision to lay mines around Haiphong harbor and celebrate the memory of Guernica with a fresh round of saturation bombing in North Vietnam.

Humphrey disagreed, of course—along with Mayor Daley—but in fact neither one of them had any choice. The war in Vietnam will be a key issue in November, and Senator Henry Jackson of Washington has already demonstrated—with a series of humiliating defeats in the primaries—what fate awaits any Democrat who tries to agree with Nixon on The War.

But Humphrey seems not quite convinced. On the morning before the Wisconsin primary he appeared on the *Today* show, along with all the other candidates, and when faced with a question involving renewed escalation of the bombing in Vietnam, he lined up with Jackson and Wallace—in clear opposition to McGovern and Lindsay, who both said we should get the hell out of Vietnam at once. Big Ed, as usual, couldn't make up his mind.

Since then—after watching Jackson suck wind all over the Midwest—Hubert has apparently decided to stick with Dick Daley on Vietnam. But he has not explained, yet, how he plans to square his late-blooming dovishness with Boss Meany—who could croak Humphrey's last chance for the nomination with a single phone call.

Meany's hired hacks and goon squads are just about all Hubert can count on these days, and even his Labor friends are having their problems. Tony Boyle, for instance, is headed for prison on more felony counts than I have space to list here. Boyle, former president of the United Mine Workers Union, was recently cracked out of office by the Justice Dept. for gross and flagrant "misuse" of the union treasury—which involved, among other things, illegal contributions to Humphrey's presidential campaign in 1968. In addition to all this, Boyle now faces a Conspiracy-

Murder rap in connection with the contract-killing of Joseph Yablonski, who made the mistake of challenging him for the union presidency in December 1969, and paid for it a few months later when hired thugs appeared one night in his bedroom and gunned him down, along with his wife and daughter.

Hubert Humphrey's opinion of Tony Boyle was best expressed when they appeared together at the United Mine Workers Convention in Denver in 1968, and Humphrey referred to Boyle as "My friend, this great American."

For whatever it's worth, the UMW is one of the most powerful political realities in West Virginia, where Humphrey recently won his fourth primary in a row.

The Democratic Convention in Miami begins on July 10, and the only major political event between now and then is the California primary on June 6. If Humphrey loses in California—and he will, I think—his only hope for the nomination will be to make a deal with Wallace, who will come to Miami with something like 350 delegates, and he'll be looking around for somebody to bargain with.

The logical bargainee, as it were, is Hubert Humphrey, who has been running a sort of left-handed, stupid-coy flirtation with Wallace ever since the Florida primary, where he did everything possible to co-opt Wallace's position on busing without actually agreeing with it. Humphrey even went so far as to agree, momentarily, with Nixon on busing—blurting out "Oh, thank goodness!" when he heard of Nixon's proposal for a "moratorium," which amounted to a presidential edict to suspend all busing until the White House could figure out some way to circumvent the U.S. Supreme Court.

When somebody called Hubert's attention to this aspect of the problem and reminded him that he had always been known as a staunch foe of racial segregation, he quickly changed his mind and rushed up to Wisconsin to nail down the black vote by denouncing Wallace as a racist demagogue, and Nixon as a cynical opportunist for saying almost exactly the same things about busing that Humphrey himself had been saying in Florida.

There is no way to grasp what a shallow, contemptible, and hopelessly dishonest old hack Hubert Humphrey really is until you've followed him around for a while on the campaign trail. The double-standard realities of campaign journalism, however, make it difficult for even the best of the "straight/objective" reporters to write what they actually think and feel about a candidate.

Hubert Humphrey, for one, would go crazy with rage and attempt to strangle his press secretary if he ever saw in print what most reporters say about him during midnight conversations around bar-room tables in all those Hiltons and Sheratons where the candidates make their headquarters when they swoop into places like Cleveland, Pittsburgh, and Indianapolis.

And some of these reporters are stepping out of the closet and beginning to describe Humphrey in print as the bag of PR gimmicks that he is. The other day one of the *Washington Post* regulars nailed him:

"Humphrey has used the campaign slogans of John Kennedy ('let's get this country moving again') and of Wallace ('stand up for America') and some of his literature proclaims that 1972 is 'the year of the people,' a title used by Eugene McCarthy for a book about his 1968 campaign."

The Wisdom

I predict regretfully that you in California will see one of the dirtiest campaigns in the history of this state—and you have had some of the dirtiest.

—Sen. Abraham Ribicoff, speaking in San Francisco

No hope for this section. Crouse is caving in downstairs; they have him on two phones at once and even from up here I can hear the conversation turning ugly . . . so there is not much time for anything except maybe a flash round-up on the outlook for California and beyond.

George Wallace himself will not be a factor in the California primary. His handlers are talking about a last-minute write-in campaign, but he has no delegates—and the California ballot doesn't list candidates; only *delegates pledged to candidates*. So a write-in vote for Wallace won't even be counted.

Wallace is not even likely, now, to have any real bargaining at the convention. Even before he was shot—and before he won Michigan and Maryland—his only hope for real leverage in Miami depended on Humphrey coming into the convention with enough delegates of his own (something like 700–800) to bargain with Wallace from strength. But as things stand now, Humphrey and Wallace between them will not have 1,000 delegates on the first ballot—and McGovern is a pretty good bet, today, to go down to Miami with almost 1,300.

Humphrey's last chance for leverage now is to win California, and although the polls still show him ahead I doubt if even Hubert believes it. Even before his weak showings in Michigan and Maryland, one of Humphrey's main strategists—Kenny O'Donnell—was quietly leaking word to the press that Hubert didn't really *need* California to get the nomination.

This is an interesting notion—particularly after Humphrey himself had de-emphasized the importance of winning the New York primary a few days earlier. He understood, even then, that there was no point even thinking about New York unless he could win in California.

And that's not going to happen unless something very drastic happens between now and June 6. Hubert's only hope in California was a savage, all-out attack on McGovern—a desperate smear campaign focused on Grass, Amnesty, Abortion, and even Busing. And to do that he would have to consciously distort McGovern's positions on those issues . . . which is something he would find very hard to do, because Humphrey and McGovern have been close personal friends for many years.

I have said a lot of foul things about Hubert, all deserved, but I think I'd be genuinely surprised to see him crank up a vicious and groundless attack on an old friend. His California managers have already said they will try to do it, with or without his approval—but Hubert knows he could never carry that off. In Ohio he got away with letting Jackson do his dirty work, and in Nebraska he let his supporters smear McGovern in a Catholic newspaper, the *True Voice* . . . but Hubert himself never got down in the ditch; he stayed on what he likes to call "the high road."

But he won't have that option in California. His only hope for winning out there is to go flat out on the Low Road.

Maybe he will, but I doubt it. The odds are too long. McGovern would probably win anyway—leaving Humphrey to rot in the history books for generations to come.

The Campaign Trail: Fear and Loathing in California: Traditional Politics with a Vengeance

July 6, 1972

In my own country I am in a far-off land.
I am strong but have no force or power
I win all yet remain a loser
At break of day I say goodnight
When I lie down I have a great fear of falling.

—François Villon

There is probably some long-standing "rule" among writers, journalists, and other word-mongers that says: "When you start stealing from your own work you're in bad trouble." And it may be true.

I am growing extremely weary of writing constantly about politics. My brain has become a steam-vat; my body is turning to wax and bad flab; impotence looms; my fingernails are growing at a fantastic rate of speed—they are turning into claws; my standard-size clippers will no longer cut the growth, so now I carry a set of huge toenail clippers and sneak off every night around dusk, regardless of where I am—in any city, hamlet, or plastic hotel room along the campaign trail—to chop another quarter of an inch or so off of all ten fingers.

People are beginning to notice, I think, but fuck them. I am beginning to notice some of *their* problems, too. Drug dependence is out in the open now: some people are getting heavy into downers—reds, Quaaludes, Tuinals—and others are gobbling speed, booze, Maalox, and other strange medications with fearsome regularity. The 1972 presidential campaign is beginning to feel more and more like the second day of a Hells Angels Labor Day picnic.

And we are only halfway home: five more months . . . the moment I finish this goddamn thing, I have to rush up to New York for the June 20 primary, then back to Washington to get everything packed for the move to Colorado . . . and after that to Miami for the Democratic Convention, which is shaping up very fast these days as one of the most brutal and degrading animal acts of our time.

After Miami the calendar shows a bit of a rest on the political front—but not for me: I have to go back out to California and ride that goddamn fiendish Vincent Black Shadow again, for the road tests. The original plan was to deal with the beast in my off-hours during the California primary coverage, but serious problems developed.

Ten days before the election—with McGovern apparently so far ahead that most of the press people were looking for ways to *avoid* covering the final week—I drove out to Ventura, a satellite town just north of L.A. in the San Fernando Valley, to pick up the bugger and use it to cover the rest of the primary. Greg Jackson, an ABC newscaster who used to race motorcycles, went along with me. We were both curious about this machine. Chris Bunche, editor of *Choppers* magazine, said it was so fast and terrible that it made the extremely fast Honda 750 seem like a harmless toy.

This proved to be absolutely true. I rode a factory-demo Honda for a while, just to get the feel of being back on a serious road-runner again . . . and it seemed just fine: very quick, very powerful, very easy in the hands, one-touch electric starter. A very civilized machine, in all, and I might even be tempted to buy one if I didn't have the same gut distaste for Hondas that the American Honda management has for *Rolling Stone*. They don't like the image. "You meet the nicest people on a Honda," they say—but according to a letter from American Honda to the *Rolling Stone* ad manager, none of these *nicest people* have much stomach for a magazine like this one.

Which is probably just as well; because if you're a safe, happy, *nice* young Republican, you probably don't want to read about things like dope, rock music, and politics anyway. You want to stick with *Time*, and for weekend recreation do a bit of the laid-back street-cruising on your big fast Honda 750 . . . maybe burn a Sportster or a Triumph here & there, just for the *fun* of it: but nothing serious, because when you start that kind of thing you don't meet many *nice people*.

• • •

Jesus! Another tangent, and right up front, this time—the whole *lead*, in fact, completely fucked.

What can I say? Last week I blew the whole thing. Total failure. Missed the deadline, no article, no wisdom, no excuse . . . Except one: yes, I was savagely and expertly duped by one of the oldest con trips in politics.

By Frank Mankiewicz, of all people. That scurvy, rumpled, treacherous little bastard . . . If I were running for president I would hire Mankiewicz to run my campaign, but as a journalist I wouldn't shed a tear if I picked up tomorrow's paper and saw where nine thugs had caught poor Frank in an alley near the Capitol and cut off both of his big toes, making it permanently impossible for him to keep his balance for more than five or six feet in any direction.

The image is horrible: Mankiewicz gets a phone call from Houston, saying the Texas delegation is on the verge of selling out to a Humphrey-Wallace coalition . . . he slams down the phone and lunges out of his cubicle in "McGovern for President" headquarters, bouncing off the door-jamb and then grabbing the Coke machine in order to stay upright—then lunging again into Rick Stearns' office to demand a detailed breakdown on the sex lives and bad debts of every member of the Texas delegation . . . then trying to catch his breath, gasping for air from the terrible exertion, and finally lunging back down the hall to his own cubicle.

It is very hard to walk straight with the big toes gone; the effect is sort of like taking the keel off a sailboat—it becomes impossibly top-heavy, wallowing crazily in the swells, not even the sea-anchor will hold it upright . . . and the only way a man can walk straight with no big toes is to use a very complex tripod mechanism, five or six retractable aluminum rods strapped to each arm, moving around like a spider instead of a person.

Ah . . . this seems to be getting heavy. Very harsh and demented language. I have tried to suppress these feelings for more than a week, but every time I sit down at a typewriter they foam to the surface. So it is probably better—if for no other reason than to get past this ugly hang-up and into the rest of the article—to just blow it all out and take the weight off my spleen, as it were, with a brief explanation.

• • •

Morning again in downtown Los Angeles; dawn comes up on this city like a shitmist. Will it burn off before noon? Will the sun eventually poke through? That is the question they'll be asking each other down there on the Pool Terrace below my window a few hours from now. I'm into my eighteenth day as a resident of the Wilshire Hyatt House Hotel, and I am getting to know the dreary routine of this place pretty well.

Outside of that pigsty in Milwaukee, this may be the worst hotel in America. The Sheraton-Schroeder remains in a class of its own: passive incompetence is one thing, but aggressive Nazi hostility on the corporate level is something else again. The only thing these two hotels have in common is that the Sheraton (ITT) chain got rid of them: the Schroeder was sold to a local business magnate, and this grim hulk ended up as a part of the Hyatt House chain.

As far as I know there was no pool in the Schroeder. Maybe a big grease pit or a scum vat of some kind on the roof, but I never saw a pool. There were rumors of a military-style S&M gallery in the basement, with maybe an icewater plunge for the survivors, but I never saw that one either. There was no way to deal with management personnel in the Schroeder unless your breath smelled heavily of sauerbraten . . . and in fact one of the happiest things about my life, these days, is that my memories of life in the Sheraton-Schroeder are becoming mercifully dim. The only open sore that remains from that relationship is the trouble I'm still having with the IBM typewriter-rental service in Milwaukee—with regard to the $600 Selectric typewriter I left behind on the desk when I checked out. It was gone when the IBM man came around to pick it up the next morning, and now they want me to pay for it.

Right. Another contribution to the Thousand-Year Reich: "We will march on a road of bones . . ." Tom Paxton wrote a song about it. And now I get these harsh letters from Milwaukee: "Herr Docktor Thompson—Der Typewriting machine you rented hass disappeared! And you will of course pay!"

No. Never in hell. Because I have a receipt for that typewriter.

• • •

But first things first. We were talking about motorcycles; Jackson and I were out there in Ventura fucking around with a 750 Honda and an experimental prototype of the new Vincent—a 1000-cc brute that proved out to be so awesomely fast that I didn't even have time to get scared of it before I found myself coming up on a highway stoplight at 90 miles an hour and then skidding halfway through the intersection with both wheel-brakes locked.

A genuinely hellish bike. Second gear peaks around 65—cruising speed on the freeways—and third winds out somewhere between 95 and 100. I never got to fourth, which takes you up to 120 or so—and after that you shift into fifth.

Top speed is 140, more or less, depending on how the thing is tuned—but there is nowhere in Los Angeles County to run a bike like that. I managed to get it back from Ventura to McGovern's downtown headquarters hotel, staying mainly in second gear, but the vibration almost fused my wrist bones, and boiling oil from the breather pipes turned my right foot completely black. Later, when I tried to start it up for another test run, the backlash from the kick-starter almost broke my leg. For two days afterward I limped around with a golf-ball-size blood-bruise in my right arch.

Later in the week I tried the bastard again, but it stalled on a ramp leading up to the Hollywood Freeway and I almost broke my hand when I exploded in a stupid, screaming rage and punched the gas tank. After that, I locked it up and left it in the hotel parking lot—where it sat for many days with a "McGovern for President" tag on the handlebars.

George never mentioned it, and when I suggested to Gary Hart that the senator might like to take the machine out for a quick test-ride and some photos for the national press, I got almost exactly the same reaction that Mankiewicz laid on me in Florida when I suggested that McGovern could pick up a million or so votes by inviting the wire-service photographers to come out and snap him lounging around on the beach with a can of beer in his hand and wearing my Grateful Dead T-shirt.

Looking back on it, I think that was the moment when my relationship with Mankiewicz turned sour. Twenty-four hours earlier I had showed up at his house in Washington with what John Prine calls "an illegal smile" on my face—and the morning after that visit he found himself sitting next to me on the plane to Florida and listening to some lunatic spiel about how his man should commit political suicide by irreparably identifying himself as the candidate of the Beachbums, Weirdos, and Boozers.

The Samoan Tragedy

The Villon quote was lifted from a book I wrote a few years ago on outlaw motorcycle gangs, and at the time it seemed like a very apt little stroke—reaching back into time and French poetry for a reminder that a sense of doomed alienation on your own turf is nothing new.

But why use the same quote to lead off another one of these rambling screeds on American politics in 1972? On the California Democratic primary? The McGovern campaign?

There has to be a reason. And there is, in fact—but I doubt if I'm up to explaining it right now. All I can say for sure is that I walked into the room and stared at the typewriter for a long time . . . knowing I'd just spent seventeen days and $2,000 in California lashing together this thirty-three-pound satchel of notes, tapes, clippings, propaganda, etc. . . . and also knowing that somewhere in one of these goddamn drawers is a valid contract that says I have to write a long article, immediately, about whatever happened out there.

How long, O Lord, how long? Where will it end?

All I ever wanted out of this grueling campaign was enough money to get out of the country and live for a year or two in peaceful squalor in a house with a big screen porch looking down on an empty white beach, with a good rich coral reef a few hundred yards out in the surf and *no neighbors*.

Some book reviewer whose name I forgot recently called me a "vicious misanthrope" . . . or maybe it was a "cynical misanthrope" . . . but either way, he (or she) was right; and what got me this way was *politics*. Everything that is wrong-headed, cynical & vicious in me today traces straight back to that evil hour in September of '69 when I decided to get heavily involved in the political process . . .

But that is another story. What worries me now—in addition to this still-unwritten saga of the California primary—is the strong possibility that my involvement in politics has become so deep and twisted that I can no longer think rationally about that big screen porch above the beach except in terms of an appointment as governor of American Samoa.

I coveted that post for many years. For a while it was my only ambition. I pursued it relentlessly, and at one point in either 1964 or '65 it seemed within my grasp. Larry O'Brien, now the chairman of the Democratic Party, was the man in charge of pork-barrel/patronage appointments at the time, and he gave me excellent reason to believe my application was on the verge of bearing fruit. I was living at the Holiday Inn in Pierre, South Dakota, when the good news arrived. It came on a Wednesday, as I recall, by telegram. The manager of the Inn was ecstatic; he called a cab immediately and sent me downtown to a dry-goods store where I bought six white sharkskin suits—using a Sinclair Oil card, which was subsequently revoked and caused me a lot of trouble.

I never learned all the details, but what was finally made clear—in the end, after a bad communications breakdown—was that O'Brien had pulled a fast one on me. As it turned out, he never had any intention of making me governor of American Samoa, and when I finally realized this it made me very bitter and eventually changed my whole life.

Like George Metesky—the "Mad Bomber" who terrorized New York for fifteen years to get even with Con Edison for overcharging him on his light bill and finally cutting off his electricity—I changed my whole lifestyle and channeled my energies into long-range plotting for vengeance on O'Brien and the Democratic Party. Instead of going into government service in the South Pacific, I fled Pierre, S.D., in a junk Rambler and drove to San Francisco—where I fell in with the Hells Angels and decided to become a writer instead of a diplomat.

Several years later I moved to Colorado and tried to live quietly. But I never forgot O'Brien. In the solitude of the Rockies I nursed a lust for vengeance . . . saying nothing to anyone, until suddenly in the summer of '69 I saw an opportunity to cripple the Democratic Party in Aspen.

This took about fifteen months, and by the time it was done, I was hopelessly hooked again on the politics of vengeance. The next step would have to be national. O'Brien was riding high in Washington, commanding a suite of offices in the Watergate and reluctantly gearing up to send a party with no real candidate and a $9 million debt from '68 into a hopeless battle with Nixon—a battle that would not only humiliate the candidate (The Man from Maine, they said), but also destroy the party by plunging it into a state of financial and ideological bankruptcy from which it would never recover.

Wonderful, I thought. I won't even have to *do* anything. Just watch, and write it all down.

• • •

That was six months ago. But things are different now—and in the strange calm of those first few days after the votes were counted in California, I began to see that George McGovern had scrambled my own carefully laid plans along with all the others—except his—and that I was suddenly facing the very distinct possibility that I might have to drag myself into a voting booth this November and actually pull the lever for the presidential candidate of the Democratic Party. O'Brien's party. That same gang of corrupt and genocidal bastards who not only burned me for six white sharkskin suits eight years ago in South Dakota and chased me through the streets of Chicago with clubs & tear gas in August of '68, but also forced me to choose for five years between going to prison or chipping in 20 percent of my income to pay for napalm bombs to be dropped on people who never threatened me with anything; and who put my friends in jail for refusing to fight an undeclared war in Asia that even Mayor Daley is now opposed to . . .

Ah . . . careful, careful: that trip has been done. No point getting off on another violent tangent. And besides, now that the Republicans are running The War, the Democrats are against it . . . or at least *some* of them are against it, including such recent converts as Ed Muskie and Hubert Humphrey. But it is also worth noting that the only Democrat to survive this hellish six-month gauntlet of presidential primaries is also the only genuine anti-war candidate.

Six months ago McGovern was dismissed by the press and the pols as a "one-issue candidate." And to a certain extent they were right. He has branched out a bit since then, but The War in Vietnam is still the only issue in McGovern's jumbled arsenal that he never has to explain, defend, or modify. All he has to do is start talking about Vietnam, and the crowd begins cheering and clapping.

For a "one-issue candidate," George McGovern has done pretty well. Four years ago Gene McCarthy was another "one-issue candidate"—the same issue poor McGovern is stuck with today—and if McCarthy had somehow managed to put together the kind of political organization that McGovern is riding now, he would be the incumbent president and the '72 campaign would be a very different scene.

Gene Pokorny, one of McGovern's key managers, who also worked for McCarthy in '68, describes the difference between the two campaigns as "the difference between an organization and a happening." . . . Which is probably true, but that "happening" dumped a Democratic president and made McCarthy the front-runner all the way to California, where he lost to Robert Kennedy by only 3 percentage points. They were still counting the votes when Sirhan Sirhan fired a bullet into Kennedy's head.

What if McCarthy had won California? Would Sirhan have gone after him, instead of Kennedy? . . . Like Artie Bremer, who stalked Nixon for a while, then switched to Wallace. Assassins, like politicians and journalists, are not attracted to losers.

"That's One Story You'll Never Hear"

Strange speculation . . . and worth pursuing, no doubt, on a day when I have more time. Is the governor's mansion in American Samoa on a cliff above the beach? Does it have a big screen porch? Sometime soon I will have to speak with Mankiewicz about this. I don't look forward to it, but perhaps we can work something out if we handle the whole thing by telephone.

Some people are easier to deal with at a distance, and Frank is apparently one of them. His whole manner changes when you confront him in person. It is very much like dealing with a gila monster who was only pretending to be asleep when you approached him—but the instant you enter his psychic territory, a radius of about six feet, he will dart off in some unexpected direction and take up a new stance, fixing you with a lazy unblinking stare and apparently trying to make up his mind whether to dart back and sink a fang in your flesh or just sit there and wait till you move on.

This is the way Mankiewicz behaved when I ran across him around midnight, a week or so before Election Day, in the hallway outside the McGovern pressroom in the Wilshire Hyatt House Hotel and asked him if he could help me out with some details on a story I'd just picked up in a strip joint called The Losers on La Cienega Boulevard—a very strange tale about Hubert Humphrey keeping a private plane on standby at a nearby landing strip, ready to take off at any moment for Vegas and return the same night with a big bag of cash, which would then be rushed to Humphrey headquarters at the Beverly Hilton and used to finance a bare-knuckle media blitz against McGovern during the last days of the campaign.

The story was at least secondhand by the time I heard it, but the source seemed reliable, and I was eager to learn more . . . but there was no point in calling Humphrey on a thing like this, so I brooded on it for a while and finally decided—for reasons better left unexplained, at this point—that the only two people even half likely to know anything about such a bizarre story as this one were Mankiewicz and Dick Tuck.

But a dozen or so phone calls failed to locate either one of them, so I wandered up to the pressroom to get a free drink and check the bulletin board for a message of some kind from Tim Crouse, who had gone off about six hours earlier to find a bottle of schnapps and continue his research on How the Press Covers the Campaign. The project had already stirred up a surprising amount of outspoken resentment among the objects of his study, and now he had gone out to get crazy on German whiskey with a bunch of people who thought he was planning to skewer them in the public prints.

The pressroom was crowded: two dozen or so ranking media wizards, all wearing little egg-shaped ID tags from the Secret Service: Leo Sauvage/*Le Figaro*, Jack Perkins/NBC, R. W. Apple/*NY Times* . . . the McGovern campaign went big-time, for real, in California. No more of that part-time, secondary coverage. McGovern was suddenly the front-runner, perhaps the next president, and virtually every room in the hotel was filled with either staff or media people . . . twelve new typewriters in the press suite, ten phones, four color TV sets, a well-stocked free bar, even a goddamn Mojo Wire.

(Footnote: aka "Xerox Telecopier." We have had many inquiries about this. "Mojo Wire" was the name originally given the machine by its inventor, Raoul Duke. But he signed away the patent, in the throes of a drug frenzy, to Xerox board chairman Max Palevsky, who claimed the invention for himself and re-named it the "Xerox Telecopier." Patent royalties now total $100 million annually, but Duke receives none of it. At Palevsky's insistence he remains on the *Rolling Stone* payroll, earning $50 each week, but his "sports column" is rarely printed and he is formally barred by court order, along with a Writ of Permanent Constraint, from Palevsky's house & grounds.)

But Crouse was nowhere in sight. I stood around for a while, trying to piece together another grisly unsubstantiated rumor about "heavy pols preparing to take over the whole McGovern campaign" . . . Several people had chunks of the story, but nobody had a real key, so I left to go back down to my room to work for a while.

That was when I ran into Mankiewicz, picking a handful of thumbtacked messages off the bulletin board outside the door.

"I have a very weird story for you," I said.

He eyed me cautiously. "What is it?"

"Come over here," I said, motioning him to follow me down the corridor to a quiet place . . . Then I told him what I had heard about Humphrey's midnight air-courier to Vegas. He stared down at the carpet, not seeming particularly interested—but when I finished, he looked up and said, "Where'd you *hear* that?"

I shrugged, sensing definite interest now. "Well, I was talking to some people over at a place called The Losers, and—"

"With Kirby?" he snapped.

"No," I said. "I went over there looking for him, but he wasn't around." Which was true. Earlier that day Kirby Jones, McGovern's press secretary, had told me he planned to stop by The Losers Club later on, because Warren Beatty had recommended it highly . . . but when I stopped by around midnight there was no sign of him.

Mankiewicz was not satisfied. "Who was there?" he asked. "Some of *our* people? Who was it?"

"Nobody you'd know," I said. "But what about this Humphrey story? What can you tell me about it?"

"Nothing," he said, glancing over his shoulder at a burst of yelling from the pressroom. Then: "When's your next issue coming out?"

"Thursday."

"Before the election?"

"Yeah, and so far I don't have anything worth a shit to write about—but this thing sounds interesting."

He nodded, staring down at the floor again, then shook his head. "Listen," he said. "You could cause a lot of trouble for us by printing a thing like that. They'd know where it came from, and they'd jerk our man right out."

"What man?"

He stared at me, smiling faintly.

At this point the story becomes very slippery, with many loose ends and dark spots—but the nut was very simple: I had blundered almost completely by accident on a flat-out byzantine spook story. There was nothing timely or particularly newsworthy about it, but when your deadline is every two weeks you don't tend to worry about things like scoops and newsbreaks. If Mankiewicz had broken down and admitted to me that night that he was actually a Red Chinese agent and that McGovern had no pulse, I wouldn't have known how to handle it—and the tension of trying to keep that kind of heinous news to myself for the next four days until *Rolling Stone* went to press would almost certainly have caused me to lock myself in my hotel room with eight quarts of Wild Turkey and all the ibogaine I could get my hands on.

But this strange tale about Humphrey & Vegas had very little news value. Its only real value, in fact, was the rare flash of contrast it provided to the insane tedium of the surface campaign. Important or not, this was something very different: midnight flights to Vegas, Mob money funneled in from Vegas to pay for Hubert's TV spots; spies, runners, counterspies; cryptic phone calls from airport phone booths . . . Indeed; the dark underbelly of big-time politics. A useless story, no doubt, but it sure beat the hell out of getting back on that goddamn press bus and being hauled out to some shopping center in Gardena and watching McGovern shake hands for two hours with lumpy housewives.

Unfortunately, all I really knew about what I called the U-13 story was the general outline and just enough key points to convince Mankiewicz that I might be irresponsible enough to go ahead and try to write the thing anyway. All I knew—or *thought* I knew—at that point, was that somebody very close to the top of the Humphrey campaign had made secret arrangements for a night flight to Vegas, in order to pick up a large bundle of money from unidentified persons presumed to be sinister, and that this money would be used by Humphrey's managers to finance another one of Hubert's eleventh-hour fast-finish blitzkriegs.

Even then, a week before the vote, he was thought to be running almost 10 points behind McGovern—and since the average daily media expenditure for each candidate was roughly $30,000 a day, Humphrey would need at least twice that amount to pay for the orgy of exposure he would need to overcome a 10-point lead. No less than a quick $500,000.

The people in Vegas were apparently willing to spring for it, because the plane was already chartered and ready to go when McGovern's headquarters got word of the flight from their executive-level spy in the Humphrey campaign. His identity remains a mystery—in the public prints, at least—but the handful of people aware of him say he performed invaluable services for many months.

His function in the U-13 gig was merely to call McGovern hq. and tell them about the Vegas plane. At this point, my second- or third-hand source was not sure what happened next. According to the story, two McGovern operatives were instantly dispatched to keep around-the-clock watch on the plane for the next seventy-two hours, and somebody from McGovern headquarters called Humphrey and warned him that they knew what he was up to.

In any case, the plane never took off, and there was no evidence in the last week of the campaign to suggest that Hubert got a last-minute influx of money, from Vegas or anywhere else.

• • •

That is as much of the U-13 story as I could piece together without help from somebody who knew the details—and Mankiewicz finally agreed, insisting the whole time that he knew nothing about the story except that he didn't want to see it in print before Election Day, that if I wanted to hold off until the next issue he would put me in touch with somebody who would tell me the whole story, for good or ill.

"Call Miles Rubin," he said, "and tell him I told you to ask him about this. He'll fill you in."

That was fine, I said. I was in no special hurry for the story anyway. So I let it ride for a few days, missing my deadline for that issue . . . and on Wednesday I began trying to get hold of Miles Rubin, one of McGovern's top managers for California. All I knew about Rubin, before I called, was that several days earlier he had thrown *Washington Post* correspondent David Broder out of his office for asking too many questions—less than twenty-four hours before Broder appeared on Rubin's TV screen as one of the three interrogators on the first Humphrey-McGovern debate.

My own experience with Rubin turned out to be just about par for the course. I finally got through to him by telephone on Friday, and explained that Mankiewicz had told me to call him and find out the details of the U-13 story. I started to say we could meet for a beer or two sometime later that afternoon and he could—

"Are you kidding?" he cut in. "That's one story you're never going to hear."

"What?"

"There's no point even talking about it," he said flatly. Then he launched into a three-minute spiel about the fantastic honesty and integrity that characterized the McGovern campaign from top to bottom, and why was it that people like me didn't spend more time writing about The Truth and The Decency and The Integrity, instead of picking around the edges for minor things that weren't important anyway?

"Jesus Christ!" I muttered. Why argue? Getting anything but pompous bullshit and gibberish out of Rubin would be like trying to steal meat from a hammerhead shark.

"Thanks," I said, and hung up.

That night I found Mankiewicz in the pressroom and told him what had happened.

He couldn't understand it, he said. But he would talk to Miles tomorrow and straighten it out.

I was not optimistic; and by that time I was beginning to agree that the U-13 story was not worth the effort. The Big Story in California, after all, was that McGovern was on the brink of locking up a first-ballot nomination in Miami—and that Hubert Humphrey was about to get stomped so badly at the polls that he might have to be carried out of the state in a rubber sack.

The next time I saw Mankiewicz was on the night before the election, and he seemed very tense, very strong into the gila monster trip . . . and when I started to ask him about Rubin he began ridiculing the story in a *very loud voice*, so I figured it was time to forget it.

Several days later I learned the reason for Frank's bad nerves that night. McGovern's fat lead over Humphrey, which had hovered between 14 and 20 percentage points for more than a week, had gone into a sudden and apparently uncontrollable dive in the final days of the campaign. By election eve it had shrunk to 5 points, and perhaps even less.

The shrinkage crisis was a closely guarded secret among McGovern's top command. Any leak to the press could have led to disastrous headlines on Tuesday morning. Election Day . . . "McGovern Falters; Humphrey Closing Gap . . ." a headline like that in either the *Los Angeles Times* or the *San Francisco Chronicle* might have thrown the election to Humphrey, by generating a last-minute Sympathy/Underdog turnout and whipping Hubert's field workers into a frenzied "get out the vote" effort.

But the grim word never leaked, and by noon on Tuesday an almost visible wave of relief rolled through the McGovern camp. The dike would hold, they felt, at roughly 5 percent.

The coolest man in the whole McGovern entourage on Tuesday was George McGovern himself—who had spent all day Monday on airplanes, racing from one critical situation to another. On Monday morning he flew down to San Diego for a major rally; then to New Mexico for another final-hour rally on the eve of the New Mexico primary (which he won the next day—along with New Jersey and South Dakota) . . . and finally on Monday night to Houston for a brief, unscheduled appearance at the National Governors Conference, which was rumored to be brewing up a "stop McGovern" movement.

After defusing the crisis in Houston he got a few hours' sleep before racing back to Los Angeles to deal with another emergency: his twenty-two-year-old daughter was having a premature baby and first reports from the hospital hinted at serious complications.

But by noon the crisis had passed and somewhere sometime around one, he arrived with his praetorian guard of eight Secret Service agents at a friend's house in Bel Air, where he immediately changed into swimming trunks and dove into the pool. The day was gray and cool, no hint of sun and none of the other guests seemed to feel like swimming.

For a variety of tangled reasons—primarily because my wife was one of the guests in the house that weekend—I was there when McGovern arrived. So we talked for a while, mainly about the Mankiewicz situation, and it occurred to me afterward that it was the first time he'd ever seen me without a beer can in my hand or babbling like a loon about Freak Power, election bets, or some other twisted subject . . . but he was kind enough not to mention this.

It was a very relaxed afternoon. The only tense moment occurred when I noticed a sort of narrow-looking man with a distinctly predatory appearance standing off by himself at one end of the pool and glowering down at the white telephone as if he planned to jerk it out by the root if it didn't ring within ten seconds and tell him everything he wanted to know.

"Who the hell is *that*?" I asked, pointing across the pool at him.

"That's Miles Rubin," somebody replied.

"Jesus," I said. "I guess I should have known."

Moments later my curiosity got the better of me, and I walked over to Rubin and introduced myself. "I understand they're going to put you in charge of press relations after Miami," I said as we shook hands.

He shook his head and said something I didn't understand, then hurried away. For a moment I was tempted to call him back and ask if I could feel his pulse. But the moment passed, and I jumped into the pool instead.

• • •

The rest of that day disintegrated into chaos, drunkenness, and the kind of hysterical fatigue that comes from spending too much time racing from one place to another and being shoved around in crowds. McGovern won the Democratic primary by exactly 5 percent—45–40—and Nixon came from behind in the GOP race to nip [John] Ashbrook by 87–13.

The Campaign Trail: In the Eye of the Hurricane

July 20, 1972

The St. Louis Lawyer & the Fixer-Man

On the face of it, McGovern seems to have everything under control now. Less than twenty-four hours after the New York results were final, chief delegate-meister Rick Stearns announced that George was over the hump. The New York blitz was the cincher, pushing him over the 1,350 mark and mashing all but the flimsiest chance that anybody would continue to talk seriously about a "Stop McGovern" movement in Miami. The Humphrey-Muskie axis had been desperately trying to put something together with aging diehards like Wilbur Mills, George Meany, and Mayor Daley—hoping to stop McGovern just short of 1,400—but on the weekend after the NY sweep George picked up another 50 or so from the last of the non-primary state caucuses and by Sunday, June 25, he was only 100 votes away from the 1,509 that would zip it all up on the first ballot.

At that point the number of officially "uncommitted" delegates was still hovering around 450, but there had already been some small-scale defections to McGovern, and the others were getting nervous. The whole purpose of getting yourself elected as an Uncommitted delegate is to be able to arrive at the Convention with bargaining power. Ideology has nothing to do with it.

If you're a lawyer from St. Louis, for instance, and you manage to get yourself elected as an Uncommitted delegate from Missouri, you will hustle down to Miami and start scouting around for somebody to make a deal with . . . which won't take long, because every candidate still in the running for anything at all will have dozens of his own personal fixers roaming around the hotel bars and buttonholing Uncommitted delegates to find out what they want.

If your price is a lifetime appointment as a judge on the U.S. Circuit Court, your only hope is to deal with a candidate who is so close to that magic 1,509 figure that he can no longer function in public because of uncontrollable drooling. If he is stuck around 1,400, you will probably not have much luck getting that bench appointment . . . but if he's already up to 1,499 he won't hesitate to offer you the first opening on the U.S. Supreme Court . . . and if you catch him peaked at 1,505 or so, you can squeeze him for almost anything you want.

The game will get heavy sometimes. You don't want to go around putting the squeeze on people unless you're absolutely clean. No skeletons in the closet; no secret vices . . . because if your vote is important and your price is high, the Fixer-Man will have already checked you out by the time he offers to buy you a drink. If you bribed a traffic court clerk two years ago to bury a drunk driving charge, the Fixer might suddenly confront you with a photostat of the citation you thought had been burned.

When that happens, you're fucked. Your price just went down to zero, and you are no longer an Uncommitted delegate.

There are several other versions of the Reverse-Squeeze: the fake hit-and-run; glassine bags found in your hotel room by a maid; grabbed off the street by phoney cops for statutory rape of a teenage girl you never saw before . . .

• • •

Every once in a while you might hit on something with real style, like this one: on Monday afternoon, the first day of the convention, you—the ambitious young lawyer from St. Louis with no skeletons in the closet and no secret vices worth worrying about—are spending the afternoon by the pool at the Playboy Plaza, soaking up sun and gin/tonics, when you hear somebody calling your name. You look up and see a smiling, rotund chap about thirty-five years old coming at you, ready to shake hands.

"Hi there, Virgil," he says. "My name's J. D. Squane. I work for Senator Bilbo and we'd sure like to count on your vote. How about it?"

You smile, but say nothing—waiting for Squane to continue. He will want to know your price.

But Squane is staring out to sea, squinting at something on the horizon . . . then he suddenly turns back to you and starts talking very fast about how he always wanted to be a riverboat pilot on the Mississippi, but politics got in the way . . . "And now, goddamn it, we must get these last few votes . . ."

You smile again, itching to get serious. But Squane suddenly yells at somebody across the pool, then turns back to you and says: "Jesus, Virgil, I'm really sorry about this, but I have to run. That guy over there is delivering my new Jensen Interceptor." He grins and extends his hand again. Then: "Say, maybe we can talk later on, eh? What room are you in?"

"1909."

He nods. "How about seven, for dinner? Are you free?"

"Sure."

"Wonderful," he replies. "We can take my new Jensen for a run up to Palm Beach . . . It's one of my favorite towns."

"Mine too," you say. "I've heard a lot about it."

He nods. "I spent some time there last February . . . but we had a bad act, dropped about twenty-five grand."

Jesus! Jensen Interceptor; twenty-five grand . . . Squane is definitely big-time.

"See you at seven," he says, moving away.

• • •

The knock comes at 7:02—but instead of Squane it's a beautiful silver-haired young girl who says J. D. sent her to pick you up. "He's having a business dinner with the senator and he'll join us later at the Crab House."

"Wonderful, wonderful—shall we have a drink?"

She nods. "Sure, but not here. We'll drive over to North Miami and pick up my girlfriend . . . but let's smoke this before we go."

"Jesus! That looks like a cigar!"

"It is!" she laughs. "And it'll make us both crazy."

• • •

Many hours later. 4:30 AM. Soaking wet, falling into the lobby, begging for help: no wallet, no money, no ID. Blood on both hands and one shoe missing, dragged up to the room by two bellboys . . .

Breakfast at noon the next day, half sick in the coffee shop—waiting for a Western Union money order from the wife in St. Louis. Very spotty memories from last night.

"Hi there, Virgil."

J. D. Squane, still grinning. "Where were you last night, Virgil? I came by right on the dot, but you weren't in."

"I got mugged—by your girlfriend."

"Oh? Too bad. I wanted to nail down that ugly little vote of yours."

"Ugly? Wait a minute . . . That girl you sent; we went someplace to meet you."

"Bullshit! You double-crossed me, Virgil! If we weren't on the same team I might be tempted to lean on you."

Rising anger now, painful throbbing in the head. "Fuck you, Squane! I'm on *nobody's* team! If you want my vote you know damn well how to get it—and that goddamn dope-addict girlfriend of yours didn't help any."

Squane smiles heavily. "Tell me, Virgil—what was it you wanted for that vote of yours? A seat on the federal bench?"

"You're goddamn fuckin'-A right! You got me in bad trouble last night, J. D. When I got back here, my wallet was gone and there was blood on my hands."

"I know. You beat the shit out of her."

"What?"

"Look at these photographs, Virgil. It's some of the most disgusting stuff I've ever seen."

"Photographs?"

Squane hands them across the table.

"Oh my God!"

"Yeah, that's what *I* said, Virgil."

"No! This can't be me! I never saw that girl! Christ, she's only a child!"

"That's why the pictures are so disgusting, Virgil. You're lucky we didn't take them straight to the cops and have you locked up." Pounding the table with his fist. "That's *rape*, Virgil! That's *sodomy*! With a child!"

"No!"

"*Yes*, Virgil—and now you're going to pay for it."

"How? What are you talking about?"

Squane smiling again. "Votes, my friend. Yours and five others. Six votes for six negatives. Are you ready?"

Tears of rage in the eyes now. "You evil sonofabitch! You're blackmailing me!"

"Ridiculous, Virgil. Ridiculous. I'm talking about coalition politics."

"I don't even *know* six delegates. Not personally, anyway. And besides, they all *want* something."

Squane shakes his head. "Don't *tell* me about it, Virgil. I'd rather not hear. Just bring me six names off this list by noon tomorrow. If they all vote right, you'll never hear another word about what happened last night."

"What if I can't?"

Squane smiles, then shakes his head sadly. "Your life will take a turn for the worse, Virgil."

It Takes a Junkie to Know One

Ah, bad craziness . . . a scene like that could run on forever. Sick dialogue comes easy after five months on the campaign trail. A sense of humor is not considered mandatory for those who want to get heavy into presidential politics. Junkies don't laugh much; their gig is too serious—and the political junkie is not much different on that score than a smack junkie.

The high is very real in both worlds, for those who are into it—but anybody who has ever tried to live with a smack junkie will tell you it can't be done without coming to grips with the spike and shooting up yourself.

Politics is no different. There is a fantastic adrenaline high that comes with total involvement in almost any kind of fast-moving political campaign—especially when you're running against big odds and starting to feel like a winner.

As far as I know, I am the only journalist covering the '72 presidential campaign who has done any time on the other side of that gap—both as a candidate and a backroom pol, on the local level—and despite all the obvious differences between running on the Freak Power ticket for sheriff of Aspen and running as a well-behaved Democrat for president of the United States, the roots are surprisingly similar . . . and whatever real differences exist are hardly worth talking about, compared to the massive, unbridgeable gap between the cranked-up reality of living day after day in the vortex of a rolling campaign—and the fiendish ratbastard tedium of covering that same campaign as a journalist, from the outside looking in.

For the same reason that nobody who has never come to grips with the spike can ever understand how far away it really is across that gap to the place where the smack junkie lives . . . there is no way for even the best and most talented journalist to know what is really going on inside a political campaign unless he has been there himself.

Very few of the press people assigned to the McGovern campaign, for instance, have anything more than a surface understanding of what is really going on in the vortex . . . or if they do, they don't mention it, in print or on the air: and after spending half a year following this goddamn zoo around the country and watching the machinery at work, I'd be willing to bet pretty heavily that not even the most privileged ranking insiders among the campaign press corps are telling much less than they know.

The Campaign Trail: Fear & Loathing in Miami: Old Bulls Meet the Butcher

August 17, 1972

Back in February it was still considered very shrewd and avant-garde to assume that the most important factor in a presidential campaign was a good "media candidate." If he had Star Quality, the rest would take care of itself. The Florida primary turned out to be a funeral procession for would-be "media candidates." Both Lindsay and Muskie went down in Florida—although not necessarily because they geared their pitch to TV; the real reason, I think, is that neither one of them understood how to *use* TV . . . or maybe they knew, but just couldn't pull it off. It is hard to be super-convincing on the tube, if everything you say reminds the TV audience of a Dick Cavett commercial for Alpo dog food. George McGovern has been widely ridiculed in the press as "the ideal anti-media candidate." He looks wrong, talks wrong, and even acts wrong—by conventional TV standards. But McGovern has his own ideas about how to use the tube. In the early primaries he kept his TV exposure to a minimum—for a variety of reasons that included a lack of both money and confidence—but by the time he got to California for the showdown with Hubert Humphrey, McGovern's TV campaign was operating on the level of a very specialized art form. His thirty-minute biography—produced by Charlie Guggenheim—was so good that even the most cynical veteran journalists said it was the best political film ever made for television . . . and Guggenheim's sixty-second spots were better than the bio film. Unlike the early front-runners, McGovern had taken his time and learned how to use the medium—instead of letting the medium use him.

Sincerity is the important thing on TV. A presidential candidate should at least *seem* to believe what he's saying—even if it's all stone crazy. McGovern learned this from George Wallace in Florida, and it proved to be a very valuable lesson. One of the crucial moments of the '72 primary campaign came on election night in Florida, March 14, when McGovern—who had finished a dismal sixth, behind even Lindsay and Muskie—refused to follow their sour example and blame his poor showing on that Evil Racist Monster, George Wallace, who had just swept every county in the state. Moments after both Lindsay and Muskie had appeared on all three networks to denounce the Florida results as tragic proof that at least half the voters were ignorant dupes and Nazis, McGovern came on and said that although he couldn't agree with some of the things Wallace said and stood for, he sympathized with the people who'd voted for "The Governor" because they were "angry and fed up" with some of the things that are happening in this country.

"I feel the same way," he added. "But unlike Governor Wallace, I've proposed *constructive solutions* to these problems."

Nobody applauded when he said that. The two hundred or so McGovern campaign workers who were gathered that night in the ballroom of the old Waverly Hotel on Biscayne Boulevard were not in a proper mood to cheer any praise for George Wallace. Their candidate had just been trounced by what they considered a dangerous bigot—and now, at the tail end of the loser's traditional concession statement, McGovern was saying that he and Wallace weren't really that far apart.

It was not what the ballroom crowd wanted to hear at that moment. Not after listening to both Lindsay and Muskie denounce Wallace as a cancer in the soul of America . . . but McGovern wasn't talking to the people in that ballroom; he was making a very artful pitch to potential Wallace voters in the other primary states. Wisconsin was three weeks away, then Pennsylvania, Ohio, Michigan—and Wallace would be raising angry hell in every one of them. McGovern's brain trust, though, had come up with the idea that the Wallace vote was "soft"—that the typical Wallace voter, especially in the North and Midwest, was far less committed to Wallace himself than to his thundering, gut-level appeal to rise up and smash all the "pointy-headed bureaucrats in Washington" who'd been fucking them over for so long.

The root of the Wallace magic was a cynical, showbiz instinct for knowing exactly which issues would whip a hall full of beer-drinking factory workers into a frenzy—and then doing exactly that, by howling down from the podium that he had an instant, overnight cure for all their worst afflictions: Taxes? Nigras? Army worms killing the turnip crop? Whatever it was, Wallace assured his supporters that the solution was actually real simple, and that the only reason they had any hassle with the government at all was because those greedy bloodsuckers in Washington didn't *want* the problems solved, so they wouldn't be put out of work.

• • •

George Wallace is one of the worst charlatans in politics, but there is no denying his talent for converting frustration into energy. What McGovern sensed in Florida, however—while Wallace was stomping him, along with all the others—was the possibility that Wallace appealed instinctively to a lot more people than would actually vote for him. He was stirring up more anger than he knew how to channel. The frustration was there, and it was easy enough to convert it—but what then? If Wallace had taken himself seriously as a presidential candidate—as a Democrat or anything else—he might have put together the kind of organization that would have made him a genuine threat in the primaries, instead of just a spoiler.

McGovern, on the other hand, had put together a fantastic organization—but until he went into Wisconsin, he had never tried to tap the kind of energy that seemed to be flowing, perhaps by default, to Wallace. He had given it some thought while campaigning in New Hampshire, but it was only after he beat Muskie in two blue-collar hard-hat wards in the middle of Manchester that he saw the possibility of a really mind-bending coalition: a weird mix of peace freaks and hard hats, farmers and film stars, along with urban blacks, rural Chicanos, the "youth vote" . . . a coalition that could elect almost anybody.

Muskie had croaked in Florida, allowing himself to get crowded over on the Right with Wallace, Jackson, and Humphrey—then finishing a slow fourth behind all three of them. At that point in the race, Lindsay's presumptuous blueprint was beginning to look like prophecy. The New Hampshire embarrassment had forced Muskie off-center in a mild panic, and now the party was popularized. The road to Wisconsin was suddenly clear in both lanes, fast traffic to the Left and the Right.

The only mobile hazard was a slow-moving hulk called "The Muskie Bandwagon," creeping erratically down what his doom-stricken Media Manager called "that yellow stripe in the middle of the road."

The only other bad casualty, at that point, was Lindsay. His Wisconsin managers had discovered a fatal flaw in the blueprint: nobody had bothered to specify the name of the candidate who would seize all that high ground on the Left, once Muskie got knocked off center. Whoever drew it up had apparently been told that McGovern would not be a factor in the later stages of the race. After absorbing two back-to-back beatings in New Hampshire and Florida, he would run out of money and be dragged off to the nearest glue factory . . . or, failing that, to some cut-rate retirement farm for old liberals with no charisma.

But something went wrong, and when Lindsay arrived in Wisconsin to seize that fine high ground on the Left that he knew, from his blueprint, was waiting for him—he found it already occupied, sealed off and well-guarded on every perimeter, by a legion of hard-eyed fanatics in the pay of George McGovern.

Gene Pokorny, McGovern's twenty-five-year-old field organizer for Wisconsin, had the whole state completely wired. He had been on the job, full time, since the spring of '71—working off a blueprint remarkably similar to Lindsay's. But they were not quite the same. The main difference was painfully obvious, yet it was clear at a glance that both drawings had been done from the same theory. Muskie would fold early on, because The Center was not only indefensible but probably nonexistent . . . and after that the Democratic race would boil down to a quick civil war, a running death-battle between the Old Guard on the Right and a gang of Young Strangers on the Left.

The name slots on Lindsay's blueprint were still empty, but the working assumption was that the crunch in California would come down to Muskie on the Right and Lindsay on the Left.

Pokorny's drawing was a year or so older than Lindsay's, and all the names were filled in—all the way to California, where the last two slots said "McGovern" and "Humphrey." The only other difference between the two was that Lindsay's was unsigned, while Pokorny's had a signature in the bottom right-hand corner: "Hart, Mankiewicz & McGovern—architects."

• • •

Even Lindsay's financial backers saw the handwriting on the wall in Wisconsin. By the time he arrived, there was not even any low ground on the Left to be seized. The Lindsay campaign had been keyed from the start on the assumption that Muskie would at least have the strength to retire McGovern before he abandoned the Center. It made perfect sense, on paper—but 1972 had not been a vintage year for paper wisdom, and McGovern's breakthrough victory in Wisconsin was written off as "shocking" and "freakish" by a lot of people who should have known better.

Wisconsin was the place where he found a working model for the nervous coalition that made the rest of the primary campaign a downhill run. Wisconsin effectively eliminated every obstacle but the corpse of Hubert Humphrey—who fought like a rabid skunk all the way to the end; cranked up on the best speed George Meany's doctors could provide for him, taking his cash and his orders every midnight from Meany's axe-man Al Barkan; and attacking McGovern savagely, day after day, from every treacherous angle Big Labor's sharpest researchers could even crudely define for him . . .

It was a nasty swan song for Hubert. He'd been signing those IOUs to Big Labor for more than twenty years, and it must have been a terrible shock to him when Meany called them all due at the same time.

But how? George Meany, the seventy-year-old quarterback of the "Stop McGovern Movement," is said to be suffering from brain bubbles at this stage of the game. Totally paralyzed. His henchmen have kept him in seclusion ever since he arrived in Florida five days ago, with a bad case of The Fear. He came down from AFL-CIO headquarters in Washington by train, but had to be taken off somewhere near Fort Lauderdale and rushed to a plush motel where his condition deteriorated rapidly over the weekend, and finally climaxed on Monday night when he suffered a terrible stroke while watching the Democratic Convention on TV.

The story is still shrouded in mystery, despite the best efforts of the five thousand ranking journalists who came here to catch Meany's last act, but according to a wealthy labor boss who said he was there when it happened—the old man went all to pieces when his creature, Hubert Humphrey, lost the crucial "California challenge."

He raged incoherently at the Tube for eight minutes without drawing a breath, then suddenly his face turned beet red and his head swelled up to twice its normal size. Seconds later—while his henchmen looked on in mute horror—Meany swallowed his tongue, rolled out of his chair like a log, and crawled through a plate glass window.

The Young Bulls Take Charge; Cronkite and the Wizards Take a Fall; Humphrey Croaked and the Squeeze Play Explained on the Beach

What happened in Miami was far too serious for the kind of random indulgence that Gonzo Journalism needs. The Real Business happened, as usual, on secret-numbered telephones or behind closed doors at the other end of long hotel corridors blocked off by sullen guards. There were only two crucial moments in Miami—two potential emergencies that might have changed the outcome—and both of them were dealt with in strict privacy.

The only real question in Miami was whether or not McGovern might be stripped of more than half of the 271 delegates he won in the California primary—and that question was scheduled to come up for a vote by the whole convention on Monday night. If the "ABM Movement" could strip 151 of those delegates away, McGovern might be stopped—because without them he had anywhere from 10 to 50 votes less than the 1,509 that would give him the nomination on the first ballot. But if McGovern could hold his 271 California delegates, it was all over.

The "ABM Movement" (Anybody but McGovern) was a coalition of desperate losers, thrown together at the last moment by Big Labor chief George Meany and his axe-man, Al Barkan. Hubert Humphrey was pressed into service as the front man for ABM, and he quickly signed up the others: Big Ed, Scoop Jackson, Terry Sanford, Shirley Chisholm—all the heavies.

The ABM movement came together, officially, sometime in the middle of the week just before the convention, when it finally became apparent that massive fraud, treachery, or violence was the only way to prevent McGovern from getting the nomination . . . and what followed, once this fact was accepted by all parties involved, will hopefully go down in history as one of the most shameful episodes in the history of the Democratic process.

It was like a scene from the final hours of the Roman Empire: everywhere you looked, some prominent politician was degrading himself in public. By noon on Sunday both Humphrey and Muskie were so desperate that they came out of their holes and appeared—trailing a mob of photographers and TV crews—in the lobby of the Fontainebleau, the nexus hotel about five hundred yards down the beach from the Doral, racing back and forth from one caucus or press conference to another, trying to make any deal available—on any terms—that might possibly buy enough votes to deny McGovern a first-ballot victory.

The ABM strategy—a very shrewd plan, on paper—was to hold McGovern under the 1,500 mark for two ballots, forcing him to peak without winning, then confront the convention with an alternative (ABM) candidate on the third ballot—and if that failed, try *another* ABM candidate on the fourth ballot, then yet another on the fifth, etc. . . . on into infinity, for as many ballots as it would take to nominate somebody acceptable to the Meany-Daley axis.

The name didn't matter. It didn't even make much difference if He, She, or It couldn't possibly beat Nixon in November . . . the only thing that mattered, to the Meany-Daley crowd, was *keeping control of the party*; and this meant the nominee would have to be some loyal whore with more debts to Big Labor than he could ever hope to pay . . . somebody like Hubert Humphrey, or a hungry opportunist like Terry Sanford.

Anybody but George McGovern—the only candidate in Miami that week who would be under no obligation to give either Meany or Daley his private number if he ever moved into the White House.

• • •

But all that noxious bullshit went by the boards in the end. The ABM got chewed up like green hamburger on opening night. They were beaten stupid at their own game by a handful of weird-looking kids who never even worked up a sweat. By midnight on Monday it was all over. Once McGovern got a lock on those 271 delegates, there was never any doubt about who would get the nomination on Wednesday.

The bedrock truths of the McGovern convention were not aired on TV—except once, very briefly, on Monday night; but it hardly mattered, because all three networks missed it completely. When the deal went down, Walter Cronkite saw green and called it red, John Chancellor opted for yellow, and ABC was already off the air.

What happened, in a nut, was a surprise parliamentary maneuver—cooked up by over-ambitious strategists in the Women's Caucus—forcing a premature showdown that effectively decided whether or not McGovern would get the nomination. The crisis came early, at a time when most of the TV/press people were still getting their heads ready to deal with all the intricate possibilities of the vote on the ABM challenge to McGovern's California delegates . . . and when Larry O'Brien announced a pending roll-call vote on whether or not the South Carolina delegation included enough women, very few people on the Floor or anywhere else understood that the result of that roll-call might determine exactly how many delegates would later vote for McGovern on the California challenge, and then on the First Ballot.

On the evidence, less than a dozen of the five thousand "media" sleuths accredited to the convention knew exactly what was happening at the time. When McGovern's young strategists deliberately lost that vote, almost everybody who'd watched it—including Walter Cronkite—concluded that McGovern didn't have a hope in hell of winning any roll-call vote from that point on: which meant the ABM could beat him on the California challenge, reducing his strength even further, and they stop him cold on the first ballot.

Humphrey's campaign manager, Jack Chestnut, drew the same conclusion—a glaring mistake that almost immediately became the subject of many crude jokes in McGovern's pressroom at the Doral, where a handful of resident correspondents who'd been attached to the campaign on a live-in basis for many months were watching the action on TV with press secretary Dick Dougherty and a room full of tense staffers—who roared with laughter when Cronkite, far up in his soundproof booth two miles away in the convention hall, announced that CBS was about to switch to McGovern headquarters in the Doral, where David Schumacher was standing by with a firsthand report and at least one painfully candid shot of McGovern workers reacting to the news of this stunning setback.

The next scene showed a room full of laughing, whooping people. Schumacher was grinning into his microphone, saying: "I don't want to argue with you, Walter—but why are these people cheering?"

Schumacher then explained that McGovern had actually won the nomination by *losing* the South Carolina vote. It had been a test of strength, no doubt—but what had never been explained to the press or even to most of McGovern's own delegates on the floor was that he had the option of "winning" that roll-call by going either up or down . . . and the only way the ABM crowd could have won was by juggling their votes to make sure the South Carolina challenge *almost* won, but not quite. This would have opened the way for a series of potentially disastrous parliamentary moves by the Humphrey-led ABM forces.

"We had to either win decisively or lose decisively," Rick Stearns explained later. "We couldn't afford a close vote."

Stearns, a twenty-eight-year-old Rhodes Scholar from Stanford, was McGovern's point man when the crisis came. His job in Miami—working out of a small white trailer full of telephones behind the convention hall—was to tell Gary Hart, on the floor, exactly how many votes McGovern could muster at any given moment, on any question—and it was Stearns who decided, after only ten out of fifty states had voted on the South Carolina challenge, that the final tally might be too close to risk. So he sent word to Hart on the floor, and Gary replied: "Okay, if we can't win big—let's lose it."

The Late, Late Show; Time to Flee Again

It was somewhere around eight thirty or nine on Sunday evening when I dragged myself off the plane from Miami. The '72 Democratic Convention was over. McGovern had wrapped it up just before dawn on Friday, accepting the bloody nomination with an elegant, finely crafted speech that might have had quite an impact on the national TV audience . . . (*Time* correspondent Hugh Sidey called it "perhaps as pure an expression as George McGovern has ever given of his particular moralistic sense of the nation") . . . but the main, middle-American bulk of the national TV audience tends to wither away around midnight, and anybody still glued to the tube at three thirty AM Miami time was probably too stoned or twisted to recognize McGovern anyway.

A few hundred ex-Muskie/Humphrey/Jackson delegates had lingered long enough to cheer Ted Kennedy's bland speech, but they started drifting away when George came on—hurrying out the exits of the air-conditioned hall, into the muggy darkness of the parking lot to fetch up a waiting cab and go back to whichever one of the sixty-five official convention hotels they were staying in . . . hoping to catch the tail end of a party or at least one free drink before getting a few hours' sleep and then heading back home on one of the afternoon planes: back to St. Louis, Altoona, Butte . . .

By sundown on Friday the "political hotels" were almost empty. In the Doral Beach—McGovern's oceanfront headquarters hotel—Southern Bell Telephone workers were dragging what looked like about five thousand miles of multicolored wires, junction boxes, and cables out of the empty Press/Operations complex on the mezzanine. Down in the lobby, a Cuban wedding (Martinez-Hernandez: 8:30–10:30) had taken over the vast, ornately sculptured Banquet Room that twenty-four hours earlier had been jammed with hundreds of young, scruffy-looking McGovern volunteers, celebrating the end of one of the longest and most unlikely trips in the history of American politics . . . it was a quiet party, by most convention standards: free beer for the troops, bring your own grass, guitar-minstrels working out here and there; but not much noise, no whooping & shouting, no madness . . .

I was trapped in the Doral for ten days, shuttling back & forth between the hotel and the convention hall by any means available: taxi, my rented green convertible, and occasionally down the canal in the fast white "staff taxi" speedboat that McGovern's people used to get from the Doral to the hall by water, whenever Collins Avenue was jammed up with sightseer traffic . . . and in retrospect, I think that boat trip was the only thing I did all week that I actually enjoyed.

There was a lot of talk in the press about "the spontaneous outburst of fun and games" on Thursday night—when the delegates, who had been so deadly serious for the first three sessions, suddenly ran wild on the floor and delayed McGovern's long-awaited acceptance speech until three thirty by tying the convention in knots with a long outburst of frivolous squabbling over the vice presidential nomination. *Newsweek* described it as "a comic interlude, a burst of silliness on the part of the delegates whose taut bonds of decorum and discipline seemed suddenly to snap, now that it didn't make any difference."

There was not much laughter in Miami, on the floor or anywhere else, and from where I stood, that famous "comic interlude" on Thursday night looked more like the first scattered signs of mass Fatigue Hysteria, if the goddamn thing didn't end soon. What the press mistook for relaxed levity was actually a mood of ugly restlessness that by three o'clock on Friday was bordering on rebellion. All over the floor I saw people caving in to the lure of booze, and in the crowded aisle between the California and Wisconsin delegations a smiling freak with a bottle of liquid THC was giving free hits to anybody who still had the strength to stick their tongue out.

Each candidate was entitled to a fifteen-minute nominating speech and two five-minute seconding speeches. The nightmare dragged on for four hours, and after the first forty minutes there was not one delegate in fifty, on the floor, who either knew or cared who was speaking. No doubt there were flashes of eloquence, now and then: probably Mike Gravel and Sissy Farenthold said a few things that might have been worth hearing, under different circumstances . . . but on that long Thursday night in Miami, with Sen. Tom Eagleton of Missouri waiting nervously in the wings to come out and accept the vice presidential nomination that McGovern had sealed for him twelve hours earlier, every delegate in the hall understood that whatever these other seven candidates were saying up there on the rostrum, they were saying for reasons that had nothing to do with who was going to be the Democratic candidate for vice president in November . . . and it was *not* going to be ex–Massachusetts governor "Chub" Peabody, or a grinning dimwit named Stanley Arnold from New York City who said he was The Businessman's Candidate, or some black Step 'n' Fetchit–style Wallace delegate from Texas called Clay Smothers.

But these brainless bastards persisted nonetheless, using up half the night and all the prime time on TV, debasing the whole convention with a blizzard of self-serving gibberish that drove whatever was left of the national TV audience to bed or the *Late Late Show*.

• • •

Thursday was not a good day for McGovern. By noon there was not much left of Wednesday night's Triumphant Warrior smile. He spent most of Thursday afternoon grappling with a long list of vice presidential possibilities, and by two, the Doral lobby was foaming with reporters and TV cameras. The name had to be formally submitted by 3:59 PM, but it was 4:05 when Mankiewicz finally appeared to say McGovern had decided on Senator Thomas Eagleton of Missouri.

There is a very tangled story behind that choice, but I don't feel like writing it now. My immediate reaction was not enthusiastic, and the staff people I talked to seemed vaguely depressed—if only because it was a concession to "the Old Politics," a nice-looking Catholic boy from Missouri with friends in the Labor Movement. His acceptance speech that night was not memorable—perhaps because it was followed by the long-awaited appearance of Ted Kennedy, who had turned the job down.

Kennedy's speech was not memorable either: "Let us bury the hatchet, etc. . . . and Get Behind the Ticket." There was something hollow about it, and when McGovern came on, he made Kennedy sound like an old-timer.

Later that night, at a party on the roof of the Doral, a McGovern staffer asked me who I would have chosen for VP. I finally said I would have chosen Ron Dellums, the black congressman from Berkeley.

"Jesus Christ!" he said. "That would be suicide!"

I shrugged.

"Why Dellums?" he asked.

"Why not?" I said. "He offered it to Mayor Daley before he called Eagleton."

"No!" he shouted. "Not Daley! That's a lie!"

"I was in the room when he made the call," I said. "Ask anybody who was there—Gary, Frank, Dutton—they weren't happy about it, but they said he'd be good for the ticket."

He stared at me. "What did Daley say?" he asked finally.

I laughed. "Christ, you *believed* that, didn't you?"

He had, for just an instant. After all, there was a lot of talk about "pragmatism" in Miami, and Illinois was a key state . . . I decided to try the Daley rumor on other staff people, to see their reactions.

But I never got around to it. I forgot all about it, in fact, until flipping through my notebook on the midnight jet from Atlanta. I came across a statement by Ron Dellums. It depressed me, for some reason, but it seems like a good way to end this goddamn thing. Dellums writes pretty good, for a politician. It's part of the statement he distributed when he switched his support from Shirley Chisholm to McGovern:

> *The great bulk of that coalition committed to change, human freedom, and justice in the country has moved actively and powerfully behind the candidacy of Senator McGovern. That coalition of hope, conscience, morality, and humanity—of the powerless and the voiceless—that did not exist in 1964, that expressed itself in outrage and frustration in 1968, and in 1972 began to form and welded itself imperfectly but courageously and lifted a man to the brink of the Democratic nomination for the Presidency of the United States, and within a short but laborious step from the Presidency of the United States. The coalition that has formed behind Senator McGovern has battled the odds, baffled the pollsters, and beat the bosses. It is my conviction that when that total coalition of the victims in this country is ever formed, this potential for change would be unheralded, for it could pose a real alternative to expediency and status quo politics in America.*
>
> —Ron Dellums, July 9, 1972

The Campaign Trail: More Fear and Loathing in Miami: Nixon Bites the Bomb

September 28, 1972

The summer is over, the harvest is in, and we are not saved.

—Isaiah circa 8:21

Miami Beach, August 28, 1972—Earlier tonight I drove down the beach to a place called Dixie's Doll House, for two six-packs of Ballantine ale. The place was full of old winos, middle-aged hookers, and aging young hustlers who looked like either junkies or Merchant Marine rejects; bearded geeks in gray T-shirts staggering back and forth along the bar, six nasty-looking pimps around a blue-lit pool table in the rear, and right next to me at the bar a ruined platinum-blonde Cuban dazzler snarling drunkenly at her nervous escort for the night: "Don't gimmie that horseshit, baby! I don't want a goddamn *one-dollar* dinner! I want a *ten-dollar* dinner!"

Life gets heavy here on the Beach from time to time. So I paid $2.70 each for my six-packs and then wheeled my big red Chevy Impala convertible back home to the Fontainebleau, about forty blocks north through the balmy southern night to the edge of the fashionable section.

"Bobo," the master pimp and carmeister who runs what they call "the front door" here in these showplace beachfront hotels, eyed me curiously as I got out of the car and started dragging wet brown bags full of beer bottles out of the backseat. "You gonna need the car again tonight?" he asked.

"Probably," I said. "But not for a while. I'll be up in the room until about midnight." I looked at my watch. "The Rams–Kansas City game is on in three minutes. After that, I'll work for a while and then go out for something to eat."

He jerked the car door open, sliding fast behind the wheel to take it down to the underground garage. With his hand on the shift lever he looked up at me: "You in the mood for some company?"

"No," I said. "I'm way behind. I'll be up all night with that goddamn typewriter. I shouldn't even take time to watch the game on TV."

He rolled his eyes and looked up at what should have been the sky, but which was actually the gold-glazed portico roof above the entrance driveway: "Jesus, what kind of work do you *do*? Hump typewriters for a living? I thought the convention was over!"

I paused, tucking the wet beer bags under the arm of my crusty brown leather jacket. Inside the lobby door about twenty feet away I could see what looked like a huge movie-set cocktail party for rich Venezuelans and high-style middle-aged Jews: my fellow guests in the Fontainebleau. I was not dressed properly to mingle with them, so my plan was to stride swiftly through the lobby to the elevators and then up to my hideout in the room.

The Nixon convention had finished on Thursday morning, and by Saturday the hundreds of national press/media people who had swarmed into this pompous monstrosity of a hotel for convention week were long gone. A few dozen stragglers had stayed on through Friday, but by Saturday afternoon the style and tone of the place had changed drastically, and on Sunday I felt like the only nigger in the governor's box on Kentucky Derby Day.

Bobo had not paid much attention to me during the convention, but now he seemed interested. "I know you're a reporter," he said. "They put 'press' on your house-car tag. But all the rest of those guys took off yesterday. What keeps *you* here?"

I smiled. "Christ, am I the only one left?"

He thought for a moment, then shook his head. "No, there's you and two others. One guy has that white Lincoln Continental—"

"He's not press," I said quickly. "Probably one of the GOP advance men, getting things settled with the hotel."

He nodded. "Yeah, he acted like he was part of the show. Not like a reporter." He laughed. "You guys are pretty easy to spot, you know that?"

"Balls," I said. "Not me. Everybody else says I look like a cop."

He looked at me for a moment, tapping his foot on the accelerator to keep the engine up. "Yeah," he said. "I guess so. You could pass for a cop as long as you kept your mouth shut."

"I'm usually pretty discreet," I said.

He smiled. "Sure you are. We've all noticed it. That other press guy that's still here asked me who you were the other day, when you were bad-mouthing Nixon . . ."

"What's his name?" I was curious to know who else in the press corps would endure this kind of shame and isolation.

"I can't remember now," Bobo said. "He's a tall guy with gray hair and glasses. He drives a blue Ford station wagon."

I wondered who it could be. It would have to be somebody with a very compelling reason to stay on, in this place. Everybody with good sense or a reasonable excuse had left as soon as possible. Some of the TV network technicians had stayed until Saturday, dismantling the maze of wires and cables they'd set up in the Fontainebleau before the convention started. They were easy to spot because they wore things like Levi's and sweatshirts—but by Sunday I was the only guest in the hotel not dressed like a PR man for Hialeah Racetrack on a Saturday night in mid-season.

It is not enough, in the Fontainebleau, to look like some kind of a weird and sinister cop; to fit in here, you want to look like somebody who just paid a scalper $200 for a front row seat at the Johnny Carson show.

Bobo put the car in gear, but kept his foot on the brake pedal and asked: "What are you writing? What did all that bullshit come down to?"

"Jesus," I said. "That's just what I've been trying to put together upstairs. You're asking me to compress about two hundred hours of work into sixty seconds."

He grinned. "You're on *my* time now. Give it a try. Tell me what happened."

I paused in the driveway, shifting the beer bags to my other arm, and thought for a moment. "Okay," I said. "Nixon sold out the party for the next twenty years by setting up an Agnew-Kennedy race in '76, but he knew exactly what he was doing and he did it for the same reason he's done everything else since he first got into politics—to make sure he gets elected."

He stared at me, not grasping it.

I hesitated, trying to put it all in a quick little capsule. "Okay," I said finally, "the reason Nixon put Agnew and the Goldwater freaks in charge of the party this year is that he knows they can't win in '76—but it was a good short-term trade; they have to stay with him this year, which will probably be worth a point or two in November—and that's important to Nixon, because he thinks it's going to be close: fuck the polls. They always *follow* reality instead of predicting it . . . But the *real* reason he turned the party over to the Agnew-Goldwater wing is that he knows most of the old-line Democrats who just got stomped by McGovern for the nomination wouldn't mind seeing George get taken out in '72 if they know they can get back in the saddle if they're willing to wait four years."

Bobo laughed, understanding it instantly. Pimps and hustlers have a fine instinct for politics. "What you're saying is that Nixon just cashed his whole check," he said. "He doesn't give a flying fuck what happens once he gets reelected—because once he wins, it's all over for him anyway, right? He can't run again . . ."

"Yeah," I said, pausing to twist the top off one of the ale bottles I'd been pulling out of the bag. "But the thing you want to understand is that Nixon has such a fine understanding of the way politicians think that he *knew* people like Daley and Meany and Ted Kennedy would go along with him—because it's in *their* interest now to have Nixon get his second term, in exchange for a guaranteed Democratic victory in 1976."

"God damn!" he said. "That's beautiful! They're gonna trade him four years now for eight later, right? Give Nixon his last trip in '72, then Kennedy moves in for eight years in '76 . . . Jesus, that's so rotten I really have to admire it." He chuckled. "Boy, I thought *I* was cynical!"

"That's not cynical," I said. "That's pure, nut-cutting politics . . . And I advise you to stay out of it; you're too sensitive."

He laughed and hit the accelerator, leaping away with a sharp screech of rubber and just barely missing the taillight of a long gold Cadillac as he turned down the ramp.

I pushed through the revolving door and crossed the vast lobby to the elevators, still sipping my ale as I thought about what I'd just said. Had

Nixon really sold the party down the river? Was it a conscious act, or pure instinct? Had he made a deal with Meany during one of their golf games? Was Daley in on it? Ted Kennedy? Who else?

I finished the ale and dropped the empty bottle into a huge spittoon full of blue gravel. Two elderly women standing next to me looked disgusted, but I ignored them and wandered over to the door of the world-renowned Poodle bar and cocktail lounge. It was almost empty. An imitation Glenn Miller band was playing the "Tennessee Waltz," but nobody was dancing. Three nights ago, the Poodle had been so crowded that it was difficult to get through the door. Every high-powered hot-rod journalist in the western world had made the scene here last week. At least that's what Sally Quinn told me, and she knows about things like that.

I went back to the elevators and found one ready to go. The sight of my ale bottle in the spittoon reminded me of Nixon again . . . Who else might be in on that deal? I picked a *Miami Herald* off a stack in the rear of the elevator, then handed the matron $1.

"Twenty-five cents," she said briskly, bringing the car to a stop at my floor . . . but before she could hand me the change I stepped out and waved back at her. "Nevermind," I said. "I'm rich." Then I hurried down the hall to my room and bolted the door.

The game had already started, but there was no score. I dumped my ale bottles in the Styrofoam cooler, then opened one and sat down to watch the action and brood on Nixon's treachery. But first I concentrated on the game for a while. It is hard to understand how somebody else thinks unless you can get on their wavelength: get in tune with their patterns, their pace, their connections . . . and since Nixon is a known football addict, I decided to get my head totally into the rhythm of this exhibition game between the Rams and Kansas City before attempting the jump into politics.

Very few people understand this kind of logic. I learned it from a Brazilian psychiatrist in the Mato Grosso back in 1963. He called it "Rhythm Logic," in English, because he said I would never be able to pronounce it in the original Jibaro. I tried it once or twice, but the Jibaro language was too much for me—and it didn't make much difference anyway. I seemed to have an instinct for Rhythm Logic, however, so I picked it up very quickly. But I have never been able to explain it, except in terms of music, and typewriters are totally useless when it comes to that kind of translation.

In any case, by the end of the first quarter I felt ready. By means of intense concentration on *every detail* of the football game, I was able to "derail" my own inner brain waves and re-pattern them temporarily to the inner brain wave rhythms of a serious football fanatic. The next step, then, was to bring my "borrowed" rhythms into focus on a subject quite different from football—such as presidential politics.

In the third and final step, I merely concentrated on a pre-selected problem involving presidential politics, and attempted to solve it subjectively . . . although the word "subjectively," at this point, had a very different true meaning. Because I was no longer reasoning in the rhythms of my own inner brain waves, but in the rhythms of a football addict.

At that point, it became almost unbearably clear to me that Richard Nixon had in fact sold the Republican Party down the tube in Miami. Consciously, perhaps, but never quite verbally. Because the rhythms of his own inner brain waves convinced his conscious mind that in fact he had no choice. Given the safe assumption that the most important objective in Richard Nixon's life today is minimizing the risk of losing the 1972 election to George McGovern, simple logic decreed that he should bend all his energies to that end, at all costs. All other objectives would have to be subjugated to Number One.

By halftime, with the Rams trailing by six, I had established a firm scientific basis for the paranoid gibberish I had uttered, an hour or so earlier, while standing in the hotel driveway and talking with Bobo the night-pimp. At the time, not wanting to seem ignorant or confused, I had answered his question with the first wisdom capsule that popped into my mind . . . But now it made perfect sense, thanks to Rhythm Logic, and all that remained were two or three secondary questions, none of them serious.

• • •

The pervasive sense of gloom among the press/media crowd in Miami was only slightly less obvious than the gungho, breast-beating arrogance of the Nixon delegates themselves. That was the real story of the convention: the strident, loutish confidence of the whole GOP machinery, from top to bottom. Looking back on that week, one of my clearest memories is that maddening "FOUR MORE YEARS!" chant from the Nixon Youth gallery in the convention hall. NBC's John Chancellor compared the Nixon Youth cheering section to the Chicago "sewer workers" who were herded into the Stockyards convention hall in Chicago four years ago to cheer for Mayor Daley. The Nixon Youth people were not happy with Chancellor for making that remark on camera. They complained very bitterly about it, saying it was just another example of the "knee-jerk liberal" thinking that dominates the media.

But the truth is that Chancellor was absolutely right. Due to a strange set of circumstances, I spent two very tense hours right in the middle of that Nixon Youth mob on Tuesday night, and it gave me an opportunity to speak at considerable length with quite a few of them . . .

What happened, in a nut, was that I got lost in a maze of hallways in the back reaches of the convention hall on Tuesday night about an hour or so before the roll-call vote on Nixon's chances of winning the GOP nomination again this year . . . I had just come off the convention floor, after the Secret Service lads chased me away from the First Family box where I was trying to hear what Charleton Heston was saying to Nelson Rockefeller, and in the nervous wake of an experience like that, I felt a great thirst rising . . . so I tried to take a shortcut to the Railroad Lounge, where free beer was available to the press; but I blew it somewhere along the way, ended up in a big room jammed with Nixon Youth workers, getting themselves ready for a "spontaneous demonstration" at the moment of climax out there on the floor . . . I was just idling around in the hallway, trying to go north for a beer, when I got swept up in a fast-moving mob of about two thousand people heading south at good speed, so instead of fighting the tide, I just let myself be carried along to wherever they were going . . .

Which turned out to be the "Ready Room," in a far corner of the hall, where a dozen or so people wearing red hats and looking like small-town high-school football coaches were yelling into bullhorns and trying to whip this herd of screaming sheep into shape for the "spontaneous" demonstration, scheduled for 10:33 PM.

It was a very disciplined scene. The red-hatted men with the bullhorns did all the talking. Huge green plastic "refuse" sacks full of helium balloons were distributed, along with handfuls of New Year's Eve party noisemakers and hundreds of big cardboard signs that said things like: "Nixon Now!" . . . "Four More Years!" . . . "No Compromise!"

Most of the signs were freshly printed. They looked exactly like the "We Love Mayor Daley" signs that Daley distributed to his sewer workers in Chicago in 1968: red and blue ink on a white background . . . but a few, here and there, were hand-lettered, and mine happened to be one of these. It said, "Garbage Men Demand Equal Time." I had several choices, but this one seemed right for the occasion.

Actually, there was a long and active time lag between the moment when I was swept into the Ready Room and my decision to carry a sign in the spontaneous demonstration. What happened in that time lag was that they discovered me early on, and tried to throw me out—but I refused to go, and that's when the dialogue started. For the first ten minutes or so I was getting very ominous Hells Angels flashbacks—all alone in a big crowd of hostile, cranked-up geeks in a mood to stomp somebody—but it soon became evident that these Nixon Youth people weren't ready for that kind of madness.

Our first clash erupted when I looked up from where I was sitting on the floor against a wall in the back of the room and saw Ron Rosenbaum from the *Village Voice* coming at me in a knot of shouting Nixon Youth wranglers. "No press allowed!" they were screaming. "Get out of here! You can't stay!"

They had nailed Rosenbaum at the door—but, instead of turning back and giving up, he plunged into the crowded room and made a beeline for the back wall, where he'd already spotted me sitting in peaceful anonymity. By the time he reached me, he was gasping for breath and about six fraternity/jock types were clawing at his arms. "They're trying to throw me out!" he shouted.

I looked up and shuddered, knowing my cover was blown. Within seconds, they were screaming at me, too. "You crazy bastard," I shouted at Rosenbaum. "You *fingered* me! Look what you've done!"

"No press!" they were shouting. "OUT! Both of you!"

I stood up quickly and put my back to the wall, still cursing Rosenbaum. "That's right!" I yelled. "Get that bastard out of here! No press allowed!"

Rosenbaum stared at me. There was shock and repugnance in his eyes—as if he had just recognized me as a lineal descendant of Judas Iscariot. As they muscled him away, I began explaining to my accusers that I was really more of a political observer than a journalist. "Have *you* run for office?" I snapped at one of them. "No! I thought not, goddamn it! You don't have the look of a man who's been to the wall. I can see it in your face!"

He was taken aback by this charge. His mouth flapped for a few seconds, then he blurted out: "What about *you*? What office did *you* run for?"

I smiled gently. "Sheriff, my friend. I ran for sheriff, out in Colorado—and I lost by just a hair. And it was the *liberals* who put the screws to me! Right! Are you surprised?"

He was definitely off balance.

"That's why I came here as an *observer*," I continued. "I wanted to see what it was like on the inside of a *winning* campaign."

It was just about then that somebody noticed my "press" tag was attached to my shirt by a blue and white McGovern button. I'd been wearing it for three days, provoking occasional rude comments from hotheads on the convention floor and various hotel lobbies—but this was the first time I'd felt called upon to explain myself. It was, after all, the only visible McGovern button in Miami Beach that week—in Flamingo Park or anywhere else—and now I was trying to join a spontaneous Nixon Youth demonstration that was about to spill out onto the floor of the very convention that had just nominated Richard Nixon for reelection, against McGovern.

They seemed to feel I was mocking their efforts in some way . . . and at that point the argument became so complex and disjointed that I can't possibly run it all down. It is enough to say that we finally compromised: if I refused to leave without violence, then I was damn well going to have to carry a sign in the spontaneous demonstration—and also wear a plastic red, white, and blue Nixon hat. They never came right out and said it, but I could see they were uncomfortable at the prospect of all three network TV cameras looking down on their spontaneous Nixon Youth demonstration and zeroing in—for their own perverse reasons—on a weird-looking, thirty-five-year-old speed freak with half his hair burned out from overindulgence, wearing a big blue McGovern button on his chest, carrying a tall cup of "Old Milwaukee" and shaking his fist at John Chancellor up in the NBC booth—screaming: "You dirty bastard! You'll *pay* for this, by God! We'll rip your goddamn teeth out! KILL! KILL! Your number just came up, you Communist son of a bitch!"

I politely dismissed all suggestions that I remove my McGovern button, but I agreed to carry a sign and wear a plastic hat like everybody else. "Don't worry," I assured them. "You'll be proud of me. There's a lot of bad blood between me and John Chancellor. He put acid in my drink last month at the Democratic Convention, then he tried to humiliate me in public."

"Acid? Golly, that's terrible! What kind of acid?"

"It felt like Sunshine," I said.

"Sunshine?"

"Yeah. He denied it, of course—But hell, he *always* denies it."

"Why?" a girl asked.

"Would *you* admit a thing like that?" I said.

She shook her head emphatically. "But I wouldn't do it, either," she said. "You could *kill* somebody by making them drink acid—why would he want to kill *you*?"

I shrugged. "Who knows? He eats a lot of it himself." I paused, sensing confusion . . . "Actually, I doubt if he really wanted to kill me. It was a hell of a dose, but not *that* strong." I smiled. "All I remember is the first rush: it came up my spine like nine tarantulas . . . drilled me right to the bar stool for two hours; I couldn't speak, couldn't even blink my eyes."

"Boy, what kind of acid does that?" somebody asked.

"Sunshine," I said. "Every time."

By now several others had picked up on the conversation. A bright-looking kid in a blue gabardine suit interrupted: "Sunshine acid? Are you talking about LSD?"

"Right," I said.

Now the others understood. A few laughed, but others muttered darkly, "You mean John Chancellor goes around putting LSD in people's drinks? He takes it himself? . . . He's a dope addict? . . ."

"Golly," said the girl. "That explains a lot, doesn't it?"

By this time I was having a hard time keeping a straight face. These poor, ignorant young waterheads. Would they pass this weird revelation on to their parents when they got back home to Middletown, Shaker Heights, and Orange County? Probably so, I thought. And then their parents would write letters to NBC, saying they'd learned from reliable sources that Chancellor was addicted to LSD-25—supplied to him in great quantities, no doubt, by Communist agents—and demanding that he be jerked off the air immediately and locked up.

I was tempted to start babbling crazily about Walter Cronkite: that he was heavy into the white slavery trade—sending agents to South Vietnam to adopt orphan girls, then shipping them back to his farm in Quebec to be lobotomized and sold into brothels up and down the Eastern seaboard . . .

But before I could get into this one, the men in the red hats began shouting that the magic moment was on us. The Ready Room crackled with tension; we were into the countdown. They divided us into four groups of about five hundred each and gave the final instructions. We were to rush onto the floor and begin chanting, cheering, waving our signs at the TV cameras, and generally whooping it up. Every other person was given a big garbage bag full of twenty-five or thirty helium balloons, which they were instructed to release just as soon as they reached the floor. Our entrance was timed precisely to coincide with the release of the thousands of non-helium balloons from the huge cages attached to the ceiling of the hall . . . so that our balloons would be *rising* while the others were *falling*, creating a sense of mass euphoria and perhaps even weightlessness for the prime-time TV audience.

Indeed. I was ready for some good, clean fun at that point, and by the time we got the signal to start moving I was seized by a giddy conviction that we were all about to participate in a spectacle that would go down in history.

They herded us out of the Ready Room and called a ragged kind of cadence while we double-timed it across the wet grass under the guava trees in back of the hall, and finally burst through a well-guarded access door held open for us by Secret Service men just as the balloons were released from the ceiling . . . it was wonderful; I waved happily to the SS man as I raced past him with the herd and then onto the floor. The hall was so full of balloons that I couldn't see anything at first, but then I spotted Chancellor up there in the booth and I let the bastard have it. First I held up my "Garbage Men Demand Equal Time" sign at him. Then, when I was sure he'd noticed the sign, I tucked it under my arm and ripped off my hat, clutching it in the same fist I was shaking angrily at the NBC booth and screaming at the top of my lungs: "You evil scum-sucker! You're *through*! You limp-wristed Nazi moron!"

I went deep into the foulest backwaters of my vocabulary for that trip, working myself into a flat-out screeching hate-frenzy for five or six minutes and drawing smiles of approval from some of my fellow demonstrators. They were dutifully chanting the slogans that had been assigned to them in the Ready Room—but I was really *into it*, and I could see that my zeal impressed them.

• • •

But a little bit of that bullshit goes a long way, and I quickly tired of it. When I realized that my erstwhile buddies were settling into the "*Four more years*!" chant, I figured it was time to move on.

Which was not easy. By this time, the whole crowd was facing the TV booths and screaming in unison. People were trampling each other to get up front and make themselves heard—or at least to get on camera for the homefolks—and the mood of that crowd was not receptive to the sight of a McGovern button in their midst, so I moved against the tide as gently as possible, keeping my elbows close down on my ribs and shouting "Chancellor to the Wall!" every thirty seconds or so, to keep myself inconspicuous.

By the time I got to the "periodical press" exit, I was almost overcome with a sense of *déjà vu*. I had seen all this before. I had been right in the middle of it before—but when?

Then it came to me. Yes. In 1964, at the Goldwater convention in San Francisco, when poor Barry unloaded that fateful line about "Extremism in the defense of liberty is no vice," etc.... I was on the floor of the Cow Palace when he laid that one on the crowd, and I remember feeling genuinely frightened at the violent reaction it provoked. The Goldwater delegates went completely amok for fifteen or twenty minutes. He hadn't even finished the sentence before they were on their feet, cheering wildly. Then, as the human thunder kept building, they mounted their metal chairs and began howling, shaking their fists at

Huntley and Brinkley up in the NBC booth—and finally they began picking up those chairs with both hands and bashing them against chairs other delegates were still standing on.

It was a memorable performance, etched every bit as clearly in the gray folds of my brain as the police beatings I saw at the corner of Michigan and Balbo four years later . . . but the Nixon convention in Miami was not even in the same league with Chicago in '68. The blinding stench of tear gas brought back memories, but only on the surface. Around midnight on Wednesday, I found myself reeling around completely blind on Washington Avenue in front of the convention hall, bumping against cops wearing black rubber gas masks and running demonstrators clutching wet towels over their faces. Many of the cops were wearing khaki flak jackets and waving three-foot hickory pick-handles . . . but nobody hit me, and despite the gas and the chaos, I never felt in danger. Finally, when the gas got so bad that I no longer knew what direction I was moving in, I staggered across somebody's lawn and began feeling my way along the outside of the house until I came to a water faucet. I sat down on the grass and soaked my handkerchief under the tap, then pressed it on my face, without rubbing, until I was able to see again. When I finally got up, I realized that at least a dozen cops had been standing within twenty feet of me the whole time, watching passively and not offering any help—but not beating me into a bloody, screaming coma, either.

That was the difference between Chicago and Miami. Or at least one of the most significant differences. If the cops in Chicago had found me crawling around in somebody's front yard, wearing a "press" tag and blind from too much gas, they'd have broken half my ribs and then hauled me away in handcuffs for "resisting arrest." I saw it happen so often that I still feel the bile rising when I think about it.

A Vicious Attack on the Demonstrators . . .
The Silent Siege of the Fontainebleau . . .
"These People Should Go Back Where They Belong"

On Tuesday afternoon my car disappeared. I left it on the street in front of the hotel while I went in to pick up my swimming trunks, and when I came back out, it was gone. To hell with it, I thought, it was time to get out of Miami.

I went up to my room and thought for a while, sitting with my back to the typewriter and staring out the window at the big ocean-going yachts and luxury houseboats tied up across the street at the piers along Indian Creek. Last week they'd been crawling with people, and many cocktail parties. Every time the Fontainebleau lobby started buzzing with rumors about another crowd of demonstrators bearing down on the hotel from the direction of Flamingo Park, the boats across Collins Avenue would fill up with laughing Republican delegates wearing striped blazers and cocktail dresses. There was no better place, they said, for watching the street action. As the demonstrators approached the front entrance to the hotel, they found themselves walking a gauntlet of riot-equipped police on one side, and martini-sipping GOP delegates on the other.

One yacht—the *Wild Rose,* out of Houston—rumbled back and forth, just offshore, at every demonstration. From the middle of Collins Avenue, you could see the guests lounging in deck chairs, observing the action through high-powered field glasses, and reaching around from time to time to accept a fresh drink from crewmen wearing white serving jackets with gold epaulets.

The scene on the foredeck of the *Wild Rose* was so gross, so flagrantly decadent, that it was hard to avoid comparing it with the kind of blood-thirsty arrogance normally associated with the last days of the Roman Empire: here was a crowd of rich Texans, floating around on a $100,000 yacht in front of a palatial Miami Beach hotel, giggling with excitement at the prospect of watching their hired gladiators brutalize a mob of howling, half-naked Christians. I half expected them to start whooping for blood and giving the thumbs-down signal.

Nobody who was out there on the street with the demonstrators would be naive enough to compare them to "helpless Christians." With the lone exception of the Vietnam Veterans Against the War, the demonstrators in Miami were a useless mob of ignorant, chicken-shit ego-junkies whose only accomplishment was to embarrass the whole tradition of public protest. They were hopelessly disorganized, they had no real purpose in being there, and about half of them were so wasted on grass, wine, and downers that they couldn't say for sure whether they were raising hell in Miami, or San Diego.

Five weeks earlier, these same people had been sitting in the lobby of the Doral, calling George McGovern a "lying pig" and a "warmonger." Their target-hotel this time was the Fontainebleau, headquarters for the national press and many TV cameras. If the Rolling Stones came to Miami for a free concert, these assholes would build their own fence around the bandstand—just so they could have something to tear down and then "crash the gates."

During both conventions, Flamingo Park was known as "Quaalude Alley," in deference to the brand of downers favored by most demonstrators. Quaalude is a mild sleeping pill, but—consumed in large quantities, along with wine, grass, and adrenaline—it produces the same kind of stupid, mean-drunk effect as Seconal ("Reds"). The Quaalude effect was so obvious in Flamingo Park that the "Last Patrol" caravan of Vietnam Vets—who came here in motorcades from all parts of the country—refused to even set up camp with the other demonstrators. They had serious business in Miami, they explained, and the last thing they needed was a public alliance with a mob of stoned street crazies and screaming teenyboppers.

The Vets made their camp in a far corner of the park, then sealed it off with a network of perimeter guards and checkpoints that made it virtually impossible to even enter that area unless you knew somebody inside. There was an ominous sense of dignity about everything the VVAW did in Miami. They rarely even hinted at violence, but their very presence was menacing—on a level that the Yippies, Zippies, and SDS street crazies never even approached, despite all their yelling and trashing.

The most impressive single performance in Miami during the three days of the GOP Convention was the VVAW march on the Fontainebleau on Tuesday afternoon. Most of the press and TV people were either down at the convention hall, covering the "liberals vs. conservatives" floor-fight over rules for seating delegates in 1976—or standing around in the boiling mid-afternoon sun at Miami International Airport, waiting for Nixon to come swooping out of the sky in Air Force One.

My own plan for that afternoon was to drive far out to the end of Key Biscayne and find an empty part of the beach where I could swim by myself in the ocean, and not have to talk to anybody for a while. I didn't give a fuck about watching the rules fight, a doomed charade that the Nixon brain trust had already settled in favor of the conservatives . . . and I saw no point in going out to the airport to watch three thousand well-rehearsed "Nixon Youth" robots "welcome the president."

Given these two depressing options, I figured Tuesday was as good a day as any to get away from politics and act like a human being for a change—or better still, like an animal. Just get off by myself and drift around naked in the sea for a few hours . . .

But as I drove toward Key Biscayne with the top down, squinting into the sun, I saw the vets . . . They were moving up Collins Avenue in dead silence; 1,200 of them dressed in battle fatigues, helmets, combat boots . . . a few carried full-size plastic M-16s, many peace symbols, girlfriends walking beside vets being pushed along the street in slow-moving wheelchairs, others walking jerkily on crutches . . . But nobody spoke; all the "stop, start" . . . "fast, slow" . . . "left, right" commands came from "platoon leaders" walking slightly off to the side of the main column and using hand signals.

One look at that eerie procession killed my plan to go swimming that afternoon. I left my car at a parking meter in front of the Cadillac Hotel and joined the march . . . No, "joined" is the wrong word; that was not the kind of procession you just walked up and "joined." Not without paying some very heavy dues: an arm gone here, a leg there, paralysis, a face full of lumpy scar tissue . . . all staring straight ahead as the long silent column moved between rows of hotel porches full of tight-lipped Senior Citizens, through the heart of Miami Beach.

The silence of the march was contagious, almost threatening. There were hundreds of spectators, but nobody said a word. I walked beside the column for ten blocks, and the only sounds I remember hearing were the soft thump of boot leather on hot asphalt and the occasional rattling of an open canteen top.

• • •

The Fontainebleau was already walled off from the street by five hundred heavily armed cops when the front ranks of the Last Patrol arrived, still marching in total silence. Several hours earlier, a noisy mob of Yippie/Zippie/SDS "non-delegates" had shown up in front of the Fontainebleau and been met with jeers and curses from GOP delegates and other partisan spectators, massed behind the police lines . . . But now there was no jeering. Even the cops seemed deflated. They watched nervously from behind their face-shields as the VVAW platoon leaders, still using hand signals, funneled the column into a tight semicircle that blocked all three northbound lanes of Collins Avenue. During earlier demonstrations—at least six in the past three days—the police had poked people with riot sticks to make sure at least one lane of the street stayed open for local traffic, and on the one occasion when mere prodding didn't work, they had charged the demonstrators and cleared the street completely.

But not now. For the first and only time during the whole convention, the cops were clearly off balance. The vets could have closed all six lanes of Collins Avenue if they'd wanted to, and nobody would have argued. I have been covering anti-war demonstrations with depressing regularity since the winter of 1964, in cities all over the country, and I have never seen cops so intimidated by demonstrators as they were in front of the Fontainebleau hotel on that hot Tuesday afternoon in Miami Beach.

There was an awful tension in that silence. Not even that pack of rich sybarites out there on the foredeck of the *Wild Rose* could stay in their seats for this show. They were standing up at the rail, looking worried, getting very bad vibrations from whatever was happening over there in the street. Was something *wrong* with their gladiators? Were they spooked? And why was there no noise?

After five more minutes of harsh silence, one of the VVAW platoon leaders suddenly picked up a bullhorn and said: "We want to come inside."

Nobody answered, but an almost visible shudder ran through the crowd. "Oh my God!" a man standing next to me muttered. I felt a strange tightness coming over me, and I reacted instinctively—for the first time in a long, long while—by slipping my notebook into my belt and reaching down to take off my watch. The first thing to go in a street fight is always your watch, and once you've lost a few, you develop a certain instinct that lets you know when it's time to get the thing off your wrist and into a safe pocket.

I can't say for sure what I would have done if the Last Patrol had tried to crack the police line and seize control of the Fontainebleau—but I have a fair idea, based on instinct and rude experience, so the unexpected appearance of Congressman Pete McCloskey on that scene calmed my nerves considerably. He shoved his way through the police line and talked with a handful of the VVAW spokesmen long enough to convince them, apparently, that a frontal assault on the hotel would be suicidal.

One of the platoon leaders smiled faintly and assured McCloskey that they'd never had any intention of attacking the Fontainebleau. They didn't even *want* to go in. The only reason they asked was to see if the Republicans would turn them away in front of network TV cameras—which they did, but very few cameras were on hand that afternoon to record it. All the network floor crews were down at the convention hall, and the ones who would normally have been on standby alert at the Fontainebleau were out at the airport filming Nixon's arrival.

No doubt there were backup crews around somewhere—but I suspect they were up on the roof, using very long lenses; because in those first few moments when the vets began massing in front of the police line, there was no mistaking the potential for real violence . . . and it was easy enough to see, by scanning the faces behind those clear plastic riot masks, that the cream of the Florida State Highway Patrol had no appetite at all for a public crunch with 1,200 angry Vietnam veterans.

Whatever the outcome, it was a guaranteed nightmare situation for the police. Defeat would be bad enough, but victory would be intolerable. Every TV screen in the nation would show a small army of heavily armed Florida cops clubbing unarmed veterans—some on crutches and others in wheelchairs—whose only crime was trying to enter Republican Convention headquarters in Miami Beach. How could Nixon explain a thing like that? Could he slither out from under it?

Never in hell, I thought—and all it would take to make a thing like that happen, right now, would be for one or two vets to lose control of themselves and try to crash through the police line; just enough violence to make *one* cop use his riot stick. The rest would take care of itself.

Ah, nightmares, nightmares . . . Not even Sammy Davis Jr. could stomach that kind of outrage. He would flee the Nixon compound within moments after the first news bulletin, rejecting his newfound soul brother like a suckfish cutting loose from a mortally wounded shark . . . and the next day's *Washington Post* would report that Sammy Davis Jr. had spent most of the previous night trying to ooze through the keyhole of George McGovern's front door in suburban Maryland.

Right . . . but none of this happened. McCloskey's appearance seemed to soothe both the crowd and the cops. The only violent act of the afternoon occurred moments later when a foul-mouthed twenty-year-old blonde girl named Debby Marshal tried to ram her way through the crowd on a 125 Honda. "Get out of my way!" she kept shouting. "This is ridiculous! These people should go back where they belong!"

The vets ignored her, but about halfway through the crowd she ran into a nest of press photographers, and that was as far as she went. An hour later she was still sitting there, biting her lips and whining about how "ridiculous" it all was. I was tempted to lean over and set her hair on fire with my Zippo, but by that time the confrontation had settled down to a series of bullhorn speeches by various vets. Not much of what was said could be heard more than fifteen feet from the bullhorn, however, because of two army helicopters that suddenly appeared overhead and filled the whole street with their noise. The only vet speaker who managed to make himself plainly understood above the chopper noise was an ex-marine sergeant from Massapequa named Ron Kovic, who spoke from a wheelchair because his legs are permanently paralyzed.

I would like to have a transcript or at least a tape of what Kovic said that day, because his words lashed the crowd like a wire whip. If Kovic had been allowed to speak from the convention hall podium, in front of network TV cameras, Nixon wouldn't have had the balls to show up and accept the nomination.

No . . . I suspect that's wishful thinking. Nothing in the realm of human possibility could have prevented Richard Nixon from accepting that nomination. If God himself had showed up in Miami and denounced Nixon from the podium, hired gunsels from the Committee for the Re-Election of the President would have quickly had him arrested for disturbing the peace.

Vietnam veterans like Ron Kovic are not welcome in Nixon's White House. They tried to get in last year, but they could only get close enough to throw their war medals over the fence. That was perhaps the most eloquent anti-war statement ever made in this country, and that Silent March on the Fontainebleau on August 22 had the same ugly sting to it.

There is no anti-war or even anti-establishment group in America today with the psychic leverage of the VVAW. Not even those decadent swine on the foredeck of the *Wild Rose* can ignore the dues Ron Kovic and his buddies have paid. They are golems, come back to haunt us all—even Richard Nixon, who campaigned for the presidency in 1968 with a promise that he had "a secret plan" to end the war in Vietnam.

Which was true, as it turns out. The plan was to end the war just in time to get himself reelected in 1972.

Four more years.

The Campaign Trail: The Fat City Blues

October 26, 1972

Hear me, people: We have now to deal with another race—small and feeble when our fathers first met them, but now great and overbearing. Strangely enough they have a mind to till the soil and the love of possession is a disease with them. These people have made many rules that the rich may break but the poor may not. They take their tithes from the poor and weak to support the rich and those who rule.

—Chief Sitting Bull, speaking at the
Powder River Conference in 1877

If George McGovern had a speechwriter half as eloquent as Sitting Bull, he would be home free today—instead of 22 points behind and racing around the country with both feet in his mouth. The Powder River Conference ended ninety-five years ago, but the old chief's baleful analysis of the White Man's rape of the American continent was just as accurate then as it would be today if he came back from the dead and said it for the microphones on prime-time TV. The ugly fallout from the American Dream has been coming down on us at a pretty consistent rate since Sitting Bull's time—and the only real difference now, with Election Day '72 only a few weeks away, is that we seem to be on the verge of *ratifying* the fallout and forgetting the Dream itself.

Sitting Bull made no distinction between Democrats and Republicans—which was probably just as well, in 1877 or any other year—but it's also true that Sitting Bull never knew the degradation of traveling on Richard Nixon's press plane; he never had the bilious pleasure of dealing with Ron Ziegler, and he never met John Mitchell, Nixon's king fixer.

If the old Sioux Chief had ever done these things, I think—despite his angry contempt for the White Man and everything he stands for—he'd be working overtime for George McGovern today.

These past two weeks have not been calm ones for me. Immediately after the Republican Convention in Miami, I dragged myself back to the Rockies and tried to forget about politics for a while—just lie naked on the porch in the cool afternoon sun and watch the aspen trees turning gold on the hills around my house; mix up a huge cannister of gin and grapefruit juice, watch the horses nuzzling each other in the pasture across the road, big logs in the fireplace at night; Herbie Mann, John Prine, and Jesse Colin Young booming out of the speakers . . . zip off every once in a while for a fast run into town along a back road above the river: to the health center gym for some volleyball, then over to Benton's gallery to get caught up on whatever treacheries the local greedheads rammed through while I was gone, watch the late TV news and curse McGovern for poking another hole in his own boat, then stop by the Jerome on the way out of town for a midnight beer with Solheim.

After two weeks on that peaceful human schedule, the last thing I wanted to think about was the grim, inescapable spectre of two more frenzied months on the campaign trail. Especially when it meant coming back here to Washington, to start laying the groundwork for a long and painful autopsy job on the McGovern campaign. What went wrong? Why had it failed? Who was to blame? And, finally, what next?

That was one project. The other was to somehow pass through the fine eye of the White House security camel and go out on the campaign trail with Richard Nixon, to watch him waltz in—if only to get the drift of his thinking, to watch his moves, his eyes. It is a nervous thing to consider: not just four *more* years of Nixon, but Nixon's *last four years in politics*—completely unshackled, for the first time in his life, from any need to worry about who might or might not vote for him the next time around.

If he wins in November, he will finally be free to do whatever he wants . . . or maybe "wants" is too strong a word for right now. It conjures up images of Papa Doc, Batista, Somoza; jails full of bewildered "political prisoners" and the constant cold-sweat fear of jackboots suddenly kicking your door off its hinges at four in the morning.

There is no point in kidding ourselves about what Richard Nixon really *wants* for America. When he stands at his White House window and looks out on an anti-war demonstration, he doesn't see "dissenters," he sees *criminals*. Dangerous parasites, preparing to strike at the heart of the Great American System that put him where he is today.

• • •

There may not be much difference between Democrats and Republicans; I have made that argument myself—with considerable venom, as I recall—over the past ten months . . . But only a blind geek or a waterhead could miss the difference between McGovern and Richard Nixon. Granted, they are both white men; and both are politicians—but the similarity ends right there, and from that point on the difference is so vast that anybody who can't see it deserves whatever happens to them if Nixon gets reelected due to apathy, stupidity, and laziness on the part of potential McGovern voters.

The tragedy of this campaign is that McGovern and his staff wizards have not been able to dramatize what is really at stake on November 7. We are not looking at just another dim rerun of the '68 Nixon-Humphrey trip, or the LBJ-Goldwater fiasco in '64. Those were both useless drills. I voted for Dick Gregory in '68, and for "No" in '64 . . . but this one is different, and since McGovern is so goddamn maddeningly inept with the kind of words he needs to make people understand what he's up to, it will save a lot of time here—and strain on my own weary head, to remember Bobby Kennedy's ultimate characterization of Richard Nixon, in a speech at Vanderbilt University in the spring of '68, not long before he was murdered.

"*Richard Nixon*," he said, "*represents the dark side of the American spirit*."

I don't remember what else he said that day. I guess I could look it up in the *New York Times* speech morgue, but why bother? That one line says it all.

Anybody who doubts it should go out and catch the president's act, the next time he swoops into the local airport. Watch the big silver-and-blue custom-built 707 come booming down the runway and roll up in front of the small but well-disciplined crowd of Nixon Youth cheerleaders singing the "Nixon Now" song, waving their freshly printed red-white-and-blue "Re-Elect the President" signs and then pausing, in perfect spontaneous unison, before intimidating every TV crew on the runway with the stylish "Four more years!" chant.

Watch the president emerge from the belly of the plane, holding hands with the aging Barbie doll known as his wife, and ooze down the rolling VIP stairway while the 105th Division Rolling Thunder Women & Children Classic Napalm U.S. Army Parade Band whips the crowd higher & higher with a big-beat rendition of "God Save the Freaks."

See the generals strut down from the plane behind the president. Take a long look at the grinning "local dignitaries" who are ushered out, by armed guards, to greet him. See the White House press corps over there about two hundred yards away, herded into that small corral behind heavy ropes stretched around red-white-and-blue painted oil drums. Why are they smiling?

The McGovern campaign appears to be fucked, at this time. A spectacular Come From Behind win is still possible—on paper and given the right circumstances—but the underlying realities of the campaign itself would seem to preclude this. A cohesive, determined campaign with the same kind of multi-level morale that characterized the McGovern effort in the months preceding the Wisconsin primary might be a good bet to close a 20-point gap on Nixon in the last month of this grim presidential campaign.

As usual, Nixon has peaked too early—and now he is locked into what is essentially a Holding Action. Which would be disastrous in a close race, but—even by Pat Caddell's (partisan) estimate—Nixon could blow 20 points off his lead in the next six weeks and still win. (Caddell's figures seem in general agreement with those of the most recent Gallup poll, ten days ago, which showed that Nixon could blow 30 points off his lead and still win.)

My own rude estimate is that McGovern will steadily close the gap between now and November 7, but not enough. If I had to make book right now, I would try to get McGovern with 7 or 8 points, but I'd probably go with 5 or 6, if necessary. In other words, my guess at the moment is that McGovern will lose by a popular vote margin of 5.5 percent—and probably far worse in the electoral college.

The tragedy of this is that McGovern appeared to have a sure lock on the White House when the sun came up on Miami Beach on the morning of Thursday, July 13. Since then he has crippled himself with a series of almost unbelievable blunders—Eagleton, Salinger, O'Brien, etc.—that have understandably convinced huge chunks of the electorate, including at least half of McGovern's own hard-core supporters, that the candidate is a gibbering dingbat. His behavior since Miami has made a piecemeal mockery of everything he seemed to stand for during the primaries.

Possibly I'm wrong on all this. It is still conceivable—to me, at least—that McGovern might actually win. In which case I won't have to worry about my P.O. Box at the Woody Creek general store getting jammed up with dinner invitations from the White House. But what the hell? Mr. Nixon never invited me, and neither did Kennedy or LBJ.

I survived those years of shame, and I'm not especially worried about enduring four more. I have a feeling that my time is getting short anyway, and I can think of a hell of a lot of things I'd rather find in my mailbox than an invitation to dinner in the Servants' Quarters.

Let those treacherous bastards eat by themselves. They deserve each other.

Terminal Campaign Bloat?

Ah, Jesus! The situation is out of hand again. The sun is up, the deal is down, and that evil bastard Mankiewicz just jerked the kingpin out of my finely crafted saga for this issue. How long, O Lord, how long? My brain has gone numb from this madness. After squatting for thirteen days in this scum-crusted room on the top floor of the Washington Hilton—writing feverishly, night after night, on the homestretch realities of this goddamn wretched campaign—I am beginning to wonder what in the name of Twisted Jesus ever possessed me to come here in the first place. What kind of madness lured me back to this stinking swamp of a town?

Am I turning into a politics junkie? It is not a happy thought—particularly when I see what it's done to all the others. After two weeks in Woody Creek, getting back on the press plane was like going back to the cancer ward. Some of the best people in the press corps looked so physically ravaged that it was painful to even see them, much less stand around and make small talk.

Many appeared to be in the terminal stage of Campaign Bloat, a gruesome kind of false-fat condition that is said to be connected somehow with failing adrenaline glands. The swelling begins within twenty-four hours of that moment when the victim first begins to suspect that the campaign is essentially meaningless. At that point, the body's entire adrenaline supply is sucked back into the gizzard, and nothing either candidate says, does, or generates will cause it to rise again . . . and without adrenaline, the flesh begins to swell; the eyes fill with blood and grow smaller in the face, the jowls puff out from the cheekbones, the neck-flesh droops, and the belly swells up like a frog's throat . . . The brain fills with noxious waste fluids, the tongue is rubbed raw on the molars, and the basic perception antennae begin dying like hairs in a bonfire.

I would like to think—or at least *claim* to think, out of charity if nothing else—that Campaign Bloat is at the root of this hellish angst that boils up to obscure my vision every time I try to write anything serious about presidential politics.

But I don't think that's it. The real reason, I suspect, is the problem of coming to grips with the idea that Richard Nixon will almost certainly be reelected for another four years as president of the United States. If the current polls are reliable—and even if they aren't, the sheer size of the margin makes the numbers themselves unimportant—Nixon will be reelected by a huge majority of Americans who feel he is not only more honest and more trustworthy than George McGovern, but also more likely to end the war in Vietnam.

The polls also indicate that Nixon will get a comfortable majority of the Youth Vote. And that he might carry all fifty states.

Well . . . maybe so. This may be the year when we finally come face to face with ourselves; finally just lay back and say it—that we are really just a nation of 220 million used car salesmen with all the money we need to buy guns, and no qualms at all about killing anybody else in the world who tries to make us uncomfortable.

The tragedy of all this is that George McGovern, for all his mistakes and all of his imprecise talk about "new politics" and "honesty in government," is really one of the few men who've run for president of the United States in this century who really understands what a fantastic monument to all the best instincts of the human race this country might have been, if we could have kept it out of the hands of greedy little hustlers like Richard Nixon.

McGovern made some stupid mistakes, but in context they seem almost frivolous compared to the things Richard Nixon does every day of his life, on purpose, as a matter of policy and a perfect expression of everything he stands for.

Jesus! Where will it end? How low do you have to stoop in this country to be president?

Ask Not for Whom the Bell Tolls . . .

November 9, 1972

Due to circumstances beyond my control, I would rather not write anything about the 1972 presidential campaign at this time. On Tuesday, November 7, I will get out of bed long enough to go down to the polling place and vote for George McGovern. Afterward, I will drive back to the house, lock the front door, get back in bed, and watch television as long as necessary. It will probably be a while before The Angst lifts—but whenever it happens I will get out of bed again and start writing the mean, cold-blooded bummer that I was not quite ready for today. Until then, I think Tom Benton's "Re-elect the President" poster says everything that needs to be said, right now, about this malignant election. In any other year I might be tempted to embellish the Death's Head with a few angry flashes of my own. But not in 1972. At least not in the sullen numbness of these final hours before the deal goes down—because words are no longer important at this stage of the campaign; all the best ones were said a long time ago, and all the right ideas were bouncing around in public long before Labor Day.

That is the one grim truth of this election most likely to come back and haunt us: the options were clearly defined, and all the major candidates except Nixon were publicly grilled, by experts, who demanded to know where they stood on every issue from Gun Control and Abortion to the Ad Valorem Tax. By mid-September both candidates had staked out their own separate turfs, and if not everybody could tell you what each candidate stood for, *specifically,* almost everyone likely to vote in November understood that Richard Nixon and George McGovern were two very different men: not only in the context of politics, but also their personalities, temperaments, guiding principles, and even their basic lifestyles . . .

There is almost a yin/yang clarity in the difference between the two men; a contrast so stark that it would be hard to find any two better models, in the national politics arena, for the legendary *duality*—the congenital Split Personality and polarized instincts—that almost everybody except Americans has long since taken for granted as the key to our National Character. This was not what Richard Nixon had in mind when he said last August that the 1972 presidential election would offer voters "the clearest choice of this century," but on a level he will never understand he was probably right . . . and it is Nixon himself who represents that dark, venal, and incurably violent side of the American character that almost every other country in the world has learned to fear and despise. Our Barbie doll president, with his Barbie doll wife and his boxful of Barbie doll children is also America's answer to the monstrous Mr. Hyde. He speaks for the werewolf in us; the bully, the predatory shyster who turns into something unspeakable, full of claws and bleeding string-warts, on nights when the moon comes too close . . .

At the stroke of midnight in Washington, a drooling red-eyed beast with the legs of a man and the head of a giant hyena crawls out of its bedroom window in the South Wing of the White House and leaps fifty feet down to the lawn . . . pauses briefly to strangle the chow watchdog, then races off into the darkness . . . toward the Watergate, snarling with lust, loping through the alleys behind Pennsylvania Avenue and trying desperately to remember which one of those four hundred iron balconies is the one outside Martha Mitchell's apartment . . .

Ah . . . nightmares, nightmares. But I was only kidding. The president of the United States would never act that weird. At least not during football season. But how would the voters react if they knew the president of the United States was presiding over "a complex, far-reaching, and sinister operation on the part of White House aides and the Nixon campaign organization . . . involving sabotage, forgery, theft of confidential files, surveillance of Democratic candidates and their families, and persistent efforts to lay the basis for possible blackmail and intimidation."

Well, that ugly description of Nixon's staff operations comes from a

New York Times editorial on Thursday, October 12. But neither Nixon nor anyone else felt it would have much effect on his steady 2–1 lead over McGovern in all the national polls. Four days later the *Times*/Yankelovich poll showed Nixon ahead by an incredible 20 points (57 percent to 37 percent, with 16 percent undecided) over the man Bobby Kennedy described as "the most decent man in the Senate."

"Ominous" is not quite the right word for a situation where one of the most consistently unpopular politicians in American history suddenly skyrockets to Folk Hero status while his closest advisors are being caught almost daily in Nazi-style gigs that would have embarrassed Adolph Eichmann.

How long will it be before "demented extremists" in Germany, or maybe Japan, start calling us a Nation of Pigs? How would Nixon react? "No comment"? And how would the popularity polls react if he just came right out and admitted it?

Memo from the Sports Desk & Rude Notes from a Decompression Chamber in Miami

August 2, 1973

There is no joy in Woody Creek tonight—at least not in the twisted bowels of this sinkhole of political iniquity called the Owl Farm—because, two thousand miles away in the swampy heat of Washington, D.C., my old football buddy, Dick Nixon, is lashing around in bad trouble . . . The vultures are coming home to roost—like he always feared they would, in the end—and it hurts me in a way nobody would publish if I properly described it, to know that I can't be with him on the sweaty ramparts today, stomping those dirty buzzards like Davy Crockett bashing spics off the walls of the Alamo.

"Delta Dawn . . . What's that flower you have on?"

Fine music on my radio as dawn comes up on the Rockies . . . But suddenly the music ends and ABC (American Entertainment Network) News interrupts: Martha Mitchell is demanding that "Mister President" either resign or be impeached, for reasons her addled tongue can only hint at . . . and Charles "Tex" Colson, the president's erstwhile *special counsel*, is denying all statements & sworn testimony, by anybody, linking him to burglaries, fire-bombings, wire-tappings, perjuries, payoffs, and other routine felonies in connection with his job at the White House . . . and President Nixon is relaxing, as it were, in his personal beach-front mansion at San Clemente, California, surrounded by the scuzzy remnants of his once imperial guard . . . Indeed, you can almost hear the rattle of martini-cups along the airwaves as Gerald Warren—Ron Ziegler's doomed replacement—cranks another hastily rewritten paragraph (Amendment No. 67 to Paragraph No. 13 of President Nixon's original statement denying everything) . . . into the overheated Dex machine to the White House, for immediate release to the national media . . . and the White House pressroom is boiling with guilt-crazed journalists, ready to pounce on any new statement like a pack of wild African dogs, to atone for all the things they knew but never wrote when Nixon was riding high . . .

Why does Nixon use the clumsy Dex, instead of the Mojo? Why does he drink martinis, instead of Wild Turkey? Why does he wear boxer shorts? Why is his life a grim monument to everything plastic, de-sexed, and nonsensual? When I look at Nixon's White House, I have a sense of *absolute* personal alienation. The president and I seem to disagree on almost *everything*—except pro football, and Nixon's addiction to that has caused me to view it with a freshly jaundiced eye, or what the late John Foster Dulles called "an agonizing reappraisal." Anything Nixon likes *must* be suspect. Like cottage cheese and catsup . . .

"The Dex machine." Jesus! Learning that Nixon and his people use *this*—instead of the smaller, quicker, more versatile (and portable) Mojo Wire—was almost the final insult: coming on the heels of the Gross Sense of Injury I felt when I saw that my name was not included on the infamous "Enemies of the White House" list.

I would almost have preferred a vindictive tax audit to that kind of crippling exclusion. Christ! What kind of waterheads compiled that list? How can I show my face in the Jerome Bar when word finally reaches Aspen that I wasn't on it?

Fortunately, the list was drawn up in the summer of '71—which partially explains why my name was missing. It was not until the autumn of '72 that I began referring to the president, in nationally circulated print, as a Cheapjack Punk and a Lust-Maddened Werewolf, whose very existence was (and remains) a bad cancer on the American political tradition. Every ad the publishers prepared for my book on the 1972 campaign led off with a savage slur on all that Richard Nixon ever hoped to represent or stand for. The man is a walking embarrassment to the human race—and especially, as Bobby Kennedy once noted, to that high, optimistic potential that fueled men like Jefferson and Madison, and which Abe Lincoln once described as "the last, best hope of man."

There is slim satisfaction in the knowledge that my exclusion from the (1971) list of "White House enemies" has more to do with timing and Ron Ziegler's refusal to read *Rolling Stone* than with the validity of all the things I've said and written about that evil bastard.

I was, after all, the only accredited journalist covering the 1972 presidential campaign to compare Nixon with Adolf Hitler . . . I was the only one to describe him as a congenital thug, a fixer with the personal principles of a used-car salesman. And when these distasteful excesses were privately censured by the docile White House press corps, I compounded my flirtation with Bad Taste by describing the White House correspondents as a gang of lame whores & sheep without the balls to even argue with Ron Ziegler—who kept them all dancing to Nixon's bogus tune until it became suddenly fashionable to see him for the hired liar he was and has been all along.

The nut of my complaint here—in addition to being left off The List—is rooted in a powerful resentment at not being recognized (not even by Ziegler) for the insults I heaped on Nixon *before* he was laid low. This is a matter of journalistic ethics—or perhaps even "sportsmanship"—and I take a certain pride in knowing that I kicked Nixon before he went down. Not afterward—though I plan to do *that*, too, as soon as possible.

And I feel no more guilt about it than I would about setting a rat trap in my kitchen, if it ever seemed necessary—and certainly no more guilt than I know Nixon would feel about hiring some thug like Gordon Liddy to set me up for a felony charge, if my name turned up on his List.

When they update the bugger, I plan to be on it. My attorney is even now preparing my tax records, with an eye to confrontation. When the next list of "White House enemies" comes out, I want to be on it. My son will never forgive me—ten years from now—if I fail to clear my name and get grouped, for the record, with those whom Richard Milhous Nixon considered dangerous.

Dick Tuck feels the same way. He was sitting in my kitchen, watching the TV set, when Sam Donaldson began reading The List on ABC-TV.

"Holy shit!" Tuck muttered. "We're not *on* it."

"Don't worry," I said grimly. "We *will* be."

"What can we *do*?" he asked.

"Kick out the jams," I said. "Don't worry, Dick. When the next list comes out, we'll *be there*. I guarantee that."

MEMO:

FROM:
Raoul Duke, Sports Editor

TO:
Main/Edit Control

C.C.:
Legal, Finance, Security, et al.

SUBJECT:
Imminent emergence of Dr. Thompson from the Decompression Chamber in Miami, and probable inability of the Sports Desk or anyone else to control his movements at that time . . . especially in connection with his ill-conceived plan to move the National Affairs desk back to Washington and bring Ralph Steadman over from England to cause trouble at the Watergate hearings . . .

EDITORS' NOTE:

The following intra-corporate memo arrived by Mojo Wire from Colorado shortly before deadline time for this issue. It was greeted with mixed emotions by all those potentially afflicted . . . and because of the implications, we felt a certain obligation to lash up a quick, last-minute explanation . . . primarily for those who have never understood the real function of Raoul Duke (whose official title is "sports editor"), and also for the many readers whose attempts to reach Dr. Thompson by mail, phone, & other means have not borne fruit.

The circumstances of Dr. Thompson's removal from the Public World have been a carefully guarded secret for the past several months. During the last week of March—after a strange encounter with Henry Kissinger while on "vacation" in Acapulco—Dr. Thompson almost drowned when his scuba tanks unexplainably ran out of air while diving for black coral off the Yucatán Coast of Mexico, at a depth of some three hundred feet. His rapid emergence from these depths—according to witnesses—resulted in a near-fatal case of the bends, and an emergency-chartered/night-flight to the nearest decompression chamber, which happened to be in Miami.

Dr. Thompson was unconscious in the decompression chamber—a round steel cell about twelve feet in diameter—for almost three weeks. When he finally regained his wits, it was impossible to speak with him, except by means of a cracked loudspeaker tube & brief handwritten notes held up to the window. A television set was introduced into The Chamber at his insistence and, by extremely complicated maneuvering, he was able to watch the Watergate hearings . . . but, due to the dangerous differences in pressurization, he was unable to communicate anything but garbled notes on his impressions to Duke, his long-time friend and associate, who flew to Miami immediately, at his own expense.

When it became apparent that Dr. Thompson would be in The Chamber indefinitely, Duke left him in Miami—breathing easily in The Chamber with a TV set & several notebooks—and returned to Colorado, where he spent the past three months handling The Doktor's personal & business affairs, in addition to organizing the skeletal framework for his 1974 senate race.

It was a familiar role for Duke, who has been Dr. Thompson's close friend & adviser since 1968—after fourteen years of distinguished service in the CIA, the FBI, and the Pittsburgh (Pa.) Police Intelligence Unit. His duties, since hiring on with Dr. Thompson, have been understandably varied. He has been described as "a weapons expert," a "ghost-writer," a "bodyguard," a "wizard," and a "brutal fixer."

"Compared to the things I've done for Thompson," Duke says, "both Gordon Liddy and Howard Hunt were stone *punks*."

It is clear, from this memo, that Duke has spent a good bit of his time in Colorado watching the Watergate hearings on TV—but it is also clear that his tentative conclusions are very different from the ones Dr. Thompson reached, from his admittedly singular vantage point in that decompression chamber in downtown Miami.

The editors of *Rolling Stone* would prefer not to comment on *either* of these viewpoints at this time, nor to comment on the nightmare/blizzard of expense vouchers submitted, by Duke, in connection with this dubious memo. In accordance with our long tradition, however, we are placing the Public Interest (publication of Duke's memo, in this case) on a plane far above and beyond our inevitably mundane haggling about the cost of breakfast and lunch.

What follows, then, is a jangled mix of Duke's official communications with this office, and Thompson's "Watergate Notes" (forwarded to us, by Duke) from his decompression chamber in Miami. The chronology is not entirely consistent. Duke's opening note, for instance, reflects his concern & alarm with Dr. Thompson's decision to go directly from Miami—once the doctors have confirmed his ability to function in normal air-pressures—to the harsh & politically volatile atmosphere in Washington, D.C. Unlike Duke, he seems blindly obsessed with the day-to-day details of the Watergate hearings . . . and what is also clear from this memo is that Dr. Thompson has maintained regular contact (despite all medical and physical realities, according to the doctors in charge of his Chamber in Miami) with his familiar, campaign trail allies, Tim Crouse and Ralph Steadman. An invoice received only yesterday from the manager of the Watergate Hotel indicates that somebody has reserved a top-floor river-view suite, under the names of "Thompson, Steadman & Crouse" . . . four adjoining rooms at $277 a day, with a long list of special equipment and an unlimited in-house expense authorization.

Needless to say, we will . . . but, why mention that now? The dumb buggers are already into it, and *something* is bound to emerge. We can save the bargaining for later . . .

—The Editors

DUKE MEMO No. 9, July 2, 1973

Gentlemen:

This will confirm my previous warnings in re: the dangerously unstable condition of Dr. Thompson, whose most recent communications leave no doubt in my mind that he still considers himself the National Affairs Editor of *Rolling Stone*—and in that capacity he has somehow made arrangements to fly immediately from Miami to Washington, upon his release, to "cover" the remaining episodes of the Watergate hearings. I have no idea what he really means by the word "cover"—but a phone-talk late last night with his doctors gave me serious pause. He will leave The Chamber at the end of this week, and he's talking in terms of "saturation coverage." According to the doctors, there is no way to communicate with him in The Chamber except by notes held up to the glass window—but I suspect he has a phone in there, because he has obviously communicated at length with Crouse, Steadman, Mankiewicz, and several others. A person resembling Crouse was seen loitering around The Chamber last Monday night around three thirty . . . and a call to Steadman's agent in London confirmed that Ralph has left his hide-out in the south of France and is booked on a Paris-Washington flight next Thursday, the day before Thompson's release.

Mankiewicz denies everything, as usual, but I talked to Sam Brown in Denver yesterday, and he said the word around Washington is that Frank is "acting very nervous" and also ordering Wild Turkey "by the case" from Chevy Chase Liquors. This indicates, to me, that Frank knows something. He has probably been talking to Crouse, but Tim's number in Boston won't answer, so I can't confirm anything there.

• • •

Dr. Squane, the Bends Specialist in Miami, says Thompson is "acceptably rational"—whatever that means—and that they have no reason to keep him in The Chamber beyond Friday. My insistence that he be returned at once to Colorado—under guard if necessary—has not been taken seriously in Miami. The bill for his stay in The Chamber—as you know—is already over $3,000, and they are not anxious to keep him there any longer than absolutely necessary. I got the impression, during my talk with Doc Squane last night, that Thompson's stay in The Chamber has been distinctly unpleasant for the staff. "I'll never understand why he didn't just wither up and die," Squane told me. "Only a *monster* could survive that kind of trauma."

I sensed disappointment in his voice, but I saw no point in arguing. We've been through this before, right? And it's always the same gig. My only concern for right now—as Thompson's de facto personal guardian—is to make sure he doesn't get involved in serious trouble, if he's serious about going to Washington.

Which he *is*, I suspect—and that means, if nothing else, that he'll be running up huge bills on the *Rolling Stone* tab. Whether or not he will write anything coherent is a moot point, I think, because *whatever* he writes—if anything—will necessarily be long out of date by the time it appears in print. Not even the *Washington Post* and the *New York Times*, which arrive daily (but three days late) out here in Woody Creek, can compete with the spontaneous, brain-boggling horrors belching constantly out of the TV set.

Last Saturday afternoon, for instance, I was sitting here very peacefully—minding the store, as it were—when the tube suddenly erupted with a genuinely *obscene* conversation between Mike Wallace and John Ehrlichman.

I was sitting on the porch with Gene Johnston—one of Dr. Thompson's old friends and ex-general manager of the Aspen *Wall Poster*—when Sandy called us inside to watch the show. Ehrlichman's face was so awful, so obviously mired in a lifetime of lies and lame treachery, that it was just about impossible to watch him in our twisted condition.

"Jesus Christ, *look* at him!" Johnston kept muttering. "Two months ago, that bastard was *running the country*." He opened a beer and whacked it down on the table. "I never want to hear the word 'paranoid' again, goddamn it! Not after seeing *that* face!" He reeled toward the front door, shaking his head and mumbling: "Goddamn! I can't *stand* it!"

I watched the whole thing, myself, but not without problems. It reminded me of *Last Exit to Brooklyn*—the rape of a bent whore—but I also knew Dr. Thompson was watching the show in Miami, and that it would fill him with venom & craziness. Whatever small hope we might have had of keeping him away from Washington during this crisis was burned to a cinder by the Wallace-Ehrlichman show. It had the effect of reinforcing Thompson's conviction that Nixon has cashed his check—and that possibility alone is enough to lure him to Washington for the death-watch.

My own prognosis is less drastic, at this point in time [*sic*], but it's also a fact that I've never been able to share The Doktor's obsessive political visions—for good or ill. My job has to do with nuts & bolts, not terminal vengeance. And it also occurs to me that there is nothing in the Watergate revelations, thus far, to convince anyone but a stone partisan fanatic that we will all be better off when it's finished. As I see it, we have already reaped the *real* benefits of this spectacle—the almost accidental castration of dehumanized power-mongers like Haldeman, Ehrlichman, and Tom Charles Huston, that vicious young jackal of a lawyer from Indianapolis that Nixon put in charge of the Special Domestic Intelligence operation.

Dumping thugs like these out of power for the next three years gives us all new room to breathe, for a while—which is just about all we can hope for, given the nature of the entrenched (Democratic) opposition. Nixon himself is no problem, now that all his ranking thugs have been neutralized. Just imagine what those bastards might have done, given three more years on their own terms.

Even a casual reading of White House memorandums in re: Domestic Subversives & Other White House Enemies (Bill Cosby, James Reston, Paul Newman, Joe Namath, et al.) is enough to queer the faith of any American less liberal than Mussolini. Here is a paragraph from one of his (September 21, 1970) memos to Harry "Bob" Haldeman:

"What we cannot do in a courtroom via criminal prosecutions to curtail the activities of some of these groups, IRS [the Internal Revenue Service] could do by administrative action. Moreover, valuable intelligence-type information could be turned up by IRS as a result of their field audits . . ."

Dr. Thompson—if he were with us & certifiably de-pressurized at this point in time—could offer some firsthand testimony about how the IRS and the Treasury Department were used, back in 1970, to work muscle on Ideological Enemies like himself . . . and if Thompson's account might be shrugged off as "biased," we can always compel the testimony of Aspen police chief Dick Richey, whose office safe still holds an illegal sawed-off shotgun belonging to a U.S. Treasury Department undercover agent from Denver who fucked up in his efforts to convince Dr. Thompson that he should find a quick reason for dropping out of electoral politics. That incident came up the other afternoon at the Jerome Bar in Aspen, when Steve Levine, a young reporter from Denver, observed that "Thompson was one of the original victims of the Watergate syndrome—but nobody recognized it then; they called it paranoia."

Right . . . But that's another story, and we'll leave it for The Doktor to tell. After three months in the Decompression Chamber, he will doubtless be cranked up to the fine peaks of frenzy. His "Watergate notes from The Chamber" show a powerful, brain-damaged kind of zeal that will hopefully be brought under control in the near future . . . and I'm enclosing some of them here, as crude evidence to show he's still functioning, despite the tragic handicap that comes with a bad case of the bends.

In closing, I remain . . . Yrs. in Fear & Loathing:
Raoul Duke, Spts. Ed

Editor's note: What follows is the unfinished midsection of Dr. Thompson's Notes from the Decompression Chamber. This section was written in his notebook on the day after convicted Watergate burglar James McCord's appearance before the Ervin committee on national TV. It was transcribed by a nurse who copied Dr. Thompson's notes as he held them up, page by page, through the pressure-sealed window of his Chamber. It is not clear, from the text, whether he deliberately wrote this section with a "Woody Creek, Colorado," dateline, or whether he planned to be there by the time it was printed.

In either case, he was wrong. His case of the bends was severe, almost fatal. And even upon his release there is no real certainty of recovery. He might have to reenter the Decompression Chamber at any time, if he suffers a relapse.

None of which has any bearing on what follows—which was published exactly as he wrote it in The Chamber:

Jesus, where will it end? Yesterday I turned on my TV set—hungry for some decent upbeat news—and here was an ex–Army Air Force colonel with nineteen years in the CIA under his belt admitting that he'd willfully turned himself into a common low-life burglar because he thought the attorney general and the president of the U.S. had more or less *ordered* him to. Ex-colonel McCord felt he had a duty to roam around the country burglarizing offices and ransacking private/personal files—because the security of the U.S.A. was at stake.

Indeed, we were in serious trouble last year—and for five or six years before that, if you believe the muck those two vicious and irresponsible young punks at the *Washington Post* have raked up.

"Impeachment" is an ugly word, they say. *Newsweek* columnist Shana

Alexander says "all but the vulture-hearted want to believe him ignorant." A week earlier, Ms. Alexander wrote a "love letter" to Martha Mitchell: "You are in the best tradition of American womanhood, defending your country, your flag . . . but most of all, defending your man."

Well . . . shucks. I can hardly choke back the tears . . . and where does that leave Pat Nixon, who apparently went on a world cruise under a different name the day after McCord pulled the plug and wrote that devastating letter to Judge Sirica.

The public prints—and especially *Newsweek*—are full of senile gibberish these days. Stewart Alsop wakes up in a cold sweat every morning at the idea that Congress might be forced to impeach "the president."

For an answer to that, we can look to Hubert Humphrey—from one of the nine speeches he made during his four-and-a-half-hour campaign for Democratic candidate George McGovern in the waning weeks of last November's presidential showdown—Humphrey was talking to a crowd of hard hats in S.F., as I recall, and he said, "My friends, we're not talking about reelecting the president—we're talking about reelecting Richard Nixon."

Even a blind pig finds an acorn now and then. Humphrey's voice just belched out of my radio, demanding that we *get to the bottom of this Watergate mess*, but meanwhile we have to make sure the Ruskies understand that we all stand firmly behind the president.

Right. As far behind him as possible, if GOP standard-bearers like B. Goldwater and Hugh Scott are any measure of the party's allegiance to the frightened unprincipled little shyster they were calling—when they nominated him for re-canonization ten months ago in Miami—"one of the greatest presidents in American History." We will want those tapes for posterity because we won't hear their like again—from Scott, Goldwater, Duke Wayne, Martha, Sammy Davis, Senator Percy, or anyone else. Not even George Meany will join a foursome with Richard Nixon these days. The hallowed halls of the White House no longer echo with the happy sound of bouncing golf balls. Or footballs either, for that matter . . . or any other kind.

The hard-nosed super-executives Nixon chose to run this country for us turned on each other like rats in a slumfire when the first signs of trouble appeared. What we have seen in the past few weeks is the incredible spectacle of a president of the United States either firing or being hastily abandoned by all of his hired hands and cronies—all the people who put him where he is today, in fact, and now that they're gone he seems helpless. Some of his closest "friends" and advisers are headed for prison, his once-helpless Democratic Congress is verging on mutiny, the threat of impeachment looms closer every day, and his coveted "place in history" is even now being etched out in acid by eager Harvard historians.

Six months ago Richard Nixon was Zeus himself, calling firebombs and shitrains down on friend and foe alike—the most powerful man in the world, for a while—but all that is gone now, and nothing he can do will ever bring a hint of it back. Richard Nixon's seventh crisis will be his last. He will go down with Harding and Grant as one of America's classically rotten presidents.

Which is exactly what he deserves—and if saying that makes me "one of the vulture-hearted," by Ms. Alexander's lights . . . well . . . I think I can live with it. My grandmother was one of those stunned old ladies who cried when the Duke of Windsor quit the Big Throne to marry an American commoner back in 1936. She didn't know the Duke or anything about him. But she knew—along with millions of other old ladies and closet monarchists—that a Once and Future King had a duty to keep up the act. She wept for her lost illusions—for the same reason Stewart Alsop and Shana Alexander will weep tomorrow if President Richard M. Nixon is impeached and put on trial by the U.S. Senate.

Our congressmen will do everything possible to avoid it, because most of them have a deep and visceral sympathy, however denied and reluctant, for the "tragic circumstances" that led Richard Nixon to what even Evans and Novak call "the brink of ruin." The loyal opposition has not distinguished itself in the course of this long-running nightmare. Even Nixon's oldest enemies are lying low, leaving the dirty work to hired lawyers and faceless investigators. Senators Kennedy, McGovern, and Fulbright are strangely silent, while Humphrey babbles nonsense and Muskie hoards his energy for beating back personal attacks by Strom Thurmond. The only politicians talking publicly about the dire implications of the Watergate iceberg are those who can't avoid it—the four carefully selected eunuch/Democrats on the Senate Select Investigating Committee and a handful of panicked Republicans up for reelection in 1974.

The slow-rising central horror of "Watergate" is not that it might grind down to the reluctant impeachment of a vengeful thug of a president whose entire political career has been a monument to the same kind of cheap shots and treachery he finally got nailed for, but that we might somehow fail to learn something from it.

Already—with the worst news yet to come—there is an ominous tide of public opinion that says whatever Nixon and his small gang of henchmen and hired gunsels might have done, it was probably no worse than what other politicians have been doing all along, and still are.

Anybody who really believes this is a fool—but a lot of people seem to, and that evidence is hard to ignore. What almost happened here—and what was only avoided because the men who made Nixon president and who were running the country in his name knew in their hearts that they were all mean, hollow little bastards who couldn't dare turn their backs on each other—was a takeover and total perversion of the American political process by a gang of cold-blooded fixers so incompetent that they couldn't even pull off a simple burglary . . . which tends to explain, among other things, why twenty-five thousand young Americans died for no reason in Vietnam while Nixon and his brain trust were trying to figure out how to admit the whole thing was a mistake from the start.

Fear and Loathing at the Watergate: Mr. Nixon Has Cashed His Check

September 27, 1973

I have just finished making out a report addressed to somebody named Charles R. Roach, a claims examiner at the Mid-Atlantic Regional Headquarters of Avis Rent a Car in Arlington, Virginia. It has to do with a minor accident that occurred on Connecticut Avenue, in downtown Washington, shortly after George [McGovern] and his wife had bade farewell to the last staggering guests at the party he'd given on a hot summer night in July commemorating the first anniversary of his seizure of the presidential nomination in Miami.

The atmosphere of the party itself had been amazingly loose and pleasant. Two hundred people had been invited—twice that many showed up—to celebrate what history will record, with at least a few asterisks, as one of the most disastrous presidential campaigns in American history. Midway in the evening I was standing on the patio, talking to Carl Wagner and Holly Mankiewicz, when the phone began ringing and whoever answered it came back with the news that President Nixon had just been admitted to the nearby Bethesda Naval Hospital with what was officially announced as "viral pneumonia."

Nobody believed it, of course. High-powered journalists like Jack Germond and Jules Witcover immediately seized the phones to find out what was *really* wrong with Nixon . . . but the rest of us, no longer locked into deadlines or the fast-rising terrors of some tomorrow's Election Day, merely shrugged at the news and kept on drinking. There was nothing unusual, we felt, about Nixon caving in to some real or even psychosomatic illness. And if the truth was worse than the news . . . well . . . there would be nothing unusual about that either.

One of the smallest and noisiest contingents among the two hundred invited guests was the handful of big-time journalists who'd spent most of last autumn dogging McGovern's every lame footstep along the campaign trail, while two third-string police reporters from the *Washington Post* were quietly putting together the biggest political story of 1972 or any other year—a story that had already exploded, by the time of McGovern's "anniversary" party, into a scandal that has even now burned a big hole for itself in every American history textbook written from 1973 till infinity.

• • •

One of the most extraordinary aspects of the Watergate story has been the way the press has handled it: what began in the summer of 1972 as one of the great media-bungles of the century has developed, by now, into what is probably the most thoroughly and most professionally covered story in the history of American journalism.

When I boomed into Washington last month to meet Steadman and set up the National Affairs desk once again, I expected—or in retrospect, I *think* I expected—to find the high-rolling *news-meisters* of the capital press corps jabbering blindly among themselves, once again, in some stylish sector of reality far-removed from the Main Nerve of "the story" . . . like climbing aboard Ed Muskie's Sunshine Special in the Florida primary and finding every media star in the nation sipping Bloody Marys and convinced they were riding the rails to Miami with "the candidate" . . . or sitting down to lunch at the Sioux Falls Holiday Inn on Election Day with a half-dozen of the heaviest press wizards and coming away convinced that McGovern couldn't possibly lose by more than 10 points.

My experience on the campaign trail in 1972 had not filled me with a real sense of awe, vis-à-vis the wisdom of the national press corps . . . so I was seriously jolted when I arrived in Washington to find that the bastards had this Watergate story nailed up and bleeding from every extremity—from "Watergate" and all its twisted details, to ITT, the Vesco case, Nixon's lies about the financing for his San Clemente beach-mansion, and even the long-dormant "Agnew Scandal."

There was not a hell of a lot of room for a Gonzo Journalist to operate in that high-tuned atmosphere. For the first time in memory, the

Washington press corps was working very close to the peak of its awesome but normally dormant potential. The *Washington Post* has a half dozen of the best reporters in America working every tangent of the Watergate story like wild-eyed junkies set adrift, with no warning, to find their next connection. The *New York Times*, badly blitzed on the story at first, called in hot rods from its bureaus all over the country to overcome the *Post*'s early lead. Both *Time*'s and *Newsweek*'s Washington bureaus began scrambling feverishly to find new angles, new connections, new leaks, and leads in this story that was unraveling so fast that *nobody* could stay on top of it . . . And especially not the three (or four) TV networks, whose whole machinery was geared to visual/action stories rather than skillfully planted tips from faceless lawyers who called on private phones and then refused to say anything at all in front of the cameras.

The only standard-brand visual "action" in the Watergate story had happened at the very beginning—when the burglars were caught in the act by a squad of plain-clothes cops with drawn guns—and that happened so fast that there was not even a still photographer on hand, much less a TV camera.

The network news moguls are not hungry for stories involving weeks of dreary investigation and minimum camera possibilities—particularly at a time when almost every ranking TV correspondent in the country was assigned to one aspect or another of a presidential campaign that was still boiling feverishly when the Watergate break-in occurred on June 17. The Miami conventions and the Eagleton fiasco kept the Watergate story backstage all that summer. Both the networks and the press had their "first teams" out on the campaign trail until long after the initial indictments—Liddy, Hunt, McCord, et al.—on September 15. And by Election Day in November, the Watergate story seemed like old news.

It was rarely if ever mentioned among the press people following the campaign. A burglary at the Democratic National Headquarters seemed relatively minor compared to the action in Miami. It was a "local" (Washington) story, and the "local staff" was handling it . . . but I *had* no local staff, so I made the obvious choice.

Except on two occasions, and the first of these still haunts me. On the night of June 17, I spent most of the evening in the Watergate Hotel:

from about eight o'clock until ten I was swimming laps in the indoor pool, and from ten thirty until a bit after one I was drinking tequila in the Watergate bar with Tom Quinn, a sports columnist for the now-defunct *Washington Daily News.*

Meanwhile, upstairs in room 214, Hunt and Liddy were already monitoring the break-in, by walkie-talkie, with ex-FBI agent Alfred Baldwin in his well-equipped spy-nest across Virginia Avenue in room 419 of the Howard Johnson's Motor Lodge. Jim McCord had already taped the locks on two doors just underneath the bar in the Watergate garage, and it was probably just about the time that Quinn and I called for our last round of tequila that McCord and his team of Cubans moved into action—and got busted less than an hour later.

All this was happening less than one hundred yards from where we were sitting in the bar, sucking limes and salt with our Sauza Gold and muttering darkly about the fate of Duane Thomas and the pigs who run the National Football League.

• • •

Neither Bob Woodward nor Carl Bernstein from the *Post* were invited to McGovern's party that night—which was fitting, because the guest list was limited to those who had lived through the day-to-day nightmare of the '72 campaign . . . People like Frank Mankiewicz, Miles Rubin, Rick Stearns, Gary Hart, and even *Newsweek* correspondent Dick Stout, whose final dispatch on the doomed McGovern campaign very nearly got him thrown out of the Dakota Queen II at thirty thousand feet over Lincoln, Nebraska, on the day before the election.

This was the crowd that had gathered that night in July to celebrate his last victory before the Great Disaster—the slide that began with Eagleton and ended, incredibly, with "Watergate." The events of the past six months had so badly jangled the nerves of the invited guests—the staffers and journalists who had been with McGovern from New Hampshire all the way to Sioux Falls on Election Day—that nobody really wanted to go to the party, for fear that it might be a funeral and a serious bummer.

By the end of the evening, when the two dozen bitter-enders had forced McGovern to break out his own private stock—ignoring the departure of the caterers and the dousing of the patio lights—the bulk of the conversation was focused on which one or ones of the Secret Service men assigned to protect McGovern had been reporting daily to Jeb Magruder at CREEP (the Committee for the Re-election of the President), and which one of the ten or twelve journalists with access to the innards of George's strategy had been on CREEP's payroll at $1,500 a month. This journalist—still publicly unknown and un-denounced—was referred to in White House memos as "Chapman's Friend," a mysterious designation that puzzled the whole Washington press corps until one of the president's beleaguered ex-aides explained privately that "Chapman" is a name Nixon used, from time to time, in the good old days when he was able to travel around obscure Holiday Inns under phony names . . .

R. Chapman, Pepsi-Cola salesman, New York City . . . with a handful of friends carrying walkie-talkies and wearing white leather shoulder-holsters . . . But what the hell? Just send a case of Pepsi up to the suite, my man, and don't ask questions; your reward will come later—call the White House and ask for Howard Hunt or Jim McCord; they'll take care of you.

Right. Or maybe Tex Colson, who is slowly and surely emerging as the guiding light behind Nixon's whole arsenal of illegal, immoral, and unethical "black advance" or "dirty tricks" department. It was Colson who once remarked that he would "walk over his grandmother for Richard Nixon" . . . and it was Colson who hired head "plumber" Egil "Bud" Krogh, who in 1969 told Daniel X. Friedman, chairman of the psychiatry department at the University of Chicago: "Anyone who opposes us, we'll destroy. As a matter of fact, anyone who doesn't support us, we'll destroy."

Colson, the only one of Nixon's top command to so far evade Watergate's legal noose, is the man who once told White House cop Jack Caulfield to put a firebomb in the offices of the staid/liberal Brookings Institution, in order to either steal or destroy some documents he considered incriminating. Colson now says he was "only joking" about the firebomb plan, but Caulfield took it so seriously that he went to then White House counsel John Dean and said he refused to work with Colson any longer, because he was "crazy."

• • •

Crazy? Tex Colson?

Never in hell. "He's the meanest man in American politics," says Nixon's speechwriter Pat Buchanan, smiling lazily over the edge of a beer can beside the pool outside his Watergate apartment. Buchanan is one of the few people in the Nixon administration with a sense of humor. He is so far to the right that he dismisses Tex Colson as a "Massachusetts liberal." But for some reason, Buchanan is also one of the few people—perhaps the only one—on Nixon's staff who has friends at the other end of the political spectrum. At one point during the campaign I mentioned Buchanan at McGovern headquarters, for some reason, and Rick Stearns, perhaps the most hardline left-bent ideologue on McGovern's staff, sort of chuckled and said, "Oh yeah, we're pretty good friends. Pat's the only one of those bastards over there with any principles." When I mentioned this to another McGovern staffer, he snapped: "Yeah, maybe so . . . like Joseph Goebbels had principles."

My own relationship with Buchanan goes back to the New Hampshire primary in 1968 when Nixon was still on the dim fringes of his political comeback. We spent about eight hours one night in a Boston hotel room, finishing off a half gallon of Old Crow and arguing savagely about politics: as I recall, I kept asking him why a person who seemed to have good sense would be hanging around with Nixon. It was clear even then that Buchanan considered me stone crazy, and my dismissal of Nixon as a hopeless bum with no chance of winning anything seemed to amuse him more than anything else.

About eight months later, after one of the strangest and most brutal years in American history, Richard Nixon was president and Pat Buchanan was one of his top two speechwriters along with Ray Price, the house moderate. I didn't see Pat again until the McGovern campaign in '72 when Ron Ziegler refused to have me on the Nixon press plane, and Buchanan intervened to get me past the White House guard and into what turned out to be a dull and useless seat on the plane with the rest of the White House press corps. It was also Buchanan who interviewed Garry Wills, introducing him into the Nixon campaign of 1968—an act of principle that resulted in an extremely unfriendly book called *Nixon Agonistes*.

So it seemed entirely logical, I thought—going back to Washington in the midst of this stinking Watergate summer—to call Buchanan and see if he felt like having thirteen or fourteen drinks on some afternoon when he wasn't at the White House working feverishly in what he calls "the bunker." Price and Buchanan write almost everything Nixon says, and they are busier than usual these days, primarily figuring out what *not* to say. I spent most of one Saturday afternoon with Pat lounging around a tin umbrella table beside the Watergate pool and talking lazily about politics in general. When I called him at the White House the day before, the first thing he said was "Yeah, I just finished your book."

"Oh Jesus," I replied, thinking this naturally meant the end of any relationship we'd ever have. But he laughed. "Yeah, it's one of the funniest things I've ever read."

One of the first things I asked him that afternoon was something that had been simmering in my head for at least a year or so, and that was how he could feel comfortable with strange friends like me and Rick Stearns, and particularly how he could possibly feel comfortable sitting out in the open—in plain sight of the whole Watergate crowd—with a known monster whose affection for Richard Nixon was a matter of fairly brutal common knowledge—or how he felt comfortable playing poker once or twice a week sometimes with Rick Stearns, whose political views are almost as diametrically opposed to Buchanan's as mine are. He shrugged it off with a grin, opening another beer. "Oh, well, we ideologues seem to get along better than the others. I don't agree with Rick on anything at all that I can think of, but I like him and I respect his honesty."

A strange notion, the far left and far right finding some kind of odd common ground beside the Watergate pool, and particularly when one of them is a top Nixon speechwriter, spending most of his time trying to keep the Boss from sinking like a stone in foul water, yet now and then laughingly referring to the White House as The Bunker.

After the sixth or seventh beer, I told him about our abortive plot several nights earlier to seize Colson out of his house and drag him down Pennsylvania Avenue tied behind a huge gold Oldsmobile Cutlass. He laughed and said something to the effect that "Colson's so tough, he might like it." And then, talking further about Colson, he said, "But you know he's not really a conservative."

And that's what seems to separate the two GOP camps, like it separates Barry Goldwater from Richard Nixon. Very much like the difference between the Humphrey Democrats and the McGovern Democrats. The ideological wing versus the pragmatists, and by Buchanan's standards, it's doubtful that he even considers Richard Nixon a conservative.

My strange and violent reference to Colson seemed to amuse him more than anything else. "I want to be very clear on one thing," I assured him. "If you're thinking about having me busted for conspiracy on this, remember that I've already deliberately dragged you into it." He laughed again and then mentioned something about the "one overt act" necessary for a conspiracy charge, and I quickly said that I had no idea where Tex Colson even lived and didn't really want to know, so that even if we'd wanted to drag the vicious bastard down Pennsylvania Avenue at sixty miles per hour behind a gold Oldsmobile Cutlass, we had no idea, that night, where to find him, and about halfway into the plot we crashed into a black and gold Cadillac on Connecticut Avenue and drew a huge mob of angry blacks who ended all thought of taking vengeance on Colson. It was all I could do to get out of that scene without getting beaten like a gong for the small crease our rented Cutlass had put in the fender of the Cadillac.

• • •

Which brings us back to that accident report I just wrote and sent off to Mr. Roach at Avis Mid-Atlantic Headquarters in Arlington. The accident occurred about three thirty in the morning when either Warren Beatty or Pat Caddell opened the door of a gold Oldsmobile Cutlass I'd rented at Dulles airport earlier that day, and banged the door against the fender of a massive black & gold Cadillac roadster parked in front of a late-night restaurant on Connecticut Avenue called Anna Maria's. It seemed like a small thing at the time, but in retrospect it might have spared us all—including McGovern—an extremely nasty episode.

Because somewhere in the late hours of that evening, when the drink had taken hold and people were jabbering loosely about anything that came into their heads, somebody mentioned that "the worst and most vicious" of Nixon's backstairs White House hit men—Charles "Tex" Colson—was probably the only one of the dozen or more Nixon/

CREEP functionaries thus far sucked into "the Watergate scandal" who was not likely to do any time, or even be indicted.

It was a long, free-falling conversation, with people wandering in and out, over a time span of an hour or so—journalists, pols, spectators—and the focus of it, as I recall, was a question that I was trying to get some bets on: How many of the primary Watergate figures would actually serve time in prison?

The reactions ranged from my own guess that only Magruder and Dean would live long enough to serve time in prison, to Mankiewicz's flat assertion that "everybody except Colson" would be indicted, convicted, sentenced, and actually hauled off to prison.

(Everybody involved in this conversation will no doubt deny any connection with it—or even hearing about it, for that matter—but what the hell? It did, in fact, take place over the course of some two or three days, in several locations, but the seed of the speculation took root in the final early morning hours of McGovern's party . . . although I don't remember that George himself was involved or even within earshot at any time. He has finally come around to the point where his friends don't mind calling him "George" in the friendly privacy of his own home, but that is not quite the same thing as getting him involved in a felony-conspiracy/attempted murder charge that some wild-eyed, Nixon-appointed geek in the Justice Department might try to crank up on the basis of a series of boozy conversations among journalists, politicians, and other half-drunk cynics. Anybody who has spent any time around late-night motel bars with the press corps on a presidential campaign knows better than to take their talk seriously . . . but after reading reviews of my book on the '72 campaign, it occurs to me that some people will believe almost *anything* that fits their preconceived notions.)

And so much for all that.

• • •

What will Nixon do now? That is the question that has every Wizard in Washington hanging by his or her fingernails—from the bar of the National Press Club to the redwood sauna in the Senate gymnasium to the hundreds of high-powered cocktail parties in suburbs like Bethesda, McLean, Arlington, Cabin John, and especially in the leafy white ghetto of the district's northwest quadrant. You can wander into Nathans tavern at the corner of M Street & Wisconsin in Georgetown and get an argument about "Nixon's strategy" without even mentioning the subject. All you have to do is stand at the bar, order a Bass ale, and look interested: the hassle will take care of itself; the very air in Washington is electric with the vast implications of "Watergate."

Thousands of big-money jobs depend on what Nixon does next; on what Archibald Cox has in mind; on whether "Uncle Sam's" TV hearings will resume full-bore after Labor Day, or be either telescoped or terminated like Nixon says they should be.

The smart money says the "Watergate hearings," as such, are effectively over—not only because Nixon is preparing to mount a popular crusade against them, but because every elected politician in Washington is afraid of what the Ervin committee has already scheduled for the "third phase" of the hearings.

Phase Two, as originally planned, would focus on "dirty tricks"—a colorful, shocking, and essentially minor area of inquiry, but one with plenty of action and a guaranteed audience appeal. A long and serious look at the "dirty tricks" aspect of national campaigning would be a death-blow to the daily soap-opera syndrome that apparently grips most of the nation's housewives. The cast of characters, and the twisted tales they could tell, would shame every soap-opera scriptwriter in America.

Phase Three, campaign financing, is the one both the White House and the Senate would prefer to avoid—and, given this mutual distaste for exposing the public to the realities of campaign financing, this is the phase of the Watergate hearings most likely to be cut from the schedule. "Jesus Christ," said one Ervin committee investigator, "we'll have *Fortune*'s 500 in that chair, and every one of those bastards will take at least one congressman or senator down with him."

• • •

The axis of Nixon's new and perhaps final strategy began to surface with the first mention of "the tapes," and it has developed with the inevitability of either desperation or inspired strategy ever since. The key question is whether the "constitutional crisis" Nixon seems determined to bring down on himself by forcing the Tape Issue all the way to the Supreme Court is a crisis that was genuinely forced on him by accident—or whether it is a masterpiece of legal cynicism that bubbled up at some midnight hour many weeks ago from the depths of attorney John Wilson's legendary legal mind.

The conventional press wisdom—backed up by what would normally be considered "good evidence," or at least reliable leaks from the Ervin committee—holds that the existence of the presidential tapes & the fact that Nixon has been systematically bugging every conversation he's ever had with anybody, in any of his offices, ever since he got elected, was a secret that was only unearthed by luck, shrewdness, and high-powered sleuth-work. According to unofficial but consistently reliable sources, Alex Butterfield—current head of the Federal Aviation Administration and former "chief for internal security" at the White House—was privately interviewed "more or less on a hunch" by Ervin committee investigators, and during the course of this interview talked himself into such an untenable position while trying to explain the verbatim-accuracy of some Oval Office logs that he finally caved in and spilled the whole story about Nixon's taping apparatus.

According to one of the investigators who conducted the private interview—in the ground-floor bowels of the Ervin committee's "boiler room" in the Old Senate Office Building—Butterfield couldn't explain why the logs of Nixon's conversations in his own office were so precise that they included pauses, digressions, half sentences, and even personal speech patterns.

"When I finally asked him if maybe these logs had been transcribed from tapes," said the investigator, "he sort of slumped back in his chair and said, 'I wish you hadn't asked me that.' And then he told us the whole thing."

• • •

I was sitting in the hearing room about twenty-four hours later when word began buzzing around the press tables, just before lunch, that the next person to face the committee would be an unscheduled "mystery witness"—instead of Nixon's personal attorney, Herbert Kalmbach, who was officially scheduled to appear when Ervin and his cohorts came back from lunch. I walked across the street to the air-conditioned bar in the Capitol Hill Hotel and heard some of the press people speculating about a man named Alex Butterfield who was going to tell the committee that Nixon had made tape recordings of all the disputed conversations referred to in John Dean's testimony.

"Well, that should just about wrap it up," somebody said.

"Bullshit," said another voice. "He'll burn those tapes before he gives them to Ervin."

"Why?"

"Shit, if he thought they'd be any good to him, the committee would have had them a long time ago. [J. Fred] Buzhardt would have turned them over personally to Sam Dash five minutes after Dean finished reading his opening statement."

The conversation rambled on, punctuated by the arrival of beer and sandwiches. The only other comment that sticks in my head from that lunch break before Butterfield came on was a rumor that the "mystery witness" had been "dug up" by staffers on the *Republican* side of the Ervin committee. It hardly seemed worth wondering about at the time . . . but that was before either Butterfield or Haldeman had testified about the tapes, and also before Nixon's carefully considered announcement that he couldn't release the tapes to anybody—despite subpoenas from both the Ervin committee and the special prosecutor—for fear of undermining the whole foundation of American government.

The president has made it absolutely clear that he has no intention of releasing those tapes—not even to an elite panel of judges who would hear them in strict privacy to determine their relevance—unless the U.S. Supreme Court compels him to do so, with a "definitive order."

• • •

The reelection of Mr. Nixon, followed so quickly by the Watergate revelations, has compelled the country to re-examine the reality of our electoral process . . .

> *The unraveling of the whole White House tangle of involvement has come about largely by a series of fortuitous events, many of them unlikely in a different political context. Without these events, the*

cover-up might have continued indefinitely, even if a Democratic administration vigorously pursued the truth . . .

In the wake of Watergate may come more honest and thorough campaign reform than in the aftermath of a successful presidential campaign which stood for such reform. I suspect that after viewing the abuses of the past, voters in the future will insist on full and open debate between the candidates and on frequent, no-holds-barred press conferences for all candidates, and especially the President.

And I suspect the Congress will respond to the fact that Watergate happened with legislation to assure that Watergate never happens again. Today the prospects for further restrictions on private campaign financing, full disclosure of the personal finances of the candidates, and public finance of all federal campaigns seem to me better than ever—and even better than if a new Democratic administration had urged such steps in early 1973. We did urge them in 1972, but it took the Nixon landslide and the Watergate exposé to make the point.

I believe there were great gains that came from the pain of defeat in 1972. We proved a campaign could be honestly financed. We reaffirmed that a campaign could be open in its conduct and decent in its motivation. We made the Democratic party a place for people as well as politicians. And perhaps in losing we gained the greatest victory of all—that Americans now perceive, far better than a new President could have persuaded them, what is precious about our principles and what we must do to preserve them. The nation now sees itself through the prism of Watergate and the Nixon landslide; at last, perhaps, we see through a glass clearly.

Because of all this, it is possible that by 1976, the 200th anniversary of America's birth, there will be a true rebirth of patriotism; that we will not only know our ideals but live them; that democracy may once again become a conviction we keep and not just a description we apply to ourselves. And if the McGovern campaign advanced that hope, even in defeat, then, as I said on election night last November, "Every minute and every hour and every bone-crushing effort . . . was worth the entire sacrifice."

—George McGovern in the Washington Post, August 12, 1973

Jesus . . . Sunday morning in Woody Creek, and here's McGovern on the minitube beside my typewriter, looking and talking almost exactly like he was in those speedy weeks between the Wisconsin and Ohio primaries, when his star was rising so fast that he could barely hang onto it. The sense of *déjà vu* is almost frightening: here is McGovern speaking sharply *against the system*, once again, in response to questions from CBS's Connie Chung and Marty Nolan from the *Boston Globe*, two of the most ever-present reporters on the '72 campaign trail . . . and McGovern, brought back from the dead by a political miracle of sorts, is hitting the first gong of doom for the man who made him a landslide loser nine months ago: "When that [judicial] process is complete and the Supreme Court rules that the president must turn over the tapes—and he refuses to do so—I think the Congress will have no recourse but to seriously consider impeachment."

Cazart! The fat is approaching the fire—very slowly, and in very cautious hands, but there is no ignoring the general drift of things. Sometime between now and the end of 1973, Richard Nixon may have to bite that bullet he's talked about for so long. Seven is a lucky number for gamblers, but not for fixers, and Nixon's seventh crisis is beginning to put his first six in very deep shade. Even the most conservative betting in Washington these days has Nixon either resigning or being impeached by the autumn of '74—if not for reasons directly connected to the "Watergate scandal," then because of his inability to explain how he paid for his beach-mansion at San Clemente, or why Vice President Agnew—along with most of Nixon's original White House command staff—is under indictment for felonies ranging from extortion and perjury to burglary and obstruction of justice.

Another good bet in Washington—running at odds between two and three to one, these days—is that Nixon will crack both physically and mentally under all this pressure, and develop a serious psychosomatic illness of some kind: maybe another bad case of pneumonia.

This is not so wild a vision as it might sound—not even in the context of my own known taste for fantasy and savage bias in politics. Richard Nixon, a career politician who has rarely failed to crack under genuine pressure, is under more pressure now than most of us will ever understand. His whole life is turning to shit, just as he reached the pinnacle . . . and every once in a while, caving in to a weakness that blooms in the cool, thinking hours around dawn, I have to admit that I feel a touch of irrational sympathy for the bastard. Not as The President: a broken little bully who would sacrifice us all to save himself—if he still had the choice—but the same kind of sympathy I might feel, momentarily, for a vicious cheap-shot linebacker whose long career comes to a sudden end one Sunday afternoon when some rookie flanker shatters both his knees with a savage crackback block.

Cheap-shot artists don't last very long in pro football. To cripple another person intentionally is to violate the same kind of code as the legendary "honor among thieves."

More linebackers than thieves believe this, but when it comes to politics—to a twenty-eight-year career of cheap shots, lies, and thievery—there is no man in America who should understand what is happening to him now better than Richard Milhous Nixon. He is a living monument to the old army rule that says: "The only *real* crime is getting caught."

This is not the first time Richard Nixon has been caught. After his failed campaign for the governorship of California in 1962 he was formally convicted—along with H. R. Haldeman, Maurice Stans, Murray Chotiner, Herb Klein, and Herb Kalmbach for almost exactly the same kind of crudely illegal campaign tactics that he stands accused of today.

But this time, in the language of the sergeants who keep military tradition alive, "he got caught every which way" . . . and "his ass went into the blades."

Not many people have ever written in the English language better than a Polack with a twisted sense of humor who called himself Joseph Conrad. And if he were with us today, I think he'd be getting a fine boot out of this Watergate story. Mr. Kurtz, in Conrad's *Heart of Darkness*, did his thing.

Mr. Nixon also did his thing.

And now, just as surely as Kurtz, "Mistah Nixon, he dead."

Letter from JSW to HST

March 7, 1973

Hunter:

1) Re-edit "The End of the Campaign Trail For Now" plus a 250 word introduction immediately. Due no later than March 12.

2) "Dr. Thompson's first-hand guide to motorcycles." Due April 23. (Remember, you must immediately send me a marked-up copy of one or two motorcycle magazines so I can set up all the demonstrations for you in L.A. right after the Yorty piece.)

3) "Sam Yorty vs The Powers of Evil" (first look at the L.A. Mayor race) Due April 9 (issue 134, expect 2500–4000 words—a column).

4) The L.A. Mayors Race—feature article due June 4 (138).

5) The N.Y. Mayors Race (long column or feature article). Due June 18 (139).

In addition I expect you to be looking into two other pieces for feature treatment:

1) The Rev. Ike
2) Professional Wrestling

Further, I would like you to let me know when you think you would like to do a long piece (or series) on Texas so I can begin to work out a schedule with Ralph Steadman. I would like the Texas article to be one or two of the leading features this fall. Please confirm.

Jann

Editor's note: None of these assignments came to fruition.

Fear and Loathing at the Super Bowl

February 28, 1974

. . . and whosoever was not found written into the book of life was cast into the lake of fire . . .

—Revelations 20:15

This was the theme of the sermon I delivered off the twentieth-floor balcony of the Hyatt Regency in Houston on the morning of Super Bowl VIII. It was just before dawn, as I recall, when the urge to speak came on me. Earlier that day I had found—on the tile floor of the men's room on the hotel mezzanine—a religious comic book titled *A Demon's Nightmare*, and it was from the text of this sleazy tract that I chose the words of my sermon.

The Houston Hyatt Regency—like others designed by architect John Portman in Atlanta and San Francisco—is a stack of one thousand rooms, built around a vast lobby at least thirty stories high, with a revolving "spindletop" bar on the roof. The whole center of the building is a tower of acoustical space. You can walk out of any room and look over the indoor balcony (twenty floors down, in my case) at the palm-shrouded, wood and naugahyde maze of the bar/lounge on the lobby floor.

Closing time in Houston is two o'clock. There are after-hours bars, but the Hyatt Regency is not one of them. So—when I was seized by the urge to deliver my sermon at dawn—there were only about twenty ant-sized people moving around in the lobby far below.

Earlier, before the bar closed, the whole ground floor had been jammed with drunken sportswriters, hard-eyed hookers, wandering geeks and hustlers (of almost every persuasion), and a legion of big and small gamblers from all over the country who roamed through the drunken, randy crowd—as casually as possible—with an eye to picking up a last-minute sucker bet from some poor bastard half mad on booze and willing to put some money, preferably four or five big ones, on "his boys."

The spread, in Houston, was Miami by 6, but by midnight on Saturday almost every one of the two thousand or so drunks in the lobby of the Regency—official headquarters and media vortex for this eighth annual Super Bowl—was absolutely sure about what was going to happen when the deal went down on Sunday, about two miles east of the hotel on the fog-soaked artificial turf of Rice University Stadium.

• • •

Ah . . . but wait! Why are we talking about gamblers here? Or thousands of hookers and drunken sportswriters jammed together in a seething mob in the lobby of a Houston hotel?

And what kind of sick and twisted impulse would cause a professional sportswriter to deliver a sermon from the book of Revelations off his hotel balcony on the dawn of Super Sunday?

I had not planned a sermon for that morning. I had not even planned to be in Houston, for that matter . . . But now, looking back on that outburst, I see a certain inevitability about it. Probably it was a crazed and futile effort to somehow explain the extremely twisted nature of my relationship with God, Nixon, and the National Football League: the three had long since become inseparable in my mind, a sort of unholy trinity that had caused me more trouble and personal anguish in the past few months than Ron Ziegler, Hubert Humphrey, and Peter Sheridan all together had caused me in a year on the campaign trail.

Or perhaps it had something to do with my admittedly deep-seated need to have public revenge on Al Davis, general manager of the Oakland Raiders . . . Or maybe an overweening desire to confess that I had been wrong, from the start, to have ever agreed with Richard Nixon about *anything*, and especially pro football.

In any case, it was apparently something I'd been cranking myself up to deliver for quite a while . . . and, for reasons I still can't be sure of, the eruption finally occurred on the dawn of Super Sunday.

I howled at the top of my lungs for almost thirty minutes, raving and screeching about all those who would soon be cast into the lake of fire for a variety of low crimes, demeanors, and general ugliness that amounted to a sweeping indictment of almost everybody in the hotel at that hour.

Most of them were asleep when I began speaking, but as a Doctor of Divinity and an ordained minister in the Church of the New Truth, I knew in my heart that I was merely a vessel—a tool, as it were—of some higher and more powerful voice.

For eight long and degrading days I had skulked around Houston with all the other professionals, doing our jobs—which was actually to do nothing at all except drink all the free booze we could pour into our bodies, courtesy of the National Football League, and listen to an endless barrage of some of the lamest and silliest swill ever uttered by man or beast . . . and finally, on Sunday morning about six hours before the opening kickoff, I was racked to the point of hysteria by a hellish interior conflict.

I was sitting by myself in the room, watching the wind & weather clocks on the TV set, when I felt a sudden and extremely powerful movement at the base of my spine. Mother of Sweating Jesus! I thought. What is it—a leech? Are there leeches in this goddamn hotel, along with everything else? I jumped off the bed and began clawing at the small of my back with both hands. The thing felt huge, maybe eight or nine pounds, moving slowly up my spine toward the base of my neck.

I'd been wondering, all week, why I was feeling so low and out of sorts . . . but it never occurred to me that a giant leech had been sucking blood out of the base of my spine all that time; and now the goddamn thing was moving up toward the base of my brain, going straight for the medulla . . . and as a professional sportswriter I knew that if the bugger ever reached my medulla I was done for.

It was at this point that serious conflict set in, because I realized—given the nature of what was coming up my spine and the drastic effect I knew it would have, very soon, on my sense of journalistic responsibility—that I would have to do two things immediately: first, deliver the sermon that had been brewing in my brain all week long, and then rush back into the room and write my lead for the Super Bowl story . . .

Or maybe write my lead first, and then deliver the sermon. In any case, there was no time to lose. The thing was about a third of the way up my spine now, and still having at good speed. I jerked on a pair of L.L. Bean walking shorts and ran out on the balcony to a nearby ice machine.

Back in the room I filled a glass full of ice and Wild Turkey, then began flipping through the pages of *A Demon's Nightmare* for some kind of spiritual springboard to get the sermon moving. I had already decided—about midway in the ice run—that I had adequate time to address the sleeping crowd and also crank out a lead before that goddamn blood-sucking slug reached the base of my brain—or, even worse, if a sharp dose of Wild Turkey happened to slow the thing down long enough to rob me of my final excuse for missing the game entirely, like last year. . . .

What? Did my tongue slip there? My fingers? Or did I just get a fine professional hint from my old buddy, Mr. Natural?

Indeed. When the going gets tough, the tough get going. John Mitchell said that—shortly before he quit his job and left Washington at ninety miles an hour in a chauffeur-driven limousine.

I have never felt close to John Mitchell, but on that rotten morning in Houston, I came as close as I ever will; because he was, after all, a pro . . . and so, alas, was I. Or at least I had a fistful of press badges that said I was.

And it was this bedrock sense of professionalism, I think, that quickly solved my problem . . . which, until that moment when I recalled the foul spectre of Mitchell, had seemed to require a frantic decision between either delivering my sermon or writing my lead, in the place of an impossibly short time.

When the going gets weird, the weird turn pro.

Who said that?

I suspect it was somebody from the *Columbia Journalism Review*, but I have no proof . . . and it makes no difference anyway. There is a bond, among pros, that needs no definition. Or at least it didn't on that Sunday morning in Houston, for reasons that require no further discussion at this point in time . . . because it suddenly occurred to me that *I had already written the lead* for this year's Super Bowl game; I wrote it last year in Los Angeles, and a quick rip through my fat manila folder of clips labeled "Football '73" turned it up as if by magic.

I jerked it out of the file, and retyped it on a fresh page slugged: "Super Bowl/Houston '74." The only change necessary was the substitution of "Minnesota Vikings" for "Washington Redskins." Except for that, the lead seemed just as adequate for the game that would begin in about six hours as it was for the one that I missed in Los Angeles in January of '73.

"The precision-jackhammer attack of the Miami Dolphins stomped the balls off the Minnesota Vikings today by stomping and hammering with one precise jack-thrust after another up the middle, mixed with pinpoint-precision passes into the flat and numerous hammer-jack stops around both ends . . ."

The jangling of the telephone caused me to interrupt my work. I jerked it off the hook, saying nothing to whoever was on the other end, and began flashing the hotel operator. When she finally cut in, I spoke very calmly. "Look," I said, "I'm a very friendly person and a minister of the gospel, to boot—but I thought I left instructions down there to put no calls—*No calls, goddamn it*!—through to this room, and especially not *now* in the middle of this orgy . . . I've been here eight days and nobody's called me yet. Why in hell would they start now? . . . What? Well, I simply can't accept that kind of flimsy reasoning, operator. Do you believe in *hell*? Are you ready to speak with Saint Peter? . . . Wait a minute now, calm down . . . I want to be sure you understand *one thing* before I get back to my business; I have some people here who *need help* . . . But I want you to know that God is Holy! He will *not allow* sin in his presence! The Bible says: 'There is none righteous. *No, not one* . . . For all have sinned and come short of the glory of God.' That's from the book of Romans, young lady . . ."

The silence at the other end of the line was beginning to make me nervous. But I could feel the sap rising, so I decided to continue my sermon from the balcony . . . and I suddenly realized that somebody was beating on my door. Jesus God, I thought, it's the manager; they've come for me at last.

But it was a TV reporter from Pittsburgh, raving drunk and demanding to take a shower. I jerked him into the room. "Nevermind the goddamn shower," I said. "Do you realize what I have on my spine?" He stared at me, unable to speak. "A giant leech," I said. "It's been there for eight days, getting fatter and fatter with blood."

He nodded slowly as I led him over to the phone. "I hate leeches," he muttered.

"That's the least of our problems," I said. "Room service won't send any beer up until noon, and all the bars are closed . . . I have this Wild Turkey, but I think it's too heavy for the situation we're in."

"You're right," he said. "I got work to do. The goddamn game's about to start. I need a shower."

"Me too," I said. "But I have some work to do first, so you'll have to make the call."

"Call?" He slumped into a chair in front of the window, staring out at the thick gray mist that had hung on the town for eight days—except now, as Super Sunday dawned, it was thicker and wetter than ever.

I gave him the phone: "Call the manager," I said. "Tell him you're Howard Cosell and you're visiting up here with a minister in 2003; we're having a private prayer breakfast and we need two-fifths of his best red wine, with a box of saltine crackers."

He nodded unhappily. "Hell, I came here for a shower. Who needs the wine?"

"It's important," I said. "You make the call while I go outside and get started."

He shrugged and dialed "O" while I hurried out to the balcony, clearing my throat for an opening run at James 2:19:

"Beware!" I shouted. "For the devils also believe, and tremble!"

I waited for a moment, but there was no reply from the lobby, twenty floors down—so I tried Ephesians 6:12, which seemed more appropriate:

"For we wrestle not," I screamed, "against flesh and blood—but against principalities, against powers, against the rulers of the darkness of this world—and, yes—against spiritual wickedness in high places!"

Still there was no response except the booming echoes of my own voice . . . but the thing on my spine was moving with new vigor now, and I sensed there was not much time. All movement in the lobby had ceased. They were all standing still down there—maybe twenty or thirty people . . . but were they *listening*? Could they *hear*?

I couldn't be sure. The acoustics of these massive lobbies are not predictable. I knew, for instance, that a person sitting in a room on the eleventh floor, with the door open, could hear—with unnerving clarity—the sound of a cocktail glass shattering on the floor of the lobby. It was also true that almost every word of Gregg Allman's "Multi-Colored Lady" played at top volume on a dual-speaker Sony TC-126 in an open-door room on the twentieth floor could be heard in the NFL pressroom on the hotel mezzanine . . . but it was hard to be sure of the timbre and carrying power of my own voice in this cavern; it sounded, to me, like the deep screaming of a bull elk in the rut . . . but there was no way to know, for sure, if I was really getting through.

"Discipline!" I bellowed. "Remember Vince Lombardi!" I paused to let that one sink in—waiting for applause, but none came. "Remember George Metesky!" I shouted. "He had discipline!"

Nobody down in the lobby seemed to catch that one, although I sensed the first stirrings of action on the balconies just below me. It was almost time for the Free Breakfast in the Imperial Ballroom downstairs, and some of the early rising sportswriters seemed to be up and about. Somewhere behind me a phone was ringing, but I paid no attention. It was time, I felt, to bring it all together . . . my voice was giving out, but despite the occasional dead spots and bursts of high-pitched wavering, I grasped the railing of the balcony and got braced for some flat-out raving:

"Revelations, Twenty-fifteen!" I screamed. "Say Hallelujah! Yes! Say Hallelujah!"

People were definitely responding now. I could hear their voices, full of excitement—but the acoustics of the place made it impossible to get a good fix on the cries that were bounding back and forth across the lobby. Were they saying "Hallelujah"?

"Four more years!" I shouted. "My friend General Haig has told us that the Forces of Darkness are now in control of the Nation—and they will rule for four more years!" I paused to sip my drink, then I hit it again: "And Al Davis has told us that whosoever was not found written in the book of life was cast into the lake of fire!"

I reached around behind me with my free hand, slapping at a spot between my shoulder blades to slow the thing down.

"How many of you will be cast into the lake of fire in the next four years? *How many will survive?* I have spoken with General Haig, and—"

At this point I was seized by both arms and jerked backward, spilling my drink and interrupting the climax of my sermon. "You crazy bastard!" a voice screamed. "Look what you've done! The manager just called. Get back in the room and lock the fucking door! He's going to bust us!"

It was the TV man from Pittsburgh, trying to drag me back from my pulpit. I slipped out of his grasp and returned to the balcony. "This is Super Sunday!" I screamed. "I want every one of you worthless bastards down in the lobby in ten minutes so we can praise God and sing the national anthem!"

At this point I noticed the TV man sprinting down the hall toward the elevators, and the sight of him running caused something to snap in my brain. "There he goes!" I shouted. "He's headed for the lobby! Watch out! It's Al Davis. He has a knife!"

I could see people moving on all the balconies now, and also down in the lobby. Then, just before I ducked back in my room, I saw one of the glass-walled elevators starting down, with a single figure inside it . . . he was the most visible man in the building; a trapped and crazy animal descending slowly—in full view of everybody from the busboys in the ground-floor coffee shop to Jimmy the Greek on the balcony above me—to certain captivity by that ugly crowd at the bottom.

I watched for a moment, then hung the Do Not Disturb sign on my doorknob and double-locked the door. That elevator, I knew, would be empty when it got to the lobby. There were at least five floors, on the way down, where he could jump out and bang on a friendly door for safe refuge . . . and the crowd in the lobby had not seen him clearly enough, through the tinted-glass wall of the elevator, to recognize him later on.

And there was not much time for vengeance, anyway, on the odd chance that anyone cared.

It had been a dull week, even by sportswriters' standards, and now the day of the Big Game was finally on us. Just one more free breakfast, one more ride, and by nightfall the thing would be over.

The first media bus was scheduled to leave the hotel for the stadium at ten thirty, four hours before kickoff, so I figured that gave me some time to relax and act human. I filled the bathtub with hot water, plugged the tape recorder with both speakers into a socket right next to the tub, and spent the next two hours in a steam-stupor, listening to Rosalie Sorrels and Doug Sahm, chewing idly on a small slice of Mr. Natural, and reading the *Cocaine Papers* of Sigmund Freud.

Around noon I went downstairs to the Imperial Ballroom to read the morning papers over the limp dregs of the NFL's free breakfast, then I stopped at the free bar for a few Bloody Marys before wandering outside to catch the last bus for the stadium—the CBS special—complete with more Bloody Marys, screwdrivers, and a roving wagon-meister who seemed to have everything under control.

On the bus to the stadium, I made a few more bets on Miami. At that point I was picking up everything I could get, regardless of the points. It had been a long and jangled night, but the two things that needed to be done before game time—my sermon and my lead—were already done, and the rest of the day looked easy: just try to keep out of trouble and stay straight enough to collect on all my bets.

• • •

The consensus among the 1,600 or so sportswriters in town favored Miami by almost two to one . . . but there are only a handful of sportswriters in this country with enough sense to pour piss out of their own boots, and by Saturday night there was an obvious drift among the few "smart" ones to Minnesota, with a seven-point cushion. Paul Zimmerman of the *New York Post*, author of *A Thinking Man's Guide to Pro Football* and the sportswriting fraternity's scaled-down answer to the *Washington Post*'s political guru David Broder, had organized his traditional pressroom betting pool—where any sportswriter who felt up to it could put $1 in the pot and predict the final score (in writing, on the pressroom bulletin board, for all the world to see) . . . and whoever came closest would pick up $1,000 or so dollars.

Or at least that was the theory. But in reality there were only about four hundred writers willing to risk a public prediction on the outcome of a game that—even to an amateur like me—was so obvious that I took every bet I could get against the Vikings, regardless of the spread. As late as 10:30 on Sunday morning, I was calling bookies on both coasts, doubling and tripling my bets with every point I could get from five to seven—and by 2:35 on Sunday afternoon, five minutes after the kickoff, I knew I was home free.

Moments later, when the Dolphins drove the length of the field for another touchdown, I began collecting money. The final outcome was painfully clear less than halfway through the first quarter—and shortly after that, *Sport* magazine editor Dick Schaap reached over my shoulder in the press section and dropped two bills—a five and a twenty—in my lap.

I smiled back at him. "Jesus," I said. "Are you giving up *already*? This game is far from over, my man. Your people are only twenty-one points down, and we still have a whole half to go."

He shook his head sadly.

"You're not counting on a second-half rally?" I asked, pocketing his money.

He stared at me, saying nothing . . . then he rolled his eyes up toward the soupy mist above the stadium where the Goodyear Blimp was hovering, almost invisible in the fog.

• • •

In the increasingly rigid tradition of Super Bowl games, this one was never in doubt. The Dolphins took the opening kickoff and stomped the Viking defense like they were a gang of sick junkies. The "Purple People Eaters"—Minnesota's fabled "front four"—ate nothing but crow on that long afternoon in Houston. It was one of the dullest and most predictable football games I've ever had to sit through, on TV or anywhere else. My final score prediction in Zimmerman's pool had been Miami, 27–10—3 points high, on both sides, from the final score of 24–7. It was not close enough, apparently, to win the sportswriters' pool—but it was close enough to beat most of the bookies, wizards, and experts.

There is a definite, perverse kind of pleasure in beating the "smart money"—in sports, politics, or anything else—and the formula for doing it seems dangerously simple: take the highest odds you can get *against the conventional wisdom*—but never bet against your own instinct or the prevailing karma.

Moments after the game, standing in the sawdust-floored circus tent where the players were being led in, one by one, for mass interviews with the sporting press, I was approached by Larry Merchant, author of a recently published book called *The National Football Lottery*, a shrewd layman's analysis about how to beat the bookies by betting on pro football games. I was just finishing a long talk with Dolphins owner Joe Robbie about the relationship between national politics, pro football, and the cruel fate of our mutual friend George McGovern, when Merchant tapped me on the shoulder with one hand and handed me a $50 bill with the other. He said nothing at all. I had given him Minnesota with six and a half. The final spread was seventeen.

I smiled and stuck the bill in my wallet. Joe Robbie seemed not to notice. Gambling on the outcome of games is strictly verboten among owners, players, coaches, and all other employees of the National Football League, and being seen in public in the presence of an obvious gambling transaction makes these people very uncomfortable. The only thing worse than being seen with a known gambler is finding yourself in the white-light glare of a network TV camera in the company of an infamous drug abuser . . . and here was the owner of the winning Super Bowl team, moments after accepting the Lombardi Trophy in front of three hundred cameras, talking with obvious enthusiasm—about the likelihood of President Nixon's impeachment—to a person long-since identified by the NFL security watchdogs as both a gambler *and* a drug freak.

I half expected Robbie to jerk his coat over his head and sprint for the tent exit, but he never even blinked. He kept right on talking about the McGovern campaign, then shook my hand again and invited me out to the Dolphin victory party that night at the Marriott Motor Hotel. "Come on out and celebrate with us," he said. "It should be a nice party."

"Why not?" I said. Behind me I could hear George Kimball, bellowing in the throes of a long-delayed acid frenzy . . . and as I turned to deal with Kimball I remembered that Joe Robbie was originally a politician—a candidate for Congress, among other things, on the left-wing Farmer-Labor ticket in Minnesota—and there was something about him that suggested a sense of politics or at least political sensitivity that you rarely encounter among men who own and run professional football teams. Both Robbie and his coach, Don Shula, seem far more relaxed and given to quick flashes of humor than the kind of militaristic, puritanical jocks and PR men you normally have to deal with on the business/power levels of the NFL. This was just as obvious—especially with Shula—*before* the game, as well as after it.

In stark contrast to Shula, Viking coach Bud Grant spent most of Super Week acting like a Marine Corps drill sergeant with a terminal case of the piles. Grant's public behavior in Houston called up ominous memories of Redskin coach George Allen's frantic pre-game bitching last year in Los Angeles.

The parallel was hard to miss, and it seemed almost certain—in both cases—that the attitudes of the coaches had to either reflect or powerfully influence the attitudes of the players . . . and in high-pressure games between supposedly evenly matched teams, pre-game signs like confidence, humor, temper tantrums, and bulging eyeballs are not to be ignored when betting-time comes.

Or at least not by me . . . although there is definitely another side to that coin, and it comes up just often enough to keep the game interesting. There is a factor known among players as "flakiness," which translates roughly as a kind of "team personality," characterized by moodiness and an almost manic-depressive unpredictability both on and off the field.

Miami is decidedly *not* a flakey team; they are consistent to the point of tedium. "We're a money team," says all-pro defensive back Jake Scott. "When something has to be done, we do it." And the record is there to prove it: the Dolphins have won two straight Super Bowls and lost only two games in the past two years. One of these was a meaningless, late-season giveaway to Baltimore last season, when Shula was resting his regulars for the play-offs—and the other was a potentially ominous 12–7 loss, in the second game of this season, to the Oakland Raiders—known throughout the league as the flakiest team in pro football.

Do Not Mistake Me for Any Other Reader
I have come here to help to save the suffering. You know God works in a mysterious way. If you have faith in God, don't fail to see:

Mother Roberts
Psychic Reader and Adviser
The One and Only Gifted Healer
was born with the God-given powers to help humanity and has devoted her life to this work. Tells your friends and enemies'

names without asking a single word. She will tell you what you wish to know regarding health, marriage, love, divorce, courtship, speculations, and business transactions of all kinds.

She will tell you of any changes you should or shouldn't make, good or bad. She removes evil influences and bad luck of all kinds. She never fails to reunite the separated, cause speedy and happy marriages. She lifts you out of sorrow and darkness and starts you on the way to success, and happiness. She will give sound and important advice on all affairs of life, whatever they may be. You will find her superior to any other reader you have consulted in the past. A place to bring your friends and feel no embarrassment.

½ Price with This Slip
Open Daily and Sundays—8 AM to 10 PM
1609 W. Alabama Phone JA 3-22
No Appointment Necessary—Look for Address

Ah yes, Mother Roberts . . . I found her card on the bus and jammed it into one of my pockets, thinking that maybe I would give her a call on Monday and make an appointment. I had a lot of heavy questions to lay on her like "Why am I here, Mother Roberts? What does it all mean? Have I finally turned pro? Can this really be the end? Down and out in Houston with—

"No, I was just kidding, Mother Roberts, just putting you on—just working a bit of the test on you, right? Yes, because what I was really leading up to is this extremely central question . . . No, I'm not shy; it's just that I come from way up north where people's lips are frozen about ten months every year, so we don't get used to talking until very late in life . . . what? Old? Well, I think you just put your finger or your wand or whatever, right smack on the head of the nail, Mother Roberts, because the godawful truth of the whole matter is that I've been feeling *extremely old* this past week, and . . . What? Wait a minute now, goddamn it, I'm still getting up to the main question, which is . . . What? No, I *never* curse, Mother Roberts; that was a cry of anguish, a silent scream from the soul, because I feel in serious trouble down here in this goddamn town, and . . . Yes, I *am* a white person, Mother Roberts, and we both know there's not a damn thing I can do about it. Are you prejudiced? . . . No, let's not get into that. Just let me ask you this question, and if you can give me a straight and reasonable answer I promise I won't come out to your place . . . because what I want you to tell me, Mother Roberts—and I mean this very seriously—is why have I been in Houston for eight days without anybody offering me some cocaine? . . . Yes, cocaine, that's what I said, and just between you and me I'm damn serious about wanting some . . . What? Drugs? *Of course* I'm talking about drugs! Your ad said you could answer my questions and lift me out of sorrow and darkness." Mother Roberts hung up on me at that point.

It was not until Monday afternoon that I actually spoke with Mother Roberts on the telephone, but the idea of going over to Galveston and dealing with the whole Super Scene story from some rotten motel on the edge of the seawall had been wandering around in my head almost from the first hour after I checked into my coveted pressroom at the Hyatt Regency.

And in dull retrospect now, I wish I had done that. Almost anything would have been better than that useless week I spent in Houston waiting for the Big Game. The only place in town where I felt at home was a sort of sporadically violent strip joint called the Blue Fox, far out in the country on South Main. Nobody I talked to in Houston had ever heard of it, and the only two sportswriters who went out there with me got involved in a wild riot that ended up with all of us getting Maced by undercover vice-squad cops who just happened to be in the middle of the action when it erupted.

Ah . . . but that is another story, and we don't have time for it here. Maybe next time. There are two untold sagas that will not fit into this story: one has to do with Big Al's Cactus Room in Oakland, and the other concerns the Blue Fox in Houston.

There is also—at least in the minds of at least two dozen gullible sportswriters at the Super Bowl—the ugly story of how I spent three or four days prior to Super Week shooting smack in a $7-a-night motel room on the seawall in Galveston.

I remember telling that story one night in the press lounge at the Hyatt Regency, just babbling it off the top of my head out of sheer boredom . . . Then I forgot about it completely until one of the local sportswriters approached me a day or so later and said: "Say, man, I hear you spent some time in Galveston last week."

"Galveston?"

"Yeah," he said. "I hear you locked yourself in a motel over there and shot heroin for three days."

I looked around me to see who was listening, then grinned kind of stupidly and said, "Shucks, there wasn't much else to do, you know—so why not get loaded in Galveston?"

He shrugged uncontrollably and looked down at his Old Crow and water. I glanced at my watch and turned to leave. "Time to hit it," I said with a smile. "See you later, when I'm feeling back on my rails."

He nodded glumly as I moved away in the crowd . . . and although I saw him three or four times a day for the rest of that week, he never spoke to me again.

Most sportswriters are so blank on the subject of drugs that you can only talk to them about it at your own risk—which is easy enough, for me, because I get a boot out of seeing their eyes bulge; but it can be disastrous to a professional football player who makes the casual mistake of assuming that a sportswriter knows what he's talking about when he uses a word like "crank." Any professional athlete who talks to a sportswriter about "drugs"—even with the best and most constructive intentions—is taking a very heavy risk. There is a definite element of hysteria about drugs of any kind in pro football today, and a casual remark—even a *meaningless* remark—across the table in a friendly hometown bar can lead, very quickly, to a seat in the witness chair in front of a congressional committee.

Ah . . . drugs; that word again. It was a hard word to avoid in NFL circles last year—like the "missle gap" in the 1960 Kennedy-Nixon election, or "law and order" in 1968.

Nineteen seventy-three was a pretty dull press-year for congressmen. The Senate's Watergate Committee had managed, somehow, to preempt most of the ink and air-time . . . and one of the few congressmen who managed to lash his own special gig past that barrier was an apparently senile sixty-seven-year-old ex-sheriff and football coach from West Virginia named Harley Staggers.

Somewhere in the spastic interim between John Dean and "Bob"

Haldeman, Congressman Staggers managed to collar some story-starved sportswriter from the *New York Times* long enough to announce that his committee—the House Subcommittee on Investigations—had stumbled on such a king-hell wasps' nest of evidence in the course of their probe into "the use of drugs by athletes" that the committee was prepared—or *almost* prepared, pending further evidence—to come to grips with their natural human duty and offer up a law, very soon, that would require individual urinalysis tests on all professional athletes and especially pro football players.

Ah, Jesus . . . another bad tangent. Somewhere in the back of my mind I recall signing a contract that said I would never do this kind of thing again; one of the conditions of my turning pro was a clause about swearing off gibberish . . .

But, like Gregg Allman says: "I've wasted so much time . . . feelin' guilty . . ."

There is some kind of back-door connection in my head between Super Bowls and the Allman Brothers—a strange kind of theme-sound that haunts these goddamn stories no matter where I'm finally forced into a corner to write them. The Allman sound, and rain. There was heavy rain, last year, on the balcony of my dim-lit hotel room just down from the Sunset Strip in Hollywood . . . and more rain through the windows of the San Francisco office building where I finally typed out "the story."

And now, almost exactly a year later, my main memory of Super Bowl VIII in Houston is rain and gray mist outside another hotel window, with the same strung-out sound of the Allman Brothers booming out of the same portable speakers that I had, last year, in Los Angeles.

• • •

The floor of the Hyatt Regency men's room was always covered, about three inches deep, with discarded newspapers—all apparently complete and unread, except on closer examination you realized that every one of them was missing its sports section. This bathroom was right next to the hotel newsstand and just across the mezzanine from the crowded NFL "press lounge," a big room full of telephones and free booze, where most of the 1,600 or so sportswriters assigned to cover The Big Game seemed to spend about sixteen hours of each day during Super Week.

After the first day or so, when it became balefully clear that there was no point in anybody except the local reporters going out on the press bus each day for the carefully staged "player interviews" that Dolphin tackle Manny Fernandez described as "like going to the dentist every day to have the same tooth filled," the out-of-town writers began using the local types as a sort of involuntary "pool" . . . which was more like an old British navy press gang, in fact, because the locals had no choice. They would go out each morning to the Miami and Minnesota team hotels and dutifully conduct the daily interviews . . . and about two hours later this mass of useless gibberish would appear, word for word, in early editions of either the *Post* or the *Chronicle*.

You could see the front door of the hotel from the balcony of the press lounge, and whenever the newsboy came in with his stack of fresh papers, the national writers would make the long forty-eight-yard walk across to the newsstand and cough up fifteen cents each for their copies. Then, on the way back to the press lounge, they would stop for a piss and dump the whole paper—except for the crucial sports section—on the floor of the men's room. The place was so deep, all week, in fresh newsprint that it was sometimes hard to push the door open.

Forty yards away, on comfortable couches surrounding the free bar, the national gents would spend about two hours each day scanning the local sports sections—along with a never-ending mass of almost psychotically detailed information churned out by the NFL publicity office—on the dim chance of finding something worth writing about that day.

There never was, of course. But nobody seemed really disturbed about it. The only thing most of the sportswriters in Houston seemed to care about was having *something* to write about . . . anything at all: a peg, an angle, a quote, even a goddamn rumor.

I remember being shocked at the sloth and moral degeneracy of the Nixon press corps during the 1972 presidential campaign—but they were like a pack of wolverines on speed compared to the relatively elite sportswriters who showed up in Houston to cover the Super Bowl.

On the other hand, there really *was no story*—as the week wore on, it became increasingly obvious that we were all "just working here." Nobody knew who to blame for it, and although at least a third of the sportswriters who showed up for that super-expensive shuck knew exactly what was happening, I doubt more than five or six of them ever actually wrote the cynical and contemptuous appraisals of Super Bowl VIII that dominated about half the conversation around the bar in the press lounge.

Whatever was happening in Houston that week had little or nothing to do with the hundreds of stories that were sent out on the newswires each day. Most of the stories, in fact, were unabashed rewrites of the dozens of official NFL press releases churned out each day by the league publicity office. Most of the stories about "fantastic parties" given by Chrysler, American Express, and Jimmy the Greek were taken from press releases and written by people who had spent the previous evening at least five miles from the scenes described in their stories.

The NFL's official Super Bowl party—the "incredible Texas Hoe Down" on Friday night in the Astrodome—was as wild, glamorous, and exciting as an Elks Club picnic on Tuesday in Salina, Kansas. The official NFL press release on the Hoe Down said it was an unprecedented extravaganza that cost the league more than $100,000 and attracted people like Gene McCarthy and Ethel Kennedy . . . Which might have been true, but I spent about five hours skulking around in that grim concrete barn, and the only people I recognized were a dozen or so sportswriters from the press lounge.

• • •

It is hard to say, even now, exactly why I was so certain of an easy Dolphin victory. The only reason I didn't get extremely rich on the game was my inability to overcome the logistical problems of betting heavily, on credit, by means of frantic long-distance phone calls from a hotel room in Houston. None of the people I met in that violent, water-logged town were inclined to introduce me to a reliable bookmaker—and the people I called on both coasts, several hours before the game on Sunday morning, seemed unnaturally nervous when I asked them to use their own credit to guarantee my bets with their local bookies.

Looking back on it now, after talking with some of these people and cursing them savagely, I see that the problem had something to do with my frenzied speech pattern that morning. I was still in the grip of whatever fiery syndrome had caused me to deliver that sermon off the balcony a few hours earlier—and the hint of mad tremor in my voice, despite my attempts to disguise it, was apparently communicated very clearly to all those I spoke with on the long-distance telephone.

How long, oh Lord, how long? This is the second year in a row that I have gone to the Super Bowl and been absolutely certain—at least forty-eight hours before game time—of the outcome. It is also the second year in a row that I have failed to capitalize, financially, on this certainty. Last year, betting mainly with wealthy cocaine addicts, I switched all my bets from Washington to Miami on Friday night—and in the resulting confusion my net winnings were almost entirely canceled by widespread rancor and personal bitterness.

This year, in order to sidestep that problem, I waited until the last moment to make my bets—despite the fact that I knew the Vikings were doomed after watching them perform for the press at their star-crossed practice field on Monday afternoon before the game. It was clear, even then, that they were spooked and very uncertain about what they were getting into—but it was not until I drove about twenty miles around the Beltway to the other side of town for a look at the Dolphins that I knew, for sure, how to bet.

There are a lot of factors intrinsic to the nature of the Super Bowl that make it far more predictable than regular season games, or even play-offs—but they are not the kind of factors that can be sensed or understood at a distance of two thousand or even twenty miles, on the basis of any wisdom or information that filters out from the site through the rose-colored, booze-bent media-filter that passes for "world-wide coverage" at these spectacles.

There is a progression of understanding vis-à-vis pro football that varies drastically with the factor of *distance*—physical, emotional, intellectual, and every other way . . . Which is exactly the way it should be, in the eyes of the amazingly small number of people who own and control the game, because it is this finely managed distance factor that accounts for the high-profit mystique that blew the sacred institution of baseball off its "national pastime" pedestal in less than fifteen years.

There were other reasons for baseball's precipitous loss of popularity among everybody except old men and middle-aged sportswriters between 1959 and now—as there will be a variety of reasons to explain the certain decline of pro football between now and 1984—but if sporting historians ever look back on all this and try to explain it, there will be no avoiding the argument that pro football's meteoric success in the 1960s was directly attributable to its early marriage with network TV and a huge, coast-to-coast audience of armchair fans who "grew up"—in terms of their personal relationships to The Game—with the idea that pro football was something that happened every Sunday on the tube. The notion of driving eight miles along a crowded freeway and then paying $3 to park the car in order to pay another $10 to watch the game from the vantage point of a damp redwood bench fifty-five rows above the 19-yard line in a crowd of noisy drunks was entirely repugnant to them.

And they were absolutely right. After ten years trying it both ways—and especially after watching this last wretched Super Bowl game from a choice seat in the "press section" very high above the 50-yard line—I hope to Christ I never again succumb to whatever kind of weakness or madness it is that causes a person to endure the incoherent hell that comes with going out to a cold and rainy stadium for three hours on a Sunday afternoon and trying to get involved with what seems to be happening down there on that far-below field.

At the Super Bowl I had the benefit of my usual game-day aids: powerful binoculars, a tiny portable radio for the blizzard of audio details that nobody ever thinks to mention on TV, and a seat on the good left arm of a friend, Mr. Natural . . . But even with all these aids and a seat on the 50-yard line, I would rather have stayed in my hotel room and watched the goddamn thing on TV; or maybe in some howling-drunk bar full of heavy bettors—the kind of people who like to bet on every play, pass or run, three to one against a first down, twenty to one on a turnover . . .

• • •

When I finally fled Houston, it was a cold Tuesday afternoon with big lakes of standing water on the way to the airport. I almost missed my plane to Denver because of a hassle with Jimmy the Greek about who was going to drive us to the airport and another hassle with the hotel garage-man about who was going to pay for eight days of tending my bogus "Official Super Bowl Car" in the hotel garage . . . and I probably would not have made it at all if I hadn't run into an NFL publicity man who gave me enough speed to jerk me awake and lash the little white

Mercury Cougar out along the Dallas freeway to the airport in time to abandon it in the "Departures/Taxis Only" area and hire a man for dollars to rush my bags and sound equipment up to the Continental Airlines desk just in time to make the flight.

• • •

What was easily the most provocative quote of that whole dreary week came on the Monday after the game from Miami linebacker Doug Swift. He was talking in his usual loose "What? Me worry?" kind of way with two or three sportswriters in the crowded lobby of the Marriott. Buses were leaving for the airport, Dolphin supporters and their wives were checking out, the lobby was full of stranded luggage, and off in one of the corners, Don Shula was talking with another clutch of sportswriters and ridiculing the notion that he would ever get rid of Jim Kiick, despite Kiick's obvious unhappiness at the prospect of riding the bench again next year behind all-pro running back Mercury Morris.

Meanwhile, on the other side of the lobby, Doug Swift was going along with a conversation that had turned, along with Shula's, to money and next year's contracts. Swift listened for a while, then looked up at whoever was talking to him and said:

"You can expect to see a lot of new faces on next year's [Miami] team. A lot of important contracts are coming up for renewal, and you can bet that the guys will be asking for more than management is willing to pay."

Nobody paid much attention to the decidedly unnatural timing of Swift's matter-of-fact prediction about "a lot of new faces next year," but it was not the kind of talk designed to tickle either Shula's or Joe Robbie's rampant humours that morning. Jesus, here was the team's player representative—a star linebacker and one of the sharpest & most politically conscious people in the league—telling anyone who cared to listen, not even twelve hours after the victory party, that the embryo "Dolphin Dynasty" was already in a very different kind of trouble than anything the Vikings or the Redskins had been able to lay on them in two straight Super Bowls.

• • •

When Doug Swift made that comment about "a lot of new faces on next year's team," he was not thinking in terms of a player revolt against forced urinalysis. What he had in mind, I think, was the fact that among the Dolphin contracts coming up for renewal this year are those of Larry Csonka, Jake Scott, Paul Warfield, Dick Anderson, and Mercury Morris—all established stars earning between $30,000 and $55,000 a year right now, and all apparently in the mood to double their salaries next time around.

Which might seem a bit pushy, to some people—until you start comparing average salary figures in the National Football League against salaries in other pro sports. The average NFL salary (according to figures provided by players association general counsel Ed Garvey) is $28,500, almost five grand less than the $33,000 average for major league baseball players, and about *half* the average salary (between $50,000 and $55,000) in the National Hockey League . . . But when you start talking about salaries in the National Basketball Association, it's time to kick out the jams: the *average* NBA salary is $92,500 a year. (The NBA Players Association claims that the average salary is $100,000.)

Against this steep-green background, it's a little easier to see why Larry Csonka wants a raise from his current salary of $55,000—to $100,000 or so, a figure that he'd probably scale down pretty calmly if Joe Robbie offered him the average NBA salary of $92,500.

(A quick little sidelight on all these figures has to do with the price TV advertisers paid to push their products during time-outs and penalty squabbles at the Super Bowl: the figure announced by the NFL and whatever TV network carried the goddamn thing was $200,000 per minute. I missed the telecast, due to factors beyond my control—which is why I don't know which network sucked up all that gravy, or whether it was Schlitz, Budweiser, Gillette, or even King Kong Amyl Nitrates that coughed up $200,000 for every sixty seconds of TV exposure on that grim afternoon.)

But that was just a sidelight . . . and the longer I look at all these figures, my watch, and this goddamn stinking Mojo Wire that's been beeping steadily out here in the snow for two days, the more I tend to see this whole thing about a pending labor management crunch in the NFL as a story with a spine of its own that we should probably leave for later.

Which is sad, but what the hell? None of this tortured bullshit about the future of pro football means anything anyway. If the Red Chinese invaded tomorrow and banned the game entirely, nobody would really miss it after two or three months. Even now, most of the games are so fucking dull that it's hard to understand how anybody can even watch them on TV unless they have some money hanging on the point spread, instead of the final score.

Pro football in America is over the hump. Ten years ago it was a very hip and private kind of vice to be into. I remember going to my first 49ers game in 1965 with fifteen beers in a plastic cooler and a Dr. Grabow pipe full of bad hash. The 49ers were still playing in Kezar Stadium then, an old gray hulk at the western end of Haight Street in Golden Gate Park. There were never any sellouts, but the thirty thousand or so regulars were extremely heavy drinkers, and at least ten thousand of them were out there for no other reason except to get involved in serious violence . . . By halftime the place was a drunken madhouse, and anybody who couldn't get it on anywhere else could always go underneath the stands and try to get into the long trough of a "Men's Room" through the "Out" door; there were always a few mean drunks lurking around to punch anybody who tried that . . . and by the end of the third quarter of any game, regardless of the score, there were always two or three huge brawls that would require the cops to clear out whole sections of the grandstand.

But all that changed when the 49ers moved out to Candlestick Park. The prices doubled and a whole new crowd took the seats. It was the same kind of crowd I saw, last season, in the four games I went to at the Oakland Coliseum: a sort of half-rich mob of nervous doctors, lawyers, and bank officers who would sit through a whole game without ever making a sound—not even when some freak with a head full of acid spilled a whole beer down the neck of their gray plastic ski jackets. Toward the end of the season, when the Raiders were battling every week for a spot in the play-offs, some of the players got so pissed off at the stuporous nature of their "fans" that they began making public appeals for "cheering" and "noise."

It was a bad joke if you didn't have to live with it—and as far as I'm concerned, I hope to hell I never see the inside of another football stadium. Not even a free seat with free booze in the press box.

That gig is over now, and I blame it on Vince Lombardi. The success of his Green Bay approach in the Sixties restructured the game entirely. Lombardi never really thought about *winning*: his trip was *not losing* . . . Which worked, and because it worked, the rest of the NFL bought Lombardi's whole style: Avoid Mistakes, Don't Fuck Up, Hang Tough, and Take No Chances . . . Because sooner or later the enemy will make a mistake and then you start grinding him down, and if you play the defensive percentage you'll get inside his 30-yard line at least three times in each half, and once you're inside the 30 you want to be sure to get at least 3 points . . .

Wonderful. Who can argue with a battle plan like that? And it is worth remembering that Richard Nixon spent many Sundays, during all those long and lonely autumns between 1962 and '68, shuffling around on the field with Vince Lombardi at Green Bay Packer games.

Nixon still speaks of Lombardi as if he might suddenly appear, at any moment, from underneath one of the larger rocks on the White House lawn . . . And Don Shula, despite his fairly obvious distaste for Nixon, has adopted the Lombardi style of football so effectively that the Dolphins are now one of the dullest teams to watch in the history of pro football.

But most of the others are just as dull—and if you need any proof, find a TV set some weekend that has pro football, basketball, and hockey games on three different channels. In terms of pure action and movement, the NFL is a molasses farm compared to the fine sense of crank that comes on when you get locked into watching a team like the Montreal Canadiens or the Boston Celtics.

One of the few sharp memories I still have from the soggy week in Houston is the sight of the trophy that would go to the team that won the Big Game on Sunday. It was appropriately named after Vince Lombardi: "The Lombardi Trophy," a thick silver fist rising out of a block of black granite.

The trophy has all the style and grace of an ice floe in the North Atlantic. There is a silver plaque on one side of the base that says something about Vince Lombardi and the Super Bowl . . . but the most interesting thing about it is a word that is carved, for no apparent or at least no esthetic reason, in the top of the black marble base:

"Discipline."

That's all it says, and all it needs to say.

The '73 Dolphins, I suspect, will be to pro football what the '64 Yankees were to baseball, the final flower of an era whose time has come and gone. The long and ham-fisted shadow of Vince Lombardi will be on us for many more years . . . But the crank is gone . . .

Should we end the bugger with that?

Why not? Let the sportswriters take it from here. And when things get nervous, there's always that smack-filled $7-a-night motel room down on the seawall in Galveston.

Fear and Loathing in Limbo: The Scum Also Rises

October 10, 1974

> *. . . before I could come to any conclusion it occurred to me that my speech or my silence, indeed any action of mine, would be a mere futility. What did it matter what anyone knew or ignored? What did it matter who was manager? One gets sometimes such a flash of insight. The essentials of this affair lay deep under the surface, beyond my reach, and beyond my power of meddling.*
>
> —Joseph Conrad, *Heart of Darkness*

Well . . . this is going to be difficult. That sold-out knucklehead refugee from a 1969 "Mister Clean" TV commercial has just done what only the most cynical and paranoid kind of malcontent ever connected with national politics would have dared to predict . . .

If I followed my better instincts right now, I would put this typewriter in the Volvo and drive to the home of the nearest politician—*any* politician—and hurl the goddamn machine through his front window . . . flush the bugger out with an act of lunatic violence, then soak him down with Mace and run him naked down Main Street in Aspen with a bell around his neck and black lumps all over his body from the jolts of a high-powered "Bull Buster" cattle prod.

But old age has either mellowed me or broken my spirit to the point where I will probably not do that—at least not today, because that blundering dupe in the White House has just plunged me into a deep and vicious hole.

About five hours after I'd sent the final draft of a massive article on

The Demise of Richard Nixon off on the Mojo Wire and into the cold maw of the typesetter in San Francisco, Gerald Ford called a press conference in Washington to announce that he had just granted a "full, free, and absolute" presidential pardon, covering any and all crimes Richard Nixon may or may not have committed during the entire five and a half years of his presidency.

Ford sprung his decision with no advance warning at 10:40 on a peaceful Sunday morning in Washington, after emerging from a church service with such a powerful desire to dispense mercy that he rushed back to the White House—a short hump across Lafayette Park—and summoned a weary Sunday-morning skeleton crew of correspondents and cameramen to inform them, speaking in curiously zombielike tones, that he could no longer tolerate the idea of ex-president Nixon suffering in grief-crazed solitude out there on the beach in San Clemente, and that his conscience now compelled him to end both the suffering of Nixon and the national *angst* it was causing by means of a presidential edict of such king-sized breadth and scope as to scourge the poison of "Watergate" from our national consciousness forever.

Or at least that's how it sounded to me when I was jolted out of a sweat-soaked coma on Sunday morning by a frantic telephone call from Dick Tuck. "Ford *pardoned* the bastard!" he screamed. "I warned you, didn't I? I buried him twice, and he came back from the dead both times . . . Now he's done it again; he's running around loose on some private golf course in Palm Desert."

I fell back on the bed, moaning heavily. No, I thought. I didn't *hear* that. Ford had gone out of his way, during his first White House press conference, to impress both the Washington press corps and the national TV audience with his carefully considered refusal to interfere in any way with Special Prosecutor Leon Jaworski's legal duty to proceed on the basis of evidence and "prosecute any and all individuals." Given the context of the question, Ford's reply was widely interpreted as a signal to Jaworski that the former president should not be given any special treatment . . . And it also meshed with Ford's answer to a question in the course of his confirmation hearings in the Senate a few months earlier, when he'd said, "I don't think the public would stand for it," when asked if an appointed vice president would have the power to pardon the president who'd appointed him, if the president were removed from office under criminal circumstances.

I recalled these things Ford had said, but I was not so sure I'd heard Dick Tuck correctly—or if I'd really heard him at all. I held my right hand up in front of my eyes, trying to remember if I'd eaten anything the night before that could cause hallucinations. If so, my hand would appear to be transparent, and I would be able to see all the bones and blood vessels very clearly.

But my hand was not transparent. I moaned again, bringing Sandy in from the kitchen to find out what was wrong. "Did Tuck just call?" I asked.

She nodded: "He was almost hysterical. Ford just gave Nixon a full pardon."

I sat up quickly, groping around on the bed for something to smash. "No!" I shouted. "That's impossible!"

She shook her head. "I heard it on the radio, too."

I stared at my hands again, feeling anger behind my eyes and noise coming up in my throat: "That stupid, lying bastard! Jesus! Who votes for these treacherous scumbags! You can't even trust the dumb ones! Look at Ford! He's too goddamn stupid to arrange a deal like that! Hell, he's almost too stupid to lie."

Sandy shrugged. "He gave Nixon all the tapes, too."

"Holy shit!" I leaped out of bed and went quickly to the phone. "What's Goodwin's number in Washington? That bonehead Rotarian sonofabitch made a deal? Maybe Dick knows something."

But it was twenty-four hours later when I finally got hold of Goodwin, and by that time I had made a huge chart full of dates, names, and personal connections—all linked and cross-linked by a maze of arrows and lines. The three names on the list with far more connections than any others were Laird, Kissinger, and Rockefeller. I had spent all night working feverishly on the chart, and now I was asking Goodwin to have a researcher check it all out.

"Well," he replied, "a lot of people in Washington are thinking along those same lines today. No doubt there was some kind of arrangement, but—" He paused. "Aren't we pretty damn close to the deadline? Jesus Christ, you'll never be able to check all that stuff before—"

"Mother of babbling god!" I muttered. The word *deadline* caused my brain to seize up momentarily. Deadline? Yes. Tomorrow morning, about fifteen more hours . . . With about 90 percent of my story already set in type, one of the threads that ran all the way through it was my belief that nothing short of a nuclear war could prevent Richard Nixon's conviction. The only thing wrong with that argument was its tripod construction, and one of the three main pillars was my assumption that Gerald Ford had not been lying when he'd said more than once, for the record, that he had no intention of considering a presidential pardon for Richard Nixon "until the legal process has run its course."

Cazart! I hung up the phone and tossed my chart across the room. That rotten, sadistic little thief had done it again. Just one month earlier he had sandbagged me by resigning so close to the deadline that I almost had a nervous breakdown while failing completely . . . And now he was doing it again, with this goddamn presidential pardon, leaving me with less than twenty-four hours to revise completely a fifteen-thousand-word story that was already set in type.

It was absolutely impossible, no hope at all—except to lash as many last-minute pages as possible into the mojo and hope for the best. Maybe somebody in San Francisco would have time, when the deadline crunch came, to knit the two versions together . . . But there was no way at all to be sure, so this will be an interesting article to read when it comes off the press . . .

Indeed . . . cast your bread on the waters . . . why not?

• • •

I have very dim memories of Tuck's call. Less than five hours earlier, I had passed out very suddenly in the bathtub, after something like 133 hours of nonstop work on a thing I'd been dragging around with me for two months and revising in ragged notebooks and on rented typewriters in hotels from Key Biscayne to Laguna Beach, bouncing in and out of Washington to check the pressure and keep a fix on the timetable, then off again to Chicago or Colorado . . . before heading back to Washington again, where the pressure valves finally blew all at once in early August, catching me in a state of hysterical exhaustion and screeching helplessly for speed when Nixon suddenly caved in and quit, ambushing me on the brink of a deadline and wasted beyond the help of anything but the most extreme kind of chemotherapy.

It takes about a month to recover physically from a collapse of that magnitude, and at least a year to shake the memory. The only thing I can think of that compares to it is that long, long moment of indescribably intense sadness that comes just before drowning at sea, those last few seconds on the cusp when the body is still struggling but the mind has given up . . . a sense of absolute failure and a very clear understanding of it that makes the last few seconds before blackout seem almost peaceful. Getting rescued at that point is far more painful than drowning: recovery brings back terrifying memories of struggling wildly for breath . . .

This is precisely the feeling I had when Tuck woke me up that morning to say that Ford had just granted Nixon "full, free, and absolute" pardon. I had just written a long, sporadically rational brief, of sorts—explaining how Nixon had backed himself into a corner and why it was inevitable that he would soon be indicted and convicted on a felony "obstruction of justice" charge, and then Ford would pardon him, for a lot of reasons I couldn't agree with, but which Ford had already stated so firmly that there didn't seem to be much point in arguing about it. The logic of sentencing Nixon to a year in the same cell with John Dean was hard to argue with on either legal or ethical grounds, but I understood politics well enough by then to realize that Nixon would have to plead guilty to something like the rape/murder of a Republican senator's son before Gerald Ford would even consider letting him spend any time in jail.

I had accepted this, more or less. Just as I had more or less accepted—after eighteen months of total involvement in the struggle to get rid of Nixon—the idea that Gerald Ford could do just about anything he felt like doing, as long as he left me alone. My interest in national politics withered drastically within hours after Nixon resigned.

After five and a half years of watching a gang of fascist thugs treating the White House and the whole machinery of the federal government like a conquered empire to be used like the spoils of war for any purpose that served either the needs or whims of the victors, the prospect of some harmless, half-bright jock like Jerry Ford running a cautious, caretaker-style government for two or even six years was almost a welcome relief.

Not even the ominous sight of Vice President Nelson Rockefeller hovering a heartbeat away from the presidency had much effect on my head.

After more than ten years of civil war with the White House and all the swine who either lived or worked there, I was ready to give the benefit of the doubt to almost any president who acted half human and had enough sense not to walk around in public wearing a swastika armband.

Well . . . the goddamn thing is over now; it ended on Thursday afternoon with all the grace and meaning of a Coke bottle thrown off a third-floor fire escape on the Bowery—exploding on the sidewalk and scaring the shit out of everybody in range, from the ones who got righteously ripped full of glass splinters to the swarm of "innocent bystanders" who still don't know what happened . . .

. . . And probably never will; there is a weird, unsettled, painfully incomplete quality about the whole thing. All over Washington tonight is the stench of a massive psychic battle that *nobody* really won. Richard Nixon has been broken, whipped, and castrated all at once, but even for me there is no real crank or elation in having been a front-row spectator at the final scenes, the Deathwatch, the first time in American history that a president has been chased out of the White House and cast down in the ditch with all the other geeks and common criminals . . .

Looking back on the final few months of his presidency, it is easy to see that Nixon was doomed all along—or at least from that moment when Special Prosecutor Archibald Cox first decided to force a showdown on the "executive privilege" question by sending a U.S. marshal over to the White House with a subpoena for some of the Oval Office tapes.

Nixon naturally defied that subpoena, but not even the crazed firing of Cox, [Elliot] Richardson, and [William] Ruckelshaus could make it go away. And when Jaworski challenged Nixon's right to defy that subpoena in the U.S. Supreme Court, the wheels of doom began rolling. And from that point on, it was clear to all the principals except Nixon himself that the Unthinkable was suddenly inevitable; it was only a matter of time . . . And it was just about then that Richard Nixon began losing his grip on reality.

Within hours after Jaworski and Nixon's "Watergate lawyer" James

St. Clair had argued the case in a special session of the court, I talked to Pat Buchanan and was surprised to hear that Nixon and his wizards in the White House were confident that the verdict would be five to three in their favor. Even Buchanan, who thinks rationally about 79 percent of the time, apparently believed—less than two weeks before the court ruled unanimously *against* Nixon—that five of the eight justices who would have to rule on that question would see no legal objection to ratifying Nixon's demented idea that anything discussed in the president's official office—even a patently criminal conspiracy—was the president's personal property, if he chose to have it recorded on his personal tape-recording machinery.

The possibility that even some of the justices The Boss himself had appointed to the court might not cheerfully endorse a concept of presidential immunity that mocked both the U.S. Constitution and the Magna Carta had apparently been considered for a moment and then written off as too farfetched and crazy even to worry about by all of Nixon's personal strategists.

It is still a little difficult to believe, in fact, that some of the closest advisers to the president of a constitutional democracy in the year nineteen hundred and seventy-four might actually expect the highest court in *any* constitutional democracy to crank up what is probably the most discredited precedent in the history of Anglo-American jurisprudence—the "divine right of kings"—in order to legalize the notion that a president of the United States or any other would-be democracy is above and beyond "the law."

That Nixon and his personal gestapo actually believed this could happen is a measure of the insanity quotient of the people Nixon took down in the bunker with him when he knew the time had come to get serious.

• • •

But even as they raved, you could hear a hollow kind of paranoid uncertainty in their voices, as if they could already feel the ebb tide sucking around their ankles—just as Nixon must have felt it when he walked alone on the beach at San Clemente a few weeks earlier, trudging slowly along in the surf with his pantlegs rolled up while he waited in angry solitude for the results of the Supreme Court vote on his claim of "executive privilege." That rush of sucking water around his ankles must have almost pulled him out to sea when Ziegler called down from the big dune in front of La Casa Pacifica: "Mister President! Mister President! We just got the news! The vote was unanimous—eight to zero."

Nixon whoops with delight: he stops in his water-filled tracks and hurls out both arms in the twin-victory sign. "Wonderful!" he shouts. "I *knew* we'd win it, Ron! Even without that clown Renchburg [Rehnquist]. It wasn't for nothing that I appointed those other dumb farts to the court!"

Ziegler stares down at him, at this doomed scarecrow of a president down there on the edge of the surf. Why is he grinning? Why does he seem so happy at this terrible news?

"No!" Ziegler shouts. "That is not what I meant. That is not what I meant at all!" He hesitates, choking back a sob. "The vote was eight to zero, Mister President—*against* you."

"What?" The scarecrow on the beach goes limp. His arms collapse, his hands flap crazily around the pockets of his wet pants. "Those dirty bastards!" he screams. "We'll break their balls!"

"Yes *sir!*" Ziegler shouts. "They'll wish they'd never been born!" He jerks a notebook out of his inside coat pocket and jots: "Break their balls."

• • •

Ah, poor Ron. I knew him well enough. It was Ziegler, in fact, who tipped me off many months ago that Nixon was finished. This was back in July, in that lull before the storm when the wizards in Washington were beginning to nod glumly at each other whenever somebody suggested that the impeachment drive seemed to be faltering and that maybe Nixon was bottoming out, that in fact he had already bounced off the bottom and was preparing to take the offensive once again.

These were the salad days of early summer, before the fateful Supreme Court decision, when Nixon's Goebbels—ex–White House "communications director" Ken Clawson—was creating a false dawn over the White House by momentarily halting Nixon's yearlong slide in the public opinion polls with a daily drumbeat of heavy, headline-grabbing attacks on "professional Nixon haters" in the press, and "unprincipled, knee-jerk liberals in Congress." At that point in time, most of Nixon's traditional allies were beginning to hear the death shrieks of the banshee floating over the White House lawns at night, and even Billy

Graham had deserted him. So Clawson, in a stroke of cheap genius, put a sybaritic Jesuit priest and a mentally retarded rabbi on the payroll and sent them forth to do battle with the forces of Evil.

Father John McLaughlin, the Jesuit, reveled joyfully in his role as "Nixon's priest" for a month or so, but his star faded fast when it was learned he was pulling down more than $25,000 a year for his efforts and living in a luxury apartment at the Watergate. His superiors in the church were horrified, but Father John McLaughlin gave them the back of his hand and, instead, merely cranked up his speechmaking act. In the end, however, not even Clawson could live with the insistent rumor that the Good Jesuit Father was planning to marry his girlfriend. This was too much, they say, for the rigid sensibilities of General Haig, the White House chief of staff, whose brother was a legitimate priest in Baltimore. McLaughlin disappeared very suddenly, after six giddy weeks on the national stage, and nothing has been heard of him since.

But Clawson was ready for that. No sooner had the priest been deep-sixed than he unveiled another holy man—the Rabbi Baruch Korff, a genuine dingbat with barely enough sense to tie his own shoes, but who eagerly lent his name and his flakey presence to anything Clawson aimed him at. Under the banner of something called the "National Citizens Committee for Fairness to the Presidency," he "organized" rallies, dinner parties, and press conferences all over the country. One of his main financial backers was Hamilton Fish Sr., a notorious fascist and the father of New York Congressman Hamilton Fish Jr., one of the Republican swing votes on the House Judiciary Committee who quietly voted for impeachment.

> *Only a month ago, the storms of destiny seemed to be subsiding for President Nixon. Among the Knowledgeable in Washington, the conviction was growing that the impeachment campaign against him had spent its moment . . . [But] it is now clear that the Knowledgeable were wrong, that they mistook a break in the clouds for lasting sunshine . . .*
>
> —R. W. Apple Jr., *New York Times*, July 28, 1974

In fact, however, Nixon was already doomed by the time the Rodino committee got around to voting. The unanimous Supreme Court vote on the question of "executive privilege" with regard to the sixty-four disputed tapes was the beginning of the end. Nixon had known all along that the release of those tapes would finish him—but he had consistently lied about their contents: not only to the press and the public, but also to his wife and his daughters and all the hard-core loyalists on his staff. He lied about the tapes to Barry Goldwater and Jerry Ford, to Hugh Scott and John Rhodes, to Al Haig and Pat Buchanan, and even to his own attorney, James St. Clair—who was stupid enough, like the others, to have believed him when he swore that the tapes he refused to let anybody listen to would finally prove his innocence.

At that point, almost every journalist in Washington assigned to the Nixon Deathwatch had been averaging about two hours' sleep a night since the beginning of summer. Many were weak and confused, succumbing to drink or drugs whenever possible. Others seemed to hover from day to day on the brink of terminal fatigue. Radio and TV reporters in the White House pressroom were reduced to tearing articles out of the nearest newspaper and reading them verbatim straight over the air—while the newspaper and magazine people would tape the live broadcasts and then transcribe them word for word under their own bylines. By the end of July, the prospect of having to cover an impeachment debate in the House and then a trial in the Senate for three or four months without relief was almost unbearable. As August began and Nixon still showed no signs of giving up, there was more and more talk of "the suicide option."

Sometime around dawn on the Friday morning of Richard Milhous Nixon's last breakfast in the White House I put on my swimming trunks and a red rain parka, laced my head with some gray Argentine snuff, and took an elevator down to the big pool below my window in the National Affairs Suite at the Washington Hilton. It was still raining, so I carried my portable TV set, a notebook, and four bottles of Bass ale in a waterproof canvas bag.

The lower lobby was empty, except for the night watchman—a meaty black gentleman whose main duty was to keep people like me out of the pool at night, but we had long since come to a friendly understanding on this subject. It was against the rules to swim when the pool was closed, but there was no rule to prevent a Doctor of Divinity from going out there to meditate on the end of the diving board.

"Mornin', Doc," said the watchman. "Up a little early, ain't you? Especially on a nasty day like this."

"Nasty?" I replied. "What are you—some kind of goddamn Uncle Tom Republican? Don't you know who's leaving town today?"

He looked puzzled for a moment, then his face cracked into a grin. "You're right, by God! I almost forgot. We finally got rid of that man, didn't we, Doc?" He nodded happily. "Yes sir, we finally got rid of him."

I reached into my bag and opened two Bass ales. "This is a time for celebration," I said, handing him one of the bottles. I held mine out in front of me: "To Richard Nixon," I said. "May he choke on the money he stole."

The watchman glanced furtively over his shoulder before lifting his ale for the toast. The clink of the two bottles coming together echoed briefly in the vast, deserted lobby.

"See you later," I said. "I have to meditate for a while, then hustle down to the White House to make sure he really leaves. I won't believe it until I see it with my own eyes."

The flat surface of the pool was pocked with millions of tiny raindrops beating steadily down on the water. There was a chain lock on the gate, so I climbed over the fence and walked down to the deep end, where I located a dry spot under a tree near the diving board. The *CBS Morning News* would be on in about twenty minutes; I turned on the TV set, adjusted the aerial, and turned the screen so I could see it from the pool about twenty feet away. It was a system I'd worked out last summer at the Senate Watergate hearings: after every two laps, I could look over the edge of the pool and check the screen to see if Hughes Rudd's face had appeared yet. When it did, I would climb out of the water and lie down on the grass in front of the set—turn up the sound, light a cigarette, open a fresh Bass ale, and take notes while I watched the tiny screen for a general outline of whatever action Sam Ervin's Roman circus might be expected to generate that day.

I stayed out there by the pool for almost two hours, sliding into the water to swim a few laps and then back out to stretch out on the grass to make a note now and then on the news. Not much was happening, except for a few kinky interviews down by the White House gate with people who claimed to have been on the Deathwatch for three days and nights without sleeping . . . But very few of them could even begin to explain why they were doing it. At least half the crowd around the White House during those last few days looked like people who spend every weekend prowling the demolition derby circuit.

The only other action on the news that Friday morning was an occasional rerun of Nixon's official resignation speech from the night before. I had watched it with Craig Vetter in the Watergate bar. It seemed like a good place to be on that night, because I had also been there on the night of June 17, 1972—while the Watergate burglary was happening five floors above my head.

But after I'd watched Nixon's speech for the third time, a strange feeling of nervousness began working on me, and I decided to get out of town as soon as possible. The movie was over—or at least it would be over in two or three hours. Nixon was leaving at ten o'clock, and Ford would be sworn in at noon. I wanted to be there on the White House lawn when Nixon was lifted off. That would be the end of *my* movie.

It was still raining when I left, and the pool was still empty. I put the TV set back in the canvas bag and climbed over the gate by the lifeguard shack. Then I stopped and looked back for a moment, knowing I would never come back to this place, and if I did it would not be the same. The pool would be the same, and it would be easy enough to pick up a case of Bass ale or a battery TV set . . . And I could even come down here on rainy summer mornings and watch the morning news . . .

No . . . even with the pool and the ale and the grass and the portable TV set, the morning news will not be the same without the foul spectre of Richard Nixon glaring out of the tube. But the war is over now, and he lost . . . Gone but not forgotten, missed but not mourned; we will not see another one like him for quite a while. He was dishonest to a fault, the truth was not in him, and if it can be said that he resembled any other living animal in this world, it could only have been the hyena.

• • •

I took a cab down to the White House and pushed through the sullen mob on the sidewalk to the guardhouse window. The cop inside glanced at my card, then looked up—fixing me with a heavy-lidded Quaalude stare for just an instant, then nodded and pushed his buzzer to open the gate. The pressroom in the West Wing was empty, so I walked outside to the Rose Garden, where a big olive-drab helicopter was perched on the lawn, about one hundred feet out from the stairs. The rain had stopped, and a long red carpet was laid out on the wet grass from the White House door to the helicopter. I eased through the crowd of photographers and walked out, looking back at the White House, where Nixon was giving his final address to a shocked crowd of White House staffers. I examined the aircraft very closely, and I was just about to climb into it when I heard a loud rumbling behind me; I turned around just in time to see Richard and Pat coming toward me, trailing their daughters and followed closely by Gerald Ford and Betty. Their faces were grim and they were walking very slowly; Nixon had a glazed smile on his face, not looking at anybody around him, and walked like a wooden Indian full of Thorazine.

His face was a greasy death mask. I stepped back out of his way and nodded hello, but he didn't seem to recognize me. I lit a cigarette and watched him climb the steps to the door of the helicopter . . . Then he spun around very suddenly and threw his arms straight up in the famous twin-victory signal; his eyes were still glazed, but he seemed to be looking over the heads of the crowd at the White House.

Nobody was talking. A swarm of photographers rushed the plane as Nixon raised his arms—but his body had spun around too fast for his feet, and as his arms went up I saw him losing his balance. The grimace on his face went slack, then he bounced off the door and stumbled into the cockpit. Pat and Ziegler were already inside; Ed Cox and Tricia went in quickly without looking back; and a marine in dress blues shut the door and jumped away as the big rotor blades began turning and the engine cranked up to a dull, whining roar.

I was so close that the noise hurt my ears. The rotor blades were invisible now, but the wind was getting heavier; I could feel it pressing my eyeballs back into their sockets. For an instant I thought I could see Richard Nixon's face pressed up to the window. Was he smiling? Was it Nixon? I couldn't be sure. And now it made no difference.

The wind blast from the rotors was blowing people off balance now;

photographers were clutching their equipment against their bodies, and Gerald Ford was leading his wife back toward the White House with a stony scowl on his face.

I was still very close to the helicopter, watching the tires. As the beast began rising, the tires became suddenly fat; there was no more weight on them . . . The helicopter went straight up and hovered for a moment, then swooped down toward the Washington Monument and then angled up into the fog. Richard Nixon was gone.

• • •

The end came so suddenly and with so little warning that it was almost as if a muffled explosion in the White House had sent up a mushroom cloud to announce that the scumbag had been passed to what will have to pose for now as another generation. The main reaction to Richard Nixon's passing—especially among journalists who had been on the Deathwatch for two years—was a wild and wordless orgasm of long-awaited relief that tailed off almost instantly to a dull, postcoital sort of depression that still endures.

Within hours after Nixon's departure, every bar in downtown Washington normally frequented by reporters was a sinkhole of gloom. Several hours after Gerald Ford was sworn in, I found ex-Kennedy speechwriter Dick Goodwin in a bar not far from the *Rolling Stone* office across the street from the White House. He was slumped in a booth by himself, staring blankly into his drink like a man who had just had his teeth ripped out by a savage bill collector.

"I feel totally drained," he said. "It's like the circus just left town. This is the end of the longest-running continuous entertainment this city ever had." He waved his arm at the waitress for another drink. "It's the end of an era. Now I know how all those rock freaks felt when they heard the Beatles were breaking up."

I felt the same way. All I wanted to do was get the hell out of town as soon as possible. I had just come from the White House pressroom, where a smoglike sense of funk—or "smunk," as somebody over there might describe it—had settled on the room within minutes after Ford took the oath. The Deathwatch was finally over; the evil demon had been purged and the Good Guys had won—or at least the Bad Guys had lost, but that was not quite the same thing.

We all knew it was coming—the press, the Congress, the "public," all the backstage handlers in Washington, and even Nixon's own henchmen—but we all had our own different timetables, and when his balloon suddenly burst on that fateful Monday in August, it happened so fast that none of us were ready to deal with it. The Nixon presidency never really had time to *crumble*, except in hazy retrospect . . . In reality, it *disintegrated*, with all the speed and violence of some flimsy and long-abandoned gazebo suddenly blasted to splinters by chain lightning.

• • •

Like the black teenage burglars who are terrorizing chic Georgetown these days, Nixon conquered so easily that he soon lost any fear of being caught. Washington police have noted a strange pattern involving burglaries in Georgetown and other posh neighborhoods in the white ghetto of the city's northwest sector: a home that has been robbed once is far more likely to be hit again than a home that has never been hit at all. Once they spot an easy mark, the burglars get lazy and prefer to go back for seconds and even thirds, rather than challenge a new target.

The police seem surprised at this pattern, but, in fact, it's fairly traditional among amateurs—or at least among the type I used to hang around with. About fifteen years ago, when I was into that kind of thing, I drifted into Lexington, Kentucky, one evening with two friends who shared my tastes; we moved into an apartment across the street from a gas station which we broke into and robbed on three consecutive nights.

On the morning after the first hit, we stood transfixed at the apartment window, drinking beer and watching the local police "investigating" the robbery . . . And I remember thinking, now that poor fool over there has probably never been hit before, and what he's thinking now is that his odds of being hit again anytime soon are almost off the board. Hell, how many gas stations have ever been robbed two nights in a row?

So we robbed it again that night, and the next morning we stood at the window drinking beer and watched all manner of hell break loose between the station owner and the cops around the gas pumps across the street. We couldn't hear what they were saying, but the proprietor was waving his arms crazily and screaming at the cops, as if he suspected *them* of doing it.

Christ, this is wonderful, I thought. If we hit the bugger again tonight he'll go stark raving mad tomorrow morning when the cops show up . . . which was true: on the next morning, after three consecutive robberies, the parking lot of that gas station was like a war zone, but this time the cops showed up with reinforcements. In addition to the two police cruisers, the lot filled up with chromeless, dust-covered Fords and crew-cut men wearing baggy brown suits and shoes with gum-rubber soles. While some of them spoke earnestly with the proprietor, others dusted the doorknobs, window latches, and the cash register for fingerprints.

It was hard to know, from our window across the street, if we were watching the FBI, local detectives, or insurance agency investigators at work . . . But in any case, I figured they'd have the whole station ringed with armed guards for the next few nights, so we decided to leave well enough alone.

About six in the evening, however, we stopped there and had the tank filled up with ethyl. There were about six bony-faced men hanging around the office, killing the time until dark by studying road maps and tire-pressure charts. They paid no attention to us until I tried to put a dime in the Coke machine.

"It ain't workin'," one of them said. He shuffled over and pulled the whole front of the machine open, like a broken refrigerator, and lifted a Coke bottle out of the circular rack. I gave him the dime and he dropped it into his pocket.

"What's wrong with the machine?" I asked, remembering how hard it had been to rip the bastard open with a crowbar about twelve hours earlier to reach the money box.

"No concern of yours," he muttered, lighting up a Marvel and staring out at the pump where the attendant was making change for a $10 bill after cleaning our windshield and checking the oil. "Don't worry," he said. "There's some folks gonna be a lot worse off than that there machine before this night's out tonight." He nodded. "This time we're *ready* for them sonsabitches."

And they were. I noticed a double-barreled shotgun standing in a corner by the rack full of oil cans. Two big coon hounds were asleep on the greasy linoleum floor, with their collar chains looped around the base of the chewing gum machine. I felt a quick flash of greed as I eyed the glass bulb filled with all those red, white, blue, and green gum balls. We had looted the place of almost everything else, and I felt a pang of regret at having to leave the gum machine untouched: all those pennies just sitting there with nobody to fondle them . . .

But in retrospect, I think that moment was the beginning of wisdom for me. We had pushed our luck far enough with that place, and the world was full of colorful gum-ball machines. There was a weird and menacing edge in the man's voice that it took me a long time to forget.

We drove downtown and cruised around drinking warm beer for a while, then we robbed a crowded liquor store on Main Street by starting a fight with the clerks and then cleaning out the cash register while they struggled to defend themselves.

We got less than $200 out of that one, as I recall—about the same as we'd picked up from three hits on the gas station—and on the way out of town I remember thinking that maybe I could do something a little better in this life than robbing gas stations and liquor stores. After taking enough crazy risks to put all three of us in prison for at least five years, we had about $135 apiece to show for it, and about half of that was already spent on gas, food, beer, and hiring winos to buy whiskey for us because we were too young to get served, and the winos were charging double for anything they bought for us.

That weekend crime spree in Lexington was my last haul, as they say; I even gave up shoplifting, which altered my lifestyle pretty severely for a while, because it had taken me several years to master the kind of skill and mental attitude it takes to walk into a jewelry store and come out with six watches, or in the front door of a tavern and hassle the bartender with a false ID long enough to let a friend slip out the back door with a case of Old Forester . . . But when I quit that gig, I quit it completely; and after fifteen years on the wagon, my skills are so hopelessly atrophied that now I can't even steal a newspaper from an open rack on the street.

Ah . . . mother of jabbering god, how in the hell did I get off on that tangent about teenage street crime? This is supposed to be a deep and serious political essay about Richard Nixon . . .

Although maybe that wasn't such a tangent after all. The original point, I think, had to do with the street-punk mentality that caused Nixon to push his luck so far that it was finally almost impossible *not* to get himself busted. For a while, he had the luck and arrogance of a half-smart amateur. From their base in the White House, Nixon and the L.A. account execs he brought with him treated the old-line Washington power structure with the same kind of contempt that the young burglars casing Georgetown seem to have for the forts of the rich and powerful—or that I had for that poor bastard who owned the gas station in Lexington.

This is a very hard thing for professional cops, journalists, or investigators to cope with. Like doctors and lawyers, most of the best minds in police work have been trained since puberty to think in terms of patterns and precedents: anything original tends to have the same kind of effect on their investigative machinery as a casually mutilated punch card fed into a computer. The immediate result is chaos and false conclusions . . . But both cops and computers are programmed to know when they've been jammed by a wild card or a joker, and in both cases there are usually enough competent technicians standing by to locate the problem and get the machinery working again pretty quickly.

Right . . . and now we have gone off on a dangerous compound tangent. And it has mushroomed into something unmanageable . . . But before we zoom off in whatever direction might come next, it would be unfair not to mention that the *Times* was the first paper to break the Pentagon Papers story, a command decision that forced Nixon and his would-be enforcers to come out in the open with fangs bared, snarling threats to have everybody connected with the publication of the Pentagon Papers either lashed into jail or subpoenaed into so many courtrooms that all their minds would snap before they finally wound up in the poorhouse.

As it turned out, however, the *Times* management strapped on its collective balls and announced that they were prepared to go to the mat with Nixon on that one—a surprisingly tough stance that was almost instantly backed up by influential papers like the *Los Angeles Times*, the *Washington Post,* and the *St. Louis Post-Dispatch* . . . And the appearance of that solid front, however shaky, caused serious turmoil in the White House. Spiro Agnew was pried loose from his kickback racket and sent out on the stump to stir up the Silent Majority against the "radiclibs" and "liberal elitists" of the "eastern media establishment"—the "nattering nabobs of negativism."

Jesus! Those were the days, eh?

The headline in today's *Washington Post* says Richard Nixon is "lonely and depressed" down there in his exile hideout in San Clemente. Jesus! How much more of this cheapjack bullshit can we be expected to take from that stupid little gunsel? Who gives a fuck if he's lonely and depressed out there in San Clemente? If there were any such thing as true justice in this world, his rancid carcass would be somewhere down around Easter Island right now, in the belly of a hammerhead shark.

But, no—he is sitting out there in the imitation-leather-lined study of his oceanside estate, still guarded constantly by a detail of Secret Service agents and still communicating with the outside world through an otherwise unemployable $40,000-a-year mouthpiece named Ron Ziegler . . . and still tantalizing the national press with the same kind of shrewdly programmed leaks that served him so well in the last months of his doomed presidency . . .

"He's terribly depressed, with much to be depressed about," says a friend. "Anyone would be depressed in his situation. I don't mean he's going off the deep end. I just mean that everything happened to him, seemingly all at once, and he doesn't know what to do about it."

Well . . . shucks. I'd be tempted to put my mind to the task of helping the poor bastard figure out "what to do about" this cruel nutcracker that he somehow stumbled into . . . but I have a powerful suspicion that probably that gang of mean niggers in Washington has already solved Nixon's problem for him. They are going to indict the bastard and try to put him on trial.

Nixon knows this. He is not the kind of lawyer you'd want to hire for anything serious, but the reality of his situation vis-à-vis the Watergate grand jury is so bleak that even *he* has to grasp it . . . and this is the reason, I think, for the more or less daily front-page comments on his half-mad and pathetically crippled mental condition. He has devised another one of his famous fourth-down game breakers—the same kind of three-fisted brainstorm that climaxed with his decision to defuse the whole impeachment process by releasing his own version of "the tapes," or the time he figured out how to put a quick lid on the Watergate burglary investigation by blaming the whole thing on John Dean.

According to one Washington topsider, widely respected as an unimpeachable source and a shrewd judge of presidential character: "Dick Nixon is in a league all by himself when you're talking about style and grace under pressure. His instincts when the crunch comes are absolutely amazing."

Nobody will argue with that—although his strategy since leaving the White House has been marked by an unnatural focus on subtlety. The savage warrior of old now confronts us in the guise of a pitiful, frightened old pol—a whipped and broken man, totally at the mercy of his enemies and baffled by the firestorm of disasters that drove him out of the White House.

Which may even be partially true: He will probably go to his grave believing he was not *really* guilty of anything except underestimating the power of his enemies . . . But the fact remains that Jaworski will very likely break the news of Nixon's formal indictment before this article appears on the newsstands, and when that happens there will be only one man in the country with the power to arbitrarily short-circuit the legal machinery that in theory could land Richard Nixon in the same cell block with John Dean.

That man is Gerald Ford, but he will have a hard time justifying a blanket presidential pardon for an admitted felon without at least the *appearance* of a groundswell of public sympathy to back him up.

It will be a carefully orchestrated public relations campaign in the classic Nixon tradition. Ziegler will hold daily press briefings and read finely crafted descriptions of the former president's pitiful condition from the typewriter of Ray Price, Nixon's former chief speechwriter at the White House. Both Price and Pat Buchanan, the left and right forks of Nixon's tongue ever since he decided to make his move on the White House back in 1965, showed up at the San Clemente fortress in early September, both insisting they had just come out to say hello and "check up on the old man." As it happened, however, they both appeared about the same time rumors began surfacing in New York about a $2 million advance that Nixon had been offered for his memoirs.

Neither Price nor Buchanan claimed to know anything definite about the book offer, but in New York Spiro Agnew's literary agent was telling everybody who asked that the Nixon deal could be closed momentarily for at least $2 million, and maybe more.

That is a hell of a lot of money for *anybody's* memoirs—even people who might reasonably be expected to tell the truth. But even a ridiculously fraudulent version of his five and a half wretched years in the White House and his own twisted view of the scandal that finished him off would be an automatic best seller if the book-buying public could be conned somehow into believing Richard Nixon was actually the author.

Meanwhile, with either Price or Buchanan or both standing ready to write his memoirs for him, Nixon was pondering an offer from *Reader's Digest* to sign on as a "consulting editor" at a salary of $100,000 a year . . . And Thursday of that week, President Ford made headlines by urging the Congress to appropriate $850,000 to cover Nixon's pension, living expenses, and other costs of the painful transition from the White House to San Clemente. When the $850,000 runs out, he will have to scrimp until July 1 of next year, when he will pick up another $400,000 that will have to last him until July 1, 1976. For as long as he lives, Richard Nixon will be on the federal dole for $400,000 a year—$60,000 pension, $96,000 to cover his personal staff salaries, $40,000 for travel, $21,000 to cover his telephone bills, and $100,000 for "miscellaneous."

On top of his $300,000 annual expense account, Nixon's twenty-four-hour-a-day Secret Service protection will cost the taxpayers between $500 and $1,000 a day for as long as he lives—a conservative figure, considering the daily cost of things like helicopters, patrol boats, walkie-talkies, and car telephones, along with salaries and living expenses for ten or twelve full-time agents. There is also the $40,000 a year Ron Ziegler still commands as a ranking public servant. Add another $30,000 to $50,000 each for personal aides like Stephen Bull and Rose Mary Woods, plus all their living and travel expenses—and the cost of maintaining Richard Nixon in exile adds up to something like $750,000 a year . . . and these are merely the *expenses*. His personal income will presumably derive from things like the $2 million advance on his memoirs, his $100,000-a-year stipend from *Reader's Digest*, and the $5,000 a crack he can average, with no effort at all, on the year-round lecture circuit.

So . . . what we are looking at here is a millionaire ex-president and admitted felon: a congenital thief and pathological liar who spent twenty-eight years on the public sugar tit and then quit just in time to avoid the axe. If he had fought to the bitter end, as he'd promised Julie he would "as long as even one senator believes in me," he risked losing about 95 percent of the $400,000 annual allowance he became qualified for under the "Former Presidents Act" by resigning . . . But a president who gets impeached, convicted, and dragged out of the White House by U.S. marshals is not covered by the Former Presidents Act. If Nixon had fought to the end and lost—which had become absolutely inevitable by the time he resigned—he would have forfeited all but about $15,000 a year from the federal dole . . . So, in retrospect, the reason he quit is as easy to see as the numbers on his personal balance sheet. The difference between resignation and being kicked out of office was about $385,000 a year for the rest of his life.

Most of this annual largesse will come, one way or another, out of the pockets of the taxpayers. *All* of the taxpayers. Even George and Eleanor McGovern will contribute a slice of their income to Richard Nixon's retirement fund . . . And so will I, unless Jaworski can nail the bastard on enough felony counts to strip him not only of his right to vote, like Agnew, but also his key to the back door of the Federal Treasury—which is not very likely now that Ford has done everything but announce the date for when he will grant the pardon.

• • •

Few people had been told, officially, about the president's new tape toy; the only people who knew about it, officially, were Nixon, Haldeman, Larry Higby, Steve Bull, Alex Butterfield, and the three Secret Service agents responsible for keeping it in order . . . But unofficially almost everybody with personal access to the Oval Office had either been told on the sly or knew Richard Nixon well enough so they didn't need to be told . . . In any case, there is enough testimony in the files of the Senate Watergate Committee to suggest that most of them had their own recording systems and taped most of what they said to each other anyway.

Neither John Ehrlichman nor Charles Colson, for instance, were "officially" aware of the stunningly sophisticated network of hidden bugs that the Technical Security Division of the Secret Service had constructed for President Nixon. According to Alex Butterfield's testimony in closed hearings before the House Judiciary Committee, Nixon told chief SS agent Wong to have his electronics experts wire every room, desk, lamp, phone, and mantelpiece inside the White House grounds where the president was likely ever to utter a word of more than one syllable on any subject.

I've been using tape recorders in all kinds of journalistic situations for almost ten years, all kinds of equipment, ranging from ten-inch studio reels to raisin-sized minibugs—but I have never even *seen* anything like the system the Secret Service experts rigged up for Nixon in the White House. In addition to dozens of wireless, voice-activated mikes about the size of a pencil eraser that he had built into the woodwork, there were also custom-built sensors, delay mechanisms, and "standby" switches wired into telephones that either Bull or Butterfield could activate.

In the Cabinet Room, for instance, Nixon had microphones built into the bases of the wall lamps that he could turn on or off with harmless-looking buzzers labeled "Haldeman" and "Butterfield" on the rug underneath the cabinet table in front of his chair. The tapes and recording equipment were installed in a locked closet in the basement of the West Wing, but Nixon could start the reels rolling by simply pressing on the floor buzzer marked "Butterfield" with the toe of his shoe—and to stop the reels, putting the machinery back on standby, he could step on the "Haldeman" button . . .

Any serious description of Nixon's awesome tape-recording system would take thousands of words and boggle the minds of most laymen, but even this quick capsule is enough to suggest two fairly obvious but rarely mentioned conclusions: Anybody with this kind of a tape system, installed and maintained twenty-four hours a day by Secret Service electronics experts, is going to consistently produce extremely high quality voice reproductions. And since the White House personnel office can hire the best transcribing typists available and provide them with the best tape-transcribing machinery on the market, there is only one conceivable reason for those thousands of maddening, strategically spotted "unintelligibles" in the Nixon version of the White House Tapes. Any Kelly Girl agency in the country would have given Nixon his money back if their secretaries had done that kind of damage to his transcripts. Sloppiness of that magnitude can only be deliberate, and Nixon is known to have personally edited most of those tape transcripts before they were typed for the printer . . . Which doesn't mean much, now that Nixon's version of the transcripts is no longer potential evidence but sloppy artifacts that are no longer even interesting to read except as an almost criminally inept contrast to the vastly more detailed and coherent transcripts that House Judiciary Committee transcribers produced from the same tapes. The only people with any reason to worry about either the implications of those butchered transcripts or the ham-fisted criminal who did the final editing job are the editors at whichever publishing house decides to pay Richard Nixon $2 million for his presidential memoirs, which will be heavily dependent on that vast haul of Oval Office tapes that Gerald Ford has just decreed are the personal property of Richard Nixon. He will have the final edit on *those* transcripts, too—just before he sends the final draft of his memoirs to the printer. The finished book will probably sell for $15, and a lot of people will be stupid enough to buy it.

The second and more meaningful aspect vis-à-vis Nixon's tape system has to do with the way he used it. Most tape freaks see their toys as a means to bug other people, but Nixon had the SS technicians install almost every concealed bug in his system with a keen eye for its proximity to Richard Nixon.

According to Butterfield, Nixon was so obsessed with recording every move and moment of his presidency for the history books that he often seemed to be thinking of nothing else. When he walked from the White House to his office in the Executive Office Building (EOB), for instance, he would carry a small tape recorder in front of his mouth and maintain a steady conversation with it as he moved in his stiff-legged way across the lawn . . . And although we will never hear those tapes, the mere fact that he was constantly making them, for reasons of his own, confirms Alex Butterfield's observation that Richard Nixon was so bewitched with the fact that he really was *the president* that his only sense of himself in that job came from the moments he could somehow record and squirrel away in some safe place, for tomorrow night or the ages.

There is a bleeding kind of irony in this unnatural obsession of Nixon's with his place in history when you realize what must have happened to his mind when he finally realized, probably sometime in those last few days of his doomed presidency, just exactly what kind of place in history was even then being carved out for him.

In the way it is usually offered, the sleazy little argument that "Nixon has been punished enough" is an ignorant, hack politician cliché . . . But that image of him walking awkward and alone across the White House lawn at night, oblivious to everything in front or on either side of him except that little black and silver tape recorder that he is holding up to his lips, talking softly and constantly to "history," with the brittle intensity of a madman: when you think on that image for a while, remember that the name Nixon will seem to give off a strange odor every time it is mentioned for the next three hundred years, and in every history book written from now on, "Nixon" will be synonymous with shame, corruption, and failure.

No other president in American history has been driven out of the White House in a cloud of disgrace. No other president has been forced to preside over the degrading collapse of his own administration or been forced to stand aside and watch helplessly—and also guiltily—while some of his close friends and ranking assistants are led off to jail. And finally, no president of the United States has ever been so vulnerable to criminal prosecution, so menaced by the threat of indictment and trial, crouched in the dock of a federal courtroom and so obviously headed for prison that only the sudden grant of presidential pardon from the man he appointed to succeed him could prevent his final humiliation.

These are the stinking realities that will determine Richard Nixon's place in American history . . . And in this ugly context, the argument that "Richard Nixon has been punished enough" takes on a different meaning. He will spend many nights by himself in his study out there in San Clemente, listening over and over to those tapes he made for the ages and half remembering the feel of thick grass on the Rose Garden lawn adding a strange new spring to his walk, even making him talk a bit louder as he makes his own knotty, plastic kind of love to his sweet little Japanese bride, telling it over and over again that he really *is* The President, The Most Powerful Man in the World—and goddamn it, you better never forget that!

• • •

Richard Nixon is free now. He bargained wisely and well. His arrangement with Ford has worked nicely, despite that week or so of bad feeling when he had to get a little rough with Jerry about the pardon, threatening to call in the *L.A. Times* man and play that quick little tape of their conversation in the Oval Office—the one where he offered to make Jerry the vice president in exchange for a presidential pardon whenever he asked for it—and he had known, by then, that he would probably need it a lot sooner than Jerry realized. Once their arrangement was made (and taped), Nixon just rode for as long as he could, then got off in time to sign up for his lifetime dole as a former president.

He will rest for a while, then come back to haunt us again. His mushwit son-in-law, David Eisenhower, is urging him to run for the U.S. Senate from California in 1976, and Richard Nixon is shameless enough to do it. Or if not in the Senate, he will turn up somewhere else. The only thing we can be absolutely sure of, at this point in time, is that we are going to have Richard Milhous Nixon to kick around for at least a little while longer.

Saigon

With both Hunter and Jann Wenner scouting around for the next epic story for Hunter to cover, Vietnam soon emerged as the obvious elephant in the room, with Saigon on the brink of falling. Hunter waltzed in to the war with thousands of dollars duct-taped to his torso, made a few tentative trips to combat zones, and spent the rest of his time drinking in his hotel's courtyard with the other war correspondents before fleeing to a hotel by the beach in Laos as Saigon became engulfed in chaos. Hunter's Vietnam epic was never written; whether due to stress, fear, exhaustion, or a profound kind of writer's block, Hunter's confrontation with his generation's defining war produced only these brief notes and correspondence.

Letter from JSW to HST, 4/22/75

Hunter,

My many years of experience in war coverage and running military press corps, involvement in revolutions, and general talent for blitzkrieg action, tells me that you should make your own decision as to when to leave Saigon for a safe zone. I do not want coverage of Saigon after the official evacutaion and do not want you to stay unless you personally want to. Your insurance expires once the embassy closes. I cannot afford twenty-five grand for a post-evacuation piece. Think it would be unwise and unsafe for you to stay since you don't know the city or the local citizens or have any time-tested credentials with the soon-to-be new centers.

It's impossible for us to get a phone call through, otherwise

I would have certainly called up for a speed-crazed chat about what you should do in a situation with which I'm totally familiar, and . . . Jesus, the overseas operator just said that all Saigon numbers beginning with nine are now completely out . . . So I guess we can't have that telephone call, and I was looking forward to negotiating the prices and the expenses on the piece.

Would like you to return to San Francisco rather than write in Hong Kong or visit Laos since the piece is on the last days of the American Empire in Saigon, and seeing the half-mad ambassador fleeing with the flag under his arm would make a nice kicker. If you go through Hong Kong, wire and call from there and we can settle deadlines then.

In closing, I wish I was there with you, facing the problem.

Jann

Interdicted Dispatch from the Global Affairs Desk

May 22, 1975

We won a military victory over the French and we'll win it over the Americans too. Yes, their Dien Bien Phu is still to come, and it will come. The Americans will lose the war on the day when their military might is at its maximum and the great machine they've put together can't move any more . . . Because all that money and strength will be a stone around their neck. It's inevitable.

—General Vo Nguyen Giap, 1969

It is 3:55 on a hot, wet Sunday morning in Saigon, and I am out of ice again. It has been raining most of the night, and the patio bar here in the Hotel Continental closed early. The paper in my notebook is limp, and the blue and white tiles on my floor are so slick with humidity that not even these white-canvas, rubber-soled basketball shoes can provide enough real traction for me to pace back and forth in the classic, high-speed style of a man caving in to The Fear.

This empty silver ice bucket is the least of my problems tonight; all I have to do to get it filled is go out in the darkened hallway and wake up any of the three or four tiny, frail-looking old men in white pajamas who are sleeping uneasily out there on green bamboo mats behind the circular staircase leading down to the lobby. The slightest noise or touch will wake them instantly; and after sleeping outside my room for almost a week, they have learned to live with my nightly ice problem in the same spirit of tolerant fatalism that I have learned to live with the nightly thumping sound of artillery fire outside my window, five or six miles to the south. It is a sound I have never heard before—not even from a safe distance—so I can never be sure if the faraway, deep-rumbling explosions that rattle the ice in my bucket every night are "outgoing" or "incoming."

There has been a noticeable lack of distant artillery fire tonight—which is probably an ominous sign, because it means the Viet Cong and North Vietnamese troops that already surround this doomed volcano of a city on three sides are no doubt spending these peaceful, early morning hours rolling their doomsday 130-mm siege cannons into place out there in the mud just north of Saigon's defense line around Bien Hoa and the remnants of what was once the biggest U.S. Air Force base outside the continental U.S. The ARVN Eighteenth Division that was supposed to protect Bien Hoa—just fifteen miles north of Saigon, on a four-lane concrete highway—has apparently been ground into hamburger in the weeklong battle for Xuan Loc. Latest reports from the front, as it were, say that two of the Eighteenth's three regiments no longer exist, for one reason or another, and that the third is down to an effective fighting strength of five hundred men.

Last week—just before I was forced to fly up to Hong Kong for an emergency medulla transplant—the ARVN Eighteenth Division consisted of three regiments of two thousand men each, and they were making a surprisingly strong stand at Xuan Loc, in a battle that most military experts considered both the beginning and the end of "The Battle for Saigon."

Well . . . If that's true, we are in serious trouble down here. I can ponder the big map of Vietnam on the wall of the *Rolling Stone* Global Affairs Suite in the Hotel Continental and see that the distance between Bien Hoa and Saigon is just about the width of a Dunhill cigarette or maybe a penlight-size transistor radio battery, which is not very far—on the map or the highway or any other way you want to measure it. There is no doubt at all in the minds of the veteran war correspondents who now occupy almost every room in the Continental and also the Caravelle—about two hundred yards across Lam Son Square from my window—that the streets of Saigon could be full of VC sappers and NVA tanks at any moment . . . Which also means we might all find ourselves jolted out of bed by a chain-lightning blast of explosions outside or even inside the hotel at any moment, and the dawn streets of Saigon will be full of round-eyed, long-nosed journalists running like crazed rats toward one of the "assembly points for emergency conditions" on the list just published yesterday by the U.S. Embassy.

These fourteen newly designated assembly points are mostly tall buildings with spacious rooftops in downtown Saigon, to which we can all flee and be picked up by U.S. Marine helicopters and ferried out to one of the Seventh Fleet aircraft carriers waiting offshore, then whisked off to the safety of the U.S. Naval Base at Subic Bay in the Philippines.

This is all stone madness, of course. If an incoming rocket blew the lobby of this hotel out from under me right now, I would quickly consult the emergency evacuation instructions and see that my "assembly point" is "3 Phan Van Dat"—which means absolutely nothing to me; it might as well be the address of a Coptic massage parlor in Macao, or maybe a street nickname for the number-three son of a once-proud South Vietnamese family, who recently turned to opium and bought himself a few suits of tailor-made, black-silk pajamas.

Probably some of the veteran war correspondents, sleeping heavily now in their high-ceilinged, tile-floored rooms up and down the dark hallway from mine, know exactly what "3 Phan Van Dat" means . . . But I am the only English-speaking person awake in the Continental at this hour, and even if I rushed out in the hall and began kicking savagely on every door I can reach—screaming: "Banzai! The jig is up!"—it wouldn't cause much of a rumble, because at least half the denizens of this elegant old French colonial hotel tonight are either drunk, stoned, or helplessly paralyzed by opium.

The nine o'clock curfew imposed on Saigon by General Nguyen Van Thieu's shaky government had a bad effect on the city's social life. All bars, restaurants, and other public nightspots are closed by eight thirty—so the employees can get home before nine, when squads of young ARVN soldiers and ill-tempered military police begin roaming the downtown streets with orders to shoot anybody still moving around.

The object of the curfew is to discourage any VC sappers or other bomb-throwing terrorist types who might otherwise feel free to skulk around at night and cause trouble. But one of the most painfully visible side effects of the curfew has been to make us all prisoners from nine at night until six in the morning in whatever hotel we're staying in: and after a month or so of this, a lot of people are starting to cave in to almost any vice or noxious habit they can get their hands on. The styles of overindulgence seem to vary—in tandem with the political viewpoints—from one hotel to another. The Continental, for instance, is generally considered to be full of "pinkos and dope fiends" by the "old Asia hands" across the square in the Caravelle, where the political style is more hawkish and the vice style tends more to booze and brawling.

Last night in the Caravelle bar, an argument between some British newspaper correspondents and a group of pilots from Flying Tiger airlines erupted into violence and a serious beating for one of the Britishers . . . while the only casualties in the Continental last night occurred in a room just up the wide spiral staircase from mine, where a half-dozen American journalists were brought to their knees by a combination of opium, Pernod, and brutal Cambodian grass.

These are some of the people I would have to wake up and depend on for guidance in the event of a sudden rocket attack. This afternoon I tried to teach some of them to use the hellishly expensive but technically simple Transceiver radio units I brought back from Hong Kong—along with about a thousand hits of Lomotil and three quarts of a powerful antinausea medicine called Emetrol—but not even the sharpest of the *Time* and *Newsweek* correspondents could cope with a basic walkie-talkie unit.

After the weekly Saturday morning Viet Cong press conference in the tightly guarded VC (or PRG) compound at Tan Son Nhut air base—Saigon's only remaining air link to the outside world—the mood of the strangely massive Caucasian press corps was so grim that many of them decided effectively to cash their U.S. Embassy PX cards by using up all their three-quart-per-month booze allotments in one final run on the PX. And since the embassy press office has still not approved my application for PX privileges, I decided to stay in the hotel with the master unit (a Sanyo Transworld Blue Impulse 7700) and establish the range effectiveness of the slave units by maintaining radio contact for as long as possible with the gaggle of flakes who planned to broadcast constantly back to the hotel from their jeep on the five-mile run through midtown Saigon traffic to the PX out by the air base.

This is the same nasty gauntlet we will all have to run when the hammer comes down and the embassy's helicopter-evacuation plan is destroyed by fear-crazed mobs and fleeing ARVN soldiers firing M-16s at the choppers from the smoking streets below . . . so it seemed like a good idea to run a field test on the radios and learn how to use them before the inevitable nightmare erupts.

But the test was a total failure. The *Time* man accidentally pushed a switch on the back of his unit and broadcast feverishly on the wrong frequency; and the *Newsweek* man failed to grasp the meaning of his "push to talk" button . . . leaving me in the hotel shouting futilely into my transmitter and receiving nothing but sporadic bursts of gibberish in Vietnamese . . . And then, about five hours later, I discovered both slave units were still turned on, a careless little oversight that drained twelve of the few remaining full-strength penlight batteries left in Saigon. There are plenty of them still for sale in the infamous "thieves' market" a few blocks away, but most of those are either used or stone dead, and that is not the kind of batteries we will need in an emergency.

Indeed, perhaps the only thing almost everybody in Saigon can agree on right now is that none of us has the vaguest goddamn idea what we will either need, do, or even attempt when the volcano finally blows all around us—and our botched trial run with the Transceiver units bodes ill for our chances of coping with things like 130-mm artillery bombs blowing hot shrapnel and chunks of human flesh all over the streets and turning downtown Saigon into an Asian replay of the Last Days of Berlin.

Even if Tan Son Nhut Airport remains functional, the inevitable panic in the streets will make it impossible for most of us to get there anyway . . . And once the airport is either closed by rocket fire or cut off by hostile mobs, our only chance for evacuation will be the air fleet of huge "Jolly Green Giant" Chinook helicopters that the embassy plans to load us into at the "secret" assembly points.

Jesus, what a nightmare! Every one of the half million or so South Vietnamese who expects to be slaughtered when the VC and the NVA finally overrun Saigon knows the exact location of these assembly points and they all keep their FM radios tuned, day and night, to the American broadcast frequency, 99.9—just like those of us hunkered down here in the Caravelle and the Continental in the middle of town—for the "secret code message" that will announce the start of the evacuation. Right: a news bulletin saying "The temperature is 105 and rising," followed by the first eight bars of "I'm Dreaming of a White Christmas."

And any Vietnamese who doesn't have an FM radio and hasn't heard about the assembly points can rush down to the shrunken "American Zone" around the big hotels along Tu Do Street and follow the first terrified round-eye he sees running along the maimed sidewalks with a suitcase in his hand. The noise of the huge Chinooks overhead will be deafening, especially when they start converging in a hail of rockets and automatic-rifle fire around the rooftops of a few tall buildings.

SX onpass Rolling Stone to Paul Scanlon, Rolling Stone, San Francisco Telex number RS 34 0337.

The phone lines are temporarily out of order here and I can't call so here is how I see the situation. I will file another 2,000 or maybe a bit more if possible, which should start reaching you Monday afternoon or Monday night and Tuesday morning.

Thanx Hunter—NTL 1520PM

SX onpass Rolling Stone HST-Saigon . . . page one. To: Paul Scanlon . . . Rolling Stone . . . San Francisco Telex number RS 34 0337. From: Hunter Thompson . . . Global Affairs Desk . . . room 9.37, Continental Hotel . . . Saigon . . . April 20, 1975.

Everybody here is becoming very edgy and kind of bone-marrow nervous. Advance units of the NVA are now only five miles out of town and they could immobilize the airport at any moment with artillery fire and that would cut us off from all access to the outside world except by Marine helicopters. It's also possible that a rocket could hit at any moment near enough to send me running over to UPI with whatever I have, hoping to get it on the wire before they begin operating under emergency conditions and not using their Telex for anything but their own copy. So if you stop receiving from me and don't understand why, check with UPI and find out if the situation here has turned weird.

Loren Jenkins, the *Newsweek* bureau chief, just sent his local fixer out to the black market to buy us two flak jackets, two helmets, and maybe a few bayonets, which are suddenly a hot item here.

I've been trying to buy a revolver, but again for obvious reasons they cannot be had for any price at this time. Some of the press vets are saying we should get some M-16s into this hotel, so the place can be defended—at least until the Marine choppers arrive—from rampaging mobs. So we are now looking at a sort of Alamo gig here in the Continental, although about half the press is against the idea because they figure any fire coming out of this hotel will merely attract fire from the uglies. I'm not sure how I feel about this at the moment, but I'm inclined to think having an M-16 around might not be a bad idea—not to use against the VC or the NVA, but against any panic-crazed mobs of deserters or savage locals who might figure the last Americans they'll ever have a chance to get even with, as it were, are the 500 or so correspondents trapped downtown in the Continental and the Caravelle. You might also advise Jann that the three-unit, triangulated walkie-talkie system I brought back from Hong Kong is now being used by other press here in the hotel and in the event of a sudden emergency it will definitely be pressed into service by the people in charge of evacuation. When Phnom Penh was evacuated, the press had to abandon everything from their personal typewriters to network TV cameras . . . Ah, Jesus . . . here comes another nasty bit: I sent Laura Palmer out to the airport a few hours ago and she just came back with a tale of woe, madness, and panic among the frightened mob of Americans out there. The evacuation planes are now running all night (this just happened) and people are being shoveled into them like coal into a furnace. I get the same frenzied reports from other correspondents who spent most of the day out there . . . We have only two hours left before curfew, and I can't get from here to UPI after nine tonight without risking being shot and the people at UPI have advised me not to take the risk because the ARVN troops and police out there in the street have orders to shoot anybody moving around and ask questions later.

We are in serious trouble down here in the eye of the hurricane. Saigon is Gen. Giap's "ultimate military objective," and he has spent the past week or so moving the elite 325th NVA "Steel Division" down from the North. The "Steel Division" is the one that cracked the French at Dien Bien Phu, and if Giap's finely honed sense of drama and timing should tell us anything right now, it is that once the 325th (check this number with UPI, if possible) is ready to roll, the fate of Saigon will be sealed. Xuan Loc is already cut off—along with some 10,000 of the

ARVN's best troops—and Bien Hoa has been under steady rocket and mortar attack for the past two days. Giap now has ten full-strength divisions surrounding Saigon, backed up with all the heavy 130s he needs and enough Russian- (and American-) built tanks to mount a final, high-speed blitzkrieg assault on Saigon any time he wants.

There are a lot of people here who think the ARVN will make a gallant last stand and hold for at least a few days at Bien Hoa before fleeing back into the city and turning it into another Da Nang scene . . . But my own feeling is that the battle for Saigon is already over, and once the Steel Division starts moving they will not even stop for a joint break until they get all the way into Saigon. And that is only a matter of hours.

. . . Jesus, I just got very repeat very reliable word that things have suddenly changed dramatically for the worse and we can expect the big move on Saigon to begin rolling tonight or tomorrow, but I can't give any details via Telex for obvious reasons . . . But you can expect my copy flow to be interdicted, as they say, at any moment from now on, and in fact you may have to use this stuff as either the ending for the piece or as some kind of intro/editor's note explaining why my story sounds so jerky, garbled, and unfinished. We are working under extreme tension here.

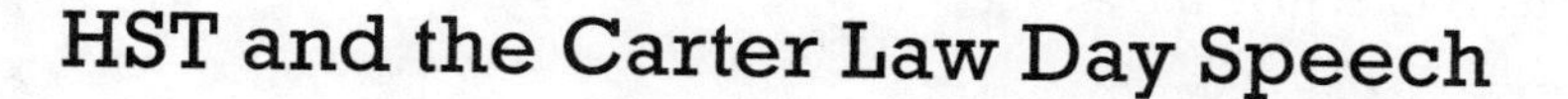

HST and the Carter Law Day Speech

Two years before his presidential run, Jimmy Carter gave a little-noticed speech at the University of Georgia. Hunter, having flown to town with Ted Kennedy, happened to be in the audience, and what he heard—in between regular trips outside to retrieve a bottle of Wild Turkey from the trunk of a Secret Service car—stunned him. For years, Hunter forced friends to listen to his audio recording of what became known as the Law Day speech, which Hunter compares to General Douglas MacArthur's "old soldiers never die" address to Congress in 1951 for sheer oratorical power. (Hunter also conducted lengthy interviews with the candidate, which President Carter recalls as being lengthy and very revealing—so much so, in fact, that the president was relieved to hear from Hunter later that he'd lost all the audiotapes.)

Letter from HST TO JSW

Oct 27 '77

Jann/

—now is the time to start pondering "The Case of James Earl Carter." A proper Job would need about 6 months, all expenses, a window looking down on the fountain and $44k.

—I've got better things to do; but, then, so did Moses.

—Somebody is going to do it, + the price will be high. All around, my own recommendations follow in order of mutual preference:

1—ignore the whole idea + keep riding the hyena
2—hire professionals to do the job
3—if all else fails, + you still want to know what a real firestorm feels like, give me a ring.

A 3-part "Assessment," beginning in Sept '78—followed by a 200-pg. book in the summer of '79—will just about make the nut—(add another $250k advance for the book, for old times sake . . .)

Okay. That's it for now.

/H

Fear & Loathing on the Campaign Trail '76: Third-Rate Romance, Low-Rent Rendezvous

June 3, 1976

It is extremely difficult to concentrate on the cheap realities of campaign '76. The idea of covering even the early stages of this cynical and increasingly retrograde campaign has already plunged me into a condition bordering on terminal despair, and if I thought I might have to stay with these people all the way to November, I would change my name and seek work as a professional alligator poacher in the swamps around Lake Okeechobee. My frame of mind is not right for another long and maddening year of total involvement in a presidential campaign . . . and somewhere in the back of my brain lurks a growing suspicion that this campaign is not right either; but that is not the kind of judgment any journalist should make at this point. At least not in print.

So for the moment I will try to suspend both the despair and the final judgment. Both will be massively justified in the next few months, I think—and until then I can fall back on the firmly held but rarely quoted conviction of most big-time Washington pols that *nobody* can function at top form on a full-time basis in more than one presidential campaign. This rule of thumb has never been applied to journalists, to my knowledge, but there is ample evidence to suggest it should be. There is no reason to think that even the best and brightest of journalists, as it were, can repeatedly or even more than once crank themselves up to the level of genuinely fanatical energy, commitment, and total concentration it takes to live in the speeding vortex of a presidential campaign from start to finish. There is not enough room on that hell-bound train for anybody who wants to relax and act human now and then. It is a gig for ambitious zealots and terminal action junkies . . . and this is especially true of a campaign like this one, which so far lacks any central, overriding issue like the war in Vietnam that brought so many talented and totally dedicated nonpoliticians into the '68 and '72 campaigns.

The issues this time are too varied and far too complex for the instant polarization of a Which Side Are You On? crusade. There will not be many ideologues seriously involved in the '76 campaign; this one is a technicians' trip, run by and for politicians . . . Which is not really a hell of a lot different from any other campaign, except that this time it is going to be painfully obvious. This time, on the two hundredth anniversary of what used to be called "the American Dream," we are going to have our noses rubbed, day after day—on the tube and in the headlines—in this mess we have made for ourselves.

> *Today, wherever in this world I meet a man or woman who fought for Spanish liberty, I meet a kindred soul. In those years we lived our best, and what has come after and what there is to come can never carry us to those heights again.*
>
> —from *The Education of a Correspondent* by Herbert Matthews

So much for the idea of a sequel to *Fear and Loathing on the Campaign Trail '72.* Barring some totally unexpected development, I will leave the dreary task of chronicling this low-rent trip to Teddy White, who is already trapped in a place I don't want to be.

But there is no way to escape without wallowing deep in the first few primaries and getting a feel, more or less, for the evidence . . . And in order to properly depress and degrade myself for the ordeal to come, I decided in early January to resurrect the National Affairs desk and set up, once again, in the place where I spent so much time in 1972 and then again in 1974. These were the boom-and-bust years of Richard Milhous Nixon, who was criminally insane and also president of the United States for five years.

> *If any person shall carnally know in any manner any brute animal, or carnally know any male or female person by the anus or by and with*

the mouth, or voluntarily submit to such carnal knowledge, he or she shall be guilty of a felony and shall be confined in the penitentiary not less than one year nor more than three years.

—Commonwealth of Virginia Anti-Sodomy Statute, 1792

One of the most difficult problems for a journalist covering a presidential campaign is getting to know the candidates well enough to make confident judgments about them, because it is just about impossible for a journalist to establish a personal relationship with any candidate who has already made the big leap from "long shot" to "serious contender." The problem becomes more and more serious as the stakes get higher, and by the time a candidate has survived enough primaries to convince himself and his staff that they will all be eating their lunches in the White House Mess for the next four years, he is long past the point of having either the time or the inclination to treat any journalist who doesn't already know him personally as anything but just another face in the campaign "press corps."

There are many complex theories about the progressive stages of a presidential campaign, but for the moment let's say there are three: Stage one is the period between the decision to run for president and the morning after the New Hampshire primary when the field is still crowded, the staff organizations are still loose and relaxed, and most candidates are still hungry for all the help they can get—especially media exposure, so they can get their names in the Gallup poll; stage two is the "winnowing out," the separating of the sheep from the goats, when the two or three survivors of the early primaries begin looking like long-distance runners with a realistic shot at the party nomination; and stage three begins whenever the national media, the public opinion polls, and Mayor Daley of Chicago decide that a candidate has picked up enough irreversible momentum to begin looking like at least a *probable* nominee, and a *possible* next president.

This three-stage breakdown is not rooted in any special wisdom or scientific analysis, but it fits both the 1972 and 1976 Democratic campaigns well enough to make the point that any journalist who doesn't get a pretty firm personal fix on a candidate while he's still in stage one might just as well go with his or her instincts all the way to Election Day in November, because once a candidate gets to stage two his whole lifestyle changes drastically.

At that point he becomes a public figure, a serious contender, and the demands on his time and energy begin escalating to the level of madness. He wakes up every morning to face a split-second, eighteen-hour-a-day schedule of meetings, airports, speeches, press conferences, motorcades, and handshaking. Instead of rambling, off-the-cuff talks over a drink or two with reporters from small-town newspapers, he is suddenly flying all over the country in his own chartered jet full of syndicated columnists and network TV stars . . . Cameras and microphones follow him everywhere he goes, and instead of pleading long and earnestly for the support of fifteen amateur political activists gathered in some English professor's living room in Keene, New Hampshire, he is reading the same cliché-riddled speech—often three or four times in a single day—to vast auditoriums full of people who either laugh or applaud at all the wrong times and who may or may not be supporters . . . And all the fat cats, labor leaders, and big-time pols who couldn't find the time to return his phone calls when he was desperately looking for help a few months ago are now ringing his phone off the hook within minutes after his arrival in whatever Boston, Miami, or Milwaukee hotel his managers have booked him into that night. But they are not calling to offer their help and support, they just want to make sure he understands that they don't plan to help or support anybody else, until they get to know *him* a little better.

It is a very mean game that these high-rolling, coldhearted hustlers play. The president of the United States may no longer be "the most powerful man in the world," but he is still close enough to be sure that nobody else in the world is going to cross him by accident. And anybody who starts looking like he might get his hands on that kind of power had better get comfortable, right from the start, with the certain knowledge that he is going to have to lean on some very mean and merciless people just to get himself elected.

Tonight, I am going to call my old friend, Pat Caddell, who is Jimmy Carter's pollster and one of the two or three main wizards in Carter's brain trust, and we will have another one of our daily philosophical chats. Jimmy Carter is always the main topic when I talk to Caddell, and we've been talking, arguing, plotting, haggling, and generally whipping on each other almost constantly, ever since this third-rate, low-rent campaign circus hit the public roads about four months ago.

That was *before* Pat went to work for Jimmy, but long after I'd been cited in about thirty-three dozen journals all over the country as one of Carter's earliest and most fervent supporters. Everywhere I went for at least the past year, from Los Angeles to Austin, Nashville, Washington, Boston, Chicago, and Key West, I've been publicly hammered by friends and strangers alike for saying that I "like Jimmy Carter." I have been jeered by large crowds for saying this; I have been mocked in print by liberal pundits and other Gucci people; I have been called a brain-damaged geek by some of my best and oldest friends; my own wife threw a knife at me on the night of the Wisconsin primary when the midnight radio stunned us both with a news bulletin from a CBS station in Los Angeles, saying that earlier announcements by NBC and ABC regarding Mo Udall's narrow victory over Carter in Wisconsin were not true, and that late returns from the rural districts were running so heavily in Carter's favor that CBS was now calling him the winner.

Sandy likes Mo Udall; and so do I, for that matter . . . I also like Jerry Jeff Walker, the Scofflaw King of New Orleans and a lot of other people I don't necessarily believe should be president of the United States. The immense concentration of power in that office is just too goddamn heavy for anybody with good sense to turn his back on. Or *her* back. Or *its* back . . . At least not as long as whatever lives in the White House has the power to fill vacancies on the U.S. Supreme Court; because anybody with that kind of power can use it—like Nixon did—to pack-crowd the Court of Final Appeal in this country with the same kind of lame, vindictive yo-yos who recently voted to sustain the commonwealth of Virginia's antisodomy statutes . . . And anybody who thinks that a 6–3 vote against "sodomy" is some kind of abstract legal gibberish that doesn't really affect *them* had better hope they never get busted for anything the Bible or any local vice-squad cop calls an "unnatural sex act." Because "unnatural" is defined by the laws of almost every state in the Union as anything but a quick and dutiful hump in the classic missionary position, for purposes of procreation only. Anything else is a *felony crime*, and people who commit felony crimes *go to prison*.

Which won't make much difference to me. I took that fatal dive off the straight and narrow path so long ago that I can't remember when I first became a felon—but I have been one ever since, and it's way too late to change now. In the eyes of The Law, my whole life has been one long and sinful felony. I have sinned repeatedly, as often as possible, and just as soon as I can get away from this goddamn Calvinist typewriter I am going to get right after it again . . . God knows, I hate it, but I can't help myself after all these criminal years. Like Waylon Jennings says, "The devil made me do it the first time. The second time, I done it on my own."

Right. And the third time, I did it because of brain damage . . . And after that: well, I figured that anybody who was already doomed to a life of crime and sin might as well learn to love it.

Anything worth all that risk and energy almost has to be beyond the reach of any kind of redemption except the power of Pure Love . . . and this flash of twisted wisdom brings us back, strangely enough, to *politics*, Pat Caddell, and the 1976 presidential campaign . . . And, not incidentally, to the fact that any Journal on any side of Wall Street that ever quoted me as saying "I like Jimmy Carter" was absolutely accurate. I have said it many times, to many people, and I will keep on saying it until Jimmy Carter gives me some good reason to change my mind—which might happen about two minutes after he finishes reading this article: but I doubt it.

I have known Carter for more than two years and I have probably spent more private, human time with him than any other journalist on the '76 campaign trail. The first time I met him—at about eight o'clock on a Saturday morning in 1974 at the back door of the governor's mansion in Atlanta—I was about two degrees on the safe side of berserk, raving and babbling at Carter and his whole bemused family about some hostile bastard wearing a Georgia State Police uniform who had tried to prevent me from coming through the gate at the foot of the long, tree-shaded driveway leading up to the mansion.

I had been up all night, in the company of serious degenerates, and when I rolled up to the gatehouse in the backseat of a taxi I'd hailed in downtown Atlanta, the trooper was not amused by the sight and sound of my presence. I was trying to act calm, but after about thirty seconds I realized it wasn't working; the look on his face told me I was not getting through to the man. He stared at me, saying nothing, while I explained from my crouch in the backseat of the cab that I was late for breakfast with "the governor and Ted Kennedy" . . . Then he suddenly stiffened and began shouting at the cabdriver: "What kind of dumb shit are you trying to *pull*, buddy? Don't you know where you *are?*"

Before the cabbie could answer, the trooper smacked the flat of his hand down on the hood so hard that the whole cab rattled. "You! Shut this engine!" Then he pointed at me: "You! Out of the cab. Let's see some identification." He reached out for my wallet and motioned for me to follow him into the gatehouse. The cabbie started to follow, but the trooper waved him back. "Stay right where you are, good buddy. I'll *get* to you." The look on my driver's face said we were both going to jail and it was my fault. "It wasn't *my* idea to come out here," he whined. "This guy told me he was invited for breakfast with the governor."

The trooper was looking at the press cards in my wallet. I was already pouring sweat, and just as he looked over at me, I realized I was holding a can of beer in my hand. "You always bring your own beer when you have breakfast with the governor?" he asked.

I shrugged and dropped it in a nearby wastebasket.

"You!" he shouted. "What do you think you're doing?"

The scene went on for another twenty minutes. There were many phone calls, a lot of yelling, and finally the trooper reached somebody in the mansion who agreed to locate Senator Kennedy and ask if he knew "some guy name of Thompson, I got him down here, he's all beered up and wants to come up there for breakfast . . ."

Jesus, I thought, that's all Kennedy needs to hear. Right in the middle of breakfast with the governor of Georgia, some nervous old darky shuffles in from the kitchen to announce that the trooper down at the gatehouse is holding some drunkard who says he's a friend of Senator Kennedy's and he wants to come in and have breakfast . . .

• • •

Which was, in fact, a lie. I had not been invited for breakfast with the governor, and up to that point I had done everything in my power to avoid it. Breakfast is the only meal of the day that I tend to view with the same kind of traditionalized reverence that most people associate with lunch and dinner.

I like to eat breakfast alone, and almost never before noon; anybody with a terminally jangled lifestyle needs at least one psychic anchor every twenty-four hours, and mine is breakfast. In Hong Kong, Dallas, or at home—and regardless of whether or not I have been to bed—breakfast is a personal ritual that can only be properly observed alone, and in a spirit of genuine excess. The food factor should always be massive: four Bloody Marys, two grapefruits, a pot of coffee, Rangoon crepes, a half pound of either sausage, bacon, or corned beef hash with diced chilies, a Spanish omelette or eggs Benedict, a quart of milk, a chopped lemon for random seasoning, and something like a slice of key lime pie, two margaritas, and six lines of the best cocaine for dessert . . . Right, and there should also be two or three newspapers, all mail and messages, a telephone, a notebook for planning the next twenty-four hours, and at least one source of good music . . . All of which should be dealt with *outside*, in the warmth of a hot sun, and preferably stone naked.

It is not going to be easy for those poor bastards out in San Francisco who have been waiting all day in a condition of extreme fear and anxiety for my long and finely reasoned analysis of "The Meaning of Jimmy Carter" to come roaring out of my faithful Mojo Wire and across two thousand miles of telephone line to understand why I am sitting here in a Texas motel full of hookers and writing at length on The Meaning of Breakfast . . . But like almost everything else worth understanding, the explanation for this is deceptively quick and basic.

After more than ten years of trying to deal with politics and politicians in a professional manner, I have finally come to the harsh understanding that there is no way at all—not even for a doctor of chemotherapy with total access to the whole spectrum of legal and illegal drugs, the physical constitution of a mule shark, and a brain as rare and sharp and original as the Sloat diamond—to function as a political journalist without abandoning the whole concept of a decent breakfast. I have worked like twelve bastards for more than a decade to be able to have it both ways, but the conflict is too basic and too deeply rooted in the nature of both politics and breakfast to ever be reconciled. It is one of those very few Great Forks in the Road of Life that cannot be avoided: like a Jesuit priest who is also a practicing nudist with a $200-a-day smack habit wanting to be the first Naked Pope (or Pope Naked the First, if we want to use the language of the church) . . . Or a vegetarian pacifist with a .44 Magnum fetish who wants to run for president without giving up his membership in the National Rifle Association or his New York City pistol permit that allows him to wear twin six-guns on *Meet the Press*, *Face the Nation*, and all of his press conferences.

There are some combinations that *nobody* can handle: shooting bats on the wing with a double-barreled .410 and a head full of jimson weed is one of them, and another is the idea that it is possible for a freelance writer with at least four close friends named Jones to cover a hopelessly scrambled presidential campaign better than any six-man team of career political journalists on the *New York Times* or the *Washington Post* and still eat a three-hour breakfast in the sun every morning.

But I had not made the final decision on that morning when I rolled up to the gatehouse of the governor's mansion in Atlanta to have breakfast with Jimmy Carter and Ted Kennedy. My reason for being there at that hour was simply to get my professional schedule back in phase with Kennedy's political obligations for that day. He was scheduled to address a crowd of establishment heavies who would convene at the University of Georgia Law School at ten thirty in the morning to officially witness the unveiling of a huge and prestigious oil portrait of former secretary of state Dean Rusk, and his tentative schedule for Saturday called for him to leave the governor's mansion after breakfast and make the sixty-mile trip to Athens by means of the governor's official airplane . . . So in order to hook up with Kennedy and make the trip with him, I had no choice but to meet him for breakfast at the mansion, where he had spent the previous night at Carter's invitation.

Oddly enough, I had also been invited to spend Friday night in a bedroom at the governor's mansion. I had come down from Washington with Kennedy on Friday afternoon, and since I was the only journalist traveling with him that weekend, Governor Carter had seen fit to include me when he invited "the Kennedy party" to overnight at the mansion instead of a downtown hotel.

But I am rarely in the right frame of mind to spend the night in the house of a politician—at least not if I can spend it anywhere else, and on the previous night I figured I would be a lot happier in a room at the Regency Hyatt House than I would in the Georgia governor's mansion. Which may or may not have been true, but regardless of all that, I still had to be at the mansion for breakfast if I wanted to get any work done that weekend, and my work was to stay with Ted Kennedy.

The scene at the gate had unhinged me so thoroughly that I couldn't find the door I'd been told to knock on when I finally got out of my cab at the mansion . . . and by the time I finally got inside I was in no shape at all to deal with Jimmy Carter and his whole family. I didn't even recognize Carter when he met me at the door. All I knew was that a middle-aged man wearing Levi's was taking me into the dining room, where I insisted on sitting down for a while, until the tremors passed.

One of the first things I noticed about Carter, after I'd calmed down a bit, was the relaxed and confident way he handled himself with Ted Kennedy. The contrast between the two was so stark that I am still surprised whenever I hear somebody talking about the "eerie resemblance" between Carter and John F. Kennedy. I have never noticed it, except every once in a while in some carefully staged photograph—and if there was ever a time when it seems like any such resemblance should have been impossible to miss, it was that morning in Atlanta when I walked into the dining room and saw Jimmy Carter and Ted Kennedy sitting about six feet apart at the same table.

Kennedy, whose presence usually dominates any room he walks into, was sitting there looking stiff and vaguely uncomfortable in his dark blue suit and black shoes. He glanced up as I entered and smiled faintly, then went back to staring at a portrait on the wall on the other side of the room. Paul Kirk, his executive wizard, was sitting next to him, wearing the same blue suit and black shoes—and Jimmy King, his executive advance man, was off in a distant corner yelling into a telephone. There were about fifteen other people in the room, most of them laughing and talking, and it took me a while to notice that nobody was talking to Kennedy—which is a very rare thing to see, particularly in any situation involving other politicians or even politically conscious people.

Kennedy was obviously not in a very gregarious mood that morning, and I didn't learn why until an hour or so later when I found myself in one of the Secret Service cars with King, Kirk, and Kennedy, running at top speed on the highway to Athens. The mood in the car was ugly. Kennedy was yelling at the SS driver for missing a turnoff that meant we'd be late for the unveiling. When we finally got there and I had a chance to talk privately with Jimmy King, he said Carter had waited until the last minute—just before I got to the mansion—to advise Kennedy that a sudden change in his own plans made it impossible for him to lend Teddy his plane for the trip to Athens. That was the reason for the tension I half noticed when I got to the mansion. King had been forced to get on the phone immediately and locate the Secret Service detail and get two cars out to the mansion immediately. By the time they arrived it was obvious that we would not get to Athens in time for the unveiling of Rusk's portrait—which was fine with me, but Kennedy was scheduled to speak, and he was very unhappy.

I refused to participate in any ceremony honoring a warmonger like Rusk, so I told King I would look around on the edge of the campus for a bar, and then meet them for lunch at the cafeteria for the Law Day luncheon . . . He was happy enough to see me go, because in the space of three or four minutes, I had insulted a half-dozen people. There was a beer parlor about ten minutes away, and I stayed there in relative peace until it was time for the luncheon.

There was no way to miss the campus cafeteria. There was a curious crowd of about two hundred students waiting to catch a glimpse of Ted Kennedy, who was signing autographs and moving slowly up the concrete steps toward the door as I approached.

I looked around the room, and indeed there was no mistaking the nature of the crowd. This was not just a bunch of good ol' boys who all happened to be alumni of the University of Georgia Law School; these were the *honored* alumni, the ranking 150 or so who had earned, stolen, or inherited enough distinction to be culled from the lists and invited to the unveiling of Rusk's portrait, followed by a luncheon with Senator Kennedy, Governor Carter, Judge Crater, and numerous other hyper-distinguished guests whose names I forget . . . And Jimmy King was right: this was not a natural habitat for anybody wearing dirty white basketball shoes, no tie, and nothing except *Rolling Stone* to follow his name on the guest list in that space reserved for titles. If it had been a gathering of distinguished alumni from the University of Georgia Medical School, the title space on the guest list would have been in front of the names, and I would have fit right in. Hell, I could even have joined a few conversations and nobody would have given a second thought to any talk about "blood on the hands."

Right. But this was Law Day in Georgia, and I was the only Doctor in the room . . . So I had to be passed off as some kind of undercover agent, traveling for unknown reasons with Senator Kennedy. Not even the Secret Service agents understood my role in the entourage. All they knew was that I had walked off the plane from Washington with Teddy, and I had been with them ever since. Nobody gets introduced to a Secret Service agent; they are expected to *know* who everybody is—and if they don't know, they act like they do and hope for the best.

It is not my wont to take undue advantage of the Secret Service. We have gone through some heavy times together, as it were, and ever since I wandered into a room in the Biltmore Hotel in New York one night during the 1972 campaign and found three SS agents smoking a joint, I have felt pretty much at ease around them . . . So it seemed only natural, down in Georgia, to ask one of the four agents in our detail for the keys to the trunk of his car so I could lock my leather satchel in a safe place, instead of carrying it around with me.

Actually, the agent had put the bag in the trunk on his own, rather than give me the key . . . But when I sat down at our table in the cafeteria and saw that the only available beverage was iced tea, I remembered that one of the things in my satchel was a quart of Wild Turkey, and I wanted it. On the table in front of me—and everyone else—was a tall glass of iced tea that looked to be the same color as bourbon. Each glass had a split slice of lemon on its rim: so I removed the lemon, poured the tea into Paul Kirk's water glass, and asked one of the agents at the next table for the key to the trunk. He hesitated for a moment, but one of the law school deans or maybe Judge Crater was already talking into the mike up there at the speakers' table, so the path of least disturbance was to give me the key, which he did . . .

And I thought nothing of it until I got outside and opened the trunk . . .

Cazart!

If your life ever gets dull, check out the trunk of the next SS car you happen to see. You won't need a key; they open just as easily as any other trunk when a six-foot whip-steel is properly applied . . . But open the bugger *carefully*, because those gentlemen keep about sixty-nine varieties of instant death inside. Jesus, I was literally staggered by the mass of weaponry in the back of that car: there were machine guns, gas masks, hand grenades, cartridge belts, tear gas canisters, ammo boxes, bulletproof vests, chains, saws, and probably a lot of other things . . . But all of a sudden I realized that two passing students had stopped right next to me on the sidewalk, and I heard one of them say, "God almighty! Look at *that* stuff!"

So I quickly filled my glass with Wild Turkey, put the bottle back in the trunk, and slammed it shut just like you'd slam any other trunk . . . and that was when I turned around to see Jimmy Carter coming at me with his head down, his teeth bared, and his eyes so wildly dilated that he looked like a springtime bat . . .

What? No. That was later in the day, on my third or fourth trip to the trunk with the iced-tea glass. I have been sitting here in a frozen, bewildered stupor for fifty or fifty-five minutes trying to figure out where that last image came from. My memories of that day are extremely vivid, for the most part, and the more I think back on it now, the more certain I am that whatever I might have seen coming at me in that kind of bent-over, fast-swooping style of the springtime bat was *not* Governor Carter. Probably it was a hunchbacked student on his way to final exams in the school of landscaping, or maybe just trying to walk fast and tie his shoes at the same time . . . Or it could have been nothing at all; there is no mention in my notebook about anything trying to sneak up on me in a high-speed crouch while I was standing out there in the street.

According to my notes, in fact, Jimmy Carter had arrived at the cafeteria not long after Kennedy—and if he attracted any attention from the crowd that had come to see Teddy, I would probably have noticed it and made at least a small note to emphasize the contrast in style—something like: "12:09, Carter suddenly appears in slow-moving crowd behind TK. No autographs, no bodyguards, and now a blue plastic suit instead of Levi's///No recognition, no greetings, just a small sandy-haired man looking for somebody to shake hands with . . ."

That is the kind of note I would have made if I'd noticed his arrival at all, which I didn't. Because it was not until around ten o'clock on the night of the New Hampshire primary, almost two years later, that there was any real reason for a journalist to make a note on the time and style of Jimmy Carter's arrival for any occasion at all, and especially not in a crowd that had come to rub shoulders with big-time heavies like Ted Kennedy and Dean Rusk. He is not an imposing figure in any way: and even now, with his face on every TV screen in the country at least five nights a week, I'd be tempted to bet $100 to anybody else's $500 that Jimmy Carter could walk—by himself and in a normal noonday crowd—from one end of Chicago's huge O'Hare Airport to the other without being recognized by anybody . . .

Ah . . . but that is not what we need to be talking about right now, is it?

The only thing I remember about the first hour or so of that luncheon was a powerful sense of depression with the life I was drifting into. According to the program, we were in for a long run of speeches, remarks, comments, etc., on matters connected with the law school. Carter and Kennedy were the last two names on the list of speakers, which meant there was no hope of leaving early. I thought about going back to the beer parlor and watching a baseball game on TV, but King warned me against it. "We don't know how long this goddamn thing is gonna last," he said, "and that's a hell of a long walk from here, isn't it?"

I knew what he was getting at. Just as soon as the program was over, the SS caravan would rush us out to the Athens airport, where Carter's plane was waiting to fly us back to Atlanta. Another big dinner banquet was scheduled for six thirty that night, and immediately after that, a long flight back to Washington. Nobody would miss me if I wanted to go to the beer parlor, King said; but nobody would miss me when the time came to leave for the airport, either.

There was no need for King and Kirk to warn me that the SS detail would have a collective nervous breakdown at the prospect of taking Senator Kennedy and the governor of Georgia through the streets of downtown Athens—or any other city, for that matter—to search for some notoriously criminal journalist who might be in any one of the half-dozen bars and beer parlors on the edge of the campus.

So there was nothing to do except sit there in the university cafeteria, slumped in my chair at a table right next to Dean Rusk's, and drink one tall glass after another of straight Wild Turkey until the Law Day luncheon ceremonies were finished. After my third trip out to the trunk, the SS driver apparently decided that it was easier to just let me keep the car keys instead of causing a disturbance every fifteen or twenty minutes by passing them back and forth . . . Which made a certain kind of fatalistic sense, because I'd already had plenty of time to do just about anything I wanted to with the savage contents of his trunk, so why start worrying now? We had, after all, been together for the better part of two days, and the agents were beginning to understand that there was no need to reach for their weapons every time I started talking about the blood on Dean Rusk's hands, or how easily I could reach over and cut off his ears with my steak knife. Most Secret Service agents have led a sheltered life, and they tend to get edgy when they hear that kind of talk from a large stranger in their midst who has managed to stash an apparently endless supply of powerful whiskey right in the middle of their trunk arsenal. That is not one of your normal, everyday situations in the SS life; and especially not when this drunkard who keeps talking about taking a steak knife to the head of a former secretary of state has a red flag on his file in the Washington SS headquarters in addition to having the keys to the SS car in his pocket.

Carter was already speaking when I came back from my fourth or fifth trip out to the car. I had been careful all along to keep the slice of lemon on the rim of the glass, so it looked like all the other iced-tea glasses in the room. But Jimmy King was beginning to get nervous about the smell. "Goddamn it, Hunter, this whole end of the room smells like a distillery," he said.

"Balls," I said. "That's blood you're smelling."

King winced, and I thought I saw Rusk's head start to swing around on me, but apparently he thought better of it. For at least two hours he'd been hearing all this ugly talk about blood coming over his shoulder from what he knew was "the Kennedy table" right behind him. But why would a group of Secret Service agents and Senator Kennedy's personal staff be talking about him like that? And why was this powerful stench of whiskey hanging around his head? Were they all drunk?

Not all—but I was rapidly closing the gap, and the others had been subjected to the fumes for so long that I could tell by the sound of their laughter that even the SS agents were acting a little weird. Maybe it was a contact drunk of some kind, acting in combination with the fumes and fiendish drone of the speeches. We were trapped in that place, and nobody else at the table liked it any better than I did.

I am still not sure when I began listening to what Carter was saying, but at some point about ten minutes into his remarks I noticed a marked difference in the style and tone of the noise coming from the speakers' table, and I found myself listening, for the first time all day. Carter had started off with a few quiet jokes about people feeling honored to pay $10 or $12 a head to hear Kennedy speak, but the only way he could get people to listen to him was to toss in a free lunch along with his remarks. The audience laughed politely a few times, but after he'd been talking for about fifteen minutes I noticed a general uneasiness in the atmosphere of the room, and nobody was laughing anymore. At that point we were all still under the impression that Carter's "remarks" would consist of a few minutes of friendly talk about the law school, a bit of praise for Rusk, an introduction for Kennedy, and that would be it . . .

But we were wrong, and the tension in the room kept increasing as more and more people realized it. Very few if any of them had supported Carter when he won the governorship, and now that he was just about finished with his four-year term and barred by law from running again, they expected him to bow out gracefully and go back to raising peanuts. If he had chosen that occasion to announce that he'd decided to run for president in 1976, the reaction would almost certainly have been a ripple of polite laughter, because they would know he was kidding. Carter had not been a bad governor, but so what? We were, after all, in Georgia; and, besides that, the South already had one governor running for president . . . Back in the spring of 1974, George Wallace was a national power; he had rattled the hell out of that big cage called the Democratic National Committee in '72, and when he said he planned to do it again in '76, he was taken very seriously.

So I would probably have chuckled along with the others if Carter had said something about running for president at the *beginning* of his "remarks" that day, but I would not have chuckled if he'd said it at the end . . . Because it was a king hell bastard of a speech, and by the time it was over he had rung every bell in the room. Nobody seemed to know exactly what to make of it, but they knew it was sure as hell not what they'd come there to hear.

I have heard hundreds of speeches by all kinds of candidates and politicians—usually against my will and for generally the same reasons I got trapped into hearing this one—but I have never heard a sustained piece of political oratory that impressed me any more than the speech Jimmy Carter made on that Saturday afternoon in May 1974. It ran about forty-five minutes, climbing through five very distinct gear changes while the audience muttered uneasily and raised their eyebrows at each other, and one of the most remarkable things about the speech is that it is such a rare piece of oratorical artwork that it remains vastly impressive, even if you don't necessarily believe Carter was sincere and truthful in all the things he said. Viewed purely in the context of rhetorical drama and political theater, it ranks with General Douglas MacArthur's "old soldiers never die" address to the Congress in 1951—which still stands as a masterpiece of insane bullshit if nothing else.

There were, however, a lot of people who believed every word and sigh of MacArthur's speech, and they wanted to make him president—just as a lot of people who are still uncertain about Jimmy Carter would want to make him president if he could figure out some way to deliver a contemporary version of his 1974 Law Day speech on network TV . . . Or, hell, even the same identical speech; a national audience might be slightly puzzled by some of the references to obscure judges, grade-school teachers, and backwoods Georgia courthouses, but I think the totality of the speech would have the same impact today as it did two years ago.

But there is not much chance of it happening . . . And that brings up another remarkable aspect of the Law Day speech: it had virtually no impact at all when he delivered it, except on the people who heard it, and most of them were more stunned and puzzled by it than impressed. They had not come there to hear lawyers denounced as running dogs of the status quo, and there is still some question in my own mind—and in Carter's too, I suspect—about what he came there to say. There was no written text of the speech, no press to report it, no audience hungry to hear it, and no real reason for giving it—except that Jimmy Carter had a few serious things on his mind that day, and he figured it was about time to unload them, whether the audience liked it or not . . .

Which gets to another interesting point of the speech: although Carter himself now says, "That was probably the best speech I ever made," he has yet to make another one like it—not even to the extent of lifting some of the best images and ideas for incorporation into his current speeches—and his campaign staff attached so little importance to it that Carter's only tape recording of his Law Day remarks got lost somewhere in the files and, until about two months ago, the only existing tape of the speech was the one I'd had copied off the original, before it was lost. I've been carrying the bastard around with me for two years, playing it in some extremely unlikely situations for people who would look at me like I was finally over the hump into terminal brain damage when I'd say they were going to have to spend the next forty-five minutes listening to a political speech by some ex-governor of Georgia.

It was not until I showed up in New Hampshire and Massachusetts for the '76 primaries and started playing my tape of the Law Day speech for a few friends, journalists, and even some of Carter's top staff people who'd never heard it that Pat Caddell noticed that almost everybody who heard the speech was as impressed by it as I was . . . But even now, after Caddell arranged to dub fifty tape copies off of my copy, nobody in Carter's brain trust has figured out what to do with them.

I am not quite sure what I would do with them myself, if I were Carter, because it is entirely possible that the very qualities that made the Law Day speech so impressive for me would have exactly the opposite effect on Carter's new national constituency. The voice I hear on my tape is the same one all those good conservative folk out there on the campaign trail have found so appealing, but very few of them would find anything familiar in what the voice is saying. The Jimmy Carter who has waltzed so triumphantly down the middle of the road through one Democratic primary after another is a cautious, conservative, and vaguely ethereal Baptist Sunday-school teacher who seems to promise, above all else, a return to normalcy, a resurrection of the national self-esteem, and a painless redemption from all the horrors and disillusion of Watergate. With President Carter's firm hand on the helm, the ship of state will once again sail a true and steady course, all the crooks and liars and thieves who somehow got control of the government during the turmoil of the Sixties will be driven out of the temple once and for all, and the White House will be so overflowing with honesty, decency, justice, love, and compassion that it might even glow in the dark.

It is a very alluring vision, and nobody understands this better than Jimmy Carter. The electorate feels a need to be cleansed, reassured, and revitalized. The underdogs of yesteryear have had their day, and they blew it. The radicals and reformers of the Sixties promised peace, but they turned out to be nothing but incompetent troublemakers. Their plans that had looked so fine on paper led to chaos and disaster when hack politicians tried to implement them. The promise of civil rights turned into the nightmare of busing. The call for law and order led straight to Watergate. And the long struggle between the Hawks and the Doves caused violence in the streets and a military disaster in Vietnam. Nobody won, in the end, and when the dust finally settled, "extremists" at both ends of the political spectrum were thoroughly discredited. And by the time the 1976 presidential campaign got under way, the high ground was all in the middle of the road.

Jimmy Carter understands this, and he has tailored his campaign image to fit the new mood almost perfectly . . . But back in May of '74 when he flew up to Athens to make his "remarks" at the Law Day ceremonies, he was not as concerned with preserving his moderate image as he is now. He was thinking more about all the trouble he'd had with judges, lawyers, lobbyists, and other minions of the Georgia establishment while he was governor—and now, with only six more months in the office, he wanted to have a few words with these people.

There was not much anger in his voice when he started talking, but halfway through the speech it was too obvious for anybody in the room to ignore. But there was no way to cut him short, and he knew it. It was the anger in his voice that first caught my attention, I think, but what sent me back out to the trunk to get my tape recorder instead of another drink was the spectacle of a southern politician telling a crowd of southern judges and lawyers that "I'm not qualified to talk to you about law, because in addition to being a peanut farmer, I'm an engineer and nuclear physicist, not a lawyer . . . But I read a lot and I listen a lot. One of the sources for my understanding about the proper application of criminal justice and the system of equities is from Reinhold Niebuhr. The other source of my understanding about what's right and wrong in this society is from a friend of mine, a poet named Bob Dylan. Listening to his records about 'The Lonesome Death of Hattie Carroll' and 'Like a Rolling Stone' and 'The Times They Are A-Changin',' I've learned to appreciate the dynamism of change in a modern society."

At first I wasn't sure I was hearing him right, and I looked over at Jimmy King. "What the hell did I just hear?" I asked.

King smiled and looked at Paul Kirk, who leaned across the table and whispered, "He said his top two advisers are Bob Dylan and Reinhold Niebuhr."

I nodded and got up to go outside for my tape recorder. I could tell by the rising anger in Carter's voice that we were in for an interesting ride . . . And by the time I got back, he was whipping on the crowd about judges who took bribes in return for reduced prison sentences, lawyers who deliberately cheated illiterate blacks, and cops who abused people's rights with something they called a "consent warrant."

"I had lunch this week with the members of the Judicial Selection Committee, and they were talking about a 'consent search warrant,' " he said. "I didn't know what a consent search warrant was. They said, 'Well, that's when two policemen go to a house. One of them goes to the front door and knocks on it, and the other one runs around to the back door and yells 'come in.' "

The crowd got a laugh out of that one, but Carter was just warming up, and for the next twenty or thirty minutes, his voice was the only sound in the room. Kennedy was sitting just a few feet to Carter's left, listening carefully but never changing the thoughtful expression on his face as Carter railed and bitched about a system of criminal justice that allows the rich and the privileged to escape punishment for their crimes and sends poor people to prison because they can't afford to bribe the judge . . .

(Jesus Babbling Christ! The phone is ringing again, and this time I know what it is for sure. Last time it was the land commissioner of Texas threatening to have my legs broken because of something I wrote about him . . . But now it is the grim reaper; he has come for my final page, and in exactly thirteen minutes that goddamn Mojo Wire across the room will erupt in a frenzy of beeping and I will have to feed it again . . . But before I leave this filthy sweatbox that is costing me $39 a day, I am going to deal with that rotten Mojo Wire. I have dreamed of smashing that fucker for five long years, but . . . Okay, okay, twelve more minutes and . . . yes . . .)

So this will have to be it . . . I would need a lot more time and space than I have to properly describe either the reality or the reaction to Jimmy Carter's Law Day speech, which was and still is the heaviest and most eloquent thing I have ever heard from the mouth of a politician. It was the voice of an angry agrarian populist, extremely precise in its judgments and laced with some of the most original, brilliant, and occasionally bizarre political metaphors anybody in that room will ever be likely to hear.

The final turn of the screw was another ugly example of crime and degradation in the legal profession, and this time Carter went right to the top. Nixon had just released his own, self-serving version of "the White House tapes," and Carter was shocked when he read the transcripts. "The Constitution charges us with a direct responsibility for determining what our government is and ought to be," he said. And then, after a long pause, he went on: "Well . . . I have read parts of the embarrassing transcripts, and I've seen the proud statement of a former attorney general who protected his boss, and now brags of the fact that he tiptoed through a minefield and came out . . . quote, clean, unquote." Another pause, and then: "You know, I can't imagine somebody like Thomas Jefferson tiptoeing through a minefield on the technicalities of the law, and then bragging about being *clean* afterward . . ."

Forty-five minutes later, on our way back to Atlanta in the governor's small plane, I told Carter I wanted a transcript of his speech.

"There is no transcript," he said.

I smiled, thinking he was putting me on. The speech had sounded like a product of five or six tortured drafts . . . But he showed me a page and a half of scrawled notes in his legal pad and said that was all he had.

"Jesus Christ," I said. "That was one of the damnedest things I've ever heard. You mean you just winged it all the way through?"

He shrugged and smiled faintly. "Well," he said, "I had a pretty good idea what I was going to say before I came up here—but I guess I was a little surprised at how it came out."

Kennedy didn't have much to say about the speech. He said he'd "enjoyed it," but he still seemed uncomfortable and preoccupied for some reason. Carter and I talked about the time he invited Dylan and some of his friends out to the governor's mansion after a concert in Atlanta. "I really enjoyed it," he said with a big grin. "It was a real honor to have him visit my home."

I had already decided, by then, that I liked Jimmy Carter—but I had no idea that he'd made up his mind, a few months earlier, to run for the presidency in 1976. And if he had told me his little secret that day on the plane back to Atlanta, I'm not sure I'd have taken him seriously . . . But if he had told me and if I had taken him seriously, I would probably have said that he could have my vote, for no other reason except the speech I'd just heard.

• • •

The Law Day speech is not the kind of thing that would have much appeal to the mind of a skilled technician, and that kind of mind is perhaps the only common denominator among the strategists, organizers, and advisers at the staff-command level of Carter's campaign. Very few of them seem to have much interest in *why* Jimmy wants to be president, or even in what he might do after he wins: their job and their meal ticket is to put Jimmy Carter in the White House, that is all they know and all they need to know—and so far they are doing their job pretty well. According to political oddsmaker Billy the Geek, Carter is now a solid three-to-two bet to win the November election—up from fifty to one less than six months ago.

"Awesome" is the mildest word I can think of to describe a campaign that can take an almost totally unknown ex-governor of Georgia with no national reputation, no power base in the Democratic Party, and not the slightest reluctance to tell Walter Cronkite, John Chancellor, and anyone else who asks that "the most important thing in my life is Jesus Christ" and to have him securely positioned, after only nine of thirty-two primaries, as an almost prohibitive favorite to win the presidential nomination of the nation's majority political party, and an even bet to win the November election against a relatively popular GOP president who has managed somehow to convince both Big Labor and Big Business that he has just rescued the country from economic disaster. If the presidential election were held tomorrow I would not bet more than three empty beer cans on Gerald Ford's chances of beating Jimmy Carter in November.

. . . What? No, cancel that bet. The Screech on the telephone just informed me that *Time* has just released a poll—on the day after the Texas primary—saying Carter would beat Ford by 48 percent to 38 percent if the election were held now. Seven weeks ago, according to *Time* via The Screech, the current figures were almost exactly reversed . . . I have never been much with math, but a quick shuffling of these figures seems to mean that Carter has picked up 20 points in seven weeks, and Ford has lost 20.

If this is true, then it is definitely time to call Billy the Geek and get something like ten cases of 66 proof Sloat ale down on Carter, and forget those three empty beer cans.

In other words, the panic is on and the last survivors of the ill-fated Stop Carter Movement are out in the streets shedding their uniforms and stacking their weapons on street corners all over Washington . . . And now another phone call from CBS correspondent Ed Bradley—who is covering Carter now after starting the '76 campaign with Birch Bayh—saying Bayh will announce at a press conference in Washington tomorrow that he has decided to endorse Jimmy Carter.

Well . . . how about that, eh? Never let it be said that a wharf rat can get off a sinking ship any faster than an 87 percent ADA liberal.

But this is no time for cruel jokes about liberals and wharf rats. Neither species has ever been known for blind courage or stubborn devotion to principle, so let the rotten go wherever they feel even temporarily comfortable . . . Meanwhile, it is beginning to look like the time has come for the rest of us to get our business straight, because the only man who is going to keep Jimmy Carter out of the White House now is Jimmy Carter.

Which might happen, but it is a hard kind of thing to bet on, because there is no precedent in the annals of presidential politics for a situation like this: with more than half the primaries still ahead of him, Carter is now running virtually unopposed for the Democratic nomination, and—barring some queer and unlikely development—he is going to have to spend the next two months in a holding action until he can go to New York in July and pick up the nomination.

I will probably nurse a few doubts of my own between now and July, for that matter, but unless something happens to convince me that I should waste any more time than I already have brooding on the evil potential that lurks, invariably, in the mind of just about *anybody* whose ego has become so dangerously swollen that he really wants to be president of the United States, I don't plan to spend much time worrying about the prospect of seeing Jimmy Carter in the White House. There is not a hell of a lot I can do about it, for one thing; and for another, I have spent enough time with Carter in the past two years to feel I have a pretty good sense of his candidacy.

I went down to Plains, Georgia, to spend a few days with him on his own turf and to hopefully find out who Jimmy Carter really was before the campaign shroud came down on him, and he started talking like a candidate instead of a human being. Once a presidential aspirant gets out on the campaign trail and starts seeing visions of himself hunkered down behind that big desk in the Oval Office, the idea of sitting down in his own living room and talking openly with some foul-mouthed, argumentative journalist carrying a tape recorder in one hand and a bottle of Wild Turkey in the other is totally out of the question.

But it was almost a year before the '76 New Hampshire primary when I talked to Carter at his home in Plains, and I came away from that weekend with six hours of taped conversation with him on subjects ranging all the way from the Allman Brothers, stock car racing, and our strongly conflicting views on the use of undercover agents in law enforcement, to nuclear submarines, the war in Vietnam, and the treachery of Richard Nixon. When I listened to the tapes again last week, I noticed a lot of things that I had not paid much attention to at the time, and the most obvious of these was the extremely detailed precision of his answers to some of the questions that he is now accused of being either unable or unwilling to answer. There is no question in my mind, after hearing him talk on the tapes, that I was dealing with a candidate who had already done a massive amount of research on things like tax reform, national defense, and the structure of the American political system by the time he announced his decision to run for president. Nor is there any question that there are a lot of things Jimmy Carter and I will never agree on. I had warned him, before we sat down with the tape recorder for the first time, that—although I appreciated his hospitality and felt surprisingly relaxed and comfortable in his home—I was also a journalist and that some of the questions I knew I was going to ask him might seem unfriendly or even downright hostile. Because of this, I said, I wanted him to be able to stop the tape recorder by means of a remote-pause button if the talk got too heavy. But he said he would just as soon not have to bother turning the tape on and off, which surprised me at the time. But now that I listen to the tapes, I realize that loose talk and bent humor are not among Jimmy Carter's vices.

They are definitely among mine, however, and since I had stayed up most of the night drinking and talking in the living room with his sons Jack and Chip Carter and their wives—and then by myself in the guest room over the garage—I was still feeling weird around noon, when we started talking "seriously," and the tape of that first conversation is liberally sprinkled with my own twisted comments about "rotten fascist bastards," "thieving cocksuckers who peddle their assess all over Washington," and "these goddamn brainless fools who refuse to serve liquor in the Atlanta airport on Sunday."

It was nothing more than my normal way of talking, and Carter was already familiar with it, but there are strange and awkward pauses here and there on the tape where I can almost hear Carter gritting his teeth and wondering whether to laugh or get angry at things I wasn't even conscious of saying at the time, but which sound on the tape like random outbursts of hostility or pure madness from the throat of a paranoid psychotic. Most of the conversation is intensely rational, but every once in a while it slips over the line, and all I can hear is the sound of my own voice yelling something like "Jesus Christ! What's that filthy smell?"

Both Carter and his wife have always been amazingly tolerant of my behavior, and on one or two occasions they have had to deal with me in a noticeably bent condition. I have always been careful not to commit any felonies right in front of them, but other than that I have never made much of an effort to adjust my behavior around Jimmy Carter or anyone else in his family—including his seventy-eight-year-old mother, Miss Lillian, who is the only member of the Carter family I could comfortably endorse for the presidency, right now, with no reservations at all.

Whoops! Well . . . we will get to that in a moment. Right now I have other things to deal with, and . . . No, what the hell? Let's get to it now, because time is running out and so is that goddamn Sloat; so now is the time to come to grips with my own "Carter Question."

It has taken me almost a year to reach this point, and I am still not sure how to cope with it . . . But I am getting there fast, thanks mainly to all the help I've been getting from my friends in the liberal community. I took more abuse from these petulant linthead bastards during the New Hampshire and Massachusetts primaries than I have ever taken from my friends on any political question since the first days of the Free Speech Movement in Berkeley, and that was nearly twelve years ago . . . I felt the same way about the first wild, violent days of the FSM as I still feel about Jimmy Carter. In both cases my initial reaction was positive, and I have lived too long on my instincts to start questioning them now. At least, not until I get a good reason, and so far nobody has been able to give me any good reason for junking my first instinctive reaction to Jimmy Carter, which was that I liked him . . . And if the editors of *Time* magazine and the friends of Hubert Humphrey consider that "bizarre," fuck them. I liked Jimmy Carter the first time I met him, and in the two years that have passed since that Law Day in Georgia I have come to know him a hell of a lot better than I knew George McGovern at this point in the '72 campaign, and I still like Jimmy Carter. He is one of the most intelligent politicians I've ever met, and also one of the strangest. I have never felt comfortable around people who talk about their feeling for Jesus, or any other deity for that matter, because they are usually none too bright . . . Or maybe "stupid" is a better way of saying it; but I have never seen much point in getting heavy with either stupid people or Jesus freaks, just as long as they don't bother me. In a world as weird and cruel as this one we have made for ourselves, I figure anybody who can find peace and personal happiness without ripping off somebody else deserves to be left alone. They will not inherit the earth, but then neither will I . . . And I have learned to live, as it were, with the idea that I will never find peace and happiness either. But as long as I know there's a pretty good chance I can get my hands on either one of them every once in a while, I do the best I can between high spots.

Oscar Zeta Acosta's Obituary

Three years after the disappearance of Oscar Acosta—presumably somewhere in Mexico—Hunter wrote an extended roast-obituary-tribute of his old friend and counselor, whom he referred to variously as his attorney, his "Samoan attorney," and, in Fear and Loathing in Las Vegas, *"Dr. Gonzo." Oscar was a familiar figure around the* Rolling Stone *office in San Francisco (he carved his middle name, "Zeta," into a wooden shelf in the men's room), and initially threatened to prevent the publication of the* Vegas *book partly due to his being described as a "three-hundred-pound Samoan," but eventually relented. To this day, no trace of Acosta has ever been found.*

Fear & Loathing in the Graveyard of the Weird: The Banshee Screams for Buffalo Meat

December 15, 1977

Nobody knows the weirdness I've seen
On the trail of the brown buffalo

—Old Black Joe

I walk in the night rain until the dawn of the new day. I have devised the plan, straightened out the philosophy, and set up the organization. When I have the 1 million Brown Buffalos on my side I will present the demands for a new nation to both the U.S. Government and the United Nations . . . and then I'll split and write the book. I have no desire to be a politician. I don't want to lead anyone. I have no practical ego. I am not ambitious. I merely want to do what is right. Once in every century there comes a man who is chosen to speak for his people. Moses, Mao, and Martin [Luther King Jr.] are examples. Who's to say that I am not such a man? In this day and age the man for all seasons needs many voices. Perhaps that is why the gods have sent me into Riverbank, Panama, San Francisco, Alpine, and Juarez. Perhaps that is why I've been taught so many trades. Who will deny that I am unique?

—Oscar Acosta, *The Autobiography of a Brown Buffalo*

Well . . . not me, old sport. Wherever you are and in whatever shape—dead or alive or even *both*, eh? That's one thing they can't take away from you . . . Which is lucky, I think, for the rest of us: because (and, yeah—let's face it, Oscar) you were not real light on your feet in this world, and you were too goddamn heavy for most of the boats you jumped into. One of the great regrets of my life is that I was never able to introduce you to my old football buddy, Richard Nixon. The main thing he feared in this life—even worse than Queers and Jews and Mutants—was people who might run amok; he called them "loose cannons on the deck," and he wanted them all put to sleep.

That's one graveyard we never even checked, Oscar, but why not? If your classic "doomed nigger" style of paranoia had any validity at all, you *must* understand that it was not just Richard Nixon who was out to get you—but all the people who thought like Nixon and all the judges and U.S. attorneys he appointed in those weird years. Were there any of Nixon's friends among all those superior court judges you subpoenaed and mocked and humiliated when you were trying to bust the grand jury selection system in L.A.? How many of those Brown Beret "bodyguards" [in the La Raza Movement] you called "brothers" were deep-cover cops or informants? I recall being seriously worried about that when we were working on that story about the killing of Chicano journalist Ruben Salazar by an L.A. County sheriff's deputy. How many of those bomb-throwing, trigger-happy freaks who slept on mattresses in your apartment were talking to the sheriff on a chili-hall pay phone every morning? Or maybe to the judges who kept jailing you for contempt of court, when they didn't have anything else?

• • •

Yeah, and so much for the "paranoid Sixties." It's time to end this bent séance—or *almost* closing time, anyway—but before we get back to raw facts and rude lawyer's humor, I want to make sure that at least one record will show that I tried and totally failed, for at least five years, to convince my allegedly erstwhile Samoan attorney, Oscar Zeta Acosta, that *there was no such thing as paranoia*: at least not in that cultural and political war zone called "East L.A." in the late 1960s and especially not for an aggressively radical "Chicano Lawyer" who thought he could stay up all night, *every* night, eating acid and throwing "Molotov cocktails" with the same people he was going to have to represent in a downtown courtroom the next morning.

There were times—all too often, I felt—when Oscar would show up in front of the courthouse at nine in the morning with a stench of fresh gasoline on his hands and a green crust of charred soap flakes on the toes of his $300 snakeskin cowboy boots. He would pause outside the courtroom just long enough to give the TV press five minutes of crazed rhetoric for the evening news, then he would shepherd his equally crazed "clients" into the courtroom for their daily war-circus with the judge. When you get into bear baiting on that level, paranoia is just another word for ignorance . . . They really *are* out to get you.

The odds on his being dragged off to jail for "contempt" were about fifty-fifty on any given day—which meant he was always in danger of being seized and booked with a pocket full of "bennies" or "black beauties" at the property desk. After several narrow escapes, he decided that it was necessary to work in the courtroom as part of a three-man "defense team."

One of his "associates" was usually a well-dressed, well-mannered young Chicano whose only job was to carry at least 100 milligrams of pure speed at all times and feed Oscar whenever he signaled; the other was not so well dressed or mannered; his job was to stay alert and be one step ahead of the bailiffs when they made a move on Oscar—at which point he would reach out and grab any pills, powders, shivs, or other evidence he was handed, then sprint like a human bazooka for the nearest exit.

This strategy worked so well for almost two years that Oscar and his people finally got careless. They had survived another long day in court—on felony arson charges, this time, for trying to burn down the Biltmore Hotel during a speech by then governor Ronald Reagan—and they were driving back home to Oscar's headquarters pad in the barrio (and maybe running sixty or sixty-five in a fifty m.p.h. speed zone, Oscar later admitted) when they were suddenly jammed to a stop by two LAPD cruisers. "They acted like we'd just robbed a bank," said Frank, looking right down the barrel of a shotgun. "They made us all lie face down on the street and then they searched the car, and—"

Yes. That's when they found the drugs: twenty or thirty white pills that the police quickly identified as "illegal amphetamine tablets, belonging to attorney Oscar Acosta."

The fat spic for all seasons was jailed once again, this time on what the press called a "high-speed drug bust." Oscar called a press conference in jail and accused the cops of "planting" him—but not even his bodyguards believed him until long after the attendant publicity had done them all so much damage that the whole "Brown Power Movement" was effectively stalled, splintered, and discredited by the time *all* charges, both arson and drugs, were either dropped or reduced to small print on the back of the blotter.

I am not even sure, myself, how the cases were finally disposed of. Not long after the "high-speed drug bust," as I recall, two of his friends were charged with murder one for allegedly killing a smack dealer in the barrio, and I think Oscar finally copped on the drug charge and pled guilty to something like "possession of ugly pills in a public place."

But by that time his deal had already gone down. None of the respectable Chicano pols in East L.A. had ever liked him anyway, and that "high-speed drug bust" was all they needed to publicly denounce everything Left of *huevos rancheros* and start calling themselves Mexican-American again. The trial of the Biltmore Five was no longer a do-or-die cause for La Raza, but a shameful crime that a handful of radical dope fiends had brought down on the whole community. The mood on Whittier Boulevard turned sour overnight, and the sight of a Brown Beret was suddenly as rare as a cash client for Oscar Zeta Acosta—the ex-Chicano lawyer.

The entire ex-Chicano political community went as public as possible to make sure that the rest of the city understood that they had known all along that this dope-addict *rata* who had somehow been one of their most articulate and certainly their most radical, popular, and politically aggressive spokesmen for almost two years was really just a self-seeking publicity dope freak who couldn't even run a bar tab at the Silver Dollar Cafe, much less rally friends or a following. There was no mention in the Mexican-American press about Acosta's surprisingly popular campaign for sheriff of L.A. County a year earlier, which had made him a minor hero among politically hip Chicanos all over the city.

No more of that dilly-dong bullshit on Whittier Boulevard. Oscar's drug bust was still alive on the Evening News when he was evicted from his apartment on three days' notice and his car was either stolen or towed away from its customary parking place on the street in front of his driveway. His offer to defend his two friends on what he later assured me were absolutely valid charges of first degree murder were publicly rejected. Not even for free, they said. A dope-addled clown was worse than no lawyer at all.

It was dumb gunsel thinking, but Oscar was in no mood to offer his help more than once. So he beat a strategic retreat to Mazatlán, which he called his "other home," to lick his wounds and start writing the Great Chicano Novel. It was the end of an era! The fireball Chicano lawyer was on his way to becoming a half-successful writer, a cult figure of sorts—then a fugitive, a freak, and finally either a permanently missing person or an undiscovered corpse.

• • •

There are not many gypsies on file at the Missing Persons Bureau—and if Oscar was not quite the classic gypsy, in his own eyes or mine, it was only because he was never able to cut that high-tension cord that kept him forever attached to his childhood home and hatchery. By the time he was twenty years old, Oscar was working overtime eight days a week at learning to live and even think like a gypsy, but he never quite jumped the gap.

Although I was born in El Paso, Texas, I am actually a small-town kid. A hick from the sticks, a Mexican boy from the other side of the tracks. I grew up in Riverbank, California; Post Office Box 303; population 3969. It's the only town in the entire state whose essential numbers have remained unchanged. The sign that welcomes you as you round the curve coming in from Modesto says The City of Action.

We lived in a two-room shack without a floor. We had to pump our water and use kerosene if we wanted to read at night. But we never went hungry. My old man always bought the pinto beans and the white flour for the tortillas in one-hundred-pound sacks which my mother used to make dresses, sheets, and curtains. We had two acres of land which we planted every year with corn, tomatoes, and yellow chiles for the hot sauce. Even before my father woke us, my old ma was busy at work making the tortillas at five a.m. while he chopped the logs we'd hauled up from the river on the weekends.

Riverbank is divided into three parts, and in my corner of the world there were only three kinds of people: Mexicans, Okies, and

Americans. Catholics, Holy Rollers, and Protestants. Peach pickers, cannery workers, and clerks. We lived on the West Side, within smelling distance of the world's largest tomato paste cannery.

The West Side is still enclosed by the Santa Fe Railroad tracks to the east, the Modesto-Oakdale Highway to the north, and the irrigation canal to the south. Within that concentration only Mexicans were safe from the neighborhood dogs, who responded only to Spanish commands. Except for Bob Whitt and Emitt Brown, both friends of mine who could cuss in better Spanish than I, I never saw a white person walking the dirt roads of our neighborhood.

—Oscar Acosta, *The Autobiography of a Brown Buffalo*, 1972

Oscar Zeta Acosta—despite any claims to the contrary—was a dangerous thug who lived every day of his life as a stalking monument to the notion that a man with a greed for the Truth should expect no mercy and give none . . .

. . . and that was the difference between Oscar and a lot of the merciless geeks he liked to tell strangers he admired: class acts like Benito Mussolini and Fatty Arbuckle.

When the great scorer comes to write against Oscar's name, one of the first few lines in the Ledger will note that he usually lacked the courage of his consistently monstrous convictions. There was more mercy, madness, dignity, and generosity in that overweight, overworked, and always overindulged brown cannonball of a body than most of us will meet in any human package even three times Oscar's size for the rest of our lives—which are all running noticeably leaner on the high side, since that rotten fat spic disappeared.

He was a drug-addled brute and a genuinely fiendish adversary in court or on the street—but it was none of *these* things that finally pressured him into death or a disappearance so finely plotted that it amounts to the same thing.

What finally cracked the Brown Buffalo was the bridge he refused to build between the self-serving elegance of his instincts and the self-destructive carnival of his reality. He was a Baptist missionary at a leper colony in Panama before he was a lawyer in Oakland and East L.A., or a radical-chic author in San Francisco and Beverly Hills . . . But whenever things got tense or when he had to work close to the bone, he was always a missionary. And that was the governing instinct that ruined him for anything else. He was a preacher in the courtroom, a preacher at the typewriter, and a flat-out awesome preacher when he cranked his head full of acid.

That's LSD-25, folks—a certified "dangerous drug" that is no longer fashionable, due to reasons of extreme and unnatural heaviness. The CIA was right about acid: some of their best and brightest operatives went over the side in the name of Top Secret research on a drug that was finally abandoned as a far too dangerous and unmanageable thing to be used as a public weapon. Not even the sacred minnock of "national security" could justify the hazards of playing with a thing too small to be seen and too big to control. The professional spook mentality was far more comfortable with things like nerve gas and neutron bombs.

But not the Brown Buffalo—he ate LSD-25 with a relish that bordered on worship. When his brain felt bogged down in the mundane nuts-and-bolts horrors of the Law or some dead-end manuscript, he would simply take off in his hot rod Mustang for a week on the road and a few days of what he called "walking with the King." Oscar used acid like other lawyers use Valium—a distinctly unprofessional and occasionally nasty habit that shocked even the most liberal of his colleagues and frequently panicked his clients.

I was with him one night in L.A. when he decided that the only way to meaningfully communicate with a judge who'd been leaning on him in the courtroom was to drive out to the man's home in Santa Monica and set his whole front lawn on fire after soaking it down with ten gallons of gasoline . . . and then, instead of fleeing into the night like some common lunatic vandal, Oscar stood in the street and howled through the flames at a face peering out from a shattered upstairs window, delivering one of his Billy Sunday–style sermons on morality and justice.

The nut of his flame-enraged text, as I recall, was this mind-bending chunk of eternal damnation from Luke 11:46—a direct quote from Jesus Christ:

"And he said, Woe unto you also, ye lawyers, for ye lade men with burdens grievous to be borne, and ye yourselves touch not the burdens with one of your fingers."

The Lawn of Fire was Oscar's answer to the Ku Klux Klan's burning cross, and he derived the same demonic satisfaction from doing it.

"Did you see his face?" he shouted as we screeched off at top speed toward Hollywood. "That corrupt old fool! I *know* he recognized me, but he'll never admit it! No officer of the court would set a judge's front yard on fire—the whole system would break down if lawyers could get away with crazy shit like this."

I agreed. It is not my wont to disagree with even a criminally insane attorney on questions of basic law. But in truth it never occurred to me that Oscar was either insane or a criminal, given the generally fascist, Nixonian context of those angry years.

In an era when the vice president of the United States held court in Washington to accept payoffs from his former vassals in the form of big wads of $100 bills—and when the president himself routinely held secretly tape-recorded meetings with his top aides in the Oval Office to plot illegal wiretaps, political burglaries, and other gross felonies in the name of a "silent majority," it was hard to feel anything more than a flash of high, nervous humor at the sight of some acid-bent lawyer setting fire to a judge's front yard at four o'clock in the morning.

I might even be tempted to justify a thing like that—but of course *it would be wrong* . . . And my attorney was Not a Crook, and, to the best of my knowledge, his mother was just as much "a saint" as Richard Nixon's.

Indeed. And now—as an almost perfect tribute to every icepick ever wielded in the name of Justice—I want to enter into the permanent record, at this point, as a strange but unchallenged fact that Oscar Z. Acosta was never disbarred from the practice of law in the state of California—and ex-president Richard Nixon *was*.

There are *some* things, apparently, that not even lawyers will tolerate; and in a naturally unjust world where the image of "Justice" is honored for being blind, even a blind pig will find an acorn once in a while.

Or maybe not—because Oscar was eventually hurt far worse by professional ostracism than Nixon was hurt by disbarment. The Great Banshee screamed for them both at almost the same time—for entirely different reasons, but with ominously similar results.

Except that Richard Nixon got rich from his crimes, and Oscar Acosta got killed. The wheels of Justice grind small and queer in this life, and if they seem occasionally unbalanced or even stupid and capricious in their grinding, my own midnight guess is that they were probably fixed from the start. And any judge who can safely slide into full-pension retirement without having to look back on anything worse in the way of criminal vengeance than a few scorched lawns is a man who got off easy.

There is, after all, considerable work and risk—and even a certain art—to the torching of a half-acre lawn without also destroying the house or exploding every car in the driveway. It would be a lot easier to simply make a funeral pyre of the whole place and leave the lawn for dilettantes.

That's how Oscar viewed arson—anything worth doing is worth doing well—and I'd watched enough of his fiery work to know he was right. If he was a King-Hell Pyromaniac, he was also a gut politician and occasionally a very skilled artist in the style and tone of his torchings.

Like most lawyers with an IQ higher than sixty, Oscar learned one definition of Justice in law school, and a very different one in the courtroom. He got his degree at some night school on Post Street in San Francisco, while working as a copy boy for the Hearst *Examiner*. And for a while he was very proud to be a lawyer—for the same reasons he'd felt proud to be a missionary and lead clarinet man in the leper colony band.

But by the time I first met him in the summer of 1967, he was long past what he called his "puppy love trip with the law." It had gone the same way of his earlier missionary zeal, and after one year of casework at an East Oakland "poverty law center," he was ready to dump Holmes and Brandeis for Huey Newton and a Black Panther style of dealing with the laws and courts of America.

When he came booming into a bar called the Daisy Duck in Aspen and announced that he was the trouble we'd all been waiting for, he was definitely into the politics of confrontation—and on all fronts: in the bars or the courts or even the streets, if necessary.

Oscar was not into serious street fighting, but he was hell on wheels in a bar brawl. Any combination of a two-hundred-fifty-pound Mexican and LSD-25 is a potentially terminal menace for anything it can reach—but when the alleged Mexican is in fact a profoundly angry Chicano lawyer with no fear at all of anything that walks on less than three legs and a de facto suicidal conviction that he *will* die at the age of thirty-three—just like Jesus Christ—you have a serious piece of work on your hands. Especially if the bastard is *already* thirty-three and a half years old with a head full of Sandoz acid, a loaded .357 Magnum in his belt, a hatchet-wielding Chicano bodyguard at his elbow at all times, and a disconcerting habit of projectile-vomiting geysers of pure red blood off the front porch every thirty or forty minutes, or whenever his malignant ulcer can't handle any more raw tequila.

This was the Brown Buffalo in the full crazed flower of his prime—a man, indeed, for all seasons. And it was somewhere in the middle of his thirty-third year, in fact, when he came out to Colorado—with his faithful bodyguard, Frank—to rest for a while after his grueling campaign for sheriff of Los Angeles County, which he lost by a million or so votes. But in defeat, Oscar had managed to create an instant political base for himself in the vast Chicano barrio of East Los Angeles—where even the most conservative of the old-line "Mexican-Americans" were suddenly calling themselves "Chicanos" and getting their first taste of tear gas at "La Raza" demonstrations, which Oscar was quickly learning to use as a fire-and-brimstone forum to feature himself as the main spokesman for a mushrooming "Brown Power" movement that the LAPD called more dangerous than the Black Panthers.

Which was probably true, at the time—but in retrospect it sounds a bit different than it did back in 1969 when the sheriff was sending out fifteen or twenty helicopter sorties a night to scan the rooftops and backyards of the barrio with huge sweeping searchlights that drove Oscar and his people into fits of blind rage every time they got nailed in a pool of blazing white light with a joint in one hand and a machete in the other.

But that is another and very long story—and since I've already written it once ("Strange Rumblings in Aztlan," *RS* 81) and came close to getting my throat slit in the process, I think we'll just ease off and pass on it for right now.

The sad tale of Oscar's fall from grace in the barrio is still rife with bad blood and ugly paranoia. He was too stunned to fight back in the time-honored style of a professional politician. He was also broke, divorced, depressed, and so deep in public disgrace in the wake of his "high-speed drug bust" that not even junkies would have him for an attorney.

In a word, he and his dream of "one million brown buffalos" were *finished* in East L.A . . . and everywhere else where it counted, for that matter, so Oscar "took off" once again, and once again with a head full of acid.

But . . .

• • •

Well . . . it is not an easy thing to sit here and keep a straight face while even considering the notion that there is any connection at all between Oscar's sorry fate and his lifelong devotion to defending the truth at all costs. There are a lot of people still wandering around, especially in places like San Francisco and East L.A., who would like nothing better than to dash out Oscar's teeth with a ball-peen hammer for all the weird and costly lies he laid on them at one point or another *in his frenzied assaults* on the way to his place in the sun. He never denied he was a lying pig who would use any means to justify his better end. Even his friends felt the sting. Yet there were times when he took himself as seriously as any other bush-league Mao or Moses, and in moments like these he was capable of rare insights and a naive sort of grace in his dealings with people that often touched on nobility. At its best, the Brown Buffalo shuffle was a match for Muhammad Ali's.

After I'd known him for only three days, he made me a solemn gift of a crude wooden idol that I am still not sure he didn't occasionally worship in secret when not in the presence of the dreaded "white-ass gabachos." In a paragraph near the end of his autobiography, he describes that strangely touching transfer far better than I can.

> *I opened my beat-up suitcase and took out my wooden idol. I had him wrapped in a bright red and yellow cloth. A San Blas Indian had given him to me when I left Panama. I called him Ebb Tide. He was made of hard mahogany. An eighteen-inch god without eyes, without a mouth, and without a sexual organ. Perhaps the sculptor had the same hang-up about drawing the body from the waist down as I'd had in Miss Rollins' fourth-grade class. Ebb Tide was my oldest possession. A string of small, yellowed wild pig's fangs hung from its neck.*

Ebb Tide still hangs on a nail just above my living room window. I can see him from where I sit now, scrawling these goddamn final desperate lines before my head can explode like a ball of magnesium tossed into a bucket of water. I have never been sure exactly what kind of luck Ebb Tide was bringing down on me, over the years—but I've never taken the little bastard down or even thought about it, so he must be paying his way. He is perched just in front of the peacock perch outside, and right now there are two high-blue reptilian heads peering over his narrow wooden shoulders.

Does anybody out there believe that?

No?

Well . . . peacocks can't live at this altitude anyway, like Doberman pinschers, sea snakes, and gun-toting Chicano missionaries with bad-acid breath.

Why does a hearse horse snicker, hauling a lawyer away?

—Carl Sandburg

Things were not going well in San Francisco or L.A. at that grim point in Oscar's time, either. To him, it must have seemed like open season on every Brown Buffalo west of the Continental Divide.

The only place he felt safe was down south on the warm foreign soil of the old country. But when he fled back to Mazatlán this time, it was not just to rest but to brood—and to plot what would be his final crazed leap for the great skyhook.

It would also turn out to be an act of such monumental perversity that not even that gentle presence of Ebb Tide could change my sudden and savage decision that the treacherous bastard should have his nuts ripped off with a plastic fork—and then fed like big meat grapes to my peacocks.

The move he made this time was straight out of Jekyll and Hyde—the Brown Buffalo suddenly transmogrified into the form of a rabid hyena. And the bastard compounded his madness by hiding out in the low-rent bowels of Mazatlán like some half-mad leper gone over the brink after yet another debilitating attack of string warts and herpes simplex lesions . . .

This ugly moment came just as my second book, *Fear and Loathing in Las Vegas*, was only a week or so away from going to press. We were in the countdown stage, and there is no way for anybody who hasn't been there to understand the tension of having a new book *almost* on the presses, but not quite there. The only thing that stood between me and publication was a last-minute assault on the very essence of the story by the publisher's libel lawyers. The book was malignant from start to finish, they said, with grievous libels that were totally indefensible. No publisher in his right mind would risk the nightmare of doomed litigation that a book like this was certain to drag us all into.

Which was true, on one level, but on another it seemed like a harmless joke—because almost every one of the most devastating libels they cited involved my old buddy, O. Z. Acosta; a fellow author, prominent Los Angeles attorney, and an officer of many courts. Specifically they advised:

> We have read the above manuscript as requested. Our principal legal objection is to the description of the author's attorney as using and offering for sale dangerous drugs as well as indulging in other criminal acts while under the influence of such drugs. Although this attorney is not named, he is identified with some detail. Consequently, this material should be deleted as libelous.
>
> In addition, we have the following specific comments:
>
> Page 3: The author's attorney's attempt to break and enter and threats (*sic*) to bomb a salesman's residence is libelous and should be deleted. Page 4: This page suggests that the author's attorney was driving at an excessive speed while drunk, all of which is libelous and should be deleted.
>
> Page 6: The incident in which the author's attorney advised the author to drive at top speed is libelous and should be deleted. The same applies to the attorney's being party to a fraud at the hotel. Page 31: The statement that the author's attorney will be disbarred is libelous and should be deleted. Page 40: The incident in which the author and his attorney impersonated police officers is libelous and should be deleted.

Page 41: The reference to the attorney's ______* being a "junkie" and shooting people is libelous and should be deleted unless it may be proven true. Page 48: The incident in which the author's attorney offers heroin for sale is libelous and should be deleted. We do not advise ______ to allow any material in this manuscript noted above as libelous to remain based upon expectancy of proving that it is true by the author's testimony. Inasmuch as the author admits being under the influence of illegal drugs at most if not all times, proof of truth would be extremely difficult through him.

* Deleted at the insistence of *Rolling Stone*'s attorney.

"Balls," I told them. "We'll just have Oscar sign a release. He's no more concerned about this 'libel' bullshit than I am.

"And besides, truth is an absolute defense against libel, anyway . . . Jesus, you don't understand what kind of a monster we're dealing with. You should read the parts I left out . . ."

But the libel wizards were not impressed—especially since we were heaping all this libelous abuse on a fellow attorney. Unless we got a signed release from Oscar, the book would not go to press.

Okay, I said. But let's do it quick. He's down in Mazatlán now. Send the goddamn thing by air express, and he'll sign it and ship it right back.

I think we are in Rats Alley
where the dead men lost their bones.

—T. S. Eliot, *The Waste Land*

Indeed. So they sent the release off at once . . . and Oscar refused to sign it—but not for any reason a New York libel lawyer could possibly understand. He was, as I'd said, not concerned at all by the libels. Of course they were all true, he said when I finally reached him by telephone at his room in the Hotel Sinaloa.

The only thing that bothered him—bothered him very badly—was the fact that I'd repeatedly described him as a three-hundred-pound Samoan.

"What kind of journalist are you?" he screamed at me. "Don't you have any respect for the truth? I can sink that whole publishing house for *defaming me*, trying to pass me off as one of those waterhead South Sea mongrels."

The libel lawyers were stunned into paranoid silence. Was it either some kind of arcane legal trick, they wondered, or was this dope-addled freak really crazy enough to insist on having himself formally identified for all time with one of the most depraved and degenerate figures in American literature?

Should his angry threats and demands conceivably be taken seriously? Was it possible that a well-known practicing attorney might not only freely admit to all these heinous crimes, but insist that every foul detail be documented as the absolute truth?

"Why not?" Oscar answered. And the only way he'd sign the release, he added, was in exchange for a firm guarantee from the lawyers that both his name and a suitable photograph of himself be prominently displayed on the book's dust cover.

They had never had to cope with a thing like this—a presumably sane attorney who flatly refused to release any other version of his clearly criminal behavior, except the abysmal naked truth. The concession he was willing to make had to do with his identity throughout the entire book as a "three-hundred-pound Samoan." But he could grit his teeth and tolerate that, he said, only because he understood that there was no way to make that many changes at that stage of the deadline without tearing up half the book. In exchange, however, he wanted a formal letter guaranteeing that he would be properly identified on the book jacket.

The lawyers would have no part of it. There was no precedent anywhere in the law for a bizarre situation like this . . . but as the deadline pressures mounted and Oscar refused to bend, it became more and more obvious that the only choice except compromise was to scuttle the book entirely . . . and if *that* happened, I warned them, I had enough plastic forks to mutilate every libel lawyer in New York.

That seemed to settle the issue in favor of a last-minute compromise, and *Fear and Loathing in Las Vegas* was finally sent to the printer with Oscar clearly identified on the back as the certified living model for the monstrous "three-hundred-pound Samoan attorney" who would soon be a far more public figure than any of us would have guessed at the time.

> *Alcohol, Hashish, Prussic Acid, Strychnine are weak dilutions. The surest poison is time.*
>
> —Emerson, *Society and Solitude*

The libel lawyers have never understood what Oscar had in mind—and, at the time, I didn't understand it myself—one of the darker skills involved in the kind of journalism I normally get involved with has to do with the ability to write the Truth about "criminals" without getting them busted—and, in the eyes of the law, *any* person committing a crime is a criminal: whether it's a Hells Angel laying an oil slick on a freeway exit to send a pursuing motorcycle cop crashing over the high side, a presidential candidate smoking a joint in his hotel room, or a good friend who happens to be a lawyer, an arsonist, and a serious drug abuser.

The line between writing truth and providing evidence is very, very thin—but for a journalist working constantly among highly paranoid criminals, it is also the line between trust and suspicion. And that is the difference between having free access to the truth and being treated like a spy. There is no such thing as "forgiveness" on that level; one fuckup will send you straight back to sportswriting—if you're lucky.

In Oscar's case, my only reason for describing him in the book as a three-hundred-pound Samoan instead of a two-hundred-fifty-pound Chicano lawyer was to protect him from the wrath of the L.A. cops and the whole California legal establishment he was constantly at war with. It would not serve either one of our interests, I felt, for Oscar to get busted or disbarred because of something I wrote about him. I had my reputation to protect.

The libel lawyers understood that much; what worried them was that I hadn't protected "my attorney" well enough to protect also the book publisher from a libel suit—just in case my attorney was as crazy as he appeared to be in the manuscript they'd just vetoed . . . or maybe he was crazy like a fox, they hinted; he was, after all, an *attorney*—who'd presumably worked just as hard and for just as many long years as *they* had—to earn his license to steal—and it was inconceivable to them that one of their own kind, as it were, would give all that up on what appeared to be a whim. No, they said, it *must* be a trap; not even a "Brown Power" *lawyer* could afford to laugh at the risk of almost certain disbarment.

Indeed. And they were at least half right—which is not a bad average for lawyers—because Oscar Z. Acosta, Chicano lawyer, very definitely could *not* afford the shitrain of suicidal publicity that he was doing everything possible to bring down on himself. There are a lot of *nice* ways to behave like a criminal—but hiring a camera to have yourself photographed doing it in the road is not one of them. It would have taken a reputation as formidable as Melvin Belli's to survive the kind of grossly illegal behavior that Oscar was effectively admitting by signing that libel release. He might as well have burned his lawyer's license on the steps of the Superior Court building in downtown L.A.

That is what the Ivy League libel lawyers in New York could not accept. They *knew* what that license was worth—at least to them; it averaged out to about $150 an hour—even for a borderline psychotic, as long as he had the credentials.

And Oscar had them—not because his father and grandfather had gone to Yale or Harvard Law; he'd paid his dues at night school, the only Chicano in his class, and his record in the courtroom was better than that of most of the colleagues who called him a disgrace to their venal profession.

Which may have been true, for whatever it's worth . . . but what none of us knew at the time of the Great Madness that came so close to making *Fear and Loathing in Las Vegas* incurably unfit for publication was that we were no longer dealing with O. Z. Acosta, attorney-at-law—but with Zeta, the King of Brown Buffalos.

• • •

In retrospect it is hard to know exactly when Oscar decided to quit the Law just as finally as he'd once quit being a Baptist missionary—but it was obviously a lot earlier than even his few close friends realized, until long after he'd already made the move in his mind, to a new and higher place. The crazy attorney whose "suicidal behavior" so baffled the N.Y. libel lawyers was only the locustlike shell of a thirty-six-year-old neoprophet who was already long overdue for his gig at the top of the Mountain.

There was no more time to be wasted in the company of lepers and lawyers. The hour had finally struck for the fat spic from Riverbank to start acting like that one man in every century "chosen to speak for his people."

None of this terminal madness was easy to see at the time—not even for me, and I knew him as well as anyone . . . But not well enough, apparently, to understand the almost desperate sense of failure and loss that he felt when he was suddenly confronted with the stark possibility that he had never *really* been chosen to speak for anybody, except maybe himself—and even that was beginning to look like a halfway impossible task, in the short time he felt he had left.

I had never taken his burning bush trip very seriously—and I still have moments of doubt about how seriously he took it himself . . . They are very *long* moments, sometimes; and as a matter of fact, I think I feel one coming on right now . . . We should have castrated that brain-damaged thief! That shyster! That blasphemous freak! He was ugly and greasy, and he still owes me thousands of dollars!

The truth was not in him, goddamn it! He was put on this earth for no reason at all except to shit in every nest he could con his way into—but only after robbing them first, and selling the babies to sand-niggers. If that treacherous fist-fucker ever comes back to life, he'll wish we'd had the good sense to nail him up on a frozen telephone pole for his thirty-third birthday present.

DO NOT COME BACK, Oscar! Wherever you are—stay there! There's no room for you here anymore. Not after all this maudlin gibberish I've written about you . . . And besides, we have Werner Erhard now. So BURROW DEEP, you bastard, and take all that poison fat with you!

Cazart! And how's that for a left-handed whipsong?

Never mind. There is no more time for questions—or answers either, for that matter. And I was never much good at this kind of thing anyway.

The first thing we do, let's kill all the lawyers.

—William Shakespeare, *King Henry VI*

Well . . . so much for whipsongs. Nobody laughed when Big Bill sat down to play. He was not into filigree when it came to dealing with lawyers.

And neither am I, at this point. That last outburst was probably unnecessary, but what the hell? Let them drink Drano if they can't take a joke. I'm tired of wallowing around in this goddamn thing.

What began as a quick and stylish epitaph for my allegedly erstwhile three-hundred-pound Samoan attorney has long since gone out of control. Not even Oscar would have wanted an obituary with no end, at least not until he was legally dead, and that will take four more years.

Until then—and probably for many years afterward—the Weird Grapevine will not wither for lack of bulletins, warnings, and other twisted rumors of the latest Brown Buffalo sightings. He will be seen at least once in Calcutta, buying nine-year-old girls out of cages on the White Slave Market . . . and also in Houston, tending bar at a roadhouse on South Main that was once the Blue Fox . . . or perhaps once again on the midnight run to Bimini; standing tall on his own hind legs in the cockpit of a fifty-foot black cigarette boat with a silver Uzi in one hand and a magnum of smack in the other, always running ninety miles an hour with no lights and howling Old Testament gibberish at the top of his bleeding lungs . . .

It might even come to pass that he will suddenly appear on my porch in Woody Creek on some moonless night when the peacocks are screeching with lust . . . Maybe so, and that is one ghost who will always be welcome in this house, even with a head full of acid and a chain of bull-maggots around his neck.

Oscar was one of God's own prototypes—a high-powered mutant of some kind who was never even considered for mass production. He was too weird to live and too rare to die—and as far as I'm concerned, that's just about all that needs to be said about him right now. Nobody really needed Oscar Zeta Acosta. Or *Rolling Stone*. Or Jimmy Carter or the Hindenburg . . . or even the Sloat diamond.

Jesus! Is there no respect in this world for the perfectly useless dead?

Apparently not . . . and Oscar *was* a lawyer, however reluctant he might have been at the end to admit it. He had a lawyer's cynical view of the Truth—which he felt was not nearly as important to other people as it was to him; and he was never more savage and dangerous than when he felt he was being lied to. He was never much interested in the *concept* of truth; he had no time for what he called "dumb Anglo abstracts."

> *Condemn'd to drudge, the meanest of the mean and furbish falsehoods for a magazine.*
>
> —Lord Byron

The truth, to Oscar, was a tool and even a weapon that he was convinced he could not do without—if only because anybody who had more of it than he did would sooner or later try to beat on him with it. Truth was Power—as tangible to Oscar as a fistful of $100 bills or an ounce of pure LSD-25. His formula for survival in a world full of rich gabacho fascists was a kind of circle that began at the top with the idea that truth would bring him power, which would buy freedom—to crank his head full of acid so he could properly walk with the King, which would naturally put him even closer to more and finer truths . . . indeed, the full circle.

Oscar believed it, and that was what finally croaked him.

I tried to warn the greedy bastard, but he was too paranoid to pay any attention . . . Because he was actually a stupid, vicious quack with no morals at all and the soul of a hammerhead shark.

We are better off without him. Sooner or later he would have had to be put to sleep anyway . . . So the world is a better place now that he's at least out of sight, if not certifiably dead.

He will not be missed—except perhaps in Fat City, where every light in the town went dim when we heard that he'd finally cashed his check.

> *One owes respect to the living; To the Dead one owes only the truth.*
>
> —Voltaire

Muhammad Ali, Parts One and Two

Hunter, an avid boxing fan, had a particular admiration for his fellow Louisville native Muhammad Ali, and what was conceived of as a fairly quick and straightforward story soon turned into another twenty-thousand-word epic—equal parts biography, explication, theorizing, and interview. While Ali was normally skeptical, suspicious, and stand-offish toward interviewers, he and Hunter did seem to find a particular rapport. Before any of this happened, though, they had to meet. Ali's promoter—a fiercely old-school bon vivant, Harold Conrad—described Hunter's entrance to Ali's hotel in Manhattan in his 1982 memoir, Dear Muffo*:*

> *He walks in late followed by the chauffeur with his luggage. I tell him Ali is waiting. He insists on checking in first.*
>
> *Now he is at the desk, reaching into his jacket for his credit card. Suddenly he is frantically going through all his pockets.*
>
> *"Holy shit, my wallet! Who the fuck took my wallet?" He screams for a bellboy to bring his luggage over, and he dumps it in the center of the lobby. One piece looks like a bedroll. Another is a strange looking satchel. There is also a tape recorder, an attaché case, and a large brown paper bag, and it's all spread out on this beautiful marble floor, right in the center of traffic.*
>
> *Thompson attacks the attaché case and turns it upside down. No wallet. Now he attacks the satchel, and his hands keep flipping things up in the air like a juggler tossing Indian clubs. First a bottle of Heineken. It caroms gently off the bag and rolls across the lobby. Then a bottle of Wild Turkey, a shoe, and another bottle of Heineken.*
>
> *By now the doctor reaches the bowels of the satchel and comes up with a shaving kit. He opens it. Eureka! There is the wallet. He had put it in his shaving kit. Doesn't everybody?*

At last he checks in, and with much trepidation I take him up to Muhammad's suite.

I don't know how the doctor did it, but he came through. The interview with Muhammad was one of the best I've ever seen, and I thought that overall "Last Tango in Vegas" was brilliant, even though he did call me a pig fucker.

Last Tango in Vegas: Fear and Loathing in the Near Room and the Far Room

May 4 and May 18, 1978

> *When I'm gone, boxing will be nothing again. The fans with the cigars and the hats turned down'll be there, but no more housewives and little men in the street and foreign presidents. It's goin' to be back to the fighter who comes to town, smells a flower, visits a hospital, blows a horn, and says he's in shape. Old hat. I was the onliest boxer in history people asked questions like a senator.*
>
> —Muhammad Ali, 1967

Life had been good to Pat Patterson for so long that he'd almost forgotten what it was like to be anything but a free-riding, first-class passenger on a flight near the top of the world . . .

It is a long, long way from the frostbitten midnight streets around Chicago's Clark and Division to the deep-rug hallways of the Park Lane Hotel on Central Park South in Manhattan . . . But Patterson had made that trip in high style, with stops along the way in London, Paris, Manila, Kinshasa, Kuala Lumpur, Tokyo, and almost everywhere else in the world on that circuit where the menus list no prices and you need at least three pairs of $100 sunglasses just to cope with the TV lights every time you touch down at an airport for another frenzied press conference and then a ticker-tape parade along the route to the presidential palace and another princely reception.

That is Muhammad Ali's world, an orbit so high, a circuit so fast and strong and with rarefied air so thin that only "The Champ," "The

Greatest," and a few close friends have unlimited breathing rights. Anybody who can sell his act for $5 million an hour all over the world is working a vein somewhere between magic and madness . . . And now, on this warm winter night in Manhattan, Pat Patterson was not entirely sure which way the balance was tipping. The main shock had come three weeks ago in Las Vegas, when he'd been forced to sit passively at ringside and watch the man whose life he would gladly have given his own to protect, under any other circumstances, take a savage and wholly unexpected beating in front of five thousand screaming banshees at the Hilton Hotel and something like sixty million stunned spectators on national network TV. The Champ was no longer The Champ: a young brute named Leon Spinks had settled that matter, and not even Muhammad seemed to know just exactly what that awful defeat would mean—for himself or anyone else; not even for his new wife and children, or the handful of friends and advisers who'd been working that high white vein right beside him for so long that they acted and felt like his family.

It was definitely an odd lot, ranging from solemn Black Muslims like Herbert Muhammad, his manager—to shrewd white hipsters like Harold Conrad, his executive spokesman, and Irish Gene Kilroy, Ali's version of Hamilton Jordan: a sort of all-purpose administrative assistant, logistics manager, and chief troubleshooter. Kilroy and Conrad are The Champ's answer to Ham and Jody—but mad dogs and wombats will roam the damp streets of Washington, babbling perfect Shakespearean English, before Jimmy Carter comes up with *his* version of Drew "Bundini" Brown, Ali's alter ego and court wizard for so long now that he can't really remember being anything else. Carter's thin-ice sense of humor would not support the weight of a zany friend like Bundini. It would not even support the far more discreet weight of a court jester like J.F.K.'s Dave Powers, whose role in the White House was much closer to Bundini Brown's deeply personal friendship with Ali than Jordan's essentially political and deceptively hard-nosed relationship with Jimmy . . . and even Hamilton seems to be gaining weight by geometric progressions these days, and the time may be just about ripe for him to have a chat with the Holy Ghost and come out as a "born-again Christian."

That might make the nut for a while—at least through the 1980 re-election campaign—but not even Jesus could save Jordan from a fate worse than any hell he'd ever imagined if Jimmy Carter woke up one morning and read in the *Washington Post* that Hamilton had pawned the great presidential seal for $500 in some fashionable Georgetown hockshop . . . or even with one of his good friends like Pat Caddell, who enjoys a keen eye for collateral.

Indeed . . . and this twisted vision would seem almost too bent for print if Bundini hadn't already raised at least the raw possibility of it by once pawning Muhammad Ali's "Heavyweight Champion of the World" gold-and-jewel-studded belt for $500—just an overnight loan from a friend, he said later; but the word got out, and Bundini was banished from The Family and the whole entourage for eighteen months when The Champ was told what he'd done.

That heinous transgression is shrouded in a mix of jive-shame and *real* black humor at this point: The Champ, after all, had once hurled his Olympic gold medal into the Ohio River, in a fit of pique at some alleged racial insult in Louisville—and what was the difference between a gold medal and a jewel-studded belt? They were both symbols of a "white devil" 's world that Ali, if not Bundini, was already learning to treat with a very calculated measure of public disrespect . . . What they shared, far beyond a very real friendship, was a shrewd kind of street-theater sense of how far out on that limb they could go, without crashing. Bundini has always had a finer sense than anyone else in The Family about where The Champ *wanted* to go, the shifting winds of his instincts, and he has never been worried about things like Limits or Consequences. That was the province of others, like Conrad or Herbert. Drew B. has always known exactly which side he was on, and so has Cassius/Muhammad. Bundini is the man who came up with "Float like a butterfly. Sting like a bee," and ever since then he has been as close to both Cassius Clay and Muhammad Ali as anyone else in the world.

Pat Patterson, by contrast, was a virtual newcomer to The Family. A two-hundred-pound, forty-year-old black cop, he was a veteran of the Chicago vice squad before he hired on as Ali's personal bodyguard. And, despite the total devotion and relentless zeal he brought to his responsibility for protecting The Champ at all times from *any* kind of danger, hassles, or even minor inconvenience, six years on the job had caused him to understand, however reluctantly, that there were at least a few people who could come and go as they pleased through the wall of absolute security he was supposed to maintain around The Champ.

Bundini and Conrad were two of these. They have been around for so long that they had once called the boss "Cassius," or even "Cash"—while Patterson had never addressed him as anything but "Muhammad" or "Champ." He had come aboard at high tide, as it were, and even though he was now in charge of everything from carrying Ali's money—in a big roll of $100 bills—to protecting his life with an ever-present chrome-plated revolver and the lethal fists and feet of a black belt with a license to kill, it had always galled him a bit to know that Muhammad's capricious instincts and occasionally perverse sense of humor made it certifiably impossible for *any* one bodyguard, or even *four*, to protect him from danger in public. His moods were too unpredictable: one minute he would be in an almost catatonic funk, crouched in the backseat of a black Cadillac limousine with an overcoat over his head—and then, with no warning at all, he would suddenly be out of the car at a red light somewhere in the Bronx, playing stickball in the street with a gang of teenage junkies. Patterson had learned to deal with The Champ's moods, but he also knew that in any crowd around The Greatest, there would be at least a few who felt the same way about Ali as they had about Malcolm X or Martin Luther King.

There was a time, shortly after his conversion to the Black Muslim religion in the mid-Sixties, when Ali seemed to emerge as a main spokesman for what the Muslims were then perfecting as the State of the Art in racial paranoia—which seemed a bit heavy and not a little naive at the time, but which the White Devils moved quickly to justify . . .

Yes. But that is a very long story, and we will get to it later. The only point we need to deal with right now is that Muhammad Ali somehow emerged from one of the meanest and most shameful ordeals any prominent American has ever endured as one of the few real martyrs of that goddamn wretched war in Vietnam and a sort of instant folk hero all over the world, except in the U.S.A.

That would come later . . .

• • •

The Spinks disaster in Vegas had been a terrible shock to The Family. They had all known it had to come *sometime*, but the scene had already been set and the papers already signed for that "sometime"—a $16 million purse and a mind-boggling, damn-the-cost television spectacle with Ali's old nemesis Ken Norton as the bogyman, and one last king-hell payday for *everybody*. They were prepared, in the back of their hearts, for that one—but not for the cheap torpedo that blew their whole ship out of the water in Vegas for no payday at all. Leon Spinks crippled a whole industry in one hour on that fateful Wednesday evening in Las Vegas—the *Muhammad Ali Industry*, which has churned out roughly $56 million in over fifteen years and at least twice or three times that much for the people who kept the big engine running all this time. (It would take Bill Walton 112 years on an annual NBA salary of $500,000 to equal that figure.)

> *I knew it was too close for comfort. I told him to stop fooling around. He was giving up too many rounds. But I heard the decision and I thought, "Well, what are you going to do? That's it. I've prepared myself for this day for a long time. I conditioned myself for it. I was young with him and now I feel old with him."*
>
> —Angelo Dundee, Ali's trainer

Dundee was not the only person who was feeling old with Muhammad Ali on that cold Wednesday night in Las Vegas. Somewhere around the middle of the fifteenth round, a whole generation went over the hump as the last Great Prince of the Sixties went out in a blizzard of pain, shock, and angry confusion so total that it was hard to even know how to feel, much less what to say, when the thing was finally over. The last shot came just at the final bell, when "Crazy Leon" whacked Ali with a savage overhand right that almost dropped The Champ in his tracks and killed the last glimmer of hope for the patented "miracle finish" that Angelo Dundee knew was his fighter's only chance. As Muhammad wandered back to his corner about six feet in front of me, the deal had clearly gone down.

The decision was anticlimactic. Leon Spinks, a twenty-four-year-old brawler from St. Louis with only seven professional fights on his record, was the new heavyweight boxing champion of the world. And the roar of the pro-Spinks crowd was the clearest message of all: that uppity nigger from Louisville had finally got what was coming to him. For fifteen long years he had mocked everything they all thought they stood for: changing his name, dodging the draft, beating the best they could hurl at him . . . But now, thank God, they were seeing him finally go down.

Six presidents have lived in the White House in the time of Muhammad Ali. Dwight Eisenhower was still rapping golf balls around the Oval Office when Cassius Clay Jr. won a gold medal for the U.S. as a light-heavyweight in the 1960 Olympics and then turned pro and won his first fight for money against a journeyman heavyweight named Tunney Hunsaker in Louisville on October 29 of that same year.

Less than four years later and almost three months to the day after John Fitzgerald Kennedy was murdered in Dallas, Cassius Clay—the "Louisville Lip" by then—made a permanent enemy of every "boxing expert" in the Western world by beating World Heavyweight Champion Sonny Liston, the meanest of the mean, so badly that Liston refused to come out of his corner for the seventh round.

That was fourteen years ago. Jesus! And it seems like fourteen months.

The Near Room

> *When he got in trouble in the ring, [Ali] imagined a door swung open and inside he could see neon orange and green lights blinking, and bats blowing trumpets and alligators playing trombones, and he could hear snakes screaming. Weird masks and actors' clothes hung on the wall, and if he stepped across the sill and reached for them, he knew that he was committing himself to destruction.*
>
> —George Plimpton, *Shadow Box*

It was almost midnight when Pat Patterson got off the elevator and headed down the corridor toward 905, his room right next door to The

Champ's. They had flown in from Chicago a few hours earlier, and Muhammad had said he was tired and felt like sleeping. No midnight strolls down the block to the Plaza fountain, he promised, no wandering around the hotel or causing a scene in the lobby.

Beautiful, thought Patterson. No worries tonight. With Muhammad in bed and Veronica there to watch over him, Pat felt things were under control, and he might even have time for a bit of refreshment downstairs and then get a decent night's sleep for himself. The only conceivable problem was the volatile presence of Bundini and a friend, who had dropped by around ten for a chat with The Champ about his run for the Triple Crown. The Family had been in a state of collective shock for two weeks or so after Vegas, but now it was the first week in March, and they were eager to get the big engine cranked up for the return bout with Spinks in September. No contracts had been signed yet, and every sportswriter in New York seemed to be on the take from either Ken Norton or Don King or both . . . But none of that mattered, said Ali, because he and Leon had already agreed on the rematch, and by the end of this year he would be the first man in history to win the heavyweight championship of the world *three times.*

Patterson had left them whooping and laughing at each other, but only after securing a promise from Hal Conrad that he and Bundini would leave early and let The Champ sleep. They were scheduled to tape a show with Dick Cavett the next day, then drive for three or four hours up into the mountains of eastern Pennsylvania to Ali's custom-built training camp at Deer Lake. Kilroy was getting the place ready for what Patterson and all the rest of The Family understood was going to be some very serious use. Ali had announced almost immediately after losing to Spinks in Vegas any talk of his "retiring from the ring was nonsense," and that soon he'd begin training for his rematch with Leon.

So the fat was in the fire: a second loss to Spinks would be even worse than the first—the end of the line for Ali, The Family, and, in fact, the whole Ali industry. No more paydays, no more limousines, no more suites and crab cocktails from room service in the world's most expensive hotels. For Pat Patterson and a lot of other people, another defeat by Spinks would mean the end of a whole way of life . . . And, worse yet, the first wave of public reaction to Ali's "comeback" announcement had been anything but reassuring. An otherwise sympathetic story in the *Los Angeles Times* described the almost universal reaction of the sporting press:

"There were smiles and a shaking of hands all around when the thirty-six-year-old ex-champion said after the fight last Wednesday night: 'I'll be back. I'll be the first man to win the heavyweight title three times.' But no one laughed out loud."

A touch of this doomsday thinking had even showed up in The Family. Dr. Ferdie Pacheco, who had been in The Champ's corner for every fight since he first won the title from Liston—except the last one—had gone on the Tom Snyder show and said that Muhammad was finished as a fighter, that he was a shadow of his former self, and that he (Pacheco) had done everything but beg Ali to retire even *before* the Spinks fight.

Pacheco had already been expelled from The Family for this heresy, but it had planted a seed of doubt that was hard to ignore. "The Doc" was no quack, and he was also a personal friend: did he know something the others didn't? Was it even *possible* that The Champ was "washed up"? There was no way to think that by looking at him, or listening to him either. He looked sharp, talked sharp, and there was a calmness, a kind of muted intensity, in his confidence that made it sound almost understated.

Pat Patterson believed—or if he didn't, there was no way that even The Champ could guess it. The loyalty of those close to Muhammad Ali is so profound that it sometimes clouds their own vision . . . But Leon Spinks had swept those clouds away, and now it was time to get serious. No more show business, no more clowning. Now they had come to the crunch.

• • •

Pat Patterson had tried not to brood on these things, but every newspaper rack he'd come close to in Chicago, New York, or anywhere else seemed to echo the baying of hounds on a blood scent. Every media voice in the country was poised for ultimate revenge on this Uppity Nigger who had laughed in their faces for so long that a whole generation of sportswriters had grown up in the shadow of a mocking, dancing presence that most of them had never half understood until now, when it seemed almost gone.

Even the rematch with Spinks was bogged down in the arcane politics of big-money boxing—and Pat Patterson, like all the others who had geared their lives to the fortunes of Muhammad Ali, understood that the rematch would have to be *soon.* Very soon. And The Champ would have to be *ready* this time—as he had not been ready in Vegas. There was no avoiding the memory of Sonny Liston's grim fate, after losing *again* to Ali in a fight that convinced even the "experts."

These things were among the dark shadows that Pat Patterson would rather not have been thinking about on that night in Manhattan as he walked down the corridor to his room in the Park Lane Hotel. The Champ had already convinced him that he would indeed be the first man to win the first Triple Crown in the history of heavyweight boxing—and Pat Patterson was far from alone in his conviction that Leon Spinks would be easy prey, next time, for a Muhammad Ali in top condition both mentally and physically. Spinks was vulnerable: the same crazy/mean style that made him dangerous also made him easy to hit. His hands were surprisingly fast, but his feet were as slow as Joe Frazier's, and it was only the crafty coaching of his trainer, the ancient Sam Solomon, that had given him the early five-round edge in Las Vegas that Ali had refused to understand until he was so far behind that his only hope was a blazing last-minute assault and a knockout or at least a few knockdowns that he was too tired, in the end, to deliver.

Leon was dead on his feet in that savage fifteenth round—but so was Muhammad Ali, and that's why Spinks won the fight . . .

Yes . . . but that is no special secret, and there will be plenty of time to deal with those questions of ego and strategy later on in this saga, if in fact we ever get there. The sun is up, the peacocks are screaming with lust, and this story is so far off the game plan that no hope of salvage exists at this time—or at least nothing less than a sweeping, all-points injunction by Judge Crater, who maintains an unlisted number so private that not even Bob Arum can reach him on short notice.

So we are left with the unhurried vision of Pat Patterson finally reaching the door of his room, number 905 in the Park Lane Hotel in Manhattan—and just as he pulls the room key out of his pocket on the way to a good night's sleep, his body goes suddenly stiff as he picks up the sound of raucous laughter and strange voices in room number 904.

Weird sounds from The Champ's suite . . . Impossible, but Pat Patterson *knows* he's stone sober and nowhere near deaf, so he drops his key back in his pocket and moves one step down the hallway, listening carefully now to these sounds he hopes are not really there . . . Hallucinations, bad nerves, almost anything but the sound of a totally unknown voice—and the voice of a "white devil," no doubt about that—from the room where Ali and Veronica are supposed to be sleeping peacefully. Bundini and Conrad had both promised to be gone at least an hour ago . . . But, no! Not this: not Bundini and Conrad and *the voice of some stranger, too*; along with the unmistakable sound of laughter from both The Champ and his wife . . . Not *now*, just when things were getting close to intolerably serious.

What was the meaning?

Pat Patterson knew what he had to do: he planted both feet in the rug in front of 904 and *knocked*. Whatever was going on would have to be cut short at once, and it was his job to do the cutting—even if he had to get rude with Bundini and Conrad.

• • •

Well . . . this next scene is so strange that not even the people who were part of it can recount exactly what happened . . . but it went more or less like this: Bundini and I had just emerged from a strategy conference in the bathroom when we heard the sudden sound of knocking on the door. Bundini waved us all into silence as Conrad slouched nervously against the wall below the big window that looked out on the snow-covered wasteland of Central Park; Veronica was sitting fully clothed on the king-size bed right next to Ali, who was stretched out and relaxed with the covers pulled up to his waist, wearing nothing at all except . . . Well, let's take it again from Pat Patterson's view from the doorway, when Bundini answered his knock:

The first thing he saw when the door opened was a white stranger with a can of beer in one hand and a lit cigarette in the other, sitting cross-legged on the bureau that faced The Champ's bed—a bad omen for sure and a thing to be dealt with at once at this ominous point in time; but the next thing Pat Patterson saw turned his face into spastic wax and caused his body to leap straight back toward the doorway like he'd just been struck by lightning.

His professional bodyguard's eyes had fixed on me just long enough to be sure I was passive and with both hands harmlessly occupied for at least the few seconds it would take him to sweep the rest of the room and see what was wrong with his $5-million-an-hour responsibility . . . and I could tell by the way he moved into the room and the look on his face that I was suddenly back at that point where any movement at all or even the blink of an eye could change my life forever. But I also knew what was coming, and I recall a split second of real fear as Pat Patterson's drop-forged glance swept past me and over to the bed to Veronica and the inert lump that lay under the sheets right beside her.

For an instant that frightened us all, the room was electric with absolute silence—and then the bed seemed to literally explode as the sheets flew away and a huge body with the hairy red face of the Devil himself leaped up like some jack-in-the-box out of hell and uttered a wild cry that jolted us all and sent such an obvious shock through Pat Patterson that he leaped backward and shot out both elbows like Kareem coming down with a rebound . . .

• • •

I waited until I was sure the Muhammad Ali party was well off the plane and up the ramp before I finally stood and moved up the aisle, fixing the stewardess at the door with a blind stare from behind two mirror lenses so dark that I could barely see to walk—but not so dark that I failed to notice a touch of mockery in her smile as I nodded and stepped past her. "Good-bye, sir," she chirped. "I hope you got an interesting story."

You nasty little bitch! I hope your next flight crashes in a cannibal country . . . But I kept this thought to myself as I laughed bitterly and stomped up the empty tunnel to a bank of pay phones in the concourse. It was New York's La Guardia Airport, around eight thirty on a warm Sunday night in the first week of March, and I had just flown in from Chicago—supposedly "with the Muhammad Ali party." But things had not worked out that way, and my temper was hovering dangerously on the far edge of control as I listened to the sound of nobody answering the phone in Hal Conrad's West Side apartment . . . That swine! That treacherous lying bastard!

We were almost to the ten-ring limit, that point where I knew I'd start pounding on things unless I hung up very quickly before we got to eleven . . . when suddenly a voice sounding almost as angry as I felt came booming over the line. "Yeah, yeah, what *is* it?" Conrad snapped. "I'm in a hell of a hurry. Jesus! I was just about into the elevator when I had to come back and answer this goddamn—"

"You crazy bastard!" I screamed, cutting into his gravelly mumbling as I slammed my hand down on the tin counter and saw a woman using the phone next to me jump like a rat had just run up her leg.

"It's *me*, Harold!" I shouted. "I'm out here at La Guardia and my whole story's fucked and just as soon as I find all my baggage I'm going to get a cab and track you down and slit your goddamn throat!"

"*Wait* a minute!" he said. "What the hell is wrong? Where's Ali? Not with *you?*"

"Are you kidding?" I snarled. "That crazy bastard didn't even know who I *was* when I met him in Chicago. I made a *goddamn fool of myself*, Harold! He looked at me like I was some kind of *autograph hound*!"

"No!" said Conrad. "I told him all about you—that you were a good friend of mine and you'd be on the flight with him from Chicago. He was *expecting* you."

"Bullshit!" I yelled. "You told me he'd be traveling alone, too . . . So I stayed up all night and busted my ass to get a first-class seat on that Continental flight that I knew he'd be catching at O'Hare; then I got everything arranged with the flight crew between Denver and Chicago, making sure they blocked off the first two seats so we could sit together . . . Jesus, Harold," I muttered, suddenly feeling very tired, "what kind of sick instinct would cause you to do a thing like this to me?"

"Where the hell is Ali?" Conrad shouted, ignoring my question. "I sent a car out to pick you up, *both* of you!"

"You mean *all* of us," I said. "His wife was with him, along with Pat Patterson and maybe a few others—I couldn't tell, but it wouldn't have made any difference; they *all* looked at me like I was weird; some kind of psycho trying to muscle into the act, babbling about sitting in Veronica's seat . . ."

"That's impossible," Conrad snapped. "He knew—"

"Well, I guess he *forgot*!" I shouted, feeling my temper roving out on the edge again. "Are we talking about *brain damage*, Harold? Are you saying he *has no memory*?"

He hesitated just long enough to let me smile for the first time all day. "This could be an *ugly* story, Harold," I said. "Ali is so punch-drunk that his memory's all scrambled? Maybe they should lift his license, eh? 'Yeah, let's croak all this talk about comebacks, Dumbo. Your memory's fucked, you're on queer street—and by the way, Champ, what are your job prospects?'"

"You son of a bitch," Conrad muttered. "Okay. To hell with all this bullshit. Just get a cab and meet us at the Plaza. I should have been there a half hour ago."

"I thought you had us all booked into the Park Lane," I said.

"Get moving and don't worry about it," he croaked. "I'll meet you at the Plaza. Don't waste any time."

"WHAT?" I screamed. "What am I doing *right now*? I have a *Friday deadline*, Harold, and this is Sunday! You call me in the middle of the goddamn night in Colorado and tell me to get on the first plane to Chicago because Muhammad Ali has all of a sudden decided he wants to talk to me—after all that lame bullshit in Vegas—so I take the *insane* risk of dumping my whole story in a parachute bag and flying off on a two-thousand-mile freakout right in the middle of a deadline crunch to meet a man in Chicago who treats me like a wino when I finally get there . . . And now you're talking to *me*, you pigfucker, about *wasting time*?"

I was raving at the top of my lungs now, drawing stares from every direction—so I tried to calm down; no need to get busted for public madness in the airport, I thought; but I was also in New York with no story and no place to work and only five days away from a clearly impossible deadline, and now Conrad was telling me that my long-overdue talk with Ali had once again "gone wrong."

"Just get in a cab and meet me at the Plaza," he was saying. "I'll pull this mess together, don't worry . . ."

I shrugged and hung up the phone. Why not? I thought. It was too late to catch a turnaround flight back to Colorado, so I might as well check into the Plaza and get rid of another credit card, along with another friend. Conrad was *trying*; I knew that—but I also knew that this time he was grasping at straws, because we both understood the deep and deceptively narrow-looking moat that eighteen years of celebrity forced Ali to dig between his "public" and his "private" personas.

It is more like a *ring* of moats than just one, and Ali has learned the subtle art of making each one seem like the last great leap between the intruder and himself . . . But there is always *one more moat* to get across, and not many curious strangers have ever made it that far.

Some people will settle happily for a smile and a joke in a hotel lobby, and others will insist on crossing two or even three of his moats before they feel comfortably "private" with The Champ . . . But very few people understand how many rings there really are:

My own quick guess would be nine; but Ali's quick mind and his instinct for public relations can easily make the third moat *seem* like the ninth; and this world is full of sporting journalists who never realized where they were until the same "private thoughts" and "spontaneous bits of eloquence" they had worked so desperately to glean from The Champ in some rare flash of personal communication that none other would ever share, appeared word for word, in cold black type, under somebody else's byline.

This is not a man who *needs* hired pros and wizards to speak for him; but he has learned how to use them so skillfully that he can save himself for the rare moments of confrontation that *interest* him . . . Which are few and far between, but anybody who has ever met Muhammad Ali on that level will never forget it. He has a very lonely sense of humor, and a sense of himself so firmly entrenched that it seems to hover, at times, in that nervous limbo between Egomania and genuine Invulnerability.

And now, as my cab moved jerkily through the snow-black streets of Brooklyn toward the Plaza Hotel, I was brooding on Conrad's deranged plot that I felt would almost certainly cause me another nightmare of professional grief and personal humiliation. I felt like a rape victim on the way to a discussion with the rapist on the Johnny Carson show. Not even Hal Conrad's fine sense of reality could take me past Moat #5—which would not be enough, because I'd made it clear from the start that I was not especially interested in anything short of at least #7 or 8.

Which struck me as far enough, for my purposes, because I understood #9 well enough to know that if Muhammad was as smart as I thought he was, I would never see or even smell that last moat.

• • •

I have known Conrad since 1962, when I met him in Las Vegas at the second Liston-Patterson fight. He was handling the press and publicity for that cruel oddity, and I was the youngest and most ignorant "sportswriter" ever accredited to cover a heavyweight championship fight . . . But Conrad, who had total control of *all access to everything*, went out of his way to overlook my nervous ignorance and my total lack of expense money—including me along with all "big names" for things like press parties, interviews with the fighters, and above all, the awesome spectacle of Sonny Liston working out on the big bag, to the tune of "Night Train," at his crowded and carpeted base camp in the Thunderbird Hotel . . . As the song moved louder and heavier toward a climax of big-band, rock & roll frenzy, Liston would step into the two-hundred-pound bag and hook it *straight up in the air*—where it would hang for one long and terrifying instant, before it fell back into place at the end of a one-inch logging chain with a vicious *clang* and a jerk that would shake the whole room.

I watched Sonny work out on that bag every afternoon for a week or so, or at least long enough to think he had to be at least nine feet tall . . . until one evening a day or so prior to the fight when I literally bumped into Liston and his two huge bodyguards at the door of the Thunderbird Casino, and I didn't even recognize The Champ for a moment because he was only about six feet tall and with nothing but the dull, fixed stare in his eyes to make him seem different from all the other rich, mean niggers a man could bump into around the Thunderbird that week.

So now, on this jangled Sunday night in New York—more than fifteen years and fifty-five thousand olive-drab tombstones from Maine to California since I first realized that Sonny Liston was three inches shorter than me—it was all coming together, or maybe coming apart once again, as my cab approached the Plaza and another wholly unpredictable but probably doomed and dumb encounter with the world of Big Time Boxing. I had stopped for a six-pack of Ballantine ale on the way in from the airport, and I also had a quart of Old Fitzgerald that I'd brought with me from home. My mood was ugly and cynical, tailored very carefully on the long drive through Brooklyn to match my lack of expectations with regard to anything Conrad might have tried to "set up" with Ali.

My way of joking is to tell the truth. That's the funniest joke in the world.

—Muhammad Ali

Indeed . . . And that is also as fine a definition of "Gonzo Journalism" as anything I've ever heard, for good or ill. But I was in no mood for joking when my cab pulled up to the Plaza that night. I was half drunk, fully cranked, and pissed off at everything that moved. My only real plan was to get past this ordeal that Conrad was supposedly organizing with Ali, then retire in shame to my $88-a-night bed and deal with Conrad tomorrow.

But this world does not work on "real plans"—mine or anyone else's—so I was not especially surprised when a total stranger wearing a *serious* black overcoat laid a hand on my shoulder as I was having my bags carried into the Plaza:

"Doctor Thompson?" he said.

"What?" I spun away and glared at him just long enough to know there was no point in denying it . . . He had the look of a rich undertaker who had once been the light-heavyweight karate champion of the Italian navy; a *very quiet* presence that was far too heavy for a cop . . . He was on *my* side.

And he seemed to understand my bad nervous condition; before I could ask anything, he was already picking up my bags and saying—with a smile as uncomfortable as my own: "We're going to the Park Lane; Mr. Conrad is waiting for you . . ."

I shrugged and followed him outside to the long black limo that was parked with the engine running so close to the front door of the Plaza that it was almost up on the sidewalk . . . and about three minutes later I was face to face with Hal Conrad in the lobby of the Park Lane Hotel, more baffled than ever and not even allowed enough time to sign in and get my luggage up to the room . . .

"What took you so goddamn long?"

"I was masturbating in the limo," I said. "We took a spin out around Sheepshead Bay and I—"

"Sober up!" he snapped. "Ali's been *waiting* for you since ten o'clock."

"Balls," I said, as the door opened and he aimed me down the hall. "I'm tired of your bullshit, Harold—and where the hell is my luggage?"

"Fuck your luggage," he replied as we stopped in front of 904 and he knocked, saying, "Open up, it's *me*."

The door swung open and there was Bundini, with a dilated grin on his face, reaching out to shake hands. "Welcome!" he said. "Come right in, Doc—make yourself at home."

I was still shaking hands with Bundini when I realized where I was—standing at the foot of a king-size bed where Muhammad Ali was laid back with the covers pulled up to his waist and his wife, Veronica, sitting next to him: they were both eyeing me with very different expressions than I'd seen on their faces in Chicago.

Muhammad leaned up to shake hands, grinning first at me and then at Conrad: "Is this *him*?" he asked. "You sure he's safe?"

Bundini and Conrad were laughing as I tried to hide my confusion at this sudden plunge into unreality by lighting two Dunhills at once, as I backed off and tried to get grounded . . . but my head was still whirling from this hurricane of changes, and I heard myself saying, "What do you mean—*Is this him*? You bastard! I should have you *arrested* for what you did to me in Chicago!"

Ali fell back on the pillows and laughed. "I'm sorry, boss, but I just couldn't *recognize* you. I knew I was supposed to meet *somebody*, but—"

"Yeah!" I said. "That's what I was trying to *tell* you. What did you think I was *there* for—an autograph?"

Everybody in the room laughed this time, and I felt like I'd been shot out of a cannon and straight into somebody else's movie. I put my satchel down on the bureau across from the bed and reached in for a beer . . . The pop-top came off with a hiss and a blast of brown foam that dripped on the rug as I tried to calm down.

"You *scared* me," Ali was saying. "You looked like some kind of a bum—or a hippie."

"What?" I almost shouted. " '*A bum*? *A hippie*?' " I lit another cigarette or maybe two, not realizing or even thinking about the gross transgressions I was committing by smoking *and* drinking in the presence of The Champ. (Conrad told me later that *nobody* smokes or drinks in the same room with Muhammad Ali—and Jesus Christ! Not—of all places—in the sacred privacy of *his own bedroom at midnight*, where I had no business being in the first place.) . . . But I was mercifully and obviously ignorant of what I was doing. Smoking and drinking and tossing off crude bursts of language are not *second* nature to me, but *first*—and my mood, at that point, was still so mean and jangled that it took me about ten minutes of foul-mouthed raving before I began to get a grip on myself.

Everybody else in the room was obviously relaxed and getting a wonderful boot out of this bizarre spectacle—which was *me*; and when the adrenaline finally burned off, I realized that I'd backed so far away from the bed and into the bureau that I was actually *sitting* on the goddamn thing, with my legs crossed in front of me like some kind of wild-eyed, dope-addled budda (Bhuddah? Buddah? Budda? . . . Ah, fuck these wretched idols with unspellable names—let's use *Budda*, and to hell with Edwin Newman) . . . and suddenly I felt just fine.

And why not?

I was, after all, the undisputed heavyweight Gonzo champion of the world—and this giggling yoyo in the bed across the room from me was no longer the champion of *anything*, or at least nothing he could get a notary public to vouch for . . . So I sat back on the bureau with my head against the mirror and I thought, Well, shit—here I am, and it's definitely a weird place to be; but not *really*, and not half as weird as a lot of other places I've been . . . Nice view, decent company, and no *real* worries at all in this tight group of friends who were obviously having a good time with each other as the conversation recovered from my flakey entrance and got back on the fast-break, bump-and-run track they were used to . . .

Conrad was sitting on the floor with his back to the big window that looks out on the savage, snow-covered wasteland of Central Park—and one look at his face told me that he was *finished working* for the night; he had worked a major miracle, smuggling a hyena into the house of mirrors, and now he was content to sit back and see what happened . . .

Conrad was as happy as a serious smoker without a serious smoke could have been right then . . . And so was I, for that matter, despite the crossfire of abuse and bent humor that I found myself caught in, between Bundini and the bed.

Ali was doing most of the talking: his mind seemed to be sort of wandering around and every once in a while taking a quick bite out of anything that caught his interest, like a good-humored wolverine . . . There was no talk about boxing, as I recall: we'd agreed to save that for the "formal interview" tomorrow morning, so this midnight gig was a bit like a warmup for what Conrad described as "the *serious* bullshit."

There was a lot of talk about "drunkards," the sacred nature of "unsweetened grapefruit," and the madness of handling money—a subject I told him I'd long since mastered: "How many acres do you own?" I kept asking him whenever he started getting too high on his own riffs. "Not as many as me," I assured him. "I'm richer than Midas, and nine times as shrewd—whole valleys and mountains of acres," I continued, keeping a very straight face: "Thousands of cattle, stallions, peacocks, wild boar, sloats . . ." And then the final twist: "You and Frazier just never learned how to handle money—but for twenty percent of the nut I can make you almost as rich as I am."

I could see that he didn't believe me. Ali is a hard man to con—but when he got on the subject of his tragic loss of "all privacy," I figured it was time for the drill.

"You really want a cure for your privacy problem?" I asked him, ripping the top out of another Ballantine Ale.

He smiled wickedly. "Sure, boss—what you got?"

I slid off the bureau and moved toward the door. "Hang on," I told him. "I'll be right back."

Conrad was suddenly alert. "Where the hell are you going?" he snapped.

"To my room," I said. "I have the ultimate cure for Muhammad's privacy problem."

"*What* room?" he asked. "You don't even know where it is, do you?"

More laughter.

"It's 1011," Conrad said, "right upstairs—but hurry back," he added. "And if you run into Pat, we never heard of you."

Pat Patterson, Ali's fearfully diligent bodyguard, was known to be prowling the halls and putting a swift arm on anything human or otherwise that might disturb Ali's sleep. The rematch with Spinks was already getting cranked up, and it was Patterson's job to make sure The Champ stayed deadly serious about his new training schedule.

"Don't worry," I said. "I just want to go up to the room and put on my pantyhose. I'll be a lot more comfortable."

The sound of raucous laughter followed me down the hall as I sprinted off toward the fire exit, knowing I would have to be fast or I'd never get back in that room—tonight *or* tomorrow.

But I knew what I wanted, and I knew where it was in my parachute bag: yes, a spectacularly hideous full-head, real-hair, $75 movie-style red devil mask—a thing so fiendishly *real* and ugly that I still wonder, in moments like these, what sort of twisted impulse caused me to even pack the goddamn thing, much less wear it through the halls of the Park Lane Hotel and back into Muhammad Ali's suite at this unholy hour of the night.

Three minutes later I was back at the door, with the mask zipped over my head and the neck-flap tucked into my shirt. I knocked twice, then leaped into the room when Bundini opened the door, screaming some brainless slogan like *"Death to the weird!"*

For a second or two there was no sound at all in the room—then the whole place exploded in wild laughter as I pranced around, smoking and drinking through the molded rubber mouth and raving about whatever came into my head.

The moment I saw the expression on Muhammad's face, I knew my mask would never get back to Woody Creek. His eyes lit up like he'd just seen the one toy he'd wanted all his life, and he almost came out of the bed after me . . .

"Okay," I said, lifting it off my head and tossing it across the room to the bed. "It's yours, my man—but let me warn you that not *everybody* thinks this thing is real funny."

("Especially *black* people," Conrad told me later. "Jesus," he said, "I just about flipped when you jumped into the room with that goddamn mask on your head. That *was* really pushing your luck.")

Ali put the mask on immediately and was just starting to enjoy himself in the mirror, when we all went stiff to the sound of harsh knocking through the door, along with the voice of Pat Patterson. "Open up," he was shouting. "What the hell is going on in there?"

I rushed for the bathroom, but Bundini was two steps ahead of me . . . Ali, still wearing the hideous mask, ducked under the covers, and Conrad went to open the door.

It all happened so fast that we all simply *froze* in position as Patterson came in like Dick Butkus on a blood scent . . . and that was when Muhammad came out of the bed with a wild cry and a mushroom cloud of flying sheets, pointing one long brown arm and a finger like Satan's own cattle prod straight into Pat Patterson's face.

And that, folks, was a moment that I'd just as soon not have to live through again. We were all lucky, I think, that Patterson didn't go for his gun and blow Muhammad away in that moment of madness before he recognized the body under the mask.

It was only a split second, but it could easily have been a hell of a lot longer for all of us if Ali hadn't dissolved in a fit of whooping laughter at the sight of Pat Patterson's face . . . And although Pat recovered instantly, the smile he finally showed us was uncomfortably thin.

The problem, I think, was not so much the mask itself and the shock it had caused him—but *why* The Champ was wearing the goddamn thing at all; where had it come from? And why? These were serious times, but a scene like this could have ominous implications for the future—particularly with Ali so pleased with his new toy that he kept it on his head for the next ten or fifteen minutes, staring around the room and saying with no hint of a smile in his voice that he would definitely wear it for his appearance on the Dick Cavett show the next day. "This is the new *me*," he told us. "I'll wear it on TV tomorrow and tell Cavett that I promised Veronica that I won't take it off until I win my title back. I'm gonna wear this ugly thing everywhere I go—even when I get into the ring with Spinks next time." He laughed wildly and jabbed at himself in the mirror. "Yes indeed!" he chuckled. "They thought I was crazy *before*, but they ain't seen *nothin'* yet."

I was feeling a little on the crazy side myself, at that point—and Patterson's accusing presence soon told us it was time to go.

"Okay, boss," Ali said to me on the way out. "Tomorrow we get serious, right? Nine o'clock in the morning. We'll have breakfast, and get *real* serious."

I agreed, and went upstairs to my room for a bit of the good smoke.

• • •

I was up at eight thirty the next day, but when I called Ali's suite, Veronica said he'd been up since seven and "was wandering around downstairs somewhere."

I found him in the restaurant, sitting at one end of a table full of cut glass and silver, dressed almost as formally as the maitre d' in a dark blue pin-striped suit and talking very seriously with a group of friends and very earnest black businessmen types who were all dressed the same way he was. It was a completely different man from the one I'd been sparring and laughing with the night before. The conversation around the table ranged from what to do about a just-received invitation to visit some new country in Africa, to a bewildering variety of endorsement offers, to book contracts, real estate, and the molecular structure of crabmeat.

It was midmorning before we finally went upstairs to his suite "to get serious." . . . And what follows is a 99 percent verbatim transcript of our conversation for almost the next two hours. Muhammad was stretched out on the bed, still wearing his "senator's suit," and balancing my tape recorder on his stomach while he talked. I was sitting cross-legged right next to him on the bed, with a bottle of Heineken in one hand, a cigarette in the other, and my shoes on the floor beside me.

The room was alive with the constant comings and goings of people bearing messages, luggage, warnings about getting to the Cavett show on time . . . and also a very alert curiosity about *me* and what I was up to. The mask was nowhere in sight, but Pat Patterson *was*—along with three or four other very serious-looking black gentlemen who listened to every word we said. One of them actually kneeled on the floor right next to the bed, with his ear about thirteen inches away from the tape recorder, the whole time we talked.

Okay, we might as well get back to what we were talking about downstairs. You said you're definitely going to fight Spinks again, right?

I can't say I'm definitely going to fight Spinks again. I think we are. I'm sure we are—but I might die, he might die.

But as far as you're concerned, you want to, you're counting on it.

Yeah, he plans to fight me. I gave him a chance, and he will give me a shot back at it. The people won't believe he's a true champion until he beats me twice. See, I had to beat Liston twice, [Ingemar] Johansson had to beat Patterson twice, but he didn't. Randy Turpin had to beat Sugar Ray [Robinson] twice, but he didn't. If he can beat me twice, then people will really believe that he might possibly be the greatest.

Okay, let me ask you . . . at what point, at what time—I was in Vegas for the fight—when did you realize that things were getting real serious?

Round twelve.

Up to then you still thought you had control.

I was told that I was probably losing, but maybe I was even. I had to win the last three, and I was too *tired* to win the last three, then I knew I was in trouble.

But you figured you could pull it off . . . up until round twelve.

Yeah, but I couldn't, 'cause he is confident, 'cause he is winning, and I had to pull it off and he was 197 and I'm 228, and that's too heavy.

Didn't you tell me downstairs at breakfast that you're going to come in at 205 next time?

I don't know what I'm going to come in at; 205 is really impossible. If I get to 220 I'll be happy. Just be eight pounds lighter . . . I'll be happy. I did pretty good at that weight, to be in condition around 220, even if it's 225, 223, I could do better.

Well, on a scale of one hundred, what kind of condition were you in for Spinks?

Scale of one hundred? I was eighty.

Where should you have been?

Should have been . . . ninety-eight.

Why didn't you know him better? You didn't seem ready . . .

Why didn't anybody know him? He slipped up on the press, a

ten-to-one underdog, they called him. He hadn't gone over ten rounds and only seven pro fights. What can you know about him?

Okay, let's get to another point:

This may be an odd question, but I want to ask you anyway. At the press conference after the fight I remember Leon saying, "I just wanted to beat this nigger." And it seems to me it was done with a smile, but when I heard that I felt the whole room get tense.

No, that's okay. I say the same things. We black people talk about each other that way, in a humorous way. "Ah, niggah, be quiet." "Ah—ahh. I can whop that niggah." "Niggah, you crazy." Those are our expressions. If you say it, I'll slap you. The white man can't call me nigger like they do.

So it was a joke? It struck me as a very raw note, but . . .

I can't blame you. When I beat Sonny Liston, I didn't say those words, but I was glad to win, so I can't take nothing from Spinks—he's good, he's a lot better fighter than people thought he was.

Did I hear you say that you were going up to the camp today?

I start training in about two weeks.

And that's going to be straight through for five or six months? You've never done that before, have you?

Never in my life, never more than two months. But this time I'm going to be in there five months, chopping trees, running up hills, I'll be coming in dancing! Dancing! [*Sudden grin*] I'll be winning my title for the third time . . . [*Shouting*] The greatest of all times! Of all times!! [*Laughing and jabbing*]

How good is Leon? I don't really know myself.

Leon is unexplored, unknown—and after I beat him, he'll come back and win the title and he'll hold it four or five years and he'll go down in history as one of the great heavyweights. Not the greatest, but one of the greatest.

So if you fought him one more time, you think that'd be it? Is that what you're saying?

I'm not sure that'll be it for me . . . I might take another fight—don't know yet, according to how I feel when that time comes.

Did you see Kallie Knoetze, that South African fighter? The one who beat Bobick?

I heard about him.

Me and Conrad spent a lot of time talking to him before the fight. I was trying to work up a really serious spectacle between you and him down in South Africa.

He seemed like a nice fellow.

Oh yeah, he was really eager to have you come down there and fight. Does that interest you, to fight a white cop in South Africa?

On the basis that on that day there'd be equality in the arena where I'm fighting.

But would that interest you? With all the heavy political overtones? How do you feel about something like that? Along with a million-dollar gate?

Yeah, I like it. With the approval of all the other African nations and Muslim countries. I wouldn't go against their wishes, regardless of how they made the arena that night; if the masses of the country and the world were against it, I wouldn't go. I know that I have a lot of fans in South Africa, and they want to see me. But I'm not going to crawl over other nations to go. The world would have to say: "Well, this case is special, they've given the people justice. His going is helping the freedom."

There's a dramatic quality to that thing—I can't think of any other fight that would have that kind of theater. Actually, it might even be too much *politics . . .*

What worries me is gettin' whupped by a white man in South Africa.

Oh ho! Yeah! [Nervous chuckle]

[Room breaks into laughter]

[*Laughing*] That's what the world needs . . . me getting whupped by a white man in South Africa!

[*Still laughing*]

Oh yeah . . .

Getting whupped by a white man *period*, but in South Africa? If a *white South African* fighter beat me . . . ?

I guess there'd be no way you could go down to South Africa without beating Leon first, right?

No, I got to beat Leon first. I will defeat Leon first. I will go down as the triple greatest of all time.

Oh yeah, I think you might. If you train, if you get serious.

If I get serious? I'm as serious as cancer. Is cancer serious?

Well, yeah, I didn't realize, uh . . . if you're going to start training now, that is serious, that's five months, six months.

I'm going to be *ready*!

Would it be more important next time to get faster?

No, next time it's to be in better shape, to take him more serious, to know him.

Why the hell didn't you this time?

Didn't know him.

You got some of the smartest people in the business working with you.

Didn't know him . . . See, all of my worst fights was when I fought nobodies. Jürgen Blin, Zurich, Switzerland, seven rounds with him, didn't look too good. Al Lewis, Dublin, Ireland, a nobody, went eleven rounds. Jean-Pierre Coopman, San Juan, Puerto Rico . . . a nobody.

Yeah, but Leon, you saw him fight several times, didn't you?

Amateurs, just seven . . . what can this man do with seven pro fights, never been over ten rounds . . .

But you had about fifteen or eighteen pro fights when you fought Liston the first time.

I don't know.

I think I counted them up the other day . . . nineteen maybe.

I caught him off guard too; I was supposed to have been annihilated like this boy was. But my best fights were those fights where I was the underdog: George Foreman's comeback, two Liston fights, Frazier fights, Norton . . .

Is that something in your head?

It makes you hungry, got something to work for. I'm doing good. Everything is going my way. I'm eating dinner. I'm living with my wife and my two children all up to the fight, which ain't that good. Least six weeks before the fight I should get away from my children 'cause they make you soft. You hug 'em and you kiss them, you know, you 'round babies all day. Day before the fight, I'm babysitting 'cause my wife done some shopping. She didn't mean no harm.

You can't blame it on her, though.

No. I got to get away from the babies, I got to get evil. Got to chop trees, run up hills, get in my old log cabin.

You plan to go up there to stay, at the camp, live there until the fight?

Where . . . what fight . . . ?

You say you're going to go up there and do a monk sort of trip?

No, my wife and babies would be with me, but my babies, they cry at night, and they'll be in another cabin.

I don't want to bring up any sore subject, but did you see Pacheco on the Tom Snyder show when he was talking about all athletes getting old . . . ? He seemed to come down pretty hard. He said physically it would just be impossible for you to get back in shape to beat Leon.

I was fighting years before I knew Pacheco. He got famous hanging around me. They all got known . . . popular. They'd never admit it . . .

and also Pacheco don't know me, he works in my corner, he's not my real physical doctor.

So you think you can get back in ninety-eight on a scale of a hundred?

Yeah. What I like, this is what I love . . . to do the impossible, be the underdog. Pressure makes me go. I couldn't . . . I didn't beat Frazier the first time, I didn't beat Norton the first time. I gotta beat the animal. I almost got to lose to keep going. It would be hard for me to keep getting the spirit up, what have I got to accomplish, who have I got to prove wrong?

Speaking of that, how did you ever get yourself in the situation where you had so much to lose and so little to gain by fighting Leon down there? . . .

How did I get in what?

You got yourself in an almost no-win situation there where you had very little to win and a hell of a lot to lose. It struck me as strategically bad . . .

That's the way it is, that's the way it's been ever since I held the crown. I didn't have nothing to gain by fighting [Joe] Bugner. I didn't have nothing to gain by fighting Jean-Pierre Coopman. I didn't have nothing to gain by fighting a lot of people.

You sure as hell will next time by fighting Leon. That will be real pressure.

Oh yeah, I like the pressure, need the pressure . . . the world likes . . . people like to see miracles . . . people like to see . . . people like to see underdogs that do it . . . people like to be there when history is made.

• • •

Muhammad Ali has interested a lot of different people for a lot of very different reasons since he became a media superstar and a high-energy national presence almost two decades ago . . . And he has interested me, too, for reasons that ranged from a sort of amused camaraderie in the beginning, to wary admiration, then sympathy & a new level of personal respect, followed by a dip into a different kind of wariness that was more exasperation than admiration . . . and finally into a mix of all these things that never really surfaced and came together until I heard that he'd signed to fight Leon Spinks as a "warmup" for his $16 million swan song against Ken Norton.

This was the point where my interest in Muhammad Ali moved almost subconsciously to a new and higher gear. I had seen all of Leon's fights in the 1976 Montreal Olympics, and I recall being impressed to the point of awe at the way he attacked and destroyed whatever they put in front of him. I had never seen a *young* fighter who could get away with planting *both* feet and leaning forward when he hooked with either hand.

Archie Moore was probably the last *big* fighter with that rare combination of power, reflexes, and high tactical instinct that a boxer *must* have to get away with risking moments of total commitment even occasionally . . . But Leon did it *constantly*, and in most of his fights that was *all* he did.

It was a pure *kamikaze* style: the Roving Tripod, as it were—with Leon's legs forming two poles of the tripod, and the body of his opponent forming the third. Which is interesting for at least two reasons: (1) There *is no tripod* until a punch off that stance connects with the opponent's head or body, so the effect of a miss can range from fatal to unnerving, or at the very least it will cause raised eyebrows and even a faint smile or two among the ringside judges who are scoring the fight . . . and, (2) If the punch connects solidly, then the tripod is formed and an almost preternatural blast of energy is delivered at the point of impact, especially if the hapless target is leaning as far back on the ropes as he can get with his head ducked in and forward in a coverup stance—like Ali's rope-a-dope.

A boxer who plants both feet and then leans forward to lash out with a hook has his whole weight *and also his whole balance* behind it; he cannot pull back at that point, and if he fails to connect he will not only lose points for dumb awkwardness, but he'll plunge his head out front, low and wide open for one of those close-in jackhammer combinations that usually end with a knockdown.

That was Leon's style in the Olympics, and it was a terrifying thing to see. All he had to do was catch his opponent with no place to run, then land one or two of those brain-rattling tripod shots in the first round—

and once you get stunned and intimidated like that in the first round of a three-round (Olympic) bout, there is not enough time to recover . . .

. . . or even *want* to, for that matter, once you begin to think that this brute they pushed you into the ring with has no reverse gear and would just as soon attack a telephone pole as a human being.

Not many fighters can handle that style of all-out assault without having to back off and devise a new game plan. But there is no time for devising new plans in a three-round fight—and perhaps not in ten, twelve, or fifteen rounds either, because Leon doesn't give you much time to think. He keeps coming, swarming, pounding; and he can land three or four shots from *both* directions once he gets braced and leans out to meet that third leg of the tripod.

On the other hand, those poor geeks that Leon beat silly in the Olympics were *amateurs* . . . and we are all a bit poorer for the fact that he was a *light-heavyweight* when he won that gold medal; because if he'd been a few pounds heavier he would have had to go against the elegant Cuban heavyweight champion, Teófilo Stevenson, who would have beaten him like a gong for all three rounds.

But Stevenson, the Olympic heavyweight champ in both 1972 and '76, and the only modern heavyweight with the physical and mental equipment to compete with Muhammad Ali, has insisted for reasons of his own and Fidel Castro's on remaining the "*amateur* heavyweight champion of the world," instead of taking that one final leap for the great ring that a fight against Muhammad Ali could have been for him.

Whatever reasons might have led Castro to decide that an Ali-Stevenson match—sometime in 1973 or '74, after Muhammad had won the hearts and minds of the whole world with his win over George Foreman in Zaire—was not in the interest of either Cuba, Castro, or perhaps even Stevenson himself, will always be clouded in the dark fog of politics and the conviction of people like me that the same low-rent political priorities that heaped a legacy of failure and shame on every other main issue of this generation was also the real reason why the two great heavyweight artists of our time were never allowed in the ring with each other.

This is one of those private opinions of my own that even my friends in the "boxing industry" still dismiss as the flakey gibberish of a half-smart writer who was doing okay with things like drugs, violence, and presidential politics, but who couldn't quite cut the mustard in *their* world.

Boxing.

These were the same people who chuckled indulgently when I said, in Las Vegas, that I'd take every bet I could get on Leon Spinks against Muhammad Ali at ten to one, and with anybody who was seriously into numbers I was ready to haggle all the way down to five to one, or maybe even four . . . but even at eight to one, it was somewhere between hard and impossible to get a bet down on Spinks with anybody in Vegas who was even a fifty-fifty bet to pay off in real money.

One of the few consistent traits shared by "experts" in any field is that they will almost never bet money or anything else that might turn up in public on whatever they call their convictions. That is why they are "experts." They have waltzed through that minefield of high-risk commitments that separates politicians from gamblers, and once you've reached that plateau where you can pass for an expert, the best way to stay there is to hedge all your bets, private and public, so artistically that nothing short of a thing so bizarre that it can pass for an "act of God" can damage your high-priced reputation . . .

I remember vividly, for instance, my frustration at Norman Mailer's refusal to bet money on his almost certain conviction that George Foreman was too powerful for Muhammad Ali to cope with in Zaire . . . And I also recall being slapped on the chest by an Associated Press boxing writer in Las Vegas while we were talking about the fight one afternoon at the casino bar in the Hilton. "Leon Spinks is a *dumb midget*," he snarled in the teeth of all the other experts who'd gathered on that afternoon to get each other's fix on the fight. "He has about as much chance of winning the heavyweight championship as *this guy*."

"*This guy*" was me, and the AP writer emphasized his total conviction by giving me a swift backhand to the sternum . . . and I thought: Well, you *dumb* loudmouth cocksucker, you're going to remember that stupid mistake as long as you live.

And he will. I have talked to him since on this subject, and when I said I planned to quote him *absolutely verbatim* with regard to his prefight wisdom in Vegas, he seemed like a different man and said that if I was going to quote him on his outburst of public stupidity that I should at least be fair enough to explain that he had "been with Muhammad Ali for so long and through so many wild scenes that he *simply couldn't go against him on this one.*"

Well . . . how's *that* for equal time? It's a hell of a lot more than you pompous big-time bullies ever even thought about giving me, and if you want to add anything else, there's always the Letters to the Editor page in *RS*. . . . But the next time you whack some idle bystander in the chest with one of your deeply felt expert opinions, keep in mind that you might hit somebody who will want to insist on betting real money.

• • •

Some people write their novels and others roll high enough to live them, and some fools try to do both—but Ali can barely read, much less write, so he came to that fork in the road a long time ago, and he had the rare instinct to find that one seam in the defense that let him opt for a third choice: he would get rid of words altogether and live his own movie.

A brown Jay Gatsby—not black and with a head that would never be white: he moved from the very beginning with the same instinct that drove Gatsby—an endless fascination with that green light at the end of the pier. He had shirts for Daisy, magic leverage for Wolfsheim, a delicate and dangerously vulnerable Ali-Gatsby shuttle for Tom Buchanan, and no answers at all for Nick Carraway, the word junkie.

There are two kinds of counterpunchers in this world—one learns early to live by his reactions and quick reflexes—and the other, the one with a taste for high rolling, has the instinct to make an aggressor's art of what is essentially the defensive, survivor's style of the counterpuncher.

Muhammad Ali decided one day a long time ago, not long after his twenty-first birthday, that he was not only going to be King of the World *on his own turf*, but Crown Prince on *everybody else's* . . .

Which is very, very *High* Thinking—even if you can't pull it off. Most people can't handle the action on whatever they chose or have to call their own turf; and the few who can, usually have better sense than to push their luck any further.

That was always the difference between Muhammad Ali and the rest of us. He came, he saw, and if he didn't entirely conquer—he came as close as anybody we are likely to see in the lifetime of this doomed generation.

Res ipsa loquitur.

The Palm Beach Story

In 1982, after a few years of mostly false starts, failed stories, and missed deadlines, Hunter took an assignment from the magazine to cover what was shaping up to be the most scandalous and lurid divorce trial in recent history: Herbert "Peter" Pulitzer Jr. versus his estranged wife, Roxanne, in Palm Beach, Florida. "Big names in the mud, multiple sodomies, raw treachery, bad craziness—the Pulitzer gig had everything," he wrote. Hunter embedded himself with the local culture of the idle rich, became mesmerized by both the details of the trial and what it seemed to represent ("What is a judge to make of two coke fiends who spent $441,000 last year on 'miscellaneous and unknown'?"), and delivered a piece that announced his return to form. The fact that he became lifelong friends with Roxanne Pulitzer in the process—after describing her in the piece as like "a jaded Pan Am stewardess"—is a testament to Hunter's legendary charm.

A Dog Took My Place

July 21, 1983

West Palm Beach, FLA., Dec. 28, 1982 (AP)—Herbert Pulitzer Jr., the millionaire publishing heir, won custody of his twin five-year-old sons today as a Circuit Court judge awarded less than $50,000 in alimony to Mr. Pulitzer's wife, Roxanne.

Judge Carl Harper, citing "flagrant acts of adultery and other gross marital misconduct," ordered the thirty-one-year-old Mrs. Pulitzer to move out of the couple's lakefront home in Palm Beach, where she had maintained custody of the children since the separation. Judge Harper's ruling came after an eighteen-day trial in which there had been testimony about cocaine abuse, extramarital affairs, incest, lesbianism, and late-night séances. The trial ended in November.

The decision was so aggressively harsh that even veteran courthouse reporters were shocked. "I couldn't believe it," one said afterward. "He whipped her like a dog."

All history is gossip.

—Harold Conrad

There is a lot of wreckage in the fast lane these days. Not even the rich feel safe from it, and people are looking for reasons. The smart say they can't understand it, and the dumb snort cocaine in rich discos and stomp to a feverish beat. Which is heard all over the country, or at least felt. The stomping of the rich is not a noise to be ignored in troubled times. It usually means they are feeling anxious or confused about something, and when the rich feel anxious and confused, they act like wild animals.

That is the situation in Palm Beach these days, and the natives are not happy with it. There is trouble on all fronts. Profits are down, the whole concept of personal privacy has gone up for grabs, and the president might be a fool. That is not the kind of news these people want to hear, or even think about. Municipal bonds and dividend checks are the lifeblood of this town, and the flow shall not be interrupted for any reason.

Nor shall privacy be breached. The rich have certain rules, and these are two of the big ones: maintain the privacy and the pipeline at all costs—although not necessarily in that order—it depends on the situation, they say; and everything has its price, even women.

• • •

The autumn months are slow in Palm Beach. The mansions along Ocean Boulevard are closed up and shuttered for the hurricane season, which ends sometime in December, when the rich come back to the island.

That is when the season starts, the winter social calendar. From the Patrons Opera Guild Luncheon in November at the Colony Hotel, to the premiere of the Lannan Foundation Museum in early March, the action is almost continuous: white ties and golden slippers, charity balls at the Breakers, cotillion dances at the Bath and Tennis Club, and endless cocktail parties.

"Eighty percent of the world's wealth is here during the season," said a local decorator one night over dinner at Dunhills in the heart of the off-season. "It's a very exciting scene to be part of."

The autumn months are boring, he said. But it is a nice time to be here, if you don't mind staying inside. The sea is wild, the beach is like Norway, and relentless monsoon rains lash the island day and night. Only servants go out in this kind of weather, and the only cars on the street are people taking care of business, for good or ill.

The business of Palm Beach is business, even on a rainy day in the off-season. Despite the town's image of terminal leisure and luxury, the people who live here are very aware of their money, and they tend to watch it carefully. Displays of naked greed are frowned on, and business is done discreetly—or, failing that, in private. Some people sell real estate, some spend all day on the telephone, raving at their brokers and making $1,000 a minute on the stock market, and others buy fistfuls of speedy cocaine and spend their afternoons playing frantically with each other and doing their own kind of business.

There are hideous scandals occasionally—savage lawsuits over money, bizarre orgies at the Bath and Tennis Club, or some genuine outrage like a half-mad eighty-eight-year-old heiress trying to marry her teenage Cuban butler—but scandals pass like winter storms in Palm Beach, and it has been a long time since anybody got locked up for degeneracy in this town. The community is very tight, connected to the real world by only four bridges, and is as deeply mistrustful of strangers as any lost tribe in the Amazon.

The rich like their privacy, and they have a powerful sense of turf. God has given them the wisdom, they feel, to handle their own problems in their own way. In Palm Beach there is nothing so warped and horrible that it can't be fixed, or at least tolerated, just as long as it stays in the family.

The family lives on the island, but not everybody on the island is family. The difference is very important, a main fact of life for the people who live here, and few of them misunderstand it. At least, not for long. The penalty for forgetting your place can be swift and terrible. I have friends in Palm Beach who are normally very gracious, but when word got out that I was in town asking questions about the Pulitzer divorce trial, I was shunned like a leper.

The Fastest Lane in the World

That's the way it was last fall at the start of *Pulitzer v. Pulitzer*, and not even the worst winter rains in forty years could explain why the town was so empty of locals when Palm Beach had a world-class spectacle to fill the dull days of the off-season.

The *Miami Herald* called it the nastiest divorce trial in Palm Beach history, a scandal so foul and far reaching that half the town fled to France or Majorca for fear of being dragged into it. People who normally stay home in the fall to have all their bedrooms redecorated or to put a new roof on the boathouse found reasons to visit Brazil. The hammer of Palm Beach justice was coming down on young Roxanne Pulitzer, a girl from the wrong side of the tracks who had married the town's most eligible bachelor a few years back and was now in the throes of divorce.

The trial was making ugly headlines all over the world, and nobody wanted to testify. Divorce is routine in Palm Beach, but this one had a very different and dangerous look to it. The whole lifestyle of the town was suddenly on trial, and prominent people were being accused of things that were not fashionable.

Some of the first families of Palm Beach society will bear permanent scars from the *Pulitzer v. Pulitzer* proceedings, a maze of wild charges and counterchargers ranging from public incest and orgies to witchcraft, craziness, child abuse, and hopeless cocaine addiction.

The Filthy Rich in America were depicted as genuinely *filthy*, a tribe of wild sots and sodomites run amok on their own private island and crazed all day and all night on cocaine. The very name Palm Beach, long synonymous with old wealth and aristocratic style, was coming to be associated with berserk sleaziness, a place where price tags mean nothing and the rich are always in heat, where pampered animals are openly worshipped in church and naked millionaires gnaw brassieres off the chests of their own daughters in public.

Fire in the Nuts

I arrived in Palm Beach on a rainy night in November, for no particular reason. I was on my way south to Miami, and then out to Nassau for a wedding. Black ties, big boats, high priests, fine linen, and fresh crab meat: a strange gathering of a strange clan, but it would not be happening for two weeks, so I had some time to kill, and Miami, I felt, was not the place to do it. Two weeks on the loose in Miami can change a man's life forever. It is the Hong Kong of the Western world, an extremely fast track for almost anybody, and dangerously fast for the innocent.

Anyway, I decided to stop in Palm Beach and have a look at the Pulitzer divorce proceedings, which were already infamous. The *Denver Post*, which I read for the sports, had carried enough bizarre headlines about the case to pique a layman's interest. Big names in the mud, multiple sodomies, raw treachery, bad craziness—the Pulitzer gig had everything. It was clearly a story that a man in the right mood could have fun with.

And I was *in* that mood. I needed a carnival in my life: whoop it up with the rich for a while, drink gin, drive convertibles, snort cocaine, and frolic with beautiful lesbians. Never mind the story. It would take care of itself. It was ripe in every direction.

That is a dangerous attitude to take into anything serious. It mandates a quick hit, wild quotes, and big headlines. "The good old in-and-out," as they like to say in the trade. Take it all on the rise, skim the top of the news, and run with it: let the locals do the legwork. We are, after all, professionals.

Divorce court is not a prestige beat in the newspaper business. It is a cut above writing obituaries or covering the Rotary Club, but it is basically a squalid assignment. Too much time in the courthouse can drive even cub reporters to drink. The trials are tedious, the testimony is ugly, and the people you meet on the job tend to have incurable problems.

The Palm Beach County Courthouse is not much different from others all over the country. It is just another clearinghouse on the street of broken dreams, a grim maze of long corridors full of people who would rather not be there. Young girls wearing neck braces sit patiently on wooden benches, waiting to testify against young men wearing handcuffs and jail denims. Old women weep hysterically in crowded elevators. Wild Negroes with gold teeth are dragged out of courtrooms by huge bailiffs. Elderly jurors are herded around like criminals, not knowing what to expect.

Only lawyers can smile in this atmosphere. They rush from one trial to another with bulging briefcases, followed by dull-eyed clerks carrying cardboard boxes filled with every kind of evidence, from rusty syringes to human fingers and sworn depositions from the criminally insane with serious grudges to settle.

The Pulitzer divorce trial was held in a small hearing room at the end of a hall on the third floor. The only furniture in the room was a long wooden table, a dozen chairs, and two coffee tables that were quickly converted for press seating. There was no room for spectators, and the only way to get one of the nine press seats was to be there in person at seven o'clock in the morning—or even earlier, on some days—and put your name on the list.

It was an odd situation, considering that the story unfolding inside was making daily headlines all over the world, but Judge Carl Harper said he liked it just fine. He was not especially fond of reporters anyway, and he clearly viewed the whole trial as a shame on the human race.

Under Florida law, however, he was compelled to allow one stationary TV camera in the courtroom so that the trial could be filmed for the public and watched on closed circuit in a room across the hall, where anybody who didn't feel like squatting in the courtroom all day could watch the proceedings in relative comfort, with cigarettes and doughnuts from the courthouse coffee shop. Nobody checked credentials in the TV room, and on most days there were fifteen or twenty reporters around the monitor, along with a handful of spectators who wandered in off the rain-swept streets outside.

These were the bleacher seats at the Pulitzer trial, a strange and sometimes rowdy mixture of everything from CBS-TV producers to lanky six-foot women with no bras and foreign accents who claimed to be from *Der Spiegel* and *Paris Match*. It was a lusty crowd, all in all, following the action intently, sometimes cheering, sometimes booing. It was like a crowd of strangers who came together each day in some musty public room to watch a TV soap opera like *General Hospital*. On one afternoon, when Roxanne Pulitzer lost her temper at some particularly degenerate drift in the testimony, the bleachers erupted with shouting: "Go get 'em, Roxy! Kick ass! That's it, Rox baby! Don't let 'em talk that way about you!"

The Best Piece of Ass in Palm Beach

On the surface, the story was not complex. Basically, it was just another tale of Cinderella gone wrong, a wiggy little saga of crime, hubris, and punishment:

Herbert "Pete" Pulitzer Jr., fifty-two-year-old millionaire grandson of the famous newspaper publisher and heir to the family name as well as the fortune, had finally come to his senses and cast out the evil gold digger who'd caused him so much grief. She was an incorrigible coke slut, he said, and a totally unfit mother. She stayed up all night at discos and slept openly with her dope pusher, among others. There was a house painter, a real-estate agent, a race-car driver, and a French baker—and on top of all that, she was a lesbian, or at least some kind of pansexual troilist. In six and a half years of marriage, she had humped almost everything she could get her hands on.

Finally, his attorneys explained, Mr. Pulitzer had no choice but to rid himself of this woman. She was more like Marilyn Chambers than Cinderella. When she wasn't squawking wantonly in front of the children with Grand Prix driver Jacky Ickx or accused Palm Beach cocaine dealer Brian Richards, she was in bed with her beautiful friend Jacquie Kimberly, thirty-two, wife of seventy-six-year-old socialite James Kimberly, heir to the Kleenex fortune. There was no end to it, they said. Not even when Pulitzer held a loaded .45-caliber automatic pistol to her head—and then to his own—in a desperate last-ditch attempt to make her seek help for her drug habits, which she finally agreed to do.

And *did*, for that matter, but five days in Highland Park General Hospital was not enough. The cure didn't take, Pete's attorneys charged, and she soon went back on the whiff and also back to the pusher, who described himself in the courtroom as a "self-employed handyman" and gave his age as twenty-nine.

Roxanne Pulitzer is not a beautiful woman. There is nothing especially striking about her body or facial bone structure, and at age thirty-one, she looks more like a jaded senior stewardess from Pan Am than an international sex symbol. Ten years on the Palm Beach Express have taken their toll, and she would have to do more than just sweat off ten pounds to compete for naked space in the men's magazines. Her legs are too thin, her hips are too wide, and her skin is a bit too loose for modeling work. But she has a definite physical presence. There is no mistaking the aura of good-humored outfront sexuality. This is clearly a woman who likes to sleep late in the morning.

Roxanne blew into town more than ten years ago, driving a Lincoln Continental with a sixty-foot house trailer in tow, a ripe little cheerleader just a year or so out of high school in Cassadaga, New York, a small town of nine hundred near Buffalo.

After graduation from Cassadaga High, she got a job in nearby Jamestown as a personal secretary to the general counsel for the American Voting Machine Corporation—a serious young man named Lloyd Dixon III, who eventually committed suicide. His father, who was later sent to prison, was president of AVM at the time and took such a shine to the new secretary that he hastened to marry her off to his other son, a callow youth named Peter, just back from the air force reserve, whose life would soon turn strange.

It is a long road from the outskirts of Buffalo to the inner sanctums of the Palm Beach Bath and Tennis Club, but the first long step was easy. The newlyweds hauled their trailer down to West Palm Beach, where young Peter had often spent winter vacations with the family, and set up housekeeping in a local trailer park. The first year was tranquil. They both enrolled in local colleges and lived more or less like their neighbors.

Welcome to the Palm Beach Express

What happened next is inscrutable. Roxanne can't remember and Peter Dixon won't talk about it. The marriage turned sour, and the couple soon separated. The divorce was apparently bitter, although there were no children and no real property to get bitter about. The trailer was sold to gypsies, and Roxanne got half, which she used to finance the rest of her education at West Palm Beach Junior College. After she graduated, she went immediately to work for a local insurance agency, selling policies.

That is where she met Randy Hopkins, a main player in this drama, who at the time was also selling policies, to supplement his income as an heir to the Listerine mouthwash fortune. Everybody in Palm Beach is an heir to something, and there is no point in checking them out unless you want to get married. Hopkins was the real thing, for Roxanne, and soon they were living together.

These were the weird years in Palm Beach, with a sort of late-blooming rock & roll crowd, champagne hippies who drove Porsches and smoked marijuana and bought Rolling Stones records and even snorted cocaine from time to time. Some ate LSD and ran naked on the beach until they were caught and dragged home by the police, who were almost always polite. Their parties got out of hand occasionally, and the servants wept openly at some of the things they witnessed, but it was mainly a crowd of harmless rich kids with too many drugs and a giddy faith in the notion that rock & roll might really set them free.

Which it did, for a while—and it was just about this time, in the heat of the mid-Seventies, that Roxanne Dixon, who would later gain fame in newspapers all over the world as the best piece of ass in Palm Beach, moved in with Randy Hopkins and took herself a seat on the Palm Beach Express.

One of Hopkins' good friends at the time was Pete Pulitzer, a forty-five-year-old recently divorced millionaire playboy who bore a certain resemblance to Alexander Haig on an ether binge and was known in some circles as the most eligible bachelor in town.

Pulitzer was also the owner of Doherty's, a fashionable downtown pub and late-night headquarters for the rock & roll set. Doherty's was a fast and randy place in the years when Pete owned it. John and Yoko would drop in for lunch, the bartenders were from Harvard, and Pete's patrons were anything but discreet about their predilection for dirty cocaine and a good orgy now and then.

It was the place to be seen, and Pulitzer was the man to be seen with. He had his pick of the ladies, and he particularly enjoyed the young ones.

When his friend Randy Hopkins introduced him to Roxanne one night, he liked her immediately.

Fiends

Pulitzer's final pretrial offer, the last exit before going public in court and creating an international scandal, was $45,000 a year, plus a $200,000 house in Palm Beach, along with the Porsche and the jewelry—and the children.

They were Roxanne's idea all along, said the husband. She took out her IUD without telling him, and suddenly she was pregnant with twin boys. Pete was shocked, he said. She knew all along that he didn't want any more children. He already had three, in their twenties, from a seventeen-year marriage with his first wife, Lilly, a prominent fashion designer. One daughter had been hospitalized for heroin addiction, the son was accused in the courtroom of being a drug dealer, and the other daughter, a beautiful twenty-six-year-old ex-model, with whom he allegedly committed incest when she was sixteen, was now married to a Palm Beach stockbroker.

At the age of fifty-two, Pete Pulitzer, described in *Town & Country* as a "dashing millionaire" sportsman from Palm Beach, was not anxious to have babies. There was considerable testimony on this point later during the actual trial, but Pulitzer never flinched, and nobody asked him if he'd ever considered a vasectomy. Custody of the twins was the big issue, in fact, until the final week of the trial, when Roxanne's lawyer outmaneuvered the judge and formally divulged pretrial testimony showing that Mack and Zack had been part of the husband's final out-of-court settlement offer a few months earlier, an offer Roxanne had rejected.

Most reporters covering the trial were surprised at this revelation, but it was not mentioned in stories detailing the judge's final decision, and it made no headlines in Palm Beach.

No one will emerge from this unscathed.

—Judge Carl Harper

All the evidence in the case was trundled around the courthouse in a grocery cart that some bailiff had apparently borrowed from a local supermarket. It contained everything from family tax returns to the tin trumpet Roxanne allegedly slept with while trying to communicate with the dead. The cart was parked next to a Xerox machine in the county clerk's office on all days when the court was not in session, and under the curious provisions of Florida's much-admired public-records statute, it was open to public inspection at all times. The contents of the cart were shuffled and reshuffled by so many people that not even the judge could have made any sense of it by the time the trial was over, but journalists found it a source of endless amusement. You could go in there with a satchel of cold beers on a rainy afternoon and whoop it up for hours by just treating the cart like a grab bag and copying anything you wanted for a dime a page. That was the press rate. The price to the general public was $1 a page, but nobody paid it, and the people in charge were more interested in collecting autographs than money. As long as we kept an honest page count, they left us alone.

I spent a lot of time poring over copies of the Pulitzers' personal tax returns and financial ledgers submitted as evidence by the Pulitzer family accountants, and I have made a certain amount of wild sense of it all, but not enough.

I understood, for instance, that these people were seriously rich. Family expenditures for 1981 totaled $972,980 for a family of four: one man, one woman, two four-year-old children, and a nanny who was paid $150 a week.

That is a lot of money, but so what? We are not talking about poor people here, and $1 million a year for family expenditures is not out of line in Palm Beach. The rich have special problems. The Pulitzers spent $49,000 on basic "household expenditures" in 1981 and another $272,700 for "household improvements." That is about $320,000 a year just to have a place to sleep and play house. There was another $79,600 listed for "personal expenses" and $79,000 for boat maintenance.

"Business" expenditures came in at $11,000, and there was no listing at all for taxes. As for "charity," the Pulitzers apparently followed the example of Ronald Reagan that year and gave in private, so as not to embarrass the poor.

The 441 Club, or the Rich Are Different from Us

There was, however, one item that begged for attention. The figure was $441,000, and the column was "miscellaneous and unknown."

Right. Miscellaneous and unknown: $441,000. And nobody in the courtroom even blinked. Here were two coke fiends who came into court because their marriage didn't seem to be working and the children were getting nervous.

And the servants were turning weird and on some nights there were naked people running around on the lawn and throwing rocks at the upstairs bedroom windows and people with white foam in their mouths were jacking off *like apes in the hallways . . . people screeching frantically on the telephone at four in the morning about volcanic eruptions in the Pacific that were changing the temperature of the ocean forever and causing the jet stream to move south, which would bring on a new ice age—and that's why neither one of us could get any sleep for two years, your Honor, and the sky was full of vultures so we called a plastic surgeon because her tits were starting to sag and my eyes didn't look right anymore and then we drove halfway to Miami at 100 miles an hour before we realized it was Sunday and the hospital wouldn't be open so we checked into the Holiday Inn with Jim's wife and ye gods, your Honor, this woman is a whore and I can't really tell you what it means because the children are in danger and we're afraid they might freeze in their sleep and I can't trust you anyway but what else can I do, I'm desperate—and, by the way, we spent $441,000 last year on things I can't remember.*

Welcome to cocaine country. White Line Fever. Bad craziness. What is a judge to make of two coke fiends who spent $441,000 last year on "miscellaneous and unknown"? The figure for the previous year was only $99,000, at a time when the Pulitzers' cocaine use was admittedly getting out of hand. They said they were holding it down to just a few grams a week, at that point, a relatively moderate figure among the Brotherhood of the Bindle, but the evidence suggests a genuinely awesome rate of consumption—something like thirteen grams a day—by the time they finally staggered into divorce court and went public with the whole wretched saga.

The numbers are staggering, even in the context of Palm Beach. Thirteen grams a day would kill a whole family of polar bears.

Mandatory Death Penalty for Drunk Drivers; Blame It on the Blow

> *With Mrs. Pulitzer sitting at a table only an arm's length away, Cheatham went on to say, "Your Honor, Jamie told me Roxanne was the wildest, strongest, best piece of ass that he ever had in his whole life."*
>
> —*New York Post*, October 4, 1982

That is not bad publicity in some towns, but it is definitely wrong for Palm Beach. And it is not the kind of thing most men want to read about their wives in the morning paper. A pimp might call it a windfall, but it is bad press with bells on for a fifty-two-year-old socialite known to big-time society page writers as a dashing millionaire sportsman from Palm Beach.

Or maybe not. History has judged F. Scott Fitzgerald harshly for allegedly saying to Hemingway that "the very rich are different from you and me," but perhaps he was on to something Ernest couldn't grasp.

What is the *real* price, for instance, of a seat on the Palm Beach Express? The island is more like a private club than a city. It is ten miles long and one mile wide, more or less, with a permanent population of 9,700. But these figures are too generous, and the real ones are lower by half. The real Palm Beach—the colony itself, the gilded nexus—is only about five miles long and three blocks wide, bordered on the east by a fine stretch of white beach and Atlantic Ocean, and on the west by palm trees, private piers, and million-dollar boathouses on the Intracoastal Waterway. There is North Palm Beach and South Palm Beach and the vast honky-tonk wasteland of West Palm Beach on the mainland, but these are not the people we're talking about. These are servants and suckfish, and they don't really matter in the real Palm Beach, except when they have to testify.

The Rich Have Problems Everywhere

That is the weak reed, a cruel and incurable problem the rich have never solved—how to live in peace with the servants. Sooner or later, the maid has to come in the bedroom, and if you're only paying her $150 a week, she is going to come in hungry, or at least curious, and the time is long past when it was legal to cut their tongues out to keep them from talking.

The servant problem is the Achilles' heel of the rich. The only solution is robots, but we are still a generation or so away from that, and in the meantime, it is just about impossible to hire a maid who is smart enough to make a bed but too dumb to wonder why it is full of naked people every morning. The gardener will not be comfortable with the sight of rope ladders hanging from the master-bedroom windows when he mows the lawn at noon, and any chauffeur with the brains to work a stick shift on a Rolls will also understand what's happening when you wake him up at midnight and send him across the bridge to a goat farm in Loxahatchee for a pair of mature billys and a pound of animal stimulant.

Nakedness is a way of life in Palm Beach, and the difference between a picnic and an orgy is not always easy to grasp. If a woman worth $40 million wants to swim naked in the pool with her billy goat at four in the morning, it's nobody's business but hers. There are laws in Florida against sexual congress with beasts, but not everybody feels it is wrong.

"My roommate fucks dogs at parties," said a sleek blond in her late twenties who sells cashmere and gold gimcracks in a stylish boutique on Worth Avenue. "So what? Who gets hurt by it?"

I shrugged and went back to fondling the goods on the shirt rack. The concept of victimless crimes is well understood in Palm Beach, and the logic is hard to argue. No harm, no crime. If a pretty girl from Atlanta can sleep late in the morning, have lunch at the Everglades Club, and make $50,000 tax free a year fucking dogs in rich people's bedrooms on weekends, why should she fear the police? What is the difference between bestiality and common sodomy? Is it better to fuck swine at the Holiday Inn or donkeys in a penthouse on Tarpon Island? And what's wrong with incest, anyway? It takes two hundred years of careful inbreeding to produce a line of beautiful daughters, and only a madman would turn them out to strangers. Feed them cocaine and teach them to love their stepsisters—or even their fathers and brothers, if that's what it takes to keep ugliness out of the family.

Look at the servants. They have warts and fat ankles. Their children are too dumb to learn and too mean to live, and there is no sense of family continuity. There is a lot more to breeding than teaching children good table manners, and a lot more to being rich than just spending money and wearing alligator shirts. The real difference between the Rich and the Others is not just that "they have more money," as Hemingway noted, but that money is not a governing factor in their lives, as it is with people who work for a living. The truly rich are born free, like dolphins; they will never feel hungry, and their credit will never be questioned. Their daughters will be debutantes and their sons will go to prep schools, and if their cousins are junkies and lesbians, so what? The breeding of humans is still an imperfect art, even with all the advantages.

Where are the Aryan thoroughbreds that Hitler bred so carefully in the early days of the Third Reich? Where are the best and brightest children of Bel Air and Palm Beach?

These are awkward questions in some circles, and the answers can be disturbing. Why do the finest flowers of the American Dream so often turn up in asylums, divorce courts, and other gray hallways of the living doomed? What is it about being born free and rich beyond worry that makes people crazy?

• • •

Nobody on the Palm Beach Express seemed very interested in that question. Instead, the community rallied around poor Pete Pulitzer when the deal started going down—even through eighteen days of weird courtroom testimony that mortified his friends and shocked half the civilized world. The most intimate aspects of his wild six-year marriage to an ambitious young cheerleader from Buffalo were splayed out in big headlines on the front pages of newspapers in New York, Paris, and London. Total strangers from places like Pittsburgh and Houston called his wife at home on the telephone, raving obscene proposals. Vicious lawyers subpoenaed his most private belongings and leaked whatever they pleased to giggling reporters. Any tourist with a handful of dimes could buy Xerox copies of his personal tax returns or even his medical records for ten cents a page in the Palm Beach County Courthouse. His privacy was violated so totally that it ceased to exist. At the age of fifty-two, with no real warning at all, Herbert Pulitzer became a very public figure. Every morning he would wake up and go downtown with his lawyers and hear himself accused of everything from smuggling drugs to degrading the morals of minors and even committing incest with his own daughter.

The only charge Judge Harper took seriously was Roxanne's "adultery," which was denied so many times by so many people that it came to be taken for granted.

No adultery was ever proved, as I recall, but in the context of all the other wild charges, it didn't seem to matter. With all the vile treachery among friends and cheap witchcraft and champagne troilism all day and all night in front of the servants while decent people were asleep or at least working at real jobs for sane amounts of money, what mainly emerged from the testimony was a picture of a lifestyle beyond the wildest and lewdest dreams of anything on *Dallas* or *Dynasty* or even *Flamingo Road*.

Nowhere in the record of the Pulitzer trial is there any mention of anybody who had to go to work in the morning. There were nannies and gardeners, hired boat captains and part-time stockbrokers and a Grand Prix driver and a French baker and at least one full-time dope dealer. But there was nobody who ever had to get time off from work to come in and testify.

I did the dirty boogie but they called it something else.

—Terry McDonell

He told me that if I didn't sign those documents, he would take my children. He said he had the power, the money, and the name. He said he would bury me.

—Roxanne Pulitzer in court, November 15, 1982

The husband was never pressed to confirm that quote, if only because of the general gag order imposed by Judge Harper on all parties involved in the trial, in order to prevent any loose talk with journalists until he made his decision. The order was routinely violated, but not flagrantly, and in the end it didn't make much difference. The judge performed the burial for his own reasons, which he explained in a brutal nineteen-page final opinion that destroyed Roxanne's case like a hurricane. In the end she got even less than her lawyer, Joe Farish, whose fee was reduced by two-thirds. He got $102,500 for his efforts, and the wife came away with $2,000 a month for two years, no house, no children, a warning to get a job quick, and the right to keep her own personal jewelry and her own car. The whole package came to not much more than Pulitzer had spent on the day-to-day maintenance of his boats in 1981, which his accountants listed as $79,000.

The $441,000 the couple spent that year on "miscellaneous and unknown" was four times what the wife was awarded as a final settlement after six and a half years of marriage and two children.

It was nothing at all. A little more than $100,000 on paper and in fact less than $50,000. There are dentists all over Los Angeles who pay more alimony than that.

But we are not talking about dentists here. We are talking about a dashing millionaire sportsman from Palm Beach, the town's most eligible bachelor—a wealthy jade of sorts who married an ex-cheerleader from the outskirts of Buffalo and took her to live sex shows and gave her jars of cocaine for Christmas.

In a nut, Herbert "Pete" Pulitzer rented the Best Piece of Ass in Palm Beach for six and a half years at a net cost of about $1,000 a month in alimony, and when it was over, he got the house and the children, along with everything else.

Roxanne was awarded about 10 percent of this, to be paid out over two years or until she remarries. The judge gave her two weeks to get out of the house where she'd been living for seven years, and Herbert took physical custody of the twins immediately.

Judge Harper had run the whole show with an evil glint in his eye, enduring a shitrain of perjury from both sides and day after day of relentless haggling and posturing by teams of Palm Beach lawyers and a circus parade of rich fools, dumb hustlers, and dope fiends who were all getting famous just for being in his courtroom—where smoking was not allowed, except for the judge, who smoked constantly.

That should have been the tip-off, but we missed it. The judge had made up his mind early on, and the rest was all show business, a blizzard of strange publicity that amused half the English-speaking world for a few months and in the end meant nothing at all.

Let the Trials Begin

Toward the end of the trial, it rained almost constantly. Logistics got difficult, and my suite overlooking the beach at the Ocean Hotel was lashed by wild squalls every night. It was a fine place to sleep, wild storms on the edge of the sea—warm blankets, good whiskey, color TV, roast beef hash and poached eggs in the morning . . .

Fat City, a hard place to wake up at six o'clock and drive across the long, wet bridge to the courthouse in West Palm—just to get your name on a list so that you could spend the rest of the day locked into the bowels of some sleazy divorce trial.

But it had to be done. The trial was big news on the Gold Coast, and even the common folk were concerned.

One morning, when I got there too late to make the list for a courtroom seat and too early to think straight, I found myself drifting aimlessly in a dimly lit bar on the fringes of the courthouse district—the kind of place where lawyers and bailiffs eat lunch and where the bartender has a machine pistol and the waitresses are all on probation, or maybe parole, for one reason or another . . .

The bartender was trying to find limes for a Bloody Mary when I asked him what he thought about the Pulitzer divorce case.

He stiffened, then leaned quickly across the bar to seize my bicep, wrapping his long, gray fingers around my arm like tentacles, and he said to me: "You know what I think? You know what it makes me feel like?"

"Well . . ." I said, "not really. I only came in here to have a drink and read the newspaper until my trial breaks for lunch and—"

"Never mind your goddamn trial!" he shouted, still squeezing my arm and staring intently into my eyes—not blinking, no humor.

I jerked out of his grasp, unsettled by the frenzy.

"It's not the goddamned Pulitzers!" he shouted. "It's nothing personal, but I know how those people behave, and I know how it makes me feel."

"Fuck off!" I snapped. "Who cares how you feel?"

"Like a goddamn animal!" he screamed. "Like a *beast*. I look at this scum and I look at the way they live and I see those shit-eating grins on their faces, *and I feel like a dog took my place*."

"What?" I said.

"It's a term of art," he replied, shooting his cuffs as he turned to deal with the cash register.

"Congratulations," I said. "You are now a Doctor of Torts."

He stiffened again and backed off.

"Torts?" he said. "What do you mean, *torts*?"

I leaned over the bar and smacked him hard on the side of his head.

"*That's* a tort," I said. Then I tossed him a handful of bills and asked for a cold beer to go. The man was slumped back on his rack of cheap bottles, breathing heavily. "You whoreface bastard," he said. "I'll kill you."

I reached over and grabbed him by the flesh on his cheek.

"Where *is* your dog, swinesucker? I want to see the dog that did this thing to you. I want to *kill* that dog." I snapped him away from me, and he fell back on the duckboards.

"Get out!" he screamed. "*You're* the one who should be on trial in this town! These Pulitzers are *nothing* compared to monsters like you."

"I'll be back," I said, lifting a small can of Mace out of my pocket and squirting it at him. "You'd better find a dog to take *your* place before you see me again—because I'm going to come back here and rip your nuts right off your ugly goddamn body."

The man was still screaming as I got in my car and drove off. People in the street stopped to stare—but when he begged them for help, they laughed at him.

He was a Doctor of Torts, but in the end it didn't matter. A dog had taken his place anyway.

Why Would They Testify Against Me?

Roxanne is a star now. She was on the cover of *People* and a featured celebrity guest on network TV shows like *Good Morning America*. The Best Piece of Ass in Palm Beach is a curious case these days: from the ashes of scandal and defeat, she has emerged as a cult figure of sorts, a kind of National Bitch for the Eighties.

The courts have yet to make themselves or even the law comfortably clear with regard to Roxanne's status as a public figure in terms of libel law, so I think we should watch this aspect of the story with a keen eye. Remember Mary Alice Firestone. But my own working guess is that the courts will continue to kick the shit out of Roxanne at every opportunity. Her own lawyer made her a public figure when he deposed Herbert and got all that buzzword-headline talk about cocaine and lesbians and trumpets, which he then leaked to the *Miami Herald*.

• • •

"Ten pounds," she said. "That's how much I would have to take off." We were talking about the possibility of her doing a nude spread for one of the men's magazines, something on the order of a Rita Jenrette appearance in *Playboy*, with a little less leg. Dark humor, and it was out of the question, of course, until the trial was over. What would that horny old bastard of a judge say if she suddenly turned up in a naked centerfold in some skin magazine on sale in the courthouse newsstand?

What indeed? There is much in the evidence to suggest, in fact, that the judge would not even have blinked. He had seen all he needed to see of Roxanne Pulitzer at that point, and a handful of naked pictures wasn't going to make much difference either way. She had already made her personal impression on the court, and it was not one that she and her lawyers had hoped for.

The language of Harper's final judgment in the now infamous Palm Beach divorce case of *Pulitzer v. Pulitzer* left little doubt that he had taken one long look at Roxanne and concluded that she was a raging slut, a homosexual adulteress so addicted to drugs and drink as to pose a direct threat to the welfare of her own children, who were removed at once from her custody.

The decision stripped Roxanne Pulitzer naked in a way that no *Playboy* or *Penthouse* photographer would want to put on film. The message was clear: let this be a lesson to all gold diggers.

The Death of Rock & Roll

Long after the Pulitzer divorce case was finally over—after the verdict was in and there were no more headlines, and the honor of Palm Beach had been salvaged by running Roxanne out of town; after all the lawyers had been paid off and the disloyal servants had been punished and reporters who covered the trial were finally coming down from the long-running high that the story had been for so long that some of them suffered withdrawal symptoms when it ended . . . Long after this, I was still brooding darkly on the case, still trying to make a higher kind of sense of it.

I have a fatal compulsion to find a higher kind of sense in things that make no sense at all. We are talking about hubris, delusions of wisdom and prowess that can only lead to trouble.

Or maybe we are talking about cocaine. That thought occurred to me more than once in the course of the Pulitzer divorce trial. Cocaine is the closest thing to instant hubris on the market these days, and there is plenty of it around. Any fool with an extra $100-bill in his pocket can whip a gram of cocaine into his head and make sense of just about anything.

Ah, yes. Wonderful. Thank you very much. I see it all very clearly now. These bastards have been lying to me all along. I should never have trusted them in the first place. Stand aside. Let the big dog eat.

Take my word for it, folks. I know how these things work.

• • •

In the end it was basically a cocaine trial, which it had looked to be from the start. There was no real money at stake: Peter Pulitzer ended up paying more money to lawyers, accountants, "expert witnesses," and other trial-related bozos than Roxanne would have happily settled for if the case had never gone to court in the first place. A few of the reporters covering the trial sat around a gray Formica table in the Alibi Lounge during one of the lunch breaks and figured out that the trial had cost Pulitzer about a half-million dollars in real money and perhaps a million more down the line, for no good reason at all. Here was a man who normally earned almost $700,000 a year just by answering his phone a few hours a day and paying a secretary to open his mail—something like $60,000 a month just to mind his own store, as it were—who somehow got himself whipped into such a hellish public frenzy that he didn't even have a bed to sleep in except on his boat for at least a year, and he was spending all his time raving crazily at his own lawyers at $150 an hour instead of taking care of business, which was naturally going to pieces, because all the people who worked for him, from his accountants and psychiatrists all the way down to his gardeners and deckhands, were going mad from fear and confusion and constant legal harassment by vicious lawyers and always worried about saying something by accident that might get them either fired or locked up for perjury, and in the midst of all that he let one of his hired dingbats come into court with a financial statement so careless and flagrant and arrogant that the simple fact of his filing it would have been cause for public outrage almost anywhere else in America except in Palm Beach County. There are a lot of people in this country who spend $1 million a year, and some of them pay no income tax at all. Nelson Rockefeller was one of them, for at least one year in the late Sixties or early Seventies, and there were two other years around that same time when he paid less than I did . . .

Epilogue: The Song of the Gilded Swine

It is to the poet a thing of awe to find that his story is true.

—Isak Dinesen

I am living the Palm Beach life now, trying to get the feel of it: royal palms and raw silk, cruising the beach at dawn in a red Chrysler convertible with George Shearing on the radio and a head full of bogus cocaine and two beautiful lesbians in the front seat beside me, telling jokes to each other in French . . .

We are on our way to an orgy, in a mansion not far from the sea, and the girls are drinking champagne from a magnum we brought from Dunhills, the chic and famous restaurant. There is a wet parking ticket flapping under the windshield wiper in front of me, and it bores me. I am giddy from drink, and the lesbians are waving their champagne glasses at oncoming police cars, laughing gaily and smoking strong marijuana in a black pipe as we cruise along Ocean Boulevard at sunrise, living our lives like dolphins . . .

The girls are naked now, long hair in the wind and perfumed nipples bouncing in the dull blue light of the dashboard, white legs on the red leather seats. One of them is tipping a glass of champagne to my mouth as we slow down for a curve near the ocean and very slowly and stylishly lose the rear end at seventy miles an hour and start sliding sideways with a terrible screeching of rubber past Roxanne Pulitzer's house, barely missing the rear end of a black Porsche that protrudes from her driveway . . .

The girls shriek crazily and spill champagne on themselves, and the radio is playing "The Ballad of Claus von Bülow," a song I wrote last year with Jimmy Buffett and James Brown and which makes me nine cents richer every time it gets played on the radio, in Palm Beach or anywhere else.

That is a lot of money when my people start adding it up. I am making ninety-nine cents a day out of Palm Beach alone, and ten times that much from Miami. The take from New York and L.A. is so massive that my accountant won't even discuss the numbers with me, and my agent is embarrassed by my wealth.

But not me, Jack. Not at all. I like being rich and crazy in Palm Beach on a pink Sunday morning in a new red Chrysler convertible on my way to an orgy with a magnum of French champagne and two gold-plated lesbian bimbos exposing themselves to traffic while my own song croaks from the radio and palm trees flap in the early morning wind and the local police call me "Doc" and ask after my general health when we speak to each other at stoplights on the boulevard . . .

The police are no problem in Palm Beach. We own them and they know it. They work for us, like any other servant, and most of them seem to like it. When we run out of gas in this town, we call the police and they bring it, because it is boring to run out of gas.

The rich have special problems, and running out of gas on Ocean Boulevard on the way to an orgy at six o'clock on Sunday morning is one of them. Nobody needs that. Not with naked women and huge bags of cocaine in the car. The rich love music, and we don't want it interrupted.

A state trooper was recently arrested in Miami for trying to fuck a drunk woman on the highway, in exchange for dropping all charges. But that would not happen in Palm Beach. Drunk women roam free in this town, and they cause a lot of trouble—but one thing they don't have to worry about, thank God, is the menace of getting pulled over and fondled by armed white trash wearing uniforms. We don't pay these people much, but we pay them every week, and if they occasionally forget who really pays their salaries, we have ways of reminding them.

The whole west coast of Florida is full of people who got fired from responsible jobs in Palm Beach, if only because they failed to understand the nature of the Social Contract.

Which brings us back to the story, for good or ill: not everybody who failed to understand the nature of the Social Contract has been terminally banished to the west coast. Some of them still live here—for now, at least—and every once in a while they cause problems that make headlines all over the world.

The strange and terrible case of young Roxanne Pulitzer is one of these, and that is the reason I came to Palm Beach, because I feel a bond with these people that runs deeper and stronger than mere money and orgies and drugs and witchcraft and lesbians and whiskey and red Chrysler convertibles.

Bestiality is the key to it, I think. I have always loved animals. They are different from us, and their brains are not complex, but their hearts are pure and there is usually no fat on their bodies and they will never call the police on you or take you in front of a judge or run off and hide with your money . . .

Animals don't hire lawyers.

The Taming of the Shrew

May 30, 1991

MEMO: FROM THE NATIONAL AFFAIRS DESK

To: Jann S. Wenner
From: Hunter S. Thompson
Date: April 15th, 1991
Subject: Nancy Reagan/Kitty Kelley Book Review
Comments: Cancel

The Taming of the Shrew

There are some things, Jann, that we know in our hearts are Ugly, and this book is one of them. It is old swill in a new bottle, a squalid tale from a squalid time that unfortunately seems to be ours. There is something weird about any calendar that has the Year of the Weasel happening thirteen times in a row.

Anyway, thanx for the review copy of Kelley's book on Nancy. It was good for a few laughs, but not many. And there is *meaning* in it, for sure, but not much. It is an ugly, mean little package that made me feel cheap for just reading it or even holding the thing in my hands.

This book is a monument to everything low and mean in the human spirit. It is a marketing triumph for that dingbat from Simon and Schuster, but it is far too wrong and repugnant to keep around the house, and last night I had to get rid of it. My friend Semmes Luckett took it away and jammed it into a garbage compactor, along with a case of old beer bottles. He was shocked and deeply embarrassed when he opened the book to page 14 and saw the Nancy Davis Reagan family tree, which shows that both he and Nancy are descended from the same family of Lucketts that left Maryland and fled westward around the turn of the century, when the family name came under a cloud of scandal. "My mama never talked about it," he said, "but she always left the room whenever *that woman* appeared on our TV set . . . Good Lord, I hope she never sees this book." He seized it off the table and stood up to leave. "Don't worry," he muttered. "I'll put it where it belongs."

• • •

Let's give Nancy all the credit she deserves. The Democrats have lost five out of the last six presidential elections, so maybe they can learn something from this book instead of just giggling about it. Kitty Dukakis, among others, might have put this evil handbook to good use if it had been available back in 1988. But, alas . . .

If politics is the art of controlling your environment, Nancy is a master politician and probably a lot more fun to live and work and travel with than I ever suspected. She has been the Best That She Can Be, and she has come a Very Long Way for a Size 2 Anorexic Dwarf. Jesus! What if she'd looked like Marilyn Monroe?

She (allegedly) had the morals of a slut on acid and behaved like a beast while the president was stoned day and night; and all that time she was talking about remodeling the White House in the style of Dolley Madison or Grandma Moses, she was acting like Linda Lovelace and Christine Keeler and Madame Defarge all at once.

They turned the whole East Wing of the White House into a Cave of Orgies and a dope den worse than anything in Singapore . . . It was horrible . . . and the press never noticed. They called him John Wayne, but he was weirder than Caligula, and the weirder he got, the more the voters loved him and the more respect he got from Ted Koppel.

Lyndon LaRouche was atomized and the Deviate Reverend Jim Bakker was sent to prison for forty-five years for *just dabbling* in the kind of brazen, low-rent crimes that were apparently taken for granted and pursued with relentless zeal—day and night, 366 days of the year, in full view of the servants and the Secret Service—by the folks who lived in the White House.

Just folks. No different from you or me or the Mitchell brothers. And they never claimed to be anything else, really. Just Good Ol' Dutch and What's Her Name, the maniac little sex doll who squawked openly (allegedly) with Frank Sinatra on dim-lit couches in TV studios, where she went constantly to tape public-service announcements about Just Say No.

It was a very wild act in a very fast lane, and I have to admire it for the Heaviness. It is no small thing in some circles to make headlines lewd and shocking enough to bump a new Kennedy/Palm Beach rape case off the front page of the tabloids . . . That is Strong . . . That is Charles Manson country.

Remember, they laughed at Thomas Edison. And don't forget that *Deep Throat* was a box-office hit in the same years that Nancy spent grooming her mongrel stud for the Real Derby, the biggest race of them all . . . and They Won!!! Twice!!!

• • •

So, never mind that review we were talking about. The book is a shitrain of old gossip and sleazy little stories that we read a long time ago and never quite believed . . . for good or ill.

So what if the former First Lady was a relentless fellatrix with the soul of a Pod and the style of a chicken in heat? She was, in her time, perhaps the highest and finest expression of the American Dream in action . . . and that is worth noting. Some people are Born to Win and others are spewed out like tadpoles. This is all ye know and all ye need to know—except that weasels speak English and God is a King Snake, and if Kitty Kelley and Nancy Reagan are what America is all about these days, there is light at the end of the tunnel.

But not here. I am glad to be rid of this book. It is like a bracing dose of ether on Monday Night in a Crack House. The very sight of it fills me with queasiness and shame. To read it and believe that it might be True is to wallow in the depths of personal and professional degradation.

Okay. That's about it, for now. Never send me a book like this again.

Thanx,

Hunter

Res ipsa loquitur.

Laughter in the Dark

In 1991 Hunter, seemingly spontaneously and after a lengthy hiatus from long-form writing, began faxing large chunks of copy—or "pages," as he referred to them, always "pages"—to the office. I was lucky enough to be on the receiving end of these pages, and ritually read them aloud to my boss, Bob Love, and whoever else might gather around. The story that began to emerge was both simple and complex, hilarious and disturbing; essentially, it involved Hunter witnessing a car crash in the Nevada desert and finding that the man driving the car was Supreme Court justice Clarence Thomas—who at the time was still sitting for his controversial Senate confirmation hearings amidst allegations of sexual harassment. Hunter and "the Judge"—who was traveling with two hookers—essentially fled, and spent the rest of the story locked in a twisted cat-and-mouse game with both each other and the long arm of the law. But to describe what became "Elko" as a story about Clarence Thomas is like calling the Beach Boys' "Don't Worry, Baby" a song about a drag race: technically correct, but short on inspiration.

—Corey Seymour

Letter from JSW to HST

October 29, 1991

VIA FAX
Hunter S. Thompson
Owl Farm
Woody Creek, CO 81656

Dear Hunter:

Time is running short and I'm getting worried. You have one big insert to write and a couple of transitions and it all has to be done this week.

Please call me asap.

All the best,
Jann

JSW/mm

Letter from HST assistant Deborah Fuller to JSW

2:32 pm
Tuesday 10.29.91

To: Jann
From: HST

OK—HERE ARE THE FIRST 5 PAGES/RAW COPY (OF THE 8 OR 9 PAGES) HUNTER HAS COLLAPSED FROM FATIGUE.

THE OTHER PAGES WILL BE FAXED OVER WITHIN THE HALF HOUR.

Best.
Deborah

Letter from JSW to HST

October 30, 1991

VIA FAX
Hunter S. Thompson
Owl Farm
Woody Creek, CO 81656

Dear Hunter:

Get out of the car. Get off the road. I know how you drive. Do the hotel scene. Without this, we don't have a piece. There are two nights left.

Call me when you get up.

No more driving. Orgy, please.

Best,
Jann

JSW/mm

Letter from JSW to HST

November 1, 1991

VIA FAX
Hunter S. Thompson
Owl Farm
Woody Creek, CO 81656

Dear Hunter:

Keep going. It continues to be terrific stuff. You still have to get us to Leach at the trailer court and then, escape from Elko, i.e., the airport farewell, which needs to be pretty brief.

We're almost home.

Love,
Jann

JSW/mm

Letter from HST to JSW

Friday 11/1/91

Dear Jann,

There is no hope for the satisfied mind. We all know that—but it don't worry us, eh? Or not me, anyway. No. My problem is a Diseased mind, and a body so wracked with death-germs & festering, backed-up poisons that I can barely speak or talk or even think in a straight line for more than 40 or 50 seconds at a time . . . Yes. I am deeply Sick & Wrong in many basic functions. Cazart!

For this reason I must know immediately if the Real Deadline for this Elko piece is NOW or next week or maybe sometime in March, when I expect to be recovered . . . I can get it finished & roughly wrapped by Sunday, but that will be a nasty drain on my health & it will also require some Skilled edit/assistance from yr. end. Ho, Ho. As in SUBHEADS, Bridges, Continuity, etc. If you know what I'm saying. Yes. So pls. let me know instantly on this, so I won't have to destroy what remains of my fragile health for nothing. Please.

Thanks,
Hunter

Letter from JSW to HST

December 13, 1991

VIA FAX
Hunter S. Thompson
Owl Farm
Woody Creek, CO 81656

Dear Hunter:

After the last minute, I have decided to go for an Elko cover. Ralph is sending in a portrait of you he has already done for this purpose. We should have it Sunday. If it suits, then it's a go.

Here are the cover heads. If you can improve them, please do . . . but not at any great length.

FEAR AND LOATHING IN ELKO

By Dr. Hunter S. Thompson

A Wild and Ugly Night with Judge Thomas . . . Sexual Harassment Then and Now . . . A Nasty Christmas Flashback . . . A Nation of Jailers . . .

All best,
Jann

JSW/mm

Hope you're pleased! I am!
Xxx J

Fear and Loathing in Elko

January 23, 1992

Dear Jann,

God *damn*, I wish you were here to enjoy this beautiful weather with me. It is autumn, as you know, and things are beginning to die. It is so wonderful to be out in the crisp fall air, with the leaves turning gold and the grass turning brown, and the warmth going out of the sunlight and big hot fires in the fireplace while Buddy rakes the lawn. We see a lot of bombs on TV because we watch it a lot more, now that the days get shorter and shorter, and darkness comes so soon, and all the flowers die from freezing.

Oh, God! You should have been with me yesterday when I finished my ham and eggs and knocked back some whiskey and picked up my Weatherby Mark V .300 Magnum and a ball of black opium for dessert and went outside with a fierce kind of joy in my heart because I was Proud to be an American on a day like this. It felt like a goddamn *Football Game*, Jann—it was like *Paradise* . . . You remember that *bliss* you felt when we powered down to the Farm and whipped Stanford? Well, it felt like That.

I digress. My fits of Joy are soiled by relentless flashbacks and ghosts too foul to name . . . Oh, no, don't ask Why. You could have been president, Jann, but your road was full of forks, and I think of this when I see the forked horns of these wild animals who dash back and forth on the hillsides while rifles crack in the distance and fine swarthy young men with blood on their hands drive back and forth in the dusk and mournfully call our names . . .

O Ghost, O Lost, Lost and Gone, O Ghost, come back again.

• • •

Right, and so much for autumn, the trees are diseased and the Animals get in your way and the President is usually guilty and most days are too long anyway . . . So never mind my poem. It was wrong from the start. I plagiarized it from an early work of Coleridge and then tried to put my own crude stamp on it, but I failed.

So what? I didn't want to talk about fucking *autumn*, anyway. I was just sitting here at dawn on a crisp Sunday morning, waiting for the football games to start and taking a goddamn very brief break from this blizzard of Character Actors and Personal Biographers and sickly *Paparazzi* that hovers around me these days (they are sleeping now, thank Christ—some even in my own bed). I was sitting here all alone, thinking, for good or ill, about the Good Old Days.

We were Poor, Jann. But we were Happy. Because we knew Tricks. We were Smart. Not Crazy, like they said. (No. They never called us late for dinner, eh?)

Ho, ho. Laughs don't come cheap these days, do they? The only guy who seems to have any fun in public is Prince Cromwell, my shrewd and humorless neighbor—the one who steals sheep and beats up women, like Mike Tyson.

Who knows why, Jann. Some people are too weird to figure.

You have come a long way from the Bloodthirsty, Beady-eyed news Hawk that you were in days of yore. Maybe you should try reading something besides those goddamn motorcycle magazines—or one of these days you'll find hair growing in your palms.

Take my word for it. You can only spend so much time "on the throttle," as it were . . . Then the Forces of Evil will take over. Beware . . .

Ah, but that is a different question, for now. Who gives a fuck? We are, after all, Professionals . . . But our Problem is not. No. It is the Problem of *Everyman*. It is *Everywhere*. The Question is our *Wa*; the Answer is our Fate . . . and the story I am about to tell you is horrible, Jann.

• • •

I came suddenly awake, weeping and jabbering and laughing like a loon at the ghost on my TV set . . . Judge Clarence Thomas . . . Yes, I knew him. But that was a long time ago. Many years, in fact, but I still remember it vividly . . . indeed, it has haunted me like a golem, day and night, for many years.

It seemed normal enough, at the time, just another weird rainy night out there on the high desert . . . What the hell? We were younger then. Me and *the Judge*. And *all* the others, for that matter . . . It was a Different Time. People were Friendly. We *trusted* each other. Hell, you could *afford* to get mixed up with wild strangers in those days—without fearing for your life, or your eyes, or your organs, or all of your money, or even getting locked up in prison forever. There was a sense of *possibility*. People were not so afraid, as they are now. You could run around naked without getting shot. You could check into a roadside motel on the outskirts of Ely or Winnemucca or Elko when you were lost in a midnight rainstorm—and nobody called the police on you, just to check out your credit and your employment history and your medical records and how many parking tickets you owed in California.

There were Laws, but they were not feared. There were Rules, but they were not worshipped . . . like Laws and Rules and Cops and Informants are feared and worshipped today.

Like I said: it was a different time. And I know the Judge would tell you the same thing, tonight, if he wanted to tell you the Truth, like I do.

The first time I actually met the Judge was a long time ago, for strange reasons, on a dark and rainy night in Elko, Nevada, when we both ended up in the same sleazy roadside Motel, for no good reason at all . . . Good God! What a night!

I almost forgot about it, until I saw him last week on TV . . . and then I saw it *all over again*. The horror! The *horror*! That night when the road washed out and we all got stuck out there—somewhere near Elko in a place just off the highway, called Endicott's Motel—and we almost went *really* Crazy.

• • •

It was just after midnight when I first saw the sheep. I was running about eighty-eight or ninety miles an hour in a drenching, blinding rain on U.S. 40 between Winnemucca and Elko with one light out. I was soaking wet from the water that was pouring in through a hole in the front roof of the car, and my fingers were like rotten icicles on the steering wheel.

It was a moonless night and I knew I was hydroplaning, which is dangerous . . . My front tires were no longer in touch with the asphalt or anything else. My center of gravity was too high. There was no visibility on the road, none at all. I could have tossed a flat rock a lot farther than I could see in front of me that night through the rain and the ground fog. There is a total understanding, all at once, of how the captain of the *Titanic* must have felt when he first saw the Iceberg.

And not much different from the hideous feeling that gripped me when the beam of my Long-Reach Super-Halogen headlights picked up what appeared to be a massive rock slide across the highway—right in front of me, blocking the road completely. Big white rocks and round boulders, looming up with no warning in a fog of rising steam or swamp gas . . .

The brakes were useless, the car was wandering. The rear end was coming around. I jammed it down into Low, but it made no difference, so I straightened it out and braced for a crash that would probably kill me. This is It, I thought. This is how it happens—slamming into a pile of rocks at one hundred miles an hour, a sudden brutal death in a fast red car on a moonless night in a rainstorm somewhere on the sleazy outskirts of Elko. I felt vaguely embarrassed, in that long pure instant before I went into the rocks. I remembered Los Lobos and that I wanted to call Maria when I got to Elko . . .

My heart was full of joy as I took the first hit, which was oddly soft and painless. Just a sickening *thud*, like running over a body, a corpse—or, ye fucking gods, a crippled two-hundred-pound *sheep* thrashing around in the road.

Yes. These huge white lumps were not boulders. They were *sheep*. Dead and dying sheep. More and more of them, impossible to miss at this speed, piled up on each other like bodies at the battle of Shiloh. It was like running over wet logs. Horrible, horrible . . .

And then I saw the *man*—a leaping Human Figure in the glare of my bouncing headlights, waving his arms and yelling, trying to flag me down. I swerved to avoid hitting him, but he seemed not to see me, rushing straight into my headlights like a blind man . . . or a monster from Mars with no pulse, covered with blood and hysterical.

It looked like a small black gentleman in a London Fog raincoat, frantic to get my attention. It was so ugly that my brain refused to accept it . . . Don't worry, I thought. This is only an Acid flashback. Be calm. This is not really happening.

I was down to about thirty-five or thirty when I zoomed past the man in the raincoat and bashed the brains out of a struggling sheep, which helped to reduce my speed, as the car went airborne again, then bounced to a shuddering stop just before I hit the smoking, overturned hulk of what looked like a white Cadillac limousine, with people still inside. It was a nightmare. Some fool had crashed into a herd of sheep at high speed and rolled into the desert like an eggbeater.

• • •

We were able to laugh about it later, but it took a while to calm down. What the hell? It was only an accident. The Judge had murdered some range animals.

So what? Only a racist *maniac* would run sheep on the highway in a thunderstorm at this hour of the night. "Fuck those people!" he snapped, as I took off toward Elko with him and his two female companions tucked safely into my car, which had suffered major cosmetic damage but nothing serious. "They'll never get away with this Negligence!" he said. "We'll eat them alive in court. Take my word for it. We are about to become *joint owners* of a huge Nevada sheep ranch."

Wonderful, I thought. But meanwhile we were leaving the scene of a very conspicuous wreck that was sure to be noticed by morning, and the whole front of my car was gummed up with wool and sheep's blood. There was no way I could leave it parked on the street in Elko, where I'd planned to stop for the night (maybe two or three nights, for that matter) to visit with some old friends who were attending a kind of Appalachian Conference for sex-film distributors at the legendary Commercial Hotel . . .

Never mind that, I thought. Things have changed. I was suddenly a Victim of Tragedy—injured and on the run, far out in the middle of sheep country—one thousand miles from home with a car full of obviously criminal hitchhikers who were spattered with blood and cursing angrily at each other as we zoomed through the blinding monsoon.

Jesus, I thought. Who *are* these people?

Who indeed? They seemed not to notice me. The two women fighting in the backseat were hookers. No doubt about that. I had seen them in my headlights as they struggled in the wreckage of the Cadillac, which had killed about sixty sheep. They were desperate with Fear and

Confusion, crawling wildly across the sheep . . . One was a tall black girl in a white minidress . . . and now she was screaming at the other one, a young blond white woman. They were both drunk. Sounds of struggle came from the backseat. "Get your hands off me, *Bitch*!" Then a voice cried out: "*Help* me, Judge! Help! She's *killing* me!"

What? I thought. *Judge*? Then she said it again, and a horrible chill went through me . . . *Judge*? No. That would be over the line. Unacceptable.

He lunged over the seat and whacked their heads together. "Shut up!" he screamed. "Where are your fucking *manners*?"

He went over the seat again. He grabbed one of them by the hair. "God *damn* you," he screamed. "Don't embarrass this man. He saved our lives. We owe him respect—not this goddamned squalling around like whores."

A shudder ran through me, but I gripped the wheel and stared straight ahead, ignoring this sudden horrible freak show in my car. I lit a cigarette, but I was not calm. Sounds of sobbing and the ripping of cloth came from the backseat. The man they called Judge had straightened himself out and was now resting easily in the front seat, letting out long breaths of air . . . The silence was terrifying: I quickly turned up the music. It was Los Lobos again—something about "One Time One Night in America," a profoundly morbid tune about Death and Disappointment:

A lady dressed in white
With the man she loved
Standing along the side of their pickup truck
A shot rang out in the night
Just when everything seemed right

Right. A shot. A shot rang out in the night. Just another headline written down in America . . . Yes. There was a loaded .454 Magnum revolver in a clearly marked oak box on the front seat, about halfway between me and the Judge. He could grab it in a split second and blow my head off.

"Good work, Boss," he said suddenly. "I owe you a big one for this. I was *done for*, if you hadn't come along." He chuckled. "Sure as hell, Boss, sure as hell. I was Dead Meat—killed a lot worse than what happened to those goddamn stupid sheep!"

Jesus! I thought. Get ready to hit the brake. This man is a Judge on the lam with two hookers. He has *no choice* but to kill me, and those floozies in the backseat, too. We were the only witnesses . . .

• • •

This eerie perspective made me uneasy . . . Fuck this, I thought. These people are going to get me locked up. I'd be better off just pulling over right here and killing all three of them. *Bang! Bang! Bang!* Terminate the scum.

"How far is town?" the Judge asked.

I jumped, and the car veered again. "Town?" I said. "*What* town?" My arms were rigid and my voice was strange and reedy.

He whacked me on the knee and laughed. "Calm down, Boss," he said. "I have everything under control. We're almost home." He pointed into the rain, where I was beginning to see the dim lights of what I knew to be Elko.

"Okay," he snapped. "Take a left, straight ahead." He pointed again, and I slipped the car into low. There was a red and blue neon sign glowing about a half mile ahead of us, barely visible in the storm. The only words I could make out were "No" and "Vacancy."

"Slow down!" the Judge screamed. "This is *it*! Turn! Goddamn it, turn!" His voice had the sound of a whip cracking. I recognized the tone and did as he said, curling into the mouth of the curve with all four wheels locked and the big engine snarling wildly in Compound Low and blue flames coming out of the tailpipe . . . It was one of those long perfect moments in the human driving experience that makes *everybody* quiet.

We were sliding sideways very fast and utterly out of control and coming up on a white steel guardrail at seventy miles an hour in a thunderstorm on a deserted highway in the middle of the night.

Why not? On some nights Fate will pick you up like a chicken and slam you around on the walls until your body feels like a beanbag . . . *Boom! Blood! Death!* So Long, Bubba—You knew it would End like this . . .

We stabilized and shot down the loop. The Judge seemed oddly calm as he pointed again. "This is it," he said. "This is my place. I keep a few suites here." He nodded eagerly. "We're finally safe, Boss. We can do anything we want in this place."

The sign at the gate said:

Endicott's Motel
Deluxe Suites and Waterbeds
Adults Only/No Animals

Thank God, I thought. It was almost too good to be true. A place to *dump* these bastards. They were quiet now, but not for long. And I knew I couldn't handle it when these women woke up.

The Endicott was a string of cheap-looking bungalows, laid out in a horseshoe pattern around a rutted gravel driveway. There were cars parked in front of most of the units, but the slots in front of the brightly lit places at the darker end of the horseshoe were empty.

"Okay," said the Judge. "We'll drop the ladies down there at our suite, then I'll get you checked in." He nodded. "We both need some *sleep*, Boss—or at least *rest*, if you know what I mean. Shit, it's been a long night."

I laughed, but it sounded like the bleating of a dead man. The adrenaline rush of the sheep crash was gone, and now I was sliding into pure Fatigue Hysteria.

The Endicott "Office" was a darkened hut in the middle of the horseshoe. We parked in front of it, and then the Judge began hammering on the wooden front door, but there was no immediate response . . . "Wake up, goddamn it! It's *me*—the *Judge*! Open up! This is Life and Death! I need *help*!"

He stepped back and delivered a powerful kick at the door, which rattled the glass panels and shook the whole building. "I know you're in there," he screamed. "You can't hide! I'll kick your ass till your nose bleeds!"

There was still no sign of life, and I quickly abandoned all hope. Get out of here, I thought. This is wrong. I was still in the car, half in and half out . . . The Judge put another fine snap-kick at a point just over the doorknob and uttered a sharp scream in some language I didn't recognize. Then I heard the sound of breaking glass.

I leapt back into the car and started the engine. Get away! I thought. Never mind sleep. It's flee or die, now. People get killed for doing this kind of shit in Nevada. It was far over the line. Unacceptable behavior. This is why God made shotguns . . .

I saw lights come on in the Office. Then the door swung open, and I saw the Judge leap quickly through the entrance and grapple briefly with a small bearded man in a bathrobe, who collapsed to the floor after the Judge gave him a few blows to the head . . . Then he called back to me. "Come on in, Boss," he yelled. "Meet Mr. Henry."

I shut off the engine and staggered up the gravel path. I felt sick and woozy, and my legs were like rubber bands.

The Judge reached out to help me. I shook hands with Mr. Henry, who gave me a key and a form to fill out. "Bullshit," said the Judge. "This man is my *guest*. He can have anything he wants. Just put it on my bill."

"Of course," said Mr. Henry. "Your *bill*. Yes. I have it right here." He reached under his desk and came up with a nasty-looking bundle of adding-machine tapes and scrawled Cash/Payment memos . . . "You got here just in time," he said. "We were about to notify the Police."

"*What*?" said the Judge. "Are you *nuts*?" I have a goddamn *platinum* American Express card! My credit is *impeccable*."

"Yes," said Mr. Henry. "We *know* that. We have total respect for you. Your signature is better than gold bullion."

The Judge smiled and whacked the flat of his hand on the counter. "You bet it is!" he snapped. "So get out of my goddamn *face*! You must be *crazy* to fuck with Me like this! You *fool*! Are you ready to go to *court*?"

Mr. Henry sagged. "*Please*, Judge," he said. "Don't *do* this to me. All I need is your *card*. Just let me run an *imprint*. That's all." He moaned and stared more or less at the Judge, but I could see that his eyes were not focused . . . "They're going to *fire* me," he whispered. "They want to put me in *jail*."

"Nonsense!" the Judge snapped. "I would *never* let that happen. You can always *plead*." He reached out and gently gripped Mr. Henry's wrist. "Believe me, Bro," he hissed. "You have *nothing to worry about*. You are *cool.* They will *never* lock you up! They will *Never* take you away! Not out of *my* courtroom!"

"Thank you," Mr. Henry replied. "But all I need is your card and your signature. That's the problem: I forgot to run it when you checked in."

"So what?" the Judge barked. "I'm good for it. How much do you need?"

"About twenty-two thousand dollars," said Mr. Henry. "Probably twenty-three thousand dollars by now. You've had those suites for nineteen days with total room service."

"What?" the Judge yelled. "You thieving bastards! I'll have you crucified by American Express. You are *finished* in this business. You will *never work again*! Not *anywhere in the world*!" Then he whipped Mr. Henry across the front of his face so fast that I barely saw it. "Stop crying!" he said. "Get a grip on yourself! This is embarrassing!"

Then he slapped the man again. "Is that all you want?" he said. "Only a *card*? A stupid little card? A piece of plastic *shit*?"

Mr. Henry nodded. "Yes, Judge," he whispered. "That's all. Just a stupid little card."

The Judge laughed and reached into his raincoat, as if to jerk out a gun or at least a huge wallet. "You want a *card*, whoreface? Is that *it*? Is that all you want? You filthy little scumbag! Here it *is*!"

Mr. Henry cringed and whimpered. Then he reached out to accept the Card, the thing that would set him free . . . The Judge was still grasping around in the lining of his raincoat. "What the fuck?" he muttered. "This thing has *too many pockets*! I can *feel* it, but I can't find the slit!"

Mr. Henry seemed to believe him, and so did I, for a minute . . . Why not? He was a Judge with a platinum credit card—a very high roller. You don't find many Judges, these days, who can handle a full case-load in the morning and run wild like a goat in the afternoon. That is a very hard dollar, and very few can handle it . . . but the Judge was a Special Case.

Suddenly he screamed and fell sideways, ripping and clawing at the lining of his raincoat. "Oh, Jesus!" he wailed. "I've lost my wallet! It's *gone*. I left it out there in the Limo, when we hit the fucking sheep."

"So what?" I said. "We don't need it for this. I have *many* plastic cards."

He smiled and seemed to relax. "How many?" he said. "We might need more than one."

• • •

I woke up in the bathtub—who knows how much later—to the sound of the hookers shrieking next door. The *New York Times* had fallen in and blackened the water. For many hours I tossed and turned like a crack baby in a cold hallway. I heard thumping rhythm & blues—serious rock & roll, and I knew that something wild was going on in the Judge's suites. The smell of amyl nitrite came from under the door. It was no use. It was impossible to sleep through this orgy of ugliness. I was getting worried. I was already a marginally legal person, and now I was stuck with some crazy Judge who had my credit card and owed me $23,000.

I had some whiskey in the car, so I went out into the rain to get some ice. I had to get out. As I walked past the other rooms, I looked in people's windows and feverishly tried to figure out how to get my credit card back. Then from behind me I heard the sound of a tow-truck winch. The Judge's white Cadillac was being dragged to the ground. The Judge was whooping it up with the tow-truck driver, slapping him on the back.

"What the hell? It was only property damage," he laughed.

"Hey, Judge," I called out. "I never got my card back."

"Don't worry," he said. "It's in my room—come on."

I was right behind him when he opened the door to his room, and I caught a glimpse of a naked woman dancing. As soon as the door opened, the woman lunged for the Judge's throat. She pushed him back outside and slammed the door in his face.

"Forget that credit card—we'll get some cash," the Judge said. "Let's go down to the Commercial Hotel. My friends are there, and they have *plenty* of money."

We stopped for a six-pack on the way. The Judge went into a sleazy liquor store that turned out to be a front for kinky marital aids. I offered him money for the beer, but he grabbed my whole wallet.

Ten minutes later, the Judge came out with $400 worth of booze and a bagful of triple-X-rated movies. "My buddies will like this stuff," he said. "And don't worry about the money, I told you I'm good for it. These guys carry serious cash."

The marquee above the front door of the Commercial Hotel said:

Welcome: Adult Film Presidents
Studebaker Society
Full Action Casino/Keno in Lounge

"Park right here in front," said the Judge. "Don't worry. I'm well known in this place."

Me too, but I said nothing. I have been well known at the Commercial for many years, from the time when I was doing a lot of driving back and forth between Denver and San Francisco—usually for Business reasons, or for Art, and on this particular weekend I was there to meet quietly with a few old friends and business associates from the Board of Directors of the Adult Film Association of America. I had been, after all, the Night Manager of the famous O'Farrell Theatre, in San Francisco—the "Carnegie Hall of Sex in America."

I was the Guest of Honor, in fact—but I saw no point in confiding these things to the Judge, a total stranger with no Personal Identification, no money, and a very aggressive lifestyle. We were on our way to the Commercial Hotel to borrow money from some of his friends in the Adult Film business.

What the hell? I thought. It's only rock & roll. And he was, after all, a Judge of some kind . . . Or maybe not. For all I knew he was a criminal pimp with no fingerprints, or a wealthy black shepherd from Spain. But it hardly mattered. He was good company (if you had a taste for the edge work—and I did, in those days. And so, I felt, did the Judge). He had a bent sense of fun, a quick mind, and no Fear of anything.

The front door of the Commercial looked strangely busy at this hour of night in a bad rainstorm, so I veered off and drove slowly around the block in low gear.

"There's a side entrance on Queer Street," I said to the Judge, as we hammered into a flood of black water. He seemed agitated, which worried me a bit.

"Calm down," I said. "We don't want to make a scene in this place. All we want is money."

"Don't worry," he said. "I know these people. They are friends. Money is nothing. They will be happy to see me."

We entered the hotel through the Casino entrance. The Judge seemed calm and focused until we rounded the corner and came face to face with an eleven-foot polar bear standing on its hind legs, ready to pounce. The Judge turned to jelly at the sight of it. "I've had enough of this goddamn beast," he shouted. "It doesn't belong here. We should blow its head off."

I took him by the arm. "Calm down, Judge," I told him. "That's White King. He's been dead for thirty-three years."

The Judge had no use for animals. He composed himself and we swung into the lobby, approaching the desk from behind. I hung back—it was getting late and the lobby was full of suspicious-looking stragglers from the Adult Film crowd. Private cowboy cops wearing six-shooters in open holsters were standing around. Our entrance did not go unnoticed.

The Judge looked competent, but there was something menacing in the way he swaggered up to the desk clerk and whacked the marble countertop with both hands. The lobby was suddenly filled with tension, and I quickly moved away as the Judge began yelling and pointing at the ceiling.

"Don't give me that crap," he barked. "These people are my friends. They're expecting me. Just ring the goddamn room again." The desk clerk muttered something about his explicit instructions not to . . .

Suddenly the Judge reached across the desk for the house phone. "What's the number?" he snapped. "I'll ring it myself." The clerk moved quickly. He shoved the phone out of the Judge's grasp and simultaneously drew his index finger across his throat. The Judge took one look at the muscle converging on him and changed his stance.

"I want to cash a check," he said calmly.

"A *check*?" the clerk said. "Sure thing, buster. I'll cash your goddamned check." He seized the Judge by his collar and laughed. "Let's get this Bozo out of here. And put him in jail."

I was moving toward the door, and suddenly the Judge was right behind me. "Let's go," he said. We sprinted for the car, but then the Judge stopped in his tracks. He turned and raised his fist in the direction of the hotel. "Fuck you!" he shouted. "I'm the Judge. I'll be back, and I'll bust every one of you bastards. The next time you see me coming, you'd better run."

We jumped into the car and zoomed away into the darkness. The Judge was acting manic. "Never mind those pimps," he said. "I'll have them all on a chain gang in forty-eight hours." He laughed and slapped me on the back. "Don't worry, Boss," he said. "I know where we're going." He squinted into the rain and opened a bottle of Royal Salute. "Straight ahead," he snapped. "Take a right at the next corner. We'll go see Leach. He owes me twenty-four thousand dollars."

I slowed down and reached for the whiskey. What the hell, I thought. Some days are weirder than others.

"Leach is my secret weapon," the Judge said, "but I have to watch him. He could be violent. The cops are always after him. He lives in a balance of terror. But he has a genius for gambling. We win eight out of ten every week." He nodded solemnly. "That is *four out of five*, Doc. That is *Big. Very* big. That is eighty percent of everything." He shook his head sadly and reached for the whiskey. "It's a *horrible* habit. But I can't give it up. It's like having a money machine."

"That's wonderful," I said. "What are you bitching about?"

"I'm *afraid*, Doc. Leach is a *monster*, a criminal hermit who understands nothing in life except point spreads. He should be locked up and castrated."

"So what?" I said. "Where does he live? We are desperate. We have no cash and no plastic. This freak is our only hope."

The Judge slumped into himself, and neither one of us spoke for a minute . . . "Well," he said finally. "Why not? I can handle almost anything for twenty-four big ones in a brown bag. What the fuck? Let's *do* it. If the bastard gets ugly, we'll kill him."

"Come on, Judge," I said. "Get a grip on yourself. This is only a gambling debt."

"Sure," he replied. "That's what they *all* say."

Dead Meat in the Fast Lane: The Judge Runs Amok . . . Death of a Poet, Blood Clots in the Revenue Stream . . . The Man Who Loved Sex Dolls

We pulled into a seedy trailer court behind the stockyards. Leach met us at the door with red eyes and trembling hands, wearing a soiled cowhide bathrobe and carrying a half gallon of Wild Turkey.

"Thank God you're home," the Judge said. "I can't *tell* you what kind of horrible shit has happened to me tonight . . . But now the worm has turned. Now that we have *cash*, we will crush them all."

Leach just stared. Then he took a swig of Wild Turkey. "We are doomed," he muttered. "I was about to slit my wrists."

"Nonsense," the Judge said. "We won Big. I bet the same way you did. You gave me the *numbers*. You even predicted the Raiders would stomp Denver. Hell, it was obvious. The Raiders are unbeatable on Monday night."

Leach tensed, then he threw his head back and uttered a high-pitched quavering shriek. The Judge seized him. "Get a grip on yourself," he snapped. "What's wrong?"

"I went sideways on the bet," Leach sobbed. "I went to that goddamn sports bar up in Jackpot with some of the guys from the shop. We were all drinking Mescal and screaming, and I lost my head."

Leach was clearly a bad drinker and a junkie for mass hysteria. "I got drunk and bet on the Broncos," he moaned. "Then I doubled up. We lost everything."

A terrible silence fell on the room. Leach was weeping helplessly. The Judge seized him by the sash of his greasy leather robe and started jerking him around by the stomach.

They ignored me and I tried to pretend it wasn't happening . . . It was too ugly.

There was an ashtray on the table in front of the couch. As I reached out for it, I noticed a legal pad of what appeared to be Leach's poems, scrawled with a red Magic Marker in some kind of primitive verse form. There was one that caught my eye. There was something particularly ugly about it. There was something *repugnant* in the harsh slant of the handwriting. It was about pigs.

I TOLD HIM IT WAS WRONG
By F. X. Leach
Omaha 1968

A filthy young pig
got tired of his gig

and begged for a transfer
to Texas.
Police ran him down
on the Outskirts of town
and ripped off his Nuts
With a coathanger.
Everything after that was like
coming home in a cage on the
back of a train from
New Orleans on a Saturday
night
with no money and cancer and
a dead girlfriend.
In the end it was no use
He died on his knees in a barn
yard
with all the others watching.
Res ipsa loquitur.

"They're going to kill me," Leach said. "They'll be here by midnight. I'm doomed." He uttered another low cry and reached for the Wild Turkey bottle, which had fallen over and spilled.

"Hang on," I said. "I'll get more."

On my way to the kitchen I was jolted by the sight of a naked woman slumped awkwardly in the corner with a desperate look on her face, as if she'd been shot. Her eyes bulged and her mouth was wide open and she appeared to be reaching out for me.

I leapt back and heard laughter behind me. My first thought was that Leach, unhinged by his gambling disaster, had finally gone over the line with his wife-beating habit and shot her in the mouth just before we knocked. She appeared to be crying out for help, but there was no voice.

I ran into the kitchen to look for a knife, thinking that if Leach had gone crazy enough to kill his wife, now he would have to kill me, too, since I was the only witness. Except for the Judge, who had locked himself in the bathroom.

Leach appeared in the doorway holding the naked woman by the neck and hurled her across the room at me . . .

Time stood still for an instant. The woman seemed to hover in the air, coming at me in the darkness like a body in slow motion. I went into a stance with the bread knife and braced for a fight to the death.

Then the thing hit me and bounced softly down to the floor. It was a rubber blow-up doll: one of those things with five orifices that young stockbrokers buy in adult bookstores after the singles bars close.

"Meet Jennifer," he said. "She's my punching bag." He picked it up by the hair and slammed it across the room.

"Ho, ho," he chuckled, "no more wife beating. I'm cured, thanks to Jennifer." He smiled sheepishly. "It's almost like a miracle. *These dolls saved my marriage*. They're a lot smarter than you think." He nodded gravely. "Sometimes I have to beat *two at once*. But it always calms me down, you know what I mean?"

Whoops, I thought. Welcome to the night train. "Oh, *hell yes*," I said quickly. "How do the neighbors handle it?"

"No problem," he said. "They love me."

Sure, I thought. I tried to imagine the horror of living in a muddy industrial slum full of tin-walled trailers and trying to protect your family against brain damage from knowing that every night when you look out your kitchen window there will be a man in a leather bathrobe flogging two naked women around the room with a quart bottle of Wild Turkey. Sometimes for two or three hours . . . It was horrible.

"Where is your wife?" I asked. "Is she still here?"

"Oh, yes," he said quickly. "She just went out for some cigarettes. She'll be back *any minute*." He nodded eagerly. "Oh, yes, she's very *proud* of me. We're almost reconciled. She really loves these dolls."

I smiled, but something about his story made me nervous. "How many do you have?" I asked him.

"Don't worry," he said. "I have all we need." He reached into a nearby broom closer and pulled out another one—a half-inflated Chinese-looking woman with rings in her nipples and two electric cords attached to her head. "This is Ling-Ling," he said. "She screams when I hit her." He whacked the doll's head and it squawked stupidly.

Just then I heard car doors slamming outside the trailer, then loud knocking on the front door and a gruff voice shouting, "Open up! *Police*!"

Leach grabbed a .44 Magnum out of a shoulder holster inside his bathrobe and fired two shots through the front door. "You *bitch*!" he screamed. "I should have killed you a long time ago."

He fired two more shots, laughing calmly. Then he turned to face me and put the barrel of the gun in his mouth. He hesitated for a moment, staring directly into my eyes. Then he pulled the trigger and blew off the back of his head.

The dead man seemed to lunge at me, slumping headfirst against my legs as he fell to the floor—just as a volley of shotgun blasts came through the front door, followed by harsh shouts on a police bullhorn from outside. Then another volley of buckshot blasts that exploded the TV set and set the living room on fire, filling the trailer with dense brown smoke that I recognized instantly as the smell of Cyanide gas being released by the burning plastic couch.

Voices were screaming through the smoke, "*Surrender! Hands up behind your goddamn head!* DEAD MEAT!" Then more shooting. Another deafening fireball exploded out of the living room. I kicked the corpse off my feet and leapt for the back door, which I'd noticed earlier when I scanned the trailer for "alternative exits," as they say in the business—in case one might become necessary. I was halfway out the door when I remembered *the Judge*. He was still locked in the bathroom, maybe helpless in some kind of accidental drug coma, unable to get to his feet as flames roared through the trailer . . .

Ye Fucking Gods! I thought. I can't let him burn.

Kick the door off its hinges. Yes. Whack! The door splintered and I saw him sitting calmly on the filthy aluminum toilet stool, pretending to read a newspaper and squinting vacantly up at me as I crashed in and grabbed him by one arm.

"Fool!" I screamed. "Get up! Run! They'll *murder* us!"

He followed me through the smoke and burning debris holding his pants up with one hand . . . The Chinese sex doll called Ling-Ling hovered crazily in front of the door, her body swollen from heat and her hair on fire. I slapped her aside and bashed the door open, dragging the Judge outside with me. Another volley of shotgun blasts and bullhorn yells erupted somewhere behind us. The Judge lost his footing and fell heavily into the mud behind the doomed Airstream.

"Oh, God!" he screamed, "who *is* it?"

"The *Pigs*," I said. "They've gone *crazy*. Leach is dead! They're trying to *kill* us. We have to get to the car!"

He stood up quickly. "Pigs?" he said. "*Pigs*? Trying to *kill* me?"

He seemed to stiffen, and the dumbness went out of his eyes. He raised both fists and screamed in the direction of the shooting. "You *bastards*! You *scum*! You will *die* for this. You stupid white-trash pigs!

"Are they *nuts*?" he muttered. He jerked out of my grasp and reached angrily into his left armpit, then down to his belt and around behind his back like a gunfighter trying to slap leather . . . But there was no leather there. Not even a sleeve holster.

"God*damn it*!" he snarled. "Where's my goddamn *weapon*? Oh, Jesus! I left it in the car!" He dropped into a running crouch and sprinted into the darkness, around the corner of the flaming Airstream. "Let's *go*!" he hissed. "I'll *kill* these bastards! I'll blow their fucking heads off!"

Right, I thought, as we took off in a kind of low-speed desperate crawl through the mud and the noise and the gunfire, terrified neighbors screaming frantically to each other in the darkness. The red convertible was parked in the shadows, near the front of the trailer right next to the State Police car, with its chase lights blinking crazily and voices burping out of its radio.

The Pigs were nowhere to be seen. They had apparently *rushed* the place, with guns blazing—hoping to kill Leach before he got away. I jumped into the car and started the engine. The Judge came through the passenger door and reached for the loaded .454 Magnum . . . I watched in horror as he jerked it out of its holster and ran around to the front of the cop car and fired two shots into the grille.

"*Fuck you*!" he screamed. "Take *this*, you Scum! Eat shit and die!" He jumped back as the radiator exploded in a blast of steam and scalding water. Then he fired three more times through the windshield and into the squawking radio, which also exploded.

"Hot damn!" he said as he slid back into the front seat. "Now we have them trapped!" I jammed the car into reverse and lost control in the mud, hitting a structure of some kind and careening sideways at top speed until I got a grip on the thing and aimed it up the ramp to the highway . . . The Judge was trying desperately to reload the .454, yelling at me to slow down so he could finish the bastards off! His eyes were wild and his voice was unnaturally savage.

I swerved hard left to Elko and hurled him sideways, but he quickly recovered his balance and somehow got off five more thundering shots in the general direction of the burning trailer behind us.

"Good work, Judge," I said. "They'll never catch us now." He smiled and drank deeply from our Whiskey Jug, which he had somehow picked up as we fled . . . Then he passed it over to me, and I too drank deeply as I whipped the big V-8 into passing gear and we went from forty-five to ninety in four seconds and left the ugliness far behind us in the rain.

I glanced over at the Judge as he loaded five huge bullets into the Magnum. He was very calm and focused, showing no signs of the drug coma that had crippled him just moments before . . . I was impressed. The man was clearly a Warrior. I slapped him on the back and grinned. "Calm down, Judge," I said. "We're almost home."

I knew better, of course. I was *one thousand miles* from home, and we were almost certainly doomed. There was no hope of escaping the drag-net that would be out for us, once those poor fools discovered Leach in a puddle of burning blood with the top of his head blown off. The squad car was destroyed—thanks to the shrewd instincts of the Judge—but I knew it would not take them long to send out an all-points alarm. Soon there would be angry police roadblocks at every exit between Reno and Salt Lake City . . .

So what? I thought. There were many side roads, and we had a very fast car. All I had to do was get the Judge out of his killing frenzy and find a truck stop where we could buy a few cans of Flat Black spray paint. Then we could slither out of the state before dawn and find a place to hide.

But it would not be an easy run. In the quick space of four hours we had destroyed two automobiles and somehow participated in at least one killing—in addition to all the other random, standard-brand crimes like speeding and arson and fraud and attempted murder of State Police officers while fleeing the scene of a homicide . . .

No. We had a Serious problem on our hands. We were trapped in the middle of Nevada like crazy rats, and the cops would shoot to Kill when they saw us. No doubt about that. We were Criminally Insane . . . I laughed and shifted up into Drive. The car stabilized at 115 or so . . .

The Judge was eager to get back to his women. He was still fiddling with the Magnum, spinning the cylinder nervously and looking at his watch. "Can't you go any faster?" he muttered. "How far is Elko?"

Too far, I thought, which was true. Elko was fifty miles away and there would be roadblocks. Impossible. They would trap us and probably butcher us.

Elko was out, but I was loath to break this news to the Judge. He had no stomach for bad news. He had a tendency to flip out and flog anything in sight when things weren't going his way.

It was wiser, I thought, to humor him. Soon he would go to sleep.

I slowed down and considered. Our options were limited. There would be roadblocks on every paved road out of Wells. It was a main crossroads, a gigantic full-on truck stop where you could get anything you wanted twenty-four hours a day, within reason, of course. And what we needed was not in that category. We needed to disappear. That was one option.

We could go south on 93 to Ely, but that was about it. That would be like driving into a steel net. A flock of pigs would be waiting for us, and after that it would be Nevada State Prison. To the north on 93 was Jackpot, but we would never make that either. Running east into Utah was hopeless. We were trapped. They would run us down like dogs. There were other options, but not all of them were mutual. The Judge had his priorities, but they were not mine. I understood that me and the Judge were coming up on a parting of the ways. This made me nervous. There were other options, of course, but they were all High Risk. I pulled over and studied the map again. The Judge appeared to be sleeping, but I couldn't be sure. He still had the Magnum in his lap.

The Judge was getting to be a problem. There was no way to get him out of the car without violence. He would not go willingly into the dark and stormy night. The only other way was to kill him, but that was out of the question as long as he had the gun. He was very quick in emergencies. I couldn't get the gun away from him, and I was not about to get into an argument with him about who should have the weapon. If I lost, he would shoot me in the spine and leave me in the road.

I was getting too nervous to continue without chemical assistance. I reached under the seat for my kit bag, which contained five or six spansules of Black Acid. Wonderful, I thought. This is just what I need. I ate one and went back to pondering the map. There was a place called Deeth, just ahead, where a faintly marked side road appeared to wander uphill through the mountains and down along a jagged ridge into Jackpot from behind. Good, I thought, this is it. We could sneak into Jackpot by dawn.

Just then I felt a blow on the side of my head as the Judge came awake with a screech, flailing his arms around him like he was coming out of a nightmare. "What's happening, goddamn it?" he said. "Where are we? They're after us." He was jabbering in a foreign language that quickly lapsed into English as he tried to aim the gun. "Oh, God," he screamed. "They're right on top of us. Get moving, goddamn it. I'll kill every bastard I see."

He was coming out of a nightmare. I grabbed him by the neck and put him in a headlock until he went limp. I pulled him back up in the seat and handed him a spansule of acid. "Here, Judge, take this," I said. "It'll calm you down."

He swallowed the pill and said nothing as I turned onto the highway and stood heavily on the accelerator. We were up to 115 when a green exit sign that said "Deeth No Services" loomed suddenly out of the rain just in front of us. I swerved hard to the right and tried to hang on. But it was no use. I remember the sound of the Judge screaming as we lost control and went into a full 360-degree curl and then backward at seventy-five or eighty through a fence and into a pasture.

For some reason the near-fatal accident had a calming effect on the Judge. Or maybe it was the acid. I didn't care one way or the other after I took the gun from his hand. He gave it up without a fight. He seemed to be more interested in reading the road signs and listening to the radio. I knew that if we could slip into Jackpot the back way, I could get the car painted any color I wanted in thirty-three minutes and put the Judge on a plane. I knew a small private airstrip there, where nobody asks too many questions and they'll take a personal check.

At dawn we drove across the tarmac and pulled up to a seedy-looking office marked Air Jackpot Express Charter Company. "This is it, Judge," I said and slapped him on the back. "This is where you get off." He seemed resigned to his fate until the woman behind the front desk told him there wouldn't be a flight to Elko until lunchtime.

"Where is the pilot?" he demanded.

"I am the pilot," the woman said, "but I can't leave until Debby gets here to relieve me."

"Fuck this!" the Judge shouted. "Fuck lunchtime. I have to leave *now*, you bitch."

The woman seemed truly frightened by his mood swing, and when the Judge leaned in and gave her a taste of the long knuckle, she collapsed and began weeping uncontrollably. "There's more where that came from," he told her. "Get up! I have to get out of here now."

He jerked her out from behind the desk and was dragging her toward the plane when I slipped out the back door. It was daylight now. The car was nearly out of gas, but that wasn't my primary concern. The police would be here in minutes, I thought. I'm doomed. But then, as I pulled onto the highway, I saw a sign that said, We Paint All Night.

As I pulled into the parking lot, the Jackpot Express plane passed overhead. So long, Judge, I thought to myself. You're a brutal hustler and a Warrior and a great copilot, but you know how to get your way. You will go far in the world.

• • •

That's about it for now, Jann. This story is too depressing to have to confront professionally in these morbid weeks before Christmas . . . I have only vague memories of what it's like there in New York, but sometimes I have flashbacks about how it was to glide in perfect speedy silence around the ice rink in front of NBC while junkies and federal informants in white beards and sleazy red jumpsuits worked the crowd mercilessly for nickels and dollars and dimes covered with crack residue.

Christmas hasn't changed much in twenty-two years, Jann—not even two thousand miles west and eight thousand feet up in the Rockies. It is still a day that only amateurs can love. It is all well and good for children and acid freaks to believe in Santa Claus—but it is still a profoundly morbid day for us working professionals. It is unsettling to know that one out of every twenty people you meet on Xmas will be dead this time next year . . . Some people can accept this, and some can't. That is why God made whiskey, and also why Wild Turkey comes in $300 shaped canisters during most of the Christmas season, and also why criminal shitheads all over New York City will hit you up for $100 tips or they'll twist your windshield wipers into spaghetti and urinate on your door handles.

And that's about it for now, Jann. Christmas is on us and it's all downhill from here on . . . At least until Groundhog Day, which is soon . . . So, until then, at least, take my advice, as your family doctor, and don't do *anything* that might cause either one of us to have to appear before the Supreme Court of the United States. If you know what I'm saying . . .

Yes. He is Up There, Jann. The Judge. And he will be there for a long time, waiting to gnaw on our skulls . . . Right. Put *that* in your leather pocket the next time you feel like jumping on your new motorcycle and screwing it all the way over thru traffic and passing cop cars at 140.

Remember F. X. Leach. He crossed the Judge, and he paid a terrible price . . . And so will you, if you don't slow down and quit harassing those girls in your office. The Judge is in charge now, and He won't tolerate it. Beware.

Hunter's Clinton Problem

On Friday, July 31, 1992, in the heat of that year's presidential campaign, the Rolling Stone *National Affairs team—Hunter, Jann, William Greider, P. J. O'Rourke, and Eric Etheridge—sat down with Democratic presidential candidate Bill Clinton at Doe's Eat Place in Little Rock, Arkansas. The result was a lively roundtable discussion about issues and policy, personalities and music for all involved—except, perhaps, Hunter, who walked in the place hoping for a kind of rapport with the candidate or, barring that, hoping to engage Clinton in the kind of extended, unguarded, revealing conversation that was Hunter's specialty. What he found was a polished candidate adept at playing a low-risk political strategy that was, in his eyes, no fun. Having had his early questions quickly debunked or dismissed by the candidate, Hunter simply got up from the table and headed for a perch at the bar, where he sat and watched the rest of the interview take place from a distance. From this moment on, his attitude toward candidate, and soon president, Clinton was fixed; Hunter tried to chalk it up to his policies, or even a supposed run-in decades earlier, when Hunter claimed to have driven his car across the lawn of the house that Bill and Hillary rented in Washington, DC, on his way home from a George McGovern staff party in 1972. It wasn't that complicated, really; Hunter spelled it out in the introduction to his story on the lunch meeting: "Bill Clinton has no Sense of Humor."*

Mr. Bill's Neighborhood

September 17, 1992

MEMO FROM THE NATIONAL AFFAIRS DESK

DATE: August 4th, '92
FROM: Dr. Hunter S. Thompson
SUBJECT: The Three Stooges Go to Little Rock . . . Tall Gibberish at Doe's Café . . . Where Were You When the Fun Stopped? . . . Mean Is Not Enough; Say Hello to President Clinton.

I have just returned, as you know, from a top-secret *Issues Conference* in Little Rock with our high-riding Candidate, Bill Clinton—who is also the five-term governor of Arkansas and the only living depositor in the Grameen Bank of Bangladesh who wears a *Rolling Stone* T-shirt when he jogs past the hedges at sundown.

Ah, yes—the *hedges*. How little is known of them, eh? And I suspect, in fact, that the truth will *never* be known . . . I wanted to check them out, but it didn't work. My rented Chrysler convertible turned into a kind of *Trojan Horse* in reverse—and frankly, I was deeply *afraid* to stay for even one night in Little Rock, by myself, for fear of being tracked and seized and perhaps even jailed and humiliated, on instructions from some nameless Clinton factotum.

It was ugly, Bubba. We were under intense surveillance the whole time, despite our desperate efforts to act like just another gang of Good Ol' Boys for Clinton . . . Which we were, I guess, since our eager, farseeing Editor had already decided on his formal *RS* endorsement for Clinton and already scheduled Big Bill for the cover . . . And since

Clinton and his People understood this, our efforts to deal mercilessly with the candidate were pretty much neutered from the start.

We were like the Three Stooges. Clinton already *had* the endorsement and cover, so anything he said to us—me, P.J. O'Rourke, and "Dollar Bill" Greider—was pretty much a matter of Filigree.

• • •

We flew down to Little Rock in high style. The six of us lounging around on a jet plane the size of a Greyhound bus—with only six seats, two telephones, and gold-plated fixtures in a bathroom larger than some of the editorial offices at *Rolling Stone*.

We were the Strike Force, the *Rolling Stone* Blue Ribbon Presidential Forum—zooming into Little Rock at six hundred miles an hour to confront Clinton and see who he really was.

It is hard to know exactly what an *RS* cover is worth to a front-running candidate—but there was no question at all about the shitrain of Ugliness that could happen if the luncheon got out of hand. These drunken, brain-damaged brutes might do anything.

Which is a nice kind of reputation to have, in some towns—but not in Little Rock, when you're meeting in public with the next president in full view of the national press and fourteen Secret Service watchdogs. Nobody needs a headline like "Clinton Injured in Wild Brawl with Dope Fiends: Candidate Denies Drunkenness, Cancels Bus Trip, Flees."

Well . . . that didn't happen. It was T. S. Eliot, I think, who wrote, "Between the idea/And the reality . . . Falls the Shadow."

Which turned out to be *me*.

I was the Shadow. Bill Clinton was not comfortable being in the same room with me. He is, after all, a career politician only a hundred or so days away from the presidency—provided he makes no mistakes before Election Day—and being involved in some kind of fracas in the back room of a downtown bar and grill would definitely be a Mistake.

Ah, but we're getting ahead of our story.

Let's go back about twenty hours to our Commandolike drop into the Little Rock Airport—where a huge blue and white sign, bigger than *two* Greyhound buses, said, "Little Rock Is Bush Country."

"Jesus Christ," I muttered to P.J. "What are *we* doing here?"

"Speak for yourself," he said. "I feel right at home."

"Of course," I said. "You Nazi swine."

He grinned and ate another Percodan to calm the pain in his gums.

"Do you have any more of those?" I asked him. "My broken back is killing me."

"No," he said. "I gave them all to Greider. I couldn't stand his pitiful screams any longer."

We were *all* injured. The plane was like a Civil War hospital. Bill Greider, our *éminence grise*, had ripped all the tendons out of his knee in a freak accident only two hours earlier on the Teterboro, New Jersey, tarmac and was in extreme pain.

"Don't worry, Bubba," I said to him. "I'm a doctor. Here, eat these pills." I gave him sixteen Advils, which he resisted but finally swallowed anyway.

"I can't stand pain," I said. "Not even to be *around* it."

"Thank God you're here, Doc," Bill said. "We're all in this thing together."

That elegant dictum, a testament to Brotherhood under stress, would be severely tested in the next twenty hours . . . It was one nightmare after another as we were plunged into Mr. Bill's Neighborhood.

Cazart! Yes. I see it all very clearly now. I was blind as a bat, but no longer. . . . So let me share it with you, Bubba: the fruits of my hard-earned Wisdom. Stand back!

Bill Clinton has no Sense of Humor. He eats a lot of French Fries and laughs at the wrong times and often manifests clinical signs of Schizophrenia. But he knows a good deal when he sees one, and on that murky Friday morning *we* were the good deal he was looking at—the Three Stooges, direct from New York on a big jet plane to legitimize the Deal.

Don't get me wrong, Bubba. We had *fun*, despite our various crippling injuries and my own humiliation when Clinton denounced every thought I uttered and every question I asked, as if I were criminally insane . . .

The encounter took place in the back room of an artificially degraded replica of a standard-brand southern diner called Doe's Eat Place (which I will hereafter and previously refer to as *Doe's Café*, because I like *café* and I can't stand the cuteness of the other) . . .

The *encounter* was what we had come for, the *Mano a Mano* gig with the man we all agreed would probably be the next president—unless . . . Remember Willie Horton. Remember Gary Hart. Indeed. There are many rooms in the mansion, and there will always be wreckage in the Fast Lane. This is the Nineties, Bubba, and there is no such thing as Paranoia. It's all true.

So it is probably not Fair to dismiss Clinton as a Cowardly Craven Fool for feeling a touch apprehensive when his scheduler set him up for an unprecedented and utterly unpredictable Lunch Forum . . . It was a high-risk venture, for sure, and I had to like him for doing it.

Still, it seemed clear as we sat down for a lunch of Tamales, Tuna Fish, and French Fries with the Next President that he was not real eager to be there. He behaved in a queer, distracted manner and crushed my knuckles together when we shook hands. I shouted with pain, and Jann quickly intervened, saying: "Calm down, Governor. We're on *your* side."

I nodded meekly and sat down in a tin chair at what was either the Head or the Foot of the table, thinking that the Candidate would naturally sit at the Other End, far out of reach of me.

But *no*. The creepy bastard quickly sat down *right next to me*, about two feet away, and fixed me with a sleepy-looking stare that made me very uneasy. His eyes had narrowed to slits, and at first I thought he was dozing off . . . But he appeared to be very tense, as if he were ready to pounce.

Ye gods, I thought. What's *happening* here? This is not what I had in Mind. The interview had turned weird, and so had the governor . . . No one else seemed to notice I was paralyzed with fear. But I was not totally brain-dead. Just as I felt myself on the brink of passing out, I remembered I had a *gift* for Clinton, who continued to stare at me darkly.

I reached quickly into my rumpled shirt pocket and pulled out a brand-new Vandoren tenor-saxophone reed, which had been entrusted to me by the famous photographer Fulton of Aspen, who also plays the tenor sax and had caught Clinton's act on *Arsenio*.

I got the governor's attention by gently waving the elegant little piece of cane back and forth in front of his eyes until he came vaguely alive and smiled at me. Hot damn, I thought. That was *close*. He seemed almost friendly now. I explained that the reed was a gift from a fellow musician who wished him well, then I pressed it into his outstretched palm. The Secret Service boys reacted like Dobermans when I unexpectedly made *uninvited physical contact* with the Candidate and then gave him a small, unidentifiable object to put in his mouth, but I waved them off with a friendly smile. "Relax, boys," I said. "It's only a harmless *reed*—a tribute to the governor's *art*."

What happened next was so strange that I would have shrugged it off as one of those random, paranoid hallucinations that occur now and then, even to sane people—except that I have the whole long moment on Sony Hi8 Metal-E60 videotape, and there were also five or six witnesses who later recalled the incident with stark clarity and a creepy sense of dismay that none of them wanted to talk about or even acknowledge at the time. But it was true:

Clinton stared balefully at the reed for what seemed like a very long time, like a Chimp peering into his first Mirror . . . There was a sense of puzzlement on his face as he silently pondered the thing.

It was an awkward moment, Bubba. *Very* awkward. Nobody knew how to handle it. He seemed unhappy, almost angry as he fondled the reed distractedly, saying nothing . . . Then he rolled his eyes back in his head and uttered a wild quavering cry that made my blood run cold.

The others tried to pretend that it wasn't happening. We were, after all, in the South—and in some tangled way we were also the governor's *guests*. Or maybe he was *ours*. Who knows? But there was no doubt at all that *somebody* was drifting over the line into unacceptable rudeness, and I didn't think it was me. Greider was sobbing quietly, and P.J. sagged limply in his chair. Jann began jabbering frantically about "the Generation Gap." A pall of helpless craziness came over the table, a sense of unknowable Doom . . .

Then the governor dropped the Reed on the table like it was just another half-eaten Potato scrap, brushing it blankly aside and suddenly smiling warmly at all of us, as if he had just emerged from a Pod and was happy to be among friends. "No more music," he said firmly. "Let's have some food, I'm *hungry*." Then he grasped the wicker basket of French Fries with both hands and buried his face in it, making soft snorting sounds as he rooted around in the basket trying vainly to finish it off.

I was afraid, but Jann was quick to recover. "Easy, Governor, easy," he said in a suave voice. "Let me help you with that, Bill. Hell, we're *all* hungry." He smiled and reached out for the half-empty basket of fries, as if to share the burden—but Clinton snatched it away, clutching it to his chest and turning his back on us—a horrible thing to see.

Somewhere behind me I heard a kind of hissing, moaning sound as Eric, our hapless editor, stood up and bolted out of the room, slamming between two startled SS agents, and then locked himself in the bathroom. I heard a croaking noise, then a rush of water.

Well, I thought. This is probably about as weird as it can get, without all of us going to jail, so why not relax and act normal—or at least try? These things happen. Buy the ticket, take the ride. Welcome to Mr. Bill's Neighborhood.

The Wisdom

I came away from Little Rock with mixed feelings. Bill Clinton and I did not hit it off real well, but so what? I got into politics a long time ago, and I still believe, on some days, that it can be an honorable trade . . . That is not an easy belief to hang on to after wallowing for thirty years in the belly of a Beast that has beaten and broken more good men and women than Crack and Junk Bonds combined. Politics is a mean Business, and when September rolls around in a campaign, it gets mean on a level that is beyond most people's comprehension. The White House is the most powerful office in the world, and a lot of people will tell you nothing is over the line when it finally comes down to winning or losing it. Nobody is safe and Nothing is sacred when the stakes get that high. It is the ultimate Fast Lane, and the people still on their feet in September are usually the Meanest of the Mean. The last train out of any station will not be full of Nice guys.

Look at Bush. He has worked overtime to give Politics a bad name. He is a mean-spirited wimp and a career bureaucrat who has arguably committed more high crimes and misdemeanors in and around the Oval Office than Nixon would have been Impeached for if he hadn't resigned . . . Nixon was genetically Dishonest, and so is Bush. They both represent what Bobby Kennedy called "the darker impulses of the American Spirit . . ."

And Bill Clinton does not. That is the nut of it. Clinton is a decent man and a credit to his race . . . Ho, ho. That's a joke, Bubba. Bush wouldn't laugh at it, and neither did Mr. Bill when I shook his hand and said it to him with a nice smile. He gave me another one of those weird, sleepy-eyed stares and wished me good Luck for the rest of my life.

I am now going back to the drawing board to come up with a *better* and more valid reason to *vote* for Clinton in November—which I plan to do, but my *reasons* are no more concrete today than they were on the flight down to Little Rock. I like him a little better, but there was nothing in what he said for the record to excite anybody except cops, money mongers, and elitist policy wonks. The rest is all a matter of blind faith and reading between the lines.

Let's face it, Bubba. The main reason I'll vote for Clinton is *George Bush*, and it has been that way from the start . . . There is no way around it (for me) and no reason to apologize for it. George Bush is a dangerously failed President and a half-bright top-level Nerd who has spent the last four years avoiding grocery stores and gas stations while he tried to keep tabs on the disastrous fallout from the orgy of greed and short selling that was the "Reagan Revolution."

We still have a problem with my inability to explain why I feel very strongly about voting for Clinton—except that another four years of the Reagan-Bush bund will mean the Death of Hope and the Loss of *any* sense of Possibility in Politics for a whole generation that desperately needs that fix and will wither on the vine without it.

That is reason enough to *vote* for Clinton. It helps that I like him as a person and trust him enough as a quality politician to believe that I can occasionally turn my back on him when he moves into the White House—which he *will*, I think—and I will help him in every way I can, short of guaranteeing in print that President Clinton/Gore will solve all our problems and give forty acres and a mule to everyone who votes for him.

Nobody is going to do that. And especially not George Bush. But Bill Clinton will at least *try*, and that's good enough for me. He is a high-stakes gambler, and he can take a punch better than anybody since Muhammad Ali . . .

So what the fuck? Let's kick those rat-bastards out of the temple and put one of our people in charge. We have nothing to lose except *fun* and the joy of watching a serious brawler go to war with the greedheads. Why not? Let us Rumble.

Letter to William Greider

January 27, 1994

To: William Greider
From: Hunter S. Thompson
Date: Nov. 22, 1993

Well, you sure as hell made up for that *giddiness* that gripped you *last time*, eh? Probably you started asking him about that goddamn bank in Bangladesh . . . Shit, why is it always *extremes* with you, Bill? Why can't you find a groove in the middle of the road, like me?

Anyway, it was a magic moment in American journalism—and no doubt in yr. own education, too. I wish I could have been there for it.

But then *it wouldn't have happened, eh*? No, I would have *handled* him, like a *matador*. He would have focused his dim little eyes on *me*, & you subwonkish bastards would have *roamed Free*—and he would have treated you like Girls, with flirtatious little moves & solemn nods from time to time, massaging your Main Points & playing footsie with you under the table like he did in the dimness of Doe's . . .

Jesus. How long have we fallen? So much for the Rock & Roll vote, eh? We are down with the UAW & the Wobblies.

And it's *your fault*. Screwhead. It was YOU that croaked the RAPPORT that a WHOLE GENERATION might have had with the President of the U.S. What kind of berserk hubris led you to pick some kind of stupid PERSONAL FIGHT with the

President when you *knew* that the *FATE OF GENERATIONS* was in your boneless goddamn hands? What *craziness* compelled you to SHIT in THEIR nests?

If I were you, I'd move my whole family to a farm in rural Turkey, and try to write poems for a living. That is all you have left. Sorry. Call me.

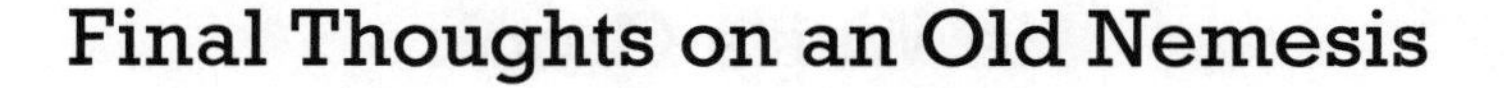

Final Thoughts on an Old Nemesis

On April 22, 1994, Richard Milhous Nixon died after suffering a severe stroke a few days earlier. At the time, Hunter was in New Orleans promoting a book, but he extended his stay to hunker down at the St. Charles Tavern, where he watched CNN incessantly and began to write the obituary of the man he'd been obsessed with for more than a quarter century. Nixon was more than Hunter's antagonist or nemesis; he was a shadow self who served as a living, breathing symbol of the dark side of the American dream, and Hunter's final send-off required him to rise to the occasion. He pulled no punches.

When Hunter next spoke to his longtime friend George McGovern—who had attended the funeral of his former opponent and ex-president of the United States out of a sense of duty—he accused him of going "in the tank" for the man who was, essentially, the enemy. According to McGovern, "He never forgave me for that."

He Was a Crook

June 16, 1994

MEMO FROM THE NATIONAL AFFAIRS DESK

Date: May 1, 1994
From: Dr. Hunter S. Thompson
Subject: The Death of Richard Nixon: Notes on the Passing of an American Monster . . . He was a liar and a quitter, and he should have been buried at sea . . . but he was, after all, the President.

And he cried mightily with a strong voice, saying, Babylon the great is fallen, is fallen, and is become the habitation of devils, and the hold of every foul spirit and a cage of every unclean and hateful bird.

—Revelation 18:2

Richard Nixon is gone now, and I am poorer for it. He was the real thing—a political monster straight out of Grendel and a very dangerous enemy. He could shake your hand and stab you in the back at the same time. He lied to his friends and betrayed the trust of his family. Not even Gerald Ford, the unhappy ex-president who pardoned Nixon and kept him out of prison, was immune to the evil fallout. Ford, who believes strongly in Heaven and Hell, has told more than one of his celebrity golf partners that "I know I will go to hell, because I pardoned Richard Nixon."

I have had my own bloody relationship with Nixon for many years, but I am not worried about it landing me in hell with him. I have already been there with that bastard, and I am a better person for it. Nixon had the unique ability to make his enemies seem honorable, and we developed a keen sense of fraternity. Some of my best friends have hated Nixon all their lives. My mother hates Nixon, my son hates Nixon, I hate Nixon, and this hatred has brought us together.

Nixon laughed when I told him this. "Don't worry," he said. "I, too, am a family man, and we feel the same way about you."

It was Richard Nixon who got me into politics, and now that he's gone, I feel lonely. He was a giant in his way. As long as Nixon was politically alive—and he was, all the way to the end—we could always be sure of finding the enemy on the Low Road. There was no need to look anywhere else for the evil bastard. He had the fighting instincts of a badger trapped by hounds. The badger will roll over on its back and emit a smell of death, which confuses the dogs and lures them in for the traditional ripping and tearing action. But it is usually the badger who does the ripping and tearing. It is a beast that fights best on its back; rolling under the throat of the enemy and seizing it by the head with all four claws.

That was Nixon's style—and if you forgot, he would kill you as a lesson to the others. Badgers don't fight fair, Bubba. That's why God made dachshunds.

• • •

Nixon was a navy man, and he should have been buried at sea. Many of his friends were seagoing people: Bebe Rebozo, Robert Vesco, William F. Buckley Jr., and some of them wanted a full naval burial.

These come in at least two styles, however, and Nixon's immediate family strongly opposed both of them. In the traditionalist style, the dead president's body would be wrapped and sewn loosely in canvas sailcloth and dumped off the stern of a frigate at least one hundred miles off the coast and at least one thousand miles south of San Diego, so the corpse could never wash up on American soil in any recognizable form.

The family opted for cremation until they were advised of the potentially onerous implications of a strictly private, unwitnessed burning of the body of the man who was, after all, the president of the United States. Awkward questions might be raised, dark allusions to Hitler and Rasputin. People would be filing lawsuits to get their hands on the dental charts. Long court battles would be inevitable—some with liberal cranks bitching about corpus delicti and habeas corpus, and others with giant insurance companies trying not to pay off on his death benefits. Either way, an orgy of greed and duplicity was sure to follow any public hint that Nixon might have somehow faked his own death or been cryogenically transferred to fascist Chinese interests on the Central Asian Mainland.

It would also play into the hands of those millions of self-stigmatized patriots like me who believe these things already.

If the right people had been in charge of Nixon's funeral, his casket would have been launched into one of those open-sewage canals that empty into the ocean just south of Los Angeles. He was a swine of a man and a jabbering dupe of a president. Nixon was so crooked that he needed servants to help him screw his pants on every morning. Even his funeral was illegal. He was queer in the deepest way. His body should have been burned in a trash bin.

• • •

These are harsh words for a man only recently canonized by President Clinton and my old friend George McGovern—but I have written worse things about Nixon, many times, and the record will show that I kicked him repeatedly long before he went down. I beat him like a mad dog with mange every time I got a chance, and I am proud of it. He was scum.

Let there be no mistake in the history books about that. Richard Nixon was an evil man—evil in a way that only those who believe in the physical reality of the Devil can understand it. He was utterly without ethics or morals or any bedrock sense of decency. Nobody trusted him—except maybe the Stalinist Chinese, and honest historians will remember him mainly as a rat who kept scrambling to get back on the ship.

It is fitting that Richard Nixon's final gesture to the American people was a clearly illegal series of 21 105-mm howitzer blasts that shattered the peace of a residential neighborhood and permanently disturbed many children. Neighbors also complained about another unsanctioned burial in the yard at the old Nixon place, which was brazenly illegal. "It makes the whole neighborhood like a graveyard," said one. "And it fucks up my children's sense of values."

Many were incensed about the howitzers—but they knew there was nothing they could do about it—not with the current president sitting about fifty yards away and laughing at the roar of the cannons. It was Nixon's last war, and he won.

The funeral was a dreary affair, finely staged for TV and shrewdly dominated by ambitious politicians and revisionist historians. The Rev. Billy Graham, still agile and eloquent at the age of 136, was billed as the main speaker, but he was quickly upstaged by two 1996 GOP presidential candidates: Sen. Bob Dole of Kansas and Gov. Pete Wilson of California, who formally hosted the event and saw his poll numbers crippled when he got blown off the stage by Dole, who somehow seized the no. 3 slot on the roster and uttered such a shameless, self-serving eulogy that even he burst into tears at the end of it.

Dole's stock went up like a rocket and cast him as the early GOP front-runner for '96. Wilson, speaking next, sounded like an Engelbert Humperdinck impersonator and probably won't even be reelected as governor of California in November.

The historians were strongly represented by the no. 2 speaker, Henry Kissinger, Nixon's secretary of state and himself a zealous revisionist with many axes to grind. He set the tone for the day with a maudlin and spectacularly self-serving portrait of Nixon as even more saintly than his mother and as a president of many godlike accomplishments—most of them put together in secret by Kissinger, who came to California as part of a huge publicity tour for his new book on diplomacy, genius, Stalin, H. P. Lovecraft, and other great minds of our time, including himself and Richard Nixon.

Kissinger was only one of the many historians who suddenly came to see Nixon as more than the sum of his many squalid parts. He seemed to be saying that History will not have to absolve Nixon, because he has already done it himself in a massive act of will and crazed arrogance that already ranks him supreme, along with other Nietzschean supermen like Hitler, Jesus, Bismarck, and the Emperor Hirohito. These revisionists have catapulted Nixon to the status of an American Caesar, claiming that when the definitive history of the twentieth century is written, no other president will come close to Nixon in stature. "He will dwarf FDR and Truman," according to one scholar from Duke University.

It was all gibberish, of course. Nixon was no more a Saint than he was a Great President. He was more like Sammy Glick than Winston Churchill. He was a cheap crook and a merciless war criminal who bombed more people to death in Laos and Cambodia than the U.S. Army lost in all of World War II, and he denied it to the day of his death. When students at Kent State University, in Ohio, protested the bombing, he connived to have them attacked and slain by troops from the National Guard.

• • •

Some people will say that words like *scum* and *rotten* are wrong for Objective Journalism—which is true, but they miss the point. It was the built-in blind spots of the Objective rules and dogma that allowed Nixon to slither into the White House in the first place. He looked so good on paper that you could almost vote for him sight unseen. He seemed so all-American, so much like Horatio Alger, that he was able to slip through the cracks of Objective Journalism. You had to get Subjective to see Nixon clearly, and the shock of recognition was often painful.

Nixon's meteoric rise from the unemployment line to the vice presidency in six quick years would never have happened if TV had come along ten years earlier. He got away with his sleazy "my dog Checkers" speech in 1952 because most voters heard it on the radio or read about it in the headlines of their local, Republican newspapers. When Nixon finally had to face the TV cameras for real in the 1960 presidential campaign debates, he got whipped like a red-headed mule. Even die-hard Republican voters were shocked by his cruel and incompetent persona. Interestingly, most people who heard those debates on the radio thought Nixon had won. But the mushrooming TV audience saw him as a truthless used-car salesman, and they voted accordingly. It was the first time in fourteen years that Nixon lost an election.

When he arrived in the White House as VP at the age of forty, he was a smart young man on the rise—a hubris-crazed monster from the bowels of the American dream with a heart full of hate and an overweening lust to be president. He had won every office he'd run for and stomped like a Nazi on all of his enemies and even some of his friends.

Nixon had no friends except George Will and J. Edgar Hoover (and they both deserted him). It was Hoover's shameless death in 1972 that led directly to Nixon's downfall. He felt helpless and alone with Hoover gone. He no longer had access to either the Director or the Director's ghastly bank of Personal Files on almost everybody in Washington.

Hoover was Nixon's right flank, and when he croaked, Nixon knew how Lee felt when Stonewall Jackson got killed at Chancellorsville. It permanently exposed Lee's flank and led to the disaster at Gettysburg.

For Nixon, the loss of Hoover led inevitably to the disaster of Watergate. It meant hiring a New Director—who turned out to be an unfortunate toady named L. Patrick Gray, who squealed like a pig in hot oil the first time Nixon leaned on him. Gray panicked and fingered White House Counsel John Dean, who refused to take the rap and rolled over, instead, on Nixon, who was trapped like a rat by Dean's relentless, vengeful testimony and went all to pieces right in front of our eyes on TV.

That is Watergate, in a nut, for people with seriously diminished attention spans. The real story is a lot longer and reads like a textbook on human treachery. They were all scum, but only Nixon walked free and lived to clear his name. Or at least that's what Bill Clinton says—and he is, after all, the president of the United States.

Nixon liked to remind people of that. He believed it, and that was why he went down. He was not only a crook but a fool. Two years after he quit, he told a TV journalist that "if the president does it, it can't be illegal."

Shit. Not even Spiro Agnew was that dumb. He was a flat-out, knee-crawling thug with the morals of a weasel on speed. But he was Nixon's vice president for five years, and he only resigned when he was caught red-handed taking cash bribes across his desk in the White House.

Unlike Nixon, Agnew didn't argue. He quit his job and fled in the night to Baltimore, where he appeared the next morning in U.S. District Court, which allowed him to stay out of prison for bribery and extortion in exchange for a guilty (no contest) plea on income-tax evasion. After that he became a major celebrity and played golf and tried to get a Coors distributorship. He never spoke to Nixon again and was an unwelcome guest at the funeral. They called him Rude, but he went anyway. It was one of those Biological Imperatives, like salmon swimming up waterfalls to spawn before they die. He knew he was scum, but it didn't bother him.

Agnew was the Joey Buttafuoco of the Nixon administration, and

Hoover was its Caligula. They were brutal, brain-damaged degenerates worse than any hit man out of *The Godfather*, yet they were the men Richard Nixon trusted most. Together they defined his presidency.

It would be easy to forget and forgive Henry Kissinger of his crimes, just as he forgave Nixon. Yes, we could do that—but it would be wrong. Kissinger is a slippery little devil, a world-class hustler with a thick German accent and a very keen eye for weak spots at the top of the power structure. Nixon was one of these, and Super K exploited him mercilessly, all the way to the end.

Kissinger made the Gang of Four complete: Agnew, Hoover, Kissinger, and Nixon. A group photo of these perverts would say all we need to know about the Age of Nixon.

• • •

Nixon's spirit will be with us for the rest of our lives—whether you're me or Bill Clinton or you or Kurt Cobain or Bishop Tutu or Keith Richards or Amy Fisher or Boris Yeltsin's daughter or your fiancée's sixteen-year-old beer-drunk brother with his braided goatee and his whole life like a thundercloud out in front of him. This is not a generational thing. You don't even have to know who Richard Nixon was to be a victim of his ugly, Nazi spirit.

He has poisoned our water forever. Nixon will be remembered as a classic case of a smart man shitting in his own nest. But he also shit in our nests, and that was the crime that history will burn on his memory like a brand. By disgracing and degrading the presidency of the United States, by fleeing the White House like a diseased cur, Richard Nixon broke the heart of the American Dream.

In Gatsby Country

Sometime around Aspen in the late Eighties, Hunter had developed an infatuation with a (married) polo player named Paula Baxt. When Hunter tried telling her to drop everything to run away with him, she offhandedly replied that she couldn't, because "polo is my life." Hunter became fixated with the phrase and the world it conjured up, and began working on a novel that he envisioned along the lines of The Great Gatsby, *which he'd continue to write, off and on, for years. In 1994 he traveled to the sport's U.S. Open on Long Island to soak up the culture and gather material. "Polo Is My Life: Fear & Loathing in Horse Country" was planned as a two-part story, although the second installment was abandoned after Hunter ran up almost $40,000 in story expenses (including $7,500 for something listed on a hotel bill as "incinerated sofa") while writing very little usable material.*

This first installment, though, was—along with "Fear and Loathing in Elko"—Hunter's last extended, evocative narrative; a surreal, gimlet-eyed inside view of the culture of a sport, as he put it, "for the filthy, aggressive rich," with guest appearances by the ghost of Averell Harriman as well as Belinda, the "all-knowing, dissolute slut horse" who is the sport's mythical, four-eyed goddess.

Letter from HST to JSW

Woody Creek
ROD & GUN CLUB
HUNTER STOCKTON THOMPSON, EXECUTIVE DIRECTOR

July 13, '94

Dear Jann,

Here is a quick memo on the story ideas we discussed on the phone yesterday. (which is not to say that my Concept of doing extensive PERFORMANCE EVALUATIONS) on a few of the *Finest Motorcycles on the American Road in the Nineties* was a failed & flawed idea . . . It has several built-in guaranteed *Fun Factors*, as in: 1) ELEGANT MOTORCYCLES on loan from the factory for me to test-drive all summer, and 2) Writing about them will be Fun to write and Fun to read, and 3) It would establish *RS* (or *MJ*) as a fount of high-end MOTORCYCLE CRITICISM—not only from me, but also from other ranking experts)

And I might do business with regard to the fee . . .

Right. And now back to POLO and MANDATORY SENTENCING—both of which are *do-able* without massive expenses or long-term grief.

I will count on you for research help on the M/S piece, and I see the POLO gig as a sort of Adventure Story: HOW I SPENT MY SUMMER VACATION, ETC. . . . ME AND RALPH GO TO POLO PRACTICE & DISCOVER THE MEANING OF LIFE. (I can start on this one *today* (Wed 7/13), and Ralph will be here next week—for a summit meeting on the nature of our Final Assignment—and you know how he loves Polo. He can't get enough of it . . .

And neither can I—because now I must immerse myself in the living, prancing, preening Human Context of a Preterhuman world of speed, money, and passion . . . "Polo Is My Life," which

I can finish by Christmas, once I get my staff/support system in place.

As a matter of fact I think I can send you a few chapters of "Polo" by Labor Day, now that I finally have time to work on it, and a professional reason to hang around Polo practice with the big-time Argentines & their sloe-eyed trophy bimbos is precisely what I need to get myself in gear.

R.S.V.P.

Hunter
HST

Letter from HST to JSW, September 22, 1994

Garden City Hotel
Please help me
I'm sick

Dear Jann,

Here is a nine (9) page running start on our Polo Project and The Nature & Fate of Democracy. Note Polo Was My Life. Details enc. You're welcome.

Tobias will have a clean copy to you before ten. He has been a big help in many ways & I think we should give him a raise . . . Corey should be fired. He went crazy out here with a sex doll & almost got me evicted . . .

Bob Love is nutty as a fruitcake if he thinks we'll have 20 real pages on this thing by "the end of the week." The BIG GAME is not until Sunday, & I'll be a victim of *Rigor Mortis* by then.

The U.S. Polo Open is the dullest spectacle since Boss Tweed died of old age with all his children watching. They were forced to, and the death took many weeks.

That is how I feel now, in this horrible morgue of a hotel. I will flee to the city tomorrow, or maybe tonight. My book has moved up to No. 13 on the NYT list and my daily expenses have increased accordingly. I can no longer live on this meager $200 a day Per Diem. [*sic*]

Okay. Let us speak. Later.

HST

*** I think this one should go as a *Memo from the Sports Desk*. We would be fools to try to bloat it up to 15K words.

Polo Is My Life:
Fear and Loathing in Horse Country

December 15, 1994

Queer for Power, Slave to Speed . . . Adventures in the Pony Business

Arms, my only ornament—my only rest, the fight.

—Cervantes, *Don Quixote*

I

Polo meant nothing to me when I was young. It was just another sport for the idle rich—golf on horseback—and on most days I had better things to do than hang around in a flimsy blue-striped tent on a soggy field far out on the River Road and drink gin with teenage girls. But that was the old days, and I have learned a lot since then. I still like to drink gin with teenage girls on a Sunday afternoon in horse country, and I have developed a natural, friendly feeling for the game.

Which is odd, because I don't play polo, and I hate horses. They are dangerously stupid beasts with brains the size of cue balls and hoofs that can crush your whole foot into bone splinters just by accidentally stepping on your toe. Some will do it on purpose. I have been on extremely mean and stupid horses that clearly wanted to hurt me. I have been run against trees by the bastards, I have been scraped against barbed-wire fences and bitten on the back of the head for no reason . . .

At the age of five, I got trapped in a stall for forty-five minutes with a huge horse named Buddy, who went suddenly crazy and kicked himself to death with terrible shrieking noises while I huddled in the urine-soaked straw right under his hoofs.

My uncle Lawless, a kindly dairy farmer, was flogging the brute across the eyes with a two-by-four and trying to get a strangle rope around his neck, but the horse was too crazy to deal with. Finally, in desperation, he ran back to the house and got a double-barreled ten-gauge shotgun—which he jammed repeatedly against the horse's lips and teeth until the beast angrily bit down on the weapon and caused both barrels to fire at once.

"So much for that one," he said as he dragged me out from under the dead animal's body. I was covered with blood and hot, steaming excrement. The brute had evacuated its bowels at the moment of death . . .

No one seemed to know why it happened. "It was a suicide," the vet said later, but nobody believed him. Uncle Lawless loved animals, and he was never able to reconcile murdering that horse with his basic Christian beliefs. He sold his farm and went into the real estate business in southern Indiana, and finally he went insane.

The main problem with horses is that they are too big to argue with when they're angry—or even bitchy, for that matter, and highbred horses are notorious for their bitchiness. Which might be cute or fey in a smaller animal, but when a beast that weighs 1,200 pounds goes crazy with some kind of stupid pique or jealousy in a room not much bigger than the handicapped stall in the Denver airport men's room, bad things will happen to anybody who tries to argue with it: fractured skulls, broken legs, split kidneys, spine damage, and permanent paralysis. The kick of a horse at close range, a hoof flicked out in anger, is like being whacked in the shins with a baseball bat. It rips flesh and shatters human bones. You will go straight to some rural Emergency Room, and you will be in a cast by nightfall . . . if you're lucky. The unlucky will limp for the rest of their lives.

Another little-known fact about horses is that the shape of their eyeballs makes them see human beings as six times their actual size and two or three times closer than they actually are. The multiples vary from horse to horse due to gene differentials, age, and eyeball size, but guaranteed pain awaits those who fail to grasp this bizarre truth of nature. Imagine how you would relate to your dog if you thought it was six times bigger than it actually is.

Fifty Years Later

On some days you find too much queerness in your Life. It happens suddenly—or at least it seems that way. But in truth it is like a boil bursting—an eruption of foul juices that were there all along and then suddenly erupted for many eyes to see.

And so it happened in the summer of '94 that I found myself happily wandering the back roads of the professional polo circuit, looking for weirdness and action. It was dumb, but so what? Dumb is a nice way to travel in some neighborhoods, and on some days, just looking for action is almost as good as finding it.

In any case, I spent many scorching long afternoons last summer driving around the mountains in my old 1976 Cadillac Fleetwood Eldorado convertible, looking for signs of people who might be engaged in some off-duty polo action—a practice drill in one place, an unscheduled game in another—back and forth in the sun along dusty narrow roads, across high-mountain pastures with humming electric fences and the occasional tin-roof animal shed every two or three miles, but on weekday afternoons there was rarely any sign of human life.

Only animals, filthy stupid animals. And the rotten blazing sun. The thirst, the anger, the crippling sense of helpless bovine dumbness when you pass the same deserted barn for the third time in forty minutes and then suddenly run out of gas on a rutted uphill grade overlooking nothing . . . The nasty rush of fear when the 5,200-pound Cadillac loses its power brakes and steering as it rolls backward down the hill and almost off a cliff.

I was looking for my homeboys, the Aspen Polo team, which was rumored to be on its way to Long Island to compete in what some people said was the Super Bowl of polo, the high-goal U.S. Open. There was even talk of *winning*, prevailing, beating the best in the world on their own turf and galloping off with the prize.

I must have been bored last summer, because I became oddly fixated with the idea. As a betting proposition, it was not as goofy as it sounded. Aspen Polo turned out to be a gang of big-time polo mercenaries who looked good enough on paper to beat anybody in the world. Doug

Matthews, the mysterious aircraft-industry tycoon from Atlanta, had stunned the polo world by brazenly hiring both of the legendary Gracida brothers, Memo and Carlos, to play on the same team, along with a twenty-three-year-old hot rod out of South Carolina named Tiger Kneece, whose lame six-goal rating was rumored to be suspiciously low.

The Gracida brothers from Mexico were both world-class ten goalers. Yes. It was not a bad bet at all—and when I learned several weeks later that the tournament was already fixed, our bet looked even better.

• • •

What polo people call "gentleman's polo" is a very different game from professional, or "high goal." The gentleman's version is an amateur horse sport, a kind of Rodeo for Rich Cowboys that is played all over the country by not many people at all—maybe .001 percent of the population, or even .0001 percent—and it is not a spectator sport. Less than .00001 percent of the U.S. population ever watches polo, and only 666 people have ever seen it on TV. Jai alai is a major sport compared with polo, and more people paid to watch the Calaveras County Frog Jumping Contest last summer than attended the prestigious month-long U.S. Polo Open on Long Island in September.

Polo is a sport for the filthy, aggressive rich and a handful of skilled professional horse athletes who roam the world and sell themselves to the highest bidder, often a different one each week and always for princely fees.

The people who pay these fees are called patrons, pronounced as in the Spanish: *patrones*. A patron hires his own players—or at least the other three—and he plays every minute of every chukker, no matter how useless he is. But make no mistake about it: patrons *are* polo; they pay all the bills and buy all the horses and support the high-goal players in the extravagant style of the polo world, which is the only style they know.

Patrons are a strange breed with no common bond except hubris. There are fewer than thirty of them in the world at any given time, and they travel a feverish high-dollar circuit, one that stretches from Palm Springs and Santa Barbara in the West to Palm Beach and Greenwich in the East, and then from England to France and back across the Atlantic to the pampas of Argentina, the mecca of high-goal polo all over the world and the sacred birthplace of Belinda, the mythical four-eyed horse goddess of polo and everything it stands for.

Belinda is lewd yet friendly; she is an all-knowing, dissolute slut horse, insanely rapacious yet very inviting and maternal at the same time. She dwells alone somewhere up in the Andes, and on moonlit nights she comes down and mingles regally with normal horses and sometimes even with the gauchos. They weep and shout at the sight of her, and a few even claim to have ridden her.

Patrons are no different. They worship Belinda for many reasons, but mainly out of fear. It was Belinda who made Argentina the ruler of the polo world and the hatchery of high-goal champions. She is capricious, however, and is said to take bribes and wantonly peddle her influence from time to time.

She usually favors Argentines, but there were rumors this year that Doug Matthews got to her first. This news sent a wave of excitement through American polo circles and ignited an anti-Argie feeding frenzy among North American patrons. The cost of entering a team in this year's U.S. Open rose to roughly $1 million, and the prize was still a bent silver cup worth less than $200. But to them it made no difference.

Eleven hard-riding patrons bit that bullet without blinking, and one of them, a mysterious black sheik from Nigeria, went so far as to "sponsor" *two* teams—which raised eyebrows here and there, but only among hard-core traditionalists. What the hell? There is nothing weird about a trainer entering two horses in the Kentucky Derby. It's called an "entry" for betting purposes, and it's done all the time.

The rules are different in horse sports, and brazen cheating is widely accepted as Normal. Hideous shenanigans that would get you barred from any other professional sport except dog racing are widely admired among horse people. Probably it is the legacy of Genghis Khan, who made his own rules and killed anybody who violated them.

There are many rules in polo—too many, in fact—but when it comes to the buying and selling of major championships, there are no rules at all. It is sleazier than pro wrestling and more expensive than a terminal cocaine habit, but the rich have warmly embraced it, and many have turned into addicts.

If there is any natural sport for the '90s in America, it is polo. It is a dangerous game ruled entirely by money and utterly without any redeeming social value. Loyalty in any form is a weakness to be jeered at, and the only thing that prevents some half-bright millionaire horse thug from buying his way to victory in the U.S. Open is ten other half-bright millionaire horse thugs who also crave to buy it and will fight to the death to prevent anyone else from winning.

A million dollars is nothing to Team Revlon or the billionaire patron Henryk de Kwiatkowski of Calumet Farm. These people fly their ponies around the world in custom-built DC-8s, luxurious airborne stables that can haul forty or fifty finely tuned horses at a time, along with fifteen or twenty grooms and usually a dozen criminal pimps on the run from Interpol or the Mafia. The polo crowd is eclectic and dangerously hagridden with narcissism and treachery, and that is the way they like it. Victory is all that matters.

The difference between a ten-goal champion and a wretched, unemployable three goaler is essentially in the diet. The best and the brightest on the high-goal circuit eat only the hearts of wild animals, while the three goalers live on horse meat. But none of them will talk about it . . .

And why should they? Many things are known in the sweaty gray world of the polo stables, but the truth is rarely spoken. The rigid code of omertà is what holds the sport together.

II

The magazine sent me an assistant, a tall, jittery young man named Tobias, who picked me up at the airport. "Welcome to New York," he said. "I have a present for you." He handed me a large gift-wrapped box containing a hideous blow-up doll named Teri, according to the information on the box—which also said she had a "real-life *vibrating* vagina" and a "luscious-lipped deep open mouth." There were other special features and a stern warning not to exceed her maximum 275-pound weight limit, or she might explode and disappear.

"You should see her tits," Tobias said. "They are bigger than Ginger Baker's head." He grinned idiotically and made a spastic jack-off motion, then loaded Teri onto the cart with all my other luggage. She was going to be part of our lives now. I knew she would be with us for a while, for good or ill. "Our car is right out in front," said Tobias. "I'll have it brought up. The hotel is not far, and I am a very skilled driver. I like to drive fast."

Everything he said turned out to be a lie, but I was not surprised. I sensed there was something deeply wrong with him. He had no idea where the car was, and I sat on the curb for an hour and a half while he searched for the Lincoln, roaming alone through the bowels of the huge parking garage.

It was another tortured hour before we got back to the hotel, and we managed to check in without incident.

"You will never drive again," I said to him. "There is something wrong with you. Don't ever touch this wheel again. From now on, I'm driving."

I was introduced to the manager as Dr. Franklin, the famous author and world-renowned polo zealot. I asked him at once for a $2,000 cash advance. "My man Tobias will handle the details," I said. "Let me know when it's done. I'll be over there in the bar."

"No problem, Doctor," he said. "I'll take care of everything." He nodded across the lobby at the elevated bar. "You just go over there and make yourself at home. I'll call Hugo and tell him you're coming."

He seemed to be snickering at me, but I ignored it.

"You'll like Hugo," he added. "He's one of our local characters. He's Swiss."

It was another lie. One look at the ugly brute of a bartender told me that he was something far worse than a Swiss. He looked like a violent hunchback from the mountains of Transylvania.

I greeted him warmly nonetheless; I tried to pretend he was normal.

"Welcome home," he said quietly. "I knew you were coming; now we'll get to know each other."

I laughed nervously, assuming he was joking, and avoided his sinister gaze.

"Never mind," I said. "I've changed my mind." I picked up my satchel and left quickly. His eyes followed me all the way to the elevator. I felt a twinge of The Fear.

When I got to the suite, I found Tobias struggling to blow up the sex doll. I quickly slapped it away from him and gave the thing to the bellboy. "This is a four-star hotel," I told him. "Get this bitch inflated and bring her back immediately." I smiled and gave him a $100 bill. "Remember me," I said with a fine smile. "I will need many things."

I looked forward to spending time at the Garden City Hotel watching football and meeting surreptitiously with emissaries from the Jimmy Carter for President Committee. They would come and go quietly, mingling with the pimps and dancers and the hard-core polo crowd.

The Garden City Hotel had a shady reputation in the old days, but now it's like a morgue. Frank Sinatra used to hang out here, and so did W. Averell Harriman. The place is full of ghosts, many of them burned alive in a series of disastrous fires that have plagued this hotel since it was built in 1874.

Yet the game went on; they all played polo: William Vanderbilt, John Pierpont Morgan, Lillian Russell, Billy Rose. Garden City was the Aspen of the Twenties, a pastoral outpost of greed, wealth, rudeness, and women who refused to wear panties. Scott Fitzgerald, no doubt, brooded in this bar just as I am today. The place has always reeked of death, from equine fever in the 1920s to human brain death in the Nineties . . . Even today there are wild boys in the elevators, cradling rubber blow-up dolls in their arms, chatting amiably with the night porters. It's a wonderful place to stay if you're dead . . . I had the time of my life. The Garden City Hotel is a fiery tomb of magic, mystery, and myth. You want fun, Bubba? This is the place to be.

• • •

The polo tournament had been running every other day for two weeks on Long Island and also at the Greenwich Polo Club, in Connecticut—only ten miles away by water across the ominous gray currents of the Sound. I thought of Jay Gatsby standing on his lawn and staring across the water at the green light at the end of Daisy's dock . . . But the Garden City Hotel is a long way from Gatsby country, and Daisy doesn't hang out here anymore. Long Island has changed drastically since Gatsby's time. Garden City was a rural hamlet back then, and when it was originally built, the hotel was so hard to reach by horse carriage from Manhattan that it seemed as far away as Cuba.

By the turn of the century, it had become a fashionable spa for the rich and famous. Teddy Roosevelt lived nearby in Oyster Bay and was often seen in the hotel bar, haranguing the local gentry to come on up to his place for a quick game of polo. But Teddy would not recognize the place now. It has burned to the ground three times and is now in its fourth incarnation. There is a disco instead of a carriage house, and Joey Buttafuoco has replaced Gatsby as the resident celebrity manqué.

By the time I got there, a rash of shocking upsets had thrown the championship up for grabs. Most of the foreigners had been humbled, and my homeboys had emerged as one of the strongest challengers. Four teams were still unbeaten going into the final week, and Aspen was one of them. They were whores, of course, and only one of them had ever set foot in the Aspen area—and that was the wily patron, Doug Matthews. But that is the way of polo, and I was the only one who seemed disturbed by it.

But not for long. I was beginning to learn that there was no need to be bothered by certain things. It is a different world, and the only way to accept it is to accept it completely . . . I was shocked at first to learn that the official headquarters of the tournament, the legendary Meadowbrook Polo Club, no longer existed except as an eerie shell of its former self. The grounds were still beautiful, and the deserted clubhouse was still elegant, but there were no polo fields, no polo ponies, no caviar brunches, no smirking, bankrupt aristocrats strutting around the terrace with half-naked Spanish courtesans on their arms. "It's a parking lot now," said club president Al Bianco Sr. when I inquired, "but we still call it the polo field."

It didn't faze me. "Of course," I said. "Good show. Now let us retire to the bar and have a mint julep."

"There is no bar," he said. "But I know a nice Italian place over in Levittown. You must come and be my guest."

"You're too kind," I said, "but I'll have to take a rain check. I have a film crew waiting back at the hotel. I have to run."

"What a pity," he said. "We'll see you tomorrow at the game?"

"You bet," I said. "We will kick ass. Those goddamn Argies are about to get what they came for. My homeboys can't lose!"

He blanched and looked away, then he pulled a plastic hip flask out of his coat and drank deeply. "What do you mean by that?" he finally asked, fixing me with a nervous smile.

"You know what I mean," I said. "I didn't come here to lose, Buster. You want to put your money where your mouth is?"

He stared down at his hands for a long moment, then shook his head. "I didn't hear that," he said. "I'll see you tomorrow at the game. Thanks for stopping by."

"The pleasure was all mine," I replied. "We are champions."

• • •

I walked across the lobby to the darkness of the Polo Lounge, which appeared to be empty. I sat down at the bar and picked up a crumpled copy of the *Sporting News*, which was open to the Dog Pages. Across the room was a big-screen Sony TV, which was tuned to the dog-racing channel. I slapped my hand on the bar and called for whiskey. I hate dog racing, and the sight of it made my mood foul. I reached into the pocket of my silk shooting jacket and pulled out a small ball of hashish, which I quickly ate.

I heard a noise behind me, and then a hand touched my shoulder. "Pardon me," said a man's voice, "are you here for the polo games?"

"You bet," I replied. "This is the big one. It's now or never."

"Who are you with?" he asked.

"Aspen Polo," I said. "My homeboys. We are undefeated. Nobody can stop us."

He nodded thoughtfully but said nothing. He was still standing slightly behind me, so shrouded in darkness that I could barely see his reflection in the mirror behind the bar. It made me nervous. For all I knew, he was a cop or maybe a professional pickpocket. But when he sat down on the stool next to me, I saw a finely dressed gray-haired man who looked like he might own a few polo ponies himself. He was wearing what appeared to be a black cashmere tuxedo jacket and patent leather boots. He was an elderly gent with deep-set eyes and a suave patrician presence—as if he'd just come back from a garden party at the old Gatsby place. I was impressed. We shook hands, and he introduced himself as Averell Harriman.

I recognized the name and felt edgy for a moment because I knew he was lying: the real Averell Harriman had been dead for quite a few years—but I smiled and shook his hand anyway. Why not? I thought. We all use borrowed names from time to time.

A minor problem arose when I accidentally signed Doug Matthews' name to a receipt for the $1,000 tip I'd given to the three hotel porters. The manager brought it to me in the bar, where I was enjoying a professional conversation with my new friend. "Why are you bothering me?" I said as I scrawled my initials on the check. "We're all on the same team anyway. There's plenty more where that came from."

• • •

Harriman was something of a historian, also a political buff. We knew some of the same people—but not many. He knew my friend George McGovern, for instance, and also Richard Nixon, but he didn't know Keith Richards or James Carville, my partners in the blood business . . . So what? I thought. I like this man. He knows things. Never mind that he looks one hundred years old. He is whiskey gentry, he is one of us.

Hugo the Swiss bartender appeared, and I asked him to get that goddamn dog racing off the TV. "Punch up the news," said Harriman. "Let's see what's developed in Haiti. I own a home there."

"Good luck," said the bartender. "You'll never see it again."

Harriman lashed out and hit him with a polo whip that had been concealed in his boot. "Shut up, Hugo! Get back where you belong." He waved the weapon at him again, and Hugo cringed. Harriman hit him again, popping the whip sharply across his back.

I took it away from him. "That's enough," I said. "He got what he deserved."

"Not yet," he muttered, sitting back down on the stool. "Hugo is a cheater. He's been cheating me for years."

I helped Hugo to his feet, but he jerked away and spit at me. "You polo bastards!" he snarled. "Your time is coming!"

I whipped him on the face with a fanlike motion that left welts all over his head, then I shoved him away toward the kitchen.

"Good show," said Harriman. "That's more like it. That was very fast work." He smiled and reached out to shake my hand. It was a graceful gesture, almost formal, as if to salute us both for doing the right thing. I understood and grasped his hand strongly in mine. I felt good about things. We were off to a good start, and I felt a new kind of attitude stirring in me—a Polo Attitude—and I knew we would soon find some action.

It came sooner than I thought. The minute Bill Clinton's face came on TV, Harriman went wild. "Oh, God," he moaned. "Not again! . . . I can't stand the sight of this skunk. He reminds me of Mussolini."

The president was somewhere in the White House, speaking nervously into the cameras at a live press conference. He was explaining his position on Haiti, which again caused an outburst from Harriman.

"Blow it out your ass!" he shouted. "You vulgar little bastard!" He shook his fist at the screen and moaned loudly.

I was shocked. There was an angry screech in his voice, and I was glad I hadn't given his weapon back to him. "Get a grip on yourself," I said sharply. "Be quiet! What the fuck is wrong with you?" It was the most violent reaction I'd ever seen to a living politician.

Harriman quickly regained his composure, but I was leery of him. I have had my own savage reactions to President Clinton—and usually for good reason—but never anywhere near the way Harriman acted. It was like he'd been stung by a wasp. I quickly put my arm around him and sat him down. He was trembling with anger, and I wasn't sure he recognized me. I had told him earlier that my name was "Ben. Ben Franklin." But that was only after he'd introduced himself as Averell Harriman.

What the hell? I thought. Fair is fair, especially here in the lobby of this goddamn creepy hotel full of high-strung polo pimps from Palm Beach and Argentina. The U.S. Open is the event of the year in the world of polo, and special rules applied. Half the crowd was traveling on false passports, but nobody cared. Even the horses were brought in illegally and put in false quarantine. It was safe to assume that anybody you met in this macho zirconium atmosphere was working at least one scam. Many were sleazy—this was, after all, a convention of horse traders—but a few were quite stylish.

I considered myself lucky to have stumbled on something no more dangerous than a skillful Averell Harriman impersonator instead of something much worse. Many people come to the Open and get cheated out of their life savings in the blink of an eye. Everything you see in this place is for sale, from fast horses and beautiful women to cheap whiskey and fat young boys.

My man Harriman was a real find in this crowd. He was good company, and he was obviously plugged in to the right people. He was brazenly weird, and I admired him for it. He was good at his work. It takes a magic kind of gall to aggressively impersonate a dead man on his own turf, especially a former governor of New York State eight years after his death. It was heavy.

My only problem with Harriman was his temper. I was still shaken by his behavior at the sight of the president on TV, and I felt I should speak with him about it. I was afraid he would get us arrested.

"You can't do that anymore," I told him. "We're both on thin ice here. You can't be threatening the president in public. We can't get away with it."

He nodded stiffly. "It's none of your goddamn business," he said. "He's been fucking my wife for many years."

"What?" I said. "Goddamn you! Stop saying that weird shit. People are watching us."

He smiled and shrugged his shoulders. "Calm down, son," he said. "You're a little jumpy today." He put an arm around me. "Don't worry, old sport," he said. "I own this place. These people work for me."

I nodded wisely, as if I'd known it all along and didn't want to embarrass him. But in truth, he was beginning to make me uneasy. He had too many irons in the fire. I had known from the start that he was a very suave hustler, but I had no problem with that . . . He was a decent sort, not without the odd moral blind spot, and I liked his morbid sense of humor. I was not entirely comfortable with his hair-trigger temper or his frequent jealous rages against the president for fucking his wife, but in my line of work, these things go with the territory. I have worked with the criminally insane all my life. These are my people, but I usually try to keep them at arm's length. It is better that way.

Harriman, on the other hand, was a very valuable source of information no matter how crazy he was. He was my man on the Island.

My man Harriman had style. I could trust him, and I felt he trusted me.

He enjoyed his reputation as an aggressively eccentric personality, and he told bizarre stories about what the hotel was like in the good old days—when mysterious fires would engulf the lobby from time to time, and prominent social figures were beaten to death in the hallways with polo mallets or found at the bottom of wells with their heads cut off. "I remember one Sunday we played a whole chukker with a small human skull that Tommy Hitchcock found in the bushes behind his stables. We had a good laugh until somebody said it might be the Lindbergh baby," he said wistfully. "But they were never able to identify it because we had bashed all its teeth out."

"That's rich," I said, but neither one of us laughed. Harriman called for more whiskey and changed the subject. "You know, I got this hotel for almost nothing," he said. "The previous owner, Mr. Hines, died horribly. The family sold out and moved to Hawaii because somebody told them there were no rats there."

"Nonsense," I said. "Hawaii is overrun with rats." I noticed the bartender staring at us, but Harriman continued.

"That was how he died," he said. "The papers called it a drowning, but I knew better." He paused and nodded darkly. "He was murdered—murdered by rats, huge pack rats, the kind with those long hairy arms and claws like a cat."

"Oh, my God," I said. "How did it happen?"

"Rats lived in the rafters above the swimming pool," he said. "Mr. Hines liked to swim laps at night for exercise." He paused again, and I saw that his hands were shaking.

"The poor son of a bitch," he said. "He never had a chance. A swarm of those filthy, hairy things fell out of the rafters and landed right on top of him in the water—he was covered with half-dead rats when they found him. They were clinging to every part of his body they could get their claws or their teeth into, just trying to stay alive."

"Jesus!" I said. "No wonder you torched the hotel."

He nodded, then stood up, and we parted. I went upstairs and took a long hot shower.

III

Polo people are very polite as a rule, and most of them seemed to like me. But they are wary of strangers, and most of our talk had to do with field conditions and horseshoes and other barnyard subjects that bored me into a stupor. I tried to get close to the horses, but when I went to the barns at night, I couldn't get any closer than the bushes across from the stables at the old Hitchcock estate, where the Australian team was quartered. They were feverish brutes, drinking heavily, and their patron was Kerry Packer, the richest man in Australia.

They were favored to win the whole thing when they got here, and people cheered when they strutted through the lobby. Then disaster struck: they lost three straight games, eliminating themselves and causing Packer to flee the country in a cloud of grief and shame. People were shocked, but it was not that unusual. "Patrons always flee and abandon their teams when they lose," explained our host, Al Bianco. "It costs about a million dollars just to enter this tournament, and they go all to pieces when they get humiliated."

"Why shouldn't they?" said tournament director Peter Rizzo. "They're full of false pride, and they got whipped. It's a terrible fate for a warrior."

• • •

Polo is not as complex as it looks, but it is every bit as dangerous. Anything that involves people riding horses at top speed and charging into each other while swinging mallets is going to be a problem for a certain percentage of participants. Broken arms and legs are common, along with dead backs and shattered eyeballs. This is not like golf or Churchill Downs or the Tennessee Walking Horse championship. Polo is a very loud, very fast contact sport, and the people who play it well are blue-chip athletes.

There are about 150 of these, however, and therein lies the problem.

The Aspen vs. Redlegs game was on Sunday, and it sucked: slow polo on a messy field, made worse by rain, heat, and a disappointing spectator turnout. The crowd of two hundred or so was a mix of horse traders, hunchbacks, and marginal types looking for Ralph Lauren. Shelby Sadler was there with two acid-crazed assistants from *Polo Magazine*. She introduced them as the Helpless Girls. They both laughed and showed me their tits . . . Just then, Joey Buttafuoco walked by, wearing a cheap imitation-linen suit that began falling apart when the rain started. My homeboys won 9–7, but nobody seemed to care. The Gracida brothers carried the attack, scoring eight of the team's nine goals. Polo is not a spectator sport, because nobody likes to watch it.

After the game I drove over to the stabling area, hoping to find some action. I was giddy from my string of gambling victories, and I wanted to buy something. People were friendly to me, but I could see that I made them uncomfortable. The whole concept of journalism is foreign to the polo world, but I went out of my way to act charming.

I was looking for my old friend Memo Gracida Sr., who once gave me refuge in Mexico. In the polo world he is a ranking legend; he sits on the right hand of God—the lewd and lovely Belinda. But nobody in the stables had ever heard of him. They knew nothing. Omertà. The code of silence. That is the way of polo.

• • •

It was long after dark when I finally got back to the hotel, where a huge party was under way. The lobby was full of teenage girls in low-cut formal dresses. "Who are these people?" I asked the manager.

"We have Jews and Koreans tonight," he said proudly. "It's a bar mitzvah on the mezzanine and a Korean wedding in the ballroom." Then he pulled me closer and whispered, "The little girls will be getting drunk pretty soon, so watch yourself."

"What?" I said. "What do you mean by *that*?"

"You know what I mean," he said. "When they get juiced up, they start wandering all over the hotel and knockin' on doors." He stared wistfully at a group of bare-shouldered young beauties across the lobby. "It worries me. Terrible things have happened in this hotel."

"I know," I said. "And they'll happen again. You can't stop it."

He hung his head, then smacked his fists together. "I know," he said quietly. "Thank God I don't have any daughters."

"You're right," I said. "They're out of control. They're *evil*." Then I gave him a $50 bill and hurried away to the elevator.

Tobias was already in the room, sorting through a pile of messages. "George Stephanopoulos called," he said. "He's not going to the ball. He says he's too nervous."

"Nonsense," I said. "He has nothing to worry about—except maybe Deborah Couples." Of course, I was speaking about the most famous woman in polo, and the only female patron.

Just then the phone rang. Tobias picked it up, then cursed and slammed it down. "Stephanopoulos again," he muttered. "What the hell's wrong with him?"

"He is drunk," I said. "He's been making an ass of himself."

Tobias laughed. "Well, get ready," he said. "He's down in the lobby, fooling around with those girls. He'll be here in a minute."

"Oh, God!" I moaned. "Don't answer the door."

I picked up the telephone and called the manager, who knew me by name. "There's a pervert down there," I said. "A wiry little Greek named George. He's already sold two of those little girls you're so worried about. Get after him!"

"You bet!" he barked. "I see him now. We'll get him, yeah, thanks for the tip."

"Good work," I said. "Beat the shit out of him."

IV

When my homeboys beat the Redlegs on Saturday, people made the sign of the stinkeye at each other behind the bleachers. Once more I heard ugly whispers of a fix. But no matter: on Sunday we will play White Birch for the championship, and I have bet many thousands of dollars. We will drive them like crippled geese across the ripped-up turf of the Bethpage polo field—me and Carlos and Memo and Doug and Tiger. "Aspen *über alles*," that is our cry. They will not even go to the Polo Ball on Friday night. It is the event of the year in our world, but there is still a genuine risk of being poisoned. It was a black-tie event, extremely private and exclusive. Only three hundred insiders were invited for dinner, and many feelings were hurt . . . but not mine. No. I was with my homeboys, and we were riding high. But I was dressed correctly nonetheless. Appearance is very important in polo. The dress code looks to be casual, but, in fact, it is very rigid, not unlike yachting. Those rumpled tan longcoats and flimsy yellow jackets they wear are not from the Gap: they are Burberry camel's-hair coats with linings of $12,000-a-yard ecru silk and supertech Gore-Tex survival jackets with French titanium zippers. It is a down-style kind of look, but it is extremely functional, and the fabrics will last forever.

It was almost eleven by the time we finally found the unmarked entrance to the Meadowbrook Club. I had whipped the big Lincoln through traffic on the turnpike for thirty or forty minutes at speeds up to 110, past an endless maze of strip malls and row homes and pizza parlors.

It was Fitzgerald's valley of ashes seventy years later and fifty times uglier. I felt an overwhelming sense of doom as we drove through it with the windows rolled up to keep out the poison gas. A brownish cloud seemed to hang over everything as far as the eye could see. Even inside the car the air smelled of deadly carbon monoxide, and a strange chemical film was forming on the windshield.

I felt frantic, and just then I spotted the darkened entrance to my club. It looked like a service road to some abandoned farm, but I turned in to it anyway. Somehow I sensed that this was the place. It felt right. It was the only driveway on the turnpike without a neon sign above it.

The small road led downhill and through a dark vale of trees. There was no sign of life anywhere—no cars, no people, no road signs—and finally I stopped the Lincoln on the side of a long, quiet hill to calm down and get my bearings.

It was a nice place to be lost, a silent forest of tall elm trees and moonlight and finely manicured grounds. I rolled down the windows and stepped out of the car. The sky was full of stars, and the air smelled sweet. I felt giddy. In the distance I could see a dense bright glow in the sky that was probably Manhattan, only eighteen miles away. But I felt a sense of great distance from it, like I'd wandered off the turnpike and gone straight through the Looking Glass and into a different time. I felt like Jay Gatsby, lost in some primitive forest on the fresh green breast of the New World.

I got back in the car and drove on, up a long hill and past two or three darkened carriage houses—and suddenly I crested a rise and came face to face with the glittering vision that had to be the Polo Ball. I was stunned. It was one of those magic moments that those of us afflicted with the Romantic Sensibility tend to nurse forever in memory. I was looking across a valley at a shimmering cluster of peaked tents, swollen with what appeared to be the most elegant party in the world. As I drew closer I could hear clarinet music and the soft laughter of women. Blue lanterns glowed in the trees around the clubhouse, and tall men moved in the shadows, sipping gin highballs and smoking thin cigars. Gatsby would have felt right at home.

I parked in the trees on the edge of the golf course, and I saw Harriman at the bar, standing alone and staring balefully out at the dancers. A wall of trees blocked my access, but I easily slipped through them, then strolled across the lawn to the tent. People smiled warmly and nodded hello, then the orchestra struck up a New Age waltz.

He was sitting with a sleek blond woman in a clinging red dress who turned out to be Deborah Couples. She was no stranger to scandal, and we bonded immediately. She was seeking a sponsor for her all-female team, and I said *Rolling Stone* would cover it.

The rest of the night was relentlessly suave. The people were very gracious, and we all drank heavily. I refused to dance with Ms. Couples for reasons of my own, so she left and began to dance wildly with a string of swarthy suitors and Argentine polo types. Harriman tried to cut in on her, but he was too drunk to dance. I decided to leave and abandon him.

The Lincoln made short work of the Jericho Turnpike at that hour of the morning, and the Polo Lounge was still open when I got back to the hotel. I saw Hugo behind the bar, hunched over the spigots like some hairy troll in a cage, and I decided to do my nightcaps by myself upstairs in the suite. Hugo lunged at me as I passed too near the railing, but I ducked and ran to the elevator. I was afraid of him.

I was weak and trembling by the time I got out of the elevator, and the hall was empty, as always. I hurried inside and quickly chained both doors, then I fell on the couch and passed out in a double-helix position for many hours.

It rained all day on Saturday, and I dropped off the polo circuit to hunker down in the suite and get involved in the football games on TV. I turned off the phones and refused to answer the door. Harriman left a message around midnight, saying he would meet me at the box before game time. The message was oddly disjointed, but I chalked it up to fatigue. I knew he had many dark things on his mind—and besides, he didn't like football. Fuck him, I thought. He's crazy. The big game was tomorrow, and I was getting very cranked up.

V

I could already see the lead: *Outlined against a gray September sky, the Four Horsemen of the Apocalypse rode again. In the Book of Revelation they were Famine, Pestilence, Destruction, and Death . . . But these were only aliases: On that frantic afternoon in the dim gray smog of Long Island, they were called Memo, Carlos, Tiger, and Doug.*

A crowd of five thousand or so had gathered to witness the championship match. We arrived early, but not early enough. The turf had turned to mush, and limos were spinning their wheels in the muddy road to the VIP entrance. Drunken gate-crashers were fighting with the police at the gate.

"Get away from here, you scum!" shouted one of the off-duty cops. "If you're looking for trouble, we'll give it to you!" He smacked one of the drunkards with a huge flashlight, and the others fell back. I aimed the big Lincoln through the opening, spinning the wheels in low gear and sending up rooster tails of mud on the crowd around the gate.

"Keep driving," said Tobias. "Don't slow down."

There was a lot of screaming behind us, and I heard whistles blowing. I turned on the windshield wipers and eased into a spot between the Gracida brothers' horse trailers. The match was about to start. I noticed Carlos standing alone in the rain, staring blankly out at the playing field, where a marching band was strutting around on the sod.

I approached him calmly and wished him good luck. "Don't worry," I said cheerfully. "We can't lose. It's in the bag. It's arranged."

"What?" he snapped. "What are you talking about?"

He seemed nervous, so I pulled out my wallet and gave him a $100 bill. "Take this for luck," I said. "This is a wonderful day for the homeboys, eh? Yes, sir, we are *champions*."

He nodded and walked to where his horse was waiting. Bugles sounded, and a roar went up from the crowd. The magic moment had come. Players galloped onto the field and held their mallets aloft like warriors charging to battle.

• • •

There were no empty seats on this day. The grandstands on both sides overflowed with the jetset cream of international polo society. The tournament had been going on for three weeks in Greenwich, as well as on Long Island, and many shocks had occurred. Most of the favorites had been eliminated: the Black Bears from Switzerland were gone, and so were the heavily favored human peacocks from Ellerston White, the fraudulent pride of Australia. The whole aristocracy of American polo had been eliminated: Pegasus, Revlon, and even the glamorous white-hat front-runners from Calumet Farm, in Kentucky. The black hats had prevailed in both brackets, but only one would survive this savage final test. The only gang that stood between my homeboys and victory was what Harriman called "those arrogant criminal swine from White Birch."

Harriman had a flair for embellishment, but his cynical, bile-fueled sentiments were widely shared by pillars of the polo establishment. Many of the oldest and most powerfully inbred families in America were mortified by the spectacle of what they called "two gangs of jailbirds" going mallet to mallet in public for the top prize in U.S. polo. "Who are these people?" one asked. "Where did they come from? We don't even know their families."

"That's because they're all curs," a woman from Palm Beach replied. "It's like having to turn your home over to a pack of colored people."

I was shocked by some of these outbursts, but Harriman said I was ignorant. "These are extremely wealthy people," he said. "Intolerance is a virtue among them, and extreme intolerance is godlike."

"That's rich," I told him. "Yesterday you said polo was the sport of Gods and Kings. No wonder you limp-wit horse freaks end up in debtors' prison."

"Please," he said. "Try not to be coarse. You embarrass me. Let's drive over to the beach and find some teenage girls."

"What?" I said. "Are you nuts? The game is about to start."

He nodded thoughtfully and then shrugged. "Oh, well," he said. "More's the pity. Maybe tomorrow."

I turned away. Harriman had given me the creeps more than once since we'd met, and the profoundly squalid image of a 102-year-old criminal man stalking innocent teenage girls on a foggy Long Island beach while they dally and laugh on the way home from school made him even more repugnant to me.

Or maybe he was only 72; it made no difference. There was something cruel and lascivious about the way he talked sometimes, and there were nights when he gave me The Fear. I was no longer sure who he was or what he was doing with me, and his incessant, violent ranting about the president screwing his wife was beginning to get on my nerves. I wanted no part of it. It is bad business to get involved in other people's domestic squabbles, and he was not the first man I'd met who thought the president was fucking his wife.

• • •

My homeboys hit the field at top speed and jumped out to a 3–1 lead after two seven-minute chukkers. Memo ran wild, scoring all three of the Aspen goals, and Tiger Kneece played defense like Deion Sanders on a good day. Even Doug Matthews was a hero.

We ran up a comfortable lead in the first half, and I spent most of the third chukker in my box, sipping absinthe and discussing the Meaning of Sport with a man named Lipsyte from the *New York Times*. He refused to gamble with me because he said he'd heard it was fixed.

"Nonsense," I told him, "you must be out of your mind. These people are pure as the driven snow. The only thing they can win here is a cheap silver cup. It is worthless."

"Bullshit," he said. "Nobody in his right mind would spend a million dollars to win anything that cheap."

"Welcome to polo," I said. "It is a sport of Gods and Kings."

By halftime the thugs from White Birch were reeling from constant attack and appeared to have lost confidence. They were acting spastic and demoralized. I figured the game was over and began working the crowd in an effort to double up on my bets. It was a wonderful feeling, and I wallowed in it, but I was careful to be discreet.

I spent most of the languid halftime break in a Lamborghini jeep parked under the VIP tower, smoking opium and eating strawberries in Devon cream with a sultry woman called Jane and some girls from Saudi Arabia.

Just then my friend Earl Biss knocked on the thick bulletproof window of the jeep. He was out on work release and had plunged deeply back into gambling. I opened the door, thinking to ask him in, but he seemed confused, and he was motioning for me to get out.

"They're ripping us to pieces," he shouted. "We're losing everything."

I hurried back to the game with him and saw to my horror that White Birch had somehow taken the lead. The score was 4–3, and my homeboys were coming apart at the seams. Memo had fouled, Tiger had missed a tap in, and Matthews was being heckled by the crowd. Our morale had collapsed. I could sense drastic change in the air. The worm had turned with a vengeance. My dream of victory seemed doomed.

The game was getting wild, and the crowd was becoming undisciplined. I went down for more gin, and when I came back to the box, I found a stranger in Harriman's seat. He looked like a foreigner, and he was so intent on the game that I had a hard time getting through to him. "Get out," I said. "This seat is taken."

He looked at me strangely, as if I were some kind of toad.

"Get out," I said again. "You don't belong here."

He continued to stare at me but said nothing. He was a handsome boy with a look of wandering royalty about him, and I could see by the glint in his eyes that he wanted to have me killed. But then he stood up and slithered lazily over the rail like a rat gone down a pipe. I felt vaguely guilty for some reason, but just then a roar went up from the crowd as Bautista Heguy, a small, speedy man sporting dreadlocks and riding a tiny horse, burst out of the pack and scored a goal for White Birch, putting them ahead 7–6 with just 1:06 on the clock. I abandoned all hope at that point and slumped down in my seat as the crowd began chanting triumphantly: "*White Birch!!! White Birch!!!*"

As the clock ticked down, I thought of leaping off the grandstand and running into the woods to avoid the fate of a Loser—which is no longer death but certain degradation . . . And then it happened—one of those magic moments in sport that no human being who saw it can ever forget. My man Carlos captured the ball and raced upfield while Memo came from the other side. The Gracida brothers were off on a Fast Break, and it was an elegant sight to see. Separately, they were each world-famous ten goalers—together they should be rated about thirty, far more than the sum of their parts.

Carlos got ridden into a corner by Mariano Aguerre and appeared to be trapped, but with eighteen seconds remaining, Carlos whirled his pony and bashed a perfect long shot at the White Birch goal some

150 yards away—across a field of torn-up sod and through the legs of seven galloping horses—that almost scored, but it drifted wide right and seemed to be going out of bounds.

We all watched it roll, utterly hypnotized, as it wandered away from its destiny and the pursuing riders slowed down to avoid mangling the crowd in the end zone. The jig was up. My homeboys had lost by a whisker—and it was at that exact moment that Carlos caught up with the ball and hit an impossible right-angle cut shot between the legs of his own horse that Doug Matthews later described as "the most exciting goal ever scored in the 2,500 years polo has been played." It curled through the goalposts like a snake going sideways. The crowd was stunned into silence, and the White Birch lads went instantly crazy with grief. They howled at each other and stabbed their mallets down into the mud.

They knew, as I did, that God was not on their side. They were doomed. Big Darkness, Soon Come; it was only a matter of time.

The sudden-death overtime period was quick and naked of drama. Memo was allegedly fouled, and Carlos lofted an easy penalty shot that won the game for my homeboys.

The crowd did not go wild—but I did, and I collected many dollars, which I quickly squandered on whips, raw silk, horse blankets, and other expensive gimcracks in the paraphernalia tents. One of the shysters conned me out of $900 for a set of gold-plated polo china that still has not been delivered. It remains a foul bone in my throat and a nasty stain in my memory. Caveat Emptor is the rule of the polo market. They are horse traders, tribal people by nature, and they wake up greedy every day of their lives. Beware.

The rest of the day was a nightmare. When I went back to the press tent to inquire about Harriman, they told me he'd been involved in a violent fracas with local police before halftime, then arrested for murder and taken away to jail. Nobody could explain it. He was apparently very well known in polo circles, and people called him a gentleman.

"I can't believe it," said a man wearing Burberry who introduced himself as the president of the Sands Point Polo Club. "He wouldn't hurt a fly; it's an outrage. He *owns* the Garden City Hotel. He was an eight goaler in his day, you know."

Whoops, I thought, get out of here. My life was about to turn weird.

These heinous charges against Harriman confirmed my worst fears. I knew he was guilty; there was no doubt in my mind about that, but I knew I couldn't just flee and turn my back on him. He was good people, and he almost seemed like a friend . . . He was a violent, murdering pervert who followed children at night on the beach, and everything he said raised disturbing questions—but I am, after all, the Founding Father of the Fourth Amendment Foundation, and I had access to the finest criminal lawyers in the world. It was the least I could do for Harriman, and I decided to do it at once. I was already late for our victory celebration in Amityville, but this was a professional emergency. I flogged the Lincoln back to the hotel with no regard for the speed limit and rushed upstairs to the suite, where I found Tobias working the telephones. "Yes," he said quickly, "it's true. They snagged him for Murder 1. I'm trying to find out where they took him."

"Call Goldstein immediately and do whatever he says. I have to run out to some Mexican place in Amityville for dinner with Doug and my homeboys. This is a night for the ages, Tobias, and I refuse to let Harriman spoil it. We'll have him out by dawn—even if he's guilty."

Then I got back on that goddamn filthy Long Island Expressway and sank into serious thinking. It was another wet night on the island. I tried to relax and act normal. What the hell? I thought. It's only rock & roll.

VI

Late Sunday night after our victory party in Amityville, I got lost driving back to the hotel with the Gracida brothers and two booze-maddened girls. All four of them were jammed into the backseat of the Lincoln, which made me nervous. They paid no attention to me, as if I were some kind of commercial chauffeur. There were sounds of whispering and struggling coming from the backseat, but I tried to ignore it. I turned up the radio volume and ate my last ball of hashish.

We had been on the road for more than an hour when I realized I was hopelessly lost. I asked for help, but nobody answered. Finally I pulled into a 7-Eleven store and left the car with its lights on and the engine running. None of my backseat people seemed to notice as I got out of the car and walked across the parking lot and got into a waiting taxicab. Fuck those people, I thought. Let them fend for themselves.

On my way back to the hotel, I spoke to the intensely silent driver about Gatsby, and I asked him if he knew where his house was.

"I know nothing," he snapped. "I speak no English."

I sagged and fell back on the seat. I had no money; in fact, I had given it all to Tobias when I sent him to look for Harriman. I reached into my dinner jacket and pulled out my .380 Walther PPK. Maybe I should just shoot this bastard in the back of the head, I thought. But I soon got a grip on myself. Yes, I thought, I could do that, but it would be wrong. I knocked sharply on the bulletproof window between us. "Go fast," I yelled. "I am sick! Take me to the Garden City Hotel. Now!"

He seemed to understand, and we both relaxed, but it was still a long way to the hotel. Wonderful, I thought. I need some time to think. I had feelings of terrible foreboding, and I wanted to flee immediately. Long Island had broken my spirit. It is an island of poison gas surrounded by a sea of garbage, and I feared I was becoming a part of it. The time had come. The jig was up. Ten days in the flashy core of Long Island had been like ten weeks on a burning garbage scow.

Even the fabled Garden City Hotel had lost its magic for me, and I was deeply afraid of having to wake up there one morning all alone after the polo people were gone. Next week's crowd would be different. The events board in the lobby said the Critical Care Associates were coming in, along with a regional convention of lingerie and rubber merchants. I was not even tempted. It was time to leave—before something terrible happened.

The hotel lobby was empty when I came in. There was nobody behind the reception desk. On my way to the elevators, I noticed that the lights were still on in the Polo Lounge, so I decided to stop for a nightcap and see what I could find out from Hugo. I knew he hated Harriman and would be eager to pass along any vile gossip about him, especially to me. But Hugo was nowhere in sight, and when I strummed the glass rack for service, an unfamiliar face emerged from the kitchen and said he was the new bartender.

"Where is Hugo?" I asked him. "I want to speak with him immediately."

He stiffened and backed away. "Who wants to know?" he asked nervously.

"Me," I said. "I'm his family doctor."

He moaned, and a shudder went through his body.

"What's wrong?" I asked him.

"Hugo is dead," he replied in a trembling voice. "They found him in the pool, floating facedown with a big rat perched on his back. He died a horrible death."

This news shocked me, but I tried to act normal. It was a hideous image. "His back was clawed all to pieces," said the bartender. "There was a cloud of blood all around him in the water. Half of his scalp was chewed off.

"It was no accident," he continued. "Somebody had it in for him. He had a lot of enemies. He was weird."

I nodded solemnly. "You bet," I said. "I knew him well—but, Jesus, how weird do you have to be to get murdered in water by rats? What kind of monster would even think of doing a thing like that? Has anybody confessed?"

"Not yet," he said, "but they arrested your friend Mr. Harriman, and I heard they were looking for you."

"What?" I blurted. "*Who's* looking for me?"

He was trembling badly. "The goddamn stinking police. They were here about an hour ago."

I left quickly, saying nothing. My heart was pounding, and my brain was swamped by confusion. But not for long. By the time I got to the room, I knew what I had to do. I called United and booked a seat on the morning flight to Denver. It would leave LaGuardia in two hours.

There was no sign of Tobias and no time to do any packing. Fuck this mess, I thought. He can pack it all up in boxes and send it by Federal Express. I flogged a few things into my satchel and called the concierge for a fast cab to the airport. There was no other way.

I felt a certain amount of guilt about leaving Harriman alone in jail to face murder charges, but so what? I knew the Polo Attitude, and so did he. We were warriors, but he was in jail, and I wasn't—and besides, I knew he was guilty. He had murdered poor Hugo just as surely as I was now on my way to the airport at top speed in a blind panic. I couldn't help Harriman now. He was doomed, and I didn't want to be doomed with him. It would be boring, and who would take care of my ponies?

I never heard from Harriman again, but Tobias told me that his trial had been put off indefinitely for lack of evidence . . . In my heart I know that the world is a better place with Hugo dead, but I keep it to myself. You can't be too careful.

Epitaph
Veni, Vidi, Vici

Life is different for me now. I go to all the tournaments. I do my shopping at Lodsworth, I am seen with Deborah Couples, and I fly to Argentina in the winter—me and the weird Dukakis sisters. Last month it was Palm Beach; now it's the U.S. Open, and then down to Buenos Aires. We live in our own world, we live our lives like dolphins.

I am a polo person now, and I know the Polo Attitude. I smoke the finest opium, and I drive a Ducati 916. Birds sing where I walk, and my home is a magnet for children.

I have come a long way from Uncle Lawless' barn. I have my own ponies now. I whack polo balls around my yard with a thirty-inch foot mallet from Gray's, and I was named to the board of trustees at the recent Polo Ball. My neighbor De Lise is a two goaler, and we spend five hours a day in the practice cage, hitting balls against the backstop at one hundred miles per hour and trying to hook each other. It is wrong, but we do it anyway. That is the Polo Attitude—and if polo is wrong, so am I.

Memo from the National Affairs Desk. To: Dollar Bill Greider

August 24, 1995

DATE: July 6, 1995
To: Dollar Bill Greider
FROM: Hunter S. Thompson
CC: P. J. O'Rourke
SUBJECT: Dragging Me into Your Rude Political Debate with P.J.
(*rs* 712-713)

You screwhead pig! Look what you've done now. You have blasted to smithereens the once-proud *Hubristic* notion (look it up) that we of the highest rank & proudest voice of the Rock & Roll persuasion are *Smart*. You both made public fools of yourselves—and then you had the cheap, cowardly, skunklike sleaziness to blame yr. dumbness on some kind of pills that you claim I "*sent you in the mail.*"

Ah, you dilettante bastards are all the same, aren't you? *First the gibberish, then the Treachery* . . . And then you blame it on *me*.

You remind me of Hubert Humphrey after he lost his nerve. In the end he was like a desperate old carrion bird. He hovered over the lives of decent people like a vulture over a barnyard—cackling & whining & drooling as vultures will—and then finally swooping and diving and then feeding crudely in public on the dreams of the Doomed down below.

Hubert never saw it that way, of course, and I'm sure you won't either . . . Ah, Billy, we are so lonely for heroes these days, aren't we? It is like living on the Moors, waving lanterns & screeching frantically at each other in the fog that hangs over the peat moss, always weak & afraid of being suddenly attacked from behind by a huge killer hound from hell—some beast with a separate agenda like you or even P.J. . . .

But *he* didn't blame his dilettante gibberish on *me* or my "pills" like you did . . . Shame on you, Bubba. I think you owe me an apology. I have a lot of Pills, but I have *nothing* that will make a smart man act like Hubert Humphrey—and I wouldn't send it to you if I did.

Most people recognize a devious pig when they see one. But we are *not* pigs, and it brings us low when we act that way. It makes me uncomfortable to think that my best friends & allies in journalism are dumb boys. It is lonely Enough out here without that.

OK. Thanx in advance for yr. cooperation.

Doc

Timothy Leary and William S. Burroughs, R.I.P.

Though neither Timothy Leary nor William S. Burroughs was among Hunter's inner circle, he'd met and corresponded with both; several years earlier he'd driven to Lawrence, Kansas, to visit and shoot with Burroughs, and in the last weeks and months of Leary's life, he and Hunter had extended late-night telephone conversations. A proper RS *send-off for both seemed only appropriate.*

Memo from the National Affairs Desk. To: Jann S. Wenner

August 8, 1996

DATE: June 9, 1996
To: Jann S. Wenner
FROM: Hunter S. Thompson
SUBJECT: Mistah Leary, He Dead

I will miss Tim Leary—not for his wisdom or his beauty or his warped lust for combat or because of his wealth or his power or his drugs, but mainly because I won't hear his laughing voice on my midnight telephone anymore. Tim usually called around 2. It was his habit—one of many that we shared, and he knew I would be awake.

Tim and I kept the same hours. He believed, as I do, that "after midnight, all things are possible."

Just last week he called me on the phone at two thirty in the morning and said he was moving to a ranch in Nicaragua in a few days and would fax me the telephone number. Which he did. And I think he also faxed it to Dr. Kesey.

Indeed. There are many rooms in the mansion. And Tim was familiar with most of them. We will never know the range of his fiendish vision, or the many lives he was sucked into by his savage and unnatural passions.

We sometimes disagreed, but in the end we made our peace.

Tim was a Chieftain. He Stomped on the Terra, and he left his elegant hoof prints on all our lives.

He is forgotten now but not gone. We will see him soon enough. Our tribe is now smaller by one. Our circle is one link shorter. And there is one more name on the honor roll of pure warriors who saw the great light and leapt for it.

The Shootist: A Short Tale of Extreme Precision and No Fear

September 18, 1997

William had a fine taste for handguns, and later in life he became very good with them. I remember shooting with him one afternoon at his range on the outskirts of Lawrence. He had five or six well-oiled old revolvers laid out on a wooden table, covered with a white linen cloth, and he used whichever one he was in the mood for at the moment. The S&W .45 was his favorite. "This is my finisher," he said lovingly, and then he went into a crouch and put five out of six shots through the chest of a human-silhouette target about twenty-five yards away.

Hot damn, I thought, we are in the presence of a serious Shootist. Nicole had been filming it all with the Hi8, but I took the camera and told her to walk out about ten yards in front of us and put an apple on her head.

William smiled wanly and waved her off. "Never mind, my dear," he said to her. "We'll pass on that trick." Then he picked up the .454 Casull Magnum I'd brought with me. "But I will try this one," he said. "I like the looks of it."

The .454 Casull is the most powerful handgun in the world. It is twice as strong as a .44 Magnum, with a huge scope and a recoil so brutal that I was reluctant to let an eighty-year-old man shoot it. This thing will snap back and crack your skull if you don't hold it properly. But William persisted.

The first shot lifted him two or three inches off the ground, but the bullet hit the throat of the target, two inches high. "Good shot," I said. "Try a little lower and a click to the right." He nodded and braced again.

His next shot punctured the stomach and left nasty red welts on his palms. Nicole shuddered visibly behind the camera, but I told her we'd only been kidding about the apple. Then William emptied the cylinder, hitting once in the groin and twice just under the heart. I reached out to shake his hand as he limped back to the table, but he jerked it away and asked for some ice for his palms. "Well," he said, "this is a very nasty piece of machinery. I like it."

I put the huge silver brute in its case and gave it to him. "It's yours," I said. "You deserve it."

Which was true. William was a Shootist. He shot like he wrote—with extreme precision and no fear. He would have fired an M-60 from the hip that day if I'd brought one with me. He would shoot anything, and he feared nothing.

Memo from the National Affairs Desk: More Trouble in Mr. Bill's Neighborhood

March 19, 1998

The devil made me do it the first time.
The second time I done it on my own.

—Waylon Jennings

That is how it goes with politicians. The worst are relentless greedheads, and the best can't control their own lusts. Spiro Agnew took brown bags full of cash, and Bill Clinton will suffer the little children to come unto him. Some people go to jail or get impeached for these things, while others are hailed as New Age Wizards and stylish rogues with unfortunate personal addictions. One man's Innocent Child is another man's Raging Slut—and, as always in combat, one loose cannon on your own deck is more dangerous than six enemy cannons.

Welcome to Mr. Bill's Neighborhood, folks. It may be weird, but it's ours. We like it here—except for a handful of worrywarts and Sex Nazis who will never be happy anyway. They are in the Minority now, and their atavistic thinking is about to take another serious whack. They hate perverts, but so what? They hated Joey Buttafuoco, too, and he became a major folk hero and a legendary Sodomite in spite of them.

Ah, but we are not talking about Joey Buttafuoco here. We are talking about William Jefferson Clinton from Hope, Arkansas, the forty-second president of the U.S.A.

Try a booming 73 percent approval rating in the polls, Bubba—up from 51 percent before the Sex Scandal. That's not a bad bump on the charts for a lame-duck, degenerate president with a minority in both houses of Congress and a whole raft of sex-related lawsuits on his hands from women who may or may not be claiming that they were preyed upon by a brute worse than Hermann Goering or even Benjamin Franklin.

Seventy-three percent is big numbers on the campaign trail, Bubba. Very big. I would feel safe in betting heavily that there aren't too many members of this Congress who came in with 73 percent of the vote. That is a Landslide. That is Victory.

Newt Gingrich had his victory, too. Remember the Republican Revolution of 1994? Now the only people who still have any respect for it are cops, preachers, and creeps who hang out on the fringes of Klan rallies and worship Charlton Heston. And in November, Gingrich is looking at a Total Loss of personal and political power as the year 2000 looms down on us. Things happen faster and faster in the nineties.

And the difference between Winning and Losing is very big. Look what happened to the dumb bastards who accused Richard Jewell of being the "mad bomber" of the '96 Atlanta Olympics. They got shamed, humiliated, and ripped to shreds for their carelessness. Some people take these warnings seriously. I know I do. The Lewd Revolution is coming; that is the message, and Bill Clinton is only one of its messengers. Never mind what William Bennett says. Anybody who writes a best seller called *The Book of Virtues* is riding for a serious fall—and now we are back in Mr. Bill's Neighborhood, at the nexus of the Lewd Revolution . . . That is what is happening, that is the message, and anybody against it will be like King Canute trying to hold back the sea.

• • •

Bill Clinton has been worried about the nature of his Legacy in History, but he should worry no longer. He can shuck off his list of previous accomplishments: ending Welfare as we knew it, presiding over the greatest peacetime prosperity since Octavian, paying off the Federal deficit, opening up the entire hemisphere to free trade, and engineering Wall Street's great six-year Bull Run.

Most historians now agree that Clinton's lasting image will be as the president who Legalized Sodomy and set millions of Americans free from the chains of prudery and hopeless Ignorance.

Abe Lincoln freed the Slaves, Thomas Jefferson bought half of America for seventeen cents an acre, and Bill Clinton legitimized oral sex on the job. The real victim of this mess will be the vice president. It is no small thing for a sitting two-term president to leave his successor with near-record approval ratings. This means that the people are happy with the way things are and will expect more of the same. Al Gore will come under terrible pressure to maintain Clinton's standard of lewdness. Yes, we are in the midst of a revolution. Should the vice president have any questions, he would do himself a favor to look up the definition of "lewd" in the Random House dictionary:

lewd (lood) adj. **-er, -est. 1** inclined to, characterized by, or inciting lust or lechery; lascivious **2** obscene or indecent, as language or songs; salacious **3** [Obs.] a) low, ignorant, or vulgar b) base, vile, or wicked, esp. of a person c) bad, worthless, or poor, esp. of a thing.

Sounds bad, eh? Well, get ready to know it up close pretty soon, Bubba. The electorate has spoken, and it will speak again in the year 2000.

Reflections

By the late nineties, Hunter had, for the most part, shifted his energies away from writing new material, concentrating instead on ensuring his literary legacy by organizing and publishing his massive trove of thousands of letters. The first volume, The Proud Highway, *had recently been published to much acclaim, and the second,* Fear and Loathing in America, *was on the way. "Hey Rube" was a stealth move in both directions—new material, yes, but the sort of thing rarely seen from Hunter: extended, thoughtful self-reflection and unfiltered autobiography taking in everything from his regular late-night swims at his neighbor's pool in Woody Creek; childhood visits to his grandmother while growing up in Louisville; his heroes Burroughs, Kerouac, James Dean, and Robert Mitchum; and the metaphysical matter of Music as Fuel.*

Letter from HST to JSW

May 7 '98

Dear Jann,

Congratulations on the General Excellence award & all the others. It was a Sweep & I'm proud to be part of it.

How is your back?

I plan to be in NY during the week of May 20.

Enc. is the lead for a new story I'm working on, called HEY RUBE! Have a laugh & let me know if it interests you & maybe we can do some business.

Okay. I'm going out to murder a skunk now.

Soon come,
HST.

Hey Rube! I Love You: Eerie Reflections on Fuel, Madness & Music

May 13, 1999

> *Let our Lord now command thy servants to seek out a man who is a cunning player on a harp: and it shall come to pass, when the evil spirit from God is upon thee, that he shall play with his hand, and thou shalt be well.*
>
> —I Samuel 16:16

It is Sunday morning now and I am writing a love letter. Outside my kitchen window the sky is bright and planets are colliding. My head is hot and I feel a little edgy. My brain is beginning to act like a V-8 engine with the spark-plug wires crossed. Things are no longer what they seem to be. My telephones are haunted and animals whisper at me from unseen places.

Last night a huge black cat tried to jump me in the swimming pool, then it suddenly disappeared. I did another lap and noticed three men in green trench coats watching me from behind a faraway door. Whoops, I thought, something weird is happening in this room. Lay low in the water and creep toward the middle of the pool. Stay away from the edges. Don't be strangled from behind. Keep alert. The work of the Devil is never fully revealed until after midnight.

It was right about then that I started thinking about my love letter. The skylights above the pool were steamed up, strange plants were moving in the thick and utter darkness. It was impossible to see from one end of the pool to the other.

I tried to stay quiet and let the water calm down. For a moment I thought I heard another person coming into the pool, but I couldn't be sure. A ripple of terror caused me to drop deeper in the water and assume a karate position. There are only two or three things in the world more terrifying than the sudden realization that you are naked and alone and something large and aggressive is coming close to you in dark water.

• • •

It is moments like this that make you want to believe in hallucinations—because if three large men in trench coats actually *were* waiting for me in the shadows behind that door and something else was slithering toward me in the darkness, I was doomed.

Alone? No, I was *not* alone. I understood that. I had already seen three men and a huge black cat, and now I thought I could make out the shape of another person approaching me. She was lower in the water than I was, but I could definitely see it was a woman.

Of course, I thought. It must be my sweetheart, sneaking up to give me a nice surprise in the pool. Yessir, this is just like that twisted little bitch. She is a hopeless romantic and she knows this pool well. We once swam here every night and played in the water like otters.

• • •

Jesus Christ! I thought, what a paranoid fool I've been. I must have been going crazy. A surge of love went through me as I stood up and moved quickly to embrace her. I could already feel her naked body in my arms . . . Yes, I thought, love does conquer all.

• • •

But not for long. No, it took me a minute or two of thrashing around in the water before I understood that I was, in fact, completely alone in the pool. She was not here, and neither were those freaks in the corner. And there was no cat. I was a fool and a dupe. My brain was seizing up, and I felt so weak that I could barely climb out of the pool.

Fuck this, I thought, I can't handle this place anymore. It's destroying my life with its weirdness. Get away and never come back. It had mocked my love and shattered my sense of romance. This horrible experience would get me nominated for Rube of the Year in any high school class.

Dawn was coming up as I drove back down the road. On my way past the graveyard, I slowed down and tossed a quarter over the fence like I always do. There were no comets colliding, no tracks in the snow except mine, and no sounds for ten miles in any direction except Lyle Lovett on my radio and the howl of a few coyotes. I drove with my knees while I lit up a glass pipe full of hashish.

When I got home I loaded my S&W .45 auto and fired a few bursts at a beer keg in the yard, then I went back inside and started scrawling feverishly in a notebook . . . What the hell? I thought. Everybody writes love letters on Sunday morning. It is a natural form of worship, a very high art. And on some days I am very good at it.

Today, I felt, was definitely one of those days. You bet. Do it *now*. Just then my phone rang and I jerked it off the hook, but there was nobody on the line. I sagged against the fireplace and moaned, and then it rang again. I grabbed it, but again there was no voice. Oh God! I thought. Somebody is fucking with me . . . I needed music, I needed rhythm. I was determined to be calm, so I cranked up the speakers and played "Spirit in the Sky," by Norman Greenbaum.

I played it over and over for the next three or four hours while I hammered out my letter. My heart was racing and the music was making the peacocks scream. It was Sunday, and I was worshipping in my own way. Nobody needs to be crazy on the Lord's Day.

• • •

My grandmother was never crazy when we went to visit her on Sundays. She always had cookies and tea, and her face was always smiling. That was down in the West End of Louisville, near the Ohio River locks. I remember a narrow concrete driveway and a big gray car in a garage behind the house. The driveway was two concrete strips with clumps of grass growing between them. It led back through the vicious wild rose bushes to what looked like an abandoned shed. Which was true. It was abandoned. Nobody walked in that yard, and nobody drove that big gray car. It never moved. There were no tracks in the grass.

It was a LaSalle sedan, as I recall, a slick-looking brute with a powerful straight-eight engine and a floor-mounted gearshift, maybe a 1939 model. We never got it started, because the battery was dead and gasoline was scarce. There was a war on. You had to have special coupons to buy five gallons of gas, and the coupons were tightly rationed. People hoarded and coveted them, but nobody complained, because we were fighting the Nazis and our tanks needed all the gasoline for when they hit the beaches of Normandy.

Looking back on it now, I see clearly that the reason we drove down to the West End to visit my grandmother on the Lord's Day was to con her out of her gas coupons for the LaSalle. She was an old lady, and she didn't need any gasoline. But her car was still registered, and she still got her coupons every month. That was why we went to her house on Sundays.

So what—I would do the same thing myself if my mother had gasoline and I didn't. We *all* would. It is the Law of Supply and Demand—and this is, after all, the final messy year of the American century and people are getting nervous. Hoarders are coming out of the closet, muttering darkly about Y2K and buying cases of Dinty Moore beef stew. Dried figs are popular, along with rice and canned hams. I, personally, am hoarding bullets, many thousands of them. Bullets will always be valuable, especially when your lights go out and your phone goes dead and your neighbors start running out of food. That is when you will find out who your friends are. Even close family members will turn on you. After the year 2000, the only people who'll be safe to have as friends will be dead people.

• • •

I used to respect William Burroughs because he was the first white man to be busted for marijuana in my time. William was the Man. He was the victim of an illegal police raid at his home at 500 Wagner Street in Old Algiers, a low-rent suburb across the river from New Orleans, where he was settling in for a while to do some shooting and smoke marijuana.

William didn't fuck around. He was serious about everything. When the Deal went down William was There, with a gun. Whacko! *Boom!* Stand back. I *am* the Law. He was my hero a long time before I ever heard of him.

• • •

But he was not the first white man to be busted for weed in my time. No. That was Robert Mitchum, the actor, who was arrested three months earlier in Malibu at the front door of a hideaway beach house for possession of marijuana and suspicion of molesting a teenage girl on

August 31, 1948. I remember the photos: Mitchum wearing an undershirt and snarling at the cops with the sea rolling up and the palm trees blowing.

Yessir, that was my boy. Between Mitchum and Burroughs and James Dean and Jack Kerouac, I got myself a serious running start before I was twenty years old, and there was no turning back. Buy the ticket, take the ride.

So welcome to *Thunder Road*, bubba. It was one of those movies that got a grip on me when I was too young to resist. It convinced me that the only way to drive was at top speed with a car full of whiskey, and I have been driving that way ever since, for good or ill.

The girl in the photos with Mitchum looked about fifteen years old, and she was also wearing an undershirt, with an elegant little nipple jutting out. The cops were trying to cover her chest with a raincoat as they rushed through the door. Mitchum was also charged with Sodomy and Contributing to the Delinquency of a Minor.

I was having my own troubles with police in those years. In the fifth grade I was officially apprehended by the FBI for turning over a U.S. mailbox in front of a bus. Soon after that, I became a frequent detainee in various jails around the South on booze, theft, and violence charges. People called me a criminal, and about half the time they were right. I was a full-bore Juvenile Delinquent, and I had a lot of friends.

We stole cars and drank gin and did a lot of fast driving at night to places like Nashville and Atlanta and Chicago. We needed music on those nights, and it usually came on the radio—on the fifty-thousand-watt clear-channel stations like WWL in New Orleans and WLAC in Nashville.

That is where I went wrong, I guess—listening to WLAC and driving all night across Tennessee in a stolen car that wouldn't be reported for three days. That is how I got introduced to the Howlin' Wolf. We didn't know him, but we liked him and we knew what he was talking about. "I Smell a Rat" is a pure rock & roll monument to the axiom that says, "There is no such thing as paranoia." The Wolf could kick out the jams, but he had a melancholy side to him. He could tear your heart out like the worst kind of honky-tonk. If history judges a man by his heroes, like they say, then let the record show that Howlin' Wolf is one of mine. He was a monster.

Music has always been a matter of Energy to me, a question of Fuel. Sentimental people call it Inspiration, but what they really mean is Fuel.

I have always needed Fuel. I am a serious consumer. On some nights I still believe that a car with the gas needle on empty can run about fifty more miles if you have the right music very loud on the radio. A V-8 Cadillac will go ten or fifteen miles faster if you give it a full dose of "Carmelita." This has been proved many times. That is why you see so many Cadillacs parked in front of truck stops on Highway 66 around midnight. These are Speed Pimps, and they are loading up on more than gasoline. You watch one of these places for a while, and you see a pattern: a big fast car pulls up in front of the doors and a wild-looking girl gets out, stark-naked except for a fur coat or a ski parka, and she runs into the place with a handful of money, half crazy to buy some flat-out-guaranteed driving music.

It happens over and over, and sooner or later you get hooked on it, you get addicted. Every time I hear "White Rabbit," I am back on the greasy midnight streets of San Francisco, looking for music, riding a fast red motorcycle downhill into the Presidio, leaning desperately into the curves through the eucalyptus trees, trying to get to the Matrix in time to hear Grace Slick play the flute.

There was no piped-in music on those nights, no headphones or Walkmans or even a plastic windscreen to keep off the rain. But I could hear the music anyway, even when it was five miles away. Once you heard the music done right, you could pack it into your brain and take it anywhere, forever.

• • •

Yes sir. That is my wisdom and this is my song. It is Sunday and I am making new rules for myself. I will open my heart to spirits and pay more attention to animals. I will take some harp music and drive down to the Texaco station, where I can get a pork taco and read a *New York Times*. After that, I will walk across the street to the post office and slip my letter into her mailbox.

Res ipsa loquitur.

His Last Bow

While the 2004 election seems almost like a fait accompli in retrospect, it was still an all-hands-on-deck, down-to-the-wire dogfight when Hunter was writing what turned out to be his last post from the National Affairs desk—and his final Rolling Stone *story. George W. Bush wasn't declared the winner until the day after the election, when John Kerry elected not to contest the official result in Ohio, and Hunter used his bully pulpit to encourage readers to get out and vote in a direct, pragmatic way that was unlike almost anything he'd done since . . . well, since trying to muster votes for his own run for sheriff of Aspen himself some thirty-four years earlier—the foundation, of course, of his first piece for the magazine. The snake was eating its own tail.*

If there's nostalgia or sentimentality in this piece, it's in Hunter's remembrance of his first meetings with John Kerry in 1972 when they were both demonstrating against the Vietnam war in Washington, D.C., "angry and righteous," and Hunter was "trying to throw a dead, bleeding rat over a black-spike fence and onto the president's lawn." It was a brutal contrast between those "white-knuckle days of yesteryear" and the nation's contemporary political climate, in which the big question was not "whether President Bush is acting more like the head of a fascist government" but "if the people want it that way."

How bad was Dubya? Bad enough to make Hunter long for his old nemesis Tricky Dick: "If he were running for president this year against the evil Bush-Cheney gang, I would happily vote for him." Less than four months later—at the end of the football season, and one month after Bush's inauguration for a second term—Hunter would be dead.

The Fun-Hogs in the Passing Lane

November 11, 2004

Fear and Loathing, Campaign 2004

Lyndon Johnson and the Pig Farmer . . . The Stink of a Loser . . . The Drug of War . . . President Nixon, Now More Than Ever . . . Revenge of the Fun-Hogs . . . A Sacrifice to the Rat Gods

Armageddon came early for George Bush this year, and he was not ready for it. His long-awaited showdowns with my man John Kerry turned into a series of horrible embarrassments that cracked his nerve and demoralized his closest campaign advisers. They knew he would never recover, no matter how many votes they could steal for him in Florida, where the presidential debates were closely watched and widely celebrated by millions of Kerry supporters who suddenly had reason to feel like winners. Kerry came into October as a five-point underdog with almost no chance of winning three out of three rigged confrontations with a treacherous little freak like George Bush. But the debates are over now, and the victor was clearly John Kerry every time. He steamrollered Bush and left him for roadkill.

Did you see Bush on TV, trying to debate? Jesus, he talked like a donkey with no brains at all. The tide turned early, in Coral Gables, when Bush went belly up less than halfway through his first bout with Kerry, who hammered poor George into jelly. It was pitiful . . . I almost felt sorry for him, until I heard someone call him "Mister President," and then I felt ashamed.

Karl Rove, the president's political wizard, felt even worse. There is angst in the heart of Texas today, and panic in the bowels of the White

House. Rove has a nasty little problem, and its name is George Bush. The president failed miserably from the instant he got onstage with John Kerry. He looked weak and dumb. Kerry beat him like a gong in Coral Gables, then again in St. Louis and Tempe—and that is Rove's problem. His candidate is a weak-minded frat boy who cracks under pressure in front of sixty million voters.

That is an unacceptable failure for hardballers like Rove and Dick Cheney. On the undercard in Cleveland against John Edwards, Cheney came across as the cruel and sinister überboss of Halliburton. In his only honest moment during the entire debate, he vowed, "We have to make America the best place in the world to do business."

Bush signed his own death warrant in the opening round, when he finally had to speak without his TelePrompTer. It was a Cinderella story brought up to date in Florida that night—except this time the false prince turned back into a frog.

• • •

Presidential politics is a vicious business, even for rich white men, and anybody who gets into it should be prepared to grapple with the meanest of the mean. The White House has never been seized by timid warriors. There *are* no rules, and the roadside is littered with wreckage. That is why they call it the *passing lane*. Just ask any candidate who ever ran against George Bush—Al Gore, Ann Richards, John McCain—all of them ambushed and vanquished by lies and dirty tricks. And all of them still whining about it.

That is why George W. Bush is president of the United States, and Al Gore is not. Bush simply *wanted* it more, and he was willing to demolish anything that got in his way, including the U.S. Supreme Court. It is not by accident that the Bush White House (read: Dick Cheney & Halliburton Inc.) controls all three branches of our federal government today. They are powerful thugs who would far rather die than lose the election in November.

The Republican establishment is haunted by painful memories of what happened to Old Man Bush in 1992. He peaked too early and he had no response to "It's the economy, stupid."

Which has always been the case. Every GOP administration since 1952 has let the military-industrial complex loot the Treasury and plunge the nation into debt on the excuse of a wartime economic emergency. Richard Nixon comes quickly to mind, along with Ronald Reagan and his ridiculous "trickle-down" theory of U.S. economic policy. If the Rich get Richer, the theory goes, before long their pots will overflow and somehow "trickle down" to the poor, who would rather eat scraps off the Bush family plates than eat nothing at all. Republicans have never approved of democracy, and they never will. It goes back to preindustrial America, when only white male property owners could vote.

• • •

The genetically vicious nature of presidential campaigns in America is too obvious to argue with, but some people call it fun, and I am one of them. Election Day—especially a presidential election—is always a wild and terrifying time for politics junkies, and I am one of those, too. We look forward to major Election Days like sex addicts look forward to orgies. We are slaves to it.

Which is not a bad thing, all in all, for the winners. They are not the ones who bitch and whine about slavery when the votes are finally counted and the losers are forced to get down on their knees. No. The slaves who emerge victorious from these drastic public decisions go crazy with joy and plunge each other into deep tubs of chilled Cristal champagne with naked strangers who want to be close to a winner.

That is how it works in the victory business. You see it every time. The Weak will suck up to the Strong, for fear of losing their jobs and their money and all the fickle power they wielded only twenty-four hours ago. It is like suddenly losing your wife and your home in a vagrant poker game, then having to go on the road with whoremongers and beg for your dinner in public.

Nobody wants to hire a loser. Right? They stink of doom and defeat.

That is the nature of high-risk politics. *Veni Vidi Vice,* especially among Republicans. It's like the ancient Bedouin saying, As the camel falls to its knees, more knives are drawn.

• • •

Indeed, the numbers are weird today, and so is this dangerous election. The time has come to rumble, to inject a bit of fun into politics.

I look at elections with the cool and dispassionate gaze of a professional gambler, especially when I'm betting real money on the outcome.

Contrary to most conventional wisdom, I see Kerry with 5 points as a recommended risk. Kerry will win this election, if it happens, by a bigger margin than Bush finally gouged out of Florida in 2000. That was about 46 percent, plus 5 points for owning the U.S. Supreme Court—which *seemed* to equal 51 percent. Nobody really believed that, but George W. Bush moved into the White House anyway.

It was the most brutal seizure of power since Hitler burned the German Reichstag in 1933 and declared himself the new Boss of Germany. Karl Rove is no stranger to Nazi strategy, if only because it worked, for a while, and it was sure as hell fun for Hitler. But not for long. He ran out of *oil*, the whole world hated him, and he liked to gobble pure crystal hiphetamine and stay awake for eight or nine days in a row with his maps & his bombers & his dope-addled general staff.

They all loved the whiff. It is the perfect drug for War—as long as you are winning—and Hitler thought he was King of the Hill forever. He had created a new master race, and every one of them worshipped him. The new Hitler Youth loved to march and sing songs in unison and dance naked at night for the generals. They were fanatics.

That was sixty-six years ago, far back in ancient history, and things are not much different today. We still love War.

George Bush certainly does. In four short years, he has turned our country from a prosperous nation at peace into a desperately indebted nation at war. But so what? He is the president of the United States and you're not. Love it or leave it.

> *War is an option whose time has passed. Peace is the only option for the future. At present we occupy a treacherous no man's land between peace and war, a time of growing fear that our military might has expanded beyond our capacity to control it and our political differences widened beyond our ability to bridge them.*
>
> *Short of changing human nature, therefore, the only way to achieve a practical livable peace in a world of competing nations is to take the profit out of war.*
>
> —Richard Nixon, *Real Peace* (1983)

Richard Nixon looks like a flaming liberal today compared to a golem like George Bush. Indeed. Where is Richard Nixon now that we finally need him?

If Nixon were running for president today, he would be seen as a "liberal" candidate, and he would probably win. He was a crook and a bungler, but what the hell? Nixon was a barrel of laughs compared to this gang of thugs from the Halliburton petroleum organization who are running the White House today—and who will be running it this time next year, if we (the once proud, once loved and widely respected "American people") don't rise up like wounded warriors and whack those lying petroleum pimps out of the White House on November 2.

Nixon hated running for president during football season, but he did it anyway. Nixon was a professional politician, and I despised everything he stood for—but if he were running for president this year against the evil Bush-Cheney gang, I would happily vote for him.

You bet Richard Nixon would be my Man. He was a crook and a creep and a ginsot, but on some nights, when he would get hammered and wander around in the streets, he was fun to hang out with. He would wear a silk sweat suit and pull a stocking down over his face so nobody could recognize him. Then we would get in a cab and cruise down to the Watergate Hotel, just for laughs.

• • •

I watch three or four frantic network-news bulletins about Iraq every day, and it is all just fraudulent Pentagon propaganda, the absolute opposite of what it says: "U.S. Transfers Sovereignty to Iraqi Interim 'Government.' " Hot damn! Iraq is finally Free, and just in time for the election. It is a deliberate cowardly lie. We are no more giving power back to the Iraqi people than we are about to stop killing them.

Your neighbor's grandchildren will be fighting this stupid, greed-crazed Bush family "war" against the whole Islamic world for the rest of their lives, if John Kerry is not elected to be the new president of the United States in November.

The question this year is not whether President Bush is acting more and more like the head of a fascist government, but if the American people *want* it that way. That is what this election is all about. We are down to nut-cutting time, and millions of people are angry. They want a Regime Change.

Some people say that George Bush should be run down and sacrificed to the Rat gods. But not me. No, I say it would be a lot easier to just vote the bastard out of office on November 2.

Bulletin

Kerry Wins Gonzo Endorsement: Dr. Thompson Joins Democrat in Calling Bush "the Syphilis President"

"Four more years of George Bush will be like four more years of syphilis," the famed author said yesterday at a hastily called press conference near his home in Woody Creek, Colorado. "Only a fool or a sucker would vote for a dangerous loser like Bush," Dr. Thompson warned. "He hates everything we stand for, and he knows we will vote against him in November.

"I endorsed John Kerry a long time ago," he said, "and I will do everything in my power, short of roaming the streets with a meat hammer, to help him be the next president of the United States."

Which is true; I said all those things, and I will say them again. Of course I will vote for John Kerry. I have known him for thirty years as a good man with a brave heart—which is more than even the president's friends will tell you about George W. Bush, who is also an old acquaintance from the white-knuckle days of yesteryear. He is hated all over the world, including large parts of Texas, and he is taking us all down with him.

Bush is a natural-born loser with a filthy rich daddy who pimped his son out to rich oilmongers. He hates music, football, and sex, in no particular order, and he is no fun at all.

• • •

Back in June, when John Kerry was beginning to feel like a winner, I had a quick little rendezvous with him on a rain-soaked runway in Aspen, Colorado, where he was scheduled to meet with a harem of wealthy campaign contributors. As we rode to the event, I told him that Bush's vicious goons in the White House are perfectly capable of assassinating Nader and blaming it on him. His staff laughed, but the Secret Service men didn't. Kerry quickly suggested that I might make a good running mate, and we reminisced about trying to end the Vietnam War in 1972.

That was the year I first met him, at a riot on that elegant little street in front of the White House. He was yelling into a bullhorn, and I was trying to throw a dead, bleeding rat over a black-spike fence and onto the president's lawn.

We were angry and righteous in those days, and there were millions of us. We kicked two chief executives out of the White House because they were stupid warmongers. We conquered Lyndon Johnson and we stomped on Richard Nixon—which wise people said was impossible, but so what? It was fun. We were warriors then, and our tribe was strong like a river.

That river is still running. All we have to do is get out and vote, while it's still legal, and we will wash those crooked warmongers out of the White House.

Postscript:

Letter from HST to JSW

March 11, 1998

Hunter S. Thompson
Woody Creek

Dear Jann,

Please re-send the *Playboy* Interview fax I just received from you. Only one page of it came through, and the top of it is illegibile.

Also, what *issue* of *Playboy* is this from? I am about to do some business with Joe [Eszterhas] & I need to know what he's saying about me in print.

Of course I'm curious. Just seeing you and & Joe mentioned in the same paragraph gives me an atavistic rush. My memory of those days is mainly of tremendous energy & talent & rare commitment running (almost) amok, but not quite. It was like being invited into a bonfire & finding out that fire is actually your friend. Ho ho . . .

But just how hot can you stand it, brother, before your love will crack?

That was the real question in those days, I think. Or maybe it was about how much money you were being paid. Or how much fun you were having. Who knows? Some people were fried to cinders, as I recall, while others used the heat to transmogrify themselves into heroes. (Which reminds me that you still owe me a vast amount of money—and you still refuse to even discuss payment for my recent politics memo.)

Anyway, my central memory of that time is that everything we were doing seemed to *work*. Or *almost* everything. What the hell? Buy the ticket, take the ride, eh? Like an amusement park, or the Circus-Circus casino: It depended on yr. personal definition of "acceptable loss."

I know Joe considers his days at *Rolling Stone* to be an utter waste of time & talent, or maybe he just says that for his own vengeful reasons. Some people are too weird for their own good. But not me, Jann. I say thanx for the rush.

Yr. buddy, Hunter

Acknowledgments

It's important to once again acknowledge the *Rolling Stone* staffers who were—quite truly—in the trenches with Jann Wenner when Hunter filed his copy on many a midnight and beyond.

Associate editor David Felton probably logged more Thompson hours than anyone else, beginning with "Strange Rumblings in Aztlan," continuing through much of the campaign trail and Watergate coverage, and the landmark two-parter on Muhammad Ali. Ditto associate editor Charles Perry, who manned the Mojo Wire and copyedited every HST word in the San Francisco years.

Managing editor John Walsh took the reins for "Fear and Loathing at the Super Bowl," Hunter's dream assignment. Managing editor Terry McDonell lured Hunter out of a prolonged absence from *Rolling Stone* to cover the sensational Roxanne Pulitzer divorce trial. Managing editor Bob Love led the dawn patrol for Hunter's later pieces, most notably "Fear and Loathing in Elko."

A special shout-out goes to Corey Seymour and Tobias Perse, Hunter's aides-de-camp and hands-on assistants in the 1990s. Both were front and center for any number of HST antics, as well as the marathon run-up to "Polo Is My Life."

David Rosenthal, editor in chief of Simon & Schuster for thirteen years, proffered contracts and cash advances that kept Hunter afloat during his less productive periods. He handled Hunter's abuse as well as anyone, and set this anthology up at S&S.

Lynn Nesbit, Hunter's literary agent for more than thirty years, was devoted to him and played an essential role in his relationship with Jann Wenner and *Rolling Stone.* She was very much a part of the inner circle that ran the HST train.

COMSEWOGUE PUBLIC LIBRARY
3 0620 00421 4200